GEOGRAPHICAL DATA ANALYSIS

GEOGRAPHICAL DATA ANALYSIS

NIGEL WALFORD
School of Geography, Kingston University, UK

JOHN WILEY & SONS
Chichester • New York • Brisbane • Toronto • Singapore

Baffins Lane, Chichester,
West Sussex PO19 IUD, England
Telephone National Chichester (01243) 779777
International (+44) (1243) 779777

Other Wiley Editorial Offices

John Wiley & Sons, Inc., 605 Third Avenue,
New York, NY 10158-0012, USA

Jacaranda Wiley Ltd, 33 Park Road, Milton,
Queensland 4064, Australia

John Wiley & Sons (Canada) Ltd, 22 Worcester Road,
Rexdale, Ontario M9W 1L1, Canada

John Wiley & Sons (SEA) Pte Ltd, 37 Jalan Pemimpin #05-04,
Block B, Union Industrial Building, Singapore 2057

Library of Congress Cataloging-in-Publication Data

Walford, Nigel.
Geographical data analysis / Nigel Walford.
p. cm.
Includes bibliographical references and index.
ISBN 0-471-94162-X
1. Geography — Statistical methods. I. Title
G70.3.W35 1994 94-29062
910'.21 — dc20 CIP

British Library Cataloguing in Publication Data

A catalogue record for this book is available from the British Library

ISBN 0-471-94162-X

Typeset in 10/12pt Times by Laser Words, Madras
Printed and bound in Great Britain by Redwood Books Ltd,
Trowbridge, Wiltshire

To Ann
and in memory of my parents

Contents

Appendices

Preface

This book has arisen in recognition of three features which are common to many undergraduate courses in geography and cognate disciplines: first, students are usually required to undertake a methodology or techniques unit; second, at least as far as United Kingdom higher education institutions are concerned, students are often expected to carry out a small research project; and third, the connection between statistical analysis and the acquisition of geographical knowledge and understanding is sometimes obscure. Students may be deterred from statistical analysis by overemphasis on mathematical theory, by the tedium of calculation and its apparent lack of relevance to what is perceived as mainstream geography.

The book attempts to confront these problems and has three specific objectives: to explain basic statistical techniques and demonstrate their application to quantitative geography; to equip students with the knowledge and skills necessary for carrying out research projects; and to make a link between statistical analysis and the substantive topics taught as part of systematic geography units. The book follows the analytical progress of four exemplar projects, drawn from physical and human geography. Each project shows how an initial geographical question can lead to the formulation of tentative hypotheses, how data can be collected and input on computer, and then how basic statistical analyses can be undertaken. The projects exemplify both primary and secondary methods for collecting geographical data and the computer-based application of a wide range of statistical techniques. Much contemporary geographical data analysis uses computer software to carry out the number-crunching operations and the projects demonstrate two general-purpose statistical packages, MINITAB and SPSS-X. The descriptions of the software commands and procedures are, however, not intended as a substitute for careful study of the manuals, which are referenced in the bibliography.

Acknowledgements

Most books, although carrying the name of one or at most a few authors, are only produced with the aid of various forms of assistance, encouragement and support given by different individuals and organisations. This book is no exception, and the author gratefully acknowledges the diverse practical and emotional support that he has received from various quarters. Rendell Williams and Don Funnell first initiated me into the mysteries of statistical analysis, at Sussex University, back in the days when calculations were carried out on electrically powered calculators. In due course these tools were superseded by ever more powerful and more compact computers, which, while removing the drudgery of calculation, at the same time extended my horizons and expectations of what statistical analyses were possible.

One feature of the book is the use of four exemplar projects to demonstrate the different stages of a statistical investigation. The author is grateful to those students who have used preliminary versions of the analyses. The diagrams in the book itself have been produced with the assistance and expertise of several people. Thanks are offered in particular to Debbie Millard, who produced most of the figures; and to Ann Hockey, for reading the text. I also acknowledge the help received from the authorities and colleagues at Kingston University, in particular from Trevor Kennea for encouraging and supporting the project. Two anonymous referees provided useful and constructive comments on an earlier draft of the text and my thanks go to them, although as usual any remaining errors are the responsibility of the author alone. Finally, thanks go to my family and friends who have tolerated interminable references to 'the book' for the last 18 months!

Nigel Walford,
Wivenhoe, Essex
April 1994

Part I

INTRODUCTION AND PROJECT DEFINITION

Chapter 1
Introduction to data analysis and statistics in geography

1.1 STATISTICAL DATA ANALYSIS

Data analysis can be defined as the processing and interpretation of a given set of information or observations. When used as a means of carrying out scientific investigations, data analysis frequently involves the application of statistical techniques to numeric data. These techniques are useful in two ways. First, they can show that the results of research make a valuable contribution to the body of knowledge relating to a group of phenomena. They may also help to establish whether relationships between the characteristics of a set of observations are likely to be genuine. In other words, statistical techniques are capable of determining the reliability of supposedly factual information and of quantifying the relationships between a given set of phenomena. The combination of data analysis and statistical techniques can be referred to as statistical data analysis and is widely used in different academic disciplines.

Academic study, for example in geography, sociology, economics, anthropology, physics, biology and chemistry, usually attempts to establish and explain facts in a scientific fashion. Over the years, the various academic disciplines have developed a relatively arbitrary division of the characteristics of different phenomena. The identity of a particular discipline is sustained by a common interest in a coherent set of phenomena and the acceptance of a collection of unifying concepts. The search for explanation and understanding involves the development of a discourse about a particular group of phenomena. This discourse provides the structure for linking together knowledge in order to understand or explain how the various 'facts' are connected and to establish a basis from which predictions about other similar phenomena might be made.

This introductory chapter has a threefold purpose: to examine the nature of scientific enquiry as a research method in academic disciplines; to indicate why statistical data analysis is important in this methodology; and to outline the development of the scientific method and statistical analysis in geography. The next section looks at the characteristics of the scientific method in general, while Section 1.3 outlines the development of this approach in geography. The chapter concludes with an outline of the book's contents and structure.

1.2 SCIENTIFIC METHOD OF ENQUIRY

Some 30 years ago, there was a surge of interest in examining how science built up knowledge and explanation, which resulted in the publication of several of books concerned with the nature and philosophy of science (e.g. Nagel 1961; Caws 1965; Popper 1965). Any attempt to summarise these complex arguments in one introductory section of a text concerned with statistical data analysis would be pointless and presumptuous. However, a basic outline of the key issues in the debate is relevant to an understanding why statistical techniques are important.

The underlying principles of the scientific method of enquiry are rigour, replication and respectability. Over the years, there has been much debate about its precise form and it is now generally accepted that the scientific method is not a single unified approach. Instead, it comprises a series of 'alternative routes to be followed in establishing a scientific law' (Harvey 1973, p. 32). These routes divide into 'top down' and 'bottom up' approaches, as shown in Figure 1.1. The top down or deductive approach starts from a set of initial conditions, from which hypotheses are developed, and progresses, by reference to empirical evidence and previously established laws, to reach logically consistent conclusions. The bottom-up or inductive approach works in the opposite direction by moving from the measurement and observation of phenomena, through a process of ordering and classification, to the recognition of pattern and regularity. Scientists, by these alternative routes, succeed in establishing new deductive or inductive scientific laws.

Traditionally the 'hard' sciences, particularly physics and chemistry, were regarded as the archetypes of deductive scientific enquiry. The 'soft' sciences such as biology, and to some extent geography, were concerned with the classification of phenomena, as a preparation for deriving inductive laws relating to classes of plants, animals and places. Statistical analysis is an important tool in these disciplines, because it provides a basis for accepting or rejecting hypotheses and for testing the validity of empirical measurements and observations (Johnston 1979). This traditional classification of the sciences was challenged by Kuhn (1962), when he examined what scientists did in their work. He argued that two types of science could be identified. He labelled the first 'normal science', because it is what the vast majority of scientists undertake throughout their working lives. He argued that normal science involves the incremental acquisition of new knowledge about phenomena, testing and proving in accordance with the established theories of the day. When something is discovered which appears to

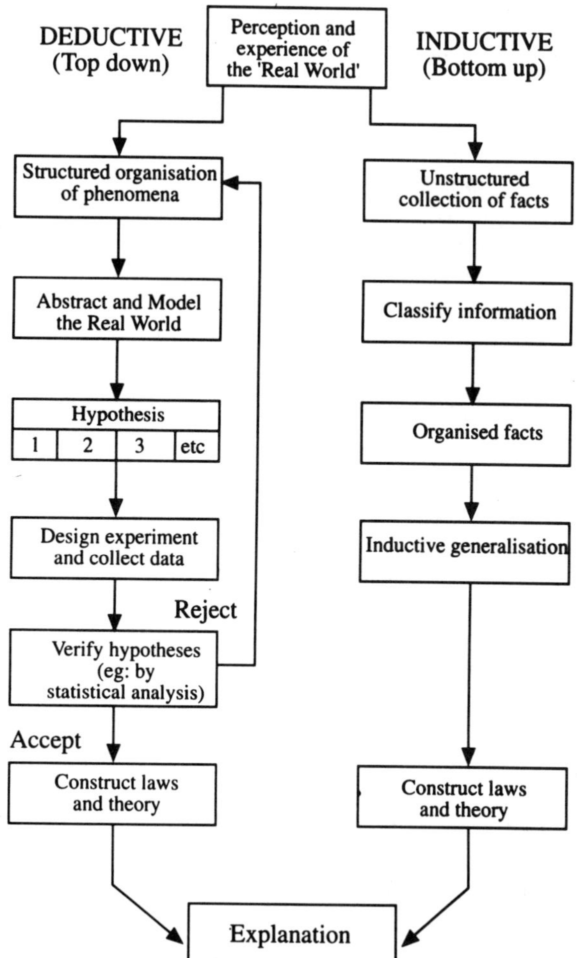

Figure 1.1 Deductive and inductive routes to scientific explanation

conflict fundamentally with the established order, the second type of science, which Kuhn called 'extraordinary research', comes into play. This revolutionary upheaval, or, as Kuhn described it, this 'paradigm shift' interrupts the period of normal science until a new order prevails.

1.3 SCIENTIFIC GEOGRAPHY

The publication of *The Structure of Scientific Revolutions* (Kuhn 1962) led members of various disciplines to search for paradigm shifts. Claims that some of the changes of direction in geography constituted such reorientations were later rejected by Johnston (1979), who failed to identify any periods of 'normal science' in geography, only 'schools of thought which wax and wane, some linked to others, some independent; but there is no consensus, no paradigm-dominance'

(p. 188). Geographers emerge from such discussions as quite content for different methodologies to operate at the same time. Thus, positivist, humanist, Marxist and structuralist positions are among those given free rein under an 'anything goes' principle.

An examination of how geographical research is carried out reveals a broad division into qualitative and quantitative approaches, which approximates to the classical inductive–deductive split. The former is believed to lack scientific rigour, whereas the latter is directly related to the scientific method and the testing of hypotheses concerning the characteristics of phenomena. The need to use numbers is likely to arise regardless of whether a qualitative or quantitative approach is adopted. Therefore, the difference between the two approaches is not about whether numerical quantities need to be calculated, but the purpose for which they are used.

Geography started to assume the role of a scientific discipline in the late 19th century, when explorers such as von Humbolt and Mackinder undertook expeditions to largely uncharted parts of the world. The tools of these early geographers were measurement and observation, followed by description, of the natural and human features of the strange lands. In the early part of the 20th century, attention switched to regional geography and the interaction and integration of all phenomena within such areas. This methodology, intrinsically qualitative in character, was not concerned with producing or referring to general laws, but focused on 'the description and interpretation of what existed in the unique locations' (Harvey 1969, p. 71).

Regional description, so much favoured in the first half of the 20th century, has not disappeared entirely from contemporary geography. However, even where a locational focus exists, the stronger interest tends to be in systematic areas of the discipline, such as transport, population, hydrology and quaternary studies. The location itself is to some extent incidental and provides a context for the outcome of different physical, chemical, biological, social and economic processes. Widespread distrust of the qualitative approach was emerging in the 1950s and 1960s and resulted in the rejection of regionalism by many geographers. In its place, they embraced statistical techniques and other forms of numerical analysis (e.g. modelling and simulation) and by their actions brought about the quantitative revolution.

Geography was not alone in adopting 'the "scientific methods" of the more prestigious hard sciences' (Johnston 1979, p. 23), although in some respects it was a follower rather than a leader. However, any initial hesitation pales into insignificance against the speed with which statistical analysis subsequently spread through the discipline. A new generation of geographers was anxious to raise geography to the status of a scientific discipline. In the preface to *Models in Geography* (Chorley and Haggett 1967), it was suggested that regional geography and the adherence to a real differentiation were under attack. Apart from a general desire to raise the discipline's status, several factors came together to promote and maintain the development of a new approach and to produce the 'quantitative revolution'. The four main factors have been:

- the availability of geographical data;
- the pace of change in geographical phenomena;
- the technical changes in the handling of information;
- a pervasive belief in the usefulness of science.

Over the last 30 years, the amount of statistical information available and the greater facility for the transfer of such data between individuals and organisations have continued to develop. The ease with which modern academic geographers can access and process large amounts of statistical data, by means of a computer terminal on their desk, may be producing a new generation of 'swivel-chair' geographers. These researchers run the risk of having little contact with the outside world to which the information relates. These changes have effectively shrunk the world to a more manageable size. It is not just geographical explorers who travel to and talk of distant places, but ordinary people in their work or their search for inspiration, relaxation and recreation. While the world has been shrinking, the pace of change appears to have accelerated. Advice to 'all practising geographers [to be] conscious [of] the speed of change in the modern world' (Freeman 1961, p. 24) is as true now as it was in the early 1960s. The effect on geography, as in many other disciplines, has been to emphasise contemporary phenomena and to consider relatively limited historical trends. The emphasis on contemporary issues has added to the value and worth of geography in an era when academic study for its own sake is increasingly regarded as an expensive luxury. The analysis of spatial patterns and of the processes of change has many applications and geographers have been quick to recognise and promote the practical value of their work. As a consequence, modern geography is less concerned with establishing its scientific credentials than with promoting its usefulness to society.

Technical improvements in the computer-based handling of numerical, graphical and cartographical data have revolutionised geography. As far as statistical analysis is concerned, the initial importance of computers as 'number-crunching' machines continues, particularly as a reduction in size of the 'geographical individual' or 'basic unit of space' (Harvey 1969, p. 73) has led to an increase in their number. For example, at the start of the quantitative revolution geographers would have been content to analyse British Population Census statistics for local authority areas (approximately 1700 in number in 1961) or for towns (Moser and Scott 1961), whereas in the early 1980s 130 000 enumeration districts were classified (Openshaw 1983). In this context, the greater processing power and storage capacity of computer hardware, and the availability of software with statistical analysis capabilities have been significant technological developments. In the period since the Second World War, traditional industries have declined, educational opportunity has expanded and a person's knowledge, rather than his or her social background, has started to become more important as a determinant of social status. The Second World War 'marked the "coming-of-age" of science and technology' (Johnston 1979, p. 23), which were accepted with a fervour that contrasted with the low regard with which they had previously been held. Quantitative techniques and statistical analysis offered a route for geography and other disciplines to achieve scientific status, and 'to be scientific was to be respectable and useful' (Johnston 1979, p. 24).

The quantitative revolution in geography, according to those writing at the time and to others reflecting on the period with the benefit of hindsight, led to 'a deep-rooted redirection of the discipline' (Billinge et al. 1984, p. 6). The effects of the quantitative revolution are manifested in modern geography in two main ways. The teaching of statistical techniques remains a key and virtually universal element in the training of new geographers. The positivist scientific approach is still the underlying methodology employed by many geographers in their research. Perhaps this persistence represents the outworking of the firm grip that the quantifiers established, in Harvey's (1973, p. 129) words, 'on the production of graduate students and on the curricula of various departments'. On the other hand, the growing interest in geographical information systems (GIS) and a resurgence of interest in spatial statistics (Campbell 1991) seem likely to buttress the quantitative approach in geography for the foreseeable future. Statistical techniques have survived a counter-reaction to the quantitative revolution because at a practical level they have something to offer Marxist, structuralist, political economic and even behaviouralist approaches.

1.4 STRUCTURE OF THE BOOK

The scientific method of enquiry and statistical data analysis are not the only valid forms of geographical methodology, although they are in common usage. The development of computers and other forms of information technology has succeeded in eliminating some of the drudgery associated with calculating statistical quantities by hand, although these machines have not removed the need to understand the principles of why statistical procedures may be required.

Training in the use of computers for carrying out statistical and other forms of data analysis is as relevant to the modern geographer as the well-established analytical skills developed in the field, laboratory and library. However, there must be many students of geography for whom statistics is an unwelcome intrusion into the study of such clearly interesting problems as soil erosion, river pollution, industrial location and urban deprivation. With these attractive topics on offer, statistics is frequently viewed as something to be avoided or at best suffered under duress. There often appears to be a suspicion that statistical analysis is not really geography. The alternative view is that without the benefit of statistical analysis, geography becomes a speculative and purely descriptive discipline, rarely able to establish reliable information about the phenomena which are observed.

The central purpose of this book is to examine the procedures of data analysis and to explain introductory-level statistical techniques. In some texts these are referred to as 'elementary' or 'basic' statistics, but these terms might imply that the techniques are simplistic. The term 'introductory', however, signifies two things: first, that the techniques are a point of entry into the realms of statistical analysis, which also has more complicated components; and second, that the principles established by the techniques are directly relevant to these more complex forms of statistical analysis.

Most statistics texts cover a similar range of techniques, but treat each one as a separate, independent procedure. The structure of this book is different. It allows the reader to see how the analysis of four sets of data progresses, and it demonstrates the circumstances in which different types of statistical technique need to be selected. These objectives are achieved by using a series of four exemplar projects in order to explain the use of statistical techniques in geographical data analysis; to demonstrate the link between the acquisition of geographical knowledge and the scientific method of investigation; and to examine the different stages in an investigation of human or physical geographic phenomena. Where appropriate, the chapters share a common structure: the broad issues are discussed; relevant statistical and analytical concepts are explained; these concepts are applied to each of the projects; and brief comparisons and contrasts between the projects are summarised. The aim of this structure is to distinguish between the general principles of the various statistical techniques and the analytical progress made with respect to each project.

The progression through the different stages of a research project is reflected in the sequence of the chapters, which proceed from the initial formulation of a research question or hypothesis that needs to be investigated (Chapter 2), through sampling and data collection (3) and input of data on to a computer (4). The chapters in Part II examine descriptive statistical analysis, including measures of central tendency and dispersion (5), frequency distributions (6) and cross-tabulations (7). Part III begins with two chapters introducing hypothesis testing (8) and the role of probability and randomness (9). The following two chapters concentrate on inferential statistical tests for single samples (10) and for two or more samples (11). Part IV covers analysis of relationships (correlation) in Chapter 12 and of causation (simple linear regression) in Chapter 13. The geographical topic of spatial statistics appears in Chapter 14, while the final chapter considers the limitations of introductory statistical techniques and briefly reviews more complex procedures.

Chapter 2
The nature of geographical data

2.1 CHARACTERISTICS OF GEOGRAPHICAL DATA

Disagreements may exist about the purpose, nature and subject-matter of geography as an academic discipline, but there is some consensus that its main focus is on the description of phenomena occurring at the earth's surface. There is also some degree of agreement that it is concerned with analysing the integration and interaction of these phenomena. Such an all-embracing definition, while perhaps intuitively pleasing, does have some practical drawbacks. It suggests that the subject-matter with which geographical investigation is concerned is everywhere. However, many geographers are no longer interested in all phenomena in a particular place, but focus on the spatial and distributional aspects of certain classes of phenomena. The transport geographer may claim to have the principal interest in any investigation of the effects of the Channel Tunnel between Britain and France. However, there are other, no doubt equally important, aspects of the Channel Tunnel that are of interest to political, population, social and environmental geographers.

This change of emphasis does not avoid the question of how to define the geographical individual or basic unit of enquiry. In the 1930s, the debate centred on the most appropriate way of defining a region. Now that the discipline is more fragmented, with the establishment of new disciplines such as biogeography, political geography, geomorphology and population geography, the problem, far from disappearing, has been multiplied many times. Is the unit of geographical analysis, for example in the case of agricultural geography, the field, the farm, the farmer, the type of farm, the agricultural region, the 'national farm' or some non-spatial entity? The answer is of course that they can all constitute legitimate subjects for geographical study provided that the analysis does not confuse the different individuals.

Another complicating factor is that very often the units of geographical analysis need to be defined not only in spatial but also in temporal terms. The current interest in global climatic change provides a salutary lesson in this respect. A basic, simplified hypothesis is that decreases in the size of glaciers may provide some indication of whether the temperature of the earth is increasing. In order to investigate this subject, it is not sufficient to refer to the extent of glaciation at different latitudes at a single point in time. It is also necessary to consider the historical aspects at several locations, so that any apparent short-term trends can be placed in the context of longer-term fluctuations, which may be entirely natural in origin. So geography is not just concerned with the contemporary distribution of phenomena, but also seeks to understand how these change over time. The temporal and spatial location of phenomena give the investigator an initial starting point for analysis and interpretation. Such spatial and temporal references, however, are not merely signposts, but carry with them certain assumptions and implicit information about the subject-matter under investigation.

Two potentially useful ways of establishing a framework for classifying geographical data relate to whether data are obtained from primary or secondary sources; and the nature of the spatial or locational information in datasets. The two classification schemes overlap and any individual geographical dataset can be categorised according to the two dimensions. A hybrid situation also exists in which simulated data are generated from a model. Such a model usually needs to be calibrated against real data in order to produce predictive results. Research projects may use a combination of various data types and sources to achieve their objectives. So it is important to be aware of the advantages and disadvantages of each.

2.1.1 Primary and secondary sources

The main basis for distinguishing between primary and secondary sources refers the relationship between the original data collector and the purpose for which they are now to be used. A primary source involves data collection at first hand by the researcher or research team. Such data may be obtained in various ways, for example by means of questionnaire survey, by measurement and recording of phenomena in the field with various types of instrumentation, by laboratory experimentation or simply by observation. Data from secondary sources will also have been collected by these various methods, but this was undertaken by another individual or organisation and then also possibly held in an archival form by a third party. Archives and central repositories of machine-readable data have become increasingly important sources for research data as the information technology revolution has progressed in recent years (Tannenbaum 1980; Hakim 1982; and Dale et al. 1988). As far as data for geographical investigations are concerned, information in other forms is also significant. These include maps, statistical abstracts, administrative records, literary and artistic documents.

The distinction between primary and secondary sources of data is important because of the extent of control which the investigator has over exactly what information is collected and how it is organised. This point has a number of repercussions. When the researchers have control over data collection a closer correspondence between the theoretical and practical definitions of concepts may be achieved. For example, the researcher may wish to define an individual as unemployed when that person is not in or seeking paid work, whereas in a secondary data source the condition of unemployment may be defined as being in receipt of state income support. The second point concerns precisely how a specific item of information is measured: for example, whether distance is recorded in 'raw' imperial or metric units, or in some grouped fashion (e.g. 0–4.9 km, 5.0–9.9 km, etc.). The third point is connected with the spatial or geographical units to which the data relate. The climatologist may wish to have a denser network of weather recording stations than actually exists in the field. An economic geographer may want to find out about people's spending patterns on a local government district basis but can only obtain regional level information. Finally, secondary sources of data may not hold the required information in the most accessible form from the researcher's point of view. For example, land-use data may be recorded on a series of printed map sheets, which makes the extraction of data for an area lying across the boundary of a number of map sheets difficult.

Primary data collection also has its problems. One particular difficulty is knowing how much reliance to place in the data. No matter how carefully the various measuring devices are set up, there always remains a chance that some or even all of the raw data will contain errors of measurement. There is also the problem of deciding how much information to collect. There appear to be two extreme strategies that the researcher could adopt: collect the minimum data necessary to obtain a reliable set of results, or obtain the maximum possible to ensure that all phenomena were observed. In practice, a middle-of-the-road path is usually taken. Another problem is that primary data collection is expensive. The typical market research company in Britain in 1994 would expect to charge a client upwards of £35.00 per interview. This figure provides a useful guide price for the real cost of surveys conducted by academic researchers. The cost of primary data collection in physical geography is more difficult to estimate, because of the wide variation in the cost of different items of equipment. Nevertheless, it is generally reasonable to assume that the costs are likely to be comparable with, if not higher than, those in human geography applications per unit of information.

Haggett (1965) suggested that about 95 per cent of articles published in human geography between 1960 and 1965 had used secondary sources of data. Shaw and Wheeler (1985) considered that in physical geography the balance between primary and secondary sources was probably the reverse. In physical geography there tends to be much more emphasis on measurement and observation in the field. However, the increased use of questionnaires and other forms of socio-economic survey technique has now probably increased the use of primary data in human geography to around 60 per cent. The data used in the exemplar projects (see Section 2.3) reflect the range of sources used in contemporary geographical research.

2.1.2 Spatial and locational references in geographical data

The emphasis placed on the spatial or locational component of geographical data has waxed and waned in the history of the discipline. Nevertheless, relatively little geographical research is carried out without some reference either to the spatial form of the phenomena or to the place to which they relate. 'Spatial form' refers to their geometrical characteristics, such as size and shape, as well as to their juxtaposition and relationship to each other. The basic geometrical units are points, lines, areas and surfaces. Most data used in geographical research relate either explicitly or implicitly to one of these units. Many of the datasets used in human geography, for example, relate to some areal feature, such as housing estates, industrial parks or administrative units; to linear features, such as transport routes; or to point features, such as factories, retail outlets or properties. A similar diversity is to be found in physical geography, where areal features include lakes and mountain ranges, linear features are exemplified by rivers and coastlines, and point features by soil or water sample sites.

An interest in where phenomena occur is a distinctive feature of geographical investigations, even when the data relate to some non-spatial entity. Datasets concerning households or people, either as individuals or groups, usually include some form of locational coding. Different types of locational referencing system can be identified in the array of datasets used in geography. In some cases a system of grid coordinates may be used, whereas in others a more basic label or name list may be all that is employed (e.g. postal code). Chapter 14 examines in more detail some of the analytic techniques that have been developed for examining the spatial component of geographical phenomena.

2.2 SCALES OF MEASUREMENT

The researcher's problems are far from over even when the individual unit of study has been identified, since there remains the question of exactly what aspects of the entities should be studied. Data items divide into two categories — *attributes* and *variables* — although to confuse the issue these terms are sometimes used interchangeably. A clear statement of the distinction between these categories defines an attribute as 'a quality . . . whereby items, individuals, objects, locations, events, etc. differ one from another' (Williams 1984, p. 4). Examples from geography include categories of land use, housing tenure, industry, employment status, soil type, climatic zone and vegetation cover. Variables, on the other hand, 'are *measured* ... they are assigned numerical values relative to some standard — the *unit of measurement*' (Williams 1984, p. 5, original emphasis). A variable is a quantity which enables individual phenomena to be measured one against another. Many variables are used in geography, including altitude, concentration of chemicals in water, population size, land value, distance and particle size.

The division of data about phenomena into attributes and variables leads to the associated question of the scales of measurement. Four scales of measurement are usually defined in ascending order of sophistication, namely *nominal, ordinal, interval* and *ratio* (Table 2.1). The first, being exclusively associated with attributes as opposed to variables, does not signify a variation in magnitude between entities but simply a qualitative difference. It is therefore strictly speaking not a scale of *measurement.* The ordinal scale ranks one entity against another with respect to a particular characteristic. This type of measurement is more common than might at first be imagined and is often useful where the researcher is dependent on secondary data. For example, some doubt is often cast on the reliability and accuracy of population counts derived from the censuses of some developing countries. It may therefore be sensible to rank countries in order of their population totals rather than treating the published figures as entirely accurate. The essence of an ordinal variable is that the individual observations are placed into ascending or descending order so that one observation has a higher or lower rank position than another.

Interval and ratio variables are often treated in the same way as far as analytic procedures are concerned, although there is an important distinction between them. The issue refers to whether the variables' units of measurement have an arbitrary or absolute zero. A common geographical variable measured on the interval scale is temperature. Here the typical unit of measurement is degrees Celsius, in which 0°C does not denote the coldest temperature that could be recorded, but is an arbitrary point on the scale, chosen simply because this happens to be the temperature at which water freezes under normal conditions. Two midday temperature measurements of 12°C and 18°C do not signify that the second day was a third as hot again as the first, it simply says that it was 6°C hotter. Many geographical variables are measured on

Table 2.1 Scales of measurement

Scale	Example	
Nominal	Housing tenure	Owner occupier, local authority tenant, privately rented, other
	Major soil types	Zonal soils, intrazonal soils, azonal soils
Ordinal	Settlement size	Village, market town, town, city, metropolitan centre
	Slope	Shallow, moderate, steep, very steep
Interval	Altitude in relation to mean sea level	−50 m, 10 m, 150 m, 2103 m, etc.
Ratio	Public expenditure	£205 621.07, £10 891 223.00, £767 809.50, etc
	River discharge in cumecs	0.54, 5.45, 9.8, 25.9, etc.

the ratio scale and therefore have an absolute zero. When measuring the discharge of a river, the unit of measurement is usually cubic metres per second (cumecs). In this case a reading of zero is not arbitrary but absolute, since it implies that the river has dried up and the flow of water has ceased. Measurements from two rivers of 10 and 20 cumecs indicate that the flow in the second case is not only 10 cumecs greater, but also twice that of the first. If the flow was to be recorded using a different unit of measurement, for example cubic feet per second, the ratio of the two values would be the same. One cubic metre equals approximately 35.31 cubic feet, so the two discharge measurements would be 353.1 and 706.2 cubic feet per second: the second value is again twice the first.

The order in which these measurement scales have been described is said to be in order of increasing sophistication because an item of information measured on the ratio scale can be converted into a less specific measurement. The reverse, however, is not possible. For example, suppose that a town has 15 petrol stations and the distance of each from a central point is measured in metres. The following set of values, shown to 1 decimal place, is obtained:

112.7, 40.6, 678.3, 15.8, 112.7, 554.9, 67.7, 889.5, 1006.5, 445.1, 112.7, 32.7, 654.5, 1322.7, 98.4

The variable, distance from the town centre, is measured on the ratio scale, since there is an absolute zero. However, distance can be converted to the ordinal scale by sorting the 15 values into either ascending or descending order. Each of the values is then assigned a rank number according to its position in the sequence. Table 2.2 shows the results of ranking the values for the petrol stations labelled A to O in ascending order.

Table 2.2 Conversion of information between measurement scales

Petrol station	Distance from town centre (m)	Ranked distance	Rank position	Nominal value*
A	112.7	15.8	1	1
B	40.6	32.7	2	1
C	678.3	40.6	3	2
D	15.8	67.7	4	1
E	112.7	98.4	5	1
F	554.9	112.7	7	2
G	67.7	112.7	7	1
H	889.5	112.7	7	2
I	1006.5	445.1	9	2
J	445.1	554.9	10	1
K	112.7	654.5	11	1
L	32.7	678.3	12	1
M	654.5	889.5	13	2
N	1322.7	1006.5	14	2
O	98.4	1322.7	15	1

*Nominal value 1 denotes 'near to centre' and 2 'far from centre'

In this example, despite measuring distance accurately to the nearest tenth of a metre, there were three petrol stations exactly the same distance from the town's central point. These were assigned the rank value 7 and the next nearest petrol station was given the value 9 because there were 8 which were nearer to the centre. Ranking the observations in this way has resulted in some information about the distance of the petrol stations from the town centre being thrown away. At the end of the exercise it is only possible to say that one petrol station is closer to the centre than another. It is not possible to say how much nearer it is either in terms of metres or as a ratio, nor whether there are any particular distances from the centre at which petrol stations tend to occur.

The next stage in collapsing distance to the simpler nominal measurement scale, also shown in Table 2.2, results in the loss of even more information about the distance of the petrol stations from the town centre. Suppose that it is only necessary to say that a petrol station is 'near to' or 'far from' the centre, with an arbitrary value of 500 m taken to define the boundary between the two categories. If this cut-off point is applied, then the petrol stations A, B, D, E, G, J, K, L and O would be defined as 'near' and C, F, H, I, M and N as 'far'. This last stage in the process has reduced the information about distance of petrol stations from the town's central point to two nominal categories. In other words, the variable has been transformed into an attribute.

The differences between the scales of measurement become important when deciding which statistical test and type of analysis to carry out. For the present, it should be noted that some types of analysis should only be used with certain types of variable or attribute. One of the basic distinctions between statistical tests is whether they require that the observations are measured on a scale where values can only occur at certain points or can take on any value along the scale. The distinction here is between *discrete* and *continuous* units of measurement, and parallels the difference between nominal and ordinal, and interval or ratio scales.

2.3 INTRODUCTION TO THE EXEMPLAR PROJECTS

Geography is a wide-ranging discipline covering many substantive areas. The four exemplar projects reflect the breadth of contemporary geographical research. Some simplification of the thematic issues represented by the projects has been necessary, nevertheless sufficient remains for them to be regarded as demonstrating some of the current themes. Four criteria were combined to select the projects. The collection of projects as a whole had to be capable of illustrating the range of introductory statistical techniques. The projects needed to exemplify relevant and contemporary issues across a range of research areas in human and physical geography. They were chosen so that both primary and secondary sources of geographical data were included. Lastly, the projects show different research objectives, including theoretical, empirical and applied questions. This section outlines the projects and the research questions which they address in the light of these criteria.

2.3.1 Land-use change

Land use has been an important theme in geographical research for many years, indeed the determination of how land is used in different places is often fundamental to understanding socio-economic patterns and processes. In the 20th century two major investigations into land use have been carried out in Britain, known as the First and Second Land Utilisation Surveys. The former was undertaken in the 1930s (Stamp 1948) and the second in the 1960s (Coleman 1961; 1978; Coleman and Maggs 1964). The results of the surveys were published as maps and statistical commentaries, which have been used, together with other information sources such as the 1950s county development plans, to examine land-use change (Best and Coppock 1962; Best 1981; Mather 1986). Contemporary data may sometimes be obtained from a local authority planning department.

Despite this earlier research, a number of important questions continue to attract the attention of geographers and planners. These typically relate to the rate and spatial extent of land-use change. The land-use project is concerned with answering the following questions:

- Which land uses have increased and which have decreased, and by how much?
- Has the amount of land-use change been greater in rural or urban fringe areas?

These are essentially empirical questions, which are concerned with establishing the characteristics and patterns of land-use change. The answers to these questions produced by the statistical analysis will not *explain* land-use change, but will attempt to establish what has happened. The first task in the project is to decide on the catcgories of land use that will be considered and the time period over which changes will be measured. It is also necessary to decide how to define rural-urban fringe areas.

The project demonstrates the use of secondary sources of data, in this case the maps produced from the two Land Utilisation Surveys, which predefine the time period over which land-use change will be measured. The second constraint imposed by the use of secondary sources is that the categories of land use available cannot be amended by the investigator. In the First Land Utilisation Survey seven categories of land use were recorded in the field and published on 1:63 360 scale Ordnance Survey maps. In the second survey a larger number of land-use categories were identified: 13 major land uses and 64 divisions. The existence of such constraints limits the scope, but does not invalidate the investigation.

Various approaches have been used to distinguish between urban and rural areas (Walford and Hockey 1991). In this project a relatively unsophisticated division is employed, which involves drawing the boundary on the basis of distance from the edge of a continuous built-up area with over 50 000 population. The urban-rural fringe area is defined as up to 5 km from the edge of the built-up area, while the rural area lies beyond the 5 km boundary. Rural-urban fringe areas are often subject to considerable development pressure and the amount of land-use change is likely to be greater than in more rural locations. An initial hypothesis could be set up to reflect this proposition which might take the following form:

> The greater pressure for development in rural-urban fringe areas is demonstrated by more rapid rates of land-use change.

More specific questions and statistical hypotheses will be examined in later chapters to illustrate how such an initial hypothesis can be investigated.

2.3.2 Chalk weathering

Geomorphologists have long been interested in the processes of erosion that bring about change in landforms and the earth's surface. The effect of such processes on limestone, and in particular on chalk landscapes in coastal and inland locations, is of considerable importance. The second project concentrates on how processes of weathering affect chalk, which has been investigated by a number of researchers in the field and in the laboratory (Potts 1970; Gerrard 1988).

One of the issues which has caused some controversy is the role played by the freezing and thawing of water in the weathering of chalk. Field observation suggests that the shattering of the chalk bedrock and the formation of debris piles occurs when exposed outcrops are subject to such temperature changes. Such chalk exposures occur on coastal cliff faces, quarries or when the bedrock is cut through for construction purposes (Figure 2.1). With such field observation as a background, the chalk weathering project is concerned with the following questions:

- What is the effect of water in freeze–thaw action on chalk?
- Does salinity of the water influence its effect on the process?

Although these are empirical questions, there is a clear sense in which they are related to some underlying theory. For example, there is the implicit assumption that freeze–thaw action contributes to the weathering process, since the frozen water may be expected to exert pressure on the rock structure and cause it to shatter. The project attempts to *explain* the effect of one variable on another and to understand limited aspects of the freeze–thaw weathering process.

These are complex questions and for the purposes of the project they are simplified and investigated by means of laboratory experimentation. This approach is frequently used in physical geography and

Figure 2.1 Apparent effect of frost action on chalk exposures (Photograph: N. Walford)

may involve setting up a number of contrasting treatments to reproduce different situations that are hypothesised to occur in the 'real world'. In this project, a structured set of experimental treatments, representing different temperature regimes, is carried out on regular blocks of pure homogeneous chalk, rather than on material collected in the field. Impurities in chalk collected in the field might have influenced the experiments. The treatments are designed to elicit information about the effect of exposing chalk alternately to temperatures above or below freezing point, in the presence of pure or saline water. The water-treated blocks are soaked for 7 days and then dried to remove any surface moisture prior to commencing a freeze–thaw cycle. The latter involves freezing the block at -5°C for 12 hours and then allowing it to thaw at +5°C for 12 hours. This freeze–thaw cycle is repeated for 14 days. The effect of the presence of water is assessed by keeping some chalk blocks constantly at these temperatures for 14 days. In all cases the blocks are placed in open-topped plastic containers so that debris can be collected. Each block is removed from its container and weighed once every 24 hours.

The project attempts to examine the contrasting changes in weight produced by the different treatments. Table 2.3 summarises the experimental design of the project which shows a total of nine different treatments being applied to the chalk blocks. Each treatment is applied to 12 blocks. One important feature of the experimental approach to research is the possibility of including one or more controls. In this case, the control treatments are for unsaturated blocks or for those kept at a constant temperature of +5°C. The experimental design in this project has been kept relatively simple, but various permutations could have been added to complicate the project further: by varying the salinity of the water, by including a third category of acidic water, by having different freeze–thaw regimes, by keeping blocks in the water either in a frozen or liquid state, and so on. A preliminary hypothesis for the project is the following:

Chalk which has been saturated with water and which is then exposed to alternate freezing and thawing, has a greater propensity to weather or erode than dry chalk which is exposed to the changing temperature regime.

Table 2.3 Chalk weathering project: experimental design

	Water present		Water absent
	Pure	Saline	
Diurnal freeze–thaw	12 blocks (1)	12 blocks (2)	12 blocks (3)
Constant −5°C	12 blocks (4)	12 blocks (5)	12 blocks (6)
Constant +5°C	12 blocks (7)	12 blocks (8)	12 blocks (9)

Note: numbers in parentheses refer to treatment type

2.3.3 River pollution

The pollution of the environment by different means has become an increasingly important topic over the last 20–30 years. Such pollution can occur in various ways, and the consequences are believed to affect human beings and the environment they live in. For example, the clustering of certain types of cancer around nuclear installations and the safety and disposal of nuclear waste have attracted some attention from geographers (Openshaw et al. 1989). Some pollutants are deliberately dumped into the environment, whereas others are transferred inadvertently. Some pollutants emerge from so-called point sources, such as factories, while others arise from a number of distributed sources, such as from the spreading of agricultural chemicals. The extent to which the pollutant becomes distributed through the environment or remains close to its source is another important issue.

Recent legislation in Britain, for example the 1990 Environmental Protection Act has attempted to limit environmental pollution. One of the main means of achieving this has involved setting maximum tolerable levels of different chemicals and organisms. The European Commission has also been involved with setting such levels with respect to water quality and the 1990 legislation was intended to contribute to the achievement of the levels in the United Kingdom. The river pollution project focuses on one small part of the overall environmental problem and relates to whether discharges into rivers from factories cause adverse changes to their chemical composition, and thus to their water quality. The project has two initial questions:

- Does pollution-control legislation help to improve the quality of water in rivers?
- To what extent does waste discharged from chemical factories increase chemical concentrations in rivers?

The project exemplifies applied research in physical geography. The first question attempts to monitor changes in the quality of freshwater in Britain's rivers. The second is mainly concerned with finding out whether factories can be blamed for pollution of rivers.

The project combines data from a secondary source, represented by a national river quality survey, with a primary source, namely water taken from rivers in the field for laboratory analysis. The quality of water in rivers has been described in England and Wales by means of government surveys, which have been carried out at five-year intervals over the last 20 years (in 1970, 1975, 1980 and 1985) and from which maps have been produced. The 1985 survey classified rivers into five categories and, since the North West Water Authority region had rivers in all of the classes, this provides a suitable area for locating the study. The problems of using data from a secondary source have already been examined. However, in the river pollution project there is the additional difficulty of trying to match such data with information collected in the field. The water taken from the rivers will be analysed in the laboratory in order to determine the concentration of selected chemicals which were used to classify rivers in the 1985 national survey and other pollutants which gave cause for concern. The aim is to link together the analytical results from the project with the official survey. The second part of the project concentrates on whether industrial plants can be blamed for increasing pollutant chemical levels. The second question is addressed by carrying out separate laboratory analyses on water taken from sites upstream and downstream of the factories discharging chemical waste.

2.3.4 Village communities

The classic study of conflict between indigenous residents and newcomers in rural settlements was published in the 1960s (Pahl 1965). The potential for such conflict has possibly increased as a result of the trend for the population of rural areas in developed countries to increase. This phenomenon, referred to as *counter-urbanisation* (Fielding 1982) or more recently as *rural repopulation*, has heightened interest in the contrasts between the two residential groups. One outcome of this conflict is the effect newcomers have on the provision of local services and facilities. Often the newcomers have greater wealth and access to private transport, and thus, despite their presence leading to an overall population increase, the decline in village-based facilities and in public transport may continue. In the eyes of the local population, newcomers may be blamed for the deterioration in lifestyle.

Studies in human geography and the social sciences frequently focus on a specific problem or area, such as the conflict between two distinct social groups. However, too many factors are often pertinent for an individual researcher to produce a definitive answer to the problem. The village communities project looks at one example of where newcomers and native residents might hold different attitudes. The example refers to a proposal by a developer to build a small industrial estate on the edge of a village which currently has a population of 8950. The settlement in question has had a high net increase in population over the last 20 years of 1.3 per cent per annum. The following questions are of interest:

- Do the indigenous or newcomer residents express stronger opposition towards the proposed development?
- What differences exist between the two groups in the means used to make their views known to the local planning authority?

The theoretical basis upon which these questions are founded reflects some general notion about group identity and allegiance, the articulateness of different groups in rural society and power relationships between social groups.

The project demonstrates the use of a primary source of data in human geography, namely the collection of data by means of a personal interview questionnaire survey. This is an important means of obtaining information concerning social, economic, demographic and related types of variable or attribute, and is widely used in geography and other disciplines. There are a number of issues to be considered when designing such a survey, which have been considered in various textbooks (see, for example, Shaw and Wheeler 1985; Barnett 1991). Four of the key considerations are highlighted here. Such surveys can be made of various types of entity including individuals, households, companies, farms, shops and local authorities. The questionnaire should elicit the required information in an efficient, but none the less sympathetic fashion with regard to the respondent. The means of asking the questions has to be considered: some surveys entail a face-to-face interview with the respondent, in others the questionnaire is delivered by post for self-completion by the respondent, and in yet others telephone interviews are carried out. Lastly, different types of question can be included, for example factual, attitudinal and verbatim response. Careful consideration of these four points is needed in the design stage of a questionnaire.

The subjects in the village communities project questionnaire are adults living in the settlement and the questions relate to the respondent and to his or her household. A face-to-face interview tends to produce more reliable answers and cuts down on the possibility of questions being misinterpreted by the respondent. Personal interviews of this type are usually more time-consuming, but can allow probing questions to be asked. One problem with the interview survey as a means for collecting data is that, if different interviewers are used, they should be thoroughly briefed so that questions are asked in a consistent fashion. The questionnaire in the village communities project is reproduced in Appendix I and includes relatively straightforward factual and attitudinal questions.

Table 2.4 Comparison of exemplar projects

	Land-use change	Chalk weathering	River pollution	Village communities
Data source	Secondary	Primary	Primary/ secondary	Primary
Main scales of measurement	Nominal/ interval/ ratio	Interval/ ratio	Ordinal/ interval/ ratio	Nominal/ ordinal
Purpose	Empirical	Theoretical	Applied	Theoretical
Geography	Human	Physical	Human/ physical	Human

Table 2.5 Scales of measurement of selected attributes/variables in exemplar projects

Scale of measurement	Land-use change	Chalk weathering	River pollution	Village communities
Nominal	Land-use category	Type of treatment	River quality indicator	Residential status
	Location category			Attitude to development
				Income in bands
Ordinal	Ranked land-use change	-	Change river quality	Distance from development
Interval	-	Temperature	-	-
Ratio	Area of land use	Weight of block	Dissolved oxygen	Length of residence

2.4 COMPARISON OF THE PROJECTS

The descriptions of the four projects show how they illustrate different aspects of the analysis of geographical data. Such contrasts relate to the use of different scales of measurement, human and physical geography, primary and secondary sources of data, and research objectives. Table 2.4 summarises the projects in terms of these contrasts. Clearly there could be some debate about the box that a particular project fits into, nevertheless the classification indicates the general focus of the project with respect to the four selection criteria. Table 2.5 gives selected details of some of the variables and attributes in each project and illustrates the different scales of measurement. It is clear that research projects in human and physical geography can include attributes and variables across the range of measurement scales. In addition to information which is obtained directly from the primary or secondary source, it is often the case that additional attributes and variables are calculated from these. The new variables may be as simple as percentages or ratios, such as persons per household, or more complex composite indicators or rank scores.

Chapter 3
Data collection: populations and samples

3.1 POPULATIONS AND SAMPLES

The previous chapter was essentially concerned with deciding what types of information to collect and how to measure different attributes and variables. The next question in designing and planning a project concerns how much information should be collected. The initial answer to this question might be to obtain as much information as possible. For example, in a project investigating how people in Bristol spend their leisure time, this approach would involve asking *all* members of *every* household about what they do when they are not sleeping, eating or at work.

Such complete counts or censuses are indeed carried out in certain circumstances, where it is essential to obtain information on 100 per cent of the observations or entities. Most countries undertake a census of population on a periodic basis, usually every 10 years, in order to produce a complete count of all members of the national population. In many countries, an agricultural census collects information on areas of crops, numbers of livestock and workers, and other agricultural variables on all farms in a country. These complete counts are expensive undertakings and so cannot be repeated frequently. The 1981 population census in the Great Britain is estimated to have cost £55 million and the 1991 census some £130 million. One important reason for carrying out a census is to provide a bench-mark or reference point against which other smaller surveys can be compared.

In statistical terms such complete counts provide information on the *population* of observations in question. The term 'population' is used regardless of whether the observations or entities in question are soil cores, road junctions, river meanders, business parks, peat bogs, settlements or any other class of phenomena which are investigated by geographers and other researchers. The results produced from the examination of statistical populations are in principle irrefutable assuming that all measurements have been made correctly, no calculation errors are present and that no under- or overcounting is detected.

If the population of hired farm workers in a country is 120 000 and a census reports that 90 000 of the total work 46 or more hours per week, then for the date and country in question this statement is not subject to question or debate. Anyone who said that the number was 90 001, 678, 111 402 or indeed any value other than 90 000 would be incorrect.

In practice, even complete counts of populations may be accurate for only a limited period of time and can be subject to some error. For example, the census of population in some countries makes its count of people according to their usual residential address on a given night; inevitably some people will not be enumerated at all, perhaps because they do not have a usual place of residence and are 'sleeping rough', or because they wilfully refuse to fill in the census questionnaire. The 1991 census of population in the United Kingdom had an estimated under-enumeration of some 1 million people. Statistical populations should be defined very carefully in terms of space and time as well as the common characteristics of the class of entities being enumerated. The statistical use of the term 'population' should not be confused with its more common use with respect to human, animal or plant populations, although in some investigations these are of course one and the same.

There are four main reasons why it may not be sensible or feasible to collect information on all members of a statistical population. The cost and time involved may exceed the data collection element of the budget for a project. For instance, anyone wishing to send a postal questionnaire with a prepaid return envelope to the population of 48 968 555 individuals present on census night in England and Wales (21–22 April 1991) would incur postal costs of £18 608 050.90 at second class postage rates (£0.19) for the outward and return postage. This scenario also raises the question of quantity versus quality in the collection of information. Postal questionnaires should be designed so that questions are unambiguous, easy to complete and relatively few in number. If these simple rules are ignored, the number of satisfactorily completed and returned questionnaires — the response rate — is liable to be low.

The complete set of observations in a population may not be available, which is a problem that arises in historical research. A researcher interested in medieval settlements relies on being able to locate those which have survived the last 600 years. The settlements which have been found do not comprise the population of medieval settlements, they are simply the ones which have been discovered. They form what is known as the *available* or *accessible population* as distinct from the *target population*. The available population is not a finite quantity in this example, since it could increase in size as additional medieval settlements are identified. A similar problem can occur in physical geography. For example, glaciologists might wish to examine englacial debris, but by definition such material is encased within a glacier. The material may be visible at the snout of the glacier, within crevasses and perhaps also along the margins, or may be examined when it melts out from the glacier. However, information about the centre can really only be obtained by means of cores, which are fairly easy to extract when the surface is accessible, but more difficult when it is steep or deeply crevassed.

In some circumstances a population of observations may in principle be available, but is infinite in number. By definition, it is therefore not possible to collect information about all of its members. There are an infinite number of points across a region's surface where soil cores could be taken, or of times in a week, day, hour, minute or second when the passengers using a transport system could be recorded. No matter how great the financial resources of the project the complete population cannot be measured in these circumstances.

Finally, the act of collecting information about the observations in a population in some situations may degrade the quality of the material obtained. The longer and more complex a questionnaire, the greater is the likelihood that the quality of responses will deteriorate during the questioning or that some people will be deterred from answering at the start. In deserts, wind action alters the profile and shape of sand dunes, and changes their position relative to each other. A researcher interested in this process might wish to map precisely their form and location over a period of time. Unfortunately, when climbing over the dunes in order to carry out the project and to take the necessary surveying measurements, there is a risk of disturbing the very phenomena that are of interest. Aerial photography could help to overcome the problem in this example, but it might not provide sufficient small-scale detail.

The first response to these apparently insuperable problems might be to abandon the research project. However, there is an alternative to such a defeatist reaction: information can be collected for a subset of the observations in the statistical population. Such a subset is known as *sample*. Provided a sample is chosen with care and thoughtful planning, its members can yield information which is just as useful as if the whole population had be measured, but at a fraction of the cost, time and effort.

3.2 SELECTING A SAMPLE

3.2.1 General issues

A sample is therefore a subset of the entities or observations in the population and is intended to be *representative* of that population. The concept of representativeness is an important one; it is not attained in equal measure by all types of sampling. A sample of entities should faithfully reproduce the statistical results that would be obtained if it was sensible or feasible to carry out the investigation on all members of the population. Such a sample is described as representative of its parent population. The problem is that we do not know which observations would faithfully and precisely reproduce the characteristics of the parent population, and if we did there would be no need to carry out the investigation.

The relationship between samples and their parent populations underpins one basic group of analytical techniques known as *inferential statistics*. When a *statistic*, such as the proportion of the observations in a sample possessing a given characteristic, is calculated, the figure is intended to be an accurate estimate of the corresponding figure in the whole population. The equivalent, actual figure in the population is known as a *parameter*. For example, if a sample survey of households in a town reports that 23 per cent live in privately rented accommodation, the inference is that 23 per cent of *all* households in that town reside under this form of tenure. The distinction between a parameter and a statistic might initially appear pedantic. Statistical analysis is littered with such rules and conventions, which at first seem designed to confuse rather than to clarify the subject. On closer examination the distinction serves a useful purpose. In this case, any reference to a statistic means that the quantity, whether a proportion, percentage, count or other measure, should only be regarded as an estimate of the corresponding value in the population. On the other hand, a parameter, having been derived from all observations in the population, should by definition be correct. Unfortunately, errors of measurement, calculation and data processing for a parameter could still lead to inaccuracy, but it would be possible for another researcher to corroborate the results. The implications of these issues for statistical analysis will be examined in due course. For the present, it is sufficient to note that samples are supposed to be representative of their parent populations.

Two further problems merit consideration in relation to sampling: which sampling method should be used; and how many items the sample should include. A wide variety of methods exist for selecting observations from a population, some of which produce more representative samples than others. So the answer to the question, which type of sampling should be used, might seem obvious: choose the method that gives the most representative results. But how can the investigator know whether a sample is representative or not, when the answer lies trapped in the elusive and inaccessible population. The number of items that should be included in a sample introduces the concept of the *sampling fraction*, which refers to the proportion of the total population included in the sample. Sometimes the precise sampling fraction cannot be computed because the population is infinitely large or has never been measured. Two intuitive responses to the sample size question are: either select the maximum number of observations that time and money will allow; or use the minimum necessary to produce reliable results. Although many people criticise political opinion polls, they have in fact satisfactorily forecast which party would win the general election in the United Kingdom on seven of the last nine occasions. These forecasts have been produced with very carefully structured samples of around 1500 voters, representing a sampling fraction of about 0.004 per cent.

Frustrating as these problems might seem, the most useful advice is to look ahead to how the data are to be analysed. If some form of

Table 3.1 Classification of sampling methods*

Non-probability	Probability
Convenience	Simple random
Judgemental	with replacement
Quota	without replacement
	Stratified random
	Cluster
	Nested
	Systematic

*For explanation see text.

inferential statistical analysis is planned, then a sampling method should be chosen which satisfies the assumptions and requirements of these techniques. Some techniques require minimum numbers of observations or that the sampling fraction is not too high, usually not greater than 10 per cent. The methods of drawing a sample are divided into two categories: non-probability and probability sampling (Table 3.1). The division relates to whether subjective judgement or random chance is the predominant factor when determining whether an observation is included or excluded from the sample.

3.2.2 Types of sample

3.2.2.1 Non-probability sampling techniques

The researcher's subjective judgement influences whether an observation is included or excluded to a varying extent in the three types of non-probability sampling. The basis for selection of individuals in *convenience sampling* is ease of access to members of the population. This type of sampling helps to overcome the problems of a very or infinitely large population, since those observations which are most conveniently measured are included. An accessibility sample is also used when preliminary information about the members of the population is non-existent or only very limited.

A researcher investigating consumer behaviour in a city's shopping centre might select observations (shoppers) for inclusion on a first-come, first-interviewed basis. If the target sample size has been set at 300, then the first 300 people who agree to take part in the survey would constitute the sample. Unfortunately, there is no way of knowing whether the sample is representative of shoppers in the city, either in general or even on the specific days when the survey was carried out. Strictly speaking, it would be misleading to claim that the results said anything significant about the population of shoppers in the city. Suppose the survey reveals that 60 respondents were women, that 45 of these were accompanied by children and that 15 of these (5 per cent of all respondents) had travelled by public transport. The researcher cannot legitimately claim that 5 per cent of the population of shoppers in the city centre were people with this combination of characteristics.

The researcher has no way of knowing how representative the sample is of the whole population. The respondents who agreed to take part in the survey are in effect volunteers and the potential for the sample being unrepresentative and biased is obvious.

The use of convenience or accessibility samples is not confined to human geography. The importance of rivers as a means of transporting weathered rock and for using this material to scour and erode the river bed has been recognised for a long time. An investigator examining this process has decided to measure and identify the size and type of rock debris along the length of a river, and, from the infinite number of points where such measurements could be made, 25 cross-sections are selected. The sites are chosen in the field because there are several stretches of the river where the gradient is steep with fast-flowing water and it would be dangerous, if not impossible, to make the necessary measurements at these locations. The term 'accessibility sample' is here used in the literal sense, as places to which the researcher can gain access.

A second non-probability sampling method, *judgemental sampling*, is frequently used when only minimal information about the parent population is available. Subjective judgement is used to decide which observations will be included in the sample, based on past experience and prior knowledge of the population. Unfortunately, statisticians have shown that people are in fact not very good at making unbiased judgements, which leads to sections of the population being over- or underrepresented. A judgemental sample could be used to examine the effects of modern agricultural practices on the environment. The researchers intend to compare the situation under intensive and extensive farming systems. Published statistical information, for example the Ministry of Agriculture, Fisheries and Food's *Farm Classification in England and Wales* (MAFF annual) reports how many holdings of particular types are found in an area, for example those predominantly involved in growing cereals or with dairying. These farm types do not indicate anything about the relative intensity of the production system in terms of the level of inputs in relation to outputs. The researchers decide to use their judgement of spatial distribution in the agricultural industry to select a sample, in which they believe intensive and extensive cereal and dairy farms are present in the correct proportions to the total population. Unfortunately, it is not possible to corroborate their judgement.

Quota sampling is essentially a combination of accessibility and judgemental sampling, and its critics claim that it suffers from the disadvantages of both systems. The starting point for selecting a quota sample is to decide on the total number of observations needed for the sample and to identify discrete groups within the population. Such groups may contain either equal or different numbers of individuals in the sample, which define their quota of observations. Equality of quota size is the result of dividing the total sample size by the number of groups. Unequal quotas are usually the result of the researcher judging the relative proportions or numbers of individuals in the different categories within the population or because certain categories of observation are required to be overrepresented in the sample. In each case, having decided on the quota of observations for each group, the researcher then sets about filling these quotas with eligible observations from the accessible members of the population.

Quota sampling can be applied in the same situations as accessibility and judgemental sampling. Suppose the investigator looking at consumer behaviour in a city centre has decided that five categories of shopper are to be equally represented in the sample — pensioners, mothers with children, children, lone working-age adults and family groups. So rather than selecting the first 300 people who agree to take part in the survey, the researcher chooses the first 60 people for each category, thus fulfilling the quota or target. If there was some prior reason for using unequal quotas, perhaps because one or two of the categories are of especial interest, then adjustments can be made to the size of the quotas. For example, suppose that pensioners and family groups are to be overrepresented, then the quotas for these groups might be increased to 90 observations, leaving the other groups with 40 individuals each.

3.2.2.2 Probability sampling techniques

The distinctive feature of sampling techniques based on probability is that an element of chance exists as to whether a particular observation is included in a sample. At first sight it might seem rather perverse to introduce chance into the selection of a representative sample of observations. Surely this would mean that any individual in the population could be selected and that the investigator has no control over which are included. Indeed, this is precisely the reason why it is sensible to use probability sampling, since this minimises the *bias* introduced into the sample by the researcher. The great value of probabilistic sampling is that each and every member of the population has an equal chance of being included. So there is no risk of an item being excluded because it was not accessible or available, or because it was judged atypical by the researcher. Subjective judgement on the part of the investigator remains to a varying extent in the various probabilistic techniques, but the presence of the chance element at some stage helps to make such samples more useful.

The most useful of the probability sampling techniques is known as *simple random sampling*. This type of sample is well suited to situations where the population size is known, since the method depends upon being able to specify a *sampling frame* or *framework*, in which each member of the population is identified and assigned a unique reference number. For example, a directory of companies or the electoral register could be used as the sampling frame. The traditional method of selecting observations for a simple random sample uses a

Figure 3.1 Random number table

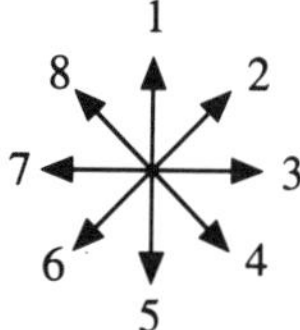

2264510204691841157322673
9145723564405001456442944
4797535840409609199986178
0515094994770646348596949
4385856721548722572657902
6856684648189730232002215
6089486312506523411920103
5687736626896579939216408
5409820518965593005167805
0495007821267287645714755
3889144304612407071384104
6819810962538339439636275
8962514105946930945815734
4474417410517393293067020
8346579065387045694927796
3916667698627035534447777
9341230841468474388082297
5605590155529871995373581
5431742640034676376576864
0251057922113435234816586
0869682671809230890843329
8968319187483511955121587
1622407440737841721843902 Starting digit **2**
4833949850037032289804018
9395011624273451332828820

Direction of movement

If the starting number is 0 or 9, or it is at the edge of the table, then reselection is necessary.

table of random numbers (see Appendix II). Such tables have been compiled so that there is no regularity or pattern in the sequence of digits. Without looking at the table, the researcher uses a pin, pen, pencil or similar object to determine a random 'point of entry' to the table. By moving through the rows, columns and diagonals of the table combinations of successive digits, either individually or in groups as large as necessary, are read off, which correspond the identification numbers of the observations to form the sample. This continues until the required number of observations have been selected. The procedure, although relatively simple, does cause confusion sometimes: it is illustrated in Figure 3.1 with a small section of a random number table. Each possible direction has been assigned a unique code, horizontal right is 3, horizontal left 7, diagonal up left 8, and so on. The single-digit value occurring at the point of entry (the bold number 2) informs the researcher in which direction to proceed through the table. In this case 2 corresponds to moving diagonally up right. Suppose there are 65 observations required for the sample, so groups of random two digit numbers are obtained. Here the numbers 23, 65 and 16 correspond to the identification numbers of the first three observations that should be included in the sample. The second group of digits encountered when moving diagonally up right was 87, which is ignored because it lies outside the range of identification numbers.

An alternative to random number tables is now widely available as a means of generating a set of numbers. Statistical software (e.g. MINITAB and SPSS-X) usually has a function which can produce a set of random numbers. In the case of MINITAB, the command sequence:

```
MTB > RANDOM 450 C1;
SUBC > INTEGER 1 6584.
```

would select 450 random numbers between 0001 and 6584 and store them in column C1. When the size of the population is infinite or there are good reasons for suspecting that the sampling frame is inaccurate or incomplete, the task of numbering each observation cannot be undertaken. In some, but by no means all, situations it is possible to adapt the simple random sampling technique to overcome this problem and still achieve a random sample.

Many geographical problems investigate phenomena that are distributed in space, such as soil types or land uses. Unfortunately, there are an infinite number of points at which to take measurements. A similar difficulty arises with information for areas, since an infinite number of boundary systems can be used to partition space. The problem of choosing a random sample of points can be overcome by overlaying a regular grid on to a map of the study area in which the points are to be located. The two axes of the grid can be labelled X and Y and a scale drawn on them (Figure 3.2). Then pairs of random numbers are chosen (see above) to represent the eastings and northings of the sample points. The degree of accuracy in this system can be varied, so that the random grid references may be composed of two, three, four or more digits, but locating points with this level of precision in the field may be difficult. In Figure 3.2 the two-digit pairs locate the larger grid squares (e.g. 67, 15), whereas the three-digit numbers identify the smaller squares (e.g. 678, 152). Also, the system cannot in fact specify an infinite number of points, since the smallest distance between two easting or northing references can only be one digit on the scale. Nevertheless, this drawback is not usually of any consequence for most practical purposes.

A further general point relating to probabilistic sampling techniques is whether items are drawn *with* or *without individual replacement*. The underlying principle of the simple random sample is that all individuals in the population have an equal probability of being selected for inclusion. No one item has any preferential position or status as far as selection is concerned. Once the first individual has been identified as a member of the sample, if that same observation is ineligible for inclusion as a subsequent member of the sample, then the probability relating to each other item in the population also being selected changes.

Figure 3.2 Selection of sample points using random coordinates

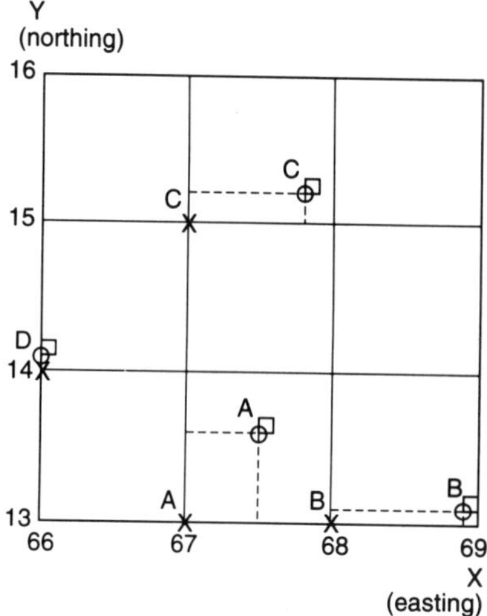

Paired Random Numbers (within range of eastings and northings)

Point	X	Y
A	67(5)	13(6)
B	68(9)	13(1)
C	67(8)	15(2)
D	66(0)	14(1)

Note: The third digits are used to locate the points more accurately, although they still refer to a square grid cell.

Suppose that a sample of 20 observations is to be selected from a population of 100 individuals. At the start of the sampling procedure each individual in the population has a 1 in a 100 chance of being a member of the sample. If the researcher has decided that no individual may enter the sample more than once, after the first observation has been chosen the probability of selection as the second item increases to 1 in 99, and of being the third to 1 in 98. In other words, the chance of an item being included improves as the sample approaches its target size. The 20th item to be chosen has a 1 in 81 probability of being selected. So all individuals in the population and in the sample *did not* experience an equal chance of being selected.

The alternative procedure is to allow individual items to be chosen more than once if random chance brings this about. At first sight this might seem to be an entirely reasonable proposition; however, such an approach may introduce further problems. In a questionnaire survey, respondents might be rather puzzled and irritated if they receive more than one request from a researcher to take part in the survey. One solution in this case might be to duplicate the questionnaire the necessary number of times in order to match the number of instances that the individual appears in the sample. However, the duration of the survey period, perhaps lasting several days, weeks or even months, might confuse the issue. During this period genuine changes in the replies to certain questions might have taken place with people changing jobs or moving into a different age group. Which set of answers should be regarded as true? Or should each one be taken as correct for the time when it was collected, with the differences being assumed to represent the dynamics of the population?

The most common solution to these questions is to undertake sampling without replacement in both human and physical geography. Provided that the population is 'large' in relation to the sample size, so that the sampling fraction is small, then the differences in probability associated with each item chosen for the sample are usually judged to be insignificant. Suppose a constant sampling fraction of 10 per cent is used. When the population size is 100, 10 items are selected, the first with probability 0.01 (1 in 10), and the last with slightly higher probability 0.010 989 01 (1 in 91), which gives a difference of 0.000 989 01. When the population is larger, for instance 100 000 individuals, the first item is selected with probability 0.000 01, while the last the probability is 0.000 011 11 (1 in 90 001). Now the difference is less, 0.000 001 11, than previously. The difference in probability between the first and last item reduces as the population size increases for a constant sampling fraction.

Simple random sampling is the basis for a number of other probabilistic techniques. *Stratified random sampling* is one of the most common and involves grouping the members of the population into classes or strata. Separate simple random samples are drawn from each stratum and the selected observations pooled together to form a single stratified random sample. The strata in the population must be mutually exclusive and exhaustive, with items able to be allocated to one class. When carrying out stratified random sampling it is presumed that the observations do genuinely vary between the strata in terms of the attributes or variables under investigation. If this was not the case then there would be no point in stratifying the population.

There are two options for deciding how the sample observations should be distributed among the strata: *proportionate* and *disproportionate quotas*. The difference between these methods relates to whether the strata have identical or different sampling fractions. The first approach is to select the same number of observations in each stratum regardless of the distribution of observations within the population. For example if the total population has 600 individuals and there are four strata, then the quota for each stratum in the sample of 80 observations is 20 items or 25 per cent. Alternatively, items in the strata are chosen in the same proportion as they occur in the population. Suppose there is a population of 400 individuals, in which 140 observations are in stratum A, 220 in stratum B and 40 in stratum C, and a sample of 60 observations is required. The number of sampled observations in the three strata would be 21 for A, 33 in B and 6 in C.

The choice between proportionate and disproportionate stratified random sampling hinges on the amount of variability within the strata. If observations are expected to be similar with respect to a given variable, then equal proportions are appropriate. However, if the items in one or more strata have a wide range of values on the variable, then the unequal sampling fractions should be used. The problem with this general rule is that there may not be enough information available about the population to choose a sample. After all, the purpose of using a sample in the first place is often because all individuals in the population cannot be measured. Nevertheless, stratified random sampling can be used very effectively when the quotas are chosen with careful regard to the structure of the population. Opinion polls are usually carried out in this way, which take into account key factors affecting electoral preferences, such as income, social class and geographical location, when determining quota sizes. Although precise predictions from these polls are typically treated with some scepticism, they have proved to be reasonably satisfactory indicators of electoral preference.

A further adaptation of the simple random sample is *cluster sampling*. The procedure entails dividing up the population into mutually exclusive and exhaustive classes, and then choosing the sample members from a random subset of these groups. The cluster sample can be chosen at random from the selected clusters or comprise all individuals in these clusters. In either case the method has the severe disadvantage that one cannot know if the sample is representative of the entire population. In a particular region, 15 of the 432 north-facing valley slopes are chosen at random to form 15 clusters and on each slope a simple random sample of 30 points is chosen and the desired biogeographical and microclimatic attributes and variables are measured. The problem here is the lack of information about the representativeness of the 15 slopes. The main difficulty is that a relatively small number of clusters are chosen from which a larger number of individual observations are specified. The chief advantage of cluster sampling is that time and money might be saved on data collection. For instance, a geographically clustered sample might reduce travel times between the locations where measurements are made. On the other hand, if the quality of the data is poorer, then the saving might not have been worthwhile.

Cluster sampling can be adapted by dividing the classes into subclasses. The process can be carried through the end point where the individual units of observation are reached. This technique is sometimes called *nested sampling*. At each stage in subdividing the classes a random selection is chosen. It does not normally produce a more representative sample, since the point at which to stop further subdivision of the classes and the definition of the classes is partly a matter of judgement. An example of nested sampling would be the selection of a random set of regions in England and Wales, then a random set of counties within the regions, then a random set of districts within the counties, then a random set of wards within the districts, then a random set of Census enumeration districts (EDs) within the wards, and finally, a random group of households within the EDs. In this situation the representativeness of the sample overall is highly influenced by the number of regions, counties and districts selected.

Systematic sampling is sometimes used in geographical studies and involves selecting observations in a regular pattern, for example addresses ending in a 5 or 0 in order to select every fifth household, or points at 1 km intervals for collecting soil samples. The procedure is useful if simple random sampling is particularly difficult or expensive. The collection of information for regularly spaced or timed observations is likely to be easier and to produce a more uniform coverage than for a randomly distributed sample of individuals. If the observations are themselves distributed at random, then a systematic sample is likely to be as reliable as a simple random one. However, if the observations have a spatial or temporal pattern in their occurrence, which happens to coincide with the chosen interval, then the sample will be biased and unrepresentative.

3.3 SAMPLING TECHNIQUES IN EXEMPLAR PROJECTS

The choice of sampling technique is an important consideration in any research project, and it sometimes lacks the attention which it merits. One of the main factors to take into account is the type of analysis that will be carried out on the data. When the different statistical techniques are examined in later chapters, it will become apparent that some should only be used when certain assumptions are satisfied. One of the most important requirements is that random sampling should be used. The sampling of observations for the exemplar projects illustrates how basic principles described in the previous section may need to be adapted to suit particular circumstances.

3.3.1 Land-use change

The study area for the land-use change project needs to include rural-urban fringe and rural areas; the boundary between these has been set at 5 km from a continuous built-up area. The study is located in a 200 km^2 area in Hertfordshire, north of London, which includes the town of Harpenden. The published map sheets (TL01/TL11) for the First and Second Land Utilisation Surveys are used for collecting the data. A representative set of locations is selected so that the land uses in the 1930s and 1960s can be measured. The categories of land use on the two series of maps are different, consequently the greater detail provided in the second survey is collapsed into seven categories which correspond approximately with those used in the first survey: arable; orchards and market gardening; grassland; woodland; heath, common and rough land; housing and gardens; and agriculturally unproductive land (including water, industry, transport, open space and derelict).

A preliminary examination of the maps and background knowledge of land-use distributions reveals the patterns to be non-random with some spatial clustering. In other words, it appears that neighbouring fields or plots of land are likely to have the same or a similar land use. The sample data should be representative of land-use change in the two types of area (rural-urban fringe and rural), and also of the overall distribution of land uses. Two separate samples are selected to achieve these objectives. First, a simple random sample comprising a set of 20 points in each of the rural-urban fringe and rural areas (sample A). The three-digit Ordnance Survey eastings and northings of these points are obtained from computer-generated random numbers constrained to lie within the range occurring on the map (eastings between 000 and 199, and northings between 100 and 199). At each sample point the land-use class is determined and its area around the point is measured to the nearest hectare by means of a transparent overlay, which is has a grid composed of hectare units. Figure 3.3a illustrates the selection of plots of land by their points and their measurements by a small grid overlay. For example, a point falling on land classified as woodland would result in the area of the entire wood being measured. Breaks of land use define the boundaries of the areal units or plots. The second sample comprises 20 randomly selected 1 km squares, which are again assigned to one of the two area types on the basis of their distance from the built-up area of Harpenden (sample B). The two-digit Ordnance Survey eastings and northings used to specify the squares are again chosen by means of computer-generated random numbers, similarly constrained by the range occurring on the map (eastings from 00 to 19, and northings from 10 to 19). Within each of the 20 squares the areas of the seven different types of land use were measured, also using a transparent grid overlay. In Figure 3.3b, one of the sampled squares is shown together with its pattern of land use. The measurement of the areas of the different land uses in both samples is to some extent approximate, since partially covered hectare squares will need to be added together. For example, if a quarter of two hectare squares and half of another hectare square are under woodland, then this would count as 1 hectare of that land use.

3.3.2 Chalk weathering

The second project is a laboratory experiment of a physical process and so it is not appropriate to specify a particular study area. Nevertheless, the question of sampling the chalk blocks to be used in the experimental design does raise certain issues. The manufacturer of the chalk blocks claims that they are 99.9 per cent pure. It is therefore reasonable to assume that there is little intrinsic difference between one block and another, although the small percentage of impurity might not be equally distributed among the population of blocks and might conceivably affect the results.

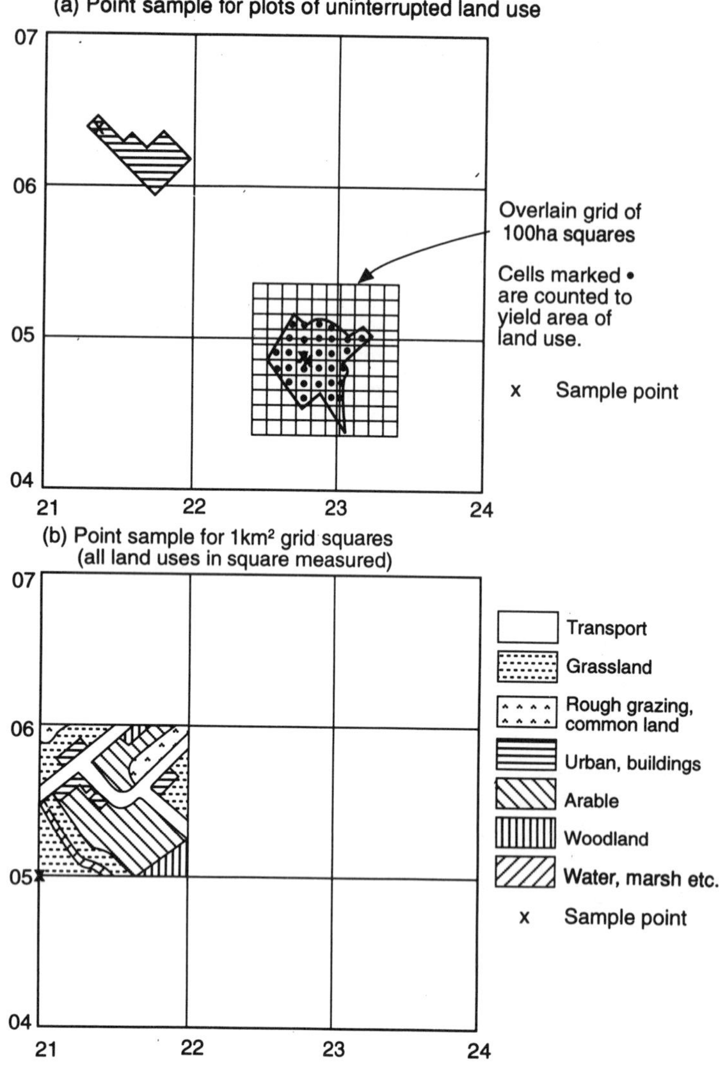

Figure 3.3 Sample points and area measurement in land-use project

A simple random sample of blocks is selected in order to avoid this difficulty. The aim of the project is to examine the effect of different treatments on the chalk. Each of the nine treatments is applied to 12 blocks, which can collectively be regarded as a sample size of 108. A box of 10 000 regular chalk blocks and a set of 120 random numbers in the range 00001 to 10 000 are obtained. The 12 spare numbers are held in reserve to allow for accidental damage to any blocks. Blocks are removed from the box one by one and those corresponding the random numbers constitute members of the sample. For example, if 01022 is one of the random numbers, then the 1022nd block taken out of the box would be included in the sample. The blocks are allocated to each of the nine treatments in turn.

3.3.3 River pollution

There are two populations under investigation in this project. The question of whether there has been an overall improvement in river quality refers to the population of rivers in England and Wales. The second question concerns whether an increase in the concentration of selected chemicals downstream from factories can be attributed to their effluent discharges; here the statistical population relates to chemical factories which are adjacent to rivers. The link between the two parts of the project arises from trying to determine whether the factories pollute rivers through raising chemical levels and consequently whether legislation to control discharges from such factories would help to improve river quality. A sample is required from each of the statistical populations in order to answer the research questions.

The sampling issues in the river pollution project are complex since the study attempts to link together information from primary and secondary sources. Furthermore, both the sites at which to abstract water for laboratory analysis and the number and frequency of water samples at each site need to be determined. The measurement of phenomena relating to rivers raises the interesting question of how to sample something which is flowing through a linear spatial feature. The usual solution is to select a number of discrete sites and then to take repeated measurements at these points. The published river-quality maps (Department of the Environment 1987) show a fivefold classification of rivers which constitute predefined strata from which to draw a sample of points (sample A) at which water samples will be collected. The key sampling question is how to choose these sites within each stratum. Unfortunately, there is an infinite number of points along the rivers and times at which the required measurements could be made. Furthermore, if the sites are chosen entirely at random, some might be dangerous, if not impossible, to reach. The previous river quality classification applies to stretches or segments of a river, and a sufficiently representative sample can be obtained by using stratified random sampling to select stretches of rivers and then choosing a convenient site on each at which to collect the water samples. All stretches of river within each stratum in the North West Water Authority region are given a unique reference number and five of these in each stratum are chosen by means of random numbers. Five water samples are collected on 10 randomly determined days over a 12-month period at an accessible site on each stretch of river, and analysed in the laboratory to determine chemical concentrations associated with the official classification scheme. Sample A thus contains 250 records representing each sample of water ($5 \times 10 \times 5$).

The second sample (B) relates to rivers that have chemical factories adjacent to them. A register of industrial companies reveals that there are 457 chemical enterprises in the North West Water Authority region and a simple random sample of 25 factories is deemed sufficient. A further five sites are randomly chosen as a control group. At each of the 30 locations five water samples are taken 250 m upstream and a further five 250 m downstream of each sample site. The water samples are analysed in the laboratory to determine the concentration of various chemicals. The intention is to detect any significant differences in chemical concentrations upstream and downstream of the factories. Sample B comprises 300 records (30 × 10) representing each water sample.

3.3.4 Village communities

The study area for the research in this project is determined by the identification of the village in which the new development is to take place. Nevertheless, it is still necessary to define precisely the boundary of the settlement. In this case the village itself, together with a handful of outlying farms and two small hamlets, includes all residents of the parish. So the parish is the taken as the study area. The issues to be considered in this project are how to establish a sampling frame and how to choose a sample which includes sufficient numbers of indigenous and newcomer residents.

In Britain, a useful sampling frame is provided by the annually updated electoral register. The information on this register is limited to name, address and ward of residence for people of voting age (18 and over). Unfortunately, some people fail to complete the electoral registration form and are consequently omitted from the published register. Both the indigenous and newcomer groups or strata in the population should be adequately represented. So the sampling frame needs to show not only who lives in the parish, but also how long they have lived there. A newcomer is defined as a resident who has moved into the parish within the previous 10 years, and the names on the electoral registers for the last 10 years are examined in order to identify the newcomers and the indigenous residents. In practice, there are problems with constructing such migration histories from electoral registers. The registers do not indicate an elector's age, so when a new name appears it is difficult to determine if the person is the son or daughter of an existing resident who has become eligible to vote, someone who has decided to register for the first time, or a migrant to the area. If the new name is shown as resident at the same address and possessing the same surname as someone already in the parish, then it might reasonably be concluded that the person was not a newcomer.

In view of these difficulties, a simpler sampling strategy is adopted. A simple random sample is generated using the latest electoral register as a sampling frame. Published sources of population statistics indicate that the parish's population is 8950 and approximately 20 per cent of the total are children (aged under 18), who are disregarded for the purposes of the project. A fairly high sampling fraction, 5 per cent, is used in an attempt to ensure that both newcomer and indigenous residents are adequately represented. This produces a target sample of 358 individuals (5 per cent of the 7160 people aged 18 or over). A slight discrepancy is noted between the estimated number of people aged 18 and over and the total on the electoral register, 7160 as opposed to 7103. The difference is judged to be acceptable, although no information is available about the missing 57 individuals. Once these details of the sample have been decided, individuals appearing on the electoral register are assigned a unique identification number and 358 random numbers between 0001 and 7103 are selected, corresponding to the people to whom the questionnaire will be administered. The respondents to the survey will be classified retrospectively as newcomer or indigenous residents on the basis of a question on length of residence.

3.4 COMPARISON OF PROJECTS

Various adaptations of the basic simple random sampling method dominate the approaches adopted in the four projects, although the first sample in the river pollution project does involve a certain amount of accessibility sampling. Table 3.2 summarises the sampling procedures used and the target numbers of observations. The term 'target numbers' is used because there may be a certain amount of non-response, which is a problem frequently associated with human geography and the social sciences, where for example individuals, households or companies refuse to take part in a survey. However, it is also possible for a particular observation which has been chosen for inclusion in the sample of a physical geography project, to elude the researcher. One of the chalk blocks in the sample might shatter after being accidentally dropped on the floor of the laboratory. For whatever reason non-response may arise, it presents the investigator with a dilemma: accept

Table 3.2 Comparison of samples in exemplar projects

	Land-use change	Chalk weathering	River pollution	Village communities
Type of sample	A. Stratified random B. Simple random	Simple random	A. Stratified random (accessibility) B. Simple random	Simple random
Target size	A. 40 B. 20	108	A. 250 B. 300	358
Observations	A. Plots of land B. Grid squares	Chalk blocks	A. Water samples from river sections B. Water samples from points on rivers	Individual adults

a reduced sample size for analysis or top up the sample with additional, similarly selected members of the population. Both options clearly distort the sample. The most sensible course of action, which has been adopted for all four exemplar projects, is to select a target sample size that is large enough to compensate for some non-response. For example, in the case of the chalk weathering project 12 extra blocks were randomly selected as reserves.

Chapter 4
Inputting geographical data on to the computer

4.1 COMPUTERS AND DATA ANALYSIS

'The most probable reason' for geography students seeming to dislike statistics 'is the perceived association between statistics and tedious calculation' (Mather 1991, p. 52). Such an association may indeed be part of the reason, but another significant factor is that the connection between statistics and thematic geography is often not made sufficiently clear. The exemplar projects in this book help to demonstrate that statistical techniques are part and parcel of accumulating and confirming geographical knowledge. In order to understand the operation of such techniques, it is important that the basic calculations are explained. However, computers rather than calculators are now the main tools for carrying out statistical computations, especially with large datasets. This chapter therefore examines how these machines operate and how geographical data can be entered, stored and manipulated.

People's reactions to using computers range from boundless enthusiasm to utter abhorrence. On the one hand, they are seen as answering our statistical and data-handling problems, whereas, on the other, they are viewed as creating more problems than they solve. The approach adopted to computers in this book is that they are a useful and valuable tool to help undertake statistical analyses, to manipulate data and to present results. In a similar vein as far as the teaching of statistics is concerned, computers are regarded as a means for undertaking statistical analysis and eliminating the tedium of hand calculation. The potential problems with using computers for these purposes should nevertheless be considered before their operation is discussed any further.

The use of computers may well remove the tedium of hand calculation, but they can introduce new problems. A computer is sometimes regarded as necessarily providing the correct answer to a question, but it will only do so if valid raw data are entered in the first place. Computers act on instructions, issued by human operators, to carry out various types of procedure on data items stored in specific locations. Unfortunately, such instructions are inevitably subject to the vagaries of human error. If the data entered into the computer contain mistakes then the results of data processing will also contain errors. Suppose a computer is instructed to add the numbers held in two storage locations together and then to divide the sum by the constant 4. If one pair of numbers should be 9 and 11, giving the answer 5 (i.e. 9 + 11/4), but 11 has been incorrectly entered as 21, then the computer will report the result of 7.5 (i.e. 9 + 21/4).

Another difficulty with using computers is that statistical analysis may become almost too easy. A computer can easily produce some descriptive statistics (see Chapter 5), generate a particular inferential test statistic (see Chapters 10 and 11), or compute correlation coefficients (see Chapter 12) for all possible combinations of variables in a dataset. It is a different question to understand what these mean and whether they are appropriate. Mather (1991) anticipates a time when a special type of computer system, known as an expert or intelligent knowledge-based system, will reduce the amount of statistical theory that a geographer or other non-professional statistician needs in order to carry out statistical analysis. Such a system would be capable of storing the 'wide-ranging knowledge covering the nature of the [statistical] techniques and the assumptions on which they are based' (Mather 1991, p. 28) so that the non-expert could focus on the substantive research topic under investigation. The use of computers, even with such an expert facility, far from removing the 'thinking stage' of a geographical project, demands that the analyst focuses on this part of the research even more clearly.

Access to greater computing power and data storage capacity has changed the way in which geographical information is processed. When computers first started to be used in geography and other disciplines, literature on the subject of computing tended to be rather inaccessible and specialised. Most academics wishing to use computers were forced to struggle along the learning curve and to develop an expertise in using package software to carry out statistical analysis and information-handling operations. There were of course exceptions to this rule, with some geographers becoming involved in the writing of computer software for carrying out specific operations on spatial data (e.g. Coppock 1965; Waugh and McCalden 1983). The increased use of computers in recent years has produced two effects: a pool of people with increasingly sophisticated computing skills and a growing curiosity to understand how computers work.

Geographers have already been introduced to the basics of computers and the breadth of their use in the discipline (Maguire 1989; Mather 1991). Little would be gained from repeating these details here and readers are referred to these texts for a more comprehensive introduction to the subject. However, there are certain key aspects of how computers work in relation to their handling of information which are appropriately examined in a data-analysis text. The following sections should therefore be viewed simply as an aid to understanding this process, rather than as an exhaustive introduction to the subject.

Computers are essentially sophisticated machines for carrying out various operations on or manipulations of machine-readable data. As such their three main functions are:

- data input and storage;
- data manipulation and management;
- information output.

The basis of this division relates to functions which are undertaken in respect of the data and information held on the computer. The term 'data' sometimes only refers to numerical and textual information that has already been converted into a machine-readable form. In this book the term 'data' (and in its singular, 'datum') is employed in a slightly broader sense to denote unprocessed numbers and text whether or not held in a computerised form. 'Information', in contrast, signifies data that have been processed in some way, for example by the calculation of summary statistics or new variables. It is useful to distinguish between three categories of data and information held on a computer. The computerised version of the data, which are to be analysed, is sometimes known as the *raw data*, because it is held in an unprocessed form. The second type is the result of processing and manipulating the raw data. The third category relates to the final results which are intended to be output from the computer system. The various connections between these different types of data in the context of statistical analysis are illustrated in a generalised form in Figure 4.1, which relates to the following discussion of the three functions.

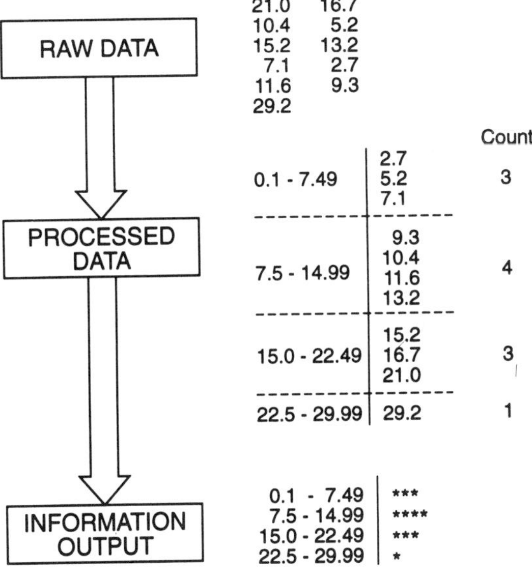

Figure 4.1 Raw data, processed data and information

4.1.1 Data input and storage

Data input and storage are considered together for two reasons. Raw data which are converted into a machine-readable form are frequently used more than once, often on separate occasions and possibly on different computers. Unless the computer user wishes to re-enter the data each time, it is necessary to store them in a computerised form for access on subsequent occasions. The process of entering data into a computer necessarily means that they are stored, albeit in a temporary fashion. For example, a word-processed letter, which will be sent to one person, has to be stored during the time that it takes to type it in, to make any corrections and then to print it out. If the raw data will be reaccessed, then they have to be stored in a computer file.

Computer systems are usually categorised on the basis of their processing power, their ability to enable separate but simultaneous data-manipulation operations and the number of users who can access the system at the same time. The mainframe computer and the personal or portable computer lie at the two extremes of the spectrum. A mainframe computer is a multi-user system, which permits data-processing operations using different software (see below) to be carried out simultaneously. Such systems were introduced into educational institutions during the 1960s and early 1970s, although access was initially rather limited. Mainframe computer systems provided the main computing resource for academic researchers and teachers until the mid-1980s. Their role has now diminished and they function as 'heavy-duty' number-crunching and database-manipulation machines. In the age of networked personal computers, it is salutary to recall that as recently as 10 years ago mainframe systems were used for elementary text formatting work, which was the precursor of contemporary word processing. Personal computers, which developed rapidly during the 1980s, have successfully distributed computing power to the desktop. Nowadays microcomputers can easily be linked together by means of networks, which provide gateways into large mainframe systems and access to remote sites. Between the two extremes on the spectrum of computer systems many different permutations are available, in particular mini-systems and workstations. Nevertheless, the basic hardware components of a computer system are a central processing unit with associated memory and data-storage devices, such as hard disks, tape and floppy disk drives; a means of data entry and display, typically in the combination of a keyboard and visual display unit; and some form of output device, such as a printer.

From the point of view of the student embarking on a computer-based statistics course, the typical computing laboratory in a college or university will have one of two configurations. On the one hand, the system might comprise a series of independent 'dumb terminals', which do not have any processing power in their own right, but are connected to a mainframe and its various output or peripheral devices.

However, the increasingly common alternative is a system comprising a series of personal computers which can be similarly linked to a mainframe or local area network, or be used independently as stand-alone computers.

Before analysis can commence, the raw data have to be entered or input on to the computer. Various ways of achieving this exist including direct entry, transfer from another computer system or by some form of automated recording instrument. Direct entry of data usually involves typing at the keyboard, although other methods such as digitising or scanning can be used with geographical data. Entry via the keyboard involves the user typing in the raw data (numbers or text) as they appear on a questionnaire, coding or recording sheet. The computer will make the necessary translation into an internal representation of the numbers and characters (see Mather 1991, pp. 6–9). The data can either be entered into a file or directly into the package software with which they will be analysed. In the past the latter option would often have restricted the user to the specific software, although this is now less of a problem. Raw data, for example remotely sensed images or census statistics, can also be transferred on to the analyst's computer from another system by means of portable storage media such as floppy disks, magnetic tapes, CD ROMs and optical video disks. These media have become increasingly interchangeable among the hardware produced by different manufacturers. Raw data can also be obtained from a remote computer system over a network, such as the Joint Academic Network (JANET), which links together the universities and research institutes in the United Kingdom and has international connections.

4.1.2 Data manipulation and management

Before looking at data management and manipulation, it is necessary to consider a further category of information, which also resides on a computer system. This category refers to the sets of instructions known as programs or software. From the data-analysis point of view, there are two types of software: the operating system, which is necessary for a computer to function; and applications packages or programs, which manipulate and manage data. Applications software includes packages for word processing, statistical analysis, graphics, database management, financial analysis and other purposes. During the 1960s and early 1970s, the statistical analyst may have had to write a program in order to carry out a specific type of analysis. Nowadays 'packaged' or 'off-the-shelf' software has become widely and cheaply available for many different applications areas.

Statistical analysis is therefore one of several purposes for which computers may be used to manipulate and manage raw data. Others include the retrieval of textual or numeric information, the maintenance of administrative and financial databases, and the presentation of information by means of computer graphics. Statistical data analysis on computers involves three main operations: the organisation of the raw data in such a way that they can be easily accessed and interpreted; the creation of new variables by carrying out some form of classification or mathematical computation of the original ones; and the calculation of various statistical quantities according to defined mathematical formulae, which are usually embedded within the software.

From a conceptual point of view, the simplest and most typical structure or layout for organising a collection of data items is as a rectangular matrix of rows and columns. Normally the rows represent the observations or items and the columns denote the attributes or variables which have been measured (Figure 4.2). The applications software manipulates the contents of these rows and columns according to the user's instructions. The term 'logical record' defines 'a collection of related data items that describe a particular object or entity' (McFadden and Hoffer 1988, p. 10) and usually refers to an entire row or 'slice' through the matrix. When each entity has a substantial number of data items, as

Figure 4.2 Rectangular data matrix

(a) Simple Data Matrix

```
Columns                    111111111112222222222223
                 1234567890123456789001234567890

Row/case 1       2461229617122831331131757
Row/case 2       6952081062413221533172024
Row/case 3       810624910172677115238106241011
Row/case 4       232724282436312274131213
Row/case 5       58619671619231185241077241919
Row/case 6       362110714112434310353111111
Row/case 7       38516385161658215302151515
Row/case 8       78621686207997259872477
```

(b) Fixed Format Data Matrix

```
 2 4 612 2 9 61712 2 8 3 13 311 317 5 7
 6 9 520 810 62413 2 2 1  5 3 3 1 72024
 810 624 9101726 7 711 5 23 810 6241011
 2 3 2 7 2 4 2 824 3 6 3 12 2 7 4131213
 5 8 619 6 716192311 8 5 2410 7 7241919
 3 6 211 0 7141124 3 4 3 10 3 5 3111111
 3 8 516 3 8 51616 5 8 2 15 3 0 2151515
 7 8 621 6 8 620 7 9 9 7 25 9 8 724 7 7
```

Space used to right-justify single digit numbers in two digit variables

(c) Comma separated variables

```
,2,4,6,12,2,9,6,17,12,2,8,3,13,3,11,3,17,5,7,
,6,9,5,20,8,10,6,24,13,2,2,1,5,3,3,1,7,20,24,
,8,10,6,24,9,10,17,26,7,7,11,5,23,8,10,6,24,10,11,
,2,3,2,7,2,4,2,8,24,3,6,3,12,2,7,4,13,12,13,
,5,8,6,19,6,7,16,19,23,11,8,5,24,10,7,7,24,19,19,
,3,6,2,11,0,7,14,11,24,3,4,3,10,3,5,3,11,11,11,
,3,8,5,16,3,8,5,16,16,5,8,2,15,3,0,2,15,15,15,
,7,8,6,21,6,8,6,20,7,9,9,7,25,9,8,7,24,7,7,
```

in a large socio-economic survey, it may be necessary for the logical record to occupy more than one physical record. A physical record can be thought of as a row containing a predetermined number of boxes or computer locations in which characters can be stored.

In addition to organising the records, the applications software also has to recognise groups of characters in columns whose contents form numbers or text (words). Obviously all numbers and words do not contain the same number of characters. Suppose that in a survey of companies the size of the workforce is a number containing between one and four digits, for example 5, 44, 906 and 3763. The software must be able to recognise groups of characters on a physical record as constituting the variable 'size of workforce'. When data are entered into a computer file, which is a collection of physical records, the user has to ensure that the software correctly identifies a particular group of characters. The two most common ways of achieving this are either to enter the data in a fixed format (Figure 4.2(b)) or in free field format with a delimiter, such as a space or comma, between the groups (Figure 4.2(c)). When the data are entered directly into the statistical software, then default settings usually exist, for example relating to how many decimal places are stored.

Once the data have been entered it is important to be able to make any changes, corrections or additions. The task of editing is simplified if the user can easily identify how the computer has stored the groups of characters. The normal practice is to label the groups of characters with column or variable names, such as 'Workers'. When attributes or categorised continuous scale variables are included in a dataset, these are often given numeric codes with labels attached to them. For example, in a survey of the plants in an area, rather than computerising the full names each time they occur, it would be more sensible to give each name a code number and to enter these codes on the data records. In this way the names themselves would only need to be typed in once as labels, which reduces potential errors, and saves time and computer storage. Careful organisation and planning of how the data analysis will be organised can prevent difficulties and confusion later.

The creation of new variables is also an important function of statistical software. For example, total weekly household expenditure might be generated in this way by adding together the values for a series of variables denoting expenditure on individual types of product, such as food, housing, leisure, transport, etc. Another example is where a continuous variable, such as distance, is collapsed into a small number of discrete groups, for instance 0–9.9 km, 10–19.9 km, etc. The new variables can be stored alongside the original ones and used in the statistical analysis.

The calculation of various measures and quantities is obviously one of the main functions of statistical software. In order to undertake these calculations, the software contains a library of mathematical formulae. This is both an advantage and a disadvantage. It is advantageous because the analyst does not have to type in the formula for a particular statistic. One disadvantage is that the formulae for calculating population and sample statistics are sometimes slightly different; unfortunately, some statistical software does not recognise the distinction and therefore applies the same formula regardless of the circumstances. However, statistical analysis carried out on a computer rather than by hand will in the long run almost certainly reduce the time required and provide the analyst with a wider range of techniques.

4.1.3 Information output

The final results comprise the information arising from the manipulation and statistical analysis of the original and new variables. It is usually these results that the investigator wishes to examine in order to discuss the issues addressed by the project. The presentation of these results can be achieved in either a graphic, cartographic, numeric or textual form. The simplest method involves reading the information from the visual display unit. However, in most cases a more permanent record is required, necessitating the use of additional computer hardware and saving the results in a separate file. A permanent record of the results or listing file can be obtained on paper by using a printer attached to the computer system. In a similar way, a graphic representation of the results can be sent to a printer or plotter.

Sometimes the results of data analysis are saved in a form that enables them to be transferred to different applications software or to an entirely separate computer system. The process involves creating a file containing the information to be transferred on some portable medium, such those outlined in Section 4.1.1. Alternatively, the information can be sent via a computer network. The transfer of data in these various ways is now relatively straightforward, since standards have been established for data interchange. These standards have removed some of the 'package dependence' which previously existed.

4.2 COMPUTERS AND GEOGRAPHICAL DATA

The general issues associated with the entry, manipulation and output of computerised information apply to geographical data as much as to those associated with any other subject area. However, there are certain special points to be examined, mainly relating to the wide range of data sources used in geography and to the locational and temporal components of geographical data. The specific points are considered in relation to the three principal functions of a computer system already identified. The emphasis again is on introducing the key questions concerning computers and geographical data rather than repeating the details adequately provided elsewhere (Maguire 1989; Mather 1991).

4.2.1 Geographical data input and storage

The principal distinguishing characteristic of geographical data is that not only the attributes and variables about the observations are relevant, but also their location. Furthermore, location is more than an additional variable, since the relative location and spatial relationships, for example describing the connectivity and adjacency of geographical features, are important. The latter are referred to as the *topological properties* of geographical objects. These properties of phenomena are examined in many branches of geography, for example by biogeographers researching plant associations and by urban geographers investigating social segregation.

Three basic spatial features can be identified which form a hierarchy (Figure 4.3), namely points, lines and areas. At the bottom of the hierarchy are *point* features, of which there are an infinite number on the surface of the earth. Each point can be located by means a pair of x and y coordinates, such as longitude and latitude, or easting and northing. Point locations are used in geography in two ways. The first way is as a shorthand reference for an area, so that a map might show the locations of towns as a scatter of points. The second is as a precise locational reference, for example the site at which certain measurements are made. Individual points can be joined together to form the second type of spatial feature, a *line*. The minimum number of points needed to define a line over a short distance is two, in which case the line is necessarily straight. However, if more than two points are used, then the line may be curved and the parts of the line between individual

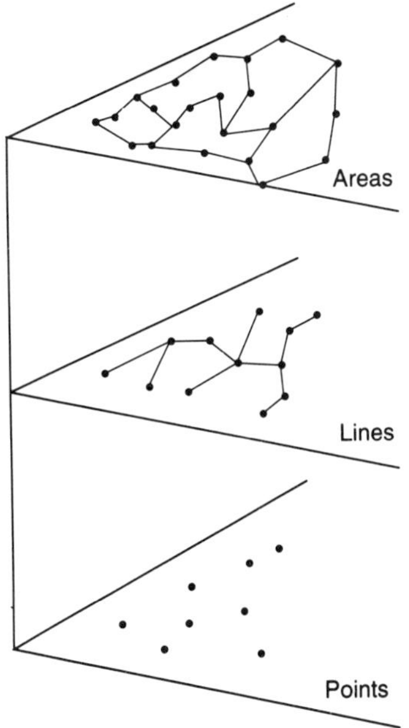

Figure 4.3 Spatial features: points, lines and areas

points are known as *segments*. The start and end points of a line and the points at which three or more lines join are called *nodes*. When a series of lines form an enclosing boundary they create the third type of spatial feature, an *area* or *polygon*. In this case the number of pairs of x and y co-ordinates is variable, since it depends on the number of lines and segments.

Introductory texts in the developing field of Geographical Information Systems (e.g. Burrough 1986; Maguire 1989; Star and Estes 1991) have elaborated the details of the data structures available for representing these three types of spatial feature on a computer. In essence, there are two forms of representation, the *raster* and *vector* systems. These are illustrated in Figure 4.4 in respect of cartographic and statistical information.

The raster system is based on covering the region of interest with a regular grid, usually, but not necessarily, composed of squares. Each square is either full or empty with regard to the presence or absence of the information being represented. In Figure 4.4(a) the squares required to create the cartographic and statistical images are shaded according to whether they form, in the one case, part of the road and forest or, in the other, bars in the histogram. Each cell or pixel in the grid possesses both a value and positional information. The value may be as simple as 0 and 1 to denote the presence or absence of a topographic feature (road, river or administrative boundary), or may be an integer coded attribute corresponding to a classification (e.g. different types of soil), or a variable with a continuous numerical range (e.g. altitude, depth or population). The positional information identifies the location of individual cells with respect to the coordinates of the whole grid, which is usually related to a topographic grid referencing system in mapping applications, such as the National Grid.

The vector system of representation creates a graphical image of the mappable features in an area or of the form of statistical diagrams by means of pairs of coordinates, which identify their constituent points, lines and areas. Such a system also implies that a grid referencing system is being used, but generally of a much finer size. Each pair of coordinates identifies the location of a particular point in terms of the grid. Figure 4.4(b) illustrates how the same cartographic and statistical information as shown in Figure 4.4(a) could be represented under the vector system. All the points within the area covered by the grid are potentially 'known to the system', since its maximum and minimum extent are defined in respect of the x and y axes, but it is only necessary for those points to be encoded where the feature is present. The example illustrates that the vector system is more economical in terms of the amount of information which needs to be computerised. Under the raster system the map or statistical chart is stored by means of reference to the full set of squares. The vector representation of the same information requires fewer pairs of coordinates.

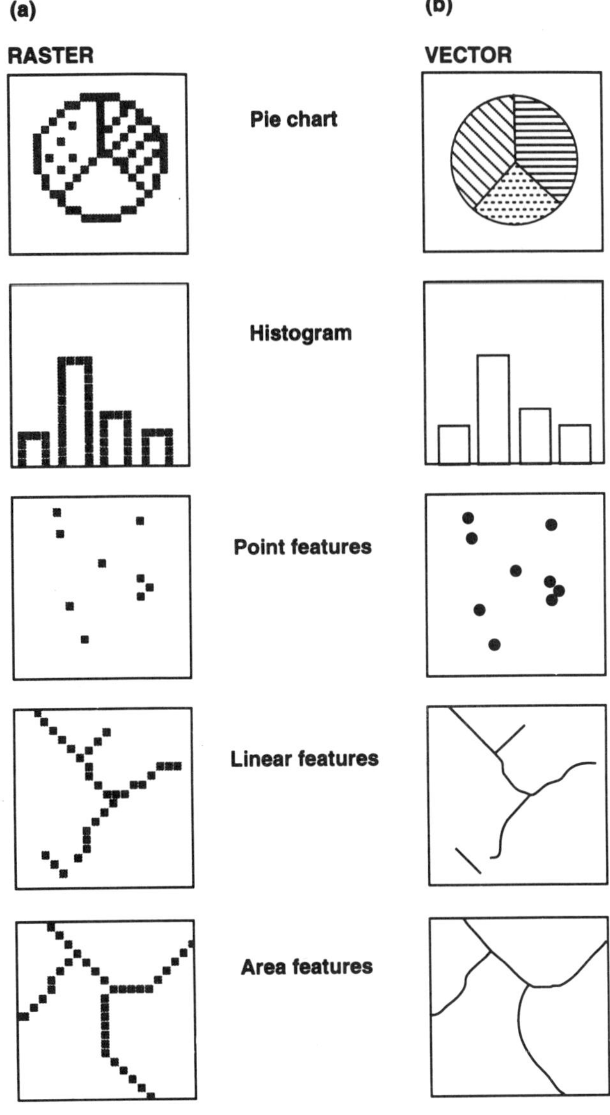

Figure 4.4 Raster and vector representation of graphic images

The raster and vector forms of graphic image representation were initially believed to be so distinct that they formed a basis for a discrete categorisation of hardware and software. More recently algorithms have been developed for converting spatial data between the two systems and they are no longer regarded as mutually exclusive. The differences are essentially technological and not conceptual (Burrough 1986). In recent years, many of these difficulties have been overcome and the debate has shifted to looking for ways of integrating raster and vector data, and identifying and combining their relative strengths, rather than asserting that one is superior to the other. The vector system is particularly useful when topological information about the spatial features is required. Satellite remote sensing and image processing systems use the raster form of graphical representation.

Some map data are already available in a digital computerised form. However, at the present time the large majority only exists as printed or hard-copy maps. Two types of computer hardware known as 'digitisers' and 'scanners' may be used to convert such secondary data sources into a machine-readable form. Digitising involves using a cursor to register pairs of x and y coordinates for the various points and lines on a map and creates vector data files. The process is time-consuming and prone to error, especially when carried out manually, although semi-automated systems have been developed, for example by the Laserscan company of Cambridge. Some software has the advantage of enabling topological relationships to be captured at the digitising stage.

Scanning a map document represents a cheaper but potentially less detailed and accurate method for computerising geographical features. A beam of light is passed across the map recording information for a myriad of tiny, regularly- spaced, rectangular points. Each of these units is given a digital value depending upon the amount of light reflected back by the different colours on the map. At one extreme, a value of 0 indicates black, while a value of 255 denotes white. Spatial features are recognised by the association of similar digital values for a series of cells, for example a string of adjacent units with the same value might indicate a linear feature, although the intelligence to know whether the line denotes a river, road, railway or power line has to be added to the data by the human operator at a later stage.

4.2.2 Geographical data manipulation and management

The manipulation and management of geographical data raise a number of new issues. The first question concerns how the spatial data representing the points, lines and areas are related to the corresponding attributes and variables. There are essentially three systems. The simplest, which is only really used for point data, treats the pair of coordinates as two additional variables embedded in the data file. The computer data files containing the population census small area statistics, which include the Cartesian coordinates for the centroid of each enumeration district, provide an example.

The second method stores the geographical data records in a separate data file, which is linked with the thematic information in two main ways. The most straightforward, but possibly more error-prone, method involves maintaining the logical and/or physical records in the two (or more files) in the same sequential order. Suppose there is geographical data file in which the logical records contain the pairs of x and y coordinates delimiting parish boundaries and a separate thematic data file, for example counts of different socio-economic characteristics. In order to manipulate these two related data files successfully using a sequential matching system, the logical records must be in the same order.

In other words if the fifth logical record in the attribute file is for St John's Without parish, then the fifth logical record in the geographical boundary file must be for the same parish. Any mismatching would obviously produce spurious output. The second method requires an identifer or key to be present in each file. This key creates a link between the two types of data file and does not require that the logical records are stored in the same order in each.

The representation of geographical features may also be implied by the nature of the dataset. This mainly applies to raster-encoded data in which the geographical location of the spatial units is inferred from their position in a regular grid. If the dimensions of the grid and its origin in terms of eastings and northings and its unit size are known, the location of any other point can be determined from a randomly selected point. For example, suppose there is a grid composed of 20 rows of 30 columns and the United Kingdom National Grid 10-metre reference for the coordinates of the origin at the bottom left-hand corner of the grid is 034189 563572. Moving east by 12 grid squares and north by 8 from this position will necessarily mean that the square at that location has the National Grid reference 034201 563580.

Another issue concerning the manipulation of geographical data arises from the fact that both types of data file may need to be analysed statistically. Spatial statistics are examined in some detail later (Chapter 14). For the present it is worth noting that geographers may investigate the patterns of the geographical features themselves, while other disciplines are usually only interested in analysing thematic attributes and variables. Spatial statistics were developed during the quantitative revolution of the 1950s and 1960s with the popularisation of such techniques as nearest-neighbour analysis and Lorenz curves.

4.2.3 Geographical information output

The final results produced by the manipulation of geographical data may be output in the same way as other forms of analysis, but frequently a cartographic presentation is also used. Computer-drawn or digital maps have been produced in a primitive fashion on the standard lineprinter since the 1960s. However, recent developments in both computer hardware and software have resulted in these facilities becoming more widely available. Cartographic output can be generated in much the same way as statistical results, for example on a computer screen, by sending information directly from the computer to an output device or by creating a file prior to printing or plotting.

The output of geographical information can be achieved with variable levels of quality, which largely depend on the nature and cost of the output device being used (for details see Mather 1991, pp. 105–119). The raster and vector data models are also relevant for the output of geographical data. The comparatively low quality of the standard lineprinter map means that these devices are now less important than they used to be. Pen plotters probably produce the highest-quality maps and are available for a range of paper sizes, with various pen colours. They operate by obeying coded instructions sent by the mapping software on the computer, such as to draw a straight line from one pair of x and y coordinates to another, or a text character at a specific location. Relatively cheap alternatives to pen plotters include 'black and white' or colour dot matrix and inkjet printers.

4.3 COMPUTERISING THE EXEMPLAR PROJECT DATA

The four projects exemplify the general and specific aspects of computerising geographical data and provide practical examples of how to organise and structure the data files for attributes and variables. Each software product has its own particular characteristics and command details. It is outside the scope of this book to introduce, let alone explain, all the package software currently used in geographical investigations. However, the projects do demonstrate certain packages and illustrate the general procedures, although even in these cases precise instructions for running the software on particular computer systems may vary from the details provided here. The full software manuals should be consulted for a comprehensive discussion of the different commands. The raw data for each project are provided in Appendix III. The following subsections include illustrative extracts from the projects' datasets.

4.3.1 Land-use change

There are two raw data files for the land-use change project reflecting the separate samples (A and B), which have been computerised with similar structures. In sample A, the data for 40 randomly selected plots of land are computerised with a rectangular data structure. The rows or logical records represent a single plot with the following attributes and variables:

Easting of sample point in plot
Northing of sample point in plot
Urban/rural locality code
Land-use code 1930s
Plot area 1930s
Land-use code 1960s
Plot area 1960s

The data can therefore be viewed as a rectangular matrix comprising 40 rows by 7 columns. The second sample has a similar general structure comprising 20 logical records representing the sample squares, each of which has 14 variables for the seven land-use categories in the 1930s and 1960s. The details of the variables are as follows:

Lower left easting of grid square
Lower left northing of grid square
Urban/rural locality code
Arable area 1930s
Market gardening area 1930s
Grassland area 1930s
Woodland area 1930s
Heathland, moorland and rough grazing area 1930s
Housing and gardens area 1930s
Agriculturally unusable land area 1930s
Arable area 1960s
Market gardening area 1960s
Grassland area 1960s
Woodland area 1960s
Heathland, moorland and rough grazing area 1960s
Housing and gardens area 1960s
Agriculturally unusable land area 1960s

MINITAB is used to analyse the data for the land-use project samples. There are two ways of entering data into MINITAB, either by means of separate file or directly into the software. The latter procedure is followed in this instance, with MINITAB running on a VAX computer with the VMS operating system. Table 4.1 logs the sequence of steps involved in computerising and saving the data for land-use samples A and B, although only the first three and the final data rows are shown in each case. Starting from the point where the user has followed local instructions for logging on to the computer system, the first task is to 'load up' the software, which causes the MINITAB prompt to appear on the screen, thus:

MTB >

This prompt indicates that MINITAB is expecting a command. The convention used in Table 4.1 and other MINITAB logs is that words in capital letters are commands, while column headings, filenames and other situations where the user can exercise choice, are shown in lower-case letters. In practice, when running MINITAB upper- and lower-case letters can be used interchangeably. The command keywords must be spelt as given in Table 4.1 and in other similar 'logs', although they can be abbreviated to the first four characters. The command OUTFILE 'land01' opens a file on the computer which will be called LAND01.LIS. The file extension, .LIS, is automatically generated by MINITAB. This file will contain everything appearing on the screen and can be printed out after the session, provided that the file is closed with the NOOUTFILE command.

The next step defines the seven columns for sample A, one for each attribute or variable, which are known as C1 C2 C3 C4 C5 C6 C7, with the READ command. This command will cause the software to

Table 4.1 Entering and storing land-use project data samples A and B in MINITAB

```
MTB > OUTFILE 'land01'
MTB > READ C1 C2 C3 C4 C5 C6 C7
DATA > 166,103,1,3,35,1,25
DATA > 176,2,1,7,3,3
DATA > 049,107,2,5,6,4,1
  ...
DATA > 070,180,2,3,31,1,19
DATA > END
MTB > NAME C1 'Easting'
MTB > NAME C2 'Northing'
MTB > NAME C3 'Urb/Rur'
MTB > NAME C4 'Uscod30s'
MTB > NAME C5 'Area30s'
MTB > NAME C6 'Uscod60s'
MTB > NAME C7 'Area60s'
MTB > PRINT C1 - C7
MTB > SAVE 'landa01'
MTB > READ C1 - C17
DATA > 03,14,2,31,8,19,36,2,0,4,52,0,4,38,0,0,6
DATA > 00,14,2,36,5,38,9,8,1,3,45,0,39,7,3,1,5
DATA > 15,16,1,30,28,24,9,0,3,6,35,32,14,4,0,5,10
  ...
DATA > 19,15,2,49,2,23,19,0,1,6,54,1,15,18,0,2,10
DATA > END
MTB > NAME C1 'Easting'
MTB > NAME C2 'Northing'
MTB > NAME C3 'Urb/Rur'
MTB > NAME C4 'Arab30s'
MTB > NAME C5 'MkGd30s'
MTB > NAME C6 'Gras30s'
MTB > NAME C7 'Wood30s'
MTB > NAME C8 'Heat30s'
MTB > NAME C9 'Hous30s'
MTB > NAME C10 'AgUn30s'
MTB > NAME C11 'Arab60s'
MTB > NAME C12 'MkGd60s'
MTB > NAME C13 'Gras60s'
MTB > NAME C14 'Wood60s'
MTB > NAME C15 'Heat60s'
MTB > NAME C16 'Hous60s'
MTB > NAME C17 'AgUn60s'
MTB > NOOUTFILE
MTB > SAVE 'landb01'
MTB > STOP
```

switch into input mode, which is indicated by a different prompt:

DATA >

This prompt enables the 40 rows of data to be entered, with each item in the correct order and separated by a comma or space, and the RETURN key pressed at the end of each series of seven items. After entering the 40th row, type END and then RETURN after the

DATA > prompt to indicate completion of data input and to switch back to command mode. The command PRINT C1 – C7 displays the contents of columns C1 to C7. The series of NAME commands labels each column with a brief description of its contents. The command SAVE 'landa01' stores or saves the data together with the column names into a MINITAB worksheet file, called LANDA01.MTW, on the user's disk area for subsequent use. The data for sample B are entered with a similar sequence of commands, including saving a separate worksheet called LANDB01.MTW. Finally, NOOUTFILE closes the results file and STOP finishes the MINITAB session. The results file appears on the user's disk area and can be printed from a VAX computer running VMS thus:

$PRINT LAND01.LIS

4.3.2 Chalk weathering

The raw data for the chalk weathering project are more straightforward, since the observations do not possess any geographical reference. The data are structured as a rectangular matrix of 108 rows representing each block, 12 blocks for each of the nine treatments, by 16 columns. The columns contain the following information:

Block number
Treatment type
Weight at time 0
Weight at time 1
Weight at time 2
Weight at time 3
Weight at time 4
Weight at time 5
Weight at time 6
Weight at time 7
Weight at time 8
Weight at time 9
Weight at time 10
Weight at time 11
Weight at time 12
Weight at time 13
Weight at time 14

The statistical analysis for this project is also carried out within MINITAB. However, the raw data are entered differently. First, the data are input on to the computer by creating a text file using an 'editor' or word-processing program on the computer rather than by direct input of the rows and columns to the analysis software. This data file is then read into MINITAB. Second, the data are organised in a fixed format as depicted in Figure 4.2(b). The editor or word processor is used to create a raw data file in which the fixed alignment of characters is replicated. For example, all decimal points for one variable are placed one beneath the other. Since there are a wide variety of editors and word processors, only a broad outline of the procedures rather than precise instructions for creating the raw data file is given. Most editors and word processors have a command mode and an input mode. The command mode enables the text to be changed, movement up and down the file, the saving and retrieval of files. Input mode allows characters to be typed into the file.

Once MINITAB has been loaded, the data file is read in using the commands shown in Table 4.2. The OUTFILE and NOOUTFILE commands respectively open and close the results file called CHWEAT01.LIS. The project illustrates the use of a subcommand. A command, READ is this instance, which is terminated by a semicolon (;), informs the software that a subcommand will follow, which in turn is ended by a full stop (.). In the chalk weathering project the variables are READ into columns C1 – C17 of the MINITAB worksheet from the raw data file called CHWEAT.DAT, which is named between single quotations marks ('CHWEAT.DAT'). The positions of the characters forming the variables are specified by means of the FORMAT subcommand, thus:

SUBC > FORMAT (F3.0,F1.0,15(F5.2)).

The specification provided instructs the software to read the first three characters on a record as column C1, the next single character as C2,

Table 4.2 Entering and storing chalk weathering project data in MINITAB

```
MTB > OUTFILE 'chweat01'
MTB > READ 'chweat.dat' C1 – C16;
SUBC > FORMAT (F3.0,F1.0,15(F5.2)).
MTB > NAME C1 'BlockNo'
MTB > NAME C2 'Treatmt'
MTB > NAME C3 'Time0'
MTB > NAME C4 'Time1'
MTB > NAME C5 'Time2'
MTB > NAME C6 'Time3'
MTB > NAME C7 'Time4'
MTB > NAME C8 'Time5'
MTB > NAME C9 'Time6'
MTB > NAME C10 'Time7'
MTB > NAME C11 'Time8'
MTB > NAME C12 'Time9'
MTB > NAME C13 'Time10'
MTB > NAME C14 'Time11'
MTB > NAME C15 'Time12'
MTB > NAME C16 'Time13'
MTB > NAME C17 'Time14'
MTB > PRINT C1 – C17
MTB > SAVE 'chweat01'
MTB > NOOUTFILE
MTB > STOP
```

and then 15 groups each composed of 5 characters with the last two characters being placed to the right of the decimal point. A series of NAME commands provide titles for the columns, which are then saved along with the data for later use in a file called CHWEAT01.MTW.

4.3.3 River pollution

The river pollution project investigates two related issues in applied physical geography by means of separate samples (A and B). The observations in each sample are sites on rivers at which water is abstracted for laboratory analysis. Both samples generate a set of raw data containing attributes and variables from the chemical analysis and a small set of contextual climatic data, together with the coordinate references of the location of each sample site. Data analysis for the project is also carried out with MINITAB.

The two datasets can be viewed as having a simple rectangular structure of rows and columns. Each of the 250 rows in sample A represents a single water sample from the 10 sites in the five quality classes in the North West region on five randomly selected days. The variables for sample A are:

Easting of sample site
Northing of sample site
1985 water-quality class
Day code number
Sample number
1985 flow class
Dissolved oxygen
Biochemical oxygen demand
Ammonia
Precipitation in previous 24 hours
Mean temperature in previous 24 hours

Sample B has 300 rows denoting the ten water samples for the 30 sites (five upstream and five downstream).

Easting of sample site
Northing of sample site
Site number
Upstream or downstream sample
Sample number
Factory present/absent
1985 water-quality class
1985 flow class
Dissolved oxygen
Biochemical oxygen demand
Ammonia
Precipitation in previous 24 hours
Copper concentration (ppm)

Table 4.3 Entering and storing river pollution project data samples A and B in MINITAB

```
MTB > OUTFILE 'river01'
MTB > READ C1 - C11
DATA > 374,467,1,1,1,4,82.4,1.234,0.0078,25.1,8.5,
DATA > 374,467,1,1,2,4,77.8,2.765,0.0812,25.1,8.5
  ...
DATA > 366,476,5,10,4,6,6.5,13.456,1.5001,18.5,11.5
DATA > 366,476,5,10,5,6,4.8,16.456,1.7721,18.5,11.5
DATA > END
MTB > NAME C1 'Easting'
MTB > NAME C2 'Northing'
MTB > NAME C3 'Class'
MTB > NAME C4 'Day'
MTB > NAME C5 'Sample'
MTB > NAME C6 'Flow'
MTB > NAME C7 'DisO'
MTB > NAME C8 'BOD'
MTB > NAME C9 'NH4'
MTB > NAME C10 'Precn'
MTB > NAME C11 'Temp'
MTB > PRINT C1 - C11
MTB > SAVE 'rivera01'
MTB > READ C1 - C16
DATA > 377,514,1,1,1,1,1,5,85.4,2.341,0.2134,0.550,0.001,14.6,3.4,11.5
DATA > 377,514,1,1,1,1,1,5,85.4,2.341,0.2134,0.550,0.001,14.6,3.4,11.5
  ...
DATA > 359,471,30,2,4,2,5,2,5.6,18.634,1.0562,5.990,0.053,27.6,6.2,9.6
DATA > 359,471,30,2,4,2,5,2,5.6,18.634,1.0562,5.990,0.053,27.6,6.2,9.6
DATA > END
MTB > NAME C1 'Easting'
MTB > NAME C2 'Northing'
MTB > NAME C3 'Site'
MTB > NAME C4 'UpDown'
MTB > NAME C5 'Sample'
MTB > NAME C6 'SiteType'
MTB > NAME C7 'Class'
MTB > NAME C8 'Flow'
MTB > NAME C9 'DisO'
MTB > NAME C10 'BOD'
MTB > NAME C11 'NH4'
MTB > NAME C12 'Copper'
MTB > NAME C13 'Mercury'
MTB > NAME C14 'Zinc'
MTB > NAME C15 'Precn'
MTB > NAME C16 'Temp'
MTB > PRINT C1 - C16
MTB > NOOUTFILE
MTB > SAVE 'riverb01'
MTB > STOP
```

Mercury concentration (ppm)
Zinc concentration (ppm)
Mean temperature in previous 24 hours

The sequence of MINITAB commands used to enter the two samples is essentially the same as for the land-use project with the OUTFILE, READ, NAME and SAVE commands performing the same functions (see Table 4.3). Two MINITAB worksheets are created, RIVERA01.MTW and RIVERB01.MTW, which contain the data for samples A and B respectively.

4.3.4 Village communities

The village communities project benefits from having a fairly large sample size, 358 individuals, which will enable a number of statistical techniques for nominal data to be used. The rectangular data matrix has 358 rows with 29 attributes or variables for each. The geographical component of the data is limited to the distance of the respondents' housing from the proposed development. Computerising the raw data illustrates two further aspects of data analysis: first, the use of free rather than fixed field format; and second, the use of another statistical package.

The software used for this project is the Statistical Package for the Social Sciences version 10 (SPSS-X), also running on a VAX mainframe with the VMS operating system. This package is particularly popular with human geographers and other social scientists, although its data-manipulation and data-analysis capabilities are equally applicable to other fields of investigation. The software can be operated in three different ways, either interactively, where a command is issued and an immediate response is obtained, or by means of command or control files or in batch mode when instructions are submitted to and executed by the computer without the direct intervention of the user. Although interactive use is perhaps more convenient in some respects, operation by means of a control file simplifies the explanation of the function of the different commands. A control file is created on the computer using an editor or word processor and contains a sequence of commands and optionally the data which are to be read in. The data may also be read in from a separate file of the type described for the chalk weathering project. Once the control file is complete and correct, SPSS-X is loaded and instructed to obey the commands. The complete control file of commands required to read in and store the data for the village communities project is given in Table 4.4, with the first three and the last data record included for illustrative purposes. The command file includes the data records between the BEGIN DATA and END DATA commands. Unlike the chalk weathering project, the characters on the data records are not aligned in regular position, but are separated into groups by commas. When reading in the file, the software recognises these commas as delimiters between the attributes or variables.

Table 4.4 Command file for entering and storing the village communities project data in SPSS-X

```
FILE HANDLE SF / NAME = 'VILLAG01.SF'
DATA LIST FREE
  /INTERNO LENGRES MOVEREAS VILLATT1 VILLATT2 NPERSONS TENURE
  AVAILCAR AGE ECONPOSN SEX VILLWORK TRAVWORK HSLDINC HSGTOFM
  NFRIENDS EMPOPPS INCEMOPP HEARPROP FAVPROP DISCHSLD DISCVILL
  DISCOTHR PROPNEWS PROPMTNG MTGEFFCT WELCDEVP WLDATTEN
  WHATEFCT
VARIABLE LABELS
  INTERNO 'Interview Number'
  /LENGRES 'Length of Residence in Village'
  /MOVEREAS 'Reason for Moving to Village'
  /VILLATT1 'Attraction 1' /VILLATT2 'Attraction 2'
  /NPERSONS 'Size of Household' /TENURE 'Housing Tenure'
  /AVAILCAR 'Availability of Car' /AGE 'Age of Respondent'
  /ECONPOSN 'Economic Position of Respondent'
  /SEX 'Sex of Respondent' /VILLWORK 'Work in the Village'
  /TRAVWORK 'Means of Travel to Work'
  /HSLDINC 'Total Annual Household Income'
  /HSGTOFM 'Distance from Cowpers Farm'
  /NFRIENDS 'Number of Friends'
  /EMPOPPS 'Sufficient Employment for Young'
  /INCEMOPP 'Increase Employment Opportunities'
  /HEARPROP 'Heard of Proposal'
  /FAVPROP 'In Favour of Proposal'
  /DISCHSLD 'Discussed in Household'
  /DISCVILL 'Discussed in Village'
  /DISCOTHR 'Discussed with Others'
  /PROPNEWS 'Proposal in Newspaper'
  /PROPMTNG 'Attended Public Meeting'
  /MTGEFFCT 'Meeting had an effect'
  /WELCDEVP 'Would welcome Development'
  /WLDATTEN 'Would have attended Meeting'
  /WHATEFCT 'Effect on Village'
VALUE LABELS MOVEREAS 1 'Retirement' 2 'Employment' 3 'Social'
  4 'Other' 8 'Don t Know' / VILLATT1 VILLATT2 1 'Size'
  2 'Facilities' 3 'People' 4 'Appearance' 5 'Other'
  8 'Don t Know' / TENURE 1 'Own Outright'
  2 'Own with Mortgage' 3 'Rent from LA or Hsg Assn'
  4 'Rent Privately' 5 'Tied to Work' 6 'Other' 8 'Don t Know'
  / AGE 1 '18-24 Years' 2 '25-44 Years' 3 '45-54 Years'
  4 '55-64 Years' 5 '65 Years and Over' /ECONPOSN
  1 'Employer or Self-Empld' 2 'Employee Full-time'
  3 'Employee Part-time' 4 'Unemployed' 5 'Housewife-husband'
  6 'Retired' 7 'Other' 8 'Don t Know' /SEX 1 'Male' 2 'Female'
  /TRAVWORK 1 'Car Driver' 2 'Car passenger' 3 'Bus' 4 'Train'
  5 'Cycle' 6 'Other' 8 'Don t Know' /HSLDINC
  1 'Less than 10 K' 2 '10 to less than 20 K'
  3 '20 to less than 30 K' 4 '30 to less than 40 K'
  5 '40 to less than 50 K' 6 '50 K and Over' 8 'Don t Know'
  /INCEMOPP 1 'Relax Develpt Restrns' 2 'Encourage Expansion'
  3 'Improve Transport' 4 'None of These' 8 'Don t Know'
  /WHATEFCT 1 'Increase Population' 2 'Provide Jobs for Young'
  3 'Increase Traffic' 4 'Impair Character' 5 'Save Facilities'
  8 'Don t Know' /AVAILCAR VILLWORK HEARPROP EMPOPPS FAVPROP
```

Table 4.4 *(continued)*

```
  DISCHSLD DISCVILL DISCOTHR PROPNEWS PROPMTNG MTGEFFCT
  WELCDEVP WLDATTEN 1 'Yes' 2 'No' 8 'Don t Know'
MISSING VALUES ALL (9)
BEGIN DATA
1,15,9,9,9,1,2,1,4,3,1,2,1,1,400,7,1,9,1,2,2,2,2,2,2,9,9,9,1,
2,2,3,3,8,3,2,1,3,5,2,9,9,2,1900,11,1,9,2,9,9,9,9,9,9,2,2,4,
3,34,9,9,9,2,3,1,5,6,2,9,9,2,1850,5,1,9,1,2,1,2,2,2,1,2,9,9,1,
  . . .
358,14,9,9,9,3,2,1,5,6,1,9,9,3,950,7,1,9,1,2,2,1,2,1,2,2,9,9,3
END DATA
SAVE OUTFILE = SF
FINISH
```

Table 4.4 shows three types of SPSS-X command. The FILE HANDLE and the SAVE commands give instructions about operations which are to be carried out on files. The FILE HANDLE command attaches a short name or mnemonic to a file, such as the raw data or, as here, the saved data (system) file. This temporary name is used as a shorthand reference to the file during a particular run of SPSS-X. A FILE HANDLE command has two parts separated by a forward slash (/) delimiter. In this example, the short name 'output' corresponds to the saved data file, VILLAG01.SF, which will be created by the SPSS-X run. The SAVE command instructs the software to carry out the operation of saving the data into a system file on the user's disk area. This file can be reaccessed for undertaking subsequent analyses and also incorporates various definitional information describing the structure, contents and coding of the data.

A second group of SPSS-X commands, represented here solely by DATA LIST, informs the software about the structure and type of raw data, and assigns variable names. The keyword FREE indicates that the attributes and variables are separated by a delimiter rather than to be found in precise column locations. The command requires the user to assign variable names (with a maximum of eight characters) to the attributes and variables. If other types of data format are used, the DATA LIST will require additional information (see SPSS-X documentation for details). The DATA LIST command in this case also illustrates the general syntax requirement that if a command line extends over two or more lines, it is necessary to indent the second and subsequent lines by at least one space.

The third group of commands, including here VARIABLE LABELS, VALUE LABELS and MISSING VALUES, provides information about the variables and their values; in each case a forward slash (/) separates the variables names. These commands are optional, but provide greater clarity. The VARIABLE LABEL command enables the user to supply a description of up to 40 characters for the variables. The VALUE LABEL command performs a similar function with respect to the values included in an attribute, by providing a descriptive label for each value.

For example, the VALUE LABEL command in Table 4.4 specifies that in the case of TENURE, a value of 1 denotes that the property is owned outright, 2 that it is being bought with a mortgage, 3 that it is rented from a local authority or housing association, and so on. In some investigations, the data for certain attributes and variables may be incorrect or missing. For example, some questions may be unanswered or the responses may be unclear. When this happens it is often useful to exclude such cases from the calculation of statistics relating to those variables. SPSS-X enables three missing-values codes to be assigned to variables, which allows differentiation of the reason for non-response.

The procedure for running this file of commands through SPSS-X will vary between computer installations. In the case of mainframe VAX computer running the VMS operating system, the typical form of the instruction issued at the monitor-level prompt ($) is:

```
$SPSSX VILLAGE.SPS/OUTPUT = VILLAGE.LIS
```

This instruction loads up the software, SPSSX being the name given to the package when it was installed, specifies that the commands should be read from a file called VILLAGE.SPS and the results put into a file called VILLAGE.LIS.

One drawback with the SPSS-X software is its habit of producing warning and error messages which may be difficult for the novice user to interpret. These messages are usually caused by mistakes, which occur when typing in the data or commands, which produce inconsistencies and cause the software to become 'confused'. For example, if a variable name is typed incorrectly as TEMURE instead of TENURE when it is first defined, then any subsequent command which uses the correct spelling will generate an error. The only satisfactory answer to this potential difficulty is to ensure that the data and commands are entered correctly in the first place.

Table 4.5 Comparison of data entry for exemplar projects

	Land-use change	Chalk weathering	River pollution	Village communities
Statistical software	MINITAB	MINITAB	MINITAB	SPSS-X
Data entry	Direct	Via file	Direct	Via control file
Data structure	Rectangular	Rectangular	Rectangular	Rectangular
Geographical element	Embedded	Not applicable	Embedded	Indirect
Number of columns/ variables	A.7 B.17	17	A.11 B.16	29

4.4 COMPARISON OF EXEMPLAR PROJECTS

The exemplar projects have illustrated different aspects of computerising geographical data. The contrasts relate to the different software and methods of data entry. Table 4.5 summarises the projects in terms of these contrasts. Whether or not the projects could have been designed differently, alternative methods for computerising their data could have been devised. The book concentrates on two general-purpose statistical packages, MINITAB and SPSS-X, but other software could have been used, including Statistical Analysis System (SAS) and for some techniques database or spreadsheet software, such as dBase and Quattro Pro. More complex data structures could have been defined for some of the projects, particularly the data for the chalk weathering and river pollution studies, which lend themselves to a hierarchical structure.

Part II

STATISTICAL ANALYSIS I

Chapter 5
Descriptive statistics

5.1 PURPOSE OF DESCRIPTIVE STATISTICS

Descriptive statistics forms one of the two main branches of statistical techniques, the other being inferential statistics which is covered in Part III. Descriptive statistics is concerned either with calculating some numerical quantity or with producing a frequency distribution in order to describe one, some or all of the attributes and variables contained in a dataset. At this point inferential statistics will simply be defined as a set of techniques which is used to determine if these descriptive, numerical quantities and frequency distributions are significant or not. There is, therefore, a close connection between the two branches of statistics. This chapter examines numerical quantities as descriptive statistics, while Chapters 6 and 7 consider univariate and bivariate frequency distributions, respectively. The initial sections of this and subsequent chapters examine the theoretical issues and the mathematical background for the statistical techniques, while the subsequent sections concentrate on applying these to the exemplar projects using the MINITAB or SPSS-X computer software.

Descriptive statistical measures can be calculated for both population and sample data. When calculated for a population, the measures are known as parameters; when for a sample, they are known as statistics. As its name implies, the purpose of descriptive statistics is to describe in numerical terms individual attributes and variables. When an investigator first collects a set of raw data, it may be difficult to assimilate the information it contains. The problem is similar to that which arises when reading a book or journal article for the first time. Asked afterwards what the book or article was about, the reader might be able to remember certain key ideas and even certain factual detail, but not all the relevant information. For example, perhaps those points which were repeated a few times or maybe those which were a little idiosyncratic or out of the ordinary will be recalled. In other words, the reader has attempted to summarise or describe the book or article by means of a few key phrases or ideas.

It would be misleading to push the analogy too far. However, the purpose of descriptive statistics is similar: namely, to condense an unorganised and potentially large set of numerical data to a smaller set of summary measures. The following series of numbers illustrates the general problem of coping with a mass of unorganised numerical data. The variable in question is the area (in hectares) of a sample of 52 farms in Yorkshire, England.

> 456.8, 45.6, 20.5, 7.8, 250.2, 134.6, 75.8, 96.7, 13.6, 100.8, 1254.0, 112.5, 19.5, 20.5, 6.4, 555.2, 60.3, 156.9, 854.8, 60.3, 1041.3, 15.7, 19.4, 86.0, 425.6, 50.8, 5.3, 788.5, 65.4, 39.1, 88.7, 4.5, 16.2, 39.0, 19.5, 40.5, 115.6, 88.7, 20.3, 34.6, 156.5, 40.5, 62.6, 657.2, 55.1, 40.5, 25.0, 14.5, 443.6, 6.7, 13.8, 202.5

Having read through the numbers at normal speed, as though they were words, try to answer the following questions without referring back to the numbers:

- What is the size of the largest farm?
- How many farms lie between 50 and 150 ha?
- Which farm sizes occur more than once?

Even with relatively few values to remember the identification of key features of the farm sizes is difficult when presented in this way. Scanning the numbers again and knowing the questions, it is not too difficult to identify the largest farm (1254.0 ha).

The simplest method of summarising a collection of data is to reorder or sort the values from lowest to highest:

> 4.5, 5.3, 6.4, 6.7, 7.8, 13.6, 13.8, 14.5, 15.7, 16.2, 19.4, 19.5, 19.5, 20.3, 20.5, 20.5, 25.0, 34.6, 39.0, 39.1, 40.5, 40.5, 40.5, 45.6, 50.8, 55.1, 60.3, 60.3, 62.6, 65.4, 75.8, 86.0, 88.7, 88.7, 96.7, 100.8, 112.5, 115.6, 134.6, 156.5, 156.9, 202.5, 250.2, 425.6, 443.6, 456.8, 555.2, 657.2, 788.5, 854.8, 1041.3, 1254.0

It is now much easier to answer the questions posed above and to make some summary statements about the data: for example, that the smallest farm is 4.5 ha and the largest 1254.0 ha; that there are 15 farms between 50 and 150 ha; and that the most frequent size is 40.5 ha (3 farms). It is also possible to see that farm size clusters around certain values. In other words, the variable is unevenly spread between the smallest and largest values. For example, there are six farms (over 10 per cent) for which the area lies between 19.4 and 20.5 ha. Equally, there are few farms (only four) with more than 750 ha, even though this size is only a little over half way between the smallest and largest. The sorting of the values in this way helps to clarify the information. Nevertheless, the data still include considerable detail, some of which may obscure the key features. For this reason, descriptive statistics is also sometimes known as *data reduction.*

Table 5.1 Descriptive statistics and scales of measurement

Measure of:	Nominal	Ordinal	Ratio/ interval
Central tendency	Mode	Mode or median	Mean
Dispersion	Interquartile range	Interquartile range	Variance or standard deviation

5.2 MEASURES OF CENTRAL TENDENCY AND DISPERSION

The two main groups of summary measures are known as measures of *central tendency* and measures of *dispersion*. Both sets of measures are numerical quantities which, in the former case, denote a central value within a specific set of numbers, and, in the latter, the spread of values in the set. The three important measures of central tendency are the *mode*, *median* and *mean*. The main dispersion measures are known as the *range*, *interquartile range*, *variance* and *standard deviation*. The two sets of measures complement each other by reporting different characteristics of a set of numbers. The selection of an appropriate measure depends to a large extent on the scale of measurement that was used when the data were collected. Table 5.1 summarises which central tendency and dispersion measures should be used with each of the four scales of measurement.

There are two further measures which can be calculated: *skewness* and *kurtosis*. These summarise the distribution of values. Skewness describes the extent to which a set of values is balanced or symmetrically distributed on either side of the mean. Kurtosis signifies whether the distribution of values is highly peaked or relatively flat; the former indicates that the values are clustered close together, while the latter suggests that they are more spread out.

5.2.1 Mode, median and mean

The mode is defined as the most frequently occurring value within a given set of numbers and is usually obtained by counting rather than by calculation. The modal size in the sample of Yorkshire farms listed above is therefore 40.5 ha, which occurs three times, although it should be noted that four other sizes (19.5, 20.5, 60.3 and 88.7 ha) each have a count of two observations. If two adjacent values occur the same number of times, the question arises as to whether there are two modes (i.e. both values) or one which is mid-way between them. Suppose there had also been three farms with 39.1 ha of land, as well as three with 40.5 ha. Usually the mode would be stated as 39.8 ha, although it could legitimately be argued that there are two modes, namely 39.1 ha and 40.5 ha. If no value occurs more than once, then a mode cannot be recorded.

The median is the value that lies at the mid-point of an ordered set of numbers. It is obtained by sorting the values into either ascending or descending order, counting the total number of observations and then identifying the value in the middle. If there is an odd number of observations, then the median will necessarily be one of the recorded values. However, if there is an even number, then the median value lies mid-way between the two observations in the middle, and will not be one of the recorded values when the two middle observations are different. The sample of Yorkshire farms contained 52 observations and therefore, by partitioning the values into two groups, the median lies mid-way between the 26th and 27th observations. In this case, the median farm size is 57.7 ha. If an additional farm were included in the sample, bringing the total to 53, then the median would be value of the 27th observation.

The arithmetic mean is the measure of central tendency which is commonly referred to as the 'average'. There are in fact several means which can be calculated, although the arithmetic mean is by far the most important. The procedure involves summing all the values for a variable (x) and then dividing by the total number of observations (n), thus:

$$\bar{x} = \frac{\sum x}{n}$$

The Greek letter sigma ($\sum$) is a mathematical symbol which gives the instruction to sum all the individual values of the variable x. The symbol $\bar{x}$ (x bar) denotes the mean of a sample. The sum of the areas for the 52 Yorkshire farms is 9026.0 ha, which gives a mean of 173.6 ha. Slightly different symbols are used in many statistical formulae to distinguish between the calculation of a population parameter and a sample statistic. Population parameters are often known by a letter from the Greek alphabet. For a population mean, the letter μ (pronounced 'mu') is used and the formula becomes

$$\mu = \frac{\sum X}{N}$$

where upper-case letters, here X and N, also signify that the calculations apply to a population rather than a sample.

The arithmetic mean possesses two important properties which are demonstrated in Table 5.2. First, if $\bar{x}$ is subtracted from each x value, then the sum of these deviations or differences is zero (i.e. $\sum(x-\bar{x}) = 0$). Calculating the differences produces a series of positive and negative numbers. When these are summed, taking into account the signs, the result will always equal zero. Second, if the deviations are squared, so that positive numbers are produced, their sum will always be a minimum (i.e. $\sum(x-\bar{x})^2 = \text{minimum}$). Put another way, the sum of the squared differences of each x value from any number apart from their mean will be always be greater than the sum of the squared differences

Table 5.2 Properties of the arithmetic mean and median

x	$(x - \bar{x})$	$(x - \bar{x})^2$	$(x$ − median)	$(x$ − median)^2
4.5	−169.1	28 594.8	−53.2	2 830.2
5.3	−168.3	28 324.9	−52.4	2 745.8
6.4	−167.2	27 955.8	−51.3	2 631.7
6.7	−166.9	27 855.6	−51.0	2 601.0
7.8	−165.8	27 489.6	−49.9	2 490.0
13.6	−160.0	25 600.0	−44.1	1 944.8
13.8	−159.8	25 536.0	−43.9	1 927.2
14.5	−159.1	25 312.8	−43.2	1 866.2
15.7	−157.9	24 932.4	−42.0	1 764.0
16.2	−157.4	24 774.8	−41.5	1 722.3
19.4	−154.2	23 777.6	−38.3	1 466.9
19.5	−154.1	23 746.8	−38.2	1 459.2
19.5	−154.1	23 746.8	−38.2	1 459.2
20.3	−153.3	23 500.9	−37.4	1 398.8
20.5	−153.1	23 439.6	−37.2	1 383.8
20.5	−153.1	23 439.6	−37.2	1 383.8
25.0	−148.6	22 082.0	−32.7	1 069.3
34.6	−139.0	19 321.0	−23.1	533.6
39.0	−134.6	18 117.2	−18.7	349.7
39.1	−134.5	18 090.3	−18.6	346.0
40.5	−133.1	17 715.6	−17.2	295.8
40.5	−133.1	17 715.6	−17.2	295.8
40.5	−133.1	17 715.6	−17.2	295.8
45.6	−128.0	16 384.0	−12.1	146.4
50.8	−122.8	15 079.8	−6.9	47.6
55.1	−118.5	14 042.3	−2.6	6.8
60.3	−113.3	12 836.9	2.6	6.8
60.3	−113.3	12 836.9	2.6	6.8
62.6	−111.0	12 321.0	4.9	24.0
65.4	−108.2	11 707.2	7.7	59.3
75.8	−97.8	9 564.8	18.1	327.6
86.0	−87.6	7 673.8	28.3	800.9
88.7	−84.9	7 208.0	31.0	961.0
88.7	−84.9	7 208.0	31.0	961.0
96.7	−76.9	5 913.6	39.0	1 521.0
100.8	−72.8	5 299.8	43.1	1 857.6
112.5	−61.1	3 733.2	54.8	3 003.4
115.6	−58.0	3 364.0	57.9	3 352.4
134.6	−39.0	1 521.0	76.9	5 913.6
156.5	−17.1	292.4	98.8	9 761.4
156.9	−16.7	278.9	99.2	9 840.6
202.5	28.9	835.2	144.8	20 967.0
250.2	76.6	5 867.6	192.5	37 056.3
425.6	252.0	63 504.0	367.9	135 350.4
443.6	270.0	72 900.0	385.9	148 918.8
456.8	283.2	80 202.2	399.1	159 280.8
555.2	381.6	145 618.6	497.5	247 506.3
657.2	483.6	233 869.0	599.5	359 400.3
788.5	614.9	378 102.0	730.8	533 630.3
854.8	681.2	464 033.4	797.1	635 368.4
1 041.3	867.7	752 903.3	983.6	967 469.0
1 254.0	1 080.4	1 167 264.2	1 196.3	1 431 133.7
9 026.0	0.0	4 051 150.4	6 112.0	4 748 940.4

from the mean. This is shown in Table 5.2 by subtracting the median from each x value and squaring the results.

The mode, median and mean are all measures of the central tendency of a set of values, but what are their relative strengths and weaknesses? The mode is only useful when the number of possible values that might occur is limited. In the case of the farm sizes, a small number of the values occurs more than once, but if the measurements had been made to two decimal places each area might have been unique. In this situation, the mode would have been useless as a means of finding a central value, since each area occurred with equal frequency. The mode is therefore most sensibly used for coded variables or attributes. The median is rather more useful since it is the value of the middle observation within a given ordered set of numbers, although this observation may lie towards one or other end of the range of values. Unfortunately, the median only focuses on either a single value within the set, or two values which lie either side of the middle.

The mean is generally regarded as by far the most useful measure, although one of its key characteristics is both a strength and a weakness. The calculation of the mean takes into account and gives equal weight to all the values, which makes it prone to the influence of extreme values. In the case of 52 Yorkshire farms, two of them had very large sizes (over 1000 ha), which dragged the mean away from the values where the majority of farms are found. If these two farms had not been selected for inclusion in the random sample, then the sum of the remaining 50 sizes would have been 6730.7 ha and their mean would have been 134.6 ha, which is considerably smaller than the original 173.6 ha. The effect of extremes may sometimes be removed by taking the *trimmed mean*, in which an equal percentage of observations are dropped from the top and bottom when calculating the mean. The median value of the 50 farms would have become 53.0 ha, which shows far less change from the original figure of 57.7 ha. However, a further advantage of the mean over the median is that it can be calculated from totals, which is particularly useful for analysing data from secondary sources. For example, suppose that the comparison of photographic evidence for the extent of a glacier in the French Alps with contemporary field observation reveals that it retreated by 150 m between 1890 and 1990. The mean annual rate of retreat can easily be calculated as 1.5 m per year, but the median cannot be determined.

5.2.2 Ranges, variance and standard deviation

The range and the interquartile range constitute two rather crude, but nevertheless easy-to-understand measures of dispersion. The range is very simply the lowest value subtracted from the highest. So in the case of the 52 farms, the range is 1254.0 – 4.5 = 1249.5 ha. The disadvantage of the range is its focus on the extreme values, which may be unusual or atypical. The problem is similar to that encountered with the mean. If the two largest farms had been excluded, then the range would have fallen by about a third to 850.3 ha (854.8 – 4.5).

The interquartile range, and other percentile ranges, attempt to overcome this difficulty. The interquartile range divides the ranked observations into four groups of equal size, such that the lowest 25 per cent of observations are allocated to group 1, the second 25 per cent to group 2 and so on. The data values at the boundaries of these groups are known as Q_1, Q_2 and Q_3 and are determined in the same way as the median (Q_2). The interquartile range is obtained by subtracting Q_1 from Q_3. The Yorkshire farms divide into 4 groups of 13 cases: Q_1 is between the 13th and 14th observation and has the value 19.9 ha; Q_3 is between the 39th and 40th observations, and equals 145.6 ha. The interquartile range is therefore 125.7 ha (145.6 – 19.9). The main problem with the interquartile range is that 50 per cent of the observations are excluded. In this example, those farms lying between 4.5 and 19.5 ha or between 156.9 and 1254.0 ha have been omitted. Other less Draconian percentile partitions can overcome this problem, such as the exclusion of the bottom and top 10 per cent of observations, but this then raises the question why 10 per cent has been chosen as the cut-off point and not 12.5 per cent, 15 per cent or 20 per cent. In other words, the choice is arbitrary and reflects the subjective judgement of the investigator.

The solution to these problems might initially seem to lie in calculating a measure of dispersion which averages the deviation or differences about the mean. Unfortunately, the sum of the differences away from the mean is always zero (see Table 5.2). There are, however, two closely related alternatives, which improve on the range and interquartile range as measures of dispersion. These are the variance (σ^2 for populations, s^2 for samples) and the square root of the variance, called the standard deviation (σ for populations, s for samples). These measures overcome the problem of the sum of the differences about a mean always being zero, by squaring the deviations before summation. The sum of the squared differences is divided by the number of observations (N) for a population and by $n - 1$ for a sample. The variance may thus be thought of as the mean squared deviation about μ or $\bar{x}$ and the standard deviation as its square root. The formulae are:

$$\sigma^2 = \frac{\sum(X - \mu)^2}{N}$$

$$s^2 = \frac{\sum(x - \bar{x})^2}{n - 1}$$

The difference in denominator between the formulae for a population and a sample might seem a little curious. However, it has been shown that if n rather than $n - 1$ is used for a sample there is a systematic tendency for the sample variance to underestimate the true population variance. This undesirable characteristic is overcome by dividing by $n - 1$.

The squared differences and their sum for the sample of Yorkshire farms were given in Table 5.2.

$$s^2 = \frac{\sum(x-\bar{x})^2}{n-1} = \frac{4\,051\,150.4}{(52-1)} = 79\,434.3$$

The calculation of a variance in this manner can be tedious and prone to error if there are more than a few observations. Alternative formulae can be derived, which, although apparently more complicated, are in fact easier to use because the individual deviations from the mean are not required:

$$\sigma^2 = \frac{\sum X^2 - \frac{(\sum X)^2}{N}}{N}$$

$$s^2 = \frac{\sum x^2 - \frac{(\sum x)^2}{n}}{n-1}$$

The term $\sum X^2$ requires the summation of the squared X values, while $(\sum X)^2$ indicates the sum of the X values squared. The same result is obtained when applying the alternative formula to the sample of Yorkshire farms:

$$s^2 = \frac{\sum x^2 - \frac{(\sum x)^2}{n}}{n-1} = \frac{5\,617\,855.8 - \frac{9026^2}{52}}{52-1} = 79\,434.3$$

In Table 5.3 the raw data for the original sample of farms in Yorkshire are shown alongside a similar sample of 52 farms in Lancashire, referred to by the symbol y. Mean farm size in the two samples is identical ($\bar{x} = \bar{y} = 173.6$ ha). A cursory examination of the data reveals that the variability or dispersion of the individual values is very different. Each sample has some extreme values, but the Lancashire farms appear to be more concentrated around the mean. The variance provides a simple quantitative measure of the extent of this variability. Calculated according to the alternative formula, the variance of the Lancashire sample is:

$$s^2 = \frac{\sum x^2 - \frac{(\sum x)^2}{n}}{n-1} = \frac{2\,811\,634.2 - \frac{9026^2}{52}}{52-1} = 24\,410.4$$

The values 79 434.3 and 24 410.4 indicate that the Yorkshire sample is more variable or dispersed than the Lancashire one. Although unlikely, a variance of zero indicates that all the values in the set are identical. In general terms, the larger the variance the greater the spread of data values.

The variance is clearly an important measure with which to compare different populations and samples. However, one drawback is that its

Table 5.3 Dispersion of values in two samples

x	x^2	y	y^2
4.5	20.3	2.4	5.8
5.3	28.1	3.7	13.7
6.4	41.0	10.5	110.3
6.7	44.9	16.2	262.4
7.8	60.8	20.3	412.1
13.6	185.0	22.1	488.4
13.8	190.4	34.3	1 176.5
14.5	210.3	35.6	1 267.4
15.7	246.5	41.2	1 697.4
16.2	262.4	46.5	2 162.3
19.4	376.4	56.0	3 136.0
19.5	380.3	66.7	4 448.9
19.5	380.3	69.2	4 788.6
20.3	412.1	75.3	5 670.1
20.5	420.3	88.6	7 845.0
20.5	420.3	103.2	10 650.2
25.0	625.0	113.0	12 769.0
34.6	1 197.2	113.0	12 769.0
39.0	1 521.0	122.7	15 055.3
39.1	1 528.8	123.2	15 178.2
40.5	1 640.3	128.5	16 512.2
40.5	1 640.3	136.7	18 686.9
40.5	1 640.3	139.8	19 544.0
45.6	2 079.4	140.0	19 600.0
50.8	2 580.6	140.0	19 600.0
55.1	3 036.0	142.4	20 277.8
60.3	3 636.1	145.8	21 257.6
60.3	3 636.1	156.7	24 554.9
62.6	3 918.8	160.8	25 856.6
65.4	4 277.2	175.5	30 800.3
75.8	5 745.6	175.8	30 905.6
86.0	7 396.0	180.3	32 508.1
88.7	7 867.7	181.2	32 833.4
88.7	7 867.7	184.3	33 966.5
96.7	9 350.9	187.4	35 118.8
100.8	10 160.6	191.2	36 557.4
112.5	12 656.3	195.3	38 142.1
115.6	13 363.4	196.3	38 533.7
134.6	18 117.2	196.4	38 573.0
156.5	24 492.3	202.5	41 006.3
156.9	24 617.6	203.2	41 290.2
202.5	41 006.3	205.0	42 025.0
250.2	62 600.0	212.3	45 071.3
425.6	181 135.4	218.5	47 742.3
443.6	196 781.0	222.1	49 328.4
456.8	208 666.2	235.3	55 366.1
555.2	308 247.0	306.5	93 942.3
657.2	431 911.8	460.6	212 152.4
788.5	621 732.3	557.1	310 360.4
854.8	730 683.0	560.0	313 600.0
1 041.3	1 084 305.7	610.6	372 832.4
1 254.0	1 572 516.0	714.2	510 081.6
9 026.0	5 617 856.5	9 026.0	2 811 634.2

value is not given in the same units as those in which the variable was originally measured, but in squared units. The standard deviation, which is the square root of the variance, overcomes this disadvantage. The formulae for the standard deviation of a population and of a sample are therefore a simple adaptation of those for the variance:

$$\sigma = \sqrt{\frac{\sum(X-\mu)^2}{N}} = \sqrt{\sigma^2}$$

$$s = \sqrt{\frac{\sum(x-\bar{x})^2}{n-1}} = \sqrt{s^2}$$

The interpretation of the standard deviation is essentially the same as the variance: the smallest possible value is zero, and the lower the value the less the dispersion in data values. Not surprisingly, the standard deviation of the Yorkshire farms (281.8 ha) is larger than that for the Lancashire farms (156.2 ha), indicating that the latter are less variable.

5.2.3 Skewness and kurtosis

Two final descriptive measures, skewness and kurtosis, are concerned with the shape of the distribution of values, and as such are perhaps more appropriately considered in the next chapter. Nevertheless, they can be calculated for the raw, ungrouped data and so are introduced at this stage. Skewness describes the extent to which a set of values is slanted in one direction or the other about the mean. Referring to Table 5.3, it is apparent that the numerical balance of the individual values about the mean is different for the two samples. In the case of the Yorkshire sample, 41 of the 52 farm areas fall below the mean of 173.6 ha, while the Lancashire farms are more evenly distributed, with 29 less than and 23 greater than the mean. However, skewness refers not only to the number of observations on either side of the mean, but also to the magnitude of the differences. Recall that the sum of the individual differences about the mean is always zero, and so this cannot be used as the basis of a skewness statistic. The square of the differences is already in use for calculating the variance, so the cube is used for skewness. There are a number of ways of defining skewness, although the most useful is known as *momental skewness*, with the following formulae for the population (β_1) and sample (b_1) measures:

$$\beta_1 = \frac{\sum(X-\mu)^3}{N\sigma^3}$$

$$b_1 = \frac{\sum(x-\bar{x})^3}{ns^3}$$

The numerator produces the sum of the cubed differences, while the denominator is the cube of the standard deviation multiplied by N or n. The contrast between the Yorkshire and Lancashire samples is quantified by their having skewness statistics of 2.23 and 1.72, respectively. If the sign of the statistic is negative, then there are more values greater than the mean and the distribution is skewed to the right whereas a positive sign denotes that there are more values less than the mean and distribution is skewed to the left. Zero skewness indicates a perfectly symmetrical distribution. A high skewness statistic not only indicates that the values are more slanted in one direction, but values at one extreme exert a disproportionate influence.

The measurement of kurtosis concerns the 'peakedness' of the data values, which is a characteristic of both severely skewed or symmetrical distributions. The formula for the kurtosis statistic is similar to that for skewness, except that the differences and the standard deviation are raised to fourth power rather than to the third, for a population (γ_2) and sample (g_2) thus:

$$\gamma_2 = \frac{\sum (X - \mu)^4}{N\sigma^4}$$

$$g_2 = \frac{\sum (x - \bar{x})^4}{ns^4}$$

The value of the kurtosis parameter or statistic centres on the value 3, which indicates a symmetrical distribution, while figures below and above 3 respectively denote relatively flat and peaked distributions. In the case of the two groups of farms, the kurtosis statistics are 7.30 for the Yorkshire sample and 5.78 for the Lancashire one. These values signify that both samples are peaked, but this shape is more pronounced in the former.

5.3 DESCRIPTIVE STATISTICS FOR THE EXEMPLAR PROJECTS

The previous section has looked at the mathematical background for the calculation of various descriptive statistical measures. It is now appropriate to compute these quantities for the projects with the MINITAB and SPSS-X software. Identical operations will not be repeated for each project, since the purpose is to choose the most appropriate measures (see Table 5.1) and to demonstrate the different software commands. The aim is to exemplify the range of facilities in the statistical packages for generating these descriptive measures, rather than to present the full project results.

5.3.1 Land-use change

The MINITAB worksheets for samples A and B contain attributes, such as the locality type code, and variables, the areas of land use recorded on the ratio scale in hectares. Referring to Table 5.1, the former require the mode as a measure of central tendency, while the mean, variance and standard deviation are suitable for the area variables. Table 5.4 presents a list of the commands needed to generate the desired descriptive

Table 5.4 Computation of central tendency and dispersion measures for land use project samples A and B in MINITAB (Results output is given in Box 5.1)

```
MTB > OUTFILE 'land02'
MTB > RETRIEVE 'landa01'
MTB > DESCRIBE C5 C7
MTB > DESCRIBE C5;
SUBC > BY C4.
MTB > TALLY C4
MTB > TALLY C4;
SUBC > ALL.
MTB > RETRIEVE 'landb01'
MTB > DESCRIBE C4 – C10
MTB > DESCRIBE C11 – C17;
SUBC > BY C3.
MTB > NOOUTFILE
MTB > STOP
```

statistics for the data in samples A and B, although the two worksheets cannot be accessed simultaneously.

The first task is to load MINITAB and use the RETRIEVE command to access the worksheet files containing the rows and columns of data, LANDA01.MTW for sample A and LANDB01.MTW for sample B. These files have to be retrieved separately, although the results can be placed in the same file. Once MINITAB has been loaded, the OUTFILE command is used to open a new results file (LAND02), and the first worksheet can be retrieved. Data manipulation commands in MINITAB operate on specified rows and columns, as already illustrated with the PRINT command in Chapter 4. When using MINITAB interactively the statistical output is reported on the computer screen and stored in the results file, provided that the OUTFILE and NOOUTFILE commands are given. There are two main ways in which MINITAB can produce descriptive statistics. The simpler method is used for this project, while the alternative is demonstrated with the river pollution study.

The DESCRIBE command produces a predetermined set of descriptive statistics, either for a single column or a group of columns:

```
MTB > DESCRIBE C5 C7
```

The headings on the output from the command (Box 5.1) are largely self-explanatory, although some abbreviations are used: N for number of rows, TRMEAN for trimmed mean, STDEV for standard deviation, SEMEAN for standard error of the mean (for explanation see Chapter 10), MIN for minimum and MAX for maximum value. The range can be calculated from the latter two figures, while the interquartile range can obtained from Q_1 from Q_3, which are provided. Descriptive statistics can also be produced for groups of rows according to a coded attribute by using DESCRIBE with the subcommand BY, thus:

Box 5.1 (*opposite*) Selection of descriptive statistics for land-use project samples A and B (MINITAB output)

```
MTB > RETRIEVE 'landa01'
  WORKSHEET SAVED 3/18/1993    Worksheet retrieved from file: landa01.MTW
MTB > DESCRIBE C5 C7
               N       MEAN    MEDIAN    TRMEAN     STDEV    SEMEAN
Area30s       40      29.02     25.00     27.25     22.89      3.62
Area60s       40      47.78     27.00     43.14     53.49      8.46

             MIN        MAX        Q1        Q3
Area30s     2.00     100.00      9.25     43.00
Area60s     1.00     178.00      9.00     54.50

MTB > DESCRIBE C5;
SUBC > BY C4.
           Uscod30s       N      MEAN    MEDIAN    TRMEAN     STDEV    SEMEAN
Area30s           1      15     35.13     30.00     32.46     26.83      6.93
                  2       5     16.40     17.00     16.40      8.93      3.99
                  3      10     43.40     44.00     44.13     17.64      5.58
                  4       5     18.20     17.00     18.20      9.73      4.35
                  5       2      9.00      9.00      9.00      4.24      3.00
                  6       1      2.00      2.00      2.00         *         *
                  7       2      3.50      3.50      3.50      0.71      0.50

           Uscod30s     MIN       MAX        Q1        Q3
Area30s           1    5.00    100.00     10.00     50.00
                  2    6.00     27.00      7.50     25.00
                  3   16.00     65.00     29.00     65.00
                  4    5.00     30.00      9.50     27.50
                  5    6.00     12.00         *         *
                  6    2.00      2.00         *         *
                  7    3.00      4.00         *         *

MTB > TALLY C4

Uscod30s    COUNT
     1         15
     2          5
     3         10
     4          5
     5          2
     6          1
     7          2
    N=         40

MTB > TALLY C4;
SUBC > ALL.
Uscod30s    COUNT    CUMCNT    PERCENT    CUMPCT
  1            15        15      37.50     37.50
  2             5        20      12.50     50.00
  3            10        30      25.00     75.00
  4             5        35      12.50     87.50
  5             2        37       5.00     92.50
  6             1        38       2.50     95.00
  7             2        40       5.00    100.00
N=             40

MTB > RETRIEVE 'landb01'
  WORKSHEET SAVED   3/28/1993 Worksheet retrieved from file: landb01.MTW
MTB > DESCRIBE C4 - C10
```

(continued)

Box 5.1 (*continued*)

	N	MEAN	MEDIAN	TRMEAN	STDEV	SEMEAN
Arab30s	20	36.15	36.00	36.22	13.69	3.06
MkGd30s	20	6.45	5.00	5.61	6.82	1.52
Gras30s	20	29.60	27.00	29.22	12.42	2.78
Wood30s	20	12.25	9.00	11.44	9.22	2.06
Heat30s	20	4.75	2.50	3.33	7.50	1.68
Hous30s	20	3.30	1.50	2.44	5.09	1.14
AgUn30s	20	7.50	6.00	6.89	5.39	1.20

	MIN	MAX	Q1	Q3
Arab30s	8.00	63.00	27.25	47.25
MkGd30s	0.00	28.00	2.25	7.75
Gras30s	11.00	55.00	19.25	37.75
Wood30s	3.00	36.00	5.25	17.00
Heat30s	0.00	35.00	1.25	5.00
Hous30s	0.00	22.00	0.00	5.75
AgUn30s	1.00	25.00	4.00	9.75

```
MTB > DESCRIBE C11 – C17;
SUBC > BY C3.
```

	UrbRur	N	MEAN	MEDIAN	TRMEAN	STDEV	SEMEAN
Arab60s	1	10	41.70	46.00	42.75	18.71	5.92
	2	10	46.00	50.00	45.88	18.48	5.84
MkGd60s	1	10	5.60	2.50	3.00	9.78	3.09
	2	10	1.70	0.50	0.62	3.68	1.16
Gras60s	1	10	18.70	19.00	17.88	10.27	3.25
	2	10	26.70	23.50	25.75	18.32	5.79
Wood60s	1	10	7.10	4.00	5.37	8.28	2.62
	2	10	11.00	8.00	8.88	11.13	3.52
Heat60s	1	10	3.10	0.00	0.38	8.76	2.77
	2	10	2.70	1.50	2.38	3.23	1.02
Hous60s	1	10	9.60	4.50	5.25	16.22	5.13
	2	10	2.90	2.00	2.00	3.84	1.22
AgUn60s	1	10	14.20	11.50	12.50	9.33	2.95
	2	10	8.70	9.50	8.62	4.08	1.29

	UrbRur	MIN	MAX	Q1	Q3
Arab60s	1	9.00	66.00	29.75	55.50
	2	19.00	74.00	27.25	57.25
MkGd60s	1	0.00	32.00	0.00	6.75
	2	0.00	12.00	0.00	1.25
Gras60s	1	5.00	39.00	8.75	26.00
	2	4.00	57.00	10.75	41.50
Wood60s	1	0.00	28.00	2.00	11.25
	2	1.00	33.00	2.00	17.25
Heat60s	1	0.00	28.00	0.00	1.00
	2	0.00	8.00	0.00	5.75
Hous60s	1	0.00	54.00	0.00	9.50
	2	0.00	13.00	0.75	3.50
AgUn60s	1	4.00	38.00	10.00	15.00
	2	2.00	16.00	5.75	10.75

```
MTB > NOOUTFILE
```

```
MTB > DESCRIBE C5;
SUBC > BY C4.
```

The functions of the semicolon (;) and full stop (.) were discussed in Chapter 4. The mode is the most suitable measure of central tendency to use with the land-use code and locality type attributes. The mode can be obtained through MINITAB's TALLY command:

```
MTB > TALLY C4
```

This command counts the number of times each value occurs in a column (or columns) and reports the result in the form of a univariate frequency table (see Chapter 6). By default the command simply displays the absolute counts. However, specifying ALL or any of the keywords COUNTS, PERCENTS, CUMCOUNTS or CUMPERCENTS in a subcommand enables percentage and cumulative frequencies to be produced.

The analysis of the project datasets (Box 5.1) reveals that, in the case of sample A, the mean area of land plots rose from 29.02 ha in the 1930s to 47.78 ha in the 1960s. Furthermore, the mean areas of arable and grass plots in the 1930s were 35.13 ha and 43.40 ha, respectively. Sample B indicates that in the 1930s the mean areas of arable and grass per square kilometre were 36.15 ha and 29.60 ha, respectively. Considering the differences between the urban-rural and the rural localities, it is not surprising that the areas of market gardening, housing and agriculturally unproductive land are greater in the former, although the higher mean figure for heath and rough grazing is interesting. In contrast, grid squares in the rural area had larger areas of arable and grass land. An examination of the standard deviations for the land uses in the two types of area gives some indication of the dispersion of values. For instance, dispersion of arable land areas is similar in the two localities, whereas grassland is more variable in the rural area.

5.3.2 Chalk weathering

The dataset for the chalk weathering project was saved as the MINITAB worksheet CHWEAT01.MTW. The sequence of commands for generating the basic descriptive statistical output is given in Table 5.5. Each

Table 5.5 Computation of central tendency and dispersion measures for chalk weathering project in MINITAB (Results output is given in Box 5.2)

```
MTB > OUTFILE 'chweat02'
MTB > RETRIEVE 'chweat01'
MTB > LET C18 = C3 – C10
MTB > LET C19 = C3 – C17
MTB > DESCRIBE C18 C19;
MTB > BY C2.
MTB > SAVE 'chweat02'
MTB > NOOUTFILE
MTB > STOP
```

row represents a chalk block, and columns C3 to C17 are the weights on 15 different occasions. While the mean weight of either all or specific groups of the blocks at any particular time might be interesting, it is perhaps more useful to examine the loss of weight by blocks undergoing different treatments. For example, there might be differences in mean weight loss after 7 days and 14 days.

Once the worksheet has been retrieved, the first task is to calculate the difference in the weight of the blocks after 7 and 14 days and to store the results in two new columns (C18 and C19). Such mathematical calculations are undertaken in MINITAB thus:

```
MTB > LET C18 = C3 - C10
MTB > LET C19 = C3 - C17
```

Using the DESCRIBE command on C18 and C19 with BY C2 (treatment type) as the subcommand produces descriptive statistics which give some indication of the effects of the different treatments. The worksheet has been amended during a MINITAB session by the addition of two new columns and is saved with either the same or preferably a new filename (CHWEAT02.MTW) so that the additional columns are kept.

The results of these descriptive analyses (Box 5.2) show that over the first 7 days the loss of weight was relatively similar for blocks undergoing the various treatments, with the mean for the freeze–thaw regimes in pure and saline water at 4.9 g and 4.1 g and with reasonably similar standard deviations, although examination of the minimum and maximum values shows a range of around 10 g. The contrast between the effects of the different treatments becomes more marked after 14 days, with reductions of 17.6 g and 21.3 g, respectively, for the freeze–thaw regimes with pure and saline water saturated blocks. Interestingly, the standard deviations for weight loss after 14 days are mostly larger than for after 7 days, which perhaps suggests that the contrasting effects of the treatments becomes more pronounced with time.

5.3.3 River pollution

The worksheets for the river pollution study are retrieved separately, as in the case of the land-use project, although the results are directed to the same file. Table 5.6 logs the MINITAB session for producing descriptive statistics for these samples, using an alternative set of commands. These commands calculate specific descriptive measures, namely MEAN, STDEV, MEDIAN, MINIMUM and MAXIMUM, for the column or columns. The results are displayed on the screen in a different format to the output from the DESCRIBE command. The examples of MEAN and STDEV commands also illustrate how a descriptive statistic can be stored as a constant, which is given a number prefixed by a K, for use on a later occasion. If the mode or interquartile range is required, these have to be obtained with the TALLY or DESCRIBE commands.

Box 5.2 (*opposite*) Selection of descriptive statistics for chalk weathering (MINITAB output)

```
MTB > RETRIEVE 'chweat01'
  WORKSHEET SAVED 3/15/1993   Worksheet retrieved from file: chweat01.MTW
MTB > LET C18 = C3 - C10
MTB > LET C19 = C3 - C17
MTB > NAME C18 'Loss0-7'
MTB > NAME C19 'Loss0-14'
MTB > DESCRIBE C18 C19;
SUBC > BY C2.

           Treatmt    N      MEAN    MEDIAN    TRMEAN     STDEV    SEMEAN
Loss0-7       1      12     4.865     4.230     4.567     2.632     0.760
              2      12     4.144     3.440     3.805     3.390     0.979
              3      12     0.001     0.000     0.000     0.003     0.001
              4      12     1.825     1.620     1.812     0.524     0.110
              5      12     0.187     0.010     0.119     0.397     0.115
              6      12     0.114     0.000     0.009     0.368     0.106
              7      12     1.108     0.085     0.328     2.850     0.823
              8      12     0.287     0.250     0.247     0.275     0.079
              9      12     0.229     0.125     0.177     0.278     0.080

Loss0-14      1      12    17.632    17.565    17.463     2.443     0.705
              2      12    21.313    21.565    21.365     2.728     0.788
              3      12     1.721     1.580     1.663     1.368     0.395
              4      12     5.600     5.670     5.586     1.475     0.426
              5      12     8.943     9.230     8.982     1.985     0.573
              6      12     1.192     1.280     1.224     0.664     0.192
              7      12     1.806     1.360     1.782     0.958     0.276
              8      12     1.244     1.290     1.212     0.483     0.139
              9      12     0.736     0.740     0.730     0.490     0.141

           Treatmt      MIN       MAX        Q1        Q3
Loss0-7       1       2.310    10.400     2.608     7.295
              2       0.660    11.020     1.955     4.412
              3       0.000     0.010     0.000     0.000
              4       1.120     2.660     1.398     2.335
              5       0.000     1.060     0.000     0.080
              6       0.000     1.280     0.000     0.017
              7       0.000    10.010     0.008     0.753
              8       0.000     0.970     0.080     0.450
              9       0.000     0.980     0.033     0.348

Loss0-14      1      14.600    22.350    15.233    19.817
              2      16.670    25.440    19.057    23.563
              3       0.020     4.000     0.285     3.065
              4       3.140     8.200     4.423     6.443
              5       5.720    11.770     7.072    10.837
              6       0.050     2.020     0.730     1.760
              7       0.550     3.300     1.013     2.670
              8       0.490     2.320     0.887     1.432
              9       0.020     1.510     0.365     1.180

MTB > SAVE 'chweat02'
  Worksheet saved into file: chweat02.MTW
MTB > NOOUTFILE
```

Table 5.6 Computation of central tendency and dispersion measures for river pollution project samples A and B in MINITAB

```
MTB > OUTFILE 'river02'
MTB > RETRIEVE 'rivera01'
MTB > MEAN C7 K1
MTB > STDEV C7 K2
MTB > MEDIAN C6
MTB > MINIMUM C9
MTB > MAXIMUM C9
MTB > DESCRIBE C7 – C9;
SUBC > BY C3.
MTB > SAVE 'rivera02'
MTB > RETRIEVE 'riverb01'
MTB > DESCRIBE C9 C10;
MTB > BY C4.
MTB > NOOUTFILE
MTB > STOP
```

The descriptive analysis of the datasets (Box 5.3) indicates that rivers classified in the 'better' quality classes in 1985 had higher percentages of dissolved oxygen (C7), and lower levels for biochemical oxygen demand (C8) and ammonia (C9). In the case of sample A, the C7 mean for class 1 water samples was 84.2 per cent compared with 8.8 per cent for class 5, the C8 and C9 means were respectively 1.5 and 15.3 mg/l, and 0.15 and 1.43 mg/l. Sample B indicates that the mean percentage of dissolved oxygen (C9) is about 8 points higher upstream

Box 5.3 Selection of descriptive statistics for river pollution project samples A and B (MINITAB output)

```
MTB > RETRIEVE 'rivera01'
  WORKSHEET SAVED  3/24/1993  Worksheet retrieved from file: rivera01.MTW
MTB > MEAN C7 K1
  MEAN = 45.962
MTB > STDEV C7 K2
  ST.DEV. = 28.704
MTB > MEDIAN C6
  MEDIAN = 5.500
MTB > MINIMUM C9
  MINIMUM = 0.000
MTB > MAXIMUM C9
  MAXIMUM = 2.343
MTB > DESCRIBE C7 – C9;
  SUBC > BY C3.
          Class   N     MEAN     MEDIAN    TRMEAN    STDEV    SEMEAN
DisO        1     50    84.154   84.300    84.148    2.780    0.393
            2     50    68.172   67.750    68.157    4.958    0.701
            3     50    48.172   47.450    48.045    5.456    0.772
            4     50    20.560   19.800    20.325    6.848    0.968
            5     50     8.754    8.800     8.657    3.159    0.447
BOD         1     50     1.519    1.538     1.530    0.738    0.104
            2     50     3.681    3.556     3.682    0.997    0.141
            3     50     7.408    7.502     7.367    1.425    0.202
            4     50    13.128   13.215    13.186    2.750    0.389
            5     50    15.291   15.354    15.267    2.458    0.348
```

(continued)

Box 5.3 (*continued*)

```
NH4      1      50       0.150      0.157      0.150      0.091      0.013
         2      50       0.635      0.673      0.637      0.214      0.030
         3      50       0.792      0.853      0.813      0.211      0.029
         4      50       1.066      0.984      1.022      0.322      0.045
         5      50       1.431      1.337      1.420      0.441      0.062
       Class      MIN        MAX        Q1         Q3
DisO     1      77.800     90.100     82.325     86.125
         2      58.900     77.800     64.250     71.550
         3      38.900     58.900     43.475     51.700
         4      10.200     35.600     15.300     25.450
         5       3.400     17.600      6.275     11.050
BOD      1       0.007      2.899      1.086      2.080
         2       1.654      5.456      2.885      4.534
         3       4.772     10.561      6.019      8.451
         4       7.201     17.567     10.979     15.515
         5      10.676     20.502     13.395     17.084
NH4      1       0.000      0.302      0.081      0.228
         2       0.239      0.994      0.447      0.834
         3       0.000      1.134      0.679      0.939
         4       0.765      2.003      0.894      1.005
         5       0.564      2.343      1.002      1.801
MTB > SAVE 'rivera02'
MTB > RETRIEVE 'riverb01'
  WORKSHEET SAVED 3/28/1993  Worksheet retrieved from file: riverb01.MTW
MTB > DESCRIBE C9 C10;
SUBC > BY C4.
        UpDown    N       MEAN     MEDIAN    TRMEAN     STDEV    SEMEAN
DisO      1      150      45.15    46.10     44.85      30.14     2.46
          2      150      37.21    33.15     36.41      29.64     2.42
BOD       1      150       8.84     7.02      8.70       6.18     0.50
          2      150       8.80     6.57      8.64       6.42     0.52
        UpDown    MIN      MAX       Q1        Q3
DisO      1       4.20    93.20     13.20     73.47
          2       1.40    88.00      6.95     64.55
BOD       1       0.19    20.20      3.44     15.48
          2       0.05    21.43      3.43     15.38
MTB > NOOUTFILE
```

of the sample sites than downstream. The level of biochemical oxygen demand is similar upstream and downstream of the sites, as are the standard deviations for the two types of location.

5.3.4 Village communities

The village communities project dataset has been saved as an SPSS-X system file, which must be accessed in order to undertake any descriptive statistical analysis. The log of the SPSS-X control file (VILLAG01.SPS) is given in Table 5.7, which is run through SPSS-X to produce the results file (Box 5.4) on a VAX computer running VMS, thus:

```
$SPSSX VILLAG01.SPS/OUTPUT = VILLAG01.LIS
```

Table 5.7 Computation of central tendency and dispersion measures for village communities project in SPSS-X

```
FILE HANDLE SF / NAME = 'VILLAG01.SF'
GET FILE = SF
DESCRIPTIVES MOVEREAS VILLATT1 VILLATT2 SEX TENURE VILLWORK
  TRAVWORK WHATEFCT /STATISTICS = SKEW MIN MAX
DESCRIPTIVES LENGRES NPERSONS HSGTOFM NFRIENDS
  /STATISTICS = ALL
TEMPORARY
SELECT IF (NPERSONS EQ 1)
DESCRIPTIVES MOVEREAS VILLATT1 VILLATT2 SEX TENURE VILLWORK
  TRAVWORK WHATEFCT /STATISTICS = SKEW MIN MAX
FINISH
```

The function of the FILE HANDLE command was described in Chapter 4, namely to supply a shorthand name for the files on disk. The GET FILE = command 'gets' or loads the specified system file so that the data can be processed. Its function is similar to the RETRIEVE command in MINITAB.

The DESCRIPTIVES command is the SPSS-X equivalent of DESCRIBE and computes a collection of central tendency and dispersion measures. The command provides some flexibility for determining which attributes and variables are 'described' and which measures are computed. DESCRIPTIVES, like many other commands in SPSS-X, requires the user to specify a variable list by referring to the variable names either individually or in groups (see Table 5.7). The default set of descriptive statistics can be rejected in favour of those specifically required by the user, by including a /STATISTICS = subcommand. The simplest, but potentially most confusing, option is to ask for ALL descriptive statistics and then decide which are appropriate. However, individual measures can be selected with keywords, such as MIN, MAX, MEAN, SKEW and VARIANCE.

Statistical operations or procedures sometimes need to be undertaken on groups of cases or records. Such groups can be identified by means of a comprehensive set of conditional record selection statements, usually introduced by the command SELECT IF, followed by a logical condition. The command

SELECT IF (NPERSONS EQ 1)

selects those records or cases where the variable NPERSONS has a value of 1 (i.e. where there is one person in the household). Complex record selection instructions referring to several variable names can be created in SPSS-X. The software documentation provides detailed instructions. These data-selection commands can be applied to just the next statistical procedure by including the extra line TEMPORARY (see Table 5.7) or for the entire SPSS-X run when this is omitted. Some questions in the survey were only applicable to respondents who satisfied certain criteria, for example, the main reason for moving to

Box 5.4 (*opposite*) Selection of descriptive statistics for village communities project (SPSS-X output)

Variable	Skew	S.E. Skew	Min	Max	N	Label
MOVEREAS	.51	.29	1.00	4.00	66	Reason for Moving to Village
VILLATT1	−.14	.29	1.00	4.00	66	Attraction 1
VILLATT2	1.41	.29	1.00	8.00	66	Attraction 2
SEX	−.08	.13	1.00	2.00	358	Sex of Respondent
TENURE	1.33	.13	1.00	6.00	358	Housing Tenure
VILLWORK	−.79	.16	1.00	2.00	220	Work in the Village
TRAVWORK	.51	.16	1.00	7.00	221	Means of Travel to Work
WHATEFCT	−.13	.13	1.00	5.00	358	Effect on Village

Variable LENGRES Length of Residence in Village

Mean	23.126	S.E. Mean	.787	Std Dev	14.843
Variance	220.319	Kurtosis	−.131	S.E. Kurt	.258
Skewness	.673	S.E. Skew	.129	Range	64.000
Minimum	.00	Maximum	64.00	Sum	8233.000

Valid observations – 356 Missing observations – 2

- -

Variable NPERSONS Size of Household

Mean	2.455	S.E. Mean	.068	Std Dev	1.286
Variance	1.655	Kurtosis	.489	S.E. Kurt	.257
Skewness	.858	S.E. Skew	.129	Range	6.000
Minimum	1.00	Maximum	7.00	Sum	879.000

Valid observations – 358 Missing observations – 0

- -

Variable HSGTOFM Distance from Cowpers Farm

Mean	1532.709	S.E. Mean	76.492	Std Dev	1447.303
Variance	2094686.476	Kurtosis	1.353	S.E. Kurt	.257
Skewness	1.367	S.E. Skew	.129	Range	6650.000
Minimum	50.00	Maximum	6700.00	Sum	548710.000

Valid observations – 358 Missing observations – 0

- -

Variable NFRIENDS Number of Friends

Mean	5.876	S.E. Mean	.232	Std Dev	4.373
Variance	19.123	Kurtosis	1.229	S.E. Kurt	.258
Skewness	1.331	S.E. Skew	.129	Range	21.000
Minimum	.00	Maximum	21.00	Sum	2092.000

Valid observations – 356 Missing observations – 2

TEMPORARY
SELECT IF (NPERSONS EQ1)

Variable	Skew S.E.	Skew	Min	Max	N	Label
MOVEREAS	.12	.56	1.00	4.00	16	Reason for Moving to Village
VILLATT1	−.40	.56	1.00	4.00	16	Attraction 1
VILLATT2	1.68	.56	1.00	8.00	16	Attraction 2
SEX	.11	.25	1.00	2.00	95	Sex of Respondent
TENURE	1.59	.25	1.00	6.00	95	Housing Tenure
VILLWORK	−1.32	.31	1.00	2.00	61	Work in the Village
TRAVWORK	.66	.31	1.00	7.00	61	Means of Travel to Work
WHATEFCT	−.05	.25	1.00	5.00	95	Effect on Village

the village and views on its attractive features (variables MOVEREAS, VILLATT1 and VILLATT2) only relate to people having migrated into the village within the previous 10 years. Where this criterion is not satisfied, the cases have a 9 entered for these variables, which has been defined as the missing value (see Table 4.4). DESCRIPTIVES, like most other SPSS-X commands, will omit these cases from the calculations when carrying out the specified statistical analysis, unless their inclusion is specifically requested.

The descriptive analysis of the attributes and variables in the village communities project (Box 5.4) indicates that the mean length of residence in the village was 23.1 years, although the fairly high variance and standard deviation (220.3 and 14.8, respectively) suggest that there is considerable dispersion of values around the mean. The skewness of the four continuous variables (LENGRES, NPERSONS, HSGTOFM and NFRIENDS) is positive, in the case of the latter two markedly so, which indicates that more observations had values less than the mean. Referring to the first and final of sections of the table, which present the same set of descriptive statistics relating, respectively, to all respondents and to those living alone, it is apparent that there was greater negative skewness for the VILLWORK variable in the latter (−1.32) case than in the former (−0.79).

5.4 COMPARISON OF DESCRIPTIVE STATISTICAL ANALYSES FOR EXEMPLAR PROJECTS

The calculation of the basic descriptive statistical measures for the four projects has introduced further commands and procedures in MINITAB and SPSS-X. In conclusion, some important points and contrasts should be highlighted. It is quite easy to produce some descriptive statistics

Table 5.8 Comparison descriptive statistical analysis for exemplar projects

	Land-use change	Chalk weathering	River pollution	Village communities
Measures of:				
Central tendency	Mode Mean	Mean Median	Mode Median Mean	Mode Mean
Dispersion	Range Variance/ standard deviation	Variance/ standard deviation	Range Variance/ standard deviation	Variance/ standard deviation
Software commands(s)	DESCRIBE DESCRIBE; BY C. TALLY C	DESCRIBE; BY C.	MEAN STDEV MIN, MAX, etc.	DESCRIPTIVES /STATISTICS =

with both packages. In each case commands exist for generating a predetermined set of descriptive measures, although the researcher's full requirements may not be satisfied. Careful consideration should be given to which descriptive measures are needed. This is partly to ensure that sound analysis is undertaken, and partly because there are implications for the choice of software. This introduces the third point when planning the research, namely to ensure that software is able to do what is wanted. In many human geography and social science projects, there are often many coded attributes, for which the mode is the most appropriate measure of central tendency. The DESCRIPTIVES command in SPSS-X produces this statistic directly, whereas it has to be obtained with the TALLY command in MINITAB. Table 5.8 compares the principal features of the descriptive analyses undertaken in the four projects. Finally, the variance is not reported as a descriptive statistic in MINITAB, although it is calculated by some statistical procedures. Furthermore, the STDEV and DESCRIBE commands calculate the standard deviation with $n - 1$ as the denominator, which is, of course, incorrect if the analysis relates to a population of observations.

Chapter 6
Frequency distributions

6.1 UNIVARIATE FREQUENCY DISTRIBUTIONS

Measures of central tendency and dispersion summarise the statistical characteristics of a variable as a single value. However, the statistical description of a variable or attribute often needs to consider the complete set of values. An overview of all the values can be achieved by producing a *frequency distribution*. Frequency distributions give a better visual impression of the characteristics of the data and are an important means for organising the data into a manageable system. This chapter concentrates on univariate frequency distributions, while the next extends this to look at bivariate and multivariate frequency distributions. Univariate distributions focus on one attribute or variable at a time.

There are occasions when an investigator can only obtain data in the form of a frequency distribution, mainly when using information from a secondary source. The Population Census, for example, contains statistics in the form of frequency distributions. Only a few of the published Census statistics are univariate distributions; most are bivariate or multivariate cross-tabulations of the type examined in Chapter 7. Physical geographers also use data from secondary sources in the form of frequency distributions. One example is the Biological Records Database held by the Institute of Terrestrial Ecology in Britain. This database contains counts of different flora and fauna on a grid-square basis.

From the point of view of the statistical analysis of population or sample data, a frequency distribution displays the occurrence of a set of observations with respect to their values for a particular variable. A frequency distribution can contain either the absolute or relative frequencies of the observations possessing the different values. Absolute frequencies show the number of observations with each value. Relative frequencies present the percentage or proportion of observations. In the case of percentage frequencies, the count of observations with each value is expressed as a percentage, and so the total for the relative frequency column adds up to 100 per cent. Proportionate frequencies can be thought of simply as the percentage frequency divided by 100. For example, suppose that on 60.3 per cent of days the predominant wind direction was westerly; expressed as a proportion this would be 0.603. The sum of a proportionate frequencies column is therefore 1. It is sometimes useful to show a frequency distribution in a cumulative fashion. For example, suppose that on a further 15.5 per cent of days the predominant wind was from a northerly direction; then the cumulative total for the two directions is 75.8 per cent or 0.758.

Frequency distributions can be displayed in either a tabular or graphical form. Simple univariate distributions are easily displayed in a table, which can include the absolute, relative and cumulative frequencies. The main graphical alternative is the *histogram* or *bar chart* (see Figure 6.1(a)). The bars are drawn so that their heights are

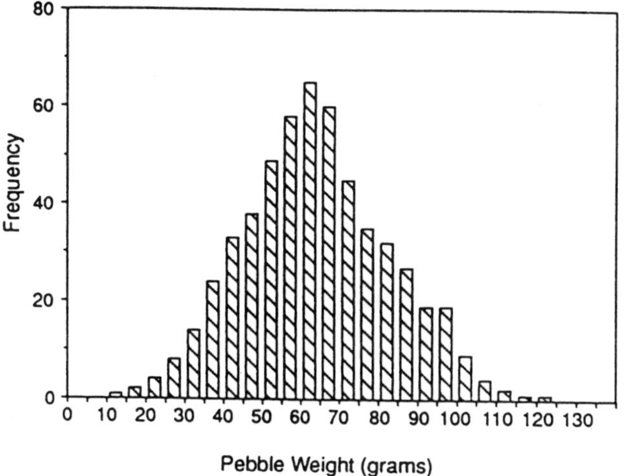

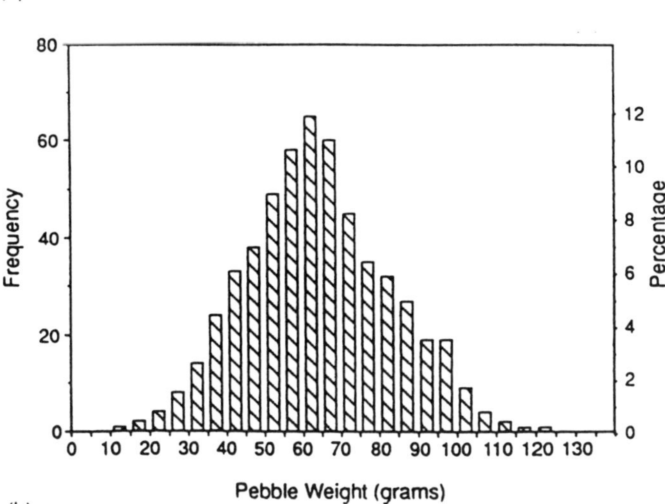

Figure 6.1 (a) One-scale and (b) two-scale histograms

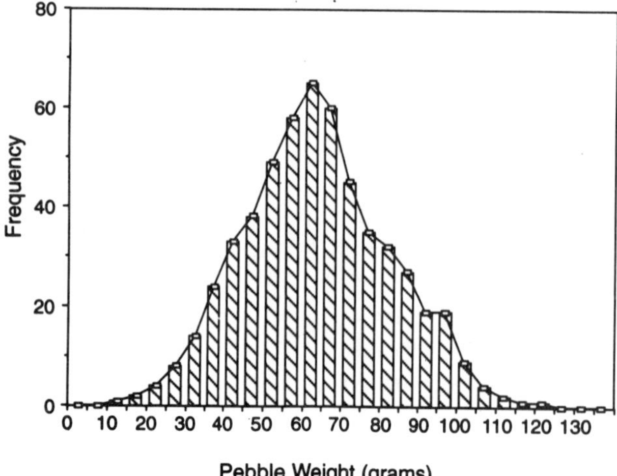

Figure 6.2 Relationship between frequency histogram and polygon

scaled in relation to the absolute frequency of observations. Sometimes a histogram is shown with different scales on two vertical axes so that the heights of the bars indicate both the absolute and relative frequencies (Figure 6.1(b)). Some statistical software represents the bars as horizontal rows of asterisks, which are simply histograms drawn on their side. More recent software, such as Quattro Pro, does not suffer from this disadvantage and allows more sophisticated graphical representations.

A second important method for graphically presenting the distribution of a continuous variable is as a *frequency polygon*. This is essentially a line graph in which the frequency count is plotted against the mid-value of each class. In Figure 6.2 such a polygon has been superimposed on the corresponding histogram. The option exists to leave the polygon hanging above the horizontal axis or to extend the lines to meet the axis at the mid-values of the classes below and above those present in the data. The latter is more visually pleasing, but possibly suggests the presence of values outside the true boundaries of the bottom and top classes. If the size of the sample and the number of classes are increased, while the class width or interval is reduced, the form of the frequency polygon will approach a smooth line, known as a *frequency curve*.

6.2 CLASSIFICATION OF CONTINUOUS VARIABLES

It is relatively straightforward to produce a frequency distribution for an attribute which is already constrained to a discrete set of nominal categories, which usually have numerical values attached to them. For example, a dichotomous question often has the code values of 1 for 'yes', 2 for 'no' and 9 for 'don't know'. Variables measured on the ordinal, interval or ratio scales present a different problem. In these situations the values need to be grouped or classified before a sensible frequency distribution can be produced. The raw data for the sample of Yorkshire farms have been classified in Table 6.1 and are shown graphically in Figure 6.3 to illustrate the effects of this form of data reduction.

The range of values in the original farm size variable has been segmented into a series of classes or groups. Such classes can be defined in a number of different ways. In this case an equal class interval has been used, which produces an unbalanced or skewed distribution of the 52 farms across the 13 classes. The cumulative percentage column shows that 78.8 per cent of the farms fall in the first two groups and 90.4 per cent in the first six. One alternative method of classification uses unequal class intervals in order to smooth out the number

Table 6.1 Classification of farm size for Yorkshire sample

Size group (ha)	Count	Cumulative count	Percentage	Cumulative percentage
0.0– 99.9	35	35	67.3	67.3
100.0– 199.9	6	41	11.5	78.8
200.0– 299.9	2	43	3.8	82.7
300.0– 399.9	0	43	0.0	82.7
400.0– 499.9	3	46	5.8	88.5
500.0– 599.9	1	47	1.9	90.4
600.0– 699.9	1	48	1.9	92.3
700.0– 799.9	1	49	1.9	94.2
800.0– 899.9	1	50	1.9	96.2
900.0– 999.9	0	50	0.0	96.2
1000.0–1099.9	1	51	1.9	98.1
1100.0–1199.9	0	52	0.0	98.1
1200.0–1299.9	1	52	1.9	100.0

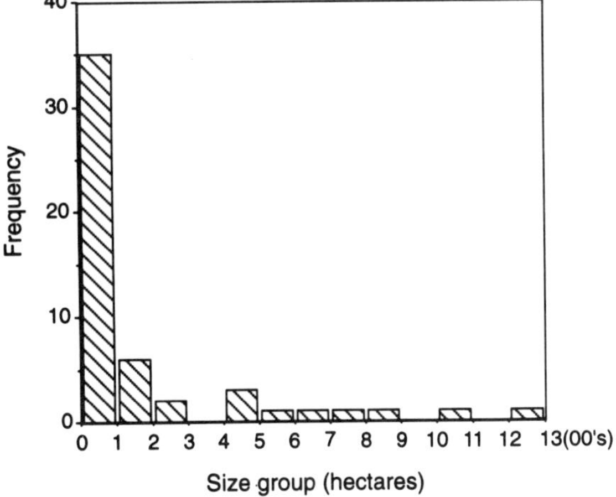

Figure 6.3 Histogram of size for sample of farms in Yorkshire

of observations per class (see Table 6.2). The farms still tend to be skewed towards the lower classes, but the effect is less pronounced (only 30.8 per cent fall in the 0.0–24.9 ha group). Another alternative is to divide the spread of values into percentile groups, in much the same way as for the calculation of the interquartile range, which is shown as the second classification in Table 6.2. The range (1249.9 ha) has been divided at the five 20 percentile points into classes with an interval of 249.9 ha. The distribution of observations remains fairly skewed, with 82.7 per cent falling in the first class (4.5–254.4 ha). The third alternative, also shown in Table 6.2, involves determining the classes in intervals in terms of units of the standard deviation (281.8 ha) away from the mean. For example, the size group 173.7–455.4 ha includes all those farms with area between the mean and the mean plus 1 standard deviation. This system has again produced a fairly skewed distribution, with 78.8 per cent of farms in the lowest group. This example illustrates how this method may produce a negative value for the lowest class boundary, which may not make sense, as in this instance. A farm cannot have a negative area, while terminating the class at 0.0 is statistically misleading.

It may be noted that in the original classification scheme (Table 6.1), some of the classes recorded zero observations. This can occur when equal classes are used and there are a few extreme values at the lower and/or upper end of the range. This problem may be alleviated by leaving the top and bottom classes open-ended. For example, a class interval of 25 ha might have been used (0.0–24.9 ha, 25.0–49.9 ha, etc.) up to 174.9 ha, and then the top group could have been 175 ha and over. The main disadvantage of this type of system is that difficulties arise in computations based on the frequency distribution. Of course, such open-ended classes are unavoidable if they exist in a distribution obtained from a secondary source.

One feature of the different classification schemes is that they are mutually exclusive, which means that an individual observation can only be assigned to one class. If the classes had been specified to the nearest whole hectare, rather than to the nearest tenth of a hectare,

Table 6.2 Comparison of alternative types of farm size classification for Yorkshire sample

Unequal size group (ha)	Count	20 percentile size group (ha)	Count	Unit standard deviation size group (ha)	Count
0.0– 24.9	16	4.5– 254.4	43	−108.2– 173.6	41
25.0– 49.9	8	254.5– 504.3	3	173.7– 455.4	4
50.0– 99.9	11	504.4– 754.2	2	455.5– 737.2	3
100.0– 149.9	4	754.5–1004.1	2	737.3–1019.0	2
150.0– 199.9	2	1004.2–1254.0	2	1019.1–1300.8	2
200.0– 499.9	5				
500.0– 999.9	4				
1000.0–1499.9	2				

then some ambiguity might have arisen. Suppose one of the farms had been 499.7 ha. With rounding this would have been allocated to a 500–599 ha group. However, if the tenth of a hectare had been taken into account, then it would have been placed in the lower group (400.0–499.9 ha). The farm sizes in Tables 6.1 and 6.2 are given to one decimal place, or 0.1 ha. Hence a class such as 200.0–299.9 ha, actually goes from 199.95–299.95 ha. The class width is, therefore, 100 ha and not 99.9 ha as might at first appear to be the case.

In Table 6.2 the number of classes varies: eight in the case of the unequal size groups, and five for the 20 percentile classes. There is no reason why the same number of classes should not have been produced. It would have been perfectly possible to divide the range of values up into 13 classes using the percentile system, in which each class spanned 7.6923 per cent of the range. Here the class interval would have been 96.2 ha. Unfortunately, there are no clear-cut and definitive rules to follow when deciding on the number of classes to use. In this example, 13 is probably too many, and a more appropriate number is six or seven. If too many categories are defined, the number of observations per class will be low. If there are too few, then differentiation between classes may be obscured.

Examination of Tables 6.1 and 6.2 and Figure 6.1 indicates clearly that the lowest class has the greatest frequency of observations. This is known as the *modal class* and is conceptually similar to the mode, although here it refers to a *range* of values which occur most often. The descriptive measures examined in Chapter 6 can be estimated for data held in a frequency distribution, although these may be less accurate than the equivalent quantities calculated from an ungrouped continuous variable. Such estimates are nevertheless useful with data obtained from secondary sources. The estimation of the value of the mode, as distinct from identifying the modal class, in a frequency distribution can be treated in a comparatively straightforward manner. The mode is defined as the mid-value of the modal class. Thus from Table 6.1 the estimate of the mode of the Yorkshire farms is 50.0 ha, which compares with a value of 40.5 ha for the ungrouped data. The most unfortunate feature of the estimated mode is the variation that can occur because of the use of different coding schemes. The alternative classification systems in Table 6.2 estimate the mode as 12.5, 129.5 and 32.7 ha, which demonstrates a weakness of the statistic. The estimated mode is really only useful if the distribution is strongly peaked and fairly symmetrical, with one of the classes dominant. The frequency distribution of farm sizes is peaked, but also highly skewed, consequently the estimated mode is still prone to quite extreme fluctuation.

The method of estimating the mean of classified values involves multiplying the count of observations in each class by the class mid-value and then dividing the sum of these products by the total number of observations. The formula for a population is:

$$\mu = \frac{\sum(FM)}{N}$$

and for a sample:

$$\bar{x} = \frac{\sum(fm)}{n}$$

where F and f denote the frequency of observations and M and m are the mid-point of each class. The mid-points are obtained by subtracting the lower limit from the upper limit, dividing by 2 and then adding the result to the lower limit. The mean of the Yorkshire sample of farms is estimated in Table 6.3 for comparison with the known true mean. The sum of the products in the final column divided by the number of observations (52) gives an estimated mean of 184.6 ha, which compares with 173.6 ha obtained by calculation from the ungrouped data. The reason for the difference between the true mean and the estimate arises because the latter assumes that the values are spread evenly within each class. In this example, the difference between the true mean and the estimate is infuenced by the skewness of the values and the size of the class interval.

One method of estimating the variance of a frequency distribution substitutes the estimate of the mean into the original variance equation. The formula for a population is:

$$\sigma^2 = \frac{\sum[F(M-\mu)^2]}{N}$$

and for a sample:

$$s^2 = \frac{\sum[f(m-\bar{x})^2]}{n-1}$$

Table 6.3 Estimation of mean from frequency distribution of Yorkshire farm sample

Size group (ha)	Count f	Class mid-value m	Count × mid-value fm
0.0– 99.9	35	49.95	1748.25
100.0– 199.9	6	149.95	899.70
200.0– 299.9	2	249.95	499.90
300.0– 399.9	0	349.95	0.00
400.0– 499.9	3	449.95	1349.85
500.0– 599.9	1	549.95	549.95
600.0– 699.9	1	649.95	649.95
700.0– 799.9	1	749.95	749.95
800.0– 899.9	1	849.95	849.95
900.0– 999.9	0	949.95	0.00
1000.0–1099.9	1	1049.95	1049.95
1100.0–1199.9	0	1149.95	0.00
1200.0–1299.9	1	1249.95	1249.95
	52		9597.40

Table 6.4 Estimation of variance from frequency distribution of Yorkshire farm sample

Size group (ha)	Count f	Class mid-value m	$m - \bar{x}$	$(m - \bar{x})^2$	$f(m - \bar{x})^2$
0.0– 99.9	35	49.95	−134.617	18 121.7367	634 260.7845
100.0– 199.9	6	149.95	−34.617	1 198.3367	7 190.0202
200.0– 299.9	2	249.95	65.383	4 274.9367	8 549.8734
300.0– 399.9	0	349.95	165.383	27 351.5367	0.0
400.0– 499.9	3	449.95	265.383	70 428.1367	211 284.4101
500.0– 599.9	1	549.95	365.383	133 504.7367	133 504.7367
600.0– 699.9	1	649.95	465.383	216 581.3367	216 581.3367
700.0– 799.9	1	749.95	565.383	319 657.9367	319 657.9367
800.0– 899.9	1	849.95	665.383	442 734.5367	442 734.5367
900.0– 999.9	0	949.95	765.383	585 811.1367	0.0
1000.0–1099.9	1	1 049.95	865.383	748 887.7367	748 887.7367
1100.0–1199.9	0	1 149.95	965.383	931 964.3367	0.0
1200.0–1299.9	1	1 249.95	1 065.383	1 135 040.9367	1 135 040.9367
	52				3 857 692.3080

The variance is calculated by subtracting the estimated mean from each class mid-value, multiplying by the frequency count of the class and then squaring the results. The sum of the squared values is divided by N for a population and by $n - 1$ for a sample. This method for estimating the variance assumes that all observations within each class possess the class mid-value. The estimated variance for the Yorkshire sample of farms is 75 641.0 to one decimal place (see Table 6.4), which compares with the true variance of 79 434.3. Although there is a difference of nearly 3800, the variance itself is so large that even a difference of this magnitude is less important than it might at first seem. An estimate of the standard deviation for a frequency distribution can be obtained by taking the square root of the estimated variance, which in this case yields a value of 275.0 ha (compared with 281.8 ha for the true sample mean).

6.3 FREQUENCY DISTRIBUTIONS AND CLASSIFICATION OF PROJECT VARIABLES

The use of statistical software to obtain frequency distributions makes certain aspects of the process more straightforward. For example, if the investigator is not quite sure which type of classification system to use, it is a relatively simple task to experiment with different methods and to compare the results. The software usually allows a certain amount of flexibility in how the classes are defined and options for controlling how the information is displayed in tabular or graphical form. Variation is found in the extent to which software packages enable estimates of the statistical measures to be calculated. If the raw unclassified data can be analysed, this is unimportant; however, difficulties arise when only frequency distribution data are available.

6.3.1 Land-use change

The data in the land-use project fall into two groups: coded attributes denoting land-use categories (sample A columns C4 and C6) and locality type (C3 in both worksheets); and variables measuring the areas of land use. The area variables have been recorded as integers, although they are continuous and therefore require some form of classification in order to produce frequency distributions. MINITAB produces univariate frequency tables and histograms by means of two separate commands. The land-use project demonstrates further use of the TALLY command to generate frequency tables. The output of bar charts or histograms in MINITAB will be discussed with respect to the chalk weathering and river pollution projects.

The log of the MINITAB session for producing frequency tables for the land-use project is given in Table 6.5. The procedure for retrieving a MINITAB worksheet and the role of the OUTFILE and NOOUTFILE commands will not be discussed further, since this aspect of using the software should be familiar by this stage. The most direct means for obtaining a univariate frequency table from a coded attribute is the TALLY command with the subcommand ALL, thus:

```
MTB > TALLY C3;
SUBC > ALL.
```

This causes the full range of absolute and relative frequencies to be generated. Again it will be noted that a semicolon (;) at the end of a command indicates that a subcommand will follow. The subcommand line itself is terminated by a full stop (.).

The production of a frequency table for a continuous variable requires that the values be coded or classified as described in Section 6.2. MINITAB's CODE command carries out this task and enables the results to be stored in a new column so that the original ungrouped data are not lost. CODE permits some flexibility in the way an interval or ratio scale variable is classified (some examples are shown in Table 6.5). In sample A, the observations represent plots of land which have been measured to the nearest hectare and can thus take on any integer value higher than 1. A classification based on equal intervals is usually preferred and a preliminary examination of the range of values suggests that an interval of 30.0 ha is suitable (i.e. 0.0–29.9 ha, 30.0–59.9 ha, 60–89.9 ha, etc.). The command

```
MTB > CODE (0:29.9) 1 (30:59.9) 2 (60:89.9) 3 ... &
(150:179.9) 6 C5 C7 INTO C8 C9
```

instructs the computer to code the raw values in columns C5 and C7 according to this scheme and store the coded results in the new columns

Table 6.5 Derivation of frequency distributions for land-use project samples A and B in MINITAB

```
MTB > OUTFILE 'land03'
MTB > RETRIEVE 'landa01'
MTB > TALLY C4 C6;
SUBC > ALL.
MTB > CODE (0:29.9) 1 (30:59.9) 2 (60:89.9) 3 (90:119.9) 4 (120:149.9) 5 &
(150:179.9) 6 C5 C7 INTO C8 C9
MTB > NAME C8 'RECARE30'
MTB > NAME C9 'RECARE60'
MTB > TALLY C8 C9;
SUBC > ALL.
MTB > SAVE 'landa02'
MTB > RESTART
MTB > RETRIEVE 'landb01'
MTB > CODE (0) 1 (1:14.9) 2 (15:29.9) 3 (30:44.9) 4 (45:59.9) 5 ++
(60:74.9) 6 C4 - C17 INTO C18 - C31
MTB > NAME C18 'ARARE30'
MTB > NAME C19 'MKGRE30'
MTB > NAME C20 'GRARE30'
MTB > NAME C21 'WOORE30'
MTB > NAME C22 'HEARE30'
MTB > NAME C23 'HSGRE30'
MTB > NAME C24 'AGURE30'
MTB > NAME C25 'ARARE60'
MTB > NAME C26 'MKGRE60'
MTB > NAME C27 'GRARE60'
MTB > NAME C28 'WOORE60'
MTB > NAME C29 'HEARE60'
MTB > NAME C30 'HSGRE60'
MTB > NAME C31 'AGURE60'
MTB > TALLY C18 - C31;
SUBC > ALL.
MTB > SAVE 'landb02'
MTB > NOOUTFILE
MTB > STOP
```

C8 and C9. These new columns will contain the values 1, 2, 3, 4, 5 or 6, with a 1 indicating that the original measurement was between 0.0 and 29.9 ha, a 2 between 30.0 and 59.9 ha, etc. The CODE command can become quite long if several classes are being defined and the ampersand (&) indicates that the command is continued on to another line.

The MINITAB log of the land-use project (Table 6.5) illustrates how the same recoding scheme may need to be applied to a number of columns, which is achieved by specifying a range of original (C4 – C17) and new columns (C18 – C31). In sample B, the area of each of the 10 land uses in the 20 grid squares has been measured for the 1930s and 1960s. These variables are stored in separate columns and the same recoding scheme is applied to each, thus:

```
MTB > CODE (0) 1 (1:14.9) 2 (15:29.9) 3 ... ++
(60:74.9) 6 C4 - C17 INTO C18 - C31
```

```
MTB > RETRIEVE 'landa01'
  WORKSHEET SAVED 3/18/1993 Worksheet retrieved from file: landa01.MTW
MTB > TALLY C4 C6;
SUBC > ALL.

Uscod30s  Count  Cumcnt  Percent  Cumpct   Uscod60s  Count  Cumcnt  Percent  Cumpct
      1     15     15     37.50    37.50       1       25     25     62.50    62.50
      2      5     20     12.50    50.00       2        1     26      2.50    65.00
      3     10     30     25.00    75.00       3        8     34     20.00    85.00
      4      5     35     12.50    87.50       4        1     35      2.50    87.50
      5      2     37      5.00    92.50       6        3     38      7.50    95.00
      6      1     38      2.50    95.00       7        2     40      5.00   100.00
      7      2     40      5.00   100.00      N =      40
     N =    40

MTB > CODE (0:29.9) 1 (30:59.9) 2 (60:89.9) 3 (90:119.9) 4 &
CONT > (120:149.9) 5 (150:179.9) 6 C5 C7 INTO C8 C9
MTB > NAME C8 'RECARE30'
MTB > NAME C9 'RECARE60'
MTB > TALLY C8 C9;
SUBC > ALL.

RECARE30  Count  Cumcnt  Percent  Cumpct   RECARE60  Count  Cumcnt  Percent  Cumpct
      1     23     23     57.50    57.50       1       21     21     52.50    52.50
      2     12     35     30.00    87.50       2       11     32     27.50    80.00
      3      4     39     10.00    97.50       4        1     33      2.50    82.50
      4      1     40      2.50   100.00       5        3     36      7.50    90.00
     N =    40                                 6        4     40     10.00   100.00
                                              N =      40

MTB > SAVE 'landa02'
  Worksheet saved into file: landa02.MTW
MTB > RESTART
MTB > RETRIEVE 'landb01'
  WORKSHEET SAVED 3/16/1993 Worksheet retrieved from file: landb01.MTW
MTB > CODE (0) 1 (1:14.9) 2 (15:29.9) 3 (30:44.9) 4 (45:59.9) 5 ++
CONT> (60:74.9) 6 C4 – C17 INTO C18 – C31
MTB > NAME C18 'ARARE30'
MTB > NAME C19 'MKGRE30'
MTB > NAME C20 'GRARE30'
MTB > NAME C21 'WOORE30'
MTB > NAME C22 'HEARE30'
MTB > NAME C23 'HSGRE30'
MTB > NAME C24 'AGURE30'
MTB > NAME C25 'ARARE60'
MTB > NAME C26 'MKGRE60'
MTB > NAME C27 'GRARE60'
MTB > NAME C28 'WOORE60'
MTB > NAME C29 'HEARE60'
MTB > NAME C30 'HSGRE60'
MTB > NAME C31 'AGURE60'
MTB > TALLY C18 – C31;
SUBC > ALL.
```

(continued)

Box 6.1 *(continued)*

ARARE30	Count	Cumcnt	Percent	Cumpct	MKGRE30	Count	Cumcnt	Percent	Cumpct
2	1	1	5.00	5.00	1	2	2	10.00	10.00
3	5	6	25.00	30.00	2	16	18	80.00	90.00
4	9	15	45.00	75.00	3	2	20	10.00	100.00
5	3	18	15.00	90.00	N =	20			
6	2	20	10.00	100.00					
N =	20								

GRARE30	Count	Cumcnt	Percent	Cumpct	WOORE30	Count	Cumcnt	Percent	Cumpct
2	1	1	5.00	5.00	2	13	13	65.00	65.00
3	11	12	55.00	60.00	3	5	18	25.00	90.00
4	6	18	30.00	90.00	4	2	20	10.00	100.00
5	2	20	10.00	100.00	N =	20			
N =	20								

HEARE30	Count	Cumcnt	Percent	Cumpct	HSGRE30	Count	Cumcnt	Percent	Cumpct
1	2	2	10.00	10.00	1	7	7	35.00	35.00
2	17	19	85.00	95.00	2	12	19	60.00	95.00
4	1	20	5.00	100.00	3	1	20	5.00	100.00
N =	20				N =	20			

AGURE30	Count	Cumcnt	Percent	Cumpct	ARARE60	Count	Cumcnt	Percent	Cumpct
2	18	18	90.00	90.00	2	2	2	10.00	10.00
3	2	20	10.00	100.00	3	2	4	10.00	20.00
N =	20				4	3	7	15.00	35.00
					5	9	16	45.00	80.00
					6	4	20	20.00	100.00
					N =	20			

MKGRE60	Count	Cumcnt	Percent	Cumpct	GRARE60	Count	Cumcnt	Percent	Cumpct
1	9	9	45.00	45.00	2	8	8	40.00	40.00
2	10	19	50.00	95.00	3	6	14	30.00	70.00
4	1	20	5.00	100.00	4	4	18	20.00	90.00
N =	20				5	2	20	10.00	100.00
					N =	20			

WOORE60	Count	Cumcnt	Percent	Cumpct	HEARE60	Count	Cumcnt	Percent	Cumpct
1	1	1	5.00	5.00	1	10	10	50.00	50.00
2	15	16	75.00	80.00	2	9	19	45.00	95.00
3	3	19	15.00	95.00	3	1	20	5.00	100.00
4	1	20	5.00	100.00	N =	20			
N =	20								

HSGRE60	Count	Cumcnt	Percent	Cumpct	AGURE60	Count	Cumcnt	Percent	Cumpct
1	5	5	25.00	25.00	2	17	17	85.00	85.00
2	14	19	70.00	95.00	3	2	19	10.00	95.00
5	1	20	5.00	100.00	4	1	20	5.00	100.00
N =	20				N =	20			

```
MTB > SAVE 'landb02'
Worksheet saved into file: landb02.MTW
MTB > NOOUTFILE
```

Box 6.1 Selection of frequency distributions for land-use project samples A and B (MINITAB output)

The class interval is smaller (15 ha) than for sample A, since the areas are constrained to less than 100 ha by the size of the grid squares. Furthermore, where a particular land use was absent the measurement 0.0 ha has been recoded to 1. The double plus (++) sign at the end of the first line has the same function as the & given previously. Once the columns have been coded, frequency tables can be produced by specifying these new columns in a TALLY command. The MINITAB log also illustrates the RESTART command, which can be used to re-load MINITAB when the user wants to RETRIEVE a new worksheet. Finally, two new MINITAB worksheets (LANDA02.MTW and LANDB02.MTW) are saved at the end of the session so that the extra columns (C8 and C9 for sample A and C18 – C31 for sample B) can be used on a later occasion.

The results of the analysis for sample A (see Box 6.1) suggest that arable land-use was the modal category in both the 1930s and 1960s, but became more important, since 25 (62.5 per cent) of the plots were under this use according to the later survey compared with 15 (37.5 per cent) in the 1930s. There is also some indication that the size of the plots increased, since 57.5 per cent were in the smallest category (0–29.9 ha) in the 1930s, whereas the equivalent figure from the 1960s survey was 52.5 per cent. It is important to note that some of the land uses have been omitted, which is a disadvantage of the sampling strategy. The second part of Box 6.1 contains the results of the frequency analysis of sample B. Comparison of the 1930s and 1960s figures suggests an expansion of arable, wood and housing land with a general reduction in grassland, market gardening and heath land.

6.3.2 Chalk weathering

The variables in the chalk weathering dataset represent the weights of the chalk blocks recorded on 15 successive days, which are held in columns C3 to C17. The data are analysed in MINITAB and, with suitable recoding of the raw weight measurements, univariate frequency tables could be produced with the TALLY command. This section, however, will examine other ways of deriving frequency distributions in MINITAB. Groups of rows in the worksheet contain the information for the different treatments, for example rows 1 to 12 are the sample blocks for treatment 1, 13 to 24 for treatment 2 and so on. Separate histograms for the 12 rows representing the blocks in each treatment would be an unsatisfactory form of graphical presentation, because of the small number of cases.

MINITAB offers an alternative presentation of a frequency distribution known as a *dotplot*. The log of the MINITAB session for producing frequency dotplots for the chalk weathering project is given in Table 6.6. A results file (CHWEAT03) is opened and the worksheet

Table 6.6 Derivation of frequency distributions for chalk weathering project in MINITAB

```
MTB > OUTFILE 'chweat03'
MTB > RETRIEVE 'chweat02'
MTB > DOTPLOT C19;
SUBC > BY C2;
SUBC > SAME.
MTB > NOOUTFILE
MTB > STOP
```

Box 6.2 Selection of frequency distributions for chalk weathering project (MINITAB output)

```
MTB > RETRIEVE 'chweat02'
WORKSHEET SAVED 3/28/1993 Worksheet retrieved from file:
  chweat02.MTW
MTB > DOTPLOT C19;
SUBC > BY C2;
SUBC > SAME.
Treatmt
   1                          :..  .:. . :    .
        +---------+---------+---------+---------+---------+-------
                                                     Loss0-14
Treatmt
   2
                                 .  . . : .  : : . .
        +---------+---------+---------+---------+---------+-------
                                                     Loss0-14
Treatmt
   3       .
        : .::. :.
        +---------+---------+---------+---------+---------+-------
                                                     Loss0-14
Treatmt
   4             .
              .  :.::.  :
        +---------+---------+---------+---------+---------+-------
                                                     Loss0-14
Treatmt
   5
                   . .... ....: .
        +---------+---------+---------+---------+---------+-------
                                                     Loss0-14
Treatmt
   6       . :
        :.:::
        +---------+---------+---------+---------+---------+-------
                                                     Loss0-14
Treatmt
   7      :  .
        .:: :..
        +---------+---------+---------+---------+---------+-------
                                                     Loss0-14
Treatmt
   8        .
          ::
         ::: .
        +---------+---------+---------+---------+---------+-------
                                                     Loss0-14
Treatmt
   9       ::
         ::::
        +---------+---------+---------+---------+---------+-------
                                                     Loss0-14
       0.0       5.0      10.0      15.0      20.0      25.0
```

CHWEAT02.MTW is retrieved. Then the DOTPLOT command is issued with respect to the total weight loss variable (C19), which was created by previous analysis, thus:

```
MTB > DOTPLOT C19;
SUBC > BY C2;
SUBC > SAME.
```

The example illustrates how two subcommands can be used to produce separate plots for the different treatment types. The BY subcommand with DOTPLOT has a similar function to the BY subcommand with the DESCRIBE, namely to undertake separate analyses on the rows according to their values in a coded column. In this instance, C2 contains a numerical code for the treatment type. The SAME subcommand forces the horizontal axes to be scaled identically irrespective of the range of values.

The output from the command enables the investigator to see whether the groups of rows, representing the different treatments, tend to be arranged separately with respect to the variable measured on the horizontal axis. The full stops and colons on the dotplots denote one and two observations, respectively. The results for the chalk weathering project (see Box 6.2) give a visual comparison of the frequency with which weight loss at the end of the experiment varies according to treatment type. There is a clear indication that the weight lost by the blocks varies considerably. The control treatments (3, 6 and 9) show only minor reductions, whereas the greatest losses, generally over 20 g, have occurred for treatment types 1 and 2, where the diurnal freeze–thaw temperature regime in pure and saline water, respectively, were applied.

6.3.3 River pollution

The majority of the columns in the MINITAB worksheets for samples A and B in the river pollution project are continuous variables measured on the ratio or interval scales, although there are some coded attributes, for example C3 and C6 in worksheet RIVERA01.MTW denote 1985 river quality and flow rate classes, respectively. The MINITAB commands used to generate a selection of histograms for this project are given in Table 6.7, which includes further use of the CODE command to create some new columns. The worksheets for samples A and B are saved into two new files in order to preserve the changes. The application of the basic HISTOGRAM command

```
MTB > HISTOGRAM C6
```

to a column containing a continuous variable will automatically divide the range of values into a series of classes. The graphical presentation of the histogram reports the mid-value of each class and the number of observations they contain is shown as rows of asterisks. If there are over 50 observations in a class, then each asterisk represents more than one observation.

Table 6.7 Derivation of frequency distributions for river pollution project samples A and B in MINITAB

```
MTB > OUTFILE 'river03'
MTB > RETRIEVE 'rivera01'
MTB > CODE (80.1:100) 1 (60.1:80) 2 (40.1:60) 3 (10.1:40) 4 &
(0.0:10.0) 5 C7 INTO C12
MTB > CODE (0:2.99) 1 (3.00:4.99) 2 (5.00:8.99) 3 &
(9.00:16.99) 4 (17.00:39.99) 5 C8 INTO C13
MTB > CODE (0:0.3999) 1 (0.4000:0.8999) 2 (0.9000:1.9999) 3 &
C9 INTO C14
MTB > NAME C12 'RecDisO'
MTB > NAME C13 'RecBOD'
MTB > NAME C14 'RecNH4'
MTB > HISTOGRAM C6 C12 C13
MTB > SAVE 'RIVERA02'
MTB > RESTART
MTB > RETRIEVE 'riverb01'
MTB > HISTOGRAM C9 – C11;
SUBC > BY C4.
MTB > CODE (80.1:100) 1 (60.1:80) 2 (40.1:60) 3 (10.1:40) 4 &
(0.0:10.0) 5 C9 INTO C17
MTB > CODE (0:2.99) 1 (3.00:4.99) 2 (5.00:8.99) 3 &
(9.00:16.99) 4 (17.00:39.99) 5 C10 INTO C18
MTB > CODE (0:0.3999) 1 (0.4000:0.8999) 2 (0.9000:1.9999) 3 &
C11 INTO C19
MTB > NAME C17 'RecDisO'
MTB > NAME C18 'RecBOD'
MTB > NAME C19 'RecNH4'
MTB > SAVE 'RIVERB02'
MTB > NOOUTFILE
MTB > STOP
```

The user can control the width, start and end points of the classes by means of two subcommands, namely INCREMENT and START. The former enables the analyst to specify the distance between the class mid-values, which is equivalent to controlling class width. The START subcommand enables the user to determine the first and optionally also the last class mid-value, which allows for certain values to be excluded from the histogram should this be required. It is also possible, as with the DOTPLOT command, to force the same scale to be used for a series of histograms and to produce a collection of histograms for groups of rows by means of using the BY subcommand. The following command sequence in Table 6.7

```
MTB > HISTOGRAM C9 – C11;
SUBC > BY C4.
```

generates a series of histograms showing the dissolved oxygen, biochemical oxygen demand and ammonia concentrations (C9 to C11) for each river quality stratum, which is held as numerical code value in column C4.

```
MTB > RETRIEVE 'rivera01'
  WORKSHEET SAVED 3/24/1993 Worksheet retrieved from file: rivera01.MTW
MTB > CODE (80.1:100) 1 (60.1:80) 2 (40.1:60) 3 (10.1:40) 4 &
CONT > (0.0:10.0) 5 C7 C12
MTB > CODE (0:2.999) 1 (3.000:4.999) 2 (5.000:8.999) 3 &
CONT > (9.000:16.999) 4 (17.000:39.999) 5 C8 C13
MTB > CODE (0:0.3999) 1 (0.4000:0.8999) 2 (0.9000:1.9999) 3 &
CONT > C10 INTO C14
MTB > HISTOGRAM C6 C12 C13
Histogram of Flow   N = 250

        Midpoint    Count
           1          10     **********
           2          25     *************************
           3          35     ***********************************
           4          40     ****************************************
           5          15     ***************
           6          40     ****************************************
           7          35     ***********************************
           8          20     ********************
           9          30     ******************************

Histogram of C12   N = 250
Each * represents 2 obs.

        Midpoint    Count
           1          46     ***********************
           2          53     ***************************
           3          49     *************************
           4          69     ***********************************
           5          33     *****************

Histogram of C13   N = 250
Each * represents 2 obs.

        Midpoint    Count
           1          65     *********************************
           2          30     ***************
           3          53     ***************************
           4          84     ******************************************
           5          18     *********

MTB > SAVE 'rivera02'
Worksheet saved into file: rivera02.MTW
MTB > RESTART
MTB > RETRIEVE 'riverb01'
  WORKSHEET SAVED 3/28/1993    Worksheet retrieved from file: riverb01.MTW
MTB > HISTOGRAM C9 – C11;
SUBC > BY C4.
```

(continued)

Box 6.3 *(continued)*

```
Midpoint   Count
    0         2   **
   10        40   ****************************************
   20        18   ******************
   30         0
   40         9   *********
   50        20   ********************
   60         7   *******
   70        19   *******************
   80        18   ******************
   90        17   *****************
```

Histogram of DisO UpDown = 2 N = 150

```
Midpoint   Count
    0        18   ******************
   10        39   ***************************************
   20         4   ****
   30        20   ********************
   40         8   ********
   50         9   *********
   60        15   ***************
   70        10   **********
   80        24   ************************
   90         3   ***
```

Histogram of BOD UpDown = 1 N = 150

```
Midpoint   Count
    0         6   ******
    2        25   *************************
    4        32   ********************************
    6        12   ************
    8        15   ***************
   10         3   ***
   12         1   *
   14        16   ****************
   16        24   ************************
   18        11   ***********
   20         5   *****
   22         0
```

Histogram of BOD UpDown = 2 N = 150

(continued)

Box 6.3 Selection of histograms for river pollution project samples A and B (MINITAB output)

A selection of histograms for samples A and B from the river pollution project is given in Box 6.3. The results of the analysis clearly indicate that most flow rate classes were adequately represented in the sample, with the exception of 1 and 5, which had two and three sites, respectively, in sample A. The second and third histograms for sample A present the distributions for dissolved oxygen and bio-

Box 6.3 (*continued*)

```
Midpoint   Count
      0        8   ********
      2       24   ************************
      4       32   ********************************
      6       15   ***************
      8       11   ***********
     10        4   ****
     12        6   ******
     14       11   ***********
     16       16   ****************
     18       14   **************
     20        8   ********
     22        1   *

Histogram of NH4   UpDown = 1   N = 150

Midpoint   Count
    0.0        1   *
    0.1        8   ********
    0.2        7   *******
    0.3        9   *********
    0.4        9   *********
    0.5        6   ******
    0.6        7   *******
    0.7       13   *************
    0.8       23   ***********************
    0.9       37   *************************************
    1.0       28   ****************************
    1.1        2   **

Histogram of NH4   UpDown = 2   N = 150

Midpoint   Count
    0.0        2   **
    0.1        5   *****
    0.2        9   *********
    0.3       10   **********
    0.4        4   ****
    0.5        9   *********
    0.6        5   *****
    0.7       10   **********
    0.8       20   ********************
    0.9       37   *************************************
    1.0       37   *************************************
    1.1        2   **
```

```
MTB > CODE (80.1:100) 1 (60.1:80) 2 (40.1:60) 3 (10.1:40) 4 &
CONT > (0.0:10.0) 5 C9 C17
MTB > CODE (0:2.99) 1 (3.00:4.99) 2 (5.00:8.99) 3 &
CONT > (9.00:16.99) 4 (17.00:39.99) 5 C10 C18
```

(*continued*)

Box 6.3 (*continued*)

```
MTB > CODE (0:0.3999) 1 (0.4000:0.8999) 2 (0.9000:1.9999) 3 &
CONT > C11 C19
MTB > SAVE 'riverb02'
Worksheet saved into file: riverb02.MTW
MTB > NOOUTFILE
```

chemical oxygen demand, with both variables recoded into five classes as shown. In each case the modal class is category 4. The remaining six histograms show separate upstream and downstream frequency distributions for dissolved oxygen, biochemical oxygen demand and ammonia for the water samples in sample B. The general shapes of the paired histograms are similar, which tends to suggest that the presence of a factory does not have much bearing on water quality in the local environment. It seems unlikely that the inclusion of the control samples will have distorted the distributions to any great extent.

6.3.4 Village communities

The various operations associated with deriving and presenting frequency distributions, which have already been described in respect of MINITAB, can also be carried out in SPSS-X, with the exception of dotplots. The principles underlying these operations are not repeated in order to concentrate on the details of the commands. In addition to generating histograms, the software is capable of generating estimates of various descriptive statistics. Most of the data from the village communities project are held as attributes, although a few are continuous variables requiring some recoding.

Table 6.8 presents the SPSS-X commands to carry out this analysis, which are stored in a control file called VILLAG02.SPS. The functions of the FILE HANDLE, GET and SAVE commands are not restated. The classification of a continuous variable or the regrouping of a coded attribute is carried out with the RECODE command, which operates in a similar fashion to the CODE command in MINITAB, although with a different syntax, thus:

```
RECODE LENGRES (0 THRU 9 = 1)(10 THRU 19 = 2)
(20 THRU 29 = 3)(30 THRU 39 = 4)(40 THRU 49 = 5)
(50 THRU 59 = 6)(60 THRU 69 = 7) INTO RELENGTH
```

Here the values in the length of residence variable LENGRES are classified into a new coded attribute called RELENGTH (standing as a mnemonic for REcoded LENGTH of residence). The syntax of the command specifies, in brackets, the lower and upper boundaries of the class with the keyword THRU used to indicate a continuous range. Each observation is assigned the appropriate value following the equals sign. If necessary, discrete or specific values can also be regrouped using a recode command, as follows:

```
RECODE ECONPOSN (1,2,3 = 1)(4,5,6,7 = 2) INTO WORK
```

Table 6.8 Derivation of frequency distributions for village communities project in SPSS-X

```
FILE HANDLE SF / NAME = 'VILLAG01.SF'
GET FILE = SF
RECODE LENGRES (0 THRU 9 = 1)(10 THRU 19 = 2)(20 THRU 29 = 3)(30 THRU 39 = 4)
  (40 THRU 49 = 5)(50 THRU 59 = 6)(60 THRU 69 = 7) INTO RELENGTH
  /ECONPOSN (1,2,3 = 1)(4,5,6,7 = 2) INTO WORK
VARIABLE LABELS RELENGTH 'Recoded length of residence'
  /WORK 'Employed'
VALUE LABELS RELENGTH 1 '0 to 9 Yrs' 2 '10 to 19 Yrs'
  3 '20 to 29 Yrs' 4 '30 to 39 Yrs' 5 '40 to 49 Yrs'
  6 '50 to 59 Yrs' 7 '60 to 69 Yrs'
  /WORK 1 'Yes' 2 'No'
FREQUENCIES VARIABLES = TENURE(1,6) ECONPOSN(1,7) EMPOPPS(1,2)
  /STATISTICS = MODE /BARCHART
TEMPORARY
SELECT IF (HEARPROP EQ 1)
FREQUENCIES VARIABLES = FAVPROP PROPMTNG(1,2) /BARCHART
FREQUENCIES VARIABLES = LENGRES NPERSONS /FORMAT = CONDENSE
  /STATISTICS = MEAN MODE SKEWNESS KURTOSIS MINIMUM MAXIMUM
  /HISTOGRAM = PERCENT
SAVE OUTFILE = SF
FINISH
```

In this example, the original economic position attribute (ECONPOSN), with seven codes, will be regrouped into an attribute with two codes which will indicate whether or not the respondent is in employment. SPSS-X provides considerable flexibility to allow complex recoding of variables to be carried out.

The main SPSS-X command used to produce univariate frequency distributions is FREQUENCIES. The software does not prevent the use of the command with unclassified variables; however, they can produce rather worthless results if there are a large number of observations and many different values present. The syntax of the command enables the analyst to specify the statistics which are required and to control the format of the output by means of subcommands. The following extract from Table 6.8 includes three FREQUENCIES commands with lists of variables for which different statistics and forms of output are requested:

```
FREQUENCIES VARIABLES = TENURE(1,6) ECONPOSN(1,7)
  EMPOPPS(1,2) /STATISTICS = MODE /BARCHART
TEMPORARY
SELECT IF (HEARPROP EQ 1)
FREQUENCIES VARIABLES = FAVPROP PROPMTNG(1,2)
  /BARCHART
FREQUENCIES VARIABLES = LENGRES NPERSONS
  /FORMAT = CONDENSE /STATISTICS = MEAN MODE
  SKEWNESS KURTOSIS MINIMUM MAXIMUM
  /HISTOGRAM = PERCENT
```

The first FREQUENCIES command operates in integer mode, with the listed variables, TENURE and ECONPOSN (economic position), having their integer value ranges shown in brackets. The absence of a FORMAT subcommand allows the default table style to be produced, showing absolute and relative frequencies and the cumulative percentage. The STATISTIC subcommand requests the mode to be printed and the graphical output is a bar chart. The SELECT IF data-selection line specifies that the second FREQUENCIES command should only apply to those cases in which HEARPROP equals 1, namely those respondents who had heard of the proposal. The preceeding command, TEMPORARY, indicates that this data-selection line only applies to the procedure which immediately follows. The variables list on the third FREQUENCIES command refers to the LENGRES and NPERSONS variables, which were recorded as continuous variables. In this case the FREQUENCIES command is used in general mode (indicated by the absence of bracketed value ranges) and the FORMAT = CONDENSE subcommand produces a more compact version of the frequency table. Various statistics and a histogram are also requested. The full details of the FREQUENCIES command are described in the software documentation. The various RECODE commands in Table 6.8 generate some new variables; it is therefore necessary to give the command

SAVE OUTFILE = SF

in order to preserve an updated version of the system file.

The results of the frequency distribution analysis of the village communities data (Box 6.4) clearly reveal that the large majority of respondents lived in households which were buying their house by means of a mortgage (58.1 per cent), with a further 11.7 per cent owning the property outright. Referring to the cumulative percentage column in the table for ECONPOSN, it is evident that just over 60 per cent of respondents were employed, with the majority in full-time employment. Retired respondents were the second largest group, with 19.0 per cent. Unemployment appears to be a relatively unimportant problem, with only 4.7 per cent of individuals in this economic position. Most of the interviewees thought that there were sufficient employment opportunities for young people. Among the respondents who had heard of the proposed development (122 people), the overwhelming majority (71.3 per cent) were opposed to it.

The condensed frequency distribution table complements the descriptive statistics for the four continuous variables discussed in Chapter 5. Some 30 per cent of the individuals interviewed had been living in the village for less than 10 years, while, at the other extreme, about 25 per cent had been resident for over 30 years. The NPERSONS variable clearly shows that one- and two-person households were dominant,

Box 6.4 Selection of frequency tables and histograms for village communities project (SPSS-X output)

TENURE Housing Tenure

Value Label	Value	Frequency	Percent	Valid Percent	Cum Percent
Own Outright	1	42	11.7	11.7	11.7
Own with Mortgage	2	208	58.1	58.1	69.8
Rent from LA or Hsg	3	52	14.5	14.5	84.4
Rent Privately	4	32	8.9	8.9	93.3
Tied to Work	5	17	4.7	4.7	98.0
Other	6	7	2.0	2.0	100.0
	Total	358	100.0	100.0	

```
        Own Outright  |***** 42
                      I
   Own with Mortgage  |**************************208
                      I
 Rent from LA or Hsg  |******* 52
                      I
      Rent Privately  |**** 32
                      I
        Tied to Work  |** 17
                      I
               Other  |* 7
                      +---------+---------+---------+---------+---------+
                      0        80       160       240       320       400
```

Mode 2.000 Valid cases 358 Missing cases 0

ECONPOSN Economic Position of Respondent

Value Label	Value	Frequency	Percent	Valid Percent	Cum Percent
Employer or Self-Emp	1	27	7.5	7.5	7.5
Employee Full-time	2	156	43.6	43.6	51.1
Employee Full-time	3	38	10.6	10.6	61.7
Unemployed	4	17	4.7	4.7	66.5
Housewife-husband	5	41	11.5	11.5	77.9
Retired	6	68	19.0	19.0	96.9
Other	7	11	3.1	3.1	100.0
	Total	358	100.0	100.0	

```
Employer or Self-Emp  |******* 27
                      I
  Employee Full-time  |***************************************156
                      I
  Employee Part-time  |**********38
                      I
          Unemployed  |**** 17
                      I
   Housewife-husband  |**********41
                      I
             Retired  |*****************68
                      I
               Other  |*** 11
                      +---------+---------+---------+---------+---------+
                      0        40        80       120       160       200
```

Mode 2.000 Valid cases 358 Missing cases 0

(continued)

Box 6.4 *(continued)*

EMPOPPS Sufficient Employment for Young

Value Label	Value	Frequency	Percent	Valid Percent	Cum Percent
Yes	1	217	60.6	60.6	60.6
No	2	141	39.4	39.4	100.0
	Total	358	100.0	100.0	

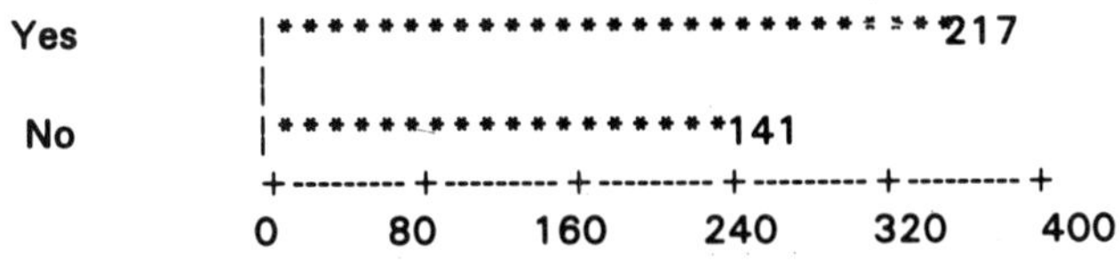

```
Yes   |****************************217
      |
No    |******************141
      +---------+---------+---------+---------+---------+
      0        80       160       240       320       400
```

Mode 1.000 Valid cases 358 Missing cases 0

FAVPROP In Favour of Proposal

Value Label	Value	Frequency	Percent	Valid Percent	Cum Percent
Yes	1	35	28.7	28.7	28.7
No	2	87	71.3	71.3	100.0
	Total	122	100.0	100.0	

```
Yes   |******************35
      |
No    |********************************************87
      +---------+---------+---------+---------+---------+
      0        20        40        60        80       100
```

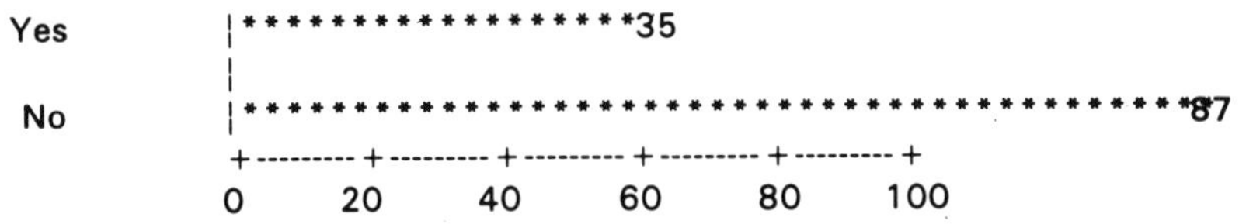

Valid cases 122 Missing cases 0

PROPMTNG Attended Public Meeting

Value Label	Value	Frequency	Percent	Valid Percent	Cum Percent
Yes	1	42	34.4	34.4	34.4
No	2	80	65.6	65.6	100.0
	Total	122	100.0	100.0	

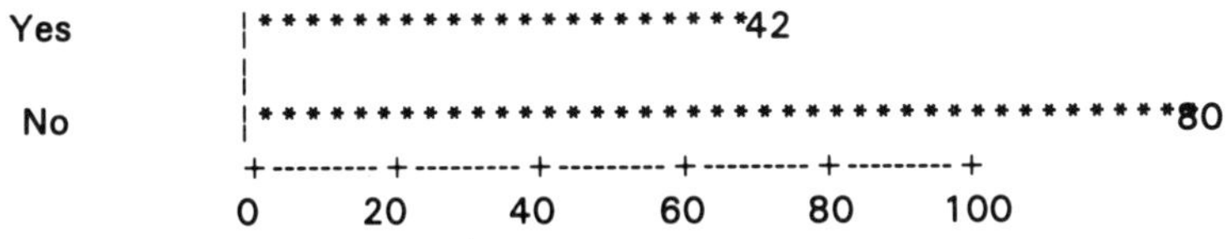

```
Yes   |*********************42
      |
No    |****************************************80
      +---------+---------+---------+---------+---------+
      0        20        40        60        80       100
```

Valid cases 122 Missing cases 0

LENGRES Length of Residence in Village

Value	Freq	Pct	Cum Pct	Value	Freq	Pct	Cum Pct	Value	Freq	Pct	Cum Pct
.00	4	1	1	21.00	15	4	52	42.00	5	1	87
1.00	6	2	3	22.00	5	1	54	43.00	2	1	88
2.00	5	1	4	23.00	14	4	58	44.00	3	1	88
3.00	9	3	7	24.00	3	1	58	45.00	7	2	90
4.00	9	3	9	25.00	10	3	61	46.00	1	0	91
5.00	9	3	12	26.00	18	5	66	47.00	4	1	92
6.00	9	3	14	27.00	8	2	69	48.00	2	1	92

(continued)

Box 6.4 (*continued*)

7.00	8	2	17	28.00	10	3	71	49.00	1	0	93
8.00	5	1	18	29.00	3	1	72	51.00	5	1	94
10.00	5	1	19	30.00	6	2	74	52.00	4	1	95
11.00	4	1	21	31.00	4	1	75	53.00	2	1	96
12.00	13	4	24	32.00	5	1	76	54.00	4	1	97
13.00	9	3	27	33.00	5	1	78	56.00	2	1	97
14.00	16	4	31	34.00	7	2	80	57.00	1	0	98
15.00	13	4	35	35.00	4	1	81	58.00	1	0	98
16.00	10	3	38	36.00	3	1	82	60.00	1	0	98
17.00	18	5	43	37.00	6	2	83	61.00	2	1	99
18.00	8	2	45	38.00	1	0	84	62.00	1	0	99
19.00	5	1	46	40.00	2	1	84	63.00	2	1	100
20.00	6	2	48	41.00	5	1	86	64.00	1	0	100

MISSING DATA

Value	Freq	Value	Freq	Value	Freq
9.00	2				

LENGRES Length of Residence in Village

```
Count  Midpoint One symbol equals approximately 1.07 occurrences

  4     -1.33   |****
 20      2.00   |*******************
 27      5.33   |*************************
 18      8.67   |*****************
 26     12.00   |************************
 39     15.33   |************************************
 37     18.67   |***********************************
 34     22.00   |********************************
 31     25.33   |*****************************
 27     28.67   |*************************
 14     32.00   |*************
 14     35.33   |*************
  9     38.67   |********
 12     42.00   |***********
 11     45.33   |**********
  7     48.67   |*******
 11     52.00   |**********
  6     55.33   |******
  3     58.67   |***
  5     62.00   |*****
  1     65.33   |*
                +----+----+----+----+----+----+----+----+----+----+
                0         3         6         9        12        15
```

Mean	23.126	Mode	17.000	Kurtosis	−.131
Skewness	.673	Minimum	.000	Maximum	64.000
Valid cases	356	Missing cases	2		

NPERSONS Size of Household

Value	Freq	Pct	Cum Pct	Value	Freq	Pct	Cum Pct	Value	Freq	Pct	Cum Pct
1.00	95	27	27	4.00	49	14	94	7.00	2	1	100
2.00	112	31	58	5.00	13	4	97				
3.00	79	22	80	6.00	8	2	99				

(*continued*)

Box 6.4 (*continued*)

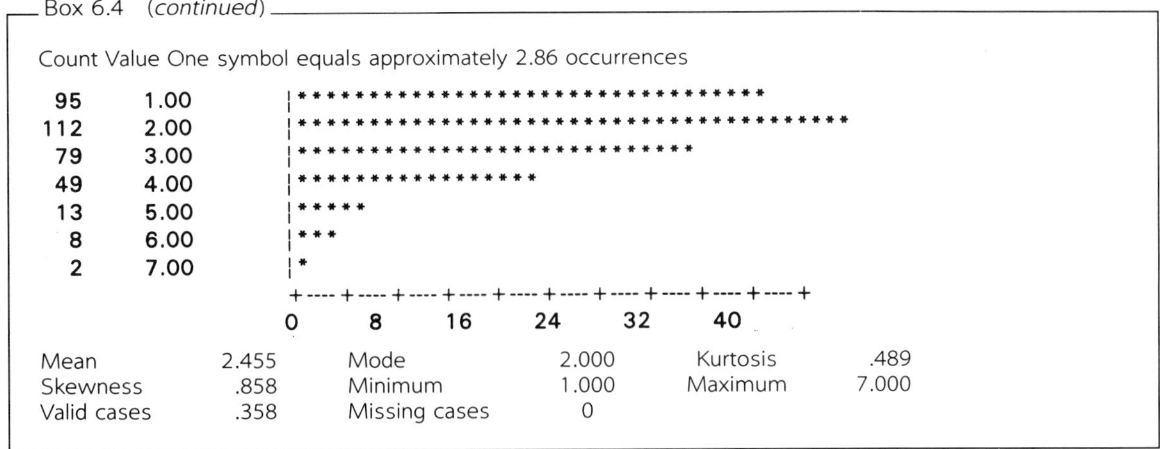

```
Count Value One symbol equals approximately 2.86 occurrences

 95    1.00     |*********************************
112    2.00     |***************************************
 79    3.00     |****************************
 49    4.00     |*****************
 13    5.00     |*****
  8    6.00     |***
  2    7.00     |*
                +----+----+----+----+----+----+----+----+----+----+
                0    8    16   24   32   40
```

Mean	2.455	Mode	2.000	Kurtosis	.489
Skewness	.858	Minimum	1.000	Maximum	7.000
Valid cases	.358	Missing cases	0		

together accounting for 58 per cent of the total. This is possibly indicative of a fairly elderly age structure, where children are no longer living with their parents.

6.4 COMPARISON OF FREQUENCY DISTRIBUTIONS IN EXEMPLAR PROJECTS

An examination of the frequency distributions for the variables and attributes in a dataset, together with the estimated measures of central tendency and dispersion, is a useful starting point for further analysis. Although in isolation these basic descriptions are often insufficient to produce a full explanation of the issues under investigation, they will help to suggest the direction in which the analysis should proceed and the more specific questions that might need to be asked.

The production of a selection of frequency distributions for the four projects has demonstrated various features of the software. By way of conclusion, a number of common points can be identified. It is usually necessary to classify or group the values in the original continuous variables, and sometimes also in the attributes, in order to produce a satisfactory frequency distribution. A certain amount of judgement and experimentation is required in order to determine the most appropriate number of classes and the scheme for defining these. It is often useful to produce frequency distributions for groups of cases, or rows in MINITAB parlance. When different schemes are used to classify the same variable, wildly different frequency distributions can result. Finally, the histogram or bar chart is the most common form of graphical display for a frequency distribution, although others may be more suited to particular circumstances.

Chapter 7
Bivariate and multivariate frequency distributions: cross-tabulation and scattergrams

7.1 BIVARIATE AND MULTIVARIATE DISTRIBUTIONS

The methods of representing and summarising a complete set of values for a single variable, examined in Chapter 6, can be extended and adapted for situations where there are two attributes or variables. These are known as bivariate distributions. Indeed, methods also exist for representing the distributions of three or more variables. However, these are only considered by way of illustration here. The main purpose of looking at bivariate (or multivariate) frequency distributions is to obtain an overview of the conjunction of the values for particular attributes or variables. More specifically, they provide a means for examining whether the values of one variable are in some way associated with those of another — in other words, whether observations are likely to possess particular combinations of values on the two (or more) variables. The second benefit of bivariate distributions is to visualise any a causal relationship which might be identified between two variables. The statistical techniques of correlation and regression, which quantify the strength, direction and nature of such relationships, are examined in Chapters 12 and 13, respectively.

An association is said to exist between two attributes or variables if the observations display a tendency to be interlinked. Suppose that employees in a sample of companies are classified in two ways: according to the type of work they do (managerial, skilled manual or unskilled manual); and with reference to the type of housing that they live in (detached, semi-detached, terraced or an apartment). If a greater proportion of the managerial employees also occupy detached housing than the overall percentage of such employees would warrant, then there might appear to be an association between the attributes: managers live in large houses. Equally, it could be claimed that a higher proportion of detached housing is occupied by managers than would be expected from their total number. In other words, the connection between the attributes or variables can be approached from either point of view, and the presence of an association does not indicate its nature or direction. It could be that a person's employment status leads him or her to live in a particular type of housing, or equally that the size of housing is tailored to household size. The notion of a causal relationship between attributes or variables is closely linked with the idea of association, but takes the connection between them one stage further. Continuing with the previous example illustrates this distinction. The connection between employment status and type of housing could be described as a causal relationship, if one of these attributes *necessarily* produced particular values in the other. For instance, if an employee's employment status *caused* him or her to live in a certain type of housing.

Bivariate and multivariate distributions are important with respect to data obtained from secondary sources, particularly those used for investigations in human geography. Again the Population Census is a prime example of this situation where the majority of the statistical output exists as bivariate or multivariate tables of information. However, a variety of secondary sources of data used by geographers occurs in this form, including Britain's monthly unemployment statistics, population estimates and agricultural census statistics. Much geographically or spatially referenced aggregate data can be considered bivariate distributions, with the locational and the substantive variables providing the two dimensions. Thus, for instance, the areas of different types of agricultural land in English counties might be considered as a count of the hectares under each use rather than as values on a continuous variable, since the figures are totals rather than denoting contiguous tracts under the same use. One of the main reasons for secondary sources of data being held as bivariate or multivariate frequency distributions is the need to preserve confidentiality. The sources of secondary data used in physical geography are perhaps less likely to exist as predefined bivariate distributions, although there are examples, for instance, the count of different types of pollution incident for geographical areas (Water Authorities Association, annual).

7.2 REPRESENTATION OF BIVARIATE DATA

The different methods of representing bivariate distributions give an overview of how observations are distributed according to the values for the two attributes or variables in question. The basic procedure for generating a bivariate distribution is analogous to a researcher going through a set of questionnaires and examining the responses to two questions. For simplicity, each question has one of three possible responses: for question I, A, B or C; for question II, 1, 2 or 3. As the researcher examines the questionnaires each is *distributed* to one of nine piles representing the combinations A1, A2, A3, B1, B2, B3, C1, C2 and C3. The numbers of questionnaires in each pile provide the frequency distribution counts.

The two main ways of representing bivariate frequency distributions are as tables and graphs, although cartographic representation may be regarded as a special case of the latter. The tabular representation is referred to as a *cross-tabulation* or a *contingency table*. One of the most common forms of graphical representation is a *scattergram* or *scatter-graph*, although adaptations of the simple bar chart used for univariate distributions are sometimes encountered. If a tabular representation is chosen, it is usually necessary to classify or group continuous variables, as in the case of producing a univariate histogram. If a graphical form of representation is used, it may not be necessary to classify continuous variables.

7.2.1 Tabular representation

A cross-tabulation shows the absolute and/or relative frequency of two or more variables. Initially only the bivariate case will be used to illustrate the important features of such tables, since this avoids the complexities of multivariate cross-tabulations. A cross-tabulation consists of a number of cells or boxes which correspond to the intersection of the different values of the two attributes. Each cell contains information relating to how frequently a particular combination of values occurs for a given set of observations. Chapter 6 included the absolute and relative frequency distribution of the size variable for the sample of Yorkshire farms (Table 6.1). The survey also included an attribute which classified the farms into the following types: dairy, arable, mixed livestock and other. In other words, there is now one coded variable and a nominal attribute for each farm. The cross-tabulation of these (Table 7.1) shows the absolute counts and relative frequencies. With the latter, it is possible to show the count as a percentage of the row, column and overall totals, or, as here, all three together. The last column and row in Table 7.1 provide the marginal totals of the cross-tabulation. These correspond to the univariate frequency distributions of the two variables considered separately. In order to avoid a large number of cells with zero observations, the upper size bands have been collapsed into a single group, greater than 700 ha. The cross-tabulation of these variables produces an eight by four table (8×4), where these numbers, respectively, refer to the number of values for farm size and farm type.

Even with only two variables, cross-tabulations can become quite lengthy and complex to describe, since it is relevant to discuss the absolute counts and the three percentages. According to Table 7.1, nearly 35 per cent of all the sample farms were in the smallest size category *and* classified as dairy farms, and these accounted for just

Table 7.1 Cross-tabulation of farm size and type of Yorkshire sample

Size group (ha)	Code	Farm type: Dairy	Arable	Mixed livestock	Other	
0.0– 99.9	1	18	4	7	6	35
		51.4	11.4	20.0	17.2	100.0
		94.7	40.0	46.7	75.0	67.3
		34.6	7.7	13.5	11.5	
100.0–199.9	2	1	1	3	1	6
		16.6	16.7	50.0	16.7	100.0
		5.3	10.0	20.0	12.5	11.6
		1.9	1.9	5.8	1.9	
200.0–299.9	3	0	1	1	0	2
		0.0	50.0	50.0	0.0	100.0
		0.0	10.0	6.7	0.0	3.8
		0.0	1.9	1.9	0.0	
300.0–399.9	4	0	0	0	0	0
		0.0	0.0	0.0	0.0	0.0
		0.0	0.0	0.0	0.0	0.0
		0.0	0.0	0.0	0.0	
400.0–499.9	5	0	2	1	0	3
		0.0	66.7	33.3	0.0	100.0
		0.0	20.0	6.7	0.0	5.9
		0.0	3.8	1.9	0.0	
500.0–599.9	6	0	0	1	0	1
		0.0	0.0	100.0	0.0	100.0
		0.0	0.0	6.7	0.0	1.9
		0.0	0.0	1.9	0.0	
600.0–699.9	7	0	1	0	0	1
		0.0	100.0	0.0	0.0	100.0
		0.0	10.0	0.0	0.0	1.9
		0.0	1.9	0.0	0.0	
> 700.0	8	0	1	2	1	4
		0.0	25.0	50.0	25.0	100.0
		0.0	0.0	13.3	0.0	7.6
		0.0	1.9	3.8	1.9	
		19	10	15	8	52
		100.0	100.0	100.0	100.0	
		36.5	19.2	28.8	15.4	100.0

Note:
Row 1 contains counts
Row 2 contains row percentages
Row 3 contains column percentages
Row 4 contains overall percentages

over 50 per cent of the 35 farms under 100 ha. The table suggests that there is a tendency for the larger farms, over 300 ha, to be classified as either arable or mixed. However, it should be noted that approximately 50 per cent of the mixed livestock farms were under 100 ha. This comparatively simple example illustrates that a written description of a cross-tabulation can be quite cumbersome and difficult to comprehend.

Table 7.2 Cross-tabulation of farm size and type of Yorkshire sample: counts and expected counts

Size group (ha)	Code	Farm type: Dairy	Arable	Mixed livestock	Other	
0.0– 99.9	1	18 12.8	4 6.7	7 10.1	6 5.4	35
100.0–199.9	2	1 2.2	1 1.2	3 1.7	1 0.9	6
200.0–299.9	3	0 0.7	1 0.4	1 0.6	0 0.3	2
300.0–399.9	4	0 0.0	0 0.0	0 0.0	0 0.0	0
400.0–499.9	5	0 1.1	2 0.6	1 0.9	0 0.5	3
500.0–599.9	6	0 0.4	0 0.2	1 0.3	0 0.2	1
600.0–699.9	7	0 0.4	1 0.2	0 0.3	0 0.2	1
> 700.0	8	0 1.5	1 0.8	2 1.2	1 0.6	4
		19	10	15	8	52

The cross-tabulation of the Yorkshire farms also illustrates the idea of 'the number of observations that would be expected'. Table 7.2 repeats the absolute counts and shows additionally the expected counts for each of the cells. The expected frequencies are the counts that would occur in each cell if the observations were distributed across all the cells in proportion to the row and column totals. The method of calculation for a particular cell involves multiplying the corresponding row and column totals (the marginal totals) and dividing their product by the total number of observations. For example, in the cell dairy by size group 0.0–99.9 ha, the expected frequency is 12.8 farms, which is obtained thus:

$$\frac{35 \times 19}{52} = \frac{665}{52} = 12.8$$

There is a difference of 5.2 between the observed and expected frequency $(18 - 12.8)$. The differences between the observed number of farms and the number expected if they were distributed in proportion to the totals are of varying orders of magnitude. The total observed and expected frequencies necessarily equal each other. A statistical test for investigating whether these differences are important will be considered later (see Chapter 11). For the present, it is sufficient to note that small dairy farms appear to be found in greater numbers than would be expected. This preliminary analysis suggests that there is an association between farm size and farm type.

Table 7.3 Multivariate cross-tabulation of Yorkshire farm sample: size by type by altitude category

Size group (ha)	Farm type: Dairy	Arable	Mixed livestock	Other	
Upland					
0.0– 99.9	14	1	4	1	20
100.0–199.9	0	0	2	1	3
200.0–299.9	0	1	1	0	2
300.0–399.9	0	0	0	0	0
400.0–499.9	0	1	1	0	2
500.0–599.9	0	0	0	0	0
600.0–699.9	0	0	0	0	0
> 700.0	0	0	1	1	2
	14	3	9	3	29
Lowland					
0.0– 99.9	4	3	3	5	13
100.0–199.9	1	1	1	0	4
200.0–299.9	0	0	0	0	0
300.0–399.9	0	0	0	0	0
400.0–499.9	0	1	0	0	1
500.0–599.9	0	0	1	0	1
600.0–699.9	0	1	0	0	1
> 700.0	0	1	1	0	3
	5	7	6	5	23

Before looking at graphical methods for representing bivariate frequency distributions, brief consideration of multivariate cross-tabulations is useful. Suppose that the survey also placed the farms into upland and lowland categories. This additional attribute provides a further dimension by which the data can be cross-tabulated (Table 7.3). In order to keep the table relatively simple, only the absolute counts are shown, although it would be possible to calculate relative frequencies in terms of row, column and overall totals as well as expected frequencies. The addition of the altitude attribute increases the number of cells in the table to 64 ($8 \times 4 \times 2$) and there are a large number of empty cells because of the small sample size. There are only 52 observations in total to be distributed among 64 cells. The emptiness of a contingency table is a problem for some statistical procedures.

7.2.2 Graphical representation

Numerous different types of graphical representation have been developed, although there are problems with trying to show more than three variables or attributes simultaneously. One of the most frequently used representations for a bivariate distribution of continuous variables is the scattergram or scattergraph. This comprises a graph with X and Y axes, which are scaled according to the units of the two variables under

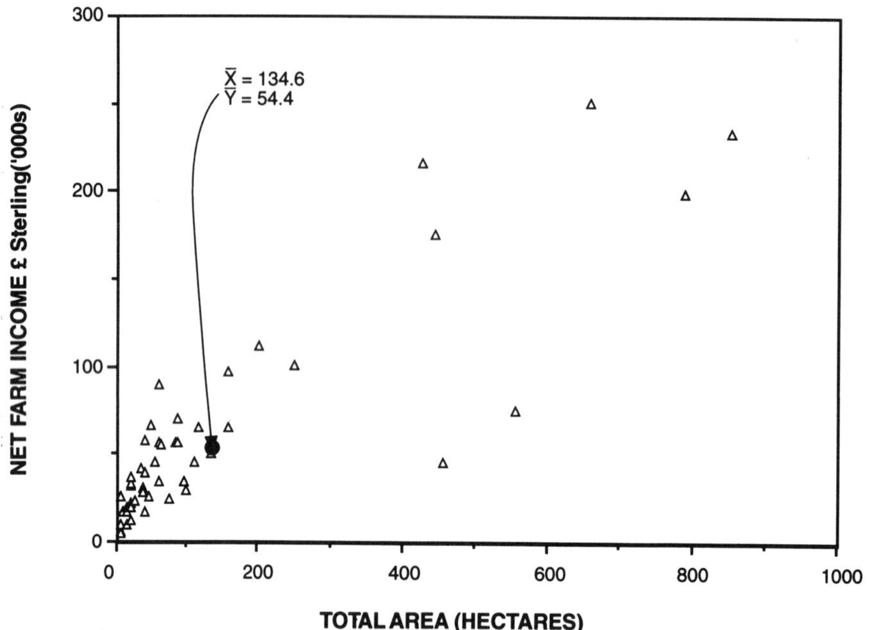

Figure 7.1 Scatterplot of size and net farm income of sample farms in Yorkshire

investigation. The intersection of the *X* and *Y* values for each observation is located by means of a symbol, such as a cross or asterisk. If two or more observations in the dataset have an identical combination of values for the two variables, then the appropriate digit (2, 3, 4, etc.) may be used in place of the asterisk to indicate the number concerned.

The important features of a scattergram are illustrated in Figure 7.1 by means of the unclassified size variable for the sample of Yorkshire farms, together with a further continuous variable, net farm income per annum. The measurement units shown on the two axes of the graph are clearly different, although both variables are measured on the ratio scale of measurement. The scattergram gives a visual impression of whether the values for two variables are associated with each other. There is some indication from Figure 7.1 that larger farms tend to have a higher net farm income, although the association is not conclusive since there are some exceptions to this general statement. Some farms have achieved high net farm-income levels with relatively small areas. In order to investigate this apparent anomaly, it would be appropriate to consider other measures of farm size, such as the monetary value of total inputs, or to introduce further variables into the analysis, such as farm type. The two variables may be causally related to each other, since farm size might control the net farm income rather than the other way around.

Scattergrams can be produced for bivariate distributions of discrete or integer variables, but a more satisfactory form of representation is an adaptation of the simple bar chart. One useful example is the back-to-back bar chart, which is illustrated in Figure 7.2 with the farm type

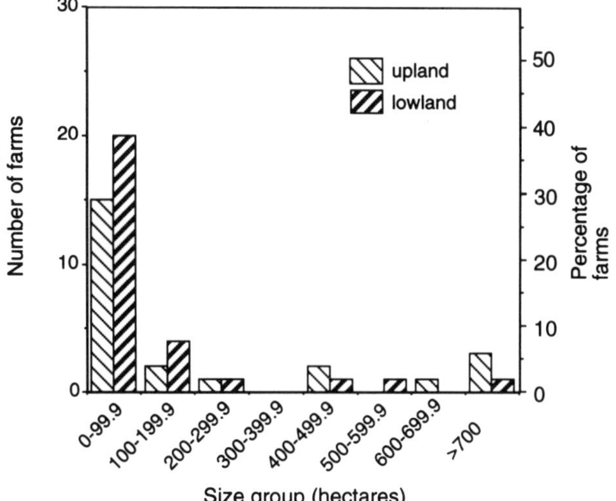

Figure 7.2 Back-to-back histogram of type and altitude of sample farms in Yorkshire

and altitude variables for the Yorkshire sample. Rather than one bar for each integer value of a single variable, there are groups of bars. Each bar within the group represents a different value on the second variable. The bars are usually distinguished by their types of shading: Figure 7.2 uses different shading for the upland and lowland altitude categories. The absolute and the relative frequencies can be shown by using separate scales on the left and right vertical axes, although the precision is not the same as with a tabular representation.

7.3 BIVARIATE DISTRIBUTIONS FOR THE EXEMPLAR PROJECTS

The intention in this section, as in previous chapters, is to demonstrate and contrast how the statistical software used to analyse the projects produces the various representations of bivariate frequency distributions. Also the ways in which the output from the specific software deviates from the 'ideal' are considered. Finally, it is worth issuing a word of caution. Some statistical software, including SPSS-X, allows variables to be cross-tabulated indiscriminately, for example all variables with each other, which can produce voluminous and unwieldy quantities of output. Some sensible selection of cross-tabulations to suit requirements should be made.

7.3.1 Land-use change

The main objectives of the land-use project are to examine change over time and differences between the rural and rural-urban fringe areas. Therefore, any difference in the amount of agricultural land lost between these types of locality should be examined. Similarly, the overall change in the area of woodland might be important. These two questions introduce a further point concerning the analysis of geographical data, namely that it is frequently necessary to calculate new variables from those which were originally collected. In this case the area measurements for the separate land uses in 1930 would be subtracted from the corresponding figures for 1960 in order to create a new set of variables measuring change.

The log of the MINITAB session in Table 7.4 illustrates these calculations and produces cross-tabulations for samples A and B. The LET command in MINITAB (see Section 5.3.2) allows arithmetic calculations to be carried out on columns, by using the basic mathematical operators +, −, * and / denoting respectively addition, subtraction, multiplication and division. A double asterisk (**) followed by a number indicates raising to the specified power (e.g. C4**2 squares the values in column C4). If necessary, various mathematical functions, such as square roots or logarithms to base 10, can be included by means of key words (SQRT and LOGTEN respectively). The LET command can be used to store constants, or, as in this case, to calculate a new column (variable). The command line

LET C10 = C7 − C5

with the worksheet for sample A causes the values held in C5 for the 1930s area measurements for each plot to be subtracted from those in C7, the corresponding 1960s figures, and the result stored in a new column, C10. In the case of sample B, a series of similar computations are carried out on the seven pairs of area measurements in order to examine the changes in individual land uses and to create columns C32 − C38. In both instances the values in these new columns are negative when there was reduction in area and positive if there was an increase. The values have been converted into discrete codes representing ranges of areal change by using the CODE command (see Section 6.3.1). The classification scheme for sample A was −100.0 to −50.1 ha, −50.0 to −0.1 ha, 0, 0.1 to 50.0 ha, 50.1 to 100.0 ha and 100.1 to 150.0 ha. In the case of sample B, where the changes were smaller, since they were constrained by the maximum of 100 ha per grid square, the classes were −20 to −10.1 ha, −10.0 to −0.1 ha, 0, 0.1 to 10.0 ha, 10.1 to 20.0 ha and 20.1 to 30.0 ha. Each scheme includes 0 as one of the groups to identify those instances where no change occurred. These reclassified variables are also stored in further new columns (C11 for sample A and C39 − C45 for sample B).

MINITAB includes a command for producing contingency tables with varying degrees of complexity. Table 7.4 includes the following simple version of the TABLE command for sample A:

MTB > TABLE C3 C11

This produces a cross-tabulation with the default layout, which gives the cell counts and the marginal totals, for the locality code (C3) with

Table 7.4 Derivation of bivariate frequency distributions for land-use project samples A and B in MINITAB

```
MTB > OUTFILE 'land04'
MTB > RETRIEVE 'landa02'
MTB > LET C10 = C7 - C5
MTB > CODE (-100:-51.1) 1 (-50:-0.1) 2 (0) 3 (0.1:50) 4 (50.1:100) &
5 (100.1:150) 6 C10 INTO C11
MTB > NAME C10 'AREACHAN'
MTB > NAME C11 'RECARECH'
MTB > DESCRIBE C10
MTB > TABLE C3 C11
MTB > SAVE 'landa03'
MTB > RETRIEVE 'landb02'
MTB > LET C32 = C11 - C4
MTB > LET C33 = C12 - C5
MTB > LET C34 = C13 - C6
MTB > LET C35 = C14 - C7
MTB > LET C36 = C15 - C8
MTB > LET C37 = C16 - C9
MTB > LET C38 = C17 - C10
MTB > CODE (-20:-10.1) 1 (-10:-0.1) 2 (0) 3 (0.1:10) 4 (10.1:20) &
5 (20.1:30) 6 (30.1:40) 7 C32 - C38 INTO C39 - C45
MTB > NAME C32 'AGRICHAN'
MTB > NAME C33 'MKGDCHAN'
MTB > NAME C34 'GRASCHAN'
MTB > NAME C35 'WOODCHAN'
MTB > NAME C36 'HEATCHAN'
MTB > NAME C37 'HSGCHAN'
MTB > NAME C38 'AGUNCHAN'
MTB > NAME C39 'REAGCH'
MTB > NAME C40 'REMGCH'
MTB > NAME C41 'REGRCH'
MTB > NAME C42 'REWOCH'
MTB > NAME C43 'REHECH'
MTB > NAME C44 'REHSCH'
MTB > NAME C45 'REAUCH'
MTB > DESCRIBE C32 - C38
MTB > TABLE C3 C39;
SUBC > ROWPERCENTS;
SUBC > COLPERCENTS;
SUBC > TOTPERCENTS;
SUBC > COUNTS.
MTB > TABLE C3 C40;
SUBC > ROWPERCENTS;
SUBC > COLPERCENTS;
SUBC > TOTPERCENTS;
SUBC > COUNTS.
MTB > TABLE C3 C44;
SUBC > ROWPERCENTS;
SUBC > COLPERCENTS;
SUBC > TOTPERCENTS;
SUBC > COUNTS.
MTB > TABLE C39 C40 C3
MTB > SAVE 'landb03'
MTB > NOOUTFILE
MTB > STOP
```

Box 7.1 (*opposite*) Selection of cross-tabulations for land-use project samples A and B (MINITAB output)

the recoded change in plot size (C11). Some slightly more complex contingency tables have been generated for sample B, which incorporate subcommands to request that the row, column and total percentages as well as the absolute counts should be included, thus:

```
MTB > TABLE C3 C39;
SUBC > ROWPERCENTS;
SUBC > COLPERCENTS;
SUBC > TOTPERCENTS;
SUBC > COUNTS.
```

This example cross-tabulates locality code (C3) with the coded column containing the change in arable land area (C39). Up to 10 columns may be specified on a TABLE command in order to produce multivariate cross-tabulations. For example,

```
MTB > TABLE C39 C40 C3
```

produces the cross-tabulation of the change in arable (C39) and market gardening (C40) land uses between the rural-urban and rural localities (C3) for sample B.

The output showing the cross-tabulations requested in Table 7.4, which has also generated the standard descriptive statistical measures for the new columns, is in Box 7.1. The results, in the case of sample A, suggest that there was relatively little difference in plot size, as shown by the recoded area change variable, RECARECH, between the urban-rural fringe and rural parts of the study area. There is perhaps some indication that greater reductions in plot size occurred in the rural-urban fringe localities, but the evidence is not conclusive. Considering the results for sample B, which examine the areal changes for each land-use separately, it is clear that grassland declined substantially (a mean change of 6.9 ha), whereas arable agricultural land increased by a mean of 7.7 ha. The cross-tabulations of change in arable agricultural land, market gardening and housing with locality type appear to indicate little differentiation between the rural-urban fringe and rural localities in the case of arable land, although market gardening declined by up to 10 ha in all rural squares and had small gains in 40 per cent of the rural-urban fringe ones. Finally, the multivariate cross-tabulation defined above emphasises the small number observations in the dataset, with a large number of empty cells.

7.3.2 Chalk weathering

The essence of the chalk weathering project is that a series of related experiments are carried out on samples of chalk blocks in order to assess their differential response to various temperature regimes. The basis of the analysis is therefore to determine whether particular types of temperature change and the presence or absence of water in the chalk are more or less likely to lead to 'frost shattering'. Two new

```
  MTB > RETRIEVE 'landa02'
    WORKSHEET SAVED   3/28/1993      Worksheet retrieved from file: landa02.MTW
  MTB > LET C10 = C7 – C5
  MTB > CODE (–100:–51.1) 1 (–50:–0.1) 2 (0) 3 (0.1:50) 4 (50.1:100) 5 &
  CONT> (100.1:150) 6 C10 INTO C11
  MTB > NAME C10 'AREACHAN'
  MTB > NAME C11 'RECARECH'
  MTB > DESCRIBE C10
               N   MEAN  MEDIAN  TRMEAN  STDEV  SEMEAN     MIN     MAX     Q1      Q3
AREACHAN      40  18.75    5.00   15.92  43.90    6.94  –56.00  141.00  –8.00   31.25
  MTB > TABLE C3 C11
ROWS:  Urb/Rur   COLUMNS:  RECARECH
            1         2         3         4        5        6       ALL
                                                                          CELL CONTENTS –
   1        0         7         3         5        2        3        20     COUNT
   2        1         6         0        11        2        0        20
ALL         1        13         3        16        4        3        40
  MTB > SAVE 'landa03'
  Worksheet saved into file: landa03.MTW
  MTB > RETRIEVE 'landb02'
    WORKSHEET SAVED   3/28/1993      Worksheet retrieved from file: landb02.MTW
  MTB > LET C32 = C11 – C4
  MTB > LET C33 = C12 – C5
  MTB > LET C34 = C13 – C6
  MTB > LET C35 = C14 – C7
  MTB > LET C36 = C15 – C8
  MTB > LET C37 = C16 – C9
  MTB > LET C38 = C17 – C1
  MTB > CODE (–20:–10.1) 1 (–10:–0.1) 2 (0) 3 (0.1:10) 4 (10.1:20) &
  CONT> 5 (20.1:30) 6 (30.1:40) 7 C32 – C38 C39 – C45
  MTB > NAME C32 'AGRICHAN'
  MTB > NAME C33 'MKGDCHAN'
  MTB > NAME C34 'GRASCHAN'
  MTB > NAME C35 'WOODCHAN'
  MTB > NAME C36 'HEATCHAN'
  MTB > NAME C37 'HSGCHAN'
  MTB > NAME C38 'AGUNCHAN'
  MTB > NAME C39 'REAGCH'
  MTB > NAME C40 'REMGCH'
  MTB > NAME C41 'REGRCH'
  MTB > NAME C42 'REWOCH'
  MTB > NAME C43 'REHECH'
  MTB > NAME C44 'REHSCH'
  MTB > NAME C45 'REAUCH'
  MTB > DESCRIBE C32 – C38
                N   MEAN   MEDIAN   TRMEAN   STDEV   SEMEAN     MIN     MAX      Q1      Q3
AGRICHAN       20   7.70     9.00     7.83    7.06     1.58   –8.00   21.00    2.75   11.75
MKGDCHAN       20  –2.80    –3.00    –2.83    3.07     0.69   –9.00    4.00   –4.75   –1.00
GRASCHAN       20  –6.90    –7.00    –6.94    4.95     1.11  –15.00    2.00  –10.75   –3.00
WOODCHAN       20  –3.20    –3.00    –3.17    3.74     0.84  –12.00    5.00   –4.75   –1.00
HEATCHAN       20  –1.85    –2.00    –2.06    3.13     0.70   –7.00    7.00   –4.00   –1.00
HSGCHAN        20   2.95     1.00     1.61    7.20     1.61   –2.00   32.00    0.00    2.75
AGUNCHAN       20   3.95     4.00     3.61    2.63     0.59    1.00   13.00    2.00    4.75
```

(continued)

Box 7.1 *(continued)*

```
MTB > TABLE C3 C39;
SUBC > ROWPERCENTS;
SUBC > COLPERCENTS;
SUBC > TOTPERCENTS;
SUBC > COUNTS.
ROWS:   UrbRur    COLUMNS:   REAGCH
          2          3          4         5         6        ALL
                                                                    CELL CONTENTS –
1        10.00       –        50.00     40.00       –      100.00     % OF ROW
         50.00       –        50.00     66.67       –       50.00     % OF COL
          5.00       –        25.00     20.00       –       50.00     % OF TBL
          1          0          5         4         0       10        COUNT
2        10.00     10.00      50.00     20.00     10.00    100.00
         50.00    100.00      50.00     33.33    100.00     50.00
          5.00      5.00      25.00     10.00      5.00     50.00
          1          1          5         2         1       10
ALL      10.00      5.00      50.00     30.00      5.00    100.00
        100.00    100.00     100.00    100.00    100.00    100.00
         10.00      5.00      50.00     30.00      5.00    100.00
          2          1         10         6         1       20
MTB > TABLE C3 C40;
SUBC > ROWPERCENTS;
SUBC > COLPERCENTS;
SUBC > TOTPERCENTS;
SUBC > COUNTS.
ROWS:   UrbRur    COLUMNS:   REMGCH
          2          3          4        ALL
                                                CELL CONTENTS –
1        60.00     20.00      20.00    100.00     % OF ROW
         37.50    100.00     100.00     50.00     % OF COL
         30.00     10.00      10.00     50.00     % OF TBL
          6          2          2       10        COUNT
2       100.00       –          –      100.00
         62.50       –          –       50.00
         50.00       –          –       50.00
         10          0          0       10
ALL      80.00     10.00      10.00    100.00
        100.00    100.00     100.00    100.00
         80.00     10.00      10.00    100.00
         16          2          2       20
MTB > TABLE C3 C44;
SUBC > ROWPERCENTS;
SUBC > COLPERCENTS;
SUBC > TOTPERCENTS;
SUBC > COUNTS.
ROWS:   UrbRur    COLUMNS:   REHSCH
          2          3          4         7        ALL
                                                          CELL CONTENTS –
1        10.00     30.00      50.00     10.00    100.00     % OF ROW
        100.00     37.50      50.00    100.00     50.00     % OF COL
          5.00     15.00      25.00      5.00     50.00     % OF TBL
          1          3          5         1       10        COUNT
```

(continued)

Box 7.1 (*continued*)

```
2            –        50.00     50.00      –       100.00
             –        62.50     50.00      –        50.00
             –        25.00     25.00      –        50.00
             0         5         5         0        10
ALL          5.00     40.00     50.00      5.00    100.00
           100.00    100.00    100.00    100.00    100.00
             5.00     40.00     50.00      5.00    100.00
             1         8        10         1        20
MTB > TABLE C39 C40 C3
CONTROL: UrbRur = 1
ROWS:      REAGCH      COLUMNS:      REMGCH
             2         3         4        ALL
                                                CELL CONTENTS –
2            1         0         0         1      COUNT
3            0         0         0         0
4            4         0         1         5
5            1         2         1         4
6            0         0         0         0
ALL          6         2         2        10
CONTROL: UrbRur = 2
ROWS:      REAGCH      COLUMNS:      REMGCH
             2         3         4        ALL
                                                CELL CONTENTS –
2            1         0         0         1      COUNT
3            1         0         0         1
4            5         0         0         5
5            2         0         0         2
6            1         0         0         1
ALL         10         0         0        10
MTB > SAVE 'landb03'
Worksheet saved into file: landb03.MTW
MTB > NOOUTFILE
```

columns, C18 and C19, which represent weight loss by the blocks after 7 and 14 days, have already been created. The company manufacturing the blocks claims that they have a uniform weight of 30 g; however, it is apparent that there are some minor variations. These can be allowed for by calculating the percentage losses of weight over 7 and 14 days. Table 7.5 indicates that two further new columns (C20 and C21), containing the final weights as a percentage of the starting weights, are obtained by means of the LET command:

LET C20 = (C18 * 100) / C4
LET C21 = (C19 * 100) / C4

Table 7.5 presents the log of the MINITAB session which produces frequency distributions for the chalk weathering project and illustrates a further adaptation of the TABLE command. Summary descriptive statistics (including the mean, standard deviation, sum, maximum and minimum) can be calculated with the TABLE command for 'associated variables'. These statistics are placed in the cells of a contingency table.

Table 7.5 Derivation of bivariate frequency distributions for chalk weathering project in MINITAB

```
MTB > OUTFILE 'chweat03'
MTB > RETRIEVE 'chweat02'
MTB > LET C20 = (C18 * 100) / C4
MTB > LET C21 = (C19 * 100) / C4
MTB > NAME C20 '%LOSS7'
MTB > NAME C21 '%LOSS14'
MTB > TABLE C2;
SUBC > COUNTS
SUBC > STATS C18 - C21.
MTB > SAVE 'chweat03'
MTB > NOOUTFILE
MTB > STOP
```

The following extract from Table 7.5

```
MTB > TABLE C2;
MTB > COUNTS;
SUBC > STATS C18 - C21.
```

produces the univariate frequency distribution table for C2 in Box 7.2. The subcommand STATS causes the number of rows, and the mean and standard deviation of the associated columns, C18 to C21, to be inserted into the cells of the table. The table has been kept relatively simple in this example and is not a cross-tabulation since only one column is specified on the TABLE command. Full information on the various subcommands associated with TABLE are contained in the software manual (Minitab 1989).

The analytical results shown in Box 7.2 help to suggest possible associations between variables, and, more specifically, how the action of temperature change and the presence or absence of water might influence the amount of 'frost shattering'. At the end of 7 days there is little to distinguish between the blocks undergoing the different types of treatment, apart from those under treatments 1 and 2, which had mean losses of 4.9 g and 4.1 g. After 14 days there is greater differentiation, with the controls (treatments 3, 6 and 9) showing only minor mean losses. In the case of percentage weight loss, it appears that the presence of the water and freeze–thaw temperature regime take effect earlier. Blocks subjected to treatments 1 and 2 had mean weight reductions of 58.9 per cent and 71.1 per cent after 14 days.

7.3.3 River pollution

The two datasets or MINITAB worksheets created for the river pollution project are characterised by having a comparatively small number of variables in relation to the number of observations (rows). Most of the columns represent variables measured on the ratio or interval scales; however, some attributes are included denoting, for example, river

```
MTB > RETRIEVE 'chweat02'
  WORKSHEET SAVED   3/28/1993      Worksheet retrieved from file: chweat02.MTW
MTB > LET C20 = (C18 * 100)/C4
MTB > LET C21 = (C19 * 100)/C4
MTB > NAME C20 '%LOSS7'
MTB > NAME C21 '%LOSS14'
MTB > TABLE C2;
SUBC > COUNTS;
SUBC > STATS C18 - C21.
ROWS: Treatmt
                  Loss0-7    Loss0-7    Loss0-7    Loss0-14   Loss0-14   Loss0-14   %LOSS7
       COUNT      N          MEAN       STD DEV    N          MEAN       STD DEV    N
 1     12         12         4.8650     2.6316     12         17.632     2.443      12
 2     12         12         4.1442     3.3899     12         21.313     2.728      12
 3     12         12         0.0008     0.0029     12          1.721     1.368      12
 4     12         12         1.8250     0.5236     12          5.600     1.475      12
 5     12         12         0.1875     0.3969     12          8.943     1.985      12
 6     12         12         0.1142     0.3676     12          1.192     0.664      12
 7     12         12         1.1075     2.8498     12          1.806     0.958      12
 8     12         12         0.2867     0.2750     12          1.244     0.483      12
 9     12         12         0.2292     0.2783     12          0.736     0.490      12
ALL    108        108        1.4178     2.4260     108         6.687     7.526      108
       % LOSS7    % LOSS7    % LOSS14   % LOSS14   % LOSS14
       MEAN       STD DEV    N          MEAN       STD DEV
 1     16.267      8.819     12         58.893     8.073
 2     13.811     11.245     12         71.100     8.986
 3      0.003      0.010     12          5.746     4.569
 4      6.085      1.741     12         18.679     4.930
 5      0.620      1.311     12         29.718     6.554
 6      0.381      1.225     12          3.975     2.219
 7      3.684      9.463     12          6.020     3.195
 8      0.956      0.918     12          4.151     1.619
 9      0.763      0.928     12          2.438     1.626
ALL     4.730      8.087     108        22.302    25.107
MTB>SAVE 'chweat03'
Worksheet saved into file: chweat03.MTW
MTB>NOOUTFILE
```

Box 7.2 Selection of cross-tabulations for chalk weathering project (MINITAB output)

quality class, flow rate and the presence or absence of an industrial unit. Cross-tabulations could be generated by the TABLE command for the continuous variables and the contextual climatic variables provided that suitable classification schemes were applied. However, it is worthwhile representing the bivariate distributions in a graphical form. There are a number of questions that could be pursued through a simple descriptive analysis of the data. For example, a scattergram of the chemical analysis variables with the climatic measurements might suggest the presence of a relationship. Similarly, there might be a connection between dissolved oxygen and biochemical oxygen demand.

MINITAB has a selection of commands which generate plots of different types, for time-series data, simple bivariate and three-way distributions. The log of the MINITAB session which produces graphical representations of the river pollution data in samples A and B using

Table 7.6 Derivation of bivariate scattergrams for river pollution project samples A and B in MINITAB

```
MTB > OUTFILE 'river04'
MTB > RETRIEVE 'rivera02'
MTB > PLOT C7 C8;
SUBC > TITLE 'RIVER POLLUTION SURVEY SAMPLE A';
SUBC > TITLE 'Dissolved Oxygen and Biochemical Oxygen Demand';
SUBC > XLABEL 'Biochemical Oxygen Demand';
SUBC > YLABEL 'Percentage Dissolved Oxygen';
SUBC > FOOTNOTE 'BOD in mg/l'.
MTB > PLOT C8 C9;
SUBC > TITLE 'RIVER POLLUTION SURVEY SAMPLE A';
SUBC > TITLE 'Biochemical Oxygen Demand and Ammonia';
SUBC > XLABEL 'Ammonia';
SUBC > YLABEL 'Biochemical Oxygen Demand';
SUBC > FOOTNOTE 'BOD in mg/l';
SUBC > FOOTNOTE 'Ammonia in mg/l'.
MTB > RETRIEVE 'riverb02'
MTB > PLOT C9 C10;
SUBC > TITLE 'RIVER POLLUTION SURVEY SAMPLE B';
SUBC > TITLE 'Dissolved Oxygen and Biochemical Oxygen Demand';
SUBC > XLABEL 'Biochemical Oxygen Demand';
SUBC > YLABEL 'Percentage Dissolved Oxygen';
SUBC > FOOTNOTE 'BOD in mg/l'.
MTB > PLOT C9 C11;
SUBC > TITLE 'RIVER POLLUTION SURVEY SAMPLE B';
SUBC > TITLE 'Percentage Dissolved Oxygen and Ammonia';
SUBC > XLABEL 'Ammonia';
SUBC > YLABEL 'Percentage Dissolved Oxygen';
SUBC > FOOTNOTE 'Ammonia in mg/l'.
MTB > NOOUTFILE
MTB > STOP
```

the PLOT command, is given in Table 7.6. The PLOT command itself is relatively straightforward: the keyword is followed by two columns, which specify the Y and X axis variables, respectively, thus:

```
MTB > PLOT C9 C10;
SUBC > TITLE 'RIVER POLLUTION SURVEY SAMPLE B';
SUBC > TITLE 'Dissolved Oxygen and Biochemical Oxygen
   Demand';
SUBC > XLABEL 'Biochemical Oxygen Demand';
SUBC > YLABEL 'Percentage Dissolved Oxygen';
SUBC > FOOTNOTE 'BOD in mg/l'.
```

In addition to the basic PLOT command, this example also demonstrates various optional subcommands, which provide some annotation for the scattergram, namely a title, *X* and *Y* axis labels and a footnote. The occurrence of each unique combination of values for the two variables is represented by an asterisk, with multiple occurrences being shown with the appropriate numerical digit up to 9, and then + is used to signify 10 or more observations with the same values.

The scattergrams produced by the series of PLOT commands for samples A and B are given in Box 7.3. The graphs suggest that lower biochemical oxygen demand occurred in those rivers where there was a greater percentage of dissolved oxygen. The third scattergram confirms that the same pattern was found in the case of sample B. The association between the concentration of ammonia and biochemical oxygen demand appears to have the reverse connection, with low values in one variable linked to low values in the other. The relationship between dissolved oxygen and ammonia, however, suggests that greater concentrations of ammonia are connected with less dissolved oxygen.

Box 7.3 Selection of two-way scattergrams for river pollution project samples A and B (MINITAB output)

```
MTB > RETRIEVE 'rivera02'
  WORKSHEET SAVED   3/31/1993      Worksheet retrieved from file: rivera02.MTW
MTB > PLOT C7 C8;
SUBC > TITLE 'RIVER POLLUTION SURVEY SAMPLE A';
SUBC > TITLE 'Dissolved Oxygen and Biochemical Oxygen Demand';
SUBC > XLABEL 'Biochemical Oxygen Demand';
SUBC > YLABEL 'Percentage Dissolved Oxygen';
SUBC > FOOTNOTE 'BOD in mg/l'.
                          RIVER POLLUTION SURVEY SAMPLE A
                  Dissolved Oxygen and Biochemical Oxygen Demand


P 90  +      *222
e     -  23579732
r     -   * *2 32    2*
c     -      * 3* *32**
e     -      **46233*2
n 60  +         * 2*2* ** *      *
t     -           2** 3 3
a     -             4* *** 522 **
g     -             3 ****342
e     -                  *  * *          **
  30  +                      * *** *    * *
D     -                  *     * *  * **2**2**
i     -                   * **   *2 3 * **** 2
s     -               *   ** 232***2*2**22223*    *
s     -                      ** 2**3** 3 *4 22* 2 *
o  0  +
       --+---------+---------+---------+---------+---------+----
        0.0       4.0       8.0      12.0      16.0      20.0
                    Biochemical Oxygen Demand    BOD in mg/l

MTB > PLOT C8 C9;
SUBC > TITLE 'RIVER POLLUTION SURVEY SAMPLE A';
SUBC > TITLE 'Biochemical Oxygen Demand and Ammonia';
SUBC > XLABEL 'Ammonia';
SUBC > YLABEL 'Biochemical Oxygen Demand';
SUBC > FOOTNOTE 'BOD in mg/l';
SUBC > FOOTNOTE 'Ammonia in mg/l'.
```

(continued)

Box 7.3 (*continued*)

RIVER POLLUTION SURVEY SAMPLE A
Biochemical Oxygen Demand and Ammonia

```
B 21.0 +                 *
i      -                3
o      -              * 2**  *         *
c      -             * 2*4   *  *    **2  * * 2 *
h      -            *** *6 2 *  *     *  *  * *
e 14.0 +               **3  **     *  * **   *     *
m      -              *225 *      * **    *  2
i      -          *    2* 5        *  *   * *
c      -            ** 222                *
a      -        *  * ***3* 2422* *
l  7.0 +   *          * 23*223
       -       **2 *  3 ***5*3
O      -        3*2 4 *232*2
x      -  223 3*2  7 2 *2 *4***
y      -  4 9*574      *     *
g  0.0 +    2 33
       --+---------+---------+---------+---------+---------+----
       0.00      0.50      1.00      1.50      2.00      2.50
              Ammonia   BOD in mg/l   Ammonia in mg/l
```

MTB > RETRIEVE 'riverb02'
WORKSHEET SAVED 3/31/1993 Worksheet retrieved from file: riverb02.MTW
MTB > PLOT C9 C10;
SUBC > TITLE 'RIVER POLLUTION SURVEY SAMPLE B';
SUBC > TITLE 'Dissolved Oxygen and Biochemical Oxygen Demand';
SUBC > XLABEL 'Biochemical Oxygen Demand';
SUBC > YLABEL 'Percentage Dissolved Oxygen';
SUBC > FOOTNOTE 'BOD in mg/l'.

RIVER POLLUTION SURVEY SAMPLE B
Dissolved Oxygen and Biochemical Oxygen Demand

```
P 90  +    * *233*
e     -  2332579*
r     -   2*324 * ***2
c     -  *  **  * 5 5*
e     -        *38443
n 60  +          2  32
t     -        **2* 2 *  **** 2
a     -        2**3* 4 *** 4 2
g     -          2 *   2 2 ** *
e     -              3 32 32*
  30  +             ** **2 * * *
D     -              2 ***            *    *
i     -                    2 *   **2 *2* **32*
s     -                   *        4*8  5*22** * *
s     -                    2*   3 * 2 3245265*55*8632  *
o  0  +                            *            *    *
      --+---------+---------+---------+---------+---------+----
      0.0       4.0       8.0      12.0      16.0      20.0
             Biochemical Oxygen Demand    BOD in mg/l
```

(*continued*)

Box 7.3 (*continued*)

```
MTB > PLOT C9 C11;
SUBC > TITLE 'RIVER POLLUTION SURVEY SAMPLE A';
SUBC > TITLE 'Percentage Dissolved Oxygen and Ammonia';
SUBC > XLABEL 'Ammonia';
SUBC > YLABEL 'Percentage Dissolved Oxygen';
SUBC > FOOTNOTE 'Ammonia in mg/l'.
           RIVER POLLUTION SURVEY SAMPLE B
         Percentage Dissolved Oxygen and Ammonia

P      -         *
e 90   +       **2* 2   ****
r      -  2*  25 323 *253*2
c      -     2*  2 *32 ****   *   **
e      -         *    2   * ***** *  *2* *
n      -            *   2*    **54  4*2  *
t 60   +                 * *  2   2    *
a      -                 * * * *  **3* **  2
g      -                 * 2 * 2   32224  2
e      -                     ** * **  4   *
       -               *         ** 23 42
D 30   +                         * * * *  4   *
i      -                  2    *   **   * *
s      -                     *   * * *6**24   *
s      -                  *      22 264*26* *
o      -                        *3 *6+647+2*
l 0    +                             * * *
       --+--------+--------+--------+--------+--------+----
       0.00     0.25     0.50     0.75     1.00     1.25
                Ammonia           Ammonia in mg/l

MTB > NOOUTFILE
```

7.3.4 Village communities

The previous projects have covered the important methods of representing bivariate and, to a limited extent, multivariate distributions. The village communities project concentrates on how similar types of output can be produced by means of the SPSS-X software. The dataset for the village communities survey contains a group of contextual attributes and variables, such as the respondents' age, type of accommodation, employment status and income category, and another group directly concerned with the issues relating to the proposed new industrial development, including length of residence, geographical location within the village, and views on employment opportunities. This small subset of the information indicates the wealth of analysis that might be undertaken and the potential for cross-tabulation and for producing scattergrams. Most of the data are already stored as attributes with integer values, although some recoding or collapsing of categories may be required (see Section 6.3.4).

The log of the SPSS-X session which generates a selection of bivariate frequency distributions for the village communities survey

Table 7.7 Derivation of bivariate frequency distributions and scattergrams for village communities project in SPSS-X

```
FILE HANDLE SF / NAME = 'VILLAG01.SF'
GET FILE = SF
CROSSTABS VARIABLES = TENURE(1,6),RELENGTH(1,6),HSLDINC(1,6),
  AGE(1,5),WORK(1,2),INCEMOPP HEARPROP FAVPROP DISCHSLD
  DISCVILL DISCOTHR PROPNEWS PROPMTNG WELCDEVP WLDATTEN(1,2)/
  TABLES = AGE BY HEARPROP,FAVPROP,DISCHSLD,DISCVILL/
  TABLES = TENURE,HSLDINC BY HEARPROP BY FAVPROP/
PLOT PLOT = LENGRES NPERSONS WITH NFRIENDS HSGTOFM
FINISH
```

is given in Table 7.7. The syntax of the command in SPSS-X which is used to create contingency tables initially might seem a rather more daunting prospect than the comparable command in MINITAB. There is, however, considerable flexibility in the form of the output that can be produced. The CROSSTABS command can operate in general and integer modes. The former can generate somewhat unwieldy and useless tables, if it is inadvertently used with continuous variables, since each different value defines a row or column in the table. The following command sequence exemplifies the integer mode:

```
CROSSTABS VARIABLES = TENURE(1,6),RELENGTH(1,6),
  HSLDINC(1,6),AGE(1,5),WORK(1,2),INCEMOPP HEARPROP
  FAVPROP DISCHSLD DISCVILL DISCOTHR PROPNEWS
  PROPMTNG WELCDEVP WLDATTEN(1,2)/
  TABLES = AGE BY HEARPROP,FAVPROP,DISCHSLD,
  DISCVILL/
  TABLES = TENURE,HSLDINC BY HEARPROP BY FAVPROP/
```

The example illustrates the two key components of the CROSSTABS command, which are introduced by the subcommands VARIABLES = and TABLES =. The first is a list of up to 200 variables with the range of values to be used in the cross-tabulation included in brackets (usually their maximum and minimum values). This information speeds up the processing of the data, since the computer is thereby informed of the dimensions of each table. The second component comprises lists of variable names, which specify the required tables, with up to 20 lists being permitted for each CROSSTABS command. The lists enable the user to investigate the distributions resulting from various combinations of variables. In this instance the last of the three lists specifies two three-way, multivariate tables. The CROSSTABS command is used in 'general mode' by omitting the VARIABLES= subcommand and only providing a list of the required cross-tabulations, which should only refer to variable names which hold integer data.

Most of the data for the village communities project is held as attributes with fairly small ranges of integer values; consequently scattergrams are inappropriate for representing the bivariate distributions. There are few variables with a wide range of values, namely length

Box 7.4 Selection of cross-tabulations and scattergrams for village communities project (SPSS-X output)

AGE Age of Respondent by HEARPROP Heard of Proposal
HEARPROP Page 1 of 1

AGE	Count	Yes 1	No 2	Row Total
1	18-24 Years	3	16	19 5.3
2	25-44 Years	17	33	50 14.0
3	45-54 Years	43	61	104 29.2
4	55-64 Years	26	73	99 27.8
5	65 Years and Ove	33	51	84 23.6
	Column Total	122 34.3	234 65.7	356 100.0

AGE Age of Respondent by FAVPROP In Favour of Proposal
FAVPROP Page 1 of 1

AGE	Count	Yes 1	No 2	Row Total
1	18-24 Years		3	3 2.5
2	25-44 Years	7	10	17 13.9
3	45-54 Years	13	30	43 35.2
4	55-64 Years	8	18	26 21.3
5	65 Years and Ove	7	26	33 27.0
	Column Total	35 28.7	87 71.3	122 100.0

(continued)

Box 7.4 (*continued*)

AGE Age of Respondent by DISCHSLD Discussed in Household
DISCHSLD Page 1 of 1

Count AGE	Yes 1	No 2	Row Total
1 18-24 Years	2	1	3 2.5
2 25-44 Years	8	9	17 13.9
3 45-54 Years	18	25	43 35.2
4 55-64 Years	9	17	26 21.3
5 65 Years and Ove	14	19	33 27.0
Column Total	48 39.3	74 60.7	122 100.0

AGE Age of Respondent by DISCVILL Discussed in Village
DISCVILL Page 1 of 1

Count AGE	Yes 1	No 2	Row Total
1 18-24 Years		3	3 2.5
2 25-44 Years	8	9	17 13.9
3 45-54 Years	22	21	43 35.2
4 55-64 Years	14	12	26 21.3
5 65 Years and Ove	15	18	33 27.0
Column Total	59 48.4	63 51.6	122 100.0

(*continued*)

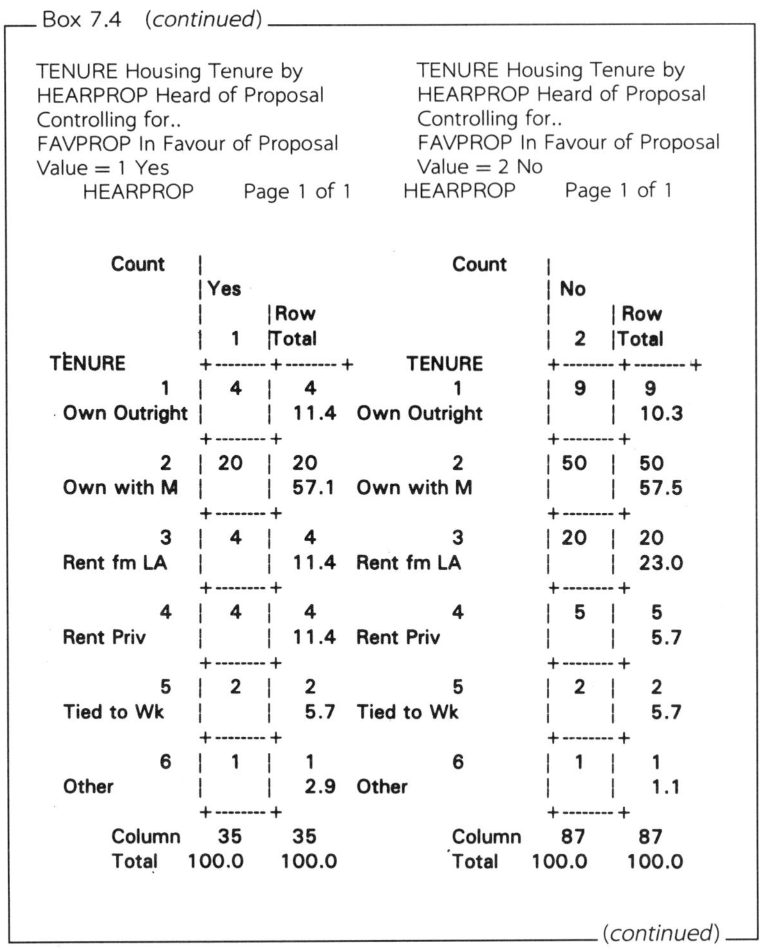

Box 7.4 *(continued)*

TENURE Housing Tenure by
HEARPROP Heard of Proposal
Controlling for..
FAVPROP In Favour of Proposal
Value = 1 Yes
HEARPROP Page 1 of 1

TENURE	Count Yes 1	Row Total
1 Own Outright	4	4 11.4
2 Own with M	20	20 57.1
3 Rent fm LA	4	4 11.4
4 Rent Priv	4	4 11.4
5 Tied to Wk	2	2 5.7
6 Other	1	1 2.9
Column Total	35 100.0	35 100.0

TENURE Housing Tenure by
HEARPROP Heard of Proposal
Controlling for..
FAVPROP In Favour of Proposal
Value = 2 No
HEARPROP Page 1 of 1

TENURE	Count No 2	Row Total
1 Own Outright	9	9 10.3
2 Own with M	50	50 57.5
3 Rent fm LA	20	20 23.0
4 Rent Priv	5	5 5.7
5 Tied to Wk	2	2 5.7
6 Other	1	1 1.1
Column Total	87 100.0	87 100.0

(continued)

of residence, number of persons in household, number of friends and distance from the proposed development, which can be displayed as scattergrams. The SPSS-X command sequence

```
PLOT PLOT = LENGRES NPERSONS WITH NFRIENDS
  HSGTOFM
```

extracted from Table 7.7 produces the four scattergraphs. The PLOT command requires at least one PLOT subcommand, which contains two lists of variables separated by the keyword WITH. Each variable in the first list is plotted against the each variable in the second. Up to 25 paired lists, separated from each other by the slash (/) delimiter, may be specified.

The output from the village communities bivariate descriptive analysis is in Box 7.4. The contingency tables generated by the CROSSTABS command by default only show the cell counts and marginal percentages, although row, column and total percentages can be obtained by means of an options command. The results from

Box 7.4 *(continued)*

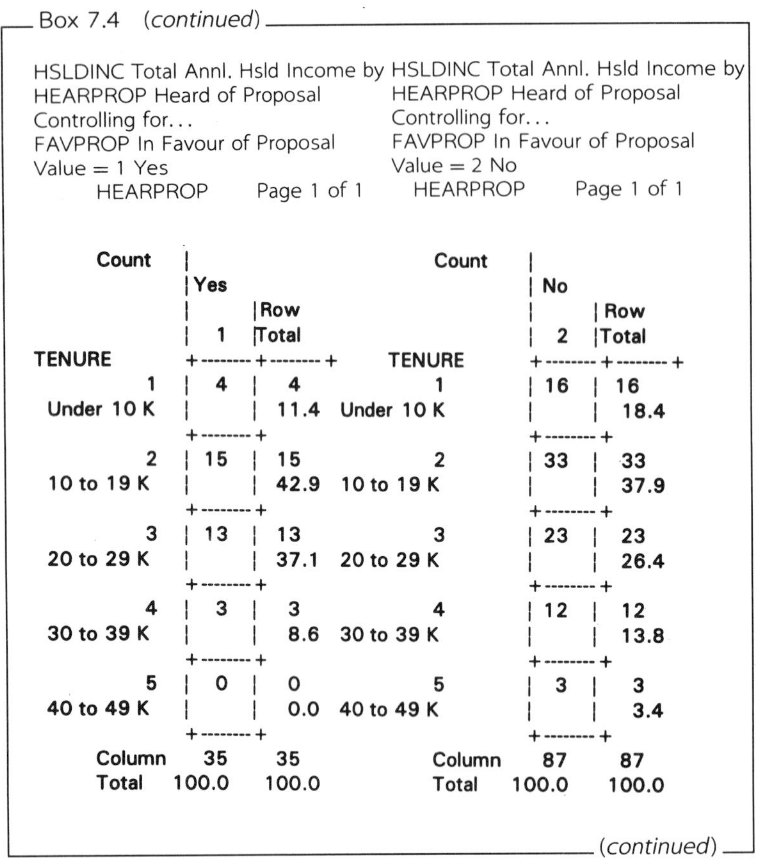

HSLDINC Total Annl. Hsld Income by
HEARPROP Heard of Proposal
Controlling for...
FAVPROP In Favour of Proposal
Value = 1 Yes
HEARPROP Page 1 of 1

TENURE	Count	Yes 1	Row Total
1	Under 10 K	4	4 11.4
2	10 to 19 K	15	15 42.9
3	20 to 29 K	13	13 37.1
4	30 to 39 K	3	3 8.6
5	40 to 49 K	0	0 0.0
	Column Total	35 100.0	35 100.0

HSLDINC Total Annl. Hsld Income by
HEARPROP Heard of Proposal
Controlling for...
FAVPROP In Favour of Proposal
Value = 2 No
HEARPROP Page 1 of 1

TENURE	Count	No 2	Row Total
1	Under 10 K	16	16 18.4
2	10 to 19 K	33	33 37.9
3	20 to 29 K	23	23 26.4
4	30 to 39 K	12	12 13.8
5	40 to 49 K	3	3 3.4
	Column Total	87 100.0	87 100.0

(continued)

the village communities survey suggest that nearly half (122) of the respondents who had heard of the proposed development were aged 55 years or more. On the other hand, interviewees who had heard of it and were in favour appeared to be in the younger age groups. People did not discuss the proposal with other household members, tending to talk about it to other people in the village. Neither of the two scattergraphs indicates a very clear association between the variables concerned. It is relevant to note that because the three variables (length of residence, number of friends and distance to Cowper's farm) are integers, the graphs display a certain regularity in the spacing of the symbols.

7.4 COMPARISON OF THE PROJECTS

The analysis of the data in the exemplar projects illustrates several important aspects of bivariate frequency distributions. The need to select the appropriate type of analysis for the data under investigation has again reappeared as a significant issue. Essentially the choice is between tabular and graphical means for representing the distributions. A tabular form is usually most suitable for attributes counted on the

Box 7.4 *(continued)*

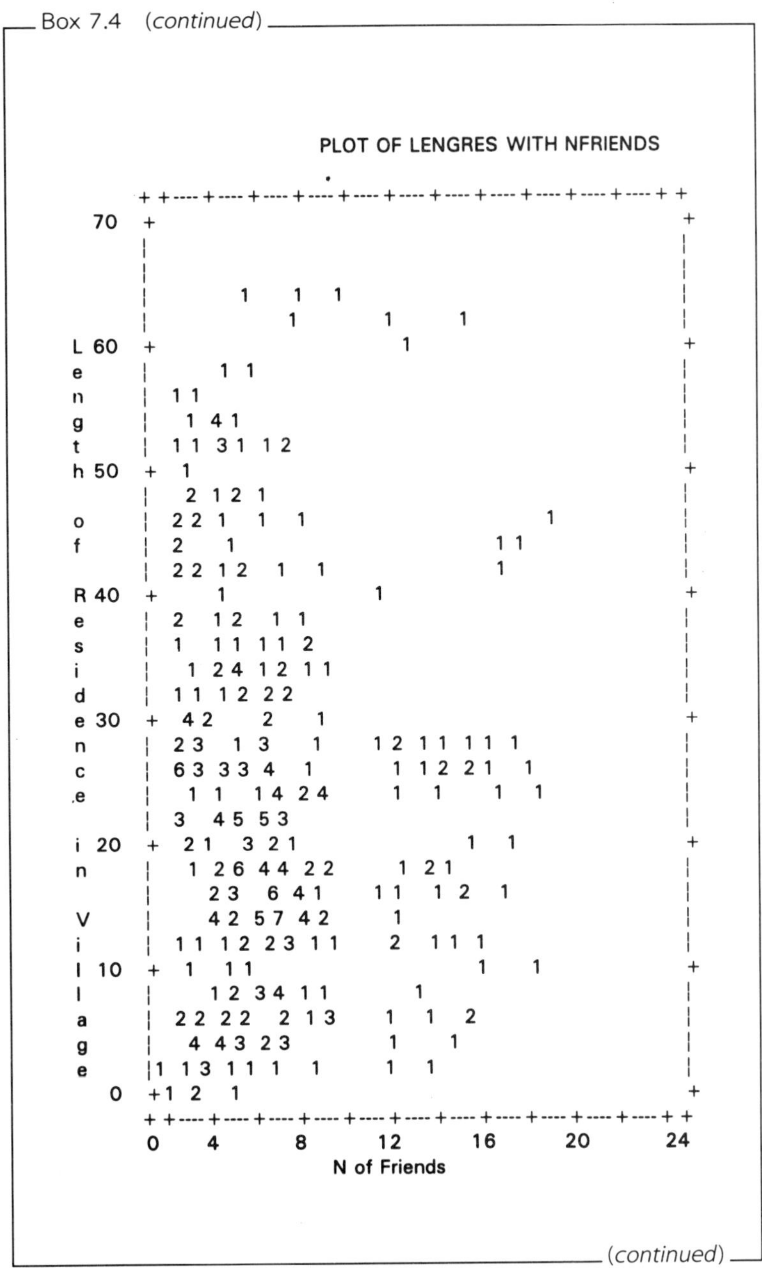

(continued)

nominal scale and for variables measured on the ordinal scale. Interval- or ratio-scale variables are more usefully presented as scattergraphs, but their values can be grouped into mutually exclusive classes, if they are to be cross-tabulated with nominal scale attributes. The MINITAB and SPSS-X software can produce cross-tabulations and scattergraphs with equal facility. The approach adopted by the two packages is different,

Box 7.4 *(continued)*

```
                     PLOT OF LENGRES WITH HSGTOFM

        + +----+----+----+----+----+----+----+----+----+----+----+ +
   70   +                                                          +
        |                                                          |
        |                                                          |
        |       1       1       1                                  |
        |  1    1            1                                     |
L  60   +            1                                             +
e       |    1                1                                    |
n       |              1                        1                  |
g       | 1   1 1        1   1      1                              |
t       |    11  1              3  1    1                          |
h  50   +            1                                             +
        | 1      1 1     1      2                                  |
o       | 111 1 11                           1    1                |
f       |     111  1  1                                            |
        | 11   2  1   1       1 1    1   1                         |
R  40   +    1                1                                    +
e       |    3 2  1       1                                        |
s       |  21    2            1          1                         |
i       |  11 111  2  1   1              1              1          |
d       | 11 1111        1   1    1                                |
e  30   +    11111 2         1           1                         +
n       | 1311 1111   2   1  1     1      11   1                   |
c       | 3133 1 21 1 1  1 2 3 1  1    1 1 1           1           |
e       |  1311 311 1  1      1       1    1           1           |
        | 1 1 21 1 2  21 11  1   1 1          2        1     1     |
i  20   + 1  12 112  1                   11                        +
n       |  1 3  31322 1   1   111   2 2   1 1                      |
        | 1  211121121       1 1 221   1    1      1               |
V       |  2 13132 11 1  1  11  1 1 1 1          11       1        |
i       |    1 111   11 121 11  1       1   1        1  1          |
l  10   +  1   1 1 1     1                                         +
l       |  11  123 1  1   1 1    1                                 |
a       | 1 14224     1  1       1         1                       |
g       | 131112   11     111   1    1 1           1               |
e       | 2 2 2  1    1 11              1                          |
    0   +     111            1                                     |
        + +----+----+----+----+----+----+----+----+----+----+----+ +
        0    1000      2000      3000      4000     5000      6000
                           Distance
```

with MINITAB working on the basis of the user requesting the inclusion of certain elements in the output (e.g. row percentages, column percentages, etc.), while SPSS-X provides the counts and all the relative frequencies unless instructed to suppress them.

The purpose of carrying out the initial descriptive analysis of the data is to suggest possible associations or causal relationships between variables. In other words, these distributions are concerned with the characteristics of and the extent to which the values of one variable are connected with those of another for the same set of observations. For reasons that will become clear in the next chapter, it has only been possible at this descriptive stage in the analysis of the projects' data to conclude that certain associations or relationships *appear* to exist. Parts III and IV demonstrate how statistical analysis can be used either to support or bring into question these conclusions.

Part III

STATISTICAL ANALYSIS II

Chapter 8
An introduction to hypothesis testing

8.1 THE ORIGIN OF HYPOTHESES

Research investigations are usually undertaken in order to answer questions. Such questions come in two main varieties: they can either be theoretical or empirical in their origins. On the one hand, the questions are derived from intellectual reflection, perhaps drawing upon past experience and general principles, and, on the other, from impressions made while observing the world around us. As scientific geographers, our aim is to establish whether our ideas can be substantiated as accurate, and, more importantly, to understand why phenomena may be associated with or related to each other. In this chapter, the processes whereby such questions become translated into formal hypotheses are examined and the general statistical procedures for testing these hypotheses outlined.

The first stage in formulating hypotheses entails stating the initial question as a research or geographical hypothesis. Even when the question arises from empirical observation, such as the apparent tendency of rivers to erode more slowly when flowing over hard rock or the coincidence of high expenditure on public services by socialist local authorities, there are implicit theoretical concepts present. What exactly do we mean by rock hardness, or erosion, or a socialist local authority, or public services? The definition of these concepts involves the researcher in translating them into more practical and precise terms. The word 'translating' is chosen deliberately, since the process involved is akin to that of converting from one language to another.

The translation produces a set of operational terms which can be incorporated into hypotheses and thus subjected to statistical testing. Once a more precise definition of the theoretical concepts has been produced, it is possible to identify the variables that should be measured in order to quantify them. In the case of the first example above, the hardness of rock minerals is traditionally defined on a scale of 1–10, indicating the extent to which the rock can be scratched by different items. Erosion is defined as the removal of particulate material from solid bedrock by various agents, including flowing water, and its subsequent deposition elsewhere. Thus if these variables are to be measured in the field, then the investigator needs to determine the hardness of the rock in the study area using the 1–10 scale and the amount of material being removed. With the second geographical hypothesis presented above, a socialist local authority can be defined as a local government council in which Labour Party councillors make up the majority of the elected representatives, and expenditure on public services refers to the amount of money actually spent in a given period, including all costs, on such items as sports centres, housing, facilities for disabled and elderly persons, and transport. Whether expenditure on these items by any particular group of authorities can be regarded as high depends either on comparing all authorities with each other and then establishing a cut-off point, or defining a standard. For example, target expenditure per person for people in different groups in the population could be set, against which each authority could be compared. The components of the geographical hypothesis have to be translated into operational terms which can be used to distinguish between the political complexions of local authorities and to identify the budgetary elements which go to make up expenditure on public services.

The second stage of hypothesis formulation involves deriving two statistical hypotheses, which are expressed in terms of the operational definitions. These statistical hypotheses are mirror images of each other. One is known as the *null hypothesis* (H_0) and the other as the *alternative hypothesis* (H_1). Most investigations require the researcher to devise several pairs of null and alternative hypotheses in order to answer the broad geographical question. For example, different stages in the analysis may build on each other, with separate null and alternative hypotheses needed at each point. In the first geographical hypothesis referred to above, it may be necessary to distinguish between fast and slow rates of erosion by rivers in general, before attempting to establish whether slower rates occur over harder rock.

The precise specification of the null and alternative hypotheses will clearly depend on the variables under investigation. In the fluvial erosion example, the null hypothesis could be phrased as follows:

H_0 The rate of erosion (variable X) by rivers over a given time period is the same for all rock types, irrespective of their hardness class (variable Y). Any observed difference in mean erosion rates between hard and soft rocks has merely arisen through chance and is not significant.

This could be expressed in symbols as

$$H_0 : \bar{x}_{\mathrm{H}} \text{ equal to } \bar{x}_{\mathrm{O}}$$

where $\bar{x}_{\mathrm{H}}$ and $\bar{x}_{\mathrm{O}}$ represent the mean rate of erosion for hard rock and all other types of rock, respectively. The alternative hypothesis could be expressed as follows:

H_1 The difference between the mean rate of erosion by rivers flowing over hard and other types of rock over a specified time period is greater that would have been expected through chance sampling variations alone.

In symbols, this could be stated as

$$H_1 : \bar{x}_H \text{ not equal to } \bar{x}_O$$

where $\bar{x}_H$ and $\bar{x}_O$ are as defined above. The form of H_0 depends on the particular research question under investigation; nevertheless reference can normally be made to some statistical quantity (such as the mean, variance or standard deviation), to the difference between the observed and expected frequencies, or to an association between two or more attributes or variables.

8.2 STATISTICAL TESTING OF NULL AND ALTERNATIVE HYPOTHESES

The techniques used for testing H_0 and H_1 come under the general heading of *inferential statistics*. The simple reason for this is that from the results of a particular test the investigator can *infer* or draw out a conclusion regarding the geographical hypothesis. The basis of all statistical tests is that if the null hypothesis is rejected then the alternative hypothesis is necessarily accepted. In other words, H_0 and H_1 are mutually exclusive and only one of them can be regarded as valid. If the results of the test are inconclusive, then further investigation is required. Suppose a suitable test was carried out with respect to H_0 and H_1 for the fluvial erosion example. If the test result suggested that H_0 should be rejected, then H_1 must necessarily be accepted. Each test produces its own *test statistic*, usually known by a letter such as Z, t, U or W. Hence the tests are often named after these letters or the statistician who devised them, for example Student's t test and Mann-Whitney U test. A test statistic is derived by calculation using a mathematical formula and its magnitude varies according to the number of observations and their values on the attribute or variable under investigation. The decision whether to accept or reject H_0 is taken with reference to the *probability* of having obtained a particular value for the test statistic. Before looking in some detail at the nature of probability statements, it is useful to outline the general procedures underlying the application of statistical tests.

The null hypothesis is always assumed to be correct until or unless shown to be unacceptable as a result of the statistical test. In other words, the investigator uses the test to put H_0 on trial and to determine whether it is probably discredited. H_0 is phrased in a deliberately cautious manner so that it is given every opportunity of passing the test and being accepted. This approach minimises the risk of H_0 being incorrectly rejected (and H_1 therefore incorrectly accepted). In most geographical investigations the consequences or penalties of incorrectly rejecting H_0 are unlikely to be very severe, but in other fields of research, such as medicine and civil engineering, the costs of making a mistake may be great. In both these cases, people's lives may be at risk. For instance, the probability of not experiencing a side-effect from a new medical treatment, or of a building not collapsing, would usually need to be higher than for a geographical research question. The analogy is sometimes made with the situation in a court of law, where 'defendants on criminal charges are assumed innocent unless proved guilty beyond reasonable doubt' (Williams 1984, p. 119). In the case of statistical tests the null hypothesis is assumed to be valid unless shown to be highly improbable.

Hypothesis testing is not about certainty but about probability. Decisions taken on the fate of null hypotheses, and by implication the corresponding alternative hypotheses, are made on the basis of *probably* selecting the right option. Unfortunately, we can never be sure that the correct decision has been made, because the right answer to the research question is unknown. If the H_0 is rejected when in fact it is true, we commit a *Type I* error. Use of a low level of significance will reduce the risk of committing this type of error, but it can never be eliminated. The level of significance gives a measure of the risk of having committed a *Type I* error. On the other hand, setting a very low level of significance runs the risk of committing a *Type II* error, which means that H_0 is accepted, when it is really false. It is scientific acceptability and convention that guides researchers towards 0.05 (5%) and 0.01 (1%) as the two most commonly used levels of significance, rather than anything intrinsically important about these values. A significance level set between 0.05 and 0.01 is generally believed to achieve a suitable compromise between the two types of error and thus produce scientifically acceptable conclusions.

Possibly the most fundamental reason for using inferential statistics arises from the uncertainty that exists over sample data. If all research investigations could be based on data for statistical populations and such populations could be continually monitored and were unchanging in their composition, there would in principle be no need to carry out statistical tests. Unfortunately this is not the case, as we have already seen in Chapter 3. Suppose a complete survey of all businesses established in the Newcastle upon Tyne Enterprise Zone since 1985 had been undertaken in a rigorous, accurate and unbiased fashion. The survey would, by virtue of being a complete enumeration, generate irrefutable statistics about these businesses. If the survey indicated that the mean number of jobs created was 35.8 per firm, then absolute confidence can be placed in this parameter. However, had the researcher decided that resources were insufficient for a complete census, or that comparisons with other enterprises zones or areas not thus designated, were desirable, then the need for statistical testing would have been introduced. A sample survey of the new businesses in the Newcastle upon Tyne Enterprise Zone might have revealed that the mean number of new jobs was 27.5. Two further sample surveys, one in the Liverpool Enterprise Zone and the other in the rest of the North of England, might indicate that the mean numbers of jobs created by new businesses were respectively 42.7 and 56.8. Yet another twist to the problem might arise from an identical sample survey in the Liverpool Enterprise Zone, which indicated that 25.6 new jobs had been created. From this wealth of apparently contradictory evidence, what can the beleaguered researcher conclude about the general effect of enterprise zone designation and its impact in Liverpool and Newcastle upon Tyne in particular?

The answer is to select an appropriate statistical test which helps to determine whether the differences are likely to be indicative of 'genuine' contrasts or to have arisen through *sampling error*. Sampling error can arise for various reasons, including imperfection in the recording instruments, misinterpretation of a question on a questionnaire, inaccurate data entry, errors in calculation or simply on account of some peculiarities in the particular set of observations which make up the sample. In all statistical tests there is a difference to be examined, either between a sample and a population, or between two or more samples. The tests are carried out to determine whether the difference is significant or not. Hence inferential tests are also referred to as *tests of significance*. The decision whether the difference is significant is taken with reference to the magnitude of the test statistic and the probability of having obtained this value. The test statistic calculated from the sample data is compared with tabulated values of the statistic, which have known probabilities derived from a mathematical probability distribution. When the statistical analysis is undertaken on a computer, the test statistic values and associated probabilities are stored in the software, and the calculated test statistic and the probability of its occurrence are reported to the investigator. The decision whether to accept or reject the null hypothesis remains with the researcher.

Statistical testing is used to determine whether a sample is significantly different from its parent population, or whether two or more samples are different from each other or come from the same population. Another important use of significance tests is quite simply to infer something about the sample's parent population. Chapter 3 suggested that there are many geographical research areas in which a sampling framework is difficult, if not impossible, to define. In such circumstances, or where nothing is known about the population, sampling may be used as a means of producing some summary descriptive statistics relating to the population. For example, a researcher recognises that there are an infinite number of sites at which soil pH could be measured in a study area and so a sample of points is selected at random. The sample mean pH value is calculated as 8.3 and the sample standard deviation is 2.1. Are these satisfactory estimates of the corresponding population parameters? If the answer is 'yes', then what is the probability of being wrong?

The approach normally adopted to answering this type of question is to use the sample data and the appropriate test to calculate *confidence limits*. In the case of a single statistic, such as a mean, these limits provide a range within which the investigator can have a chosen level of confidence that the population mean will lie. Suppose that the lower and upper 95 per cent confidence limits for soil pH were calculated as 7.7 and 9.1, respectively, noting that these are an equal interval either side of the sample mean (8.3). The investigator can conclude with 95 per cent confidence that the true population mean lies between these two values, although there is a fairly remote chance that it lies outside this range. In other words, it is highly probable that the soil in the region is alkaline (pH $>$ 7.0), but it is not possible to be absolutely certain about the mean value.

The bewildering array of statistical tests seem more designed to confuse than to enlighten the novice analyst. Each test makes certain assumptions and has specific requirements about the data and the circumstances in which it can be employed. The key criteria in selecting a suitable test relate to the type of sampling, the scales of measurement employed and the number of samples. In general terms, most tests require simple random sampling with replacement, where each item in the population has an equal probability of being included. In practice, this stringent requirement for replacement may be relaxed if the population is sufficiently large in relation to the size of the sample. Tests which require nominal or ordinal scale data are collectively known as *non-parametric*, while those used with the interval or ratio scales are referred to as *parametric* tests. Tests involving a single sample are designed to compare this with some hypothesised population or to derive confidence limits, while those intended for two or more samples facilitate comparison. Table 8.1 summarises the interplay of these criteria and indicates how the appropriate test for a particular situation can be selected. Computerised data analysis makes it all too easy to apply various tests to a set of data in an indiscriminate or 'sledgehammer' fashion. The computer will churn out some results, but whether they mean anything is another matter.

Before considering the specific null and alternative hypotheses associated with the exemplar projects, it is useful to look in a little more detail at the nature of the differences which the tests referred to in Table 8.1 can be used to investigate. Table 8.2 summarises the differences which the statistical techniques discussed in the following chapters examine. It is clear that the parametric tests focus on the mean, variance and standard deviation of the sample(s), whereas the non-parametric ones concentrate on relative frequencies of nominal or ordinal data.

Table 8.1 A structure for selecting the appropriate statistical test

	Non-parametric		Parametric
	Nominal	Ordinal	Interval/ratio
1 sample	Pearson's chi-square	Kolmogorov-Smirnov *D* test	*Z* test *t* test
1 sample of paired observations	Pearson's chi-square		Wilcoxon *W* test paired *t* test
2 samples	Pearson's chi-square	Kolmogorov-Smirnov *D* test Mann-Whitney *U* test	*t* test
More than 2 samples (*k* samples)	Pearson's chi-square	Kruskall-Wallis *H* test	Analysis of variance *F* test

Table 8.2 The differences examined by selected tests of significance

	One sample univariate tests
Z test	Difference between a sample with a mean of $\bar{x}$ from a population of known mean (μ) and standard deviation (σ).
t test	Difference between a sample with a mean of $\bar{x}$ and a standard deviation of s and a population of mean (μ).
Pearson's chi-square	Differences in the relative frequencies of a sample and a hypothesised population.
D test	Differences in the cumulative relative frequencies of a sample and a hypothesised population.
	Paired-sample univariate tests
Paired *t* test	Differences between the means of pairs of measurements.
W test	Differences between the means of pairs of measurements.
Pearson's chi-square	Differences in the relative frequencies between two paired parts of a sample.
	Two-sample univariate tests
F test	Differences in the variances of two samples.
t test	Differences in the means of two samples.
U test	Difference between the mean and variance of the samples.
D test	Differences in the cumulative relative frequencies of two ordered samples.
Pearson's chi-square	Difference in the relative frequencies between a sample grouped according to two classification schemes *or* two independent samples.
	k-sample univariate tests
Pearson's chi-square	Difference in the relative frequencies between a sample grouped according to three or more classification schemes *or* three or more independent samples.
H test	Differences between observations classified according to three or more ordered groups.
ANOVA	Differences between sample means.

8.3 FORMATION OF SPECIFIC NULL HYPOTHESES FOR PROJECTS

The formulation of the projects' research questions or geographical hypotheses was considered in Chapter 2. The following subsections translate these into suitable null hypotheses. Furthermore, in the light of the structure outlined in Table 8.1, the types of test that will be applied in each case are indicated. The projects compare the application of a range of statistical techniques with the aim of illustrating the suitability of particular tests for different situations. For example, two-sample tests would be irrelevant when the project only included one sample. Similarly, tests designed for frequency distributions should only be used with counted attributes or coded variables.

8.3.1 Land-use change

The land-use project is essentially concerned with empirical questions relating to the extent of change in the area of different land uses between the 1930s and 1960s, and in particular whether any differences can be detected between rural-urban fringe and rural areas. The use of secondary sources of data has restricted the range of land uses to seven fairly broad categories (arable, market gardening, grassland, woodland, heath and moorland, housing, and other agriculturally unproductive). There is a suggestion that the loss of countryside to urban uses has continued to erode the rural character of land proximate to built-up areas despite controls on development, especially through the implementation of green belt policies. The project examines results from two random samples, one of plots of land (A) and one of grid squares (B), in an area of Hertfordshire where some of these land-use planning issues are adjudged to be important. Pairs of measurements for the seven land uses are obtained relating to the Land Utilisation Surveys undertaken in the 1930s and 1960s.

The precise phraseology of a null hypothesis depends partly on the specific research project and partly upon the nature of the difference under investigation. The null hypotheses for the land-use change project detailed below have been phrased in a generic form to enable them to be applied to the seven land-use categories. The null hypotheses recognise that the analysis of the data concentrates partly on individual land uses and partly on the overall mix of uses. Furthermore, in some cases samples A and B are treated separately, whereas in others they are compared.

LU1 The mean areas of each land use in sample A are not significantly different from the population, which has a known mean (μ) and standard deviation (σ).

LU2 The mean areas of each land use in sample B, with standard deviations of s, are not significantly different from the population, which has a known mean (μ).

LU3 The area of each land use in the 1930s is not significantly different from that in the 1960s. Any differences have arisen purely due to sampling error.

LU4 Any differences in the areal changes of each land use, as recorded by samples A and B, have arisen entirely through sampling error and are not significant.

LU5 The apparent difference in the area of each land use between rural-urban fringe and rural locations is not significant. Chance alone accounts for the inconsistencies.

The assumptions associated with the different tests will be discussed in due course. However, it should be noted that null hypotheses LU1 and LU2 require that the published summary results for the county of Hertfordshire from the First Land Utilisation Survey are available to provide population parameters.

8.3.2 Chalk weathering

The chalk weathering project investigates selected aspects of the process of freeze–thaw weathering by focusing on the effect of different temperature regimes and on the contribution of pure or saline water. Chalk blocks kept at +5°C and without being saturated in water are treated as controls. A series of nine sub-samples comprising 12 blocks have been selected at random. The blocks have been weighed at the start and daily during the 14 days of the experiment, and weight-loss variables after 7 and 14 days have already been calculated. The statistical analysis therefore needs to consider both the inter- and intra-treatment results. Variations in weight loss between the blocks forming a single sub-sample provide the intra-group differences. Contrasts between two or more of the different types of treatment produce the inter-group differences.

There are no empirically derived population figures with which the sample results can be compared in this project, since in principle there are an infinite number of chalk blocks which could have been sampled. Therefore, the sub-samples provide estimates of the population parameters and thus some indication of the operation of freeze–thaw processes in the field. It is, however, sensible to examine whether the loss of weight by the different sub-samples is significantly different from zero, as reflected in CW2. The following null hypotheses reflect these various issues.

CW1 In the absence of any population data, the sub-samples of chalk blocks produce the best estimate of the population mean with a defined measure of confidence.

CW2 The apparent loss of weight by the chalk blocks in the different sub-samples has occurred through sampling error: the mean loss for each sub-sample is in fact zero.

CW3 The differences between the variances of the weight-loss variable for pairs of samples in the experiment (e.g. pure water and saline water sub-samples at a constant −5°C) are not significant and have arisen through sampling error.

CW4 The differences in mean weight loss between pairs of samples in the experimental design (e.g. diurnal freeze–thaw and constant +5°C after saturation in pure water) are not statistically significant. Such apparent differences as exist in the sample data can be attributed entirely to sampling error.

CW5 Variations in mean weight loss among the sub-samples are not of such magnitude as to suggest that different types of temperature regime and water treatment have any effect on the freeze–thaw weathering process. The differences are not significant.

It should, of course, be noted that CW1 is not in fact a null hypothesis, but a statement intended to investigate the validity of the sample data as an estimate for the parent population.

8.3.3 River pollution

The two main questions in this project are, first, whether there has been a change in the quality of the North West Water Authority's rivers since 1985, and second, whether discharged waste from factories can be blamed for increases in pollutant chemical levels. Two samples have been employed to investigate these questions. The first sample is stratified by river quality class as determined by the 1985 national survey, which provides bench-mark parameters against which the sample results can be tested. The abstracted water samples are chemically analysed for three variables which were critical in the 1985 classification (percentage of dissolved oxygen, biochemical oxygen demand and ammonia). The observations in the second sample (factories adjacent to rivers) have paired measurements made upstream and downstream. The water samples were analysed for the same set of chemicals in order to determine whether any differences between downstream and upstream concentrations existed: if the downstream levels were higher, the factories might be blamed for the difference.

The null hypotheses for the two samples in this project are not directly connected with each other, since each sample addresses a different issue in the river pollution debate.

RP1 The mean concentrations of the specific chemicals in the rivers differ from those reported in the national surveys only because of sampling error. The differences are not statistically significant.

RP2 The difference in the concentration of the chemicals upstream and downstream of the factories is more illusory than real, and does not indicate that discharged industrial waste from these plants is to blame for seemingly higher levels downstream.

RP3 The mean concentrations produced by the analysis of the two samples are identical, having come from a single population with mean μ and standard deviation σ. Any difference in sample means is due to chance.

RP4 The 1985 river quality and flow classification systems are independent of each other: any apparent tendency for rivers in one flow class to have a particular quality rating is entirely the result of sampling error.

RP5 Any apparent differences between the rivers in sample B with respect to river quality and flow class are not significant, and have merely emerged as a result of chance; the sample survey provides no firm evidence of an improvement in water quality.

Population mean figures used to test these hypotheses have been obtained from published reports on the 1985 survey (Department of the Environment, 1987, 1992).

8.3.4 Village communities

The village communities project is concerned with how a particular development proposal brings group allegiances and discord to the surface, thereby revealing division and potential conflict within a rural population. Rural populations are typically viewed as models of harmonious existence, but issues such as the one investigated by this project can sometimes expose hidden problems. The sample of 358 adults in the parish is sufficient to allow for the cross-tabulation of the various nominal-scale attributes.

There is a certain amount of information relating to the settlement available from the national population census, which enables some statistical comparisons to be made between the sample and its parent population. The following null hypotheses partly reflect the need to confirm the representativeness of the sample data and partly to examine the research questions.

VC1 Any differences in the relative frequencies between the sample and its parent population in respect of the limited set of common attributes have occurred through sampling error and are not significant.

VC2 The households are distributed randomly with respect to distance from the site of the proposed development.

VC3 A public meeting to explain details of the proposed development has no effect on people's attitude. The apparent differences of opinion are not statistically significant.

VC4 Attitudes towards the development are not influenced by the respondent's length of residence in the village — the newcomers and the indigenous population are indistinguishable in their views.

VC5 The relative frequencies produced when the respondents in the sample are classified according to their economic position, household tenure and attitude towards the proposed development show no sign of an association between these attributes. The frequencies are what would be expected if the sample had been distributed entirely at random.

8.4 COMPARISON OF PROJECT HYPOTHESES

The null hypotheses put forward in the previous section should be regarded as a selection given the number of variables and attributes measured in the exemplar projects. Further specific questions could be examined, but the range provided enables the key univariate statistical tests to be explained and demonstrated. In conclusion to this chapter, it is therefore useful to examine the null hypotheses of the projects in relation to the general points made in Tables 8.1 and 8.2. Table 8.3

Table 8.3 Comparison of null hypotheses and statistical tests employed in the exemplar projects

	Land-use change	Chalk weathering	River pollution	Village communities
		One-sample univariate tests		
Z test	LU1			
t test	LU2	CW2	RP1	
t confidence interval		CW1		
Pearson's chi-square				VC1
D test				VC2
		Paired-sample univariate tests		
Paired *t* test			RP2	
W test	LU3			
Pearson's chi-square				VC3
		Two-sample univariate tests		
F test		CW3		
t test		CW4	RP3	
U test	LU4			
Pearson's chi-square			RP4	VC4
		k-sample univariate tests		
Pearson's chi-square	LU5			VC5
H test			RP5	
ANOVA		CW5		

illustrates how the selection of null hypotheses detailed for the four projects relates to the different statistical tests under consideration. The alternative hypotheses, counterparts to the stated null hypotheses, have not been provided, since they are necessarily accepted when the former are rejected. Such decisions may, of course, be made in error, but the chosen level of significance gives a guide as to likelihood of making such a mistake. Additional questions and null hypotheses will be presented in respect of the bivariate and spatial statistical techniques which can be applied to the projects.

Chapter 9
An overview of probability distributions

9.1 CONCEPTUALISING PROBABILITY

The previous chapter has indicated that probability plays an important part in inferential statistics. In regular speech we use the concept of 'probability', or perhaps more often its associated parts of speech, 'probable' and 'probably', to indicate uncertainty over the likelihood of some occurrence or event. The sentences, 'I'll probably be at the theatre before 7.30 p.m.', 'He'll probably get over 50 per cent in his human geography examination' or 'It's quite probable that he took last Friday off work' demonstrate common usage of the concept and how probabilistic statements can be made about both future and past events. In the case of future events the uncertainty arises from not knowing whether the event will actually take place. With retrospective events, it results from a lack of knowledge about why something occurred.

In statistics the term *probability* is used in a slightly more refined, rigorous fashion in order to quantify whether the results obtained in a particular investigation are genuine or have been affected by sampling error. There are two underlying questions: 'What is the probability that the difference between a sample and its parent population has arisen by chance?' and 'What is the probability that a difference between two or more samples has occurred by chance?'. The numerical value representing the probability of an event or a difference is usually expressed either as a percentage or as a proportion. For example, if there are two possible outcomes (A and B) to an unbiased experiment, then theoretically each outcome has a 50 per cent or 0.5 probability of actually occurring. Probability is usually represented by the letter p, thus if $p = 0.2$, there is a 20 per cent chance of the event occurring. This example indicates the close relationship between percentages and proportions, which was discussed with respect to relative frequency distributions. Another way of referring to the probability of an event is as so many times in 100, in 1000, in 10 000, etc. So if the experiment referred to above was repeated 1000 times under identical conditions, then it is probable that *A* will be the outcome on 500 occasions and *B* on the other 500.

Before looking at three of the key probability distributions used in statistics, it is useful to examine the broad concept of an *event*. Statistically, the term refers to three types of situation:

- dichotomous outcomes, whether or not something has already taken place or will happen;
- discrete outcomes, the number of times that something has already taken place or will happen;
- continuous outcomes, the value possessed by something which has already been or will be measured.

These situations are connected with the measurement scales used for attributes and variables. Dichotomous and discrete outcomes relate to the nominal and ordinal scales. A dichotomous attribute is one in which only two outcomes are possible, for instance 'Yes' or 'No' in reply to a question, an increase or decrease in temperature, and the presence or absence of a species of plant in an area. A discrete event is one which can have more than two possible outcomes, but only integer values are permitted for the number of times a particular outcome occurs within a given set of observations. These integers may be ranked, for instance, the number of public houses in a collection of villages may be $0, 1, 2, 3, 4, \ldots, n$, but in any individual village a count of 2.65, 1.72 or any other fractional quantity of public houses is impossible. The mean number of public houses per village and their standard deviation may of course be fractional amounts. A continuous event is one measured on the ratio or interval scale, and therefore is not constrained to integer values. There are numerous examples of such variables, including the area of derelict land, the depth of the A soil horizon, the length of railway lines in a county and the altitude of the tree-line in mountainous regions.

Statements of probability, as far as statistical analysis is concerned, can be derived in two main ways: either from consideration of all possible outcomes; or on the basis of the known relative frequency of outcomes for similar past events. The former are known as *theoretical* or *a priori* probabilities, and the latter as *empirical* or *a posteriori* probabilities. The distinction is a useful one, although it should be noted that not all statisticians and logicians are agreed on its validity. For a fuller discussion of the issues involved the reader is referred to texts on the philosophy of science (e.g. Ayer 1964). The probability distributions, which underpin the various statistical tests, are constructed from mathematical formulae and indicate the relative frequency of dichotomous or discrete counts, or the values of continuous variables if they were to occur at random. Statistical tests compare the empirical or sample outcome, with its measures of central tendency and dispersion, with that derived from a probability distribution. The purpose is to determine whether any difference between them is statistically significant or has merely arisen through chance or sampling error. Unfortunately, the derivation of the probability distributions can cause a certain amount of confusion when they are first encountered. The following sections introduce three probability distributions which relate to the three situations or outcomes just described. The three theoretical distributions, the *binomial*, the *Poisson* and the *normal*, are fundamental to the tests of significance used in geography and other scientific disciplines.

9.2 THE BINOMIAL DISTRIBUTION

The binomial distribution, developed by James Bernoulli in the seventeenth century, relates to events in which there are only two possible outcomes (i.e. the dichotomous situation). However, in order to understand how the distribution works, it is important to appreciate that the event itself may occur more than once and therefore different numerical combinations of the two outcomes may ensue. The nature of the distribution is typically explained with reference to events or trials involving the tossing of a coin, where the outcome is either the head or tail uppermost. In each individual trial, it would be generally accepted that the probability of a head is 1 in 2, assuming the coin to be unbiased, in other words the probability associated with each outcome is 0.5. It is important to appreciate that, although the binomial distribution deals with individual dichotomous events, their collective outcomes do not have to have equal probabilities. The advantage of looking at coin-tossing events is that it focuses the discussion on an everyday two-outcome problem. The disadvantage is that it is unconnected to academic investigation in geography or other disciplines.

Suppose instead that the two outcomes relate to the occurrence or non-occurrence of rain on the spring and summer public holidays in England and Wales. There is, after all, a popular belief that every public holiday is blighted with rain, but perhaps it is really just a random event. In theory rain may or may not occur on each of the five public holidays (Good Friday, Easter Monday, May Day, Spring and Late Summer), which fall during the spring and summer months. Other things being equal and assuming that the occurrence of rain on one holiday is independent of the outcome on any of the other four, the probability of the occurrence of rain is 0.5 and of its non-occurrence is also 0.5, which sum to 1.0. The combination of outcomes for each year will range from the non-occurrence of rain on all five public holidays at one extreme, to its occurrence on all five days at the other. Thus in any one year, the variable X, number of public holidays in the summer with rain, can only score one of six possible values (0, 1, 2, 3, 4 or 5).

The binomial distribution can be used to define the probability or likelihood of each outcome occurring. Unlike some mathematically defined distributions, the form and shape of the binomial varies according to the length of trials in a sequence and the probability of an occurrence. In general terms, the probability of X occurrences (the number of public holidays with rain) in a sequence N trials (the number of public holidays in the summer months) is given by the term $p(X)$, which is defined by the binomial distribution as

$$p(X) = \frac{N!}{X!(N-X)!} p^X q^{N-X}$$

where p is the probability of occurrence (here 0.5 for rain) and $q(= 1 - p)$ the probability of non-occurrence. The expression

$$\frac{N!}{X!(N-X)!}$$

uses factorials to calculate the number of times that a particular combination of occurrences will result when the number of trials is known. In this example, suppose we wish to obtain the number of combinations that will result in 2 of the 5 public holidays in the summer having rain, $p(2)$ where $N = 5$; then:

$$\frac{N!}{X!(N-X)!} = \frac{5 \times 4 \times 3 \times 2 \times 1}{(2 \times 1)(3 \times 2 \times 1)} = \frac{120}{12} = 10$$

Table 9.1 Probabilities derived from binomial distribution, equal probability of outcomes ($p = 0.5$, $N = 5$)

X	$\frac{N!}{X!(N-X)!}$	p^X	$(1-p)^{(N-X)}$	$p(X)$
0	1	1.0	0.0313	0.0313
1	5	0.5	0.0625	0.1563
2	10	0.25	0.125	0.3135
3	10	0.125	0.25	0.3125
4	5	0.0625	0.5	0.1563
5	1	0.0313	1.0	0.0313

Note: 0! and anything raised to the power 0 are both 1.

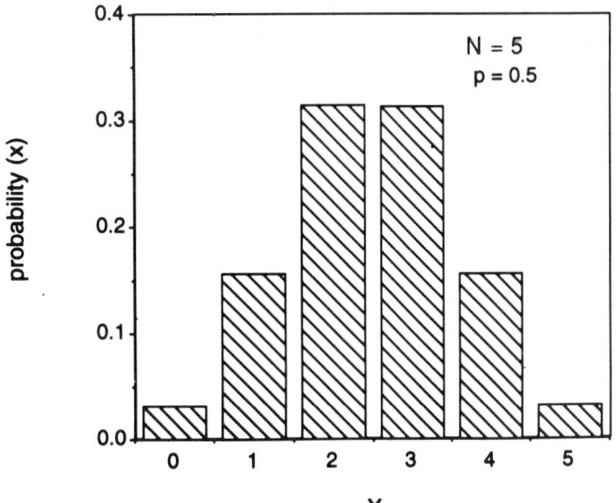

Figure 9.1 Symmetrical binomial probability distribution

There are 10 different ways in which rain could occur on two days. Substituting this information into the binomial equation thus:

$$p(2) = 10(0.5)^2(1 - 0.5)^{(5-2)}$$
$$= 10(0.25)(0.125)$$
$$= 0.3125$$

demonstrates that in each year the probability of rain occurring on two out of the five spring and summer public holidays is 0.3125. In order to complete the picture, the probabilities for all six combinations of outcomes are given in Table 9.1 and shown graphically in Figure 9.1.

Figure 9.1 illustrates that when the probabilities of occurrence/non-occurrence, success/failure, and presence/absence are identical (as in this example), the distribution of binomial probabilities is symmetrical (see final column of Table 9.1). The distribution becomes skewed when there is any difference in the probability of the two outcomes. Suppose that the probability of the occurrence of rain on public holidays is obtained from empirical observation, which may differ from theory which says that the two outcomes are equally probable. Meteorological

Table 9.2 Probabilities derived from binomial distribution, unequal probability of outcomes ($p = 0.28$, $N = 5$)

X	$\frac{N!}{X!(N-X)!}$	p^X	$(1-p)^{(N-X)}$	$p(X)$
0	1	1.0	0.1935	0.1935
1	5	0.28	0.2687	0.3762
2	10	0.0784	0.3732	0.2926
3	10	0.0220	0.5184	0.1138
4	5	0.0061	0.72	0.0221
5	1	0.0017	1.0	0.0017

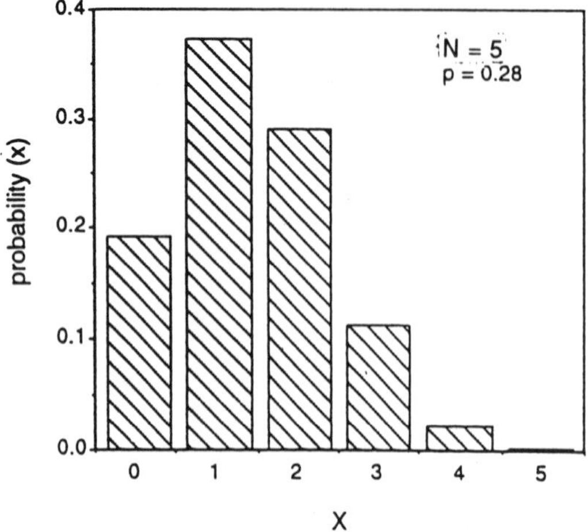

Figure 9.2 Skewed binomial probability distribution

records show that rain fell on 14 of the 50 spring and summer public holidays over the last 10 years. Thus the empirical probability of rain on a public holiday is 0.28 (14/50) and of no rain, 0.72 (36/50). Using these probability assessments, the binomial distribution of the possible outcomes becomes skewed (Table 9.2 and Figure 9.2). The effect of a lower probability for the occurrence of the event in comparison to its

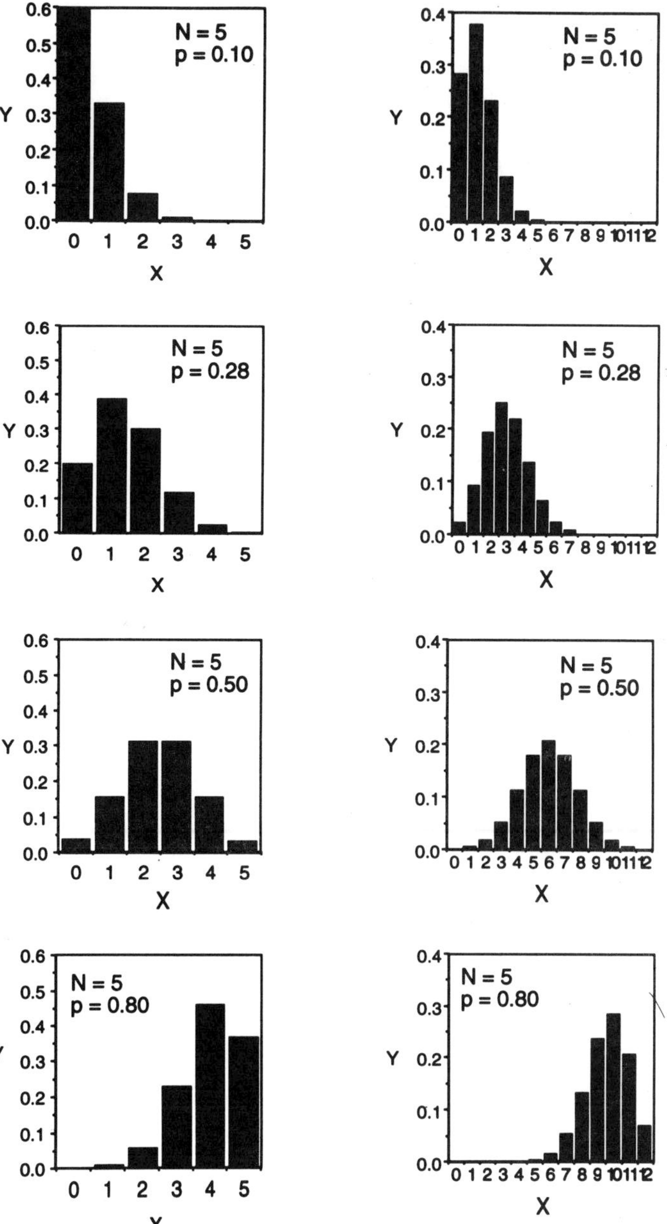

Figure 9.3 Effect of variation in probability (p) on binomial distribution

non-occurrence skews the distribution to the right. In this example the probability of four, let alone five, wet public holidays in a single year is fairly remote, in the latter case less than one year (0.17 years) in 100. The reverse effect, with a skewed distribution to the left, would be produced if the probability of the non-occurrence outcome was low compared to that of occurrence.

The shape of the distribution is also affected by length of the series of trials. For example, the previous example could be adapted to relate to the occurrence and non-occurrence of rain on the 12 days of the Wimbledon lawn tennis championship. Assuming that the probability of the two outcomes is equal ($p = 0.5$ and $q = 0.5$), there are 924 different combinations of 12 days which include 6 days with rain and according to the binomial distribution the probability of this happening is 0.2256. Figure 9.3 compares pairs binomial distributions for these two examples with various probabilities for each outcome.

Finally, the mean, variance, standard deviation and skewness of the binomial distribution can also be calculated. The mean, defined as the average number of occurrences in repeated trials of length N, is derived from

$$\mu = Np$$

which can sometimes produce a fractional figure. For example, if the empirical probability of rain on a spring or summer public holiday, based on the meteorological records, is 0.28, then the mean number of rainy days per year is $5 \times 0.28 = 1.40$. The equations for the variance, standard deviation and skewness, respectively, are:

$$\sigma^2 = Np(1 - p)$$

$$\sigma = \sqrt{Np(1 - p)}$$

$$\beta_1 = \frac{p - (1 - p)}{Np(1 - p)}$$

The variance and standard deviation are interpreted as usual. The skewness statistic, which is zero when the probabilities of the two outcomes are equal, increases as p deviates from 0.5.

9.3 THE POISSON DISTRIBUTION

The Poisson distribution is used in respect of events which have a discrete number of outcomes (i.e. they are counted as integers) and the probability of occurrence reduces as the integer count of the event increases. The outcome of the event may be dichotomous, although this is not a requirement. The Poisson distribution is particularly useful when the number of times a phenomenon occurs within a given unit of space or time is under investigation, for example the number of road junctions per kilometre grid square or the number of days in a year when the temperature rises above a specified level. In both cases the counts can be regarded as ordinal variables.

One of the most important differences between the binomial and Poisson distributions is that with the former there has to be a finite upper limit to the number of occasions on which the event can occur. The number of public holidays with rain in any one year has an upper limit of 5 (the number of spring/summer public holidays). Suppose the example was adapted to determine whether the number of days with rain in any one year was distributed at random. The binomial distribution could still be used, but the upper limit of 365 days would lead to somewhat onerous calculations. The example could also be altered in order to investigate whether the number of days with rain between Good Friday and the Late Summer Holiday was distributed at random. The binomial distribution could not be employed in this instance, since annual variations in the dates of these public holidays mean that the number of days (trials) in this period each year would be variable. The Poisson distribution constitutes a suitable alternative.

The mathematical formula for the Poisson distribution consists of a series of terms which calculate the probability corresponding to the number of occurrences (i.e. the first term provides the probability of 0 occurrences, the second 1 occurrence, the third 2, and so on). In theory the number of terms is limitless. However, it is usually only necessary to calculate the first few, since the probabilities become very small. The first four terms in the series, relating to 0, 1, 2, and 3 occurrences of an event, and the general term for X occurrences, are:

$$\mathrm{e}^{-\lambda}, \lambda\mathrm{e}^{-\lambda}, \frac{\lambda^2}{2!}\mathrm{e}^{-\lambda}, \frac{\lambda^3}{3!}\mathrm{e}^{-\lambda}, \ldots, \frac{\lambda^X}{X!}\mathrm{e}^{-\lambda}$$

There are certain common elements in each term: the symbol e denoting the base of natural logarithms (a constant which equals 2.71828...); the denominators are the factorials of the number of occurrences; and λ, the Greek letter 'lambda', which can be any positive number. Note that

$$\mathrm{e}^{-\lambda} = \frac{1}{\mathrm{e}^{\lambda}}$$

The value of λ varies from one application of the Poisson distribution to another, yet a common feature is that the calculated probabilities become progressively smaller as the number of occurrences increases. Table 9.3 and Figure 9.4 illustrate this point for λ equal to 0.5, 2.0, 5.0 and 10.0. Low values of λ produce a skewed the distribution, while higher values lead to a more symmetrical shape. The value of λ is therefore crucial in determining the calculated probabilities. The problem is to decide on a value for λ. Fortunately, one of its most important properties gives a clue. λ is numerically equal to both the mean and variance of the Poisson distribution and therefore the most convenient starting point for applying the distribution to a particular set of data is to equate λ with the mean number of actual or empirical occurrences.

Table 9.3 Effect of altering λ on Poisson distribution probabilities $p(X)$

X	$\lambda = 0.5$	$\lambda = 2.0$
0	0.606 531	0.135 335
1	0.303 265	0.270 671
2	0.075 816	0.270 671
3	0.012 636	0.180 447
4	0.001 580	0.090 224
5	0.000 158	0.036 089
6	0.000 013	0.012 030
7	0.000 001	0.003 437
8	0.000 000	0.000 859
9	0.000 000	0.000 191
10	0.000 000	0.000 038
11	0.000 000	0.000 000
12	0.000 000	0.000 000
	$\lambda = 5.0$	$\lambda = 10.0$
	0.006 738	0.000 045
	0.033 690	0.000 454
	0.084 224	0.002 270
	0.140 374	0.007 567
	0.175 467	0.018 917
	0.175 467	0.037 833
	0.146 223	0.063 055
	0.104 445	0.090 079
	0.065 278	0.112 599
	0.036 266	0.125 110
	0.018 133	0.125 110
	0.008 242	0.113 736
	0.003 434	0.094 780

The reason for applying the Poisson distribution to a set of data is essentially the same as for the binomial, namely to determine whether the observed frequency distribution of events is likely to be random. Table 9.4 shows the frequency distribution for the number of junctions involving motorways, A or B class roads per grid square in a 176 km^2 area of rural Hertfordshire. A junction is defined as where two or more roads intersect. The frequency distribution of the 111 junctions is skewed, with substantial numbers of squares with 0 or 1 junction and relatively few with 4 or 5 (see column headed 'No. of squares'). However, is the distribution of junctions random? The value of λ is taken as the mean number of junctions per grid square, $111/176 = 0.6307$, which means that $1/e^{\lambda}$ equals 1.8789. The column headed 'Poisson probabilities' in Table 9.4 gives the appropriate terms of the Poisson distribution and the calculated probabilities. For example, the probability of 3 road junctions in a square is 0.0223. The sum of the probabilities is fractionally less than 1.0 (0.0001), and this shortfall represents the probability of 6 or more junctions in a square. Multiplying each probability by the total number of squares produces the

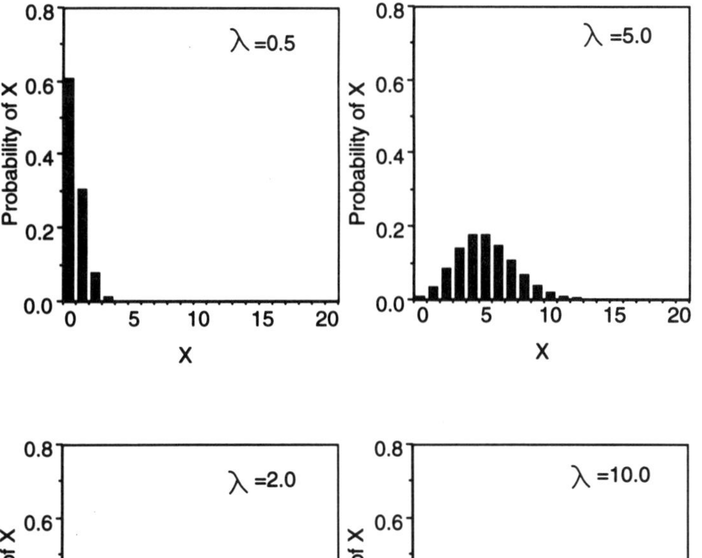

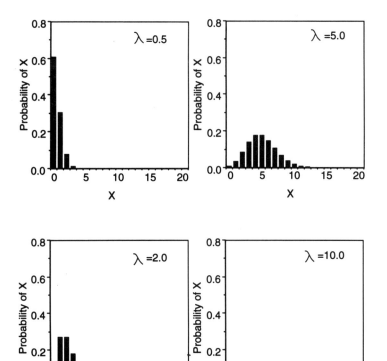

Figure 9.4 The shape of the Poisson probability distribution for different λ

Table 9.4 Poisson probabilities for the density of road junctions in rural Hertfordshire

No. of junctions per km^2	No. of squares	Poisson probabilities	Expected distribution
0	105	0.5322	93.7
1	46	0.3357	59.1
2	13	0.1058	18.6
3	10	0.0223	3.9
4	1	0.0035	0.6
5	1	0.0004	0.1
	176	0.9999	176

random frequency distribution of junctions per square as determined by the Poisson distribution, shown in the final column. There appears to be a reasonably close fit between the observed and random distributions, which suggests that the density of road junctions is largely a matter of chance. A different value of λ might have produced an even closer correspondence, but that the differences are sufficiently minor to make further experimentation unnecessary.

The numerical equality of mean and variance for the Poisson distribution and their identity with λ has already been noted. The other main descriptive measures, the standard deviation and skewness, can also be derived from the observed density of occurrences. Their respective formulae are:

$$\sigma = \sqrt{\lambda}$$

$$\beta_1 = \frac{1}{\sqrt{\lambda}}$$

These statistical measures can be interpreted in the usual fashion.

Finally, two drawbacks of the Poisson distribution should be mentioned. The element λ is of critical importance in determining the Poisson probabilities, yet its value is assumed to remain constant over time and space. Suppose, in the previous example, that the mean density of junctions was higher for one section of the map, perhaps 3.564 per grid square for a 45 km^2 area in which there were some small towns with a more complex road network. In the remaining 131 km^2 of the study area, the density was lower than the overall mean (say 0.433). It would be possible to weight the overall mean density according to these figures, thus:

$$\text{Overall mean} = [(45 \times 3.564) + (131 \times 0.433)]/176$$
$$= 1.2335$$

This might appear to offer a better alternative to the original λ, but the problem emerges of how to identify 'regions' of squares where the density of junctions appears to be uniform, which to some extent invalidates the whole exercise. The second problem with applications of the Poisson distribution is that the frequency distribution can easily be altered by varying the units of space or time for which the occurrences are recorded. The frequency distribution for the revised spatial or temporal units might still have a similarly skewed form, but the mean density of junctions (λ) may alter substantially. Suppose that the size of the grid squares in the road junctions case was increased to 4 km^2, thus reducing the total spatial units to 44, the mean density would rise to 2.5227 and, as an example, the probability of 2 junctions in 4 km^2 would be 0.2553, rather than 0.1058 in 1 km^2.

9.4 THE NORMAL DISTRIBUTION

The normal distribution relates to situations in which continuous rather than discrete outcomes are recorded for the observations under investigation: it is used when the phenomena are measured on the interval or ratio scales rather than counted. The normal distribution was first identified by the German mathematician, Karl Friedrich Gauss. The essence of the distribution is the tendency for observations to possess values which lie close to the mean rather than towards the extremes or tails of the range of values for many measured variables. The normal distribution in its ideal mathematical form is symmetrical with a convex peak created by the clustering of observations around the mean and concave tails drawn out by proportionately fewer items towards the extremes. Figure 9.5 illustrates this normal curve, which is sometimes referred to as 'bell-shaped'. The points of inflection on the curve, where it changes from convex to concave, occur at one standard deviation either side of the mean. Expressed in symbols, these points are denoted as lying at $\mu - \sigma$ and $\mu + \sigma$.

The mathematical formula from which the normal curve can be constructed is unfortunately rather daunting for the statistically faint-hearted:

$$Y = \frac{1}{\sigma\sqrt{2\pi}} e^{-1/2\left(\frac{X-\mu}{\sigma}\right)}$$

Although appearing complicated, the principle of the formula is essentially the same as with most equations, namely to calculate an unknown quantity from one or more known values. The unknown quantity in this case is the height or *ordinate* of the normal curve, Y, for different known values of X, the measured variable. The calculation of sufficient Y values enables the normal curve for a given variable to be plotted. The Y values themselves represent the frequency or number of occurrences of measurement of X. The conventional presentation of equations dictates that the known elements appear to the right of the equal sign. These terms appear somewhat confusing at first; however, by breaking them down into three groups it is possible to see that most are reasonably familiar. The first group comprises the constants π (3.141 59...) and e (2.7128...). The second group includes the mean

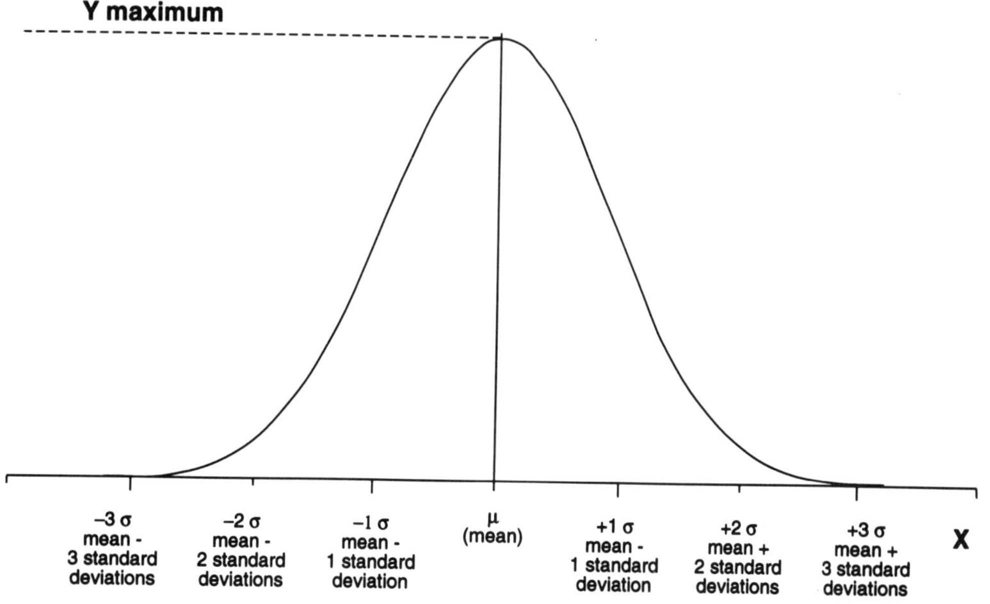

Figure 9.5 Shape of normal probability distribution

and standard deviation (μ and σ), which are calculated from the raw data for the sample or population. The third group consists of the term X, which denotes the value of the measured variable, for which the corresponding Y value is to be calculated. In theory there are an infinite number of points or values along the X axis for which Y values could be calculated. Fortunately, it is not usually necessary to carry out the calculations associated with the normal curve in order to make use of the important characteristics of the normal distribution, although it is instructive to examine how the curve is generated.

The mean and standard deviation, which have previously simply been referred to as descriptive statistics, are of crucial importance in determining the position and spread of the normal curve. Suppose that several samples of observations from a single population are measured in respect of the same variable and coincidentally the standard deviation is identical in each case, but variations are revealed in the magnitude of the sample means. The effect of this variation is to shift the normal curve along the horizontal axis (see Figure 9.6(a)), while its shape is retained. On the other hand, if the mean turns out to be constant and the standard deviation differs, the effect is either to raise or lower the peak of the normal curve in relation to vertical axis (see Figure 9.6(b)), while still maintaining the symmetrical shape. Variations in the standard deviation influence the location of the points of inflection, with a relatively large standard deviation pushing them away from the mean and thus flattening the distribution, and a smaller standard deviation having the reverse effect of producing a sharper peak.

Variations in the form of the normal curve therefore arise from inherent differences between sets of data. This problem would make it difficult to compare between samples measured in respect of the same variable were it not for the process of standardisation which can be applied to the raw data values. The difference between any X value and the mean can be expressed as Z, a *proportion of the standard deviation*, thus:

$$Z = \frac{X - \mu}{\sigma}$$

The process converts the original units of measurement into Z values or scores. An X value greater than the mean produces a positive Z, while a smaller one leads to a negative Z. These Z values are units of the standard deviation. For example, a raw data value of 234.4 for an observation in a collection where the mean is 115.2 and the standard deviation is 60.4 leads to a Z value of +1.97:

$$Z = \frac{234.5 - 115.2}{60.4} = +1.97$$

The Z value of +1.97 indicates that X is 1.97 standard deviations greater than the mean.

Furthermore, provided that the original data appear to be distributed in an approximately normal fashion, which can be estimated by examining their frequency distribution, the previous formula for the normal

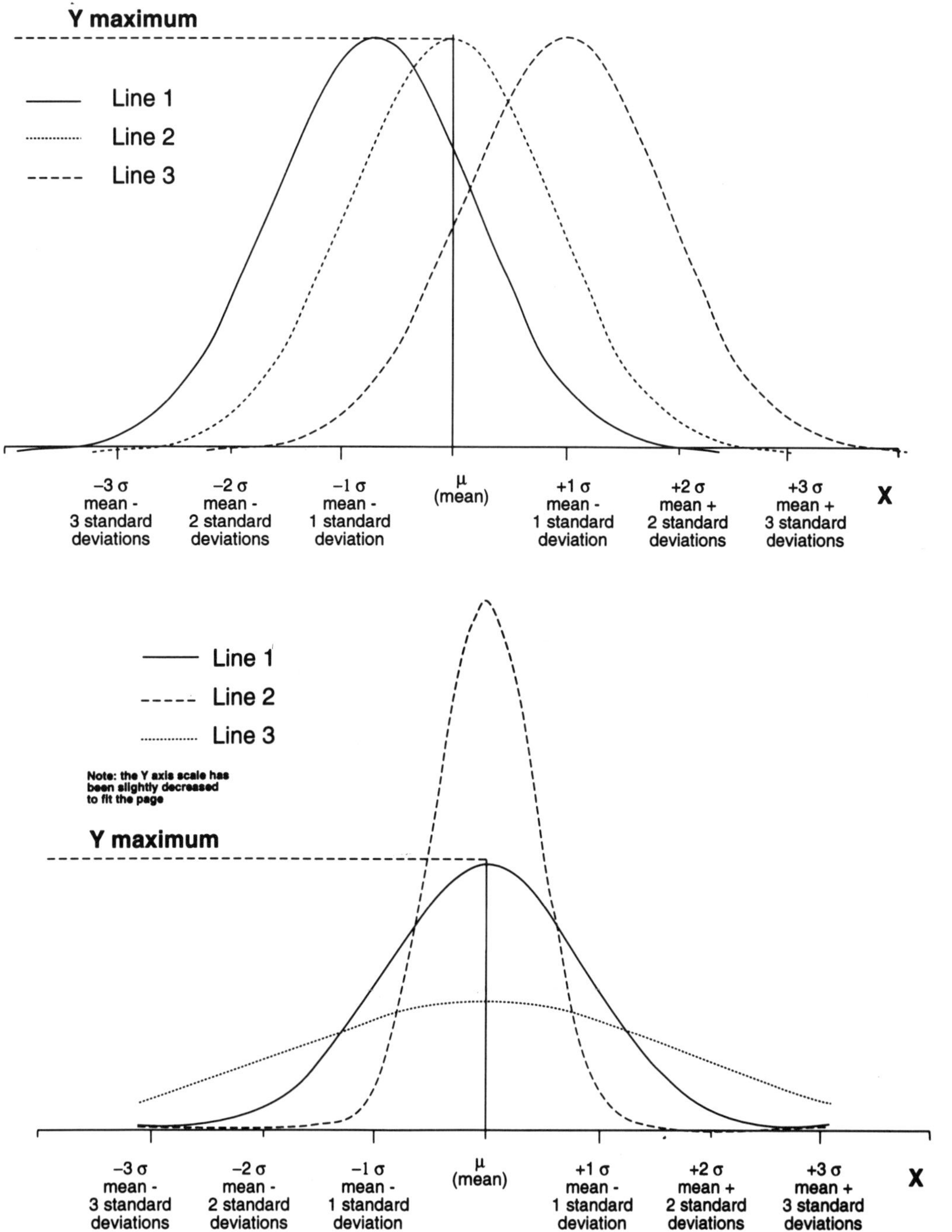

Figure 9.6 Effect of variation in (a) mean and (b) variance on the normal curve

curve can be simplified. It is possible to substitute Z in place of a term on the right-hand side of the original formula, thus:

$$Y = \frac{1}{\sqrt{2\pi}} e^{-(Z/2)^2}$$

because this term is in fact the equation for calculating Z. A consequence of this change is that all other terms in the formula involving the standard deviation equal 1.0. The use of the standardised formula for the normal curve requires that the relatively simple task of converting the raw data into Z values is carried out before the formula is applied and the standardised normal curve is plotted.

The normal curve reaches a peak above the mean and its tails approach, but never reach, the horizontal axis. Nevertheless, the area under the curve can be regarded as finite with a nominal value of 1.0, since in probability terms it contains the frequency of all possible events or values of X. Since the shape of the normal curve is symmetrical, a vertical line drawn between the mean value of X on the horizontal axis and the peak of the curve bisects the distribution. Probability statements made in relation to the normal curve refer to ranges of values on the X axis. As a simple illustration, the probability that any randomly selected value of X will lie between the mean and plus infinity is 0.5 or 50 per cent. In this particular example, it also is equally probable that any X value will fall between the mean and minus infinity.

The probabilities associated with the normal curve form the basis of decisions about whether to accept or reject the null hypothesis in several statistical tests. It is therefore important to understand how these probability statements can be made in respect of the normal curve. The software used to carry out statistical tests will usually report the probability associated with a particular test statistic. However, in order to interpret this information correctly, it is useful to consider how the task can be achieved by hand. The simplest approach is to consult tables which give the probability or proportion of the area under the standardised normal curve between any two Z values. Such tables can be prepared in different ways, and one of the more common is included as Table 1 in Appendix IV.

The probability statements associated with the normal curve can be phrased in two complementary ways:

1. What proportion or percentage of X events or values can be expected to occur between two Z scores?
2. What is the probability that any X event or value will fall between two Z scores?

These two types of question are depicted graphically in Figure 9.7. The asymmetrical shaded zone around the centre of the curve is bounded by the Z values of -0.45 and $+1.75$. What percentage of observations measured in respect of X lie within this region? What is the probability that a particular X value will lie within this area? Before trying to answer these questions accurately from the Z distribution table, it is worth analysing the general procedure. The proportion of the total area accounted for by the shaded zone can be identified and this can be equated with the percentage of all X values between $Z = -0.45$ and $Z = +1.75$, since the area under the curve equals 100 per cent of X values. For the sake of argument, imagine that the proportion turns out to be 0.3562 of the total area under the normal curve. Two implications now follow:

1. 35.62 per cent of X events or values occur between the two Z scores.
2. There is a 0.3562 probability of any X event or value falling between the two Z scores.

The percentage of X values falling outside the shaded zone is $100.00 - 35.62 (= 64.38)$, and the probability of an X value not occurring between the two Z scores is $1.0000 - 0.3562 (= 0.6438)$.

How can we determine the true answers to questions of the type posed above? The answer is by reference to the probabilities associated with the different Z values given in Appendix IV, Table 1. The figures in the body of the Z table are proportions representing the combined area of the normal curve found in its two tails, where the total area under the curve has the nominal value of 1.0. The Z distribution table gives the value of Z of 2 decimal places (2 digits to the right of the decimal point). Using the left-hand column in the table to find the first decimal place and the top row to identify the second, the proportion in the two tails is found at the intersection of the corresponding row and column. Thus, where $Z = 1.00$, the proportion of the area in the two tails is 0.3173, i.e. 0.1587 in each (0.3173/2). In the example illustrated in Figure 9.7, the two halves of the area under the normal curve should be regarded as having a nominal value of 0.5 (i.e. 1.0/2) and the shaded area as composed of two unequal parts. These parts lie either side of the central line where $Z = 0.00$ (the mean of the distribution). The

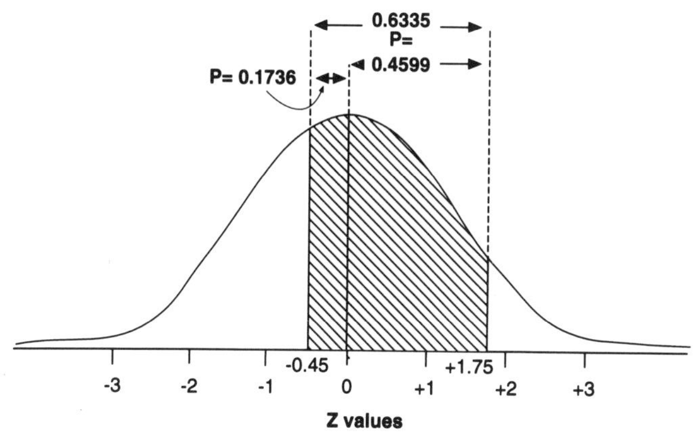

Figure 9.7 Probabilities and Z values associated with the normal curve

proportions of the curve lying in the left-hand part, between $Z = 0.00$ and $Z = -0.45$, and on the right, between $Z = 0.00$ and $Z = +1.75$, are given by the following equations:

$$\text{Left-hand side} \quad P = 0.5 - (0.6527/2) = 0.1736$$
$$\text{Right-hand side} \quad P = 0.5 - (0.0801/2) = 0.4599$$

where the probabilities (proportions) 0.6527 and 0.0801 have been obtained from Appendix IV, Table 1 with $Z = 0.45$ and 1.75. The shaded area therefore equals 0.6335 (0.1736 + 0.4599). It is now possible to conclude that 63.35 per cent of X events will occur between the two Z scores and that there is a 0.6335 probability of any X event or value falling between the two Z scores.

Using these general principles, the determination of probabilities for testing hypotheses is straightforward. The previous chapter referred to the fact that the decision on rejection or acceptance of the null hypothesis depends largely upon whether the calculated test statistic can reasonably be expected to have arisen through chance. The probability at which this decision is made is known as the level of significance, which is typically taken as either 0.05 or 0.01. Remember also that these levels of significance can easily be converted in to percentages (5 and 1 per cent, respectively). The tabulated value of the test statistic at the chosen significance level is called the *critical value*. The key question now is:

> What are the negative and positive Z scores which will define a zone outside of which 5 per cent (or 1 per cent) of X values may be expected to fall?

This question is effectively the opposite of those just considered and may be answered by using the Z table in reverse. The procedure is demonstrated with reference 0.05 level of significance. The proportion $0.95(1.00 - 0.05)$ represents a relative area under the normal curve, but because the curve is symmetrical about the mean where $Z = 0.00$, this proportion may be assigned equally between the halves, $0.95/2 = 0.475$. The Z table may be scanned to search for the value 0.475 in order to read off the corresponding Z score, which is 1.96. Thus the two Z scores of -1.96 and $+1.96$ define the tails of the distribution within which 5 per cent of the X values will occur (2.5 per cent in each tail). Or conversely, 95 per cent will fall within a central zone between these limits. The equivalent Z values for 0.99 probability are -2.576 and $+2.576$. The zones of the normal curve beyond these critical Z values, ± 1.96 and ± 2.576, are shaded in Figure 9.8. In this figure the extreme values of X are apportioned equally between the two tails of the distribution. It should be noted in passing, however, that the probability of extreme events may be allocated exclusively to one or other end of the distribution in some circumstances.

On the assumption that the variable under investigation corresponds approximately to the normal distribution, the Z scores relating to the level of significance may be converted into raw data values. If the mean

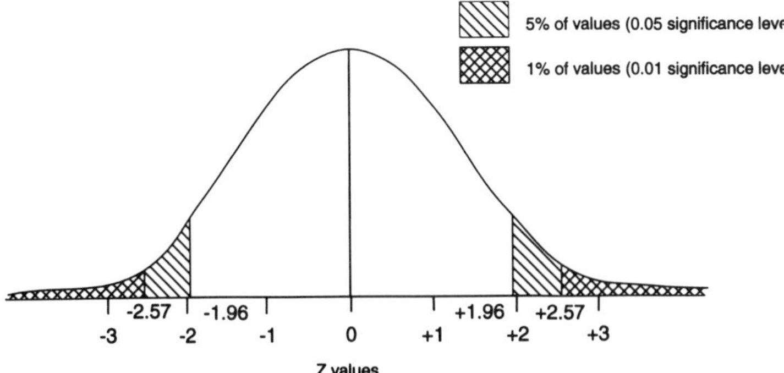

Figure 9.8 Areas of the normal curve associated with the 0.05 and 0.01 levels of significance

and standard deviation of the variable are 115.2 and 60.4, respectively, then the raw data value associated with -1.96 is calculated as:

$$-1.96 = \frac{X - 115.2}{60.4}$$
$$-118.384 = X - 115.2$$
$$X = -3.184$$

and

$$+1.96 = \frac{X - 115.2}{60.4}$$
$$118.384 = X - 115.2$$
$$X = 233.584$$

Ninety-five per cent of X values should therefore lie between 3.184 and 233.584. The size of the standard deviation is crucial in these calculations; if it was smaller the limits would be brought closer together, and if larger they would be further apart.

There are several real-world variables which might display the general characteristics of the normal distribution, clustering of values around the mean and tending towards a symmetrical shape. Geographical examples include various hydrological phenomena, population totals for certain types of administrative area, and several meteorological variables. However, one problem with the normal distribution is what to do with manifestly non-normal data, most notably variables which are severely skewed. The problem could perhaps be ignored, if many statistical tests did not assume that the variable under investigation was normally distributed, although some statisticians now attach less importance to this prerequisite.

The most common solution to this problem is to transform the raw data. Normality can be imposed on a number of positively skewed variables, those where the majority of observations occur at the lower end of the range, by taking the logarithms of the raw data. Raw data which conform to the normal distribution once transformed in this way are known as *log-normal*. The transformation cannot be applied, however, if the data contain zeros or negative values, for which there are no logarithmic equivalents. Negatively skewed variables, where most of the observations are found towards the upper end of the range, are not very common, but can sometimes be transformed by squaring the raw data values. The difficulty with transforming or *normalising* the raw data in these ways is that it can become difficult to make sense of the results in geographical terms. Thus it is may be more sensible to select an alternative, perhaps less powerful, statistical technique, which does not require the data to be normally distributed.

9.5 CONNECTION BETWEEN THE BINOMIAL, POISSON AND NORMAL PROBABILITY DISTRIBUTIONS

Despite the fact that the binomial and Poisson distributions deal with discrete data and the normal distribution with continuous variables, there are some situations in which their form and shape become similar. Close agreement is achieved in the probabilities produced by the binomial and the Poisson distributions, when the probability of the event occurring in the former is low (e.g. $p = 0.01$) and the upper finite limit on the number of occurrences is equal to λ. In the extreme case where an infinite number of occurrences are possible and the probability of an occurrence is very small, $\lambda = Np$, and the binomial and Poisson distributions are equal. There is also a relationship between the Poisson and the normal distribution. Figure 9.4 demonstrated that the Poisson distribution becomes more symmetrical as λ increases. In theory, when λ is infinitely large, the distribution is exactly normal.

The binomial and normal distributions also become similar when neither p nor q is close to zero, for instance when the probabilities of the two outcomes are approximately equal, and the number of trials, N, is very large. Suppose that the number of spring and summer public holidays was increased to 10 each year. Remembering that rain and no-rain are the two equally probable outcomes (0.5), then over a long sequence of years the most frequent occurrence will be for 5 days with rain, 4 or 6 days with rain will be slightly less frequent, 3 or 7 less common again and so on. When sufficient years are taken into account, the frequency polygon formed by joining the tops of the columns in the histogram will approximate to the normal curve. The longer the sequence of observations and the greater the number of trials, the closer it is that the frequency polygon resembles the normal curve, despite being based on discrete counts.

The next few chapters examine some of the statistical tests which use these mathematically defined probability distributions. The binomial, Poisson and normal distributions describe the scatter of random outcomes of sets of independent observations. Inferential statistics attempts to determine whether real-world variables, as opposed to the random ones depicted in probability distributions, differ significantly from these ideal types or not. If the difference is significant, then the researcher can start to develop explanations for why this might be the case. If it is not, then the distribution of the real observations can be ascribed to a random process.

Chapter 10
Inferential statistics: univariate, single-sample tests

10.1 CHARACTERISTICS OF SINGLE-SAMPLE TESTS

The definitive characteristics of univariate, single-sample tests are that one variable or attribute is under examination, and that the differences under scrutiny are between either the descriptive statistics (mean, variance and standard deviation) or frequency distribution obtained from a sample, and the corresponding quantities or distribution for an actual or hypothesised population. In most situations the individual items forming the single-sample are only measured once in respect of a particular attribute or variable; however, this is not always the case. In some investigations the observations are either measured twice for the same variable, or can be divided into two parts with separate measurements being made for each. An example of the former would be a random sample of individuals offered a free ticket for an event one evening who were asked to choose between a concert and a play. The same question was put to the sample the following evening with the assurance that, if they chose the same form of entertainment, the performance would be different. An example of an observation divided into two parts can be illustrated by a survey of married couples in which the husband and wife are separately asked their total gross annual income in order to examine the differences.

In many instances, a sample is used to estimate characteristics of the population from which it has been selected, and the mathematical procedures and probability statements associated with the tests are adapted in order to obtain confidence limits within which the value of the population parameter may be expected to fall. The known probabilities associated with the mathematically defined frequency distribution are used to determine the likelihood of the population mean lying within a range around the sample mean.

The distinguishing feature of parametric tests, whether applied to single or multiple samples, is that the populations from which samples are drawn should be approximately normally distributed (see Chapter 9). Non-parametric tests, in contrast, do not impose this requirement on the samples' parent populations, and are therefore sometimes referred to as 'distribution-free'. The division of statistical tests into parametric and non-parametric categories also reflects the scales of measurement applied to attributes and variables. Parametric tests are generally only applicable to data measured on the ratio or interval scales, whereas non-parametric tests apply to nominal- and ordinal-scale attributes.

The separation between parametric and non-parametric techniques, although not entirely free from contention and debate in the statistical literature, nevertheless forms a useful operational division for this and the following chapter. The underlying mathematical theory and the formulae used to specify the different tests can give rise to confusion, especially since the precise detail of the formulae may differ from one text to another. One response to these difficulties is to take the pragmatic course of applying a variety of tests to the available data and then selecting those results which seem 'to make some sense'. On balance, this course of action is not to be recommended and statistical tests should not be employed in such a slavish, mechanistic fashion. The following two sections explain the principles of univariate, single-sample tests divided between the parametric and non-parametric categories. The Z and t parametric tests and their confidence intervals are discussed in Section 10.2 and the Pearson's chi-square and Kolomogorov–Smirnov non-parametric tests are examined in Section 10.3. The paired t and Wilcoxon's signed ranks paired-sample tests are also considered in this chapter. Each test is introduced by an outline of its theoretical background, which is reinforced by a worked example and finally a discussion of its assumptions and limitations. Section 10.4 demonstrates the application of the tests to the projects using MINITAB and SPSS-X.

10.2 PARAMETRIC TESTS

10.2.1 The *Z* test

The calculation of Z values and the associated probabilities for a population in relation to the standardised normal curve was outlined in the previous chapter (Section 9.4). The percentage or proportion of observations falling between two Z values or, by simple conversion, between the two corresponding values of the original measurement units (e.g. hectares, mm, °C) can be determined. When dealing with a sample it is possible that sampling error may be present in the data, which could cause the sample mean to under- or overestimate the population mean. In other words, the data may contain a certain, but indeterminate, amount of distortion. So even if the sample displays the characteristics of the normal distribution, one cannot automatically assume that the population will do the same.

This problem can be overcome by means of a quantity known as the *standard error of the mean*. Any particular sample from a population, where the items have been selected with individual replacement, is just one from a potentially infinite number of samples that could have been selected. If more than one sample was taken, then their means for variable X, although different, may tend to cluster around some overall or 'super' mean value. Suppose samples 1 to k were taken from the population; then the mean of the means or the 'grand mean' ($\bar{\bar{x}}$) could be calculated and is specified in symbols as:

$$\bar{\bar{x}} = \frac{\bar{x}_1 + \bar{x}_2 + \bar{x}_3 \cdots \bar{x}_k}{k} = \sum \frac{\bar{x}}{k}$$

where k is the number of samples (not their size), and $\bar{x}$ denotes each individual sample mean. The more samples taken from a population, the more accurate the 'grand' mean becomes as an estimate of the population mean (μ), but nevertheless there is still a scatter or dispersion of sample means either side of this figure. This dispersion can be quantified as the standard deviation of the means when there is an infinite number of samples, otherwise known as the standard error of the mean, with the formula:

$$\sigma_{\bar{x}} = \frac{\sum(\bar{x} - \bar{\bar{x}})^2}{k - 1}$$

In practice, an infinite number of samples cannot be taken from a population; fortunately the standard error can easily be calculated when the population standard deviation (σ) and the sample size (n) are known:

$$\sigma_{\bar{x}} = \frac{\sigma}{\sqrt{n}}$$

When sampling without replacement is carried out, then strictly speaking a *finite population correction factor* should be added to this formula, thus:

$$\sigma_{\bar{x}} = \frac{\sigma}{\sqrt{n}} \left(\frac{N - n}{N - 1} \right)$$

unless it can be argued that the population is of infinite size.

If sufficient samples were taken then the individual means could be displayed as a distribution, which is called the *sampling distribution of the mean*. The histogram of this distribution will be normal if the parent population is also normally distributed, and it will be approximately normal even if the population is skewed. Furthermore, the larger the size of the samples the closer the sampling distribution of the mean comes to the normal distribution regardless of the shape of the parent population. These statements constitute the *central limit theorem*, which is of crucial importance in tests of significance.

The reason for using a simple random sample with a sufficiently large number of independently selected items should now be apparent. When these two conditions are satisfied the central limit theorem can be invoked and the known probabilities associated with the normal distribution can be employed. The collection of items constituting the sample in a specific project can be regarded as but one from a potentially infinite number of samples that could have been chosen. The question to be answered is whether any difference between the sample and population means is likely to have occurred through chance alone.

Section 9.4 showed how any value of a normally distributed variable (X) can be converted into a Z value, for which a probability can be ascertained from prepared tables. The Z test is used to find out the probability of having obtained the sample mean as opposed to the known population mean. The point is that, if the magnitude of the difference between the $\bar{x}$ and μ can be attributed to chance, then the researcher can confidently proceed with further analysis of the data, since there does not appear to be anything statistically idiosyncratic about the sample. If, on the other hand, the difference is statistically significant, then there may be something unusual about the sample. In another vein, if the sample observations relate to a different time or place than those in the known population, for example to a single region or 15 years earlier, then the researcher may wish to test whether any changes are significant or artefacts of sampling. The formula for converting an individual X value into a Z score:

$$Z = \frac{|X - \mu|}{\sigma}$$

can easily be transformed into the equivalent Z test formula, thus:

$$Z = \frac{|\bar{x} - \mu|}{\sigma_{\bar{x}}}$$

where the standard error ($\sigma_{\bar{x}}$) is:

$$\sigma_{\bar{x}} = \frac{\sigma}{\sqrt{n}}$$

The population mean, μ, and the grand mean, $\bar{\bar{x}}$, are assumed to be equal.

The sample of 52 Yorkshire farms was shown to be moderately skewed to the right (most farms are smaller than the mean, 173.6 ha). Suppose the population of farms in England has a mean of 88.5 ha and a standard deviation of 157.9 ha. Does sampling error (chance) alone account for a difference of 85.1 ha between the means? The null hypothesis would be that the difference has arisen because of sampling error and is not statistically significant. The significance level is set at 0.05. Substituting these values into the formulae for the standard error of the mean and the test statistic, the value of Z can be calculated:

$$\sigma_{\bar{x}} = \frac{157.9}{\sqrt{52}} = 21.897$$

and

$$Z = \frac{|173.6 - 88.5|}{21.897} = \frac{85.1}{21.897} = 3.89$$

The probability associated with $Z = 3.9$ is 0.000 096 2 from Table 1 in Appendix IV. There is no prior reason to believe that the sample mean should be either lower or higher than the population mean, therefore a two-tailed test should be used. Thus the probability (0.000 096 2) of a difference as great or greater than 85.1 is divided equally between the two tails or extremes of the normal distribution. The outcome of the test indicates that, if 100 000 samples were selected, a difference at least as great as 85.1 is likely to occur 9.62 times by chance. Since this is less than the chosen level of significance (0.05 or 5 per cent), the null hypothesis is confidently rejected and the conclusion is reached that the difference is statistically significant. The test result indicates either that the population mean and/or standard deviation are not as stated, or that Yorkshire farms are significantly larger than the entire population of English farms.

The key stages in carrying out a Z test are as follows:

1. State null hypothesis and significance level.
2. Calculate test statistic (Z, which also requires calculation of the standard error).
3. Decide whether a one- or two-tailed test is appropriate.
4. Determine the probability of obtaining the calculated Z value.
5. Decide whether to accept or reject the null hypothesis.

This sequence forms the basic set of operations for most statistical tests, although the test statistic will obviously vary.

Each statistical test makes certain assumptions about the sample and/or population data with which it may be used. Only the essential points are examined here, since other texts have already discussed the issues fully (for example, Williams 1984). The requirements of the Z test may appear so stringent as to make its application quite problematic and in some respects the Z test might be regarded as an ideal which is rarely attained in practice. These comments apply to the natural and social sciences, although their impact is particularly restrictive for the latter. In principle, the results of a test are invalid if it has been applied to data which contravene its assumptions, although some relaxation of the stringent requirements may be permissible.

There are five main points in connection with the Z test.

1. *Random sampling* is required in order to ensure that the sample mean is unbiased.
2. Items in the population should be *independent* of each other. The value of one item is not influenced in any way by the value of any other. This requirement is demanded in order to avoid problems associated with negative or positive autocorrelation. Positive

autocorrelation exists when items in the population which are close together, for example in space or time, possess similar values for the same variable. Negative autocorrelation is the opposite, with closely juxtaposed items tending to have very different values. Increasing the sample size when autocorrelation is suspected helps to alleviate the problem.

3. *Normality of sample means* is required so that the central limit theorem can be employed. This assumption may readily be made if the population is approximately normal, but is more risky when this is not the case. Theory suggests that a sufficiently large sample will also produce a sampling distribution of the mean that is nearly normal. The problem is to decide how large is sufficiently large: there is no simple answer to this question. Shaw and Wheeler (1985, p. 113) maintained that 'When large samples (n of over 30) are used the sampling distributions are normal regardless of the population'. Williams (1984, p. 135) disagrees with this assertion, regarding it as 'a dangerous generalisation' and argued that 'samples of several hundreds of items may not be sufficient' for populations which are far from normal. The assumption of normality can be a serious drawback as far as applying the Z test to geographical problems is concerned, since it is frequently unclear whether normality is present.
4. *Combined effects of* μ *and* σ are not taken into account by the Z test. By definition, the test examines the difference between the sample and population means in relation to the size of σ, although it does not identify the origin of any difference, which may be associated with dissimilarity in the standard deviations or a mixture of both.
5. *The value of* σ, the population standard deviation, which is necessary for calculating the standard error of the mean, $\sigma_{\bar{x}}$, may not be known. Unless provided by the originator or publisher of the population data, the calculation of σ may be impossible.

These issues, taken together, may make the reader wonder whether the Z test has any practical application at all. It is perhaps less helpful in some disciplines than others, and unfortunately geography falls into the former category. Nevertheless, the Z test is a useful starting point from which to examine other less robust, but also less demanding, tests.

10.2.2 The t test

The t test is closely related to the Z test, and the difference might seem somewhat trivial. In order to calculate a standard error of the mean, the population standard deviation (σ) is replaced by the equivalent sample statistic (s). This change produces a standard error which is therefore an estimate of the true parameter, which can only be generated when the population standard deviation is known. The estimated standard error is represented by a slightly different symbol $\sigma_{\hat{x}}$ or $s_{\bar{x}}$ and calculated as:

$$s_{\bar{x}} = \frac{s}{\sqrt{n}}$$

Once this change has been made, $s_{\bar{x}}$ is substituted into the formula for calculating Z in order to produce a different test statistic, known as t, thus:

$$t = \frac{|\bar{x} - \mu|}{s_{\bar{x}}}$$

The t distribution is named after the statistician William Gosset, who, writing under the pseudonym 'Student', discovered it in 1908. The important difference between the Z and t distributions arises from the fact that the $s_{\bar{x}}$ is also potentially subject to sampling error, since it is derived from a sample. Variation between the standard deviation of a sample and its parent population may produce differing quantities for the standard error. The difference between the population standard error and the estimate is likely to be larger for smaller samples.

At this point, before looking up probabilities associated with the t distribution, the idea of *degrees of freedom* should be introduced. The concept, although relatively simple, sometimes causes confusion. The degrees of freedom refer to the number of items in a sample whose values are free to alter without affecting the result of the statistical test being carried out. Suppose the five items in a sample are measured in respect of a continuous variable with the values 2.3, 3.5, 6.6, 7.4, and 10.2; the sum of the five measurements is 30, giving a mean of 6. If 4 of the values were different, say 1.4, 5.8, 7.2 and 12.1, the fifth would be fixed at 3.5 in order for the sum to remain as 30 and their mean as 6. In other words, four of the values are free to vary, but one is predetermined by the condition that their mean shall equal 6. Degrees of freedom, usually denoted by the symbol df, are defined in the case of the one-sample t test as:

$$\text{df} = n - 1$$

where n is the sample size. In bivariate statistical tests df may be defined differently, but the principle remains the same.

The strucutre of the t distribution table is different than that for Z. The Z table (see Appendix IV, Table 1) includes two pieces of information: the Z value and the corresponding probability. The t table incorporates a further dimension, namely that the probability associated with a specific t value varies according to the degrees of freedom. Instead of the numbers in the body of the table being the probabilities, these are usually the t values themselves (Appendix IV, Table 2). Each row represents different degrees of freedom (see row labels in left-hand margin) and the headings in the top margin indicate the probability associated with each column, for example 0.2, 0.1, 0.05, 0.02 and 0.01. Following a single row across the table from left to right, the value of t increases as the probability decreases. In other words, for a constant df level the probability of obtaining a high value for t by chance becomes more remote.

The t distribution is therefore not a single distribution (as with Z), but a series of similar distributions whose precise form and shape varies with sample size (Figure 10.1). The shape of the distribution is unimodal and symmetrical, but when the sample size is small the peak is depressed and the tails are elevated in comparison to the normal. Larger sample sizes produce t distributions which approximate to the normal, until when the sample size is infinite the two distributions are coincident. The broken line in Figure 10.1 represents the standardised normal curve, with the t distribution curves for df = 2 and df = 4 as solid lines for comparison. The tendency for larger samples to produce a t distribution closer to the normal is connected with the likelihood of a smaller difference between the true and estimated standard error.

The effect of sample size on the t distribution goes beyond the form and shape of the curve: the probabilities associated with identical values of t also vary. Like Z, the quantity t can be used to provide a standardising scale for the horizontal axis. In the case of the Z distribution the area under the curve and the probability linked to a particular value of Z is the same regardless of sample size. But, because sample size influences the precise form and shape of the curve for the t distribution, the probabilities for each value of t also alter. The differences between the probabilities of Z and t distributions are shown in Figure 10.2. The curve traces the t distribution with df = 10 and the standardised normal curve. The probability associated with a Z value of 1.96 was given as 0.05 (see Chapter 9), so that there is a 5 per cent chance of a sample mean from a normally distributed population lying beyond either -1.96 or $+1.96$ units of Z, represented by the innermost vertical broken lines. A t value of 1.96 with df = 10 yields a probability of 0.30, giving a 30 per cent chance of a sample mean lying in either of the tails of the distribution. A t value of 2.23 and df = 10 is required in order to reach the 0.05 level of significance, denoted by the innermost solid vertical lines.

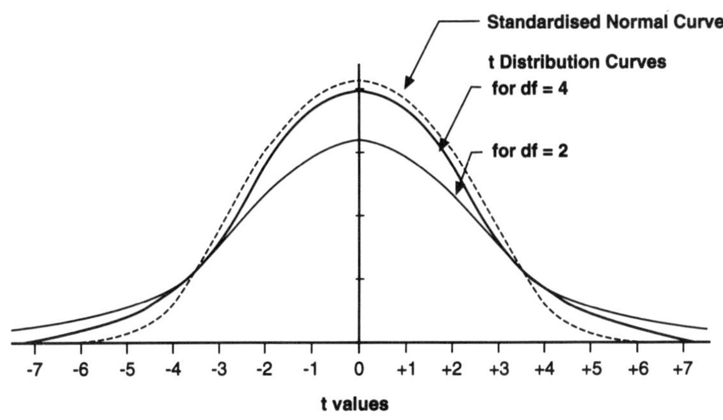

Figure 10.1 Effect of sample size on the shape of the t distribution

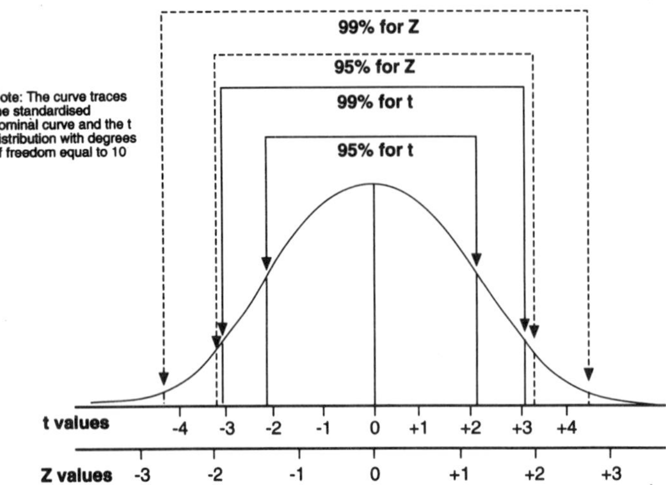

Figure 10.2 Probabilities of t distribution associated with different sample sizes

When applying the t test, the difference between the sample and population means has probably not arisen through chance or sampling error when the test statistic is equal to or greater than the tabulated value for the chosen level of significance. Suppose the sample size is 10, giving df = 9, the chosen level of significance is 0.05 and the calculated t statistic is 3.154. The critical t value in the table at the junction of the desired row and column is 2.262. Since the calculated t is greater, the difference in means would be regarded as significant at the 0.05 level, although not at the 0.01 level where the critical t value is 3.250. The probability associated with the t value at a particular degrees of freedom level relates to the two tails of the distribution and therefore should be halved if a one-tailed test is required.

The Z test suggested that the mean size of the sample of 52 Yorkshire farms was significantly different from that of the parent population. Is the same result obtained when a t test is used? The Z test requires both the population mean and standard deviation to be known; the t test is less demanding, with only the former necessary. This is a much more realistic proposition, since published secondary sources of data often provide sufficient information, such as the number of farms and the sum of their areas in this example. The mean area of all English farms has already been stated as 88.5 ha, while the sample mean is 173.6 ha, which yields a difference of 85.1 ha. The standard deviation for the sample is 281.8 ha (see Chapter 5). A suitable null hypothesis is that the difference of 85.1 ha between the population and sample means has arisen purely through chance and is not statistically significant at either the 0.05 or the 0.01 levels. Substituting the relevant figures into the formulae for the estimated standard error and the test statistic, t, thus:

$$s_{\bar{x}} = \frac{281.8}{\sqrt{52}} = 39.079$$

and

$$t = \frac{|173.6 - 88.5|}{39.079} = \frac{85.1}{39.079} = 2.178$$

produces a t test statistic of 2.178. There are 51 degrees of freedom (52 – 1) and, since no sound a priori reason is available for why the difference between the means should be in one direction rather than the other, a two-tailed test is required. Referring to Table 2 in Appendix IV, and tracing across the row for 50 degrees of freedom, since 51 is not provided, under the 0.05 column the tabulated value for t is 2.010 and under the 0.02 column it is 2.403. The test statistic (2.178) lies between these t values and the difference of 85.1 ha is unlikely to have occurred as a result of sampling error and is significant at the 0.05 level, but not at 0.01. A difference at least as great as the one obtained would occur by chance less often than 5 times in 100, but more frequently than once (or for that matter twice) in 100. Unlike the Z test, the precise probability associated with a particular t value will rarely be determined from the table.

The t test makes certain assumptions about the sample and population. As with all parametric tests the sampled items should be selected randomly and they should be independent of each other in the population. The test may tolerate modest positive autocorrelation, but if extreme the test results may be distorted. The items in the population are assumed to be normally distributed, even though the validity of this assumption may not be determined with a high level of accuracy. Some problems can arise if the population is severely non-normal.

1. A poor fit will be achieved between the theoretical t distribution and the sampling distribution of the mean, if the population is markedly skewed.
2. Sample size is again an important question and larger samples are needed to overcome the problems of highly skewed populations.
3. Skewness in the parent population also affects the symmetry of the distribution, with the probability of the t value unequally divided between the tails.

The t test, although widely used, is less robust than the Z test and should not be regarded as necessarily suitable for small samples, as some authors have suggested (Shaw and Wheeler 1985). The form and shape of the parent population is of considerable importance in determining the accuracy of the results. Unfortunately, sufficient information about the population may not be available to enable the researcher to make a judgement about the suitability of using the test. Finally, the t test does not take the population standard deviation into account and, as in the case of the Yorkshire farms sample, there might be a substantial difference between σ and s.

10.2.2.1 Paired-sample t test

A special hybrid of the t test has been devised for situations where there are pairs of measurements of the same variable for the sampled items. For example, we could take two measurements of annual lichen growth on tree trunks, one for the windward side and one for the leeward side. If the windward measurements for each sampled tree were denoted as A and those for the leeward as B, the paired-sample t test would help to determine if the difference between the A and B measurements is significant. Thus the first task is to calculate these differences, in other words to subtract the value for each B measurement from the corresponding A value to give a series of positive and negative values. If these differences were not significant, they would cancel each other out and the mean difference for the population of trees would be 0.

Suppose the farms in the Yorkshire sample had been surveyed 15 years previously, and the aim is to investigate if any change in size over this period was significant. In Table 10.1 the two sets of figures in the columns headed X_{A} and X_{B} denote respectively the current and previous areas: some farms increased, some decreased and others remained the same. Where a difference (d) is recorded, this might have arisen because of a genuine change in area, or because of errors of measurement or sampling. The null hypothesis states that the sample of differences between the pairs of measurements are purely the result of chance and have come from a population of normally distributed differences whose mean is 0. Overall the mean area was slightly less 15 years before (168.1 ha) and the sum of the differences is 284.8 ha, so there was an overall increase in area.

The basic t-test formula is adapted so that it applies to the differences, using the letter d in place of X. The mean ($\bar{d}$) and standard deviation ($s_{\bar{d}}$) of the differences are calculated, from which the standard error $\hat{\sigma}_{\bar{d}}$ is estimated, thus:

$$\hat{\sigma}_{\bar{d}} = \frac{s_{\bar{d}}}{\sqrt{n}}$$

The paired t test considers the disparity between the mean of a sample of differences and a hypothesised population mean of differences equalling 0. Thus the t-test formula given above is adapted as follows:

$$t = \frac{|\bar{d} - 0|}{\hat{\sigma}_{\bar{d}}} = \frac{|\bar{d}|}{\hat{\sigma}_{\bar{d}}}$$

to yield the statistic t. Substituting the figures for the Yorkshire farms, whose mean difference is 5.48 ha, into these formulae, the estimated standard error is

$$\hat{\sigma}_{\bar{d}} = \frac{37.32}{\sqrt{52}} = 5.18$$

and t is

$$t = \frac{|5.48 - 0|}{5.18} = 1.058$$

Table 10.1 Paired sample data from Yorkshire sample farms

X_A	X_B	d
4.5	4.5	0.0
5.3	5.7	−0.4
6.4	10.9	−4.5
6.7	6.5	0.2
7.8	1.2	6.6
13.6	13.6	0.0
13.8	20.3	−6.5
14.5	14.5	0.0
15.7	15.7	0.0
16.2	5.8	10.4
19.4	21.1	−1.7
19.5	19.7	−0.2
19.5	19.5	0.0
20.3	40.5	−20.2
20.5	25.2	−4.7
20.5	20.5	0.0
25.0	25.1	−0.1
34.6	34.6	0.0
39.0	38.7	0.3
39.1	39.1	0.0
40.5	40.5	0.0
40.5	75.3	−34.8
40.5	15.7	24.8
45.6	45.6	0.0
50.8	50.4	0.4
55.1	55.0	0.1
60.3	60.3	0.0
60.3	60.3	0.0
62.6	75.4	−12.8
65.4	20.4	45.0
75.8	45.2	30.6
86.0	86.0	0.0
88.7	88.7	0.0
88.7	35.8	52.9
96.7	90.1	6.6
100.8	95.3	5.5
112.5	112.5	0.0
115.6	115.6	0.0
134.6	134.6	0.0
156.5	108.2	48.3
156.9	153.2	3.7
202.5	202.5	0.0
250.2	250.0	0.2
425.6	450.7	−25.1
443.6	375.2	68.4
456.8	456.8	0.0
555.2	555.5	−0.3
657.2	657.2	0.0
788.5	680.1	108.4
854.8	1012.3	−157.5
1041.3	900.1	141.2
1254.0	1254.0	0.0
9026.0	8741.2	284.8

The degrees of freedom are again 51 and, referring to the t distribution (Table 2 in Appendix IV), the calculated test statistic is less than the tabulated value of t at the 0.05 level of significance ($1.058 < 2.010$). Thus the mean difference being tested, 5.48 ha, is likely to have occurred by chance considerably more often than five times in 100 and consequently the null hypothesis should be accepted. The increase in mean farm size over the 15-year period was not statistically significant and quite probably resulted from sampling error.

10.2.3 Confidence limits for Z and t

The Z and t tests have dealt with situations in which some information is known about the population from which a sample is drawn. This fortunate position does occur in geographical research, but not with as much frequency as might at first be imagined. When the population is infinite (for example, points within a study area) or theoretically finite but unable to be counted (for example, a population composed of businesses, which although finite at a specific point in time, in practice 'come and go' as companies commence and cease trading), little if any information may exist about the population and one purpose of the research is to estimate its principal statistical characteristics from a sample. Unfortunately, sampling error brings the accuracy of these estimates into question. However, boundaries or limits can be defined between which it is possible to claim that the population mean lies, with a specified degree of confidence.

What is needed therefore are two numbers, one larger and one smaller than the sample mean, which define a range within which the population mean is likely to lie with a specified probability. If these limits are far apart, for instance 650 units equidistant either side of a sample mean of 675, at 25 and 1325, then it is not very reassuring to discover that there is a 0.95 (95 per cent) probability of the population mean falling within this range. On the other hand, if the limits were relatively close together, say 25 units either side of 675 (650 and 700) and the probability is still 0.95, the sample affords a good estimate of the population and may be relied upon for further analysis. Thus the importance of a confidence interval should be assessed with respect to the width of the interval itself and its probability.

The principles and calculation of a confidence interval are similar for a number of statistical tests. In the case of the Z and t intervals the real or estimated standard error plays a crucial role. A 95 per cent confidence interval for the population mean (μ) may be calculated from the following formula:

$$\bar{x} - 1.96\sigma_{\bar{x}} \text{ to } \bar{x} + 1.96\sigma_{\bar{x}}$$

A Z value of 1.96 denotes the point at which 0.025 of the total probability lies in each tail of the distribution, so there is a 95 per cent chance of the population mean occurring between -1.96 and $+1.96$ units of Z. If a 99 per cent confidence interval is required then 2.57

would replace 1.96 in the formula. Although the population mean of English farms has already been provided (88.5 ha), the example serves to illustrate the general procedure. Substituting the relevant figures into the equation, the 95 per cent confidence interval for the mean size of farms is

$$173.6 - (1.96 \times 21.90) \text{ to } 173.6 + (1.96 \times 21.90)$$
$$130.7 \text{ ha to } 216.5 \text{ ha}$$

and the 99 per cent interval is

$$173.6 - (2.57 \times 21.90) \text{ to } 173.6 + (2.57 \times 21.90)$$
$$117.3 \text{ ha to } 229.9 \text{ ha}$$

The fact that the known population mean (88.5 ha) lies outside both of the above confidence intervals is not surprising given the result of the Z test. A confidence interval based on the Z distribution requires that the population standard deviation, and therefore its standard error, are known. In practice, it would be unusual to know σ and not μ, and thus the Z confidence interval is rarely required.

The calculation of confidence intervals based on the t distribution is much more useful. The need to take into account the degrees of freedom present in the sample adds a further minor complication to the operation. A 95 per cent confidence interval using the t distribution is calculated as:

$$\bar{x} - t_{(0.05)}\hat{\sigma}_{\bar{x}} \text{ to } \bar{x} + t_{(0.05)}\hat{\sigma}_{\bar{x}}$$

where $t_{(0.05)}$ is the tabulated value of t for the appropriate degrees of freedom. Suppose such a confidence interval is required for the Yorkshire farms sample; the degrees of freedom are 51. If the specific number of degrees of freedom does not appear as a row in the table, as in this case, the closest row with a lower t value under the appropriate column of probability should be used. The t value with 55 degrees of freedom (not shown in Appendix IV, Table 2) is 2.00 when $p = 0.05$ and 2.40 when $p = 0.01$. The 95 per cent confidence interval based on t is

$$173.6 - (2.00 \times 39.08) \text{ to } 173.6 + (2.00 \times 39.08)$$
$$95.4 \text{ to } 251.8 \text{ ha}$$

and the 99 per cent interval is

$$173.6 - (2.40 \times 39.08) \text{ to } 173.6 + (2.40 \times 39.08)$$
$$79.8 \text{ to } 267.4 \text{ ha}$$

Given the previous t-test results, it is not surprising that the known population mean (88.5 ha) lies within the second of these ranges. Comparison of the 95 and 99 per cent confidence intervals from the Z and t distributions reveals that the t intervals are wider, chiefly because of the larger standard error. The differences between the critical

Z and t values, 1.96 and 2.00 at $p = 0.05$, and 2.57 and 2.40 at $p = 0.01$, are relatively minor. If there had been fewer cases in the sample, say 10, giving df = 9, the t value would have been 2.26 and the confidence interval would have widened to between 85.2 and 261.9 ha. Thus small samples tend to produce less reliable estimates of population parameters. The assumptions and limitations relating to the Z and t statistical tests also apply if the distributions are used to calculate confidence intervals. The population should be normally distributed or the sample so large that, in the case of an interval based on the Z distribution, the sampling distribution of the mean can be assumed to be approximately normal. Items in the population should be independent of each other, and sampling with individual replacement from a finite population, or without replacement from an infinite one, should be employed.

10.3 NON-PARAMETRIC TESTS

10.3.1 Pearson's chi-square

Most non-parametric tests deal with frequency counts rather than measurements. Even if the original variables are measured on a continuous scale they usually need to be converted into grouped attributes in order to apply non-parametric tests. Probably the most important and frequently used non-parametric test is *Pearson's chi-square* or, more simply, the *chi-square test*. The test can be used with either single or multiple samples, and this section examines the basic principles of the test for the single-sample case.

Somewhat ironically, the theoretical background of the chi-square distribution, from which Pearson's chi-square test is derived, is defined in terms of measurements rather than frequencies. In Section 9.4 the conversion of any individual measurement of a normally distributed variable X into a Z value was achieved with the following formula:

$$Z = \frac{|X - \mu|}{\sigma}$$

Suppose n items are measured in respect of the variable X, denoted as $X_1, X_2, X_3, \ldots, X_n$, and the corresponding Z values are calculated for each, which can be shown in symbols as $Z_1, Z_2, Z_3, \ldots, Z_n$. The sum of the squares of the Z values produces a statistic known as chi-square (χ^2), which can be expressed as:

$$\chi^2 = (Z_1)^2 + (Z_2)^2 + (Z_3)^2 + \cdots + (Z_n)^2$$

χ^2 can take any positive value from 0 to plus infinity, and depends on the amount of deviation from the mean and the number of items. The number of X values is referred to as the degrees of freedom in chi-square and is equivalent to sample size. The variation in the form and shape of the distribution of chi-square connected with selected

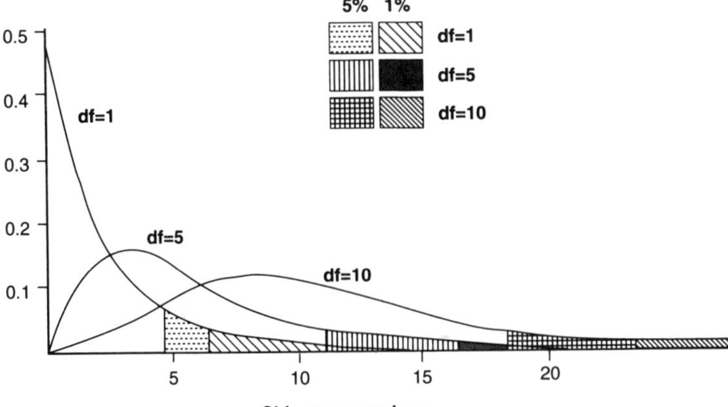

Figure 10.3 Effect of sample size on the shape of the χ^2 distribution

degrees of freedom is illustrated in Figure 10.3. As the number of items increases the distribution of chi-square becomes less and less skewed, approaching the normal when there are over 40 observations.

The values of the chi-square distribution are tabulated in a similar form to the *t* distribution, with the rows defining degrees of freedom and the columns a series of critical probability levels, while the body of the table contains chi-square values (see Appendix IV, Table 3). The probabilities for the chi-square distribution relate to the chance of obtaining a particular χ^2 value, or one greater, for a given number of degrees of freedom. For example, at 0.05 probability and with 10 degrees of freedom, the χ^2 value of 18.307 cuts off the right-hand or upper tail of the distribution. In other words, if 100 samples with 10 items each were selected, five samples would attain a χ^2 value of at least 18.307 through chance sampling. All of the probability associated with a particular chi-square value lies in one tail of the distribution, which arises because the statistic cannot be negative and the minimum possible value is 0, which represents the unlikely event that all X values are identical to their mean.

Chi-square may occasionally be used to test the difference between variances (for an explanation see Williams 1984, p. 195), but a far more important test statistic which approximates very closely to the chi-square distribution was developed by Pearson and hence is known as Pearson's chi-square. Pearson's chi-square test is used with data expressed as frequency counts for samples of n items classified and distributed among j groups. A suitable null hypothesis would state that the difference between the observed and expected frequency counts in the classes has arisen merely through chance sampling and is not statistically significant. If the observed frequency count in each class is denoted as O and the expected count as E, then the Pearson chi-square test statistic can be calculated from the formula

$$\chi^2 = \sum \frac{(O - E)^2}{E}$$

Pearson's chi-square approximates to the chi-square distribution, defined above, with $j-1$ degrees of freedom in the single-sample case, and the approximation grows closer as sample size increases. If the χ^2 test statistic is greater than the tabulated figure at the intersection of the appropriate degrees of freedom row and level of significance column, the difference between the observed and expected frequency counts is regarded as in excess of what might occur through sampling error. In this situation the null hypothesis would be rejected as untenable.

The frequency distribution of farm types in the Yorkshire sample (see Chapter 7) will now be used to illustrate the single-sample application of Pearson's chi-square test, with a significance level of 0.05. The a priori expectation is that the farms would be distributed equally across the four classes, so the hypothesised distribution is for 13 farms per class (52/4). Part A of Table 10.2 shows the observed and expected frequencies for the sample of farms, and the difference between them. The squared differences are divided by the expected frequency and the results summed to give the χ^2 statistic, 5.68. Four classes give 3 degrees of freedom (4 – 1). Referring the row where df = 3 in the chi-squared distribution table in Appendix IV, the calculated χ^2 lies somewhere between 0.2 and 0.1 probability. Thus the likelihood of the difference in the frequency distributions having occurred by chance is higher than 10 times in 100 but not as high as 20 times. The null hypothesis would have to be retained, since the probability of the test statistic having arisen by chance is greater than the significance level (0.05).

Table 10.2 Observed and expected frequency counts of farm type in Yorkshire sample

	Farm type				
	Dairy	Arable	Mixed	Other livestock	Total
Part A (see text)					
Observed	19	10	15	8	52
Expected	13	13	13	13	52
Difference	+6	−3	+2	−5	0
Squared difference	$\frac{36}{13}$	$\frac{9}{13}$	$\frac{4}{13}$	$\frac{25}{13}$	74
	= 2.8	= 0.7	= 0.3	= 1.9	= 5.7
	Pearson's chi-square = 5.68, p > 0.1				
Part B (see text)					
Observed	19	10	15	8	52
Expected	(0.6)(52) = 31.2	(0.03)(52) = 1	(0.07)(52) = 3.64	(0.3)(52) = 15.6	52
Difference	−12.2	+8.44	+11.36	−7.6	0
Squared difference	$\frac{148.9}{31.2}$	$\frac{71.2}{1.56}$	$\frac{129.1}{3.64}$	$\frac{57.8}{15.6}$	
	= 4.8	= 45.6	= 35.5	= 3.7	= 89.6
	Pearson's chi-square = 89.59, p < 0.001				

Sometimes the expected frequencies can be determined by reference to the known probability of an item falling in each class. Part B of Table 10.2 illustrates this situation when the distribution of all farms in the agricultural census is used to produce prior probabilities of the different types occurring in the sample. The proportions of farms occurring in the four categories, dairy, arable, mixed and other livestock, were 0.6, 0.03, 0.07 and 0.3, respectively. Multiplying the total number of sample farms by each proportion yields the frequency that would be expected. For instance, the proportion of dairy farms was 0.6 and the expected number in the sample is:

$$0.6 \times 52 = 31.2 \text{ dairy farms}$$

The procedure for the test is now the same as before and generates a very high Pearson's chi-square with a probability lower than 0.001. The null hypothesis, that there is no significant difference in farm type between the population and sample, would be rejected on the grounds that such a large disparity between the observed and expected frequencies would occur by chance less often than 1 in a 1000 times.

The assumptions and limitations of Pearson's chi-square test will be examined more fully in the next chapter; however, the following basic points should be noted. Simple random sampling is required and the items in the population should be independent of each other. The classes into which the items are placed should *not* contain any inherent ranking or order; they are simply nominal categories.

10.3.2 Kolmogorov–Smirnov *D* test

Statisticians disagree about the usefulness of the Kolmogorov–Smirnov test. A common application of the test involves comparing the difference between the frequencies for a ranked variable that would arise from a random probability distribution, such as the Poisson, and those which have been observed. The main problem is that Poisson distribution relies on the mean density of the observed occurrences, λ, in order to calculate the expected frequency. The critical values for the test statistic assume no such connection and that the expected frequencies are obtained independently from the sampled observations. This difficulty may be overcome by careful selection of the significance level and by exercising caution when accepting or rejecting the null hypothesis in marginal cases.

The Kolmogorov–Smirnov test is used with an ordinal variable which has been measured for a single sample. The observed and expected frequencies for the ordered classes into which the items have been placed are expressed as proportions and accumulated in order to produce two cumulative frequency distributions. The null hypothesis claims that any difference between the cumulative frequency distributions is the result of chance and entirely attributable to sampling error. The differences between the observed and expected cumulative frequency distributions are calculated for each ordered class and the largest difference produces the test statistic D. Table 4 in Appendix IV shows the probabilities associated with random values of D. The distribution of D varies according to the degrees of freedom, which equals sample size. When the sample size (n) is less than or equal to 35, the D table in Appendix IV can be used to assess the probability of the test statistic. However, if n is greater than 35, then a simple formula is used to determine the critical value of D:

$$D = \frac{1.36}{\sqrt{n}}$$

The numerator depends on the level of significance: 1.36 is used for the 0.05 level and 1.63 for 0.01. If the test statistic derived from the sample exceeds the tabulated value of D or that calculated by the formula at the chosen level of significance, then the likelihood of the difference between the two cumulative frequency distributions having arisen through chance is quite small.

The farms in the Yorkshire sample have been ranked in relation to the main farmstead's distance from the village centre (to the nearest kilometre). The variable contains the numbers 0, 1, 2, 3, 4, etc., with 0 denoting that the farmstead is located in the village. The null hypothesis states that the farms are randomly distributed with respect to distance from village centres. The Poisson distribution is used to determine the expected number of farms at different distances from their nearest village centre if they were distributed at random. The observed and expected frequency distributions for the farms are given in Table 10.3, together with the corresponding cumulative frequencies. The maximum difference between the cumulative frequencies, 0.1394, occurs with the fourth ordered class, 3 km. Since the sample size is greater than 35 the formula for the critical value of D at 0.05 significance should be used, thus:

$$D = \frac{1.36}{\sqrt{52}} = 0.189$$

Table 10.3 Expected and observed frequencies for distance of farmstead from village centre in Yorkshire sample

Ranked distance	Expected frequency	Observed frequency	Cumulative expected	Cumulative observed	Difference
0	1.48	5	0.0286	0.0962	0.0676
1	5.27	4	0.1298	0.1731	0.0433
2	9.38	3	0.3102	0.2308	0.0794
3	11.12	8	0.5240	0.3846	0.1394
4	9.89	16	0.7142	0.6923	0.0219
5	7.04	11	0.8496	0.9038	0.0542
6	4.18	3	0.9300	0.9615	0.0315
7	2.12	2	0.9708	1.0000	0.0292
8	0.95	0	0.9890	1.0000	0.0110
9	0.37	0	0.9961	1.0000	0.0039
	51.8	52			

Since the critical value of D at the 0.05 significance level, 0.189, is greater than the calculated test statistic for the sample, 0.1394, the null hypothesis is accepted. The differences between the observed and expected distributions are so insignificant that they would occur by chance in more than 5 out of 100 samples.

10.3.3 Wilcoxon signed ranks test

The Wilcoxon signed ranks test examines the difference in mean for a paired set of measurements for a continuous variable, but does not place such stringent requirements on the data as the paired t test. The pairs of measurements are for the same variable and relate to two separate sets of conditions or parts of the phenomena under investigation. The null hypothesis asserts that the measurements forming each pair differ purely through chance sampling and the mean of the differences in the population from which the sample has been drawn is 0.

The mathematical operations required to carry out the test are quite simple, although several different stages are involved. First calculate the differences between the pairs of measurements, A and B, and then rank these, ignoring the sign (+ or −) and discarding any with no difference (equal rank). Assign the rank value 1 to the smallest absolute difference, 2 to next and so on, and give the mean rank score for any adjacent identical differences. Now attach the sign of the difference to the ranks and sum independently the positive and negative rank scores. The smallest sum, irrespective of sign, provides the test statistic W. A one- or two-tailed test is carried out depending upon the nature of the difference under examination. The probability of obtaining the calculated value of W, or one smaller, through chance sampling is determined either through consulting Table 5 in Appendix IV or by converting W into Z. The W values form the rows in the table and the number of non-zero differences, n, in the group of observations which provides the test statistic W, define the columns. The body of the table contains the probabilities. When the number of non-zero differences is greater than 20, W approximates to the normal distribution and is converted to Z, thus:

$$Z = \frac{|W - \mu w|}{\sigma_w} = \frac{\left| W - \dfrac{n(n+1)}{4} \right| - \dfrac{1}{2}}{\sqrt{\dfrac{n(n+1)(2n+1)}{24}}}$$

After this transformation the approximate probability may be obtained from the Z table (Appendix IV, Table 1).

The area of 31 of the farms in the Yorkshire sample had changed over the 15-year period (see paired t-test example). The null hypothesis states that the differences between the pairs of measurements are insignificant and the sample comes from a population in which the mean difference is zero. The rank scores of the absolute differences and the signed

Table 10.4 Ranks of non-zero differences between pairs of size measurements for sample of Yorkshire farms

X_A	X_B	d	Unsigned rank	Signed rank
5.3	5.7	−0.4	8.5	−8.5
6.4	10.9	−4.5	12.0	−12.0
6.7	6.5	0.2	4.0	4.0
7.8	1.2	6.6	16.5	16.5
13.8	20.3	−6.5	15.0	−15.0
16.2	5.8	10.4	18.0	18.0
19.4	21.1	−1.7	10.0	−10.0
19.5	19.7	−0.2	4.0	−4.0
20.3	40.5	−20.2	20.0	−20.0
20.5	25.2	−4.7	13.0	−13.0
25.0	25.1	−0.1	1.5	−1.5
39.0	38.7	0.3	6.5	6.5
40.5	75.3	−34.8	24.0	−24.0
40.5	15.7	24.8	21.0	21.0
50.8	50.4	0.4	8.5	8.5
55.1	55.0	0.1	1.5	1.5
62.6	75.4	−12.8	19.0	−19.0
65.4	20.4	45.0	25.0	25.0
75.8	45.2	30.6	23.0	23.0
88.7	35.8	52.9	27.0	27.0
96.7	90.1	6.6	16.5	16.5
100.8	95.3	5.5	14.0	14.0
156.5	108.2	48.3	26.0	26.0
156.9	153.2	3.7	11.0	11.0
250.2	250.0	0.2	4.0	4.0
425.6	450.7	−25.1	22.0	−22.0
443.6	375.2	68.4	28.0	28.0
555.2	555.5	−0.3	6.5	−6.5
788.5	680.1	108.4	29.0	29.0
854.8	1012.3	−157.5	31.0	−31.0
1041.3	900.1	141.2	30.0	30.0

ranks are shown in Table 10.4. The positive and negative ranks sum respectively to 309.5 and 186.5. The latter, being smaller, constitutes the W-test statistic, but conversion into Z is required, since the number of non-zero differences exceeds 20. Substituting the appropriate figures into the formula:

$$Z = \frac{|W - \mu_W|}{\sigma_W} = \frac{\left|186.5 - \dfrac{31 \times 32}{4}\right| - \dfrac{1}{2}}{\sqrt{\dfrac{31 \times 32 \times 63}{24}}} = \frac{61}{51.03} = 1.195$$

The probability associated with $Z = 1.195$ is approximately 0.2301. A two-tailed test is required since there is no overriding reason to believe that one set of measurements would be greater than the other. The null hypothesis is retained, with the expectation that the difference would occur through chance about 23 times in 100. The fate of the null hypothesis is the same as for the paired t test carried out on the raw differences and the probabilities suggested by the two tests are similar.

The Wilcoxon signed ranks test has certain assumptions and limitations:

1. The differences are assumed to be drawn from a population of differences which are independent of each other.
2. The exclusion of zero differences is somewhat arbitrary and, given that the variable is continuous, these should not occur in any case, but do as an artifact of rounding.
3. The test is less powerful than the paired t test because rank scores rather than the real differences are used, although, as the example has demonstrated, the overall conclusion regarding the validity of the null hypothesis may be the same.

10.4 APPLICATION OF SINGLE- AND PAIRED SINGLE-SAMPLE TESTS TO EXEMPLAR PROJECTS

Sections 8.3 outlined the hypotheses for the four exemplar projects and the tests that would be applied. The following subsections demonstrate these tests using the MINITAB and SPSS-X programs, which include a range of relatively simple commands for carrying out statistical tests. The contrasts between the manual and computerised methods are highlighted, since these are a potential source of some confusion. The structure of the analytical subsections for the projects outlines the general form of the software commands for the various tests, restates the null hypotheses and then briefly reviews the test results. In most cases a single log of the computer session carrying out the tests is given in a table, while the complete results are brought together in the boxed examples.

10.4.1 Land-use change

10.4.1.1 Z test

The MINITAB command ZTEST performs the test on a specified column or columns of data. The test requires that the mean and standard deviation of the population from which the sample has been chosen are known. This information is included on the ZTEST command by means of two parameters preceding the column specifications; the values given to these parameters apply to all the columns included on the command. The general format of the command for a two-tailed Z test is:

MTB > ZTEST μ σ C4

where the known population mean and standard deviation are substituted for the symbols μ and σ. In some situations the investigator may wish to test the hypothesis that the population mean is likely to be zero; then the μ parameter is omitted from the command. If a one-tailed test is required, the ALTERNATIVE subcommand should be added:

```
MTB > ZTEST μ σ C4;
SUBC > ALTERNATIVE = K.
```

where K is either -1 or $+1$, which respectively indicate whether it is intended to test that the population mean is less than or greater than the sample mean. The output from the ZTEST command includes the sample mean and standard deviation, the standard error of the mean, the test statistic Z and its probability given to four decimal places. The command may report a negative value for Z, which is contrary to the description of the test given previously, because the formula for calculating Z in the software does not take the absolute difference between the μ and $\bar{x}$.

The MINITAB session for testing the hypotheses LU1, LU2 and LU3 in the land-use project is shown in Table 10.5. Hypothesis LU1 states:

Table 10.5 Application of univariate tests (Z, t and W tests) to land-use project samples A and B in MINITAB

```
MTB > OUTFILE 'land05'
MTB > RETRIEVE 'landa03'
MTB > COPY C5 C12;
SUBC > USE C4 = 1.
MTB > COPY C5 C13;
SUBC > USE C4 = 2.
MTB > COPY C5 C14;
SUBC > USE C4 = 3.
MTB > COPY C5 C15;
SUBC > USE C4 = 4.
MTB > COPY C5 C16;
SUBC > USE C4 = 5.
MTB > COPY C5 C17;
SUBC > USE C4 = 6.
MTB > COPY C5 C18;
SUBC > USE C4 = 7.
MTB > ZTEST 37.36 20.50 C12
MTB > ZTEST 0.12 13.20 C13
MTB > ZTEST 44.31 14.60 C14
MTB > ZTEST 6.58 12.10 C15
MTB > ZTEST 1.82 0.13 C16
MTB > ZTEST 7.04 5.09 C17
MTB > ZTEST 2.77 0.56 C18
MTB > SAVE 'landa03'
MTB > RETRIEVE 'landb03'
MTB > TTEST 37.36 C4
MTB > TTEST 0.12 C5
MTB > TTEST 44.31 C6
MTB > TTEST 6.58 C7
MTB > TTEST 1.82 C8
MTB > TTEST 7.04 C9
MTB > TTEST 2.77 C10
MTB > WTEST C32 – C38
MTB > NOOUTFILE
MTB > STOP
```

> The mean areas of each land use in sample A are not significantly different from the population, which has a known mean (μ) and standard deviation (σ).

and is examined by means of the Z test. The population means and standard deviations are obtained from published sources (e.g. Stamp 1948) — for example, the mean areas of arable and rough grazing land per square kilometre were 37.36 ha and 1.82 ha. The following extract from Table 10.5 shows that some manipulation of the columns in LANDA03.MTW is required in order to copy the 1930s areas for the different land uses into separate columns (C12 to C18) prior to carrying out the Z tests, thus:

```
MTB > COPY C5 C12;
SUBC > USE C4 = 1.
MTB > ZTEST 37.36 20.50 C12
```

In this example, the USE subcommand copies the values in C5 into C12 when C4 contains a 1, which denotes arable land.

The Z-test results for sample A in the land-use project are summarised in Box 10.1. The results indicate that for three of the six land uses (arable, grass and agriculturally unproductive) the null

Box 10.1 Summary of Z-test results for LU1 for each land use in sample A in 1930s

	μ	σ	$\bar{x}$	Z	P	Accept/ Reject H_0
Arable	37.36	20.50	35.13	0.42	0.67	Accept
Orchards & Mkt G.	0.12	13.20	16.40	2.76	0.01	Reject
Permanent Grass	44.31	14.60	43.40	0.20	0.84	Accept
Forestry & Woodland	6.58	12.10	18.20	2.14	0.03	Reject
Rough Grazing	1.82	0.13	9.00	78.11	0.00	Reject
Houses and Gardens*	7.04	5.09	3.30			
Agric. Unprod.	2.77	0.56	3.5	1.84	0.07	Accept

Sample ZTEST Output from MINITAB

```
MTB > ZTEST 37.36 20.50 C12
TEST OF MU = 37.360 VS MU N.E. 37.360
THE ASSUMED SIGMA = 20.5
          N      MEAN     STDEV    SE MEAN       Z     P VALUE
C12      15    35.133    26.827      5.293   -0.42     0.67
MTB > ZTEST 0.12 13.20 C13
TEST OF MU = 0.120 VS MU N.E. 0.120
THE ASSUMED SIGMA = 13.2
          N      MEAN     STDEV    SE MEAN       Z     P VALUE
C13       5    16.400     8.933      5.903    2.76     0.0059
```

*Only one observation prevents calculation of Z test.

hypothesis is accepted at the 0.05 level of significance. As far as market gardening, woodland and rough grazing are concerned, the null hypothesis is rejected and the conclusion is reached that there are significant differences between the sample and population means. One land use (housing) occurred only once in sample A and the test could not be carried out. The sample sizes for some of these tests are quite small and the frequency distributions tend to be slightly skewed. These features cast some doubt over the legitimacy of applying the Z test to the market gardening, woodland, heath and rough grazing and housing land uses.

10.4.1.2 t test

The MINITAB command used to perform a t test is, not surprisingly, TTEST. The value of population mean, μ, is again provided as a parameter immediately following the command and applies to all the specified columns. The parameter may be omitted if the null hypothesis assumes μ to be 0. A one- or two-tailed test may be chosen with the ALTERNATIVE subcommand, with K taking the value -1 or $+1$, thus:

MTB > TTEST μ C4;
SUBC > ALTERNATIVE = K.

The value -1 denotes that a one-tailed test should be carried out where the difference between the sample and population means is assumed to be positive, whereas $+1$ indicates the reverse. If -1 and $+1$ are omitted, a two-tailed test is performed. The output from the command includes the sample mean and standard deviation, the standard error of the mean and the calculated t statistic with its probability to four decimal places. A negative t statistic may be obtained, as with Z, contrary to the standard mathematical formula for the t test.

The second null hypothesis in the land-use project, LU2, states:

> The mean areas of each land use in sample B, with standard deviations of s, are not significantly different from the population, which has a known mean (μ).

The population means used in the series of t tests are the same as before, but the software automatically substitutes the sample standard deviations when estimating the standard errors. The areas of the seven land uses are already held in columns C4 to C10 of MINITAB worksheet LANDB03.MTW and the application of the t test with the appropriate population means as parameters (see Table 10.5) is relatively straightforward:

MTB > TTEST 37.36 C4

The output from the command includes the sample mean and standard deviation together with the standard error, the t statistic and its probability.

	μ	s	$\bar{x}$	t	P	Accept/ Reject H_0
Arable	37.36	13.69	36.15	0.40	0.70	Accept
Permanent Grass	44.31	12.42	29.60	5.29	0.00	Reject
Orchards & Mkt G.	0.12	6.82	6.45	4.15	0.00	Reject
Forestry & Woodland	6.58	9.22	12.25	2.75	0.01	Reject
Rough Grazing	1.82	4.50	4.75	1.75	0.10	Accept
Houses and Gardens	7.04	5.09	3.30	3.29	0.00	Reject
Agric. Unprod.	2.77	3.39	7.50	3.93	0.00	Reject

Sample TTEST Output from MINITAB

```
MTB > TTEST 37.36 C4
TEST OF MU = 37.360 VS MU N.E. 37.360
           N     MEAN     STDEV     SE MEAN      T      P VALUE
Arab30s   20    36.150   13.685     3.060      -0.40     0.70
MTB > TTEST 0.12 C5
TEST OF MU = 0.120 VS MU N.E. 0.120
           N     MEAN     STDEV     SE MEAN      T      P VALUE
MkGd30s   20     6.450    6.817     1.524       4.15     0.0005
```

Box 10.2 Summary of *t*-test results for LU2 for each land use in sample B in the 1930s

The results of carrying out t tests on the seven land uses in the 1930s are summarised in Box 10.2. The null hypotheses should be rejected for all but two of the land-use categories (arable and rough grazing). Broadly speaking, the results are in accord with those obtained for sample A with the Z test, although the probabilities of the test statistics are smaller and in most instances the null hypothesis would also be rejected at the 0.01 significance level. The sample size for each land use is 20 and, although some of the frequency distributions appear to depart from normality (e.g. market gardening and housing), the test results are perhaps more reliable than the previous Z tests.

10.4.1.3 Wilcoxon signed ranks test

The WTEST command in MINITAB performs a Wilcoxon signed ranks test. The analyst may choose between a one- or two-tailed test by means of the ALTERNATIVE subcommand and the general format of the command is similar to the t test (see above):

MTB > WTEST μ C4;
SUBC > ALTERNATIVE = K.

The parameter, μ, on the WTEST command denotes the hypothesised centre or mean of the differences between the observations in the population from which the sample was drawn. This is frequently omitted since the null hypothesis usually states that the centre is zero, which is the default value. The column(s) specified on the WTEST command contain the differences. A value of +1 on the ALTERNATIVE subcommand indicates a one-tailed test with H_1 greater than the hypothesised centre, −1 signifies the reverse.

The method of calculating *W* is different, but computationally equivalent, to that described in Section 10.3.2. Any sample observations equal to the hypothesised centre are disregarded and the remainder are paired with each other and the mean of each pair is calculated. The test statistic, *W*, is the number of means greater than, plus half of those equal to, the hypothesised centre. The output from WTEST reports an estimate of the population median, the number of non-zero differences and the *W* statistic with its probability.

The third null hypothesis in the land-use project, LU3, which requires a single-sample univariate test asserts:

> The area of each land use in the 1930s is not significantly different from that in the 1960s. Any differences have arisen purely due to sampling error.

The null hypothesis claims that the mean of the differences between the land uses is in fact 0 and the sample observations only indicate an increase or decrease by virtue of sampling error. The differences between the pairs of land-use area measurements in sample B have already been computed and stored in columns C32 to C38. A single WTEST command can be used to carry out the test on the seven land-use categories, thus:

MTB > WTEST C32 – C38

A summary of the results for the seven tests (Box 10.3) indicates that the null hypothesis is rejected at the 0.05 significance level in all cases. With some land uses the probabilities are very small (< 0.000) and only two land uses, rough grazing and houses and gardens, do not also have their null hypotheses rejected at the 0.01 level. The results provide clear confirmation of the importance of land-use change over the period covered by the two surveys. The application of the *W* test to the land-use data generally conforms to the test's assumptions, although there may be some autocorrelation between nearby sample squares.

10.4.2 Chalk weathering

10.4.2.1 Confidence interval based on t distribution

Several of the MINITAB commands which perform statistical tests, including ZTEST, TTEST and WTEST, have associated commands which produce confidence intervals. The TINTERVAL command, which produces confidence intervals based on the *t* distribution, will serve as an example. The general format of the command is

MTB > TINTERVAL K C5

	μ	N	W	P	Accept/ Reject H_0
Arable	0	19	179.0	0.001	Reject
Permanent Grass	0	18	16.0	0.003	Reject
Orchards & Mkt G.	0	20	6.0	0.000	Reject
Forestry & Woodland	0	19	20.0	0.003	Reject
Rough Grazing	0	18	30.0	0.017	Reject
Houses and Gardens	0	12	72.0	0.011	Reject
Agric. Unprod.	0	20	210.0	0.000	Reject

Sample WTEST Output from MINITAB

```
MTB > WTEST C32 – C38
TEST OF MEDIAN = 0.000000 VERSUS MEDIAN N.E. 0.000000
```

	N	N FOR TEST	WILCOXON STATISTIC	P-VALUE	ESTIMATED MEDIAN
AGRICHAN	20	19	179.0	0.001	8.000
MKGDCHAN	20	18	16.0	0.003	−3.000
GRASCHAN	20	20	6.0	0.000	−7.000

Box 10.3 Summary of W test results for LU3 for each land use in sample B in the 1930s to 1960s

where K is the percentage confidence interval required, for example 95 or 99, and C5 is the column containing the sample data. The output from the command includes the sample mean and standard deviation, the estimated standard error of the mean and two values within brackets which are the lower and upper confidence limits.

The sequence of MINITAB commands for examining the assertion CW1 and testing the hypothesis CW2 in the chalk weathering project is given in Table 10.6. The chalk weathering project, being based on laboratory experimentation with pure chalk blocks, does not have any empirically derived population parameters against which to test the sample data. CW1 investigates the reliability and usefulness of the sample data:

> In the absence of any population data, the sub-samples of chalk blocks produce the best estimate of the population mean with a defined measure of confidence.

Table 10.6 shows that manipulation of the chalk weathering data, using the COPY and USE command/subcommand sequence, is necessary before the t intervals can be calculated. Nine new columns (C22 to C30) are created containing the overall weight-loss figures after 14 days for treatments 1 to 9. The confidence intervals for these new columns are reported in Box 10.4. The width of the intervals at the 95 and 99 per cent levels suggest that the sub-samples are reasonably good estimators for the population. For example, in the case of treatment 1, the 95 per cent interval is 16.079 to 19.148 g and the 99 per cent is

Table 10.6 Application of *t* confidence interval and *t* test to chalk weathering project in MINITAB

```
MTB > OUTFILE 'chweat05'
MTB > RETRIEVE 'chweat03'
MTB > COPY C19 C22;
SUBC > USE C2 = 1.
MTB > COPY C19 C23;
SUBC > USE C2 = 2.
MTB > COPY C19 C24;
SUBC > USE C2 = 3.
MTB > COPY C19 C25;
SUBC > USE C2 = 4.
MTB > COPY C19 C26;
SUBC > USE C2 = 5.
MTB > COPY C19 C27;
SUBC > USE C2 = 6.
MTB > COPY C19 C28;
SUBC > USE C2 = 7.
MTB > COPY C19 C29;
SUBC > USE C2 = 8.
MTB > COPY C19 C30;
SUBC > USE C2 = 9.
MTB > TINTERVAL 95 C22 – C30
MTB > TINTERVAL 99 C22 – C30
MTB > TTEST C22 – C30
MTB > NOOUTFILE
MTB > SAVE 'chweat03'
MTB > STOP
```

Box 10.4 *t* confidence intervals (95 and 99 per cent) for CW1 in chalk weathering project (MINITAB output)

```
MTB > TINTERVAL 95 C22 – C30
             N      MEAN      STDEV     SE MEAN     95.0 PERCENT C.I.
Treat1      12    17.632      2.443      0.705     ( 16.079, 19.184)
Treat2      12    21.313      2.728      0.788     ( 19.579, 23.047)
Treat3      12     1.721      1.368      0.395     (  0.852,  2.590)
Treat4      12     5.600      1.475      0.426     (  4.663,  6.537)
Treat5      12     8.943      1.985      0.573     (  7.681, 10.204)
Treat6      12     1.192      0.664      0.192     (  0.771,  1.614)
Treat7      12     1.806      0.958      0.276     (  1.197,  2.414)
Treat8      12     1.244      0.483      0.139     (  0.937,  1.551)
Treat9      12     0.736      0.490      0.141     (  0.424,  1.047)
MTB > TINTERVAL 99 C22 – C30
             N      MEAN      STDEV     SE MEAN     99.0 PERCENT C.I.
Treat1      12    17.632      2.443      0.705     ( 15.441, 19.822)
Treat2      12    21.313      2.728      0.788     ( 18.867, 23.760)
Treat3      12     1.721      1.368      0.395     (  0.494,  2.947)
Treat4      12     5.600      1.475      0.426     (  4.278,  6.922)
Treat5      12     8.943      1.985      0.573     (  7.162, 10.723)
Treat6      12     1.192      0.664      0.192     (  0.597,  1.788)
Treat7      12     1.806      0.958      0.276     (  0.947,  2.665)
Treat8      12     1.244      0.483      0.139     (  0.811,  1.677)
Treat9      12     0.736      0.490      0.141     (  0.296,  1.175)
```

MTB > TTEST C22 – C30

TEST OF MU = 0.000 VS MU N.E. 0.000

	N	MEAN	STDEV	SE MEAN	T	P VALUE	ACCEPT/ REJECT H_0
Treat1	12	17.632	2.443	0.705	25.00	0.0000	Reject
Treat2	12	21.313	2.728	0.788	27.06	0.0000	Reject
Treat3	12	1.721	1.368	0.395	4.36	0.0011	Reject
Treat4	12	5.600	1.475	0.426	13.15	0.0000	Reject
Treat5	12	8.943	1.985	0.573	15.60	0.0000	Reject
Treat6	12	1.192	0.664	0.192	6.22	0.0001	Reject
Treat7	12	1.806	0.958	0.276	6.53	0.0000	Reject
Treat8	12	1.244	0.483	0.139	8.92	0.0000	Reject
Treat9	12	0.736	0.490	0.141	5.20	0.0003	Reject

Note: ACCEPT/REJECT H_0 has been added to MINITAB output.

Box 10.5 *t*-test results for CW2 in chalk weathering project (MINITAB Output)

15.441 to 19.822 g with a sample mean of 17.632 g. The low standard deviations for these columns also indicate a low level of dispersion.

10.4.2.2 t test

Assuming that the data satisfy the normality assumption, a series of *t* tests were carried out to examine whether the weight lost was significantly different from zero. Null hypothesis CW2 states that

> The apparent loss of weight by the chalk blocks in the different sub-samples has occurred through sampling error: the mean loss for each sub-sample is in fact zero.

A single TTEST command (see Table 10.6) referring to columns C22 to C30, but with the parameter μ omitted to signify that the hypothesised population mean is zero, performs the series of tests. The output from the command is of course the same as when used with the land-use project. The results for the nine treatments are brought together in Box 10.5. In all cases the null hypothesis is rejected given that the *P* values are extremely small in some cases too small to be shown as a precise figure. The greater *P* values are for the three control treatments (3, 5 and 9). These results confirm that loss of weight over the 14-day experimental period was significant for all treatments. Subsequent statistical analysis will examine whether the reductions for some treatments were more significant than for others.

10.4.3 River pollution

10.4.3.1 t test

The application of the *t* test to investigate null hypotheses RP1 and RP2 in the river pollution project also uses the MINITAB command TTEST (see Table 10.7). The first question is whether the differences between the concentrations of the chemicals in the sample and the 1985 river quality survey are significant. This issue is reflected in RP1, which states:

Table 10.7 Application of univariate tests (t test and paired t test) to river pollution project samples A and B in MINITAB

```
MTB > OUTFILE 'river05'
MTB > RETRIEVE 'rivera02'
MTB > COPY C3 C7 – C9 C15 – C18;
SUBC > USE C3 = 1.
MTB > COPY C3 C7 – C9 C19 – C22;
SUBC > USE C3 = 2.
MTB > COPY C3 C7 – C9 C23 – C26;
SUBC > USE C3 = 3.
MTB > COPY C3 C7 – C9 C27 – C30;
SUBC > USE C3 = 4.
MTB > COPY C3 C7 – C9 C31 – C34;
SUBC > USE C3 = 5.
MTB > TTEST 85 C16
MTB > TTEST 1.5 C17
MTB > TTEST 0.2 C18
MTB > TTEST 70 C20
MTB > TTEST 2.0 C21
MTB > TTEST 0.5 C22
MTB > TTEST 50 C24
MTB > TTEST 5.0 C25
MTB > TTEST 0.8 C26
MTB > TTEST 25 C28
MTB > TTEST 7.5 C29
MTB > TTEST 0.9 C30
MTB > TTEST 15 C32
MTB > TTEST 9.5 C33
MTB > TTEST 0.95 C34
MTB > SAVE 'rivera03'
MTB > RETRIEVE 'riverb02'
MTB > TABLE C3 C4;
SUBC > MEANS C9 – C11.
MTB > READ C30 – C35
DATA > 84.22 1.87 0.2314 79.60 1.95 0.2633
DATA > 73.92 3.87 0.6196 67.98 4.01 0.6562
DATA > 47.70 6.98 0.8342 28.10 6.25 0.8195
DATA > 15.56 12.90 0.8555 8.16 14.31 0.9280
DATA > 11.56 17.56 0.9879 4.46 18.15 0.9527
DATA > 87.42 1.62 0.2747 78.98 1.54 0.2409
DATA > 70.46 3.91 0.5861 60.54 4.08 0.6956
DATA > 46.70 7.23 0.8620 29.36 6.68 0.9472
DATA > 15.14 15.32 0.9142 7.10 12.20 0.9525
DATA > 8.96 16.66 0.9756 3.90 17.61 0.9303
DATA > 86.74 1.66 0.2324 80.38 1.72 0.2635
DATA > 70.48 4.11 0.5529 57.22 3.58 0.6497
DATA > 49.04 7.14 0.6911 30.90 5.75 0.6818
DATA > 16.10 13.70 0.8224 7.24 14.83 0.9420
DATA > 8.34 16.71 0.9235 4.56 17.28 0.9174
DATA > 85.72 1.55 0.2147 78.26 1.15 0.2387
DATA > 67.34 4.07 0.6568 50.32 4.05 0.6940
DATA > 43.92 6.37 0. 8591 31.52 6.57 0.9672
DATA > 15.82 15.34 0.8906 6.86 14.99 0.9111
DATA > 8.40 16.24 0.9281 5.24 18.22 0.9282
```

Table 10.7 *(continued)*

```
DATA > 83.96 1.67 0.2736 80.28 1.12 0.2420
DATA > 65.28 4.11 0.6648 53.04 4.10 0.7239
DATA > 44.20 6.51 0.8785 34.20 7.97 0.9031
DATA > 14.18 15.39 0.9427 8.06 14.04 0.9519
DATA > 6.52 17.47 0.9533 4.02 18.33 0.9253
DATA > END
MTB > READ C36 – C41
DATA > 85.16 1.65 0.2140 84.92 1.85 0.1451
DATA > 68.00 3.92 0.6977 66.72 3.73 0.7480
DATA > 50.72 6.45 0.8343 43.56 5.99 0.8197
DATA > 15.58 15.75 0.9441 14.52 13.46 0.8849
DATA > 7.24 16.87 0.9688 6.22 18.70 0.9626
DATA > END
MTB > LET C42 = C30 – C33
MTB > LET C43 = C31 – C34
MTB > LET C44 = C32 – C35
MTB > LET C45 = C36 – C39
MTB > LET C46 = C37 – C40
MTB > LET C47 = C38 – C41
MTB > TTEST C42 – C47
MTB > NOOUTFILE
MTB > SAVE 'riverb03'
MTB > STOP
```

The mean concentrations of the specific chemicals in the rivers differ from those reported in the national surveys only because of sampling error. They are not statistically significant.

Biochemical oxygen demand and ammonia are measured in milligrams per litre, and dissolved oxygen as a percentage. The mean values for the former are not reported precisely in the national survey report, but are shown as, for example, not greater than 1.5 mg/l for BOD in the case of class 1 rivers and not greater than 5 mg/l for class 3. As with the previous projects, some manipulation of the data in the worksheet for sample A is necessary before the *t* tests can be undertaken. The data columns containing the river-quality class and concentration figures for the three chemicals are copied across into five groups of new columns, C15 to C18, C19 to C22, C23 to C26, C27 to C30 and C31 to C34 (see Table 10.7). A series of TTEST commands are then carried out using suitable population means derived from the classification used in the 1985 survey (Department of the Environment 1987, 1992). For example, TTEST 85 C16 examines whether the sample mean for BOD in class 1 rivers was significantly different than the 85 per cent recorded for the population.

In general the results of the *t* tests (see Box 10.6) indicate that the null hypotheses should be rejected, since the *P* values associated with the test statistic are very low. Thus dissolved oxygen is significantly different from the population mean for the five quality classes. The only tests in which the null hypothesis should be accepted are water quality class 1 and BOD, and class 3 and ammonia, where the *P* values are

	Class	μ	s	$\bar{x}$	t	P	Accept/ Reject H_0
Dissolved Oxygen	1	85.0	2.78	84.15	2.15	0.036	Reject
	2	70.00	4.96	68.17	2.61	0.012	Reject
	3	50.00	4.56	48.17	2.37	0.022	Reject
	4	25.00	6.85	20.56	4.58	0.000	Reject
	5	15.00	3.16	8.75	13.98	0.000	Reject
Biochemical Oxygen Demand	1	1.50	0.74	1.52	0.18	0.860	Accept
	2	2.00	0.99	3.68	11.92	0.000	Reject
	3	5.00	1.43	7.41	11.95	0.000	Reject
	4	7.50	2.75	13.13	14.47	0.000	Reject
	5	9.50	0.32	15.29	16.66	0.000	Reject
Ammonia	1	0.20	0.09	0.15	3.81	0.000	Reject
	2	0.50	0.21	0.64	4.47	0.000	Reject
	3	0.80	0.21	0.79	0.25	0.810	Accept
	4	0.90	0.32	1.07	3.65	0.001	Reject
	5	0.95	0.44	1.43	7.07	0.000	Reject

Sample TTEST Output from MINITAB

```
MTB > TTEST 85 C16
TEST OF MU = 85.000 VS MU N.E. 85.000
            N      MEAN     STDEV    SE MEAN       T    P VALUE
DisOx1     50    84.154     2.780      0.393   -2.15    0.036
MTB > TTEST 1.5 C17
TEST OF MU = 1.500 VS MU N.E. 1.500
            N      MEAN     STDEV    SE MEAN       T    P VALUE
BOB1       50     1.519     0.738      0.104    0.18    0.86
MTB > TTEST 0.2 C18
TEST OF MU = 0.2000 VS MU N.E. 0.2000
            N      MEAN     STDEV    SE MEAN       T    P VALUE
NH41       50    0.1505    0.0918     0.0130   -3.81    0.0004
```

Box 10.6 Summary of t-test results for each chemical in river pollution project sample A

both greater than 0.80. The results suggest some improvement in river quality. The MINITAB output from the TTEST command includes a negative sign with the t-test statistic, if the sample mean is less than μ, the population mean, although this is contrary to the previously stated format of the test. The probabilities are given as proportions, although these can easily be converted into percentages.

10.4.3.2 Paired *t* test

MINITAB does not include a specific command to allow the investigator to carry out a single-sample paired t test. However, by storing the pairs of measurements in two columns, the differences can be calculated and placed in a new column, and the standard TTEST command can then be applied. Supposing that the paired measurements are held in C6 and C7, the following sequence of commands would generate the new column (C8) and carry out the paired t test:

```
MTB > LET C8 = C6 - C7
MTB > TTEST C8
```

The parameter μ is not provided, since the hypothesised mean of the differences is zero.

The second null hypothesis in the river pollution project is concerned with trying to detect any significant difference in the concentration of chemicals upstream and downstream of the factories in sample B. Even if the test results indicate a significant difference, the factories are not necessarily responsible, although they may contribute to any increase. Null hypothesis RP2 states that:

> The difference in the concentration of the chemicals upstream and downstream of the factories is more illusory than real, and does not indicate that discharged industrial waste from these plants is to blame for seemingly higher levels downstream.

The problem can be tackled with the paired t test, since the points on the rivers where the factories are located constitute the sampled items. The paired measurements comprise the mean upstream and downstream concentration of a particular chemical at each site. The variability or dispersion of the concentrations in each set of five upstream and downstream water samples was assessed by examining their means and standard deviations, and appears to be relatively minor. It is reasonable to take the mean of each set as the basis for testing the null hypothesis. In other words, the input to the test comprises 25 pairs of measurements for the factory sites, each of which comprises the upstream and downstream mean concentration. The water samples taken at the five control sites are tested in a similar way.

Some manipulation of the sample B data in the worksheet is required to restructure the information into a form suitable for the TTEST command. The following abbreviated extract from Table 10.7 shows the key points:

```
MTB > TABLE C3 C4;
SUBC > MEANS C9 - C11.
MTB > READ C30 - C35
DATA > 84.22 1.87 0.2314 79.60 1.95 0.2633
  ...
DATA > 6.52 17.47 0.9533 4.02 18.33 0.9253
DATA > END
MTB > READ C36 - C41
DATA > 85.16 1.65 0.2140 84.92 1.85 0.1451
  ...
DATA > 7.24 16.87 0.9688 6.22 18.70 0.9626
DATA > END
MTB > LET C42 = C30 - C33
MTB > LET C43 = C31 - C34
MTB > LET C44 = C32 - C35
```

```
MTB > LET C45 = C36 – C39
MTB > LET C46 = C37 – C40
MTB > LET C47 = C38 – C41
MTB > TTEST C42 – C47
```

MTB > TTEST C42 – C47

TEST OF MU = 0.000 VS MU N.E. 0.000

	N	MEAN	STDEV	SE MEAN	T	P VALUE	ACCEPT/ REJECT H_0
DisOxFac	25	−333.283	1711.214	342.243	−0.97	0.34	Accept
BODFac	25	−1.019	5.138	1.028	−0.99	0.33	Accept
NH4Fac	25	−0.286	1.310	0.262	−1.09	0.29	Accept
DisOxCtl	5	2.152	2.827	1.264	1.70	0.16	Accept
BODCtl	5	0.182	1.476	0.660	0.28	0.80	Accept
NH4Ctl	5	0.020	0.048	0.021	0.93	0.41	Accept

Note: ACCEPT/REJECT H_0 has been added to MINITAB output.

Box 10.7 Paired *t*-test results for each chemical in river pollution project sample B (MINITAB output)

The means of columns C9 to C11, which contain the data for the three chemicals used in the river-quality classification, are obtained by producing a contingency table of C3 and C4, in which the cell contents are the required values (see Section 7.3.2). The 25 pairs of mean values for each chemical for the sites with a factory are entered into six new columns with a READ command (C30 – C35), as are those for the five control sites into C36 – C41. C30 and C33 contain respectively the 25 upstream and downstream means for sites with factories for BOD, C31 and C34 the equivalent figures for dissolved oxygen, and C32 and C35 for ammonia. Unfortunately, MINITAB does not allow these means to be stored in columns automatically. A series of LET statements compute and store the differences in columns C42 to C47. Finally, *t* tests are carried out on these six columns by means of a single TTEST command.

The results of the paired *t* tests (Box 10.7) lead resoundingly to the conclusion that there is no significant difference in the concentration of the three chemicals upstream and downstream of the sample points, regardless of whether or not a factory was present. In most cases the *P* values associated with the *t* statistic for the sample are greater than 0.30. Clearly this result is somewhat disappointing, from the point of view of attributing water-quality deterioration to pollution from the factories. However, as with all tests where the null hypothesis is accepted, there remains a chance that an incorrect decision has been made.

10.4.4 Village communities

10.4.4.1 Pearson's chi-square test

SPSS-X includes a command, NPAR TESTS, which has a series of subcommands for performing various non-parametric tests. Some of the parametric tests which have been described can also be carried out in the software, but these are not relevant to the village communities project. The NPAR TESTS subcommand which carries out a one-sample Pearson's chi-square test is CHISQUARE, which tabulates an attribute into categories and calculates the Pearson's chi-square test statistic. The procedure automatically assigns equal expected frequency counts to all classes, unless this is adjusted by the EXPECTED subcommand. The general format of the command sequence is:

```
NPAR TESTS CHISQUARE = varlist(lo,hi)
  /EXPECTED = 6 7 3 4
```

The unique values for each variable specified on the variable list become categories in the corresponding contingency table, which implies that continuous variables or attributes with many integer values should be reclassified before carrying out the test. The specification of the lowest and highest value of a variable to be included in a test is optional. The numbers supplied on the EXPECTED subcommand determine the expected proportion of observations in each cell. In the example above, the software would sum the listed values, 6 + 7 + 3 + 4 = 20, and 6/20 (30 per cent) of observations would be expected in class 1, 7/20 (35 per cent) in class 2, and so on. Since the EXPECTED subcommand applies to all variables specified on the preceding variable list, multiple lists may be included on a single NPAR TESTS command. This facility is useful if the null hypothesis postulates inequality of counts among the classes. The output from the CHISQUARE subcommand includes the observed and expected frequencies, the χ^2 statistic, the degrees of freedom and, unlike MINITAB, the probability associated with the test statistic.

The log of the SPSS-X session to examine the first three null hypotheses in the village communities project is shown in Table 10.8. The first hypothesis compares the characteristics of the individuals forming the sample with the limited information about the population of individuals living in the village obtained from the Population Census. There are four comparable Census counts relating to housing tenure, the age structure, employment status and the availability of cars or vans. The null hypothesis has been expressed in a general form to cover these different variables and states:

> Any differences in the relative frequencies between the sample and its parent population in respect of the limited set of common attributes have occurred through sampling error and are not significant.

Once the system file for the village communities project has been loaded the χ^2 test is carried out, thus:

```
NPAR TESTS CHISQUARE = AGE(1,5)
  /EXPECTED = 21 18 36 15 10
```

The variable AGE contains a value from 1 to 5 representing the age group to which the respondent belonged. The numbers following the

Table 10.8 Application of univariate tests (Pearson's chi-square and Kolmogorov-Smirnov) to village communities project in SPSS-X

```
FILE HANDLE SF / NAME = 'VILLAG01.SF'
GET FILE = SF
NPAR TESTS CHISQUARE = AGE(1,5) /EXPECTED = 21 18 36 15 10
  /CHISQUARE = TENURE(1,6) /EXPECTED = 15 52 24 5 3 1
  /CHISQUARE = AVAILCAR(1,2) /EXPECTED = 81 19
  /CHISQUARE = ECONPOSN(1,7) /EXPECTED = 9 47 11 8 10 13 2
RECODE HSGTOFM (0 THRU 999 = 1)(1000 THRU 1999 = 2)(2000 THRU 2999 = 3)
  (3000 THRU 3999 = 4)(4000 THRU 4999 = 5)(5000 THRU 5999 = 6)
  (6000 THRU 6999 = 7) INTO RECDIST
NPAR TESTS K-S (POISSON) = RECDIST
SELECT IF (HEARPROP EQ 1)
COMPUTE CHANGATT = 0
IF (FAVPROP EQ 1 AND PROPMTNG EQ 1 AND MTGEFFCT EQ 1)CHANGATT = 1
IF (FAVPROP EQ 2 AND PROPMTNG EQ 1 AND MTGEFFCT EQ 1)CHANGATT = 2
IF (FAVPROP EQ 1 AND PROPMTNG EQ 1 AND MTGEFFCT EQ 2)CHANGATT = 3
IF (FAVPROP EQ 2 AND PROPMTNG EQ 1 AND MTGEFFCT EQ 2)CHANGATT = 4
NPAR TESTS CHISQUARE = CHANGATT(1,2)
SAVE OUTFILE = SF
FINISH
```

equals sign on the EXPECTED command are the percentage of the adult population found in each of the five age groups in the village's population. Thus the expected frequency for age group 1 is that 21 per cent of the sampled individuals will be aged 16–24 inclusive, 18 per cent will be in group 2 aged 25–44, and so on.

The results of the four tests (Box 10.8) report significant χ^2 values in three of the four tests, with χ^2 as high as 152.319 for age of respondent and a very low probability. The probabilities are generally very low, except in the case of car availability. The null hypothesis is rejected in favour of the alternative in the case of three of the variables. The tests suggest that the sample is in accord with the population overall as far as their access to private transport is concerned. On the other hand, it appears that the population is somewhat more elderly, and more likely to live in local authority or housing association accommodation than in the population as a whole. These characteristics should be taken into account when carrying out further analysis on the sample data.

10.4.4.2 Kolmogorov-Smirnov test

The Kolmogorov-Smirnov test is another non-parametric test which can be carried out by means of a subcommand on the NPAR TESTS command with the keyword K-S:

NPAR TESTS K-S (dis [parameters]) = varlist

where 'dis' represents the distribution which will be used to calculate expected frequencies (either UNIFORM, NORMAL or POISSON should be inserted). The optional population parameters vary according

Box 10.8 (*opposite*) Pearson's chi-square test results for VC1 in village communities project (SPSS-X output)

– – – – Chi-square Test
AGE Age of Respondent

	Category	Cases Observed	Expected	Residual
18–24 Years	1.00	19	75.18	−56.18
25–44 Years	2.00	51	64.44	−13.44
45–54 Years	3.00	105	128.88	−23.88
55–64 Years	4.00	99	53.70	45.30
65 Years and Over	5.00	84	35.80	48.20
	Total	358		

Chi-square	D.F.	Significance
152.319	4	.000

– – – – Chi-square Test
TENURE Housing Tenure

	Category	Cases Observed	Expected	Residual
Own Outright	1.00	42	53.70	−11.70
Own with Mortgage	2.00	208	186.16	21.84
Rent from LA or Hsg	3.00	52	85.92	−33.92
Rent Privately	4.00	32	17.90	14.10
Tied to Work	5.00	17	10.74	6.26
Other	6.00	7	3.58	3.42
	Total	358		

Chi-square	D.F.	Significance
36.525	5	.000

– – – – Chi-square Test
AVAILCAR Availability of Car

	Category	Cases Observed	Expected	Residual
Yes	1.00	289	289.98	−.98
No	2.00	69	68.02	.98
	Total	358		

Chi-square	D.F.	Significance
.017	1	.895

– – – – Chi-square Test
ECONPOSN Economic Position of Respondent

	Category	Cases Observed	Expected	Residual
Employer or Self-Emp	1.00	27	32.22	−5.22
Employee Full-time	2.00	156	168.26	−12.26
Employee Part-time	3.00	38	39.38	−1.38
Unemployed	4.00	17	28.64	−11.64
Housewife-husband	5.00	41	35.80	5.20
Retired	6.00	68	46.54	21.46
Other	7.00	11	7.16	3.84
	Total	358		

Chi-square	D.F.	Significance
19.228	6	.004

```
– – – Kolmogorov–Smirnov Goodness of Fit Test
RECDIST
Test distribution - Poisson        Mean: 2.1034
                  Cases: 358
                  Most extreme differences
Absolute          Positive          Negative          K-S Z          2-Tailed P
.14359            .14359            –.02972           2.717          .000
```

Box 10.9 Kolmogorov–Smirnov test result for VC2 in village communities project (SPSS-X output)

to the distribution: a single parameter is required for the Poisson, the mean, which becomes λ. If omitted, the sample mean is used. The output from the test presents the most extreme differences, the D test statistic (converted into Z) and its associated probability.

The second null hypothesis in the village communities project, VC2, refers to the geographical distribution of respondents in relation to the location of the proposed development. If the respondents were not randomly distributed throughout the village, then a locational bias might have crept into the data. The null hypothesis simply states that

> The households are distributed randomly with respect to distance from the site of the proposed development.

The Kolmogorov–Smirnov test using the Poisson distribution helps to answer this question. The HSGTOFM variable measuring the households' distance from Cowper's Farm is regrouped into a new variable, RECDIST, with 1000 m class interval, and the following NPAR TESTS command is given (see Table 10.8):

```
RECODE HSGTOFM (0 THRU 999 = 1)(1000 THRU 1999 = 2) ...
  (6000 THRU 6999 = 7) INTO RECDIST
NPAR TESTS K-S POISSON = RECDIST
```

The mean parameter is omitted and thus the sample mean is used to calculate the Poisson probabilities and expected frequencies. The test result, which is converted into Kolmogorov–Smirnov Z, shows a low probability of obtaining the maximum difference between the cumulative expected and observed frequency distributions by chance (see Box 10.9). The null hypothesis is therefore rejected.

10.4.4.3 Pearson's chi-square

The third null hypothesis in the village communities project is concerned with paired frequency counts and can be examined with Pearson's chi-square test. VC3 states that:

> A public meeting to explain details of the proposed development has no effect on people's attitude. The apparent differences of opinion are not statistically significant.

Individuals who knew about the proposed development and who attended the public meeting were asked whether their attitude changed afterwards: in other words, there are paired frequencies for a subset of cases. Individual respondents may fall into one of four categories, reflecting whether they retained their opinions or changed their minds about the development after attending the meeting. The test focuses on the latter subset of individuals: people who were against the development but became in favour and those who were initially for and then became against. The null hypothesis asserts that the number of people who changed their opinion is distributed equally between these two groups. Supposing 160 people changed their view, then the null hypothesis assumes that 80 are in the 'for'/'against' and 80 in the 'against'/'for' categories. If the test statistic is significant, then the implication is that the meeting was successful in influencing people's attitude.

Some data manipulation in SPSS-X is required before the test can be carried out to select those individuals in the complete sample who knew about the proposal and whose attendance at the meeting resulted in a change of attitude. Table 10.8 includes the following sequence of commands for this purpose:

```
SELECT IF (HEARPROP EQ 1)
COMPUTE CHANGATT = 0
IF (FAVPROP EQ 1 AND PROPMTNG EQ 1 AND MTGEFFCT
   EQ 1) CHANGATT = 1
IF (FAVPROP EQ 2 AND PROPMTNG EQ 1 AND MTGEFFCT
   EQ 1) CHANGATT = 2
IF (FAVPROP EQ 1 AND PROPMTNG EQ 1 AND MTGEFFCT
   EQ 2) CHANGATT = 3
IF (FAVPROP EQ 2 AND PROPMTNG EQ 1 AND MTGEFFCT
   EQ 2) CHANGATT = 4
NPAR TESTS CHISQUARE = CHANGATT(1,2)
```

The variables FAVPROP, PROPMTNG and MTGEFFCT identify the respondents' present attitude to the proposal, whether or not they went to the meeting and if the meeting led to a change of mind. The COMPUTE command creates a new variable signifying a change of attitude, CHANGATT, set to an initial value of 0, which may be reset to 1, 2, 3 or 4. The CHISQUARE subcommand on NPAR TESTS carries out the test on the new variable CHANGATT, with the range (1,2) limiting the analysis to the respondents who changed their views. The omission of the EXPECTED subcommand indicates that the cases will be split equally between the two classes. The results of the test (Box 10.10) suggest that the meeting had little effect on people's attitude to the proposed development. The small χ^2 value (2.13) has a high probability given only one degree of freedom. Thus the null hypothesis should be accepted on the basis of the sample evidence.

```
--- Chi-square Test
CHANGATT
                  Cases
   Category      Observed     Expected     Residual
     1.00            8          11.50        -3.50
     2.00           15          11.50         3.50
     Total          23
       Chi-square              D.F.              Significance
         2.130                  1                    .144
```

Box 10.10 Pearson's chi-square test result for VC3 in village communities project (SPSS-X output)

Table 10.9 Comparison of software commands for performing single-sample univariate tests

	MINITAB	SPSS-X
Unpaired sample		
Z test	ZTEST μ σ C... C	Not available
t test	TTEST μ C... C	T-TEST
Z/*t* confidence intervals	ZINTERVAL 95 σ C... C TINTERVAL 95 C...C	Not available
χ^2	TABLE C...C; CHISQUARE.	NPAR TESTS CHISQUARE = /EXPECTED =
D test	Not available	NPAR TESTS K-S (dis(parameters)) =
Paired sample		
Paired *t* test	TTEST C...C	T-TEST PAIRS =
W test	WTEST C...C	NPAR TESTS WILCOXON =
χ^2	TABLE C...C; CHISQUARE.	NPAR TESTS CHISQUARE = /EXPECTED =

10.5 REVIEW OF SOFTWARE COMMANDS

There are a number of similarities and contrasts between the commands in MINITAB and SPSS-X for carrying out single-sample univariate tests. Table 10.9 summarises the syntax of the software commands which carry out univariate tests, including commands which have not been discussed in the previous sections because they were inappropriate for the project data. The table does not include any additional data manipulation that may be necessary, since this will be specific to each application. Allowing for differences in syntax, there are clear similarities in the key command words used in the two packages. The probability associated with the calculated test statistic is usually provided in SPSS-X, which facilitates taking a decision about the null hypothesis in relation to the chosen significance level. Some MINITAB commands do not do this (for example, TABLE with the CHISQUARE subcommand), and reference to published statistical tables, such as those in Appendix IV, may be necessary.

Chapter 11
Inferential statistics: univariate tests for two or more samples

11.1 CHARACTERISTICS OF TESTS OF TWO OR MORE SAMPLES

Researchers are often interested in finding out if two or more populations differ from each other in some statistically significant way. As in the case of examining a single population, the difference is quantified with reference to key summary statistics, in particular the mean, variance and standard deviation, and absolute or relative frequency distributions. Do cliffs composed of chalk erode more easily than sandstone? Do farmers in upland regions have lower incomes than those in lowland areas? Is grain size more variable on the windward or leeward side of sand dunes? Do commuters travelling to work over the same distance by public or private transport suffer longer delays? Such questions can generally not be answered by investigating the population as a whole, which, as we have seen, may be too large, inaccessible or indeterminate.

Samples taken from each population estimate the population parameters and quantify any differences, and similarly sample frequency distributions emulate those for the population. The problem is to decide how much significance to attach to any observed difference. Suppose, in the chalk and sandstone cliff question, that a research project is undertaken lasting several years. Two random samples, one of chalk and the other of sandstone cliffs, are selected and regular recordings are taken to measure the rate at which the cliffs are receding. The researchers assemble all the data in their laboratory and analyse the results, discovering that the mean rate of erosion for the chalk sample is 5.34 cm per annum and for the sandstone 4.12 cm per annum. Is the difference due to chance or is it indicative of a genuine difference between the two populations? If the difference is small then the samples may in fact be regarded as having come from identical populations as far as the erosion variable is concerned. But how small is small? Perhaps the researchers consider that the means of the two samples are very similar, and therefore are likely to have come from the same population, but what about the dispersion or variability of the values for this variable?

The problem is to decide, on the basis of sample evidence, whether the two or more populations are in fact genuinely distinct and different. The apparent difference may be illusory and what were initially hypothesised as separate populations are in fact the same. The procedure for trying to unravel this question when dealing with a continuous variable is to look at the means and variances or standard deviations of the two samples. Figure 11.1 illustrates in general terms the possible combinations of similarity and dissimilarity in mean and variance between two normally distributed samples in respect of the continuous variable X. The same principles apply in the case of three or more samples ($k \geqslant 3$). Two samples with similar or identical means and variances (Figure 11.1(a)) are more likely to come from the same population rather than two distinct ones. On the other hand, even if the means are identical, but the variances are widely contrasted (Figure 11.1(b)), then the populations may well be distinct. When the sample means are clearly different, regardless of whether their variances are alike (Figures 11.1(c) and 11.1(d)), it is reasonably certain that they have come from separate populations. Thus the most important difference is between sample means, but it may only be significant when the sample variances are also taken into account.

In some research investigations two or more samples are taken from the same population. The most obvious examples occur when change over time or space is examined, and separate, but similarly selected,

Figure 11.1 Effect of similarity and dissimilarity of mean and variance in two samples

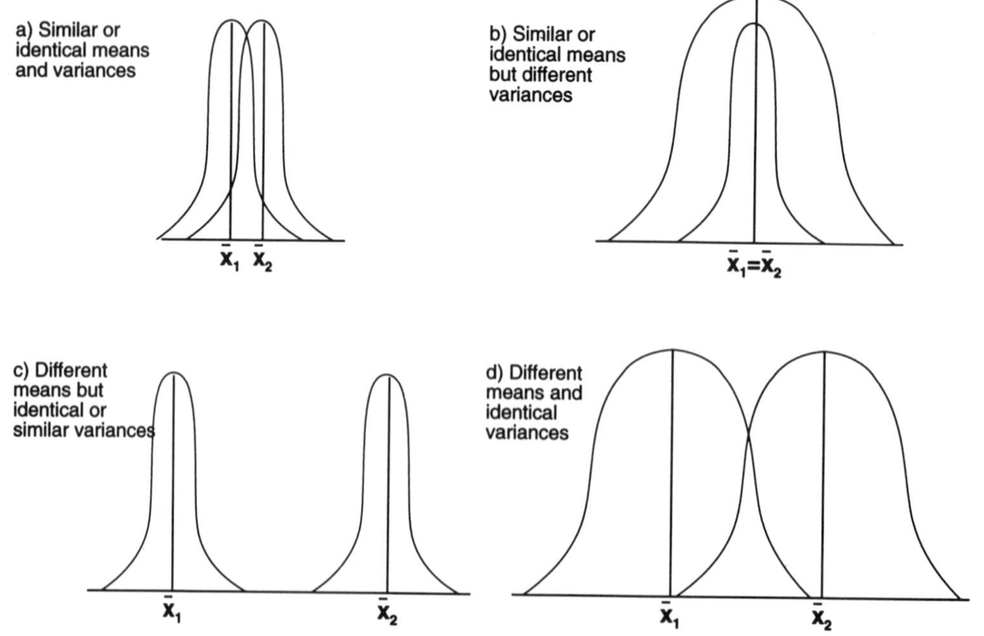

samples are drawn on different occasions. The partitioning of time and space into supposedly discrete and distinct units, such as years and weeks, countries and settlements, is largely the result of social or cultural processes rather than natural ones. Again the means and variances of the samples may be different and the problem is to establish the significance of these differences. If found to be statistically significant, the implication is that the population has genuinely changed between one time period and another, or is truly different between one area and another, in respect of the variable under study.

Not all investigations involving two or more samples deal with a continuous variable: sometimes the differences relate to the absolute or relative frequency distribution of an attribute. Is the distribution of housing tenure in Scotland different than that in England? Is the occurrence of plant species more diverse on north- or south-facing slopes? Suppose, with reference to the housing tenure question in Scotland and England, that two random samples of households are selected. The number of observations in the samples is in proportion to the total number of households in each country. The two groups of households are interviewed and households are placed into one of four categories, based on their housing tenure (owner occupier, local authority or housing association, private rented furnished, or private rented unfurnished). It is possible that not only will the number of households allocated to each cell of the contingency table be different in the two samples, but also the percentage or proportion. Are these differences such as to warrant the conclusion that the two countries have dissimilar systems of housing tenure?

The distinction within analytical techniques for two or more samples between those concerned with examining differences in descriptive or summary measures (mean and variance) and those focusing on frequency distributions reiterates the parametric and non-parametric division of statistical tests. The parametric tests considered here are the *F* test, the two-sample t test and oneway analysis of variance (Section 11.2). The non-parametric tests are Pearson's chi-square test, the Mann–Whitney *U* test and the Kruskell–Wallis *H* test (Section 11.3).

11.2 PARAMETRIC TESTS

11.2.1 *F* test

The *F* test examines the difference between two sample variances in order to determine whether their population variances can be regarded as equal. The test for equality of variance in the populations is a necessary precursor for undertaking a two-sample *t* test, which is described in the next subsection. The latter test exists in two slightly different forms and the choice of which to use depends on whether the variances of the sampled populations are assumed to be equal. The statistical problem tackled by the *F* test is whether a disparity between the two sample variances has arisen through chance or a difference in the variances of the parent populations. The F test itself indicates nothing about the means of the populations or samples.

The F test is based on the ratio between the variances of two samples. However, in order to understand how the test works, we need to start by considering two normal populations of infinite size, designated A and B, from which two samples have been taken. Suppose the means and variances for a particular variable in these populations are equal, in other words, as far as these parameters are concerned, the populations are statistically identical. Since σ_A^2 equals σ_B^2, the ratio between them necessarily equals 1. Even in the unlikely event that the two 'real-world' populations were precisely normal and infinite in size, research into their characteristics would usually be based on two random samples rather than the populations themselves. The sample variances, s_A^2 and s_B^2, may well be unequal and thus the ratio of the larger to the smaller will be greater than 1. This ratio is known as F.

Each sample is composed of items which have been randomly selected from their population and if the process of selecting the samples was repeated a second time, some items might be measured on both occasions, whereas others would not. Consequently, the second set of variances, s_1^2 and s_2^2, and the resultant F ratio may be different. The process of selecting pairs of samples from the two populations could be continued indefinitely and the F ratio values thus obtained could be plotted as a frequency distribution, known as the F distribution.

A further complication is that the two samples need not contain the same number of items. In theory, they can consist of any combination ranging from 2 items selected from population A and an infinite number from population B, to an infinite number from population A and 2 items from population B. In practical terms it would, of course, be impossible to select an infinite number of items from either population. Each combination of sample sizes would produce a different and distinctively shaped frequency distribution of F ratios (see Figure 11.2). All F distributions are asymmetrical, with their tails stretched out to the

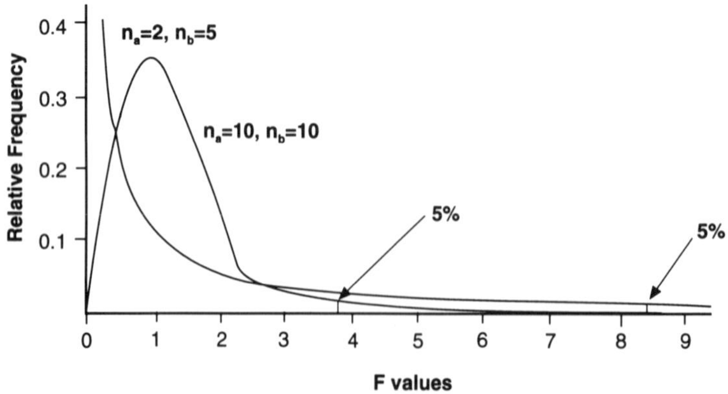

Figure 11.2 Effect of sample size combinations on the shape of the F distribution

right, indicating that large F values will occur relatively less often than smaller ones.

The implication, if s_A^2/s_B^2 does equal 1, is that sampling error is absent. When the ratio is calculated as a test statistic, the probability of obtaining the value of F through chance has to be assessed. If the probability of obtaining the calculated F value (or one greater) is equal to or less than the chosen level of significance, given the number of items in each sample, then sampling error cannot reasonably be blamed for the difference in sample variances. Conversely, if the probability is greater than the significance level, chance alone may be responsible. The table showing the F distributions (see Appendix IV, Table 6) is usually simplified, since the possible combinations of sample sizes are in theory infinite, and each value of F has a different probability for every combination. Larger differences between the sample variances produce greater F values, but the probability of a large F occurring is low.

In Chapter 5 the presence of the two largest farms in the Yorkshire sample was shown to have had the effect of inflating the mean. Suppose that the area of the two farms might have been recorded incorrectly in the survey and they are omitted from the analysis. It is important to find out whether there is a significant difference between the Yorkshire (minus the two suspect farms) and Lancashire samples. The variances for the smaller Yorkshire and the Lancashire samples are respectively 41 938.5 and 24 410.4. The null hypothesis states that the difference in variances has arisen purely through chance and is not significant at the 0.05 level: the sample data really indicate that the populations of Yorkshire and Lancashire farms have the same variance. Dividing the larger sample variance by the smaller

$$F = \frac{41\,938.5}{24\,410.4} = 1.72$$

produces an F test statistic of 1.72. The degrees of freedom for each sample are

$$\text{df} = n - 1$$

which amounts to 49 for the Yorkshire sample and 51 for the Lancashire one. A one-tailed test, which would entail halving the probability, cannot be justified in this instance. The simplified table for the F distributions only shows selected degrees of freedom, and the combination of 49 degrees of freedom for the numerator (larger variance sample, n_l) and 51 for the denominator (smaller variance sample, n_s) is not included. Thus some approximation and interpolation is required. The F value at 0.05 significance level with 50 degrees of freedom for the numerator and 60 for the denominator is 1.70, which increases to 1.83 when the denominator's degrees of freedom are reduced to 40. The test statistic, 1.72 lies in between these values, making it difficult to determine whether the null hypothesis should be rejected. Erring on the side of caution, its acceptance appears sensible, and the sample evidence therefore suggests that the two populations probably have identical variances and that the difference has occurred through sampling error.

The procedure and calculations for the F test are therefore relatively straightforward:

1. State null hypothesis and significance level.
2. Calculate the test statistic F, the larger sample variance divided by the smaller.
3. Decide whether a one- or two-tailed test is appropriate.
4. Determine the probability of obtaining the observed F value, or one greater, through chance.
5. Decide whether to accept or reject the null hypothesis.

There are three important assumptions or limitations associated with the F test:

1. The items in each sample must be randomly and independently selected from their respective populations. Sampling with replacement should be employed, allowing an item to occur more than once in the same sample, or else the populations should be of infinite size.
2. The items in the populations and the samples should be independent of each other in respect of the variable X which is being measured.
3. The populations from which the sampled items are selected are assumed to be normally distributed in respect of the variable X. Failure of one of the populations to comply with this assumption can seriously bias the results of the test, since very large and very small variances tend to occur more often if even slight skewness is present. Earlier analysis of the Yorkshire and Lancashire samples of farms has shown them to be somewhat skewed, which may well have distorted the results of the F test.

11.2.2 Two-sample *t* test

The two-sample t test is one of the most widely used statistical tests since it assesses the significance of the difference between two sample means. The theoretical starting point for the two-sample t test is similar to the F test, namely two populations of infinite size, here designated with subscripts 1 and 2. The population means (μ_1 and μ_2) and variances (σ_1 and σ_2) are known. Suppose a series of random samples is taken from population 1 each with n_1 items and a similar series is selected from population 2 with n_2 items. The difference between the means of each pair of samples is calculated ($\bar{x}_1 - \bar{x}_2$). The process of sampling from populations 1 and 2, and then calculating the difference in sample means, is repeated indefinitely.

The series of differences can be plotted as a frequency distribution, known as the *sampling distribution of the difference in means*. Summary statistics for the differences themselves can be calculated. The principle is similar to obtaining the grand mean for a series of samples drawn from a single population (see Chapter 10). In the present case, the mean of the differences between the pairs of samples equals the difference between the population means ($\mu_1 - \mu_2$). The standard error of the difference can be calculated using two alternative formulae:

$$\text{Standard error of the difference } (\sigma_{1.2}) = \sigma^2_{\bar{x}_1} + \sigma^2_{\bar{x}_2}$$

or

$$\text{Standard error of the difference } (\sigma_{1.2}) = \sqrt{\frac{\sigma_1^2}{n_1} + \frac{\sigma_2^2}{n_2}}$$

where $\sigma^2_{\bar{x}_1}$ and $\sigma^2_{\bar{x}_2}$ are the variances of the sampling distribution of the means for populations 1 and 2, respectively. In the second formula the population variances are divided by their respective sample sizes. The mean and the standard error of the difference can be calculated irrespective of the form of the distributions of X values in the two populations. These quantities do not vary with differences in the characteristics of the frequency distributions of the parent populations, which are not required to be normally distributed. However, whether the sampling distribution of the difference in means is normal is important with respect to statistical testing.

Two related factors help to determine whether or not the sampling distribution of the differences in means is normal: first, the form of the parent population distributions; and second, the number of items in the samples. The form of the distribution will be normal if the samples contain a finite number of items and their populations are normal. The same result will also occur if the samples contain an infinite number of items regardless of the distribution of the population. When the sampling distribution of the difference in means is normal the central limit theorem can be applied and the test statistic Z, with null hypothesis $\mu_1 = \mu_2$, can be calculated thus:

$$Z = \frac{|(\bar{x}_1 - \bar{x}_2) - (\mu_1 - \mu_2)|}{\sqrt{\frac{\sigma_1^2}{n_1} + \frac{\sigma_2^2}{n_2}}}$$

In these circumstances the difference in population means is zero ($\mu_1 - \mu_2 = 0$) and Z is distributed normally. The probability of having obtained the calculated value of Z value or one greater through chance sampling may be determined from the Z table in Appendix IV.

The usefulness of the single-sample Z test is hampered by the general lack of availability of the population variance (see above). The likelihood of knowing the variances for *two* populations is even more remote. Furthermore two populations are unlikely to be precisely normal and the samples will contain a finite number of observations. Provided that the sample sizes are sufficiently large, then an estimate of $Z(\hat{Z})$ can be calculated by substituting the sample variances (s_1^2 and s_2^2) in the previous formula for the standard error of the difference.

The problem is how to know what are 'sufficiently large' samples in these situations. The way out of this difficulty is to turn to the t distribution, which, although not so powerful as Z, is slightly less demanding in its data requirements. The statistic t may be calculated thus:

$$t = \frac{|\bar{x}_1 - \bar{x}_2|}{\sqrt{\dfrac{s_1^2}{n_1} + \dfrac{s_2^2}{n_2}}}$$

irrespective of sample size, provided that the populations are normally distributed. The numerator yields the absolute difference between the sample means and the denominator represents the standard error of the difference. The degrees of freedom are given by

$$\text{df} = (n_1 - 1) + (n_2 - 1)$$

The form of the two-sample t test varies slightly depending on whether the population variances are believed to be equal or not. If the variances of the parent populations are either known, or assumed on the basis of an F test, to be equal, the estimated standard error of the difference in means is given by the formula

$$s_{\bar{x}_1 - \bar{x}_2} = \sqrt{\frac{n_1 s_1^2 + n_2 s_2^2}{n_1 + n_2 - 2}} \sqrt{\frac{n_1 + n_2}{n_1 n_2}}$$

The first part of this formula calculates the 'pooled' or combined estimate of the variance, but relies on the sample variances being reasonably similar. If the population variances are known or believed to be different, then the formula for the standard error of the difference given previously should be employed.

The F test described in Section 11.2.1 for the Yorkshire and the Lancashire samples suggested that the difference between their variances was not statistically significant. Thus the second method for calculating the two-sample t-test statistic should be used. The null hypothesis states that the difference in sample means has occurred entirely through sampling error and is not statistically significant: the population means are hypothesised to be identical. Substituting the appropriate figures into the formula gives

$$t = \frac{|(\bar{x}_1 - \bar{x}_2)|}{\sqrt{\dfrac{n_1 s_1^2 + n_2 s_2^2}{n_1 + n_2 - 2}} \sqrt{\dfrac{n_1 + n_2}{n_1 n_2}}}$$

$$= \frac{|134.6 - 173.6|}{\sqrt{\dfrac{49 \times 41\,938.5 + 51 \times 24\,410.4}{49 + 51 - 2}} \sqrt{\dfrac{49 + 51}{49 \times 51}}}$$

$$= \sqrt{\frac{(3\,299\,916.9}{98}} \sqrt{\frac{100}{2499}}$$

$$= 183.501 \times 0.200\,04$$
$$= 36.7$$

with degrees of freedom

$$\text{df} = (52 - 1) + (50 - 1) = 100$$

Referring to the t-distribution table (Appendix IV, Table 2), the probability of having obtained the calculated t value or one greater through chance sampling error is higher than 0.2. So more often than 20 times in 100 the difference between the sample means will occur through random sampling error. The difference in sample means, although substantial (39.0 ha), is not significant at the 0.05 level. The null hypothesis is therefore accepted. The t-confidence interval (see Section 10.2.3) for the difference in sample means is between −57.5 and 135.5 ha in this case at the 95 per cent level.

The procedure and calculations for the two-sample t test are a little more complicated than for some tests, since two distinct forms of the test exist depending on whether there is equality of the population variances:

1. State null hypothesis and significance level.
2. Calculate the test statistic F.
3. Decide which form of the test is required and select the appropriate formula to calculate t.
4. Decide whether a one- or two-tailed test is appropriate.
5. Look up the probability of obtaining the calculated t value, or one greater, through chance.
6. Decide whether to accept or reject the null hypothesis.

The two-sample t test has certain limitations in its application. Four main points should be considered:

1. Random sampling should be employed when selecting items for both samples, and the observations should not be paired. The usual stricture regarding sampling with and without replacement applies, with the latter only permitted for infinite populations.
2. There should not be any positive or negative autocorrelation between the values of the items within each of the two populations.
3. The two populations are assumed to be normally distributed.
4. The homogeneity (similarity) of the variances of the populations has been assessed by means of an F test or is known.

A review of the Yorkshire farms example reveals that some of these assumptions may not have been rigidly applied. Sampling was random, but without replacement. This is unlikely to cause difficulties, given that sampling fraction from the finite population is relatively small. There is perhaps some possibility of positive autocorrelation in the population, with similarly sized farms clustered together. Previous analysis of the farm data has shown that the samples are skewed to the right with a preponderance of small farms, which perhaps suggests that their parent populations are not exactly normal. Statisticians have demonstrated that the t test is fairly robust even if the assumption of normality is not satisfied, although unequal samples sizes can also distort the picture. The investigator should be more concerned about the data failing to conform to the assumptions of a test if its application results in the null hypothesis being rejected. In this instance H_0 is accepted and the side of caution has been followed.

11.2.3 Oneway analysis of variance

One some occasions more than two samples need to be compared, which can be achieved by an important and very useful technique known as *analysis of variance* (frequently abbreviated to ANOVA). The technique forms the basis for a number of quite complex types of analysis involving not only several samples, but also a number of variables measured on the interval or ratio scales. A useful introduction to the technique is provided by considering the situation in which a single variable is measured for the items in three or more samples, known as *oneway ANOVA*. Analysis of variance does not indicate whether one sample is 'more different' than the others, the result of the test applies equally to all samples. The procedure addresses the simpler question of whether or not it is likely that the samples have come from the same population. A typical null hypothesis for ANOVA would state that there is no difference between the k sample/group means: $\bar{x}_1 = \bar{x}_2 = \bar{x}_3 \ldots \bar{x}_k$. The alternative hypothesis asserts that this is untrue and, by implication, that the samples are different from the populations.

Oneway ANOVA requires that the items in the samples are measured in respect of a single variable, which is defined identically in each case. Rather than focusing directly on the means themselves, the technique works by breaking down the total variance of all the items in the samples into the within- and between-groups components. These represent the variance within each group and the variance between the groups about the grand mean. The test statistic, the F ratio, is obtained as follows:

$$F = \frac{\text{Between-groups variance}}{\text{Within-groups variance}}$$

When the between-groups variance is large in relation to the within-groups variance then a high F value will result, which indicates that most of the total variance is contributed by inter-group differences (see Figure 11.3(a)). Conversely a smaller difference between the two components of the total variance produces a lower F ratio, which suggests substantial overlap among the groups (see Figure 11.3(b)).

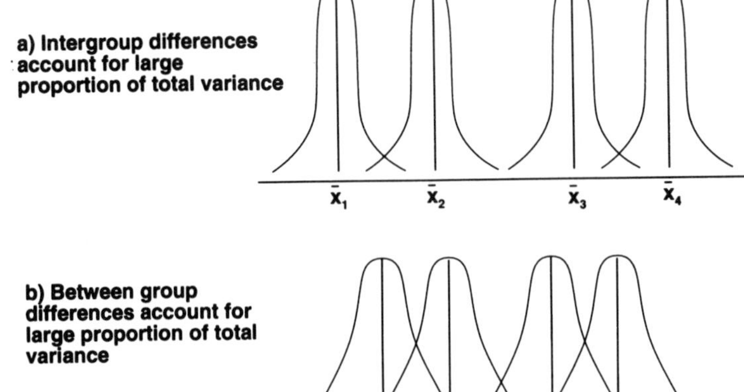

a) Intergroup differences account for large proportion of total variance
$\bar{x}_1$ $\bar{x}_2$ $\bar{x}_3$ $\bar{x}_4$
b) Between group differences account for large proportion of total variance
$\bar{x}_1$ $\bar{x}_2$ $\bar{x}_3$ $\bar{x}_4$

Figure 11.3 Variation in within- and between-groups (samples) variance (Reproduced from Shaw and Wheeler, 1985, by permission of David Fulton Publishers)

In general terms the variance of a set of numbers can be defined as the sum of the squared deviations of those numbers about their mean divided by $n-1$ (the degrees of freedom). This principle forms the basis for calculating the within- and between-groups variances (respectively s_{w}^2 and s_{b}^2), which are required for calculating the F statistic. The within-groups variance is found by first summing the squared deviations of the observations in each sample from their respective means, adding these sums together and then dividing the result by the appropriate degrees of freedom, which is the total number of observations minus the number of samples or groups $(n - k)$. This may be expressed by the following formula:

$$s_{\mathrm{w}}^2 = \frac{\sum\sum(X_{ij} - \bar{x}_j)^2}{n - k}$$

where the subscripts i and j refer respectively to the individual items in each sample and to the separate samples. The between-groups variance, s_{b}^2, is obtained by summing the squared deviations of each sample mean $(\bar{x}_1, \ldots, \bar{x}_{\mathrm{j}})$ from the mean of all observations $(\bar{x}_{\mathrm{t}})$ and dividing the result by the number of samples minus 1 $(k - 1)$, where k is the number of samples.

$$s_{\mathrm{b}}^2 = \frac{\sum n_j(\bar{x}_j - \bar{x}_{\mathrm{t}})^2}{k - 1}$$

This denominator represents the degrees of freedom, which can here be thought of as the number of sample means which are free to vary given the known value of the grand mean.

The summation of the numerators of the these two equations $(\sum\sum(X_{ij} - \bar{x}_j)^2 + \sum n_j(\bar{x}_j - \bar{x}_{\mathrm{t}})^2)$ produces a quantity known as the *total sum of squares*, but the within- and between-groups variances cannot be added to produce the total variance. The test statistic F may formally be defined as

$$F = \frac{s_b^2}{s_w^2}$$

The calculated value of F is now compared with the tabulated F distributions (Appendix IV, Table 6) with the df for the larger variance denoted as n_l and for the smaller as n_s. Failure correctly to assign the appropriate degrees of freedom to greater and lesser variances might result in an incorrect decision on the null hypothesis. If the calculated F statistic is equal to or greater than the critical value in the table at the chosen level of significance, the null hypothesis is rejected and the alternative hypothesis is necessarily accepted.

The two-sample t test has already shown that there is no significant difference between the mean area of farms in the Yorkshire and Lancashire samples. Suppose two further random sample surveys of farms were carried out in Norfolk and Surrey. The two-sample t test is no longer appropriate for examining any statistically significant difference in mean farm size between English counties, since there are now four samples. Oneway analysis of variance is a suitable substitute. The null hypothesis claims that any difference which has arisen in mean farm size in the four samples is the result of chance or sampling error: the four samples are in fact from one single population of farms in the four counties. The alternative hypothesis maintains that the differences were significant at the specified level (0.05) and that there is regional variation in farm size.

Previous calculation of the variances of the Yorkshire (excluding the two suspect farms) and Lancashire samples has supplied their contribution to the total within-group sum of squares, which are repeated under the columns headed $\sum(x_Y - \bar{x}_Y)$ and $\sum(x_L - \bar{x}_L)$ in Table 11.1. The subscripts Y and L denote the Yorkshire and Lancashire samples, respectively. The sums of squares and other necessary calculations for applying analysis of variance for these two counties, together with those for Norfolk (N) and Surrey (S), are also given in Table 11.1. In the interests of brevity only a small number of the squared deviations are shown for each sample. The within-groups variance equals 11 101.9. The between-groups variance is calculated as 82 046.2. The division of the latter by the former produces the F statistic (7.39). The degrees of freedom for the larger variance are 3 and for the smaller 202. In the table showing the F distributions (Appendix IV), the corresponding critical value of F is 3.12 at the 0.05 level of significance with degrees of freedom equal to 3 and infinity (∞). The null hypothesis can confidently be rejected at this as well as at more stringent levels of significance, since the F-test statistic is larger than the tabulated value.

The test thus provides statistical support for the conclusion that the difference in the mean area of farms across the four counties is significant. Figure 11.4 presents scattergrams of the four samples with a common X axis (in hectares), which illustrates the separation of the items between the counties. The distribution of mean farm size tends

Table 11.1 Calculations for analysis of variance on samples of farms in four English counties

	Lancashire		Norfolk		Surrey		Yorkshire	
Within-group calculations								
	x_L	$\sum(x_L - \bar{x}_L)^2$	x_N	$\sum(x_N - \bar{x}_N)^2$	x_S	$\sum(x_S - \bar{x}_S)^2$	x_Y	$\sum(x_Y - \bar{x}_Y)^2$
1	203.2	876.2	167.9	449.4	145.6	210.3	45.6	7921.0
2	140.0	1129.0	275.2	7413.2	153.0	50.4	456.8	103812.8
.	.	.	.	.	.	.	.	.
.	.	.	.	.	.	.	.	.
.	.	.	.	.	.	.	.	.
52	175.8	4.8	101.6	7656.3	202.3	1780.8	202.5	4610.4
Sum	9026.0	1269340.8	9834.6	675621.4	8322.7	87944.3	6370.0	209692.5
$\bar{x}_j$	173.6		189.1		160.1		134.6	

$$s_w^2 = \frac{1\,269\,340.8 + 675\,621.4 + 8944.3 + 209\,692.5}{206 - 4} = 11\,101.9$$

Between-group calculations

	Lancashire	Norfolk	Surrey	Yorkshire
$\bar{x}_j$	173.6	189.1	160.1	134.6
n_j	52	52	52	50
$\bar{x}_t = 166.3$				
$n_j(\bar{x}_j - \bar{x}_t)^2 =$	2771.1	27031.7	1998.9	50244.5

$$s_b^2 = \frac{2771.1 + 27\,031.7 + 1998.9 + 50\,244.5}{4 - 1} = 82\,046.2$$

$$F = \frac{s_b^2}{s_w^2} = \frac{82\,046.2}{11\,101.9} = 7.39$$

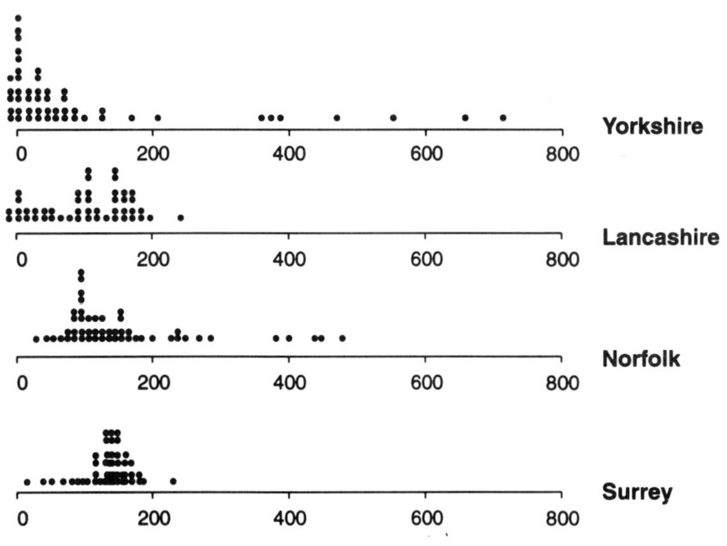

Figure 11.4 Scatterplot of size for four farm samples with different means

to reflect our intuitive understanding that farms around urban centres (represented by Surrey) are likely to be smaller and that larger enterprises are found in arable areas and those with extensive livestock enterprises (Norfolk and Lancashire). The Yorkshire farms do not neatly conform to this pattern, and would require further investigation. The breakdown of the total variance into the two components thus starts to enable some statistical explanation to be attached to the differences. The between-groups variance represents that part which may be attributed to genuine contrasts among the samples, whereas the within-groups component can be attributed to the unexplained differentiation among the items within each sample.

The calculations for oneway analysis of variance appear somewhat daunting, especially if the number of items and samples is relatively large. The procedure for the technique can be broken down into five steps:

1. State null hypothesis and significance level.
2. Calculate the within- and between-groups variance estimates.
3. Calculate the test statistic F by dividing the between groups variance by the within-groups variance.
4. Determine the probability of obtaining the calculated F value, or one greater, through chance, having due regard to the degrees of freedom.
5. Decide whether to accept or reject the null hypothesis.

Analysis of variance is a parametric procedure and therefore makes fairly stringent requirements of the data. Variables should only be measured on the interval or ratio scales and be defined in an identical fashion for each sample. Random selection should be employed when choosing items for inclusion in each sample. Furthermore, each sample of items should be normally distributed with respect to the variable in question and their variances should be reasonably similar. There is some debate among statisticians about how closely a particular set of data needs to conform to these requirements and, as we have seen with other parametric tests, a certain amount of latitude is permissible. Clearly the amount of deviation from the assumptions of the procedure is to some extent a matter of judgement.

11.3 NON-PARAMETRIC TESTS

11.3.1 Pearson's chi-square test

The previous chapter introduced the essential elements of Pearson's chi-square test, as applied to a single sample with one attribute or variable recorded, and outlined its theoretical background. The test can be applied to situations in which either a single sample of items are categorised in two or more different ways or, equivalently, where two or more samples are classified according to the same attribute. In the first case the test is used to examine whether or not the items are independent of each other with respect to the attributes. In the second the focus is on whether the samples are similarly classified with regard to the same attribute and can be thought of as a non-parametric equivalent of ANOVA. In both cases the purpose of the test is to determine if there is a significant association between the frequency distributions (see Chapter 7).

The simplest form of contingency table is where both dimensions of the table are divided into two classes, which is known as a 2×2 table. This notation may be generalised to refer to an $r \times c$ table, in which there are r rows and c columns containing a total of rc cells. If the contingency table relates to a single sample, which has been classified in two ways, the grand total of cell counts equals the sample size. If two or more samples have been categorised according to the same variable, the grand total is the sum of items in the samples combined. In the latter situation, sample membership becomes a new attribute by which the items in the total set may be classified.

A further more important distinction between these two situations is that in the single-sample case the row and column totals are free to vary randomly provided that they sum to the total number of items, unless stratified random sampling has been employed with a predetermined quota of items for one of the classifying attributes. However, in the case of two or more samples, the row totals are constrained to sum to number of items in the respective samples. Table 11.2 provides a simple illustration of this distinction. The total number of items in the 2×2 contingency tables in both parts of Table 11.2 equals 64. In Part 1 the single sample of items are classified according to their values on the attributes A and B (denoted as A1 and A2, and B1 and B2). In Part 2 of the table the two samples (1 and 2) have been categorised with regard to attribute A. In the latter case, because the sample sizes are predetermined, the rows must total 40 and 24 respectively for sample 1 and sample 2, although these 40 and 24 items may be randomly distributed between classes A1 and A2. There is a third much less common situation which should be noted. It occurs when both the row and column totals are predetermined, for instance when the sample of items has been stratified within reference to both attributes in the contingency table.

Pearson's chi-square test can be applied to these situations, although some attention needs to be given to sample size, since this influences

Table 11.2 Comparison of types of contingency table

Part 1				Part 2			
	Class A1	Class A2			Class A1	Class A2	
Class B1	16	8	20	Sample 1	25	15	40
Class B2	12	32	44	Sample 2	10	14	24
	28	36	64		35	29	64

the probabilities associated with the test statistic. The null hypothesis states that there is no association between the two classifying attributes and the categorisation of an item under one attribute is independent of its classification by the other. The null hypothesis postulates that any difference between the frequency counts that would be expected to arise if the items were distributed among the cells in proportion to the row and column totals and those that have been observed is purely the result of sampling error. Thus the first task is to calculate the expected frequencies for each cell in the table by multiplying the row and column totals for the cell in question and dividing by the grand total (see Chapter 7). The formula for Pearson's chi-square statistic given previously, also applies in the bivariate or the two-sample case, thus:

$$\chi^2 = \frac{(O - E)^2}{E}$$

The difference between the observed (O) and expected (E) frequency in each cell is squared and the result divided by the expected frequency. These quantities are summed to produce χ^2. The degrees of freedom are obtained as follows:

$$\text{df} = (r - 1)(c - 1)$$

where r and c are the numbers of rows and columns. Having due regard to whether a one- or two-tailed test is appropriate, the chi-square table (Appendix IV, Table 3) should be consulted to determine the probability of having obtained the calculated test statistic. If the probability is equal to or greater than the tabulated value at the specified significance level, then the null hypothesis may be rejected. As with most tests the significance level provides a basis for determining how often a wrong decision may have been made (e.g. 5 times in 100).

The farm survey data illustrates both applications of the test. The additional farm type attribute (see Chapter 7), demonstrates the first situation. The null hypothesis, which is to be tested at the 0.05 significance level, states that there is no association between the size of a farm and its type, and that any apparent connection revealed by the sample data is merely a consequence of random sampling effects. The number of classes used for the attributes in the contingency table (Table 11.3) has been reduced when compared with Table 7.2, because the reliability of Pearson's chi-square test is sensitive to the number of cells with very low expected frequencies. The cells in Table 11.3 show the individual elements involved in the calculation of the test statistic, which in this case sum to 12.212. There are three rows and three columns in the table thus the degrees of freedom are:

$$\text{df} = (3 - 1)(3 - 1) = 4$$

Referring to the chi-square table, at the 0.05 significance level and with 4 degrees of freedom, the critical value is 9.488; since 12.212 is

Table 11.3 Application of Pearson's chi-square test to farm size and type in Yorkshire sample

Size group (hectares)	Farm type: Dairy	Arable	Mixed Livestock and other	Total
0.0– 99.9	$\frac{(18-12.8)^2}{12.8} = 2.112$	$\frac{(4-6.7)^2}{6.7} = 1.088$	$\frac{(13-15.5)^2}{15.5} = 0.374$	35
100.0– 299.9	$\frac{(1-3.0)^2}{3.0} = 1.333$	$\frac{(2-1.6)^2}{1.6} = 0.100$	$\frac{(5-3.5)^2}{3.5} = 0.643$	8
300.0–1299.9	$\frac{(0-3.2)^2}{3.2} = 3.200$	$\frac{(4-1.7)^2}{1.7} = 3.112$	$\frac{(5-4.0)^2}{4.0} = 0.250$	9
Total	19	10	23	52

$\chi^2 = 2.112 + 1.088 + 0.374 + 1.333 + 0.1 + 0.643 + 3.2 + 3.112 + 0.25 = 12.212$

greater the null hypothesis can be discarded as unlikely. However, at the 0.01 significance level the tabulated value of chi-square is 13.277, which would lead to the null hypothesis being accepted. Nevertheless, the sample suggests that farm size and type are to some extent interdependent on each other. This conclusion does not imply any causal relationship, simply that the two attributes are not randomly distributed among farms in Yorkshire.

The second application of Pearson's chi-square test to the farm survey data considers whether the samples for the four counties exhibit any evidence of an association between size and geographical location. The null hypothesis claims that any difference between the observed and expected distribution of farms has arisen through sampling error and is not significant at the 0.05 level. The number of cells with low expected frequencies has been limited by reducing the number of farm size and type categories. The details of the calculations of each cell are incorporated in Table 11.4. The expected frequencies in the first three rows of the table are identical for each column; this has occurred because the row totals (sample sizes) are the same. In the case of the Yorkshire sample, where the original sample has been reduced by omission of the two suspect farms, the row total is 50. The test statistic, χ^2, equals 26.475, which, with 6 degrees of freedom $(4-1)(3-1)$, is clearly significant at the 0.05 and 0.01 levels (see Appendix IV, Table 3). The null hypothesis of no significant difference may be rejected in favour of the alternative.

Pearson's chi-square test leads to the same conclusion as the ANOVA carried out on the raw data. Both tests offer some statistical evidence for the claim that farm size varies across English counties. ANOVA is a more powerful technique than Pearson's chi-square, and it would normally be unnecessary to undertake both tests on the same data.

Table 11.4 Calculation of Pearson's chi-square on samples of farms in four English counties

	Farm size			
	0.1–99.9	100.0–299.9	300–1299.9	Total
Lancashire	$\frac{(15-23.22)^2}{23.22}$ = 2.912	$\frac{(31-22.47)^2}{22.47}$ = 3.242	$\frac{(6-6.31)^2}{6.31}$ 0.015	52
Norfolk	$\frac{(19-23.22)^2}{23.22}$ = 0.768	$\frac{(24-22.47)^2}{22.47}$ = 0.105	$\frac{(9-6.31)^2}{6.31}$ = 1.146	52
Surrey	$\frac{(23-23.22)^2}{23.22}$ = 0.002	$\frac{(26-22.47)^2}{22.47}$ = 0.556	$\frac{(3-6.31)^2}{6.31}$ = 1.737	52
Yorkshire	$\frac{(35-22.3)^2}{22.3}$ = 7.233	$\frac{(8-21.60)^2}{21.60}$ = 8.565	$\frac{(7-6.1)^2}{6.1}$ = 0.143	50
Total	92	89	25	206

$\chi^2 = 2.898 + 3.302 + 0.014 + 0.76 + 0.114 + 1.157 + 0.002 + 0.578 + 1.729 + 7.233 + 8.563 + 0.133 = 26.379$

Nevertheless, cross-tabulation of the data affords a more straightforward overview of the distribution of the items than a series of overlapping scattergrams (see Figure 11.4). Visual interpretation of the latter inevitably involves some perceptual partitioning or grouping of the items, in the case of the cross-tabulation this has already been carried out on a consistent basis.

The procedure of Pearson's chi-square test is relatively straightforward and does not involve any complex mathematical calculations. The five steps are as follows:

1. State null hypothesis and significance level.
2. Calculate the squared differences between the observed and expected frequency count for each cell and divide by the latter.
3. Sum the results of these calculation to yield the χ^2 test statistic;
4. Calculate the degrees of freedom and determine whether χ^2 is significant, which occurs when it is equal to or greater than the critical tabulated value.
5. Decide whether to accept or reject the null hypothesis.

The test is versatile and readily used in many geographical applications where the data do not fulfil the stringent requirements of its parametric counterparts. Despite its versatility, it makes certain assumptions and has some noteworthy limitations. In addition to requiring that the items should be selected at random (except where stratified sampling is used), and that they should be classified independently of each other, there are four points to be made.

1. A set of raw data, which does not meet the requirements of parametric statistical analysis, can be classified in any way that may seem appropriate. The number and definition of classes has a major effect on the magnitude of the χ^2 test statistic. Referring back to the farm size and type example above, suppose that the number of farm size categories had been altered so that four remained, 0.1–99.9, 100–299.9, 300–499.9 and over 500 ha, and the original set of farm types was reinstated. Pearson's chi-square statistic would equal 14.268 and, with 9 degrees of freedom, would no longer be significant at the 0.05 level, where the critical value of chi-square is 16.919. Contrary to the previous result, the null hypothesis would be accepted. Whether or not the classes are adjusted in order to produce a reliable test statistic is to some extent a matter of personal judgement. The purists would say that classes, once defined on a legitimate and justifiable basis, should be left unaltered, whereas the pragmatists might be prepared to experiment with alternative grouping systems.
2. The frequencies in a cross-tabulation are often expressed as percentages rather than raw counts, which eases interpretation of the results. It is much easier to comprehend the statement that 65 per cent of people on waiting lists for minor operations in private hospitals receive their treatment within 8 weeks compared with giving the absolute count of 750. The latter on its own has no point of reference, there is no indication whether 750 is a small or large proportion of the total. Unfortunately, Pearson's chi-square test should not be used when the data are expressed as percentage frequencies, since an inaccurate value of P (the probability) will be obtained. If the sample size is under 100 and percentages are used, P will be too low, which may result in the null hypothesis being incorrectly rejected. If the sample size is greater than 100, P will be overestimated, possibly leading to the null hypothesis being incorrectly accepted. When there are exactly 100 items in the sample there is of course no problem with referring to the absolute counts as percentages, since they are one and the same.
3. The theoretical background of Pearson's chi-square statistic is the continuous quantity chi-square (see Chapter 10). The correspondence between these distributions becomes a closer as the sample size increases until, in the unrealistic situation of infinite sample size, the probabilities of Pearson's chi-square and chi-square are equal. The implication is that larger sample sizes will lead to fewer cells with low expected frequencies. As with many of these 'statistical health warnings', there is some dispute among statisticians over precise details. What is a low expected frequency and how many cells in a table may have a low expected count, before the test is invalidated? Thus the cautions urged upon would-be users of Pearson's chi-square test may appear somewhat vague. Traditionally the minimum expected frequency was set at either 5 or 10

items per cell, with no more than 20 per cent of cells at this level. Such general guidelines are still useful, but readers are advised to consider some of the other options discussed by Williams (1984, pp. 213–14). One tempting solution to the problem is to collapse some of the categories so that rows and/or columns are combined. If the number of size categories in Table 11.3 were reduced from three to two, 0.1–99.9 and over 100.0 ha, the number cells with low expected frequencies would be cut from six to one. Furthermore, the test statistic calculates as 10.978, which is still significant at the 0.05 level with 2 degrees of freedom. Manipulating the number of cells in the table in this fashion is, as indicated above (see point 1), a rather dubious activity.

4. Pearson's chi-square test is designed for use with nominal-scale attributes or with continuous variables converted to this scale by classification. However, the test is not suitable for situations in which any form of ranking or ordering of the items is implied. The reason is that the same value of χ^2 will be obtained for a cross-tabulation regardless of the order in which the classes of the variables are presented. For example, suppose that the alphabetical sequence of the sampled counties in Table 11.4 was reversed: Yorkshire, Surrey, Norfolk and Lancashire. The same Pearson's chi-square value of 26.475 would be obtained. Alternative tests are available for considering the statistical significance of ordered classes, one of which is examined in Section 11.3.2.

11.3.2 Mann–Whitney *U* test

The Mann–Whitney *U* test is used in two situations: first, when two samples of items are ranked according a single continuous variable; and second, when a single sample is measured on one continuous variable and a dichotomous attribute which has some temporal or spatial partitioning implied in its two categories — for example, the inner and outer zones around a city centre. The loss information about the magnitude of the differences between the items, which results from the conversion of variables measured on the interval or ratio scales to ordinal variables, may have to be tolerated, if the data do not satisfy the requirements of parametric tests. The *U* test pools the two samples in order that they can be ranked according to the continuous variable and then examines the extent to which the ranks of the items in the samples are separated or interleaved. The principle is that if most items from one sample have low rank scores and those from the other have high ones, then the samples may be regarded as coming from populations which are different in respect of the variable. The test considers whether the difference in ranks between the two samples is likely to be the result of chance.

The ranked items may be summarised as a contingency table, but in order to carry out the test the rank scores of the individual items in the two samples are needed. Suppose two random samples of English

Table 11.5 Rank size of sample of towns in the North and South of England

	0.1–1.4 km	1.5–2.9 km	3.0–4.4 km	Total
North	5	3	1	9
South	2	3	7	12

towns are chosen, nine in the North and 12 in the South, and the distance across the widest points of their built-up areas is measured from land-use maps. In Table 11.5 the distance measurements have been grouped into three classes, but the rank positions of the 21 towns are required in order to carry out a U test on the data. The null hypothesis for the test claims that any difference between the ranks of the two groups of items has arisen as a consequence of random sampling error and is not statistically significant: the items have come from populations with the same mean and variance. The complete set of items is ranked according to the continuous variable, with a rank of 1 assigned to the smallest value. Ties are treated so that the mean of the ranks which would have been allocated had the items not been tied is given to each item in a series. If items 3, 4, 5 and 6 have the same value, each is assigned the rank score of 4.5. Next sum the ranks of the items (not the values) in each sample or group, designated sample A and sample B. If sample sizes are small this is a relatively simple task. However, when there is a large number of items it is sensible to calculate the sum of the ranks of the smallest sample and then subtract this value from the sum of the ranks of all the items which may be obtained from the formula:

$$\frac{(n_A + n_B)(n_A + n_B + 1)}{2}$$

where n_A and n_B are the numbers of items in samples A and B. The smaller sum of rank scores, referred as the quantity Σr, is used to calculate the test statistic U, thus:

$$U = \Sigma r - \frac{n_r(n_r + 1)}{2}$$

where n_r is the size of the sample providing Σr. The U test contrasts with most other test statistics in that low rather than high values lead to the null hypothesis being rejected.

Before consulting the tables showing the distribution of the U statistic, a decision should be made as to whether a one- or two-tailed test is required. If there is any prior reason for believing that the ranks in one sample should be different from those in the other, then a one-tailed test should be used. There are three methods for assessing the probability of U, and the choice of technique relates to the number of items in the two samples or groups. Provided neither sample contains more than 10 items, the probabilities associated with different values of U may be obtained from Table 7(a) in Appendix IV. The probabilities in the table should be doubled if a two-tailed test is required. So long as neither sample contains more than 20 items, but one has more than 10, then the alternative form of the U table in Appendix IV, Table 7(b) should be used. The body of the table shows the minimum value of U which is significant for a one- or two-tailed test at the chosen significance level associated with a particular combination of sample sizes. The table includes the most frequently required significance levels (0.05 and 0.01 for two-tailed tests, corresponding to 0.025, 0.005 for one-tailed ones). For example, when the sample yielding Σr has 10 items ($n_r = 10$) and the other (n_o) has 6, the smallest value of U which is significant at the 0.05 level is 12 for a two-tailed test. However, if this value of U had been obtained for a one-tailed test, then the probability is 0.025.

The third method of determining the probability of U is employed when both samples contain more than 20 items. In this situation the sampling distribution of U becomes approximately normal with the following mean and standard deviation:

$$\mu_U = \frac{n_A n_B}{2} \qquad \sigma_U = \sqrt{\frac{n_A n_B (n_A + n_B + 1)}{12}}$$

The probability of U can be approximated by deriving the corresponding Z value, thus:

$$Z = \frac{|U - \mu_U|}{\sigma_U}$$

and then referring to the table of the sampling distribution Z in Appendix IV, Table 1. The probabilities associated with Z values are for a two-tailed test, and should therefore be halved if a one-tailed test is required. Regardless of which method is used to estimate the probability of U, the null hypothesis is rejected if the probability is greater than the chosen level of significance.

The null hypothesis for the northern and southern towns data asserts that towns in the two areas are not significantly different from each other in respect of size, as measured by the maximum width across their built-up area. Table 11.6 shows the sorted (ranked) data for the two samples, retaining the raw unclassified values of the variable. The summation of the rank scores for each sample reveals that the sum for the northern towns is less than for the southern ones, thus $\Sigma r = 69.5$ and $n_r = 9$. Substituting the appropriate values into the formula for the U statistic:

$$U = 69.5 - \frac{9(9+1)}{2} = 69.5 - 45 = 24.5$$

Since n_o has more than 10 but less than 21 items, the second method for determining the probability of U must be used. A two-tailed test is required in this example, since there is no overriding prior reason why towns in one area should be larger than in the other. At the 0.05 level of significance, the null hypothesis is rejected, with $n_r = 9$ and

Table 11.6 Extent of built-up area of sample of towns in the North and South of England (rank position)

	North		South	
	Maximum width	Rank	Maximum width	Rank
1	0.75	1		
2	0.8	2.5		
3			0.8	2.5
4	0.9	4		
5			1.05	5
6	1.35	6		
7	1.4	7		
8	1.6	8		
9			2.0	9
10			2.5	10
11	2.7	11.5		
12	2.7	11.5		
13			2.9	13
14			3.1	14
15			3.6	16
16			3.6	16
17			3.6	16
18	3.9	18		
19			4.2	19
20			4.25	20
21			4.4	21
Rank sums		69.5		161.5

$n_o = 12$, and as far as the maximum width of towns is concerned, there is a significant difference between those in the north and south of England. At the 0.01 significance level the opposite conclusion would be reached. The sample sizes are perhaps a little too small to conclude with confidence that the mean and variance of their parent populations are different, although there is some evidence for this.

There are six main steps to the standard procedure and calculations required for the Mann–Whitney U test:

1. Establish the null hypothesis which asserts that any difference in the rank positions of the two samples is merely due to chance.
2. Sort all items according to their values on the continuous variable and assign their rank scores.
3. Sum the ranks for each sample and identify from which one the value of Σr arises.
4. Calculate the test statistic U.
5. Estimate the probability of U by selecting the most appropriate of the three methods, having due regard to whether a one- or two-tailed test is required.
6. Decide whether to accept or reject the null hypothesis.

The U test, although comparatively undemanding, does nevertheless make certain assumptions about the nature of the sample data. Simple random sampling with individual replacement (or without replacement from an infinite population) is necessary. The items should be independent of each other with respect to the continuous variable, but this does not need to be normally distributed. The test cannot be used with a nominal attribute, since there is obviously no means for ranking the items. If the populations are normally distributed and the samples sufficiently large, then the U test is almost as powerful as the t test. However, one of the advantages of the test is its applicability with very small sample sizes.

11.3.3 Kruskal–Wallis *H* test

The Kruskal–Wallis H test extends the principles of the U test into slightly more complex sampling situations. The H test examines two types of difference either between three or more samples, or for a single sample which is classified into at least three groups. In both cases the items are ranked with respect to an ordinal variable or to a sorted interval/ratio variable. The H test focuses on the inter-group contrasts and, as with the Mann–Whitney U test, benefits from being applicable to situations in which relatively few items have been sampled. The H test investigates whether the samples or groups are significantly different from each other with respect to their rank scores. In other words, when the rank scores of the complete set of items are considered, are the samples segregated or interspersed? The null hypothesis states that the differences in ranks between the groups or samples is the result of chance sampling. The alternative hypothesis claims that the differences in the samples'/groups' ranks are statistically significant and more than could reasonably be attributed to sampling error.

The calculations for the H statistic involves only simple mathematical operations, although the data manipulation may be tedious if undertaken by hand with large samples. The complete set of items are pooled and ranked overall with respect to the measured variable, taking due account of any ties that may occur. The sums of the rank scores within each of the k groups yield a series of values known as R_1, R_2, ..., R_k. These are inserted into the equation which calculates the test statistic, H:

$$H = \left(\frac{12}{n_s(n_s + 1)}\right)\left(\sum \frac{R_k}{n_k}\right) - 3(n_s + 1)$$

where n_s and n_k are the total number of items and the number within each of the k groups, respectively. The probability of having obtained the calculated value of H or one greater through chance may be determined from Appendix IV, Table 8, or, if there are at least five items in each group, the sampling distribution of H approximates to chi-square and the table for the latter statistic is used. In both methods the degrees of freedom are given by $k - 1$, where k is the number of groups. Reject the null hypothesis if the test statistic, H, is equal to or greater than the tabulated value at the chosen level of significance.

Table 11.7 Rank size and locality of sample of towns in the North and South of England and in Scotland

	0.1-1.4 km	1.5-2.9 km	3.0-4.4 km	Total
North				
Plain	3	1	0	4
Valley	2	2	1	5
South				
Plain	1	2	4	7
Valley	1	1	3	5
Scotland				
Plain	2	1	3	6
Valley	3	3	4	10
				37

Suppose that the samples of towns in the North and South of England are joined by a third sample of 16 Scottish towns, and that each town is classified according to whether its location is within a valley or on a plain. Table 11.7 summarises in tabular form the distribution of the towns according to their region, locality and maximum width. A cursory examination of the rankings for the 37 towns (Table 11.8) suggests that there may be some segregation between the difference groups. The null hypothesis states that the three regions — northern and southern England, and Scotland — are inseparable as far as the size and location of towns is concerned. The alternative hypothesis maintains that the differences are significant at the 0.05 level. The sums of the rank scores for each group of towns (see Table 11.8) are substituted into the H-test formula thus:

$$H = \left(\frac{12}{37(37+1)}\right)\left(\frac{37^2}{4} + \frac{80^2}{5} + \frac{159^2}{7} + \frac{117^2}{5} + \frac{111^2}{6} + \frac{199.5^2}{10}\right) - 3(37+1)$$

$$= \left(\frac{12}{1406}\right)(13\,985.221) - 3(37+1)$$

$$= (0.00853)(13\,985.221) - 114 = 5.294$$

The groups are sufficiently large for the probability of $H = 5.294$ to be determined from the chi-square table, although one group has only four towns. With the degrees of freedom calculated as the number of groups minus one $(6 - 1)$, it is apparent from Appendix IV, Table 3 that the probability of having obtained the value 5.29 by chance is greater than 0.50 and thus the null hypothesis is accepted. The sample evidence that town size varies regionally and according to their locality does not appear to be substantiated.

The six steps of the standard procedure for the Kruskell–Wallis H test are similar to those of the Mann–Whitney U test:

Table 11.8 Extent of built-up area and locality of sample of towns in the North and South of England and in Scotland

	North				South				Scotland			
	Plain		Valley		Plain		Valley		Plain		Valley	
	W	R	W	R	W	R	W	R	W	R	W	R
1											0.5	1
2	0.75	2										
3			0.8	3.5								
4							0.8	3.5				
5									0.85	5		
6	0.9	6										
7									1.0	7		
8					1.05	8						
9											1.3	9
10	1.35	10										
11			1.4	11.5								
12											1.4	11.5
13											1.5	13
14			1.6	14								
15											1.7	15
16					2.0	16						
17									2.3	17		
18							2.5	18				
19	2.7	19										
20	2.7	20										
21											2.8	21
22					2.9	22						
23									3.0	23		
24					3.1	24						
25									3.2	25		
26											3.4	26
27					3.6	28						
28							3.6	28				
29					3.6	28						
30											3.7	30
31			3.9	31								
32							4.2	32				
33					4.25	33						
34									4.3	34		
35							4.4	35.5				
36											4.4	35.5
37											4.5	37
Rank sums		37		80		159		117		111		199
No. in group		4		5		7		5		6		10

Note: *W* and *R* denote respectively maximum width in kilometres and rank

1. State the null hypothesis: any difference in the rank positions of the samples is merely due to chance and is not significant at the chosen level.
2. Rank the items in all the samples/groups according to their values on the continuous variable.
3. Sum the ranks for the groups designating each R_i.
4. Calculate the test statistic H.

5. Determine the approximate probability of the tests statistic H by reference to appropriate statistical table.
6. Accept or reject the null hypothesis.

The data requirements for the H test are fairly minimal. The samples should be selected at random and the items in each population should be independent of each other with respect to the continuous variable, which is not necessarily normally distributed. One potential problem concerns the number of ties that occur when the complete set of observations are ranked. If this is large (more than 25 per cent of the data), then H should be divided by the following correction factor (C):

$$C = 1 - \frac{T^3 - T}{n_s^3 - n_s}$$

where T is the number of ties and n_s the total observations. The number of ties in the towns example (5) is not greater than 25 per cent nevertheless the correction factor is:

$$C = 1 - \frac{(125 - 5)}{50\,616} = 0.998$$

Dividing 5.294 by 0.998 produces a revised H value of 5.30, which still gives a probability greater than 0.50. The test is generally tolerant of fairly low numbers of observations, although very small groups should be avoided.

11.4 APPLICATION OF TESTS FOR TWO OR MORE SAMPLES TO EXEMPLAR PROJECTS

This section parallels Section 10.4 by demonstrating how bivariate statistical techniques have been applied to the data from the exemplar projects by means of the MINITAB and SPSS-X software. The full range of statistical techniques available in the software is not covered, since the purpose is to select those which are relevant to the projects. Discussion in the following subsections focuses on the statistical analysis commands rather than the data manipulation, although the latter appears in the software logs. Some new data manipulation commands are introduced where these are required in order to facilitate the statistical analysis.

11.4.1 Land-use change

11.4.1.1 U test

Most statistical tests are carried out in MINITAB by means of a single command, which may sometimes require a subcommand, for example to perform a one-tailed test. The U-test command has the following general structure:

```
MTB > MANN-WHITNEY [K] C1 C2,
SUBC > ALTERNATIVE = -1 or +1.
```

Columns C1 and C2 contain the data for the two samples and K specifies the desired confidence interval for the population medians, which is generated automatically. The default setting for K (95 per cent) is applied if this parameter is omitted.

The calculations performed on the columns of data for the two samples, here shown as C1 and C2, are carried out slightly differently to the method described above. The Mann–Whitney test in MINITAB focuses on the difference in the medians of the two samples, η_1 and η_2 (η is the lower case of the Greek letter 'eta' and denotes a median). Suppose that two samples are measured and then independently ranked according to a continuous variable. If η_1 and η_2 are similar, then the observations are likely to be interspersed with regard to the continuous variable. In contrast, if the median values are far apart, then some segregation among the observations is indicated. These two situations provide an alternative interpretation of the U test as defined above. If the items in the two samples are pooled and their rank positions determined, the sums of the ranks for each sample may be used to test for a significant difference between the medians.

The MANN–WHITNEY command in MINITAB operates in this fashion. The smallest rank sum becomes the test statistic W, which is equivalent to the quantity obtained in the Wilcoxon signed ranks test for the difference between pairs of measurements on a single sample described in Section 10.3.3. A small value for W indicates that η_1 is greater than η_2, while a large value of W suggests the reverse. If the probability of W equals or is less than the chosen level of significance (e.g. 0.05 or 0.01), then the difference between the medians is statistically significant and the null hypothesis of no difference between the samples may be rejected. The MINITAB command provides the exact probability of W.

The two differently structured random samples in the land-use project provide information about the changes in the areas of seven land uses. The Mann–Whitney test is applied to each land use in order to investigate whether the results from the two samples are similar, as stated in null hypothesis LU4:

> Any differences in the areal changes of each land use, as recorded by samples A and B, have arisen entirely through sampling error and are not significant.

The changes in area for each land use in sample B have already been computed in the previous analysis and saved in C32 to C38 in LANDB03.MTW. The equivalent computations for sample A are now undertaken and stored in column C19, and then copied into columns C20 to C26 for each individual land-use (see Table 11.9). Some further data manipulation is necessary in order to analyse the change variables for the two samples together, since MINITAB can only RETRIEVE one

Table 11.9 Application of univariate tests for two or more samples (U and Pearson's χ^2) to land-use project samples A and B in MINITAB

```
MTB > OUTFILE 'land06'
MTB > RETRIEVE 'landa03'
MTB > LET C19 = C7 - C5
MTB > COPY C19 C20;
MTB > USE C6 = 1.
MTB > COPY C19 C21;
MTB > USE C6 = 2.
MTB > COPY C19 C22;
MTB > USE C6 = 3.
MTB > COPY C19 C23;
MTB > USE C6 = 4.
MTB > COPY C19 C24;
MTB > USE C6 = 5.
MTB > COPY C19 C25;
MTB > USE C6 = 6.
MTB > COPY C19 C26;
MTB > USE C6 = 7.
MTB > WRITE 'samplea.dat' C20 - C26
MTB > SAVE 'landa04'
MTB > RETRIEVE 'landb03'
MTB > READ 'SAMPLEA.DAT' C46 - C52
MTB > MANN-WHITNEY C32 C46
MTB > MANN-WHITNEY C33 C47
MTB > MANN-WHITNEY C34 C48
MTB > MANN-WHITNEY C35 C49
MTB > MANN-WHITNEY C36 C50
MTB > MANN-WHITNEY C37 C51
MTB > MANN-WHITNEY C38 C52
MTB > TABLE C3;
SUBC > MEANS C11 - C17.
READ > C53 - C59
DATA > 42 6 19 7 3 10 14
DATA > 46 2 27 11 3 3 9
DATA > END
MTB > CHISQUARE C53 - C59
MTB > SAVE 'landb04'
MTB > NOOUTFILE
MTB > STOP
```

worksheet at a time. The newly computed columns in LANDA03.MTW (C20 to C26) are written out to a raw data file, SAMPLEA.DAT. The second worksheet is retrieved and the data from SAMPLEA.DAT read in and subsequently saved as additional columns (C46 to C52). The current worksheet now has pairs of columns (C46 and C32, C33 and C47, etc.) containing the area change variables for each land use in samples A and B, respectively. The command to perform the Mann-Whitney test (see Table 11.9) is applied to the pairs of columns in the new worksheet, thus:

```
MTB > MANN-WHITNEY C32 C46
```

	NA	NB	A	B	W	P	Accept/ Reject H_0
Arable	24	20	9	11	416.0	0.4295	Accept
Permanent Grass	8	20	−6	−7	284.0	0.7792	Accept
Orchards & Mkt G.	Not enough data						
Forestry & Woodland	Not enough data						
Rough Grazing	Not enough data						
Houses and Gardens	3	20	0	1	246.0	0.6036	Accept
Agric. Unprod.	2	20	0.5	4.0	249.0	0.0317	Reject

Sample MANN-WHITNEY Output from MINITAB

```
MTB > MANN-WHITNEY AGRICHAN AGCHSMPA
  Mann-Whitney Confidence Interval and Test

  AGRICHAN          N = 20               Median =  9.00
  AGCHSMPA          N = 24               Median = 11.00
  Point estimate for ETA1-ETA2 is                 -6.50
  95.1 pct c.i. for ETA1-ETA2 is (-22.00,5.01)
  W = 416.0
  Test of ETA1 = ETA2 vs. ETA1 n.e. ETA2 is significant at 0.4298
  The test is significant at 0.4295 (adjusted for ties)

  Cannot reject at alpha = 0.05
  MTB > MANN-WHITNEY AGUNCHAN AGUNCSPA
  Mann-Whitney Confidence Interval and Test

  AGUNCHAN          N = 20               Median = 4.000
  AGUNCSPA          N =  2               Median = 0.500
  Point estimate for ETA1-ETA2 is                 3.000
  95.4 pct c.i. for ETA1-ETA2 is (1.000,6.001)
  W = 249.0
  Test of ETA1 = ETA2 vs. ETA1 n.e. ETA2 is significant at 0.0346
  The test is significant at 0.0317 (adjusted for ties)
```

The test could not be carried out for market gardening, woodland and rough grazing because the sample only included 1 occurrence of those land uses.

Box 11.1 Summary of Mann–Whitney test results for LU4 for change in each land use 1930s–1960s

The analytical results have been brought together into a summary table (Box 11.1) and suggest that in general the two samples provide a consistent account of land-use change. Only the U test for agriculturally unproductive land is statistically significant at the 0.05 level. The number of plots of land in sample A for three land-use categories was insufficient to apply the test. Furthermore, even for housing and agriculturally unproductive land there are only three and two observations for sample A.

11.4.1.2 Pearson's chi-square test

There are two ways of undertaking a Pearson's chi-square test in MINITAB: the first is by using the command CHISQUARE; and the second is by means of a subcommand on the TABLE command. The first is used for the land-use project and the second in the river pollution study. The CHISQUARE command works on a contingency table stored in up to seven data columns: in other words, the counts in the cells of the cross-tabulation are stored as data values in the rows and columns, and there is a maximum of seven classes for one of the variables. The general syntax of the command is

```
MTB > CHISQUARE C1 C2
```

The expected frequencies, the Pearson's chi-square statistic and the degrees of freedom are calculated by the command, but not the probability. The output from the command shows the expected frequencies and the result of each element of χ^2 (i.e. $(O - E)^2/E$ for each cell). This allows the analyst to determine the contribution of each cell to the overall χ^2. The output also includes a count of the number of cells with an expected frequency of less than 5, and, if any have an expected frequency of less than 1, χ^2 is not provided, since some statisticians would regard the test as unreliable.

The land-use project illustrates the situation in which a sample of items are classified according to two variables, namely with respect to their location (rural or rural-urban fringe) and the extent of the seven different land uses. Null hypothesis LU5 states that:

> The apparent difference in the area of each land use between urban fringe and rural locations is not significant. Chance alone accounts for the inconsistencies.

Some preliminary remarks are needed before LU5 is examined with the χ^2 test. The variables measuring the areas of the different land uses have thus far been regarded as continuous, but they can also be thought of as a frequency count of the number of hectares of each land use. This is especially the case with the sample of kilometre squares, since there may be separate, discontinuous 'pockets' of the same land use within any square.

Manipulation of the raw data is required in order to convert the information into a form suitable for use with the CHISQUARE command (see Table 11.9). The CHISQUARE command requires that the total hectare counts for each land use classified according to rural and rural-urban fringe location are presented in the form of a 2 × 7 contingency table. The following sequence of commands, taken from Table 11.9, performs the required data manipulation operations for the 1960s areas in sample B:

```
MTB > TABLE C3,
SUBC > MEANS C11 - C17.
READ > C53 - C59
DATA > 42 6 19 7 3 10 14
DATA > 46 2 27 11 3 3 9
DATA > END
MTB > CHISQUARE C53 - C59
```

```
MTB > CHISQUARE C53 - C59
  Expected counts are printed below observed counts
          C53    C54    C55     C56    C57    C58     C59   Total
  1       42     6      19      7      3      10      14     101
          44.00  4.00   23.00   9.00   3.00   6.50   11.50
  2       46     2      27      11     3      3       9      101
          44.00  4.00   23.00   9.00   3.00   6.50   11.50
  Total   88     8      46      18     6      13      23     202
  ChiSq = 0.091 + 1.000 + 0.696 + 0.444 + 0.000 + 1.885 + 0.543+
  0.091 + 1.000 + 0.696 + 0.444 + 0.000 + 1.885 + 0.543 = 9.318
  df = 6
  4 cells with expected counts less than 5.0
```

Box 11.2 Pearson's chi-square test results for LU5 for each land use in urban-fringe and rural areas (MINITAB output)

The TABLE command produced a contingency table of the mean change in each land use within the rural and rural-urban fringe areas. The seven values on the DATA entry lines were obtained from this contingency table. The mean values have been rounded to the nearest integer so that they represent counts in the contingency table. The CHISQUARE C53 – C59 command carries out the required statistical test.

The output from the CHISQUARE command (Box 11.2) shows the observed and expected frequencies and the value of Pearson's chi-square. The chi-square table provides the probability associated with the test statistic (χ^2). With 6 degrees of freedom, the χ^2 of 9.318 has a probability between 0.2 and 0.1: thus the null hypothesis is accepted. The result of the test on the land-use data suggests that in the 1960s there was no significant difference between the rural-urban fringe and rural localities in terms of the amount of each land use.

11.4.2 Chalk weathering

11.4.2.1 F test

The *F* test, which is used to examine the difference between two sample variances, is not directly available in MINITAB, although the simplicity of the test allows the necessary calculations to be carried out easily. The variances for columns of data may be obtained by squaring the standard deviations, which are produced by the DESCRIBE command, and storing the results in a new column, in this case C31, which contains the variances for six of the treatments (see extract from software log below). The pairs of variances are inspected and the larger is divided by the smaller, with the number of observations (rows) associated with the larger variance noted in order to determine the degrees of freedom. The following illustrates the general sequence of commands:

```
MTB > DESCRIBE C22 - C30
MTB > SET C31
DATA > 5.963 7.442 1.871 2.176 3.940 0.441 0.918 0.233 0.240
DATA > END
```

```
MTB > LET K1 = C31(1) / C31(4)
MTB > LET K2 = C31(2) / C31(5)
MTB > LET K3 = C31(3) / C31(6)
MTB > LET K4 = C31(4) / C31(7)
MTB > LET K5 = C31(5) / C31(8)
MTB > PRINT K1 K2 K3 K4 K5
```

The numbers in brackets on the LET commands refer to specific rows within C31; in other words, they identify individual cells within the column, and thus dictate how the variances are divided by each other. The values held in the constants K1 to K5, which are created by the LET commands are the five F-test statistics. Their probabilities may be found in the in the F distribution table (Appendix IV, Table 6) taking to account the degrees of freedom for the two samples.

The chalk weathering project includes several sub-samples which n be examined to determine the significance of any differences in eir variances. The relevant null hypothesis, CW3, does not state which vo sub-samples are compared but adopts a more general form:

> The differences between the variances of the weight-loss variable for pairs of samples in the experiment (e.g. pure water and saline water sub-samples at a constant $-5°C$) are not significant and have arisen through sampling error.

Table 11.10 Application of univariate tests for two or more samples (F, two-sample t, and ANOVA) to chalk weathering project in MINITAB

```
MTB > OUTFILE 'chweat06'
MTB > RETRIEVE 'chweat03'
MTB > DESCRIBE C22 - C30
MTB > SET C31
DATA > 5.963 7.442 1.871 2.176 3.940 0.441 0.918 0.233 0.240
DATA > END
MTB > LET K1 = C31(1) / C31(4)
MTB > LET K2 = C31(2) / C31(5)
MTB > LET K3 = C31(3) / C31(6)
MTB > LET K4 = C31(4) / C31(7)
MTB > LET K5 = C31(5) / C31(8)
MTB > PRINT K1 K2 K3 K4 K5
MTB > TWOSAMPLE C22 C25;
SUBC > POOLED.
MTB > TWOSAMPLE C23 C26;
SUBC > POOLED.
MTB > TWOSAMPLE C24 C27;
SUBC > POOLED.
MTB > TWOSAMPLE C24 C28;
SUBC > POOLED.
MTB > TWOSAMPLE C25 C29;
MTB > ONEWAY C19 C2
MTB > NOOUTFILE
MTB > STOP
```

```
MTB > LET K1 = C31(1) / C31(4)
MTB > LET K2 = C31(2) / C31(5)
MTB > LET K3 = C31(3) / C31(6)
MTB > LET K4 = C31(4) / C31(7)
MTB > LET K5 = C31(5) / C31(8)
MTB > PRINT K1 K2 K3 K4 K5
K1              2.740
K2              1.869
K3              4.243
K4              2.370
K5             16.910
```

Box 11.3 *F*-test results for CW3 for selected treatments in chalk weathering project (MINITAB output)

The software log for the chalk weathering project (Table 11.10) includes the series of MINITAB computation commands which produce the various F-test statistics. The sample size is 12 in all cases and therefore the degrees of freedom do not vary (df = 11). The probabilities of the various F statistics and the decisions on the specific null hypotheses are given in Box 11.3. The critical value of F is 3.47 at degrees of freedom of 11 and 11, which reveals that only the fifth test is significant at the 0.05 level, which relates to treatments 5 and 8.

11.4.2.2 Two-sample t test

The two-sample t test is applied to a continuous variable which satisfies the test's data requirements. The TWOSAMPLE command in MINITAB performs both versions of the two-sample t test, although due care is required to determine if the variances are likely to be equal. The command tests the null hypothesis that the means of the populations from which the samples have been drawn are equal. An optional subcommand enables a one-tailed test to be carried out, if there are grounds for believing that the mean of the first population is necessarily larger (or smaller) than that of the second. The syntax of the command is as follows:

```
MTB > TWOSAMPLE [K] C3 C5;
SUBC > ALTERNATIVE = −1 or + 1,
SUBC > POOLED.
```

In this instance the columns C3 and C5 contain the sample data, K is an optional parameter which controls the confidence level to be used: the default setting is 95 per cent. If necessary, the −1 or +1 on the ALTERNATIVE subcommand forces the direction of a one-tailed test (see Section 10.4.1.2). Finally, the POOLED subcommand selects the form of the test in which the population variances are assumed to be equal: if omitted the alternative version is used. The output from TWOSAMPLE includes the mean, standard deviation and standard error of the sample data as well as the specified confidence interval.

The degrees of freedom, the test statistic t and its probability are also printed, which avoids the necessity of referring to the t-distribution table.

The application of the two-sample t test to the data from the chalk weathering project enables the effect of each treatment to be examined independently. Null hypothesis CW4 provides a general statement of the differences under investigation and illustrates these with a particular example:

> The differences in mean weight loss between pairs of samples in the experimental design (e.g. diurnal freeze–thaw and constant +5°C after saturation in pure water) are not statistically significant. Such apparent differences as exist in the sample data can be attributed entirely to sampling error.

The information obtained from the parallel set of F tests (see Section 11.4.2.1) has determined which form of the test should be

Test:	$\bar{X}$	$\sigma_{\bar{x}}$	95 % Conf Interval	t	P	Accept/ Reject H_0
1 and	17.63	0.71	10.32,13.74	14.61	0.0000	Reject
4	5.60	0.43				
2 and	21.31	0.79	10.35,14.39	12.70	0.0000	Reject
5	8.94	0.57				
3 and	1.72	0.39	−0.38, 1.44	1.20	0.2400	Accept
6	1.19	0.19				
4 and	1.72	0.39	−1.08, 0.91	0.18	0.8600	Accept
7	1.81	0.28				
5 and	5.60	0.43	3.39, 5.32	9.72	0.0000	Reject
8	1.24	0.14				

Sample TWOSAMPLE Output from MINITAB

```
MTB > TWOSAMPLE C22 C25;
SUBC > POOLED.

TWOSAMPLE T FOR C22 VS C25
            N        MEAN       STDEV      SE MEAN
Treat1      12       17.63      2.44       0.71
Treat4      12        5.60      1.47       0.43

95 PCT CI FOR MU C22 – MU C25: (10.32, 13.74)

TTEST MU C22 = MU C25 (VS NE): T = 14.61 P = 0.0000 DF = 22

POOLED STDEV = 2.02

MTB > TWOSAMPLE C24 C27;
SUBC > POOLED.

TWOSAMPLE T FOR C24 VS C27
            N        MEAN       STDEV      SE MEAN
Treat3      12       1.72       1.37       0.39
Treat6      12       1.192      0.664      0.19

95 PCT CI FOR MU C24 – MU C27: (–0.38, 1.44)

TTEST MU C24 = MU C27 (VS NE): T = 1.20 P = 0.24 DF = 22

POOLED STDEV = 1.08
```

Box 11.4 Two-sample t-test results for CW4 for selected treatments in chalk weathering project

employed. The following extract from Table 11.10 shows two of the TWOSAMPLE tests:

```
MTB > TWOSAMPLE C22 C25;
SUBC > POOLED.
MTB > TWOSAMPLE C23 C26;
SUBC > POOLED.
```

Five two-sample t tests were carried out comparing treatments 1 and 4, 2 and 5, 3 and 6 (controls), 4 and 7, and 5 and 8. The preliminary F tests indicated that in all but the last of these, the population variances could be assumed to be equal. The results of the series of tests are shown in Box 11.4. Some statistically significant contrasts have been identified, for example between treatments 1 and 4, and 2 and 5. In two of the tests the value of t has a high probability, which indicates that the null hypothesis should be retained, for treatments 3 and 6, and 5 and 8.

11.4.2.3 Oneway analysis of variance

MINITAB has two commands which carry out a oneway analysis of variance: one is AOVONEWAY and the other ONEWAY. The first requires that the raw data for each group or sample are held in a separate column, thus the general format of the command is

```
MTB > AOVONEWAY C1 C3 C6 C14
```

where the data for the four samples are stored in columns C1, C3, C6 and C14. The ONEWAY command requires that the variable for all samples is stored in a single column and that a second column contains integer code numbers (e.g. 1, 2, 3, etc.) which identify the sample or group to which a row belongs. The syntax of the command is:

```
MTB > ONEWAY C1 C2 [C15]
```

The first column referenced on the ONEWAY command (C1) specifies where the data are stored and the second (C2) denotes the location of the sample identifiers. It is also possible to create a new column in which the residuals from the analysis of variance are stored (here shown as C15).

Both forms of the command produce an analysis of variance table, which uses slightly different terminology to the worked example given above. In MINITAB's ANOVA output the within-groups and between-groups sums of squares are respectively replaced by the terms *error* and *factor* to denote the different sources of variation between the samples. The output shows the degrees of freedom and the sum of squares associated with each source. The test statistic F and its probability are displayed, thus enabling the analyst to reach a decision on the null hypothesis in the light of the chosen level of significance without recourse to tables showing the F distributions. The output also includes

```
ANALYSIS OF VARIANCE ON Loss0-14
SOURCE       DF        SS         MS         F        p
Treatmt       8   5804.44     725.55    281.11    0.000
ERROR        99    255.52       2.58
TOTAL       107   6059.96

                                  INDIVIDUAL 95 PCT CI'S FOR MEAN
                                  BASED ON POOLED STDEV
LEVEL     N     MEAN    STDEV
                          -+---------+---------+---------+----
    1    12   17.632    2.443                          (*-)
    2    12   21.313    2.728                              (*-)
    3    12    1.721    1.368    (*-)
    4    12    5.600    1.475          (*)
    5    12    8.943    1.985             (-*)
    6    12    1.192    0.664   (-*)
    7    12    1.806    0.958    (-*)
    8    12    1.244    0.483   (-*)
    9    12    0.736    0.490   (*)
                          -+---------+---------+---------+----
POOLED STDEV =     1.607      0.0       7.0      14.0      21.0
```

Box 11.5 Oneway analysis of variance results for CW5 in chalk weathering project (MINITAB output)

the 95 per cent confidence intervals for the means of the populations from which the samples have been drawn based on their pooled standard deviation. The interpretation of these confidence intervals is essentially the same as for the one-sample case, namely they provide a range within which it is possible to be 95 per cent certain that the population means will fall. The output gives a visual impression of these intervals.

Analysis of variance is used to examine the fifth null hypothesis, CW5, which states that:

> Variations in mean weight loss among the sub-samples are not of such magnitude as to suggest that different types of temperature regime and water treatment have any effect on the freeze–thaw weathering process. The differences are not significant.

The structure of the worksheet for the chalk weathering project allows either ANOVA command to be used. Column C2 contains a numeric code denoting treatment type (the group or sub-sample identifers) for use with the ONEWAY command. Previous analysis of the data have indicated that the controls stand out from the other sub-samples by having very little weight loss. The oneway ANOVA identifies the effects produced by different temperature regimes and the presence of pure or saline water.

The ANOVA table (Box 11.5) summarises the test results. The F ratio, at 281.1, is highly significant, showing that the nine samples are highly differentiated in terms of their total weight loss at the end of the experimental period. The diagram showing the 95 per cent confidence intervals for the different groups or sub-samples clearly reveals that treatments 2 and 1, followed by 5 and 4, have the greatest reductions in weight, whereas the remaining groups showed little loss. However, as noted previously, ANOVA only tests for the presence of a difference between the groups, not its source or magnitude.

11.4.3 River pollution

11.4.3.1 Two-sample t test

The two-sample t test is employed to examine null hypothesis RP3 in the river pollution project, which asserts that:

> The mean concentrations produced by the analysis of the two samples are identical, having come from a single population with mean μ and standard deviation σ. Any difference in sample means is due to chance.

The test examines any differences between the two samples in the project. Each sample was designed to answer particular questions, but there is some overlap in the variables collected and thus it is sensible to compare their results. The log of the MINITAB session (Table 11.11) shows a similar set of operations to those carried out for the land-use project. A subset of the columns from the sample A worksheet are written out into RIVSAMPA.DAT, which is combined with the columns in the worksheet for sample B once this has been retrieved.

```
MTB > RETRIEVE 'rivera03'
MTB > WRITE 'rivsampa' C7 – C9
...
MTB > RETRIEVE 'riverb03'
MTB > READ 'rivsampa' C48 – C50
```

Box 11.6 Summary of two sample t test results for RP3 for selected chemicals in Samples A and B of river pollution project

		$\bar{X}$	$\sigma_{\bar{x}}$	95% Conf Interval	t	P	Accept/ Reject H_0
Test: Dissolved Oxygen	A	46.0	1.8	−9.70, 0.20	1.90	0.0590	Accept
	B	41.2	1.7				
BOD	A	8.21	0.36	−0.39, 1.62	1.20	0.2300	Accept
	B	8.82	0.36				
Ammonia	A	0.82	0.03	−0.16, −0.03	2.77	0.0058	Reject
	B	0.72	0.02				

Sample TWOSAMPLE Output from MINITAB

```
MTB > TWOSAMPLE DisOA DisOB;
SUBC > POOLED.

TWOSAMPLE T FOR DisOA VS DisOb
          N      MEAN     STDEV    SE MEAN
DisOA   250      46.0      28.7        1.8
DisOB   300      41.2      30.1        1.7
95 PCT CI FOR MU DisOA - MU DisOB: (−9.7, 0.2)

TTEST MU DisOA = MU DisOB (VS NE): T = −1.90 P = 0.059 DF = 548

POOLED STDEV = 29.5
```

Table 11.11 Application of univariate tests for two or more samples (two t, χ^2 and H tests) to river pollution project samples A and B in MINITAB

```
MTB > OUTFILE 'river06'
MTB > RETRIEVE 'rivera03'
MTB > WRITE 'rivsampa' C7 - C9
MTB > TABLE C3 C6;
SUBC > CHISQUARE.
MTB > RETRIEVE 'riverb03'
MTB > READ 'rivsampa' C48 - C50
MTB > DESCRIBE C48 - C50
MTB > SET C51
DATA > 823.690 31.539 0.263
DATA > END
MTB > DESCRIBE C9 - C11
MTB > SET C52
DATA > 906.492 39.523 0.081
DATA > END
MTB > LET K1 = C51(1) / C52(1)
MTB > LET K2 = C51(2) / C52(2)
MTB > LET K3 = C52(3) / C51(3)
MTB > PRINT K1 - K3
MTB > TWOSAMPLE C9 C48;
SUBC > POOLED.
MTB > TWOSAMPLE C10 C49;
SUBC > POOLED.
MTB > TWOSAMPLE C11 C50;
SUBC > POOLED.
MTB > TABLE C7 C8;
SUBC > CHISQUARE.
MTB > KRUSKELL-WALLIS C9 C7
MTB > KRUSKELL-WALLIS C10 C7
MTB > KRUSKELL-WALLIS C11 C7
MTB > KRUSKELL-WALLIS C9 C8
MTB > KRUSKELL-WALLIS C10 C8
MTB > KRUSKELL-WALLIS C11 C8
MTB > KRUSKELL-WALLIS C9 C4
MTB > KRUSKELL-WALLIS C10 C4
MTB > KRUSKELL-WALLIS C11 C4
MTB > KRUSKELL-WALLIS C12 C4
MTB > KRUSKELL-WALLIS C13 C4
MTB > KRUSKELL-WALLIS C14 C4
MTB > KRUSKELL-WALLIS C12 C7
MTB > KRUSKELL-WALLIS C12 C8
MTB > KRUSKELL-WALLIS C13 C7
MTB > KRUSKELL-WALLIS C13 C8
MTB > KRUSKELL-WALLIS C14 C7
MTB > KRUSKELL-WALLIS C14 C8
MTB > NOOUTFILE
MTB > SAVE 'riverb03'
MTB > STOP
```

The TWOSAMPLE command performs these tests on dissolved oxygen, biochemical oxygen demand and ammonia, with due regard having been taken of the preliminary F tests. These F tests suggest that the two samples are drawn from the same population and the variances are assumed to be equal. The second form of the two-sample t test, in which the samples variances are pooled, is therefore appropriate.

A table summarising the two-sample t-test results (Box 11.6) indicates that the differences between the water samples in the two surveys for percentage dissolved oxygen and biochemical oxygen demand were not significant. However, in the case of ammonia, a low probability (0.0058), which is less than the significance level of 0.05, suggests that rejection of the null hypothesis is appropriate. A difference as small as 0.10 mg/l is likely to occur by chance in only 58 out of 10 000 samples.

11.4.3.2 Pearson's chi-square test

Samples A and B in the river pollution project include the flow and river-quality class as determined by the 1985 national survey. Null hypothesis RP4 examines whether the apparent association between these attributes is statistically significant in both samples, and states:

> The 1985 river quality and flow classification systems are independent of each other: any apparent tendency for rivers in one flow class to have a particular quality rating is entirely the result of sampling error.

The sampled rivers are classed into five quality and eight flow groups, which produce a 5 by 8 cross-tabulation. The Pearson chi-square test seems an appropriate means for examining the association between the groupings. Strictly speaking, Pearson's chi-square test is unsuitable to this question, because the water-quality classes are ordered rather than simple nominal categories. The same test statistic would be obtained regardless of the sequence in which the categories are presented in the contingency table. So at best the test is capable of showing that any differences in the frequencies are significant, it would not, for example, be justifiable to conclude that faster flowing rivers were of better quality. Thus, although not entirely appropriate, for the purpose of illustration, Pearson's chi-square test is used to examine null hypothesis RP4 in samples A and B.

The software log (Table 11.11) shows the second method for carrying out this test in MINITAB, which is by means of a subcommand on the TABLE command, thus:

```
MTB > TABLE C7 C8;
SUBC > CHISQUARE.
```

where C7 and C8 define the two columns containing the attributes which are to form the contingency table. Here, in the case of sample B, the columns are the river quality and flow class. The expected frequencies and Pearson's chi-square statistic are displayed in the output,

Sample A:

```
MTB > TABLE C3 C6;
SUBC > CHISQUARE.
```

ROWS: Class COLUMNS: Flow

	1	2	3	4	5	6	7	8	9	All
1	0	5	10	10	5	10	0	0	10	50
2	0	5	10	0	0	10	15	5	5	50
3	5	5	5	10	5	5	5	0	10	50
4	0	5	5	10	5	5	10	10	0	50
5	5	5	5	10	0	10	5	5	5	50
ALL	10	25	35	40	15	40	35	20	30	50

CHI-SQUARE = 90.774 WITH D.F. = 32

CELL CONTENTS -
COUNT

Sample B:

```
MTB > TABLE C7 C8;
SUBC > CHISQUARE.
```

ROWS: Class COLUMNS: Flow

	1	2	3	4	5	6	7	8	All
1	0	0	0	20	10	10	10	10	60
2	0	0	0	0	20	40	0	0	60
3	0	0	30	29	0	1	0	0	60
4	0	10	30	0	10	10	0	0	60
5	10	48	0	0	0	2	0	0	60
ALL	10	58	60	49	40	63	10	10	300

CHI-SQUARE = 552.128 WITH D.F. = 28

CELL CONTENTS -
COUNT

Box 11.7 Summary of Pearson's chi-square results for RP4 for flow and river-quality class river pollution project in Samples A and B (MINITAB output)

together with the degrees of freedom and the number of cells with less than five observations. The probability associated with the test statistic should be obtained by reference to the chi-square table in order to reach a decision on whether to accept or reject the null hypothesis.

The results of the two tests and the contingency tables are given Box 11.7. The degrees of freedom are shown, and reference to the chi-square table (Appendix IV, Table 3) shows that the probabilities of the χ^2-test statistics for samples A and B are greater than 0.001. The null hypotheses may be rejected, with the conclusion reached that the bivariate classification of both samples by flow rate and river-quality class shows a statistically significant association, which is likely to occur by chance on less than 1 in a 1000 occasions. However, the inappropriateness of the test should be noted in relation to this conclusion.

11.4.3.3 H test

The Kruskal–Wallis H test is the non-parametric equivalent of analysis of variance and seeks to determine if three or more samples or groups are significantly different. The MINITAB command which performs an H test has a similar general structure to ONEWAY in so far as the data for the continuous variable, which will be ranked, are held in one column and a second column of integers identifies the groups or levels to which the observations belong. The command syntax is therefore relatively simple:

MTB > KRUSKAL-WALLIS C1 C2

where C1 contains the raw data for all observations and C2 the 'group identifiers'. The output from the command reports the median and the average rank score, together with a Z value for each group. The null hypothesis states that there is no difference between the groups, and the Z distribution for each is approximately normal with a mean of 0 and a variance of 1. The validity of the H statistic derived from the standard formula may be affected by the presence of ties when the complete set of observations are ranked. The correction factor, given previously, is applied automatically by MINITAB if there are ties. In this case both H and the adjusted value of H are printed together with their respective probabilities, leaving the analyst to decide on which H value to use when choosing between the null and alternative hypotheses by reference to the usual levels of significance.

The river pollution project includes primary data from the analysis of water samples and data from secondary sources in the form of the river-quality and flow class as determined by the 1985 national survey. The project is concerned with how well the classification system separates or segregates rivers according to their quality. It also investigates the extent to which pollution of rivers can be attributed to discharges from factories. These issues are reflected in null hypothesis RP5, which states that:

> Any apparent differences between the rivers in sample B with respect to river quality and flow class are not significant, and have merely emerged as a result of chance; the sample survey provides no firm evidence of an improvement in water quality.

As usual, a number of null hypotheses could be specified, relating to the classificatory chemicals (dissolved oxygen, BOD and ammonia) and the concentrations of metallic ions. The lack of detailed results from the previous river-quality survey means that the more powerful parametric tests are unavailable and thus the Kruskal-Wallis test is a suitable non-parametric substitute. The sequence of commands to perform a series of H tests on sample B is given in Table 11.11. The tests rank the continuous variables derived from the chemical analysis of the water samples and the attributes representing previous quality and flow class, and upstream or downstream location.

The results of the analysis have been assembled in Box 11.8. The tests suggest that dissolved oxygen, BOD and ammonia concentrations are strongly connected with river quality and flow class, since the probabilities for the six H tests are all very small (< 0.001). In other words, the specific null hypotheses are rejected in favour of the alternative

	H	P	Accept/ Reject H_0
Test:			
Dissolved Oxygen with			
Quality	277.18	0.000	Reject
Flow	191.01	0.000	Reject
Up/Downstream	9.84	0.000	Reject
BOD with			
Quality	277.71	0.000	Reject
Flow	190.53	0.000	Reject
Up/Downstream	0.00	0.996	Accept
Ammonia with			
Quality	215.39	0.000	Reject
Flow	148.27	0.000	Reject
Up/Downstream	0.50	0.478	Accept
Copper with			
Quality	6.13	0.191	Accept
Flow	9.83	0.200	Accept
Up/Downstream	61.48	0.000	Reject
Mercury with			
Quality	6.02	0.198	Accept
Flow	5.86	0.556	Accept
Up/Downstream	84.52	0.000	Reject
Zinc with			
Quality	18.70	0.001	Reject
Flow	27.01	0.000	Reject
Up/Downstream	142.17	0.000	Reject

Sample KRUSKELL-WALLIS Output from MINITAB

```
MTB > KRUSKELL-WALLIS C9 C7
LEVEL      NOBS    MEDIAN    AVE. RANK    Z VALUE
1            60    83.200        269.8      11.91
2            60    65.300        209.9       5.93
3            60    43.000        151.8       0.13
4            60    12.250         80.5      -6.99
5            60     6.500         40.5     -10.98
OVERALL     300                  150.5
H = 277.18 d.f. = 4 p = 0.000
H = 277.20 d.f. = 4 p = 0.000 (adj. for ties)
```

Box 11.8 Summary of *H* test results for RP5 for selected chemicals in sample B of river pollution project

hypotheses that river quality and flow class have a statistically significant association with the amount of these chemicals in the rivers of the North West Water Authority. However, the levels of these chemicals upstream and downstream of factories are not significantly different. The concentration of the three metallic ions does vary in this way, with H-test probabilities of less than 0.05 in all cases. The metallic ions do not appear to vary in association with water quality and flow class.

11.4.4 Village communities

11.4.4.1 Pearson's chi-square: two- and k-sample tests

Pearson's chi-square test can be carried out in SPSS-X by using the NPAR TESTS command, which was introduced in Chapter 10, or by means of the STATISTICS subcommand on CROSSTABS. The syntax of the CROSSTABS command was examined in Section 7.3.4 and it is relatively simple to add the necessary subcommand thus:

```
CROSSTABS VARIABLES = varlist / TABLES
                    = varlist BY varlist / STATISTICS = 1
```

The 1 on the statistics subcommand is the code number instructing the software to calculate the χ^2 statistic for each of the tables specified on the TABLES subcommand. The keyword CHISQ can be used in place of 1. Several other test statistics may be obtained by using the appropriate code numbers, but these are more specialised and outside the scope of this text. Reclassification of the raw data may be necessary before the test can be carried out, using appropriate data transformation commands (e.g. RECODE). The output includes the value of the test statistic, χ^2, its probability and the degrees of freedom, which enables the fate of the null hypothesis to be decided immediately.

The village communities project offers numerous opportunities for investigating associations between the observations (respondents), with respect to two, three, or even more, variables and attributes. These multivariate situations are computationally equivalent to examining two or more samples in respect of the same attribute. The two null hypotheses, VC4 and VC5, are simply two examples which relate to the bivariate and multivariate situations. They state, respectively, that:

> Attitudes towards the development are not influenced by the respondent's length of residence in the village — the newcomers and the indigenous population are indistinguishable in their views.

and

> The relative frequencies produced when the respondents in the sample are classified according to their economic position, household tenure and attitude towards the proposed development show no sign of an association between these attributes. The frequencies are what would be expected if the sample had been distributed entirely at random.

The former relates to a two-dimensional contingency table with attitude to the development and recoded length of residence on the axes.

Table 11.12 Application of χ^2 test for two or more samples to village communities project in SPSS-X

```
FILE HANDLE SF / NAME = 'VILLAG01.SF'
GET FILE = SF
CROSSTABS VARIABLES =
  TENURE (1,6),RELENGTH(1,6),ECONPOSN(1,7),FAVPROP(1,2) /
  TABLES = FAVPROP BY RELENGTH / TABLES = FAVPROP BY ECONPOSN BY
  TENURE / STATISTICS = CHISQ
FINISH
```

Box 11.9 Summary of Pearson's chi-square test results for VC4 and VC5 in village communities project

FAVPROP In Favour of Proposal by RELENGTH Recoded length of residence

RELENGTH Page 1 of 1

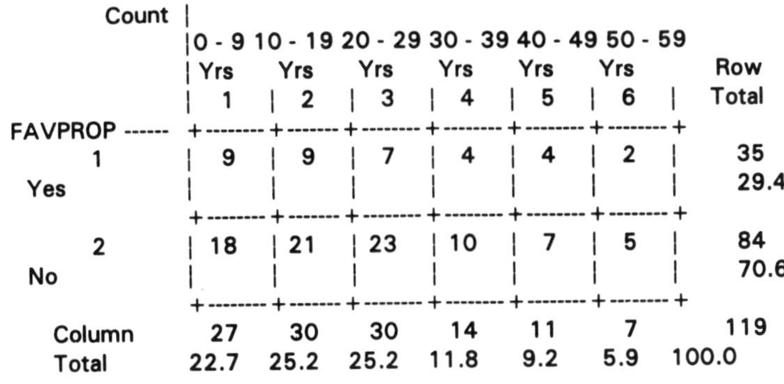

Count	0 - 9 Yrs 1	10 - 19 Yrs 2	20 - 29 Yrs 3	30 - 39 Yrs 4	40 - 49 Yrs 5	50 - 59 Yrs 6	Row Total
FAVPROP							
1 Yes	9	9	7	4	4	2	35 29.4
2 No	18	21	23	10	7	5	84 70.6
Column Total	27 22.7	30 25.2	30 25.2	14 11.8	11 9.2	7 5.9	119 100.0

Chi-square	Value	DF	Significance
Pearson	1.00209	5	.96240

Minimum Expected Frequency −2.059
Cells with Expected Frequency < 5 − 4 OF 12(33.3%)

Number of Missing Observations: 3

In Favour of Proposal by ECONPOSN Economic Position of Respondent
Controlling for... TENURE Housing Tenure Value = 1 Own Outright

ECONPOSN Page 1 of 1

Count	Emplr S-E 1	Emplee F T 2	Emplee P T 3	H'wife/ band 5	Other 7	Row Total
FAVPROP						
1 Yes	1	2	1			4 30.8
2 No	2	5		1	1	9 69.2
Column Total	3 23.1	7 53.8	1 7.7	1 7.7	1 7.7	13 100.0

Chi-square	Value	DF	Significance
Pearson	3.16402	4	.53076

Minimum Expected Frequency − .308
Cells with Expected Frequency < 5 − 10 OF 10(100.0%)

(continued)

Box 11.9 (*continued*)

FAVPROP In Favour of Proposal by ECONPOSN Economic Position of Respondent Controlling for... TENURE Housing Tenure Value = 2 Own with Mortgage

ECONPOSN Page 1 of 1

Count / FAVPROP	Emplr S-E 1	Emplee F-T 2	Emplee P T 3	Unempl 4	H'wife/ band 5	Ret'd 6	Other 7	Row Total
1 Yes	3	5	3	2	3	3	1	20 28.6
2 No	3	22	4	1	6	13	1	50 71.4
Column Total	6 8.6	27 38.6	7 10.0	3 4.3	9 12.9	16 22.9	2 2.9	70 100.0

Chi-square	Value	DF	Significance
Pearson	6.82662	6	.33718

Minimum Expected Frequency –.571
Cells with Expected Frequency < 5 – 9 OF 14(64.3%)

FAVPROP In Favour of Proposal by ECONPOSN Economic Position of Respondent Controlling for... TENURE Housing Tenure Value = 3 Rent from LA or Hsg

ECONPOSN Page 1 of 1

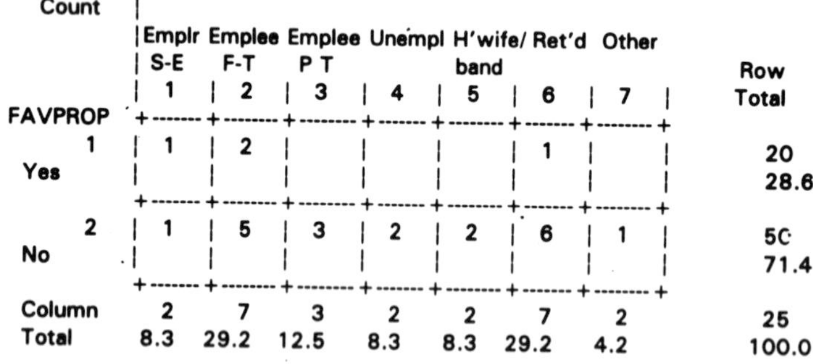

Count / FAVPROP	Emplr S-E 1	Emplee F-T 2	Emplee P T 3	Unempl 4	H'wife/ band 5	Ret'd 6	Other 7	Row Total
1 Yes	1	2				1		20 28.6
2 No	1	5	3	2	2	6	1	50 71.4
Column Total	2 8.3	7 29.2	3 12.5	2 8.3	2 8.3	7 29.2	2 4.2	25 100.0

Chi-square	Value	DF	Significance
Pearson	3.94286	6	.68441

Minimum Expected Frequency –.167
Cells with Expected Frequency < 5 – 12 OF 14(85.7%)

(*continued*)

Box 11.9 *(continued)*

FAVPROP In Favour of Proposal by ECONPOSN Economic Position of Respondent Controlling for... TENURE Housing Tenure Value = 4 Rent Privately

ECONPOSN Page 1 of 1

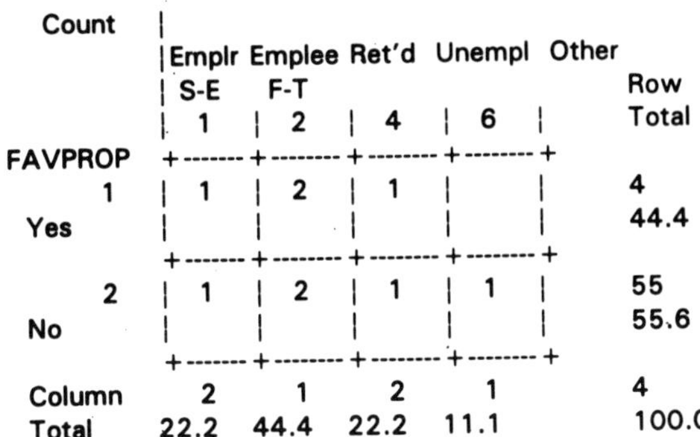

Count	Emplr S-E 1	Emplee F-T 2	Ret'd 4	Unempl Other 6	Row Total
FAVPROP					
1 Yes	1	2	1		4 44.4
2 No	1	2	1	1	55 55.6
Column Total	2 22.2	1 44.4	2 22.2	1 11.1	4 100.0

Chi-square	Value	DF	Significance
Pearson	.90000	3	.82543

Minimum Expected Frequency –.444
Cells with Expected Frequency < 5 – 8 OF 8(100.0%)

FAVPROP In Favour of Proposal by ECONPOSN Economic Position of Respondent Controlling for... TENURE Housing Tenure Value = 5 Tied to Work

ECONPOSN Page 1 of 1

Count	Emplr S-E 1	Emplee F-T 2	Ret'd Other 6	Row Total
FAVPROP				
1 Yes	1		1	2 50.0
2 No		1	1	50.0
Column Total	1 25.0	1 25.0	2 50.0	4 100.0

Chi-square	Value	DF	Significance
Pearson	2.00000	2	.36788

Minimum Expected Frequency –.500
Cells with Expected Frequency < 5 – 6 OF 6(100.0%)

(continued)

Box 11.9 (*continued*)

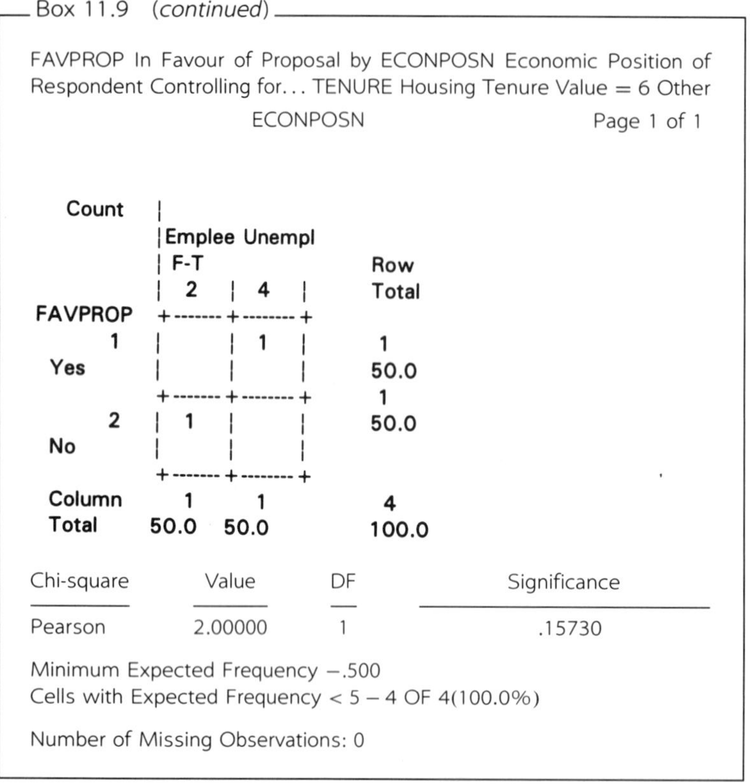

FAVPROP In Favour of Proposal by ECONPOSN Economic Position of Respondent Controlling for... TENURE Housing Tenure Value = 6 Other

```
                        ECONPOSN                      Page 1 of 1

        Count  |
               |Emplee Unempl
               | F-T               Row
               |  2   |  4  |      Total
FAVPROP        +------+-----+
            1  |      |  1  |      1
      Yes      |      |     |      50.0
               +------+-----+      1
            2  |  1   |     |      50.0
      No       |      |     |
               +------+-----+
      Column      1      1         4
      Total     50.0   50.0        100.0
```

Chi-square	Value	DF	Significance
Pearson	2.00000	1	.15730

Minimum Expected Frequency –.500
Cells with Expected Frequency < 5 – 4 OF 4(100.0%)

Number of Missing Observations: 0

The latter is a more complex, three-dimensional table. Both statistical tests can be performed on the same CROSSTABS command with different TABLES specifications. The log of the SPSS-X session is given in Table 11.12.

The tabular and statistical results of these analyses appear in Box 11.9. SPSS-X presents multivariate cross-tabulations as a series of two-dimensional tables, in this case one for each category of the third attribute. The test result for VC4 (the cross-tabulation of recoded length of residence and attitude to the proposal produces a χ^2 of 1.002) suggests that the null hypothesis should be accepted. The probability of getting this value with 5 degrees of freedom is far greater than 0.05 at 0.9624. As far as VC5 is concerned, the series of six tests between economic position and attitude to the proposal, controlling for tenure type, are not statistically significant; thus the null hypotheses are retained. It should be noted that the percentage of cells with an expected frequency of less than 5 is high in most cases.

11.4 REVIEW OF SOFTWARE COMMANDS

The range of statistical tests has been deliberately limited to those most suitable for an introductory text, consequently we have only scratched the surface of the facilities and statistics commands in the software. The discussion has revealed that there are both similarities and differences in the commands used in MINITAB and SPSS-X for carrying out univariate tests for two or more samples. The general approach adopted in MINITAB is for separate commands which perform a particular test, for example the non-parametric procedures CHISQUARE, MANN-WHITNEY and KRUSKAL-WALLIS. In contrast, the same result is achieved in SPSS-X with the general command NPAR TESTS with various subcommands to specify the required test (e.g. CHISQUARE and M-W for Mann-Whitney). Both packages include a facility for producing contingency tables with optional test statistics.

Table 11.13 summarises the software commands for carrying out the various tests which have been described in this chapter, as well as other tests which have not been examined. The variables to be tested are specified on MINITAB commands by their column number or column name. In SPSS-X, variables and attributes are always referred to on a procedural or data manipulation command by their variable name of up to eight characters, which was defined when the data were first entered

Table 11.13 Comparison of commands for performing multiple-sample univariate tests

	MINITAB	SPSS-X
Two samples		
F test	Not available	Not available
t test	TWOSAMPLE C C; ALTERNATIVE = ; POOLED.	T-TEST GROUPS = /VARIABLES =
χ^2	CHISQUARE C C	CROSSTABS VARIABLES = / /TABLES = /STATISTICS = 1
	or	or
	TABLE C. . .C; CHISQUARE.	NPAR TESTS CHISQUARE = /EXPECTED =
U test	MANN-WHITNEY [K] C C; ALTERNATIVE = .	NPAR TESTS M-W = BY
k samples		
ANOVA	AOVONEWAY C. . .C	ONEWAY BY
	or	
	ONEWAY C C	
H test	KRUSKAL-WALLIS C C	NPAR TESTS K-W = BY
χ^2	CHISQUARE C. . . C	CROSSTABS VARIABLES = / /TABLES = /STATISTICS = 1
	or	or
	TABLE C. . .C; CHISQUARE.	NPAR TESTS CHISQUARE = /EXPECTED =

in to the software. In general both packages offer a wide range of facilities for undertaking parametric and non-parametric tests, although in the case of MINITAB some rather tedious data manipulation commands may be necessary, since it is difficult to select groups of cases for inclusion on the basis of conditional statements. The data transformation and selection facilities in SPSS-X are generally more flexible in this respect.

Part IV

STATISTICAL ANALYSIS III

Chapter 12
Analysis of relationships: correlation

12.1 RELATIONSHIPS BETWEEN TWO VARIABLES

The statistical techniques discussed previously, with two exceptions, have dealt with univariate analyses. The exceptions are the Pearson's chi-square and Kruskal–Wallis tests when applied to one sample classified respectively according to two or more nominal attributes or ordinal variables. Although univariate techniques are important as a foundation for understanding the principles of statistical analysis and the ways in which this supports the accumulation of scientific knowledge, most geographical problems involve at least two variables and some may require considerably more. The analytical techniques used in these situations are known, in the former case, as *bivariate* (i.e. two variates or variables) and, in the latter, as *multivariate* (i.e. many variates or variables). Specific multivariate techniques are only introduced briefly in the concluding chapter, since a detailed exposition is outside the scope of this text. Bivariate techniques, most notably correlation and regression, provide a basis for examining more complex statistical procedures and are covered in this and the following chapter.

The main focus of attention in correlation analysis is on whether a relationship exists between two variables which have been measured for a single sample of observations. Designating the two variables as X and Y, there are generally three ways in which they can vary or be related:

1. The values of X and Y alter in tandem with each other, with low values for X associated with low values of Y and vice versa.
2. The values of X and Y vary in opposite directions, with low values of X associated with high values of Y and vice versa.
3. The values of X and Y do not vary according to a regular pattern and are randomly connected, with low values of X as likely to be associated with high values of Y as they are with low ones, and vice versa.

These are descriptions of 'ideal type' relationships which will rarely, if ever, be achieved in reality. The purpose of correlation analysis is to identify the ideal type to which a given set of observations most closely approximates and to measure the extent of the approximation.

There are several different techniques of correlation, but a common feature is that they produce a numerical quantity measuring the extent and nature of any relationship. This quantity is known as a *correlation coefficient*, and it provides a statistical description of the relationship, or lack of it, between two sets of numbers. The descriptive function of a correlation coefficient is similar to the measures of central tendency and dispersion which describe the features of a single set of numbers. In contrast to measures such as the mean, variance and standard deviation, the various types of correlation coefficient are constrained by their formulae to lie between -1.0 to $+1.0$. In other words, these are standardised measures which enable one set of data to be compared with another. A correlation coefficient of $+1.0$ relates to 'ideal type' relationship 1 outlined above, -1.0 to relationship 2 and 0.0 to relationship 3.

The interpretation of a correlation coefficient in relation to these ideal types requires that two aspects are taken into account: its magnitude and its sign. The magnitude of the coefficient quantifies the extent or strength of the *covariation* between the two sets of numbers; the closer the value approaches to either of the extremes the stronger the relationship. Thus a correlation coefficient of ± 0.9000 indicates a stronger relationship than ± 0.4000. A correlation coefficient equal to 0.0 may indicate the absence of a relationship. The sign, $-$ or $+$, attached to the coefficient denotes the direction of the relationship. A value of $+0.9000$ indicates that the numbers tend towards ideal type 1, whereas -0.9000 suggests a tendency towards ideal type 2. Correlation coefficients of $+0.4000$ and -0.4000 also signify relationships which tend towards to ideal types 1 and 2, but less strongly than for ± 0.9000.

A further point to note is that the value of the correlation coefficient for a particular set of paired data values will be the same regardless of which variable is designated as X and which as Y. It is quite feasible to restate the above ideal type descriptions to reflect this. For example, relationship 1 would become:

> The values of Y and X alter in tandem with each other, with low values for Y associated with low values of X and vice versa.

This simple point reflects an important distinction between correlation and regression. The former quantifies the relationship between two variables, whereas the latter examines whether the connection is causal. In regression analysis it is important to decide which variable is the cause and which is the effect, and then correctly designate the former as X and the latter as Y. From a computational point of view, no such distinction is necessary with correlation.

The correlation coefficient therefore provides a precise measure of the nature and extent of a relationship; however, the various types are most conveniently distinguished by means of a series of scatterplots (Figure 12.1). The perfect positive relationship (ideal type 1) is shown in Figure 12.1(a), where the paired measurements for each observation all fall along a straight line from the bottom left to top right of the graph. The reverse situation, perfect negative correlation, (ideal type 2), illustrated in Figure 12.1(e), has the observations aligned from top left to bottom right. In reality, if a positive or negative relationship is present between two sets of measurements, it is unlikely that they will form a straight line. The more usual outcome is that the observations will be scattered or dispersed on either side and, at best, will display only a general tendency towards linear alignment (Figures 12.1(b) and 12.1(d)). A correlation coefficient of precisely 0.0 is also improbable in reality, but can be achieved by the situation depicted in Figure 12.1(c). Finally, the correlation techniques examined in this chapter relate to linear relationships, in other words ideal types 1 and 2, and involve values varying in a regular pattern. Other types of relationship, for example curvilinear and cyclical, are illustrated in Figure 12.1(f) and 12.1(g). Despite the fact that the observations in both these cases display a perfect curvilinear or cyclical relationship, their linear coefficients would be 0.0. Alternative types of correlation analysis should be considered, if an examination of the scatterplot suggests that a non-linear relationship may be present.

The statistical tests examined in the last two chapters help the investigator to decide whether any difference between summary descriptive statistics (the median, mean, variance, etc.) derived from sample data and the equivalent population parameters is likely to have arisen through random sampling error. A correlation coefficient relating to a sample of observations may also be subject to error from this source. The presence of a certain type of relationship in a population is not confirmed or inferred simply by virtue of having calculated a correlation coefficient from a sample of its observations, any more than the mean of a variable from a sample necessarily provides an accurate estimate of the parent population mean. The sample may contain various types of randomly distributed errors. Tests exist which enable the investigator to determine the probability that any difference between the correlation coefficient for the sampled observations and some hypothesised value for the corresponding parameter in the parent population is due to chance. Similarly, it may be necessary to determine a confidence interval for a correlation coefficient which has been calculated from sample data in order to estimate the population parameter.

The choice of correlation technique should be based on the characteristics of the data, in particular the scale of measurement and method of sampling employed. We have already seen how the scales of measurement for a single variable can be collapsed from the more to the less sophisticated (i.e. from the ratio/interval to the ordinal and nominal). A similar exercise can be carried out for two variables and helps to

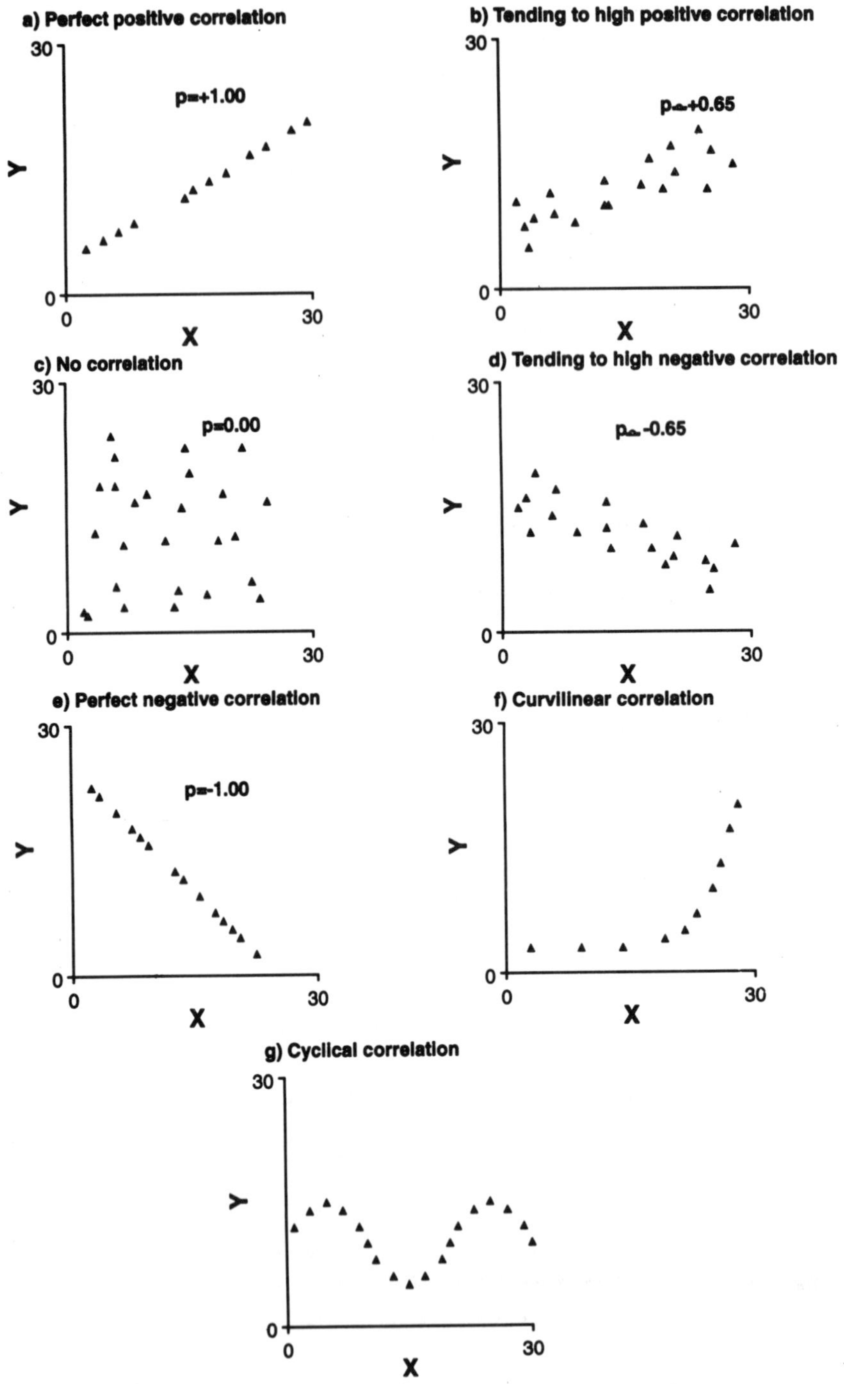

Figure 12.1 'Ideal types' of relationship between two variables

explain some of the principles of correlation and how it differs from the analysis of association which can be undertaken with contingency tables. Suppose that a sample of 30 companies in a city provide information about their total expenditure and income during a year. In simple terms it may be expected that these variables would exhibit a fairly strong positive relationship, with higher levels of investment being connected to greater financial returns. The scatterplot of the raw data in Figure 12.2(a) shows that in general terms this is indeed the case, with expenditure and income respectively recorded on the X and Y axes.

Two grids with different cell sizes, which represent alternative classifications of the raw data, have been superimposed on to the scatterplot (Figure 12.2(b)). The sizes of the grids are determined by the width of the classes applied to the variables. As the class interval becomes wider, so the number of observations per cell increases, while at the same time more information and detail are lost. Using the grid with the wider class intervals (shown in Figure 12.2(b) a contingency table has been produced and analysed by means of Pearson's chi-square test to determine whether there is any association in the frequency counts. The contingency table is shown alongside the gridded scatter plot in Figure 12.2(b). The value of χ^2 for the 3×3 contingency table is 12.895, which is considerably larger than would be expected by chance at the 0.05 level (the tabulated chi-square is 9.488 at $P = 0.05$). The null hypothesis of no difference between the observed and expected frequency distributions would be rejected.

Now imagine that the rows and columns of this 3×3 table are rearranged, while retaining the relative location of each observation within the cell in which it occurs (Figure 12.2(c)). Such a reorganisation of the rows and columns of a contingency table is entirely feasible in a genuine application of Pearson's chi-square test, since no ordering of the classes is implied. Surprising though it might seem at first, this change does not alter the observed and expected frequencies within a given cell, it only changes the relative location of the cells within the table as a whole. On the other hand, the overall scatter of observations across the underlying graph of the raw data is now completely different, with the previous indication of a relationship tending towards ideal type 1 eradicated. The correlation coefficient for the rearranged set of data would now be entirely different, whereas the value of χ^2 remains the same. The example demonstrates how the analysis of association by means of contingency tables is a less powerful statistical procedure than the examination of relationships undertaken by correlation.

12.2 TYPES OF CORRELATION ANALYSIS

Students of statistics may sometimes form the impression that correlation analysis is restricted to certain types of variable, namely those

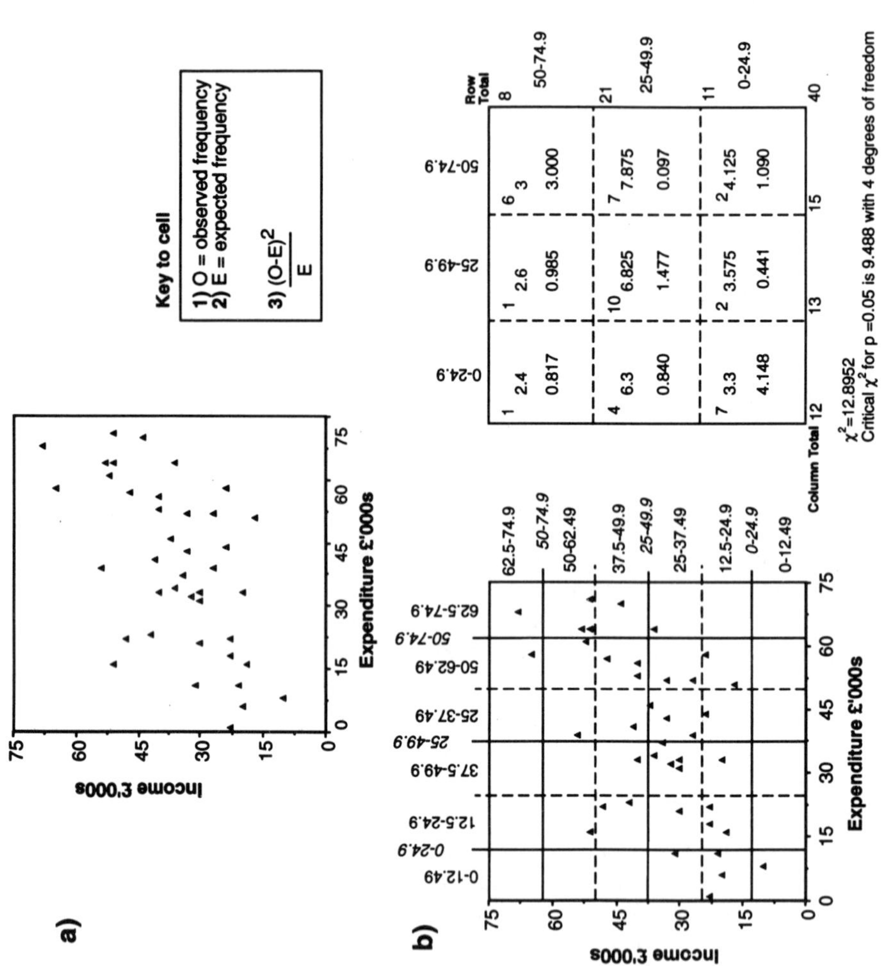

a)
Income £'000s
Expenditure £'000s
b)
Key to cell
1) O = observed frequency
2) E = expected frequency
3) (O-E)²/E
Row Total
Column Total
50-74.9
25-49.9
0-24.9
χ²=12.8952
Critical χ² for p =0.05 is 9.488 with 4 degrees of freedom

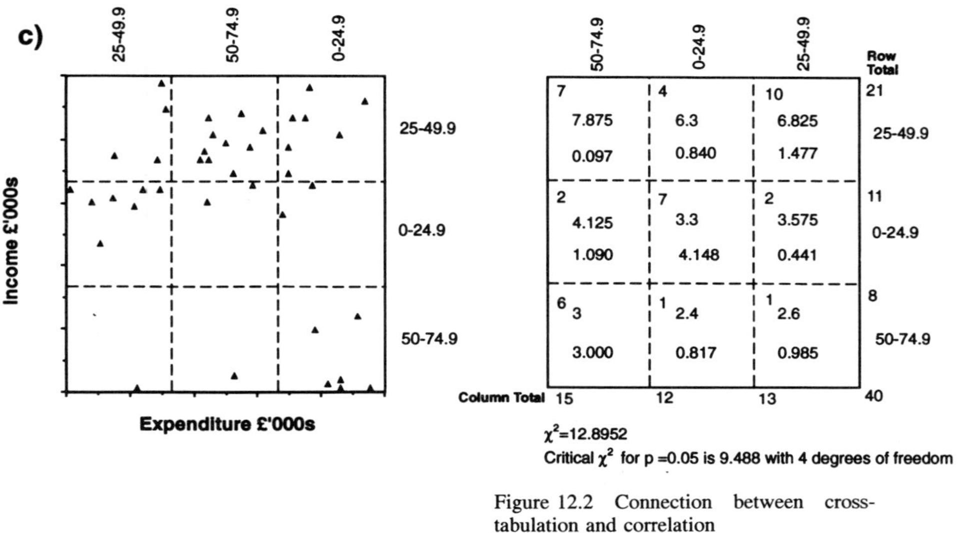

	50-74.9	0-24.9	25-49.9	Row Total	
	7 7.875 0.097	4 6.3 0.840	10 6.825 1.477	21	25-49.9
	2 4.125 1.090	7 3.3 4.148	2 3.575 0.441	11	0-24.9
	6 3 3.000	1 2.4 0.817	1 2.6 0.985	8	50-74.9
Column Total	15	12	13	40	

χ^2=12.8952

Critical χ^2 for p =0.05 is 9.488 with 4 degrees of freedom

Figure 12.2 Connection between cross-tabulation and correlation

measured on the interval or ratio scales. Furthermore, the assumptions made by the correlation technique associated with this type of variable (Pearson's product moment correlation coefficient) are sufficiently restrictive as to make such analysis of limited value for several disciplines, particularly in the social sciences. Fortunately, other less demanding types of correlation coefficient exist and some of the restrictive assumptions connected with Pearson's product moment correlation coefficient can be relaxed, especially when the sample size is large. The following sections examine three types of correlation coefficient: Pearson's product moment, Spearman's rank and the phi (ϕ) coefficient. These have been selected partly because of their inclusion in one or both of the software packages (MINITAB and SPSS-X) and partly because they cover the range of measurement scales, being used respectively for ratio/interval, ordinal and nominal data.

12.2.1 Pearson's product moment correlation coefficient

The *product moment correlation coefficient* was formulated by Karl Pearson in 1907. The coefficient is based on the notion of *covariance*, which is a development of the concept of variance, and can be conceived of as a bivariate measure of dispersion. The means of the two variables, $\bar{X}$ and $\bar{Y}$, define a central point within the set of observations, known as the *centroid*. Covariance is the mean deviation of the set of observations from their centroid. Two slightly different formulae exist for calculating the covariance, and for that matter the production moment correlation coefficient, depending on whether the data relate to a population or a sample. Population covariance is given by the formula

$$\frac{\Sigma(X - \bar{X})(Y - \bar{Y})}{N}$$

while sample covariance is given by

$$\frac{\Sigma(x - \bar{x})(y - \bar{y})}{n - 1}$$

where the two variables are represented by X and Y (lower-case x and y for a sample), N denotes the number of items in the population and n the number in a sample. The numerators of the equations are the sum of the products of the deviations of the individual X and Y values from their respective means. These quantities are not squared, which would be required if the separate variances of the two variables were being calculated. Squaring the deviations of each X and Y value from its respective mean is unnecessary when they are multiplied together before summation. The denominator for a sample is $n - 1$, because division by n leads to a biased estimate of the covariance.

The product moment correlation coefficient is represented by the symbol ρ (the Greek letter rho), or R, when used as a population parameter, but when applied to sample data the lower-case Roman letter r is almost invariably used. The covariance of the two sets of matched measurements provides the numerator for the product moment correlation coefficient formulae. The denominator in both formulae is the product of the standard deviations of the two variables. So, the formula for the population product moment correlation coeffecient is:

$$\rho = \frac{\dfrac{\Sigma(X-\bar{X})(Y-\bar{Y})}{N}}{\sqrt{\dfrac{\Sigma(X-\bar{X})^2}{N}}\sqrt{\dfrac{\Sigma(Y-\bar{Y})^2}{N}}}$$

and for a sample:

$$r = \frac{\dfrac{\Sigma(x-\bar{x})(y-\bar{y})}{n-1}}{\sqrt{\dfrac{\Sigma(x-\bar{x})^2}{n-1}}\sqrt{\dfrac{\Sigma(y-\bar{y})^2}{n-1}}}$$

The calculations involved in these equations are somewhat tedious, even if the number of observations is relatively small. An alternative set of formulae are available which entail less cumbersome data manipulation. The adjustments are similar to those made to the variance and standard deviation formulae and avoid calculation of the individual deviations. The alternative formulae are, for a population:

$$\rho = \frac{N\Sigma XY - \Sigma X\Sigma Y}{\sqrt{N\Sigma X^2 - (\Sigma X)^2}\sqrt{N\Sigma Y^2 - (\Sigma Y)^2}}$$

and for a sample:

$$r = \frac{n\Sigma xy - \Sigma x\Sigma y}{\sqrt{n\Sigma x^2 - (\Sigma x)^2}\sqrt{n\Sigma y^2 - (\Sigma y)^2}}$$

The farm size and net farm income variables for the sample of Yorkshire farms illustrate the procedure for calculating the product moment correlation coefficient (see Figure 7.1). The paired raw values of these variables (Table 12.1) suggest a reasonably strong positive relationship is present, with larger farms having higher levels of income. The sample size is 50 (the two suspiciously large farms have been omitted) and the centroid occurs at the intersection of the means: the mean area is 134.6 ha and mean net farm income is £58 428. The appropriate column totals from Table 12.1 are inserted into the simpler formula for calculating r thus:

$$r = \frac{50 \times 906\,878.38 - 6730.7 \times 2921.4}{\sqrt{50 \times 2\,961\,034.50 - 6730.7^2}\sqrt{50 \times 340\,745.56 - 2941.4^2}}$$

$$= \frac{45\,343\,919 - 19\,797\,680.98}{\sqrt{148\,051\,725.00 - 45\,302\,322.49}\sqrt{17\,037\,278.00 - 8\,651\,833.96}}$$

$$= \frac{25\,546\,238.02}{\sqrt{102\,749\,402.50}\sqrt{8\,385\,444.04}} = +0.8703$$

Table 12.1 Product moment correlation coefficient analysis for Yorkshire farms

Total Area (x)	NFI ('000s £) (y)	xy	x^2	y^2
456.8	45.6	20 830.08	208 666.23	2079.36
45.6	25.3	1 153.68	2 079.36	640.09
20.5	12.2	250.10	420.25	148.84
7.8	17.6	137.28	60.84	309.76
250.2	101.4	25 370.28	62 600.04	10 281.96
134.6	50.3	6 770.38	18 117.16	2 530.09
75.8	24.1	1 826.78	5 745.64	580.81
96.7	34.3	3 316.81	9 350.89	1 176.49
13.6	10.2	138.72	184.96	104.04
100.8	30.0	3 024.00	10 160.64	900.00
112.5	45.5	5 118.75	12 656.25	2 070.25
19.5	20.1	391.95	380.25	404.01
20.5	37.5	768.75	420.25	1 406.25
6.4	6.2	39.68	40.96	38.44
555.2	75.6	41 973.12	308 247.06	5 715.36
60.3	56.6	3 412.98	3 636.09	3 203.56
156.9	96.8	15 187.92	24 617.61	9 370.24
854.8	233.5	199 595.80	730 683.00	54 522.25
60.3	34.7	2 092.41	3 636.09	1 204.09
15.7	19.8	310.86	246.49	392.04
19.4	22.2	430.68	376.36	492.84
86.0	56.7	4 876.20	7 396.00	3 214.89
425.6	216.7	92 227.52	181 135.36	46 958.89
50.8	66.2	3 362.96	2 580.64	4 382.44
5.3	10.1	53.53	28.09	102.01
788.5	199.3	157 148.05	621 732.25	39 720.49
65.4	55.4	3 623.16	4 277.16	3 069.16
39.1	27.8	1 086.98	1 528.81	772.84
88.7	70.2	6 226.74	7 867.69	4 928.04
4.5	5.3	23.85	20.25	28.09
16.2	20.1	325.62	262.44	404.01
39.0	30.4	1 185.60	1 521.00	924.16
19.5	31.7	618.15	380.25	1 004.89
40.5	57.6	2 338.80	1 640.25	3 317.76
115.6	65.4	7 560.24	13 363.36	4 277.16
88.7	56.3	4 993.81	7 867.69	3 169.69
20.3	33.7	684.11	412.09	1 135.69
34.6	41.9	1 449.74	1 197.16	1 755.61
156.5	65.0	10 172.50	24 492.25	4 225.00
40.5	16.7	676.35	1 640.25	278.89
62.6	89.7	5 615.22	3 918.76	8 046.09
657.2	250.6	164 694.31	431 911.84	62 800.36
55.1	45.8	2 523.58	3 036.01	2 097.64
40.5	39.5	1 599.75	1 640.25	1 560.25
25.0	23.4	585.00	625.00	547.56
14.5	16.7	242.15	210.25	278.89
443.6	175.6	77 896.16	196 780.97	30 835.36
6.7	25.6	171.52	44.89	655.36
13.8	17.2	237.36	190.44	295.84
202.5	111.3	22 538.25	41 006.25	12 387.69
6730.7	2921.4	906 878.38	2 961 034.50	340 745.56

The value of r, $+0.8703$, clearly approaches the upper end of the positive range for the coefficient (the maximum possible value is $+1.0$), which indicates a strong relationship, tending towards ideal type 1 as suspected. It is worth recalling that the formula for the product moment correlation coefficient is symmetrical and r would equal $+0.8703$ regardless of which variables were designated as X and Y.

A correlation coefficient of $+0.8703$ is clearly encouraging for any researcher. The square of the correlation coefficient can be calculated (r^2) to generate a statistic known as the *coefficient of determination*, which measures the proportion of the variance explained. Thus, in the previous example, r^2 equals 0.7574, which indicates that 75.74 per cent of the total variance is explained by the correlation between the two variables. The remainder is accounted for by other variables. Any excessive enthusiasm about the strength of the correlation coefficient should be tempered by the fact that the result has been obtained from a sample of 50 farms. If the population of farms in Yorkshire had yielded a product moment correlation coefficient of $+0.8703$ from the two variables, there might well have been cause for celebration, but as it stands the coefficient is but one of many values that could have been obtained from samples containing the same or different numbers of observations. The value of ρ (the population coefficient) may well be $+0.8703$, but unless the sample statistic is tested to determine the probability of having occurred through chance, it would be unwise to attach too much significance to this conclusion.

12.2.1.2 Testing the significance of r

The focus of attention, as usual, is on the probabilities of the sampling distribution associated with the test statistic, in this case the correlation coefficient r. The sampling distribution of the test statistic is derived from a mathematical probability distribution. The importance of the normal distribution for univariate parametric tests has already been emphasised, and it is therefore perhaps not surprising that a similar mathematical model, the *bivariate normal distribution*, is central to significance testing for the product moment correlation coefficient. In the real world it is unlikely that two variables will correspond exactly to the bivariate normal distribution, in just the same way that no single variable will precisely conform to the binomial, Poisson and normal distributions. Nevertheless, the bivariate normal distribution forms a convenient and easily manipulated starting point from which to test the significance of the product moment correlation coefficient.

In formal terms, the bivariate normal distribution requires that both the *marginal* and *conditional* frequency distributions of the variables X and Y for a population of observations are normal. This somewhat confusing statement is best explained graphically. The two marginal distributions refer to the frequency distributions of variables X and Y (Figure 12.3(a)). Conditional frequency distributions exist for each different value of X, and also for each value of Y. Put another way,

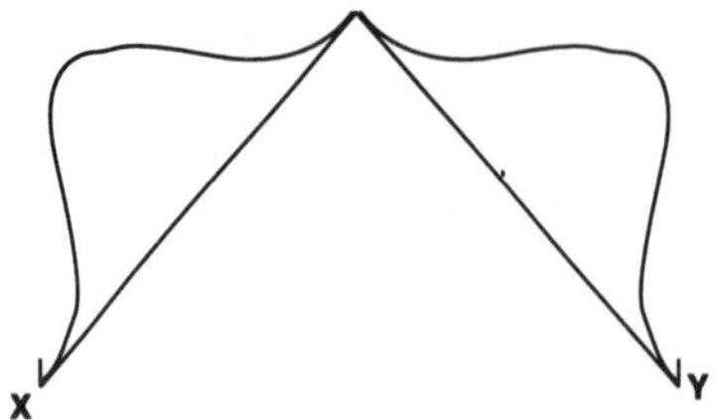

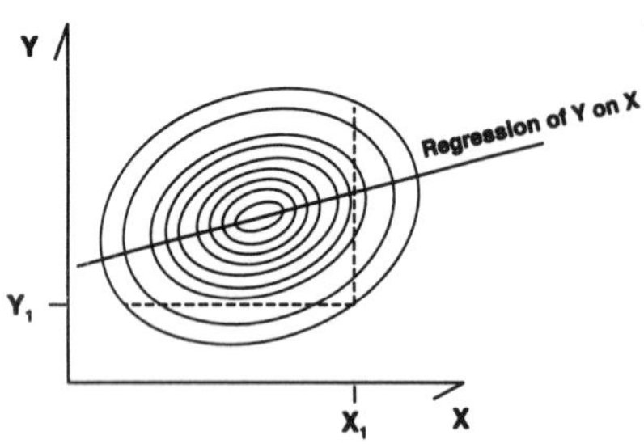

Figure 12.3 Bivariate probability distributions

at each value of X, the values of Y are normally distributed; similarly, at every value of Y, the values of X are normally distributed. There are as many conditional distributions as there are values of the continuous variables X and Y. Remembering that a frequency distribution refers to the count or number of observations possessing a particular value, or combination of values in the bivariate case, it is possible to draw a bivariate normal distribution as a contour map (Figure 12.3(b)). The contours represent heights or equal frequencies for the various combinations of X and Y values.

The univariate normal distribution has been described as 'bell-shaped', although strictly speaking it is a cross-section through the central peak of a bell shape. The bivariate normal distribution may be thought of as completing the analogy by possessing the three-dimensional form. Each vertical cross-section through the shape represented by the bivariate normal distribution is normal and symmetrical about its mean, regardless of whether it is perpendicular to one of the axes. On the other hand, horizontal sections are not necessarily circular, but are more often elliptical. The reason for this is that the marginal distributions of X and Y are required to be normal, but they are not necessarily identical. The variances and standard deviations of X and Y may be unequal, indicating differences in the dispersion or spread of values about their respective means.

The sampling distribution of r, which forms the basis for testing the significance of the correlation coefficient for a particular sample, is derived from the bivariate normal distribution. The shape of the sampling distribution varies according to sample size and the value of the population correlation coefficient, ρ, becoming progressively more normal and symmetrical (if ρ does not equal zero) as sample size increases. There are two ways in which this theory can be used to test the significance of a product moment correlation coefficient obtained from a sample.

The first method hypothesizes that ρ is 0.0, or, in other words, as far as the population of items is concerned, the two variables are uncorrelated. The null hypothesis states that the difference between $\rho(0.0)$ and r has arisen due to sampling error and is not significant. In these circumstances the probability of the coefficient r may be determined by reference to the t distribution, with the t statistic calculated as follows:

$$t = \frac{|r|\sqrt{n-2}}{\sqrt{1-r^2}}$$

The degrees of freedom are $n - 2$ and the t distribution table (Appendix IV, Table 2) should be consulted in order to reach a decision on whether to accept or reject the null hypothesis. Substituting the correlation coefficient from the Yorkshire sample into the equation, thus:

$$t = \frac{0.8703\sqrt{50-2}}{\sqrt{1-0.75742}} = \frac{6.0296}{0.4925} = 12.242$$

yields a test statistic of 12.242. Referring to the Table 2 in Appendix IV, there is an extremely low probability, less than 0.0001, of having obtained the test statistic t by chance. Thus the null hypothesis may be rejected and the correlation coefficient deemed to be significant.

The second method for testing the significance of Pearson's product moment correlation coefficient is used when the null hypothesis states that ρ is some value other than 0.0. This alternative test could be used to examine whether a sample coefficient differs significantly from that obtained in a previous census of the same population. The test involves transforming r into a quantity known as Fisher's **Z**, (sometimes shown as **Z**), which should not be confused with the Z distribution discussed previously. The transformation is carried out by means of the following:

$$\mathbf{Z} = 1.1513 \log_{10}\left(\frac{1+r}{1-r}\right)$$

The main advantages of Fisher's **Z** over r are that the correspondence between Fisher's **Z** and the normal distribution occurs with smaller sample sizes than r, and **Z** allows for the hypothesised population correlation coefficient, ρ, to be other than 0.0. The mean and standard deviation of the Fisher's **Z** distribution are:

$$\mu_{\mathbf{Z}} = 1.1513 \log_{10}\left(\frac{1+\rho}{1-\rho}\right)$$

$$\sigma_{\mathbf{Z}} = \frac{1}{\sqrt{n-3}}$$

Once r has been transformed into Fisher's $\mathbf{Z}$ the more familiar test statistic Z can be calculated as:

$$Z = \frac{|\mathbf{Z} - \mu_{\mathbf{Z}}|}{\sigma_{\mathbf{Z}}}$$

where $\mathbf{Z}$ is the transformed r coefficient, $\mu_{\mathbf{Z}}$ is the mean and $\sigma_{\mathbf{Z}}$ the standard deviation of the distribution of Fisher's $\mathbf{Z}$.

Suppose that a previous complete census of farms had produced a correlation coefficient of +0.7736 for the variables farm size and total net farm income. Is the sample correlation coefficient (+0.8703) different because the positive relationship has become stronger or is it due to sampling error? The first step in the test procedure is to transform the sample correlation r into Fisher's $\mathbf{Z}$, thus:

$$\mathbf{Z} = 1.1513 \log_{10}\left(\frac{1 + 0.8703}{1 - 0.8703}\right) = 1.1513 \log_{10}(14.4202) = 1.3343$$

A similar conversion is then carried out for the hypothesised value of the population, ρ, and the standard deviation or standard error is calculated:

$$\mu_{\mathbf{Z}} = 1.1513 \log_{10}\left(\frac{1 + 0.7736}{1 - 0.7736}\right) = 1.1513 \log_{10}(7.8339) = 1.0292$$

$$\sigma_{\mathbf{Z}} = \frac{1}{\sqrt{50 - 3}} = \frac{1}{\sqrt{47}} = 0.1459$$

The next step involves calculating the test statistic Z, thus:

$$Z = \frac{|1.3343 - 1.0292|}{0.1459} = 2.09$$

The probability associated with this Z value is obtained from the Z distribution table (Appendix IV, Table 1). The probability of obtaining a Z value of 2.09 (and therefore the difference between r and ρ) by chance is 0.0366, which is less than 0.05 but more than 0.01. Thus the decision on whether to accept or reject the null hypothesis will depend upon which level of significance is used. There is no prior reason to believe that the sample correlation coefficient should be smaller or larger than the hypothesised ρ. If there had been a reason, then a one-tailed test would have required the probability to be halved.

Product moment correlation and its associated significance testing procedures make a number of assumptions about the data.

1. Random sampling with replacement should be employed, or alternatively sampling without replacement from an infinite population where the sample size is less than 10 per cent of the population.
2. The two variables, X and Y, should be measured on either the interval or ratio scale and should conform to the bivariate normal distribution. Statisticians are unfortunately not in agreement as to

whether the product moment correlation coefficient is sufficiently robust to withstand deviation from this assumption. The usual solution to the problem is to ensure that the sample size is reasonably large, but this will not overcome the problem in some circumstances.

3. The items in the population, and therefore in the sample, should be independent of each other with respect to the variables X and Y; in other words, autocorrelation between the items should not be present for either variable.

The data from the sample of farms in Yorkshire satisfy the first of these requirements, but we have already seen that their distribution is relatively skewed and therefore likely to contravene the second. Fortunately, the sample size is reasonably large, although it does exceed 10 per cent of the population. Some positive spatial autocorrelation may be present, with similar-sized farms tending to cluster together, but the extent of this problem is undetermined.

12.2.2 Spearman's rank correlation coefficient

The potential difficulties of Pearson's product moment correlation coefficient have lead some analysts to turn to alternative, non-parametric methods of correlation analysis based on ordinal data. Spearman's rank correlation analysis produces a coefficient known as r_s. This type of correlation is used quite frequently in geographical analysis, where the data may not conform to the more stringent requirements of product moment correlation. The principle behind the technique is that a strong relationship between the variables is indicated by the items being ordered similarly with respect to the two variables and thus having similar rank scores. The ideal type relationships can be rephrased to apply to ordinal data, for example, in the case of ideal type 2:

> The rank scores of X and Y vary in opposite directions, with low ranks for X associated with high ranks for Y, and vice versa.

The procedure involved in the calculation of Spearman's rank correlation coefficient is reminiscent of the univariate tests for ordinal data, except that rather than ranking the observations from one or more samples according to a single variable, the observations from one sample are ordered with respect to two variables. The analysis requires a minimum of five observations. Tied observations are assigned the appropriate mean rank score. The differences (d) in the ranks are calculated and then squared (d^2). The sum of d^2 is used in the equation for calculating r_s:

$$r_s = 1 - \frac{6\Sigma d^2}{n(n^2 - 1)}$$

For comparison with the previous product moment correlation analysis, Spearman's rank technique has been applied to the size and net farm income variables for the sample of Yorkshire farms. The first step in the procedure is to sort and rank the farms according to each variable (see Table 12.2). The farms' rank positions on the two variables appear to be very similar: 37 farms have the same rank score in both cases, and the maximum difference is only 1. The second step is to substitute the relevant figures into the equation for Spearman's rank correlation coefficient:

$$r_s = 1 - \frac{6 \times 5.5}{50 \times (50^2 - 1)} = 1 - \frac{33}{124\,950} = +0.9997$$

The coefficient of +0.9997 shows a remarkably strong positive relationship between the two variables. Nevertheless, having been obtained from a sample, its significance should be tested.

The null hypothesis states that the two variables are in fact uncorrelated and the coefficient of +0.9997 has been achieved by chance through sampling error: the similarity of the farms' rank positions is not significant. There are two methods of testing the significance of an r_s coefficient depending on sample size.

If the sample has less than 100 observations, then Table 9 in Appendix IV should be used which shows the critical values of the coefficient for selected levels of significance. If the calculated coefficient exceeds or equals the tabulated value corresponding to the sample size and required level of significance, then the null hypothesis may safely be rejected. In this example the critical value of the coefficient corresponding to $n = 50$ and with a significance level of 0.05 (two-tailed) is ±0.279. The sample figure is far in excess of this and clearly significant.

The second method for testing the significance of r_s, which is used with larger samples, involves transforming the coefficient into a t statistic, thus:

$$t = r_s \sqrt{\frac{n-2}{1-r_s^2}}$$

Applying this conversion to the Yorkshire farms example, gives:

$$t = 0.9997 \sqrt{\frac{50-2}{1-0.9997}} = 399.88$$

Referring to the t distribution table (Appendix IV, Table 2), with $n - 2$ degrees of freedom, confirms that the null hypothesis can be rejected. Both tests lead to the conclusion that the two variables are highly correlated.

The assumptions associated with Spearman's rank correlation coefficient are relatively modest compared with some statistical procedures. The sample should be randomly selected with replacement from a finite population, although sampling without replacement is permissible from an infinite population. However, as with the product moment correlation coefficient, provided that the sample is sufficiently large and

Table 12.2 Spearman's rank correlation coefficient analysis for Yorkshire farms

Total area (x)	NFI ('000s £) (y)	Rank x	Rank y	(d)	(d^2)
4.5	5.3	1.0	1.0	0.0	0.00
5.3	6.2	2.0	2.0	0.0	0.00
6.4	10.1	3.0	3.0	0.0	0.00
6.7	10.2	4.0	4.0	0.0	0.00
7.8	12.2	5.0	5.0	0.0	0.00
13.6	16.7	6.0	6.5	−0.5	0.25
13.8	16.7	7.0	6.5	0.5	0.25
14.5	17.2	8.0	8.0	0.0	0.00
15.7	17.6	9.0	9.0	0.0	0.00
16.2	19.8	10.0	10.0	0.0	0.00
19.4	20.1	11.0	11.5	−0.5	0.25
19.5	20.1	12.5	11.5	1.0	1.00
19.5	22.2	12.5	13.0	−0.5	0.25
20.3	23.4	14.0	14.0	0.0	0.00
20.5	24.1	15.5	15.0	0.5	0.25
20.5	25.3	15.5	16.0	−0.5	0.25
25.0	25.6	17.0	17.0	0.0	0.00
34.6	27.8	18.0	18.0	0.0	0.00
39.0	30.0	19.0	19.0	0.0	0.00
39.1	30.4	20.0	20.0	0.0	0.00
40.5	31.7	22.0	21.0	1.0	1.00
40.5	33.7	22.0	22.0	0.0	0.00
40.5	34.3	22.0	23.0	−1.0	1.00
45.6	34.7	24.0	24.0	0.0	0.00
50.8	37.5	25.0	25.0	0.0	0.00
55.1	39.5	26.0	26.0	0.0	0.00
60.3	41.9	27.5	27.0	0.5	0.25
60.3	45.5	27.5	28.0	−0.5	0.25
62.6	45.6	29.0	29.0	0.0	0.00
65.4	45.8	30.0	30.0	0.0	0.00
75.8	50.3	31.0	31.0	0.0	0.00
86.0	55.4	32.0	32.0	0.0	0.00
88.7	56.3	33.5	33.0	0.5	0.25
88.7	56.6	33.5	34.0	−0.5	0.25
96.7	56.7	35.0	35.0	0.0	0.00
100.8	57.6	36.0	36.0	0.0	0.00
112.5	65.0	37.0	37.0	0.0	0.00
115.6	65.4	38.0	38.0	0.0	0.00
134.6	66.2	39.0	39.0	0.0	0.00
156.5	70.2	40.0	40.0	0.0	0.00
156.9	75.6	41.0	41.0	0.0	0.00
202.5	89.7	42.0	42.0	0.0	0.00
250.2	96.8	43.0	43.0	0.0	0.00
425.6	101.4	44.0	44.0	0.0	0.00
443.6	111.3	45.0	45.0	0.0	0.00
456.8	175.6	46.0	46.0	0.0	0.00
555.2	199.3	47.0	47.0	0.0	0.00
657.2	216.7	48.0	48.0	0.0	0.00
788.5	233.5	49.0	49.0	0.0	0.00
854.8	250.6	50.0	50.0	0.0	0.00
6370.7	2941.2				5.50

comprises no more than 10 per cent of the total population, these strictures are not binding upon the researcher. Spearman's rank correlation coefficient is less powerful than the product moment coefficient and does not take into account the magnitude of the variations between the observations, simply their rank positions.

12.2.3 Phi coefficient

The phi correlation coefficient (ϕ) represents a development of Pearson's chi-square test for cross-tabulated data, although there are some importance differences. Unlike the latter statistic, ϕ quantifies the extent and strength of any relationship between two attributes. χ^2 is concerned with the simpler question of testing for an association between the bivariate frequencies. The number of classes into which the attributes are grouped for Pearson's chi-square test is only limited by the need to ensure that number of cells with zero observations or an expected frequency of less than 5 is kept within the assumptions of the test. The ϕ coefficient deals exclusively with 2×2 contingency tables for two dichotomous attributes. For example, a specific mineral may be present or absent in a soil or a person may or may not have been on holiday within a given time period. The third important difference is that the value of ϕ is constrained to lie in the range -1.0 to $+1.0$.

The procedure for calculating the coefficient involves computations on the frequency counts in the cells of the 2×2 contingency table, in which the cells are labelled A, B, C and D (Table 12.3). Cells A and D contain those observations which possess both or neither of the characteristics. In formal terms the formula for ϕ is

$$\phi = \frac{AD - BC}{\sqrt{[(A+B)(B+C)(A+C)(B+D)]}}$$

When ϕ has been calculated for sample data, the analyst needs to test whether the coefficient is simply the result of sampling error. The null hypothesis states that the observed value of ϕ has occurred through chance and there is no relationship between the attributes. The significance of ϕ is determined by converting the statistic into chi-square and

Table 12.3 Contingency table for phi correlation coefficient

		Attribute A	
		Present/for/ yes/etc.	Absent/against/ no/etc.
Attribute B	Present/ for/yes/ etc.	A	B
	Absent/ against/no/ etc.	C	D

using the standard tabulated values for the latter and their associated probabilities as a basis for rejecting or accepting the null hypothesis. The conversion is achieved by the following formula:

$$\chi^2 = \phi^2 N$$

where N is the total number of observations. The probability of having obtained this value of χ^2 with 1 degree of freedom, since $(r-1)(c-1)$ always equals 1, may be determined from inspection of Appendix IV, Table 3.

Information from the survey of farms in Yorkshire indicates whether formal management training for farmers is related to farm profitability. Two survey questions are related to this theme: the first establishes whether the farmer has successfully completed a course in farm management, and the second classifies the net farm income according to whether it is higher or lower than the sample mean. The contingency table (Table 12.4) suggests there may be a connection between the attributes, but what is its magnitude and its significance? The null hypothesis in this case states that the true ϕ coefficient for the population of farms is in fact 0.0. Substituting the relevant frequencies from the table into the ϕ formula, as follows:

$$\phi = \frac{(11 \times 25) - (13 \times 1)}{\sqrt{[(11+13)(1+25)(11+1)(13+25)]}}$$

$$= +0.4912$$

The significance of +0.4912 is determined by conversion into χ^2 thus:

$$\chi^2 = +0.4912^2 \times 50$$

$$= 12.062$$

Referring to the table of χ^2, such a large value would be obtained less often than once in 1000 samples by chance ($p < 0.001$). The null hypothesis can safely be discarded and the ϕ correlation coefficient may be regarded as evidence of a significant, but only moderately strong positive relationship between the attributes.

The assumptions and data requirements of the ϕ coefficient are met with comparative ease in most situations. The sampled items should be

Table 12.4 Contingency table for phi correlation coefficient analysis, Yorkshire farms

		Profitability		
		Higher than mean	Lower than mean	
Management training	Received	11	13	24
	Not received	1	25	26
		12	38	50

selected randomly from their parent population. If the marginal totals of the contingency table are very dissimilar, then the value of ϕ will be restricted to a specific range, irrespective of the frequencies in the cells. The Yorkshire sample suffers slightly from this problem, although probably not to the extent that the analysis is invalidated. The design of the contingency table in terms of the order in which the categories of the two attributes are cross-tabulated affects the sign of the coefficient. A table of the type shown in Table 12.3 will produce a positive coefficient, which would also arise if the sequence of categories for *both* attributes were altered. It is therefore important to examine the form of the contingency table before calculating the correlation coefficient.

12.3 PROBLEMS OF CORRELATION

The potential problems with correlation analysis have long been identified and have been discussed in other texts (e.g. Silk 1979; Williams 1984; Shaw and Wheeler 1985). Certain of the key issues require further examination here. The diversity of applications for correlation analysis in geography means that the full range of potential problems may arise. The most fundamental difficulty is that the data may possess certain characteristics which, if ignored, might exert an undetected effect on the correlation coefficient. The essential cautionary point, as with all statistical analysis, is that the data should be carefully scrutinised by means of the elementary descriptive procedures in order to identify the possible pitfalls. In some cases the problems can be overcome by selecting a less complex type of correlation analysis.

The methods of correlation analysis discussed in this chapter have been concerned with measuring the strength of linear relationships, in which the connection between the values or frequencies of the variables is an arithmetic progression. This is the simplest type of relationship to understand, since perfect negative or positive correlation occurs when all the observations fall along a straight line. Perfect linear correlation is extremely unlikely to be found for a sample of items from a population. They will deviate to a greater or lesser extent from a straight line, even if the parent population from which they have been taken is perfectly correlated with respect to the two variables.

Once the items are scattered, it is unclear whether the observations are in fact deviating from a perfect linear or curvilinear relationship. A relationship in which all the items lie along a smooth regular curve (Figure 12.1(f)) is equally possible from a mathematical point of view. In this situation, the precise form of the curve is more difficult to determine, since many different types of curve can be defined and the scatter of observations could deviate from any one of them. So the solution to the first problem with correlation analysis is to examine carefully the pattern of the bivariate distribution by means of a scattergram in order to decide, albeit rather subjectively, whether the observations can legitimately be thought to deviate from a linear relationship.

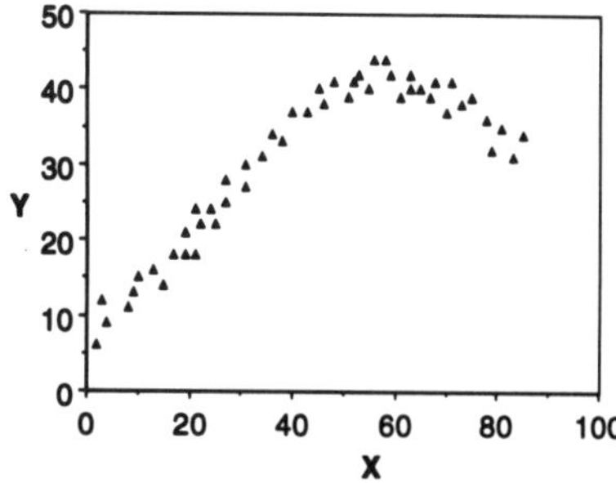

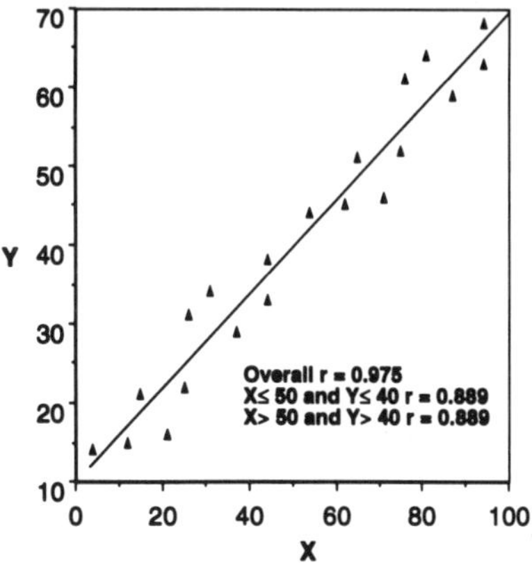

Figure 12.4 Potential problems with correlation relationships

The scatter of sampled observations may not conclusively confirm that a linear relationship is present. The *X* and *Y* values encountered in the sample may not reflect the full range occurring in the population. Two variables may exhibit a strong linear relationship in their lower values and a curvilinear one in the higher ranges, or vice versa (Figure 12.4(a)). A correlation coefficient derived for a restricted set of *X* and *Y* values may well provide a misleading interpretation of the overall situation and fail to reflect any change in the form of the relationship. Furthermore, even if a linear relationship is present throughout the ranges of *X* and *Y* values in the population, the correlation coefficient for a sample relating to only a limited subset of values may inaccurately estimate the coefficient for the population. In these circumstances a test to determine whether the sample coefficient is significantly different from 0.0 or some other specified value (see above) will ignore the fact that the population possesses the wider range of values and will thus not give a satisfactory result. Suppose a population of observations exists in which either or both of their vertical and horizontal deviations from the straight line are identical throughout its length across the full range of *X* and *Y* values (Figure 12.4(b)). A sample which relates to a limited part of the range will have a smaller correlation coefficient than one covering the full set, although for individual sections of *X* and *Y* values the coefficient will be the same.

Autocorrelation has been mentioned previously; however, the problem merits closer attention with respect to correlation analysis itself. Bivariate correlation techniques concentrate on a single sample of independent observations which are measured in respect of two variables. Correlation analysis in general is concerned with the direction and strength of the relationship between variables for a particular class or population of observations; it does not quantify the connections between observations. The fact that one observation in a population or sample has $X = 15.5$ and $Y = 134.2$ should have no bearing whatsoever on the X and Y values of any other observation. Autocorrelation occurs when such independence is absent and some or all of the items themselves are related to each other. A number of geographical phenomena display autocorrelation, since observations which are close together in time or space often tend to possess similar characteristics or measurements for variables. For example, people living on the same housing estate may have very similar social, economic and demographic characteristics. The similarities between people living in close proximity and the differences between them and the inhabitants of more distant localities may be exaggerated. The tendency for temporally or spatially proximate observations to have related values is known as 'positive autocorrelation'. The reverse (negative autocorrelation) is also possible, but much less common since it is unusual for items which are close together to have widely different values with respect to their attributes and variables.

Provided that autocorrelated populations are sampled at random, then the sample correlation coefficient can be regarded as an unbiased estimate of the population parameter. The autocorrelation in the population can be assumed to have been encapsulated by the random sample. However, autocorrelation becomes a serious problem when attempting to test the significance of a sample correlation coefficient. The standard error formulae for the various statistical tests are inaccurate if autocorrelation is present. Positive autocorrelation, especially if severe, will underestimate the true standard error and therefore lead to a larger test statistic with a correspondingly lower probability. The probability may fall below the critical significance level (0.05 or 0.01) and thus the null hypothesis would be incorrectly discarded. Negative autocorrelation will have the opposite effect of inflating the standard error and raising the probability. Unfortunately, there is no simple solution to the problem, other than to advise caution when rejecting the null hypothesis, especially if positive autocorrelation is suspected.

Autocorrelation arises when observations which are proximate in time or space are related to each other. For example, a set of observations would have a strong correlation coefficient between a variable representing their geographical location and one or more of thematic variables. Considered in this light, autocorrelation may in some respects be regarded as a special case of a more general problem known as *confounding*. By definition, bivariate correlation techniques concentrate on two variables at a time; however, the extent and direction of their relationship, as measured by a correlation coefficient, may be distorted by the effects of other variables. If these unwanted effects could be eliminated by controlling for these variables then the correlation might be sound. Unfortunately, this is not always possible, especially with measurements made in the field, for example on physical or human geographic phenomena. A correlation matrix can be produced in which all the measured variables are correlated with one another. But can the investigator be sure that all the variables which might just conceivably have an effect have been included in the dataset? If not, then some undesired influence may remain undetected.

One correlation analysis problem has received considerable attention from quantitative geographers. In general terms it is known as the *modifiable unit* or *item problem*, or in geographical parlance as the *modifiable areal unit problem* (Robinson 1956; Openshaw and Taylor 1981; Openshaw 1984). From a statistical point of view, the diverse spatial units with which geographical analysis is concerned are arbitrary divisions of continuous space, with boundaries capable of redefinition and areas combinable in a multitude of ways. In some cases the areal units form a nested hierarchy with small units being joined to form medium-sized ones, and these combined into larger areas without any overlap of the boundaries (Figure 12.5). At each stage in the process the values of the variables are averaged or the frequencies of the attributes are summed in order to obtain the measurement for the larger units. Figure 12.5(a) demonstrates the process with five areas at the smallest scale (labelled a, b, c, d and e), which respectively record 20, 36, 15,

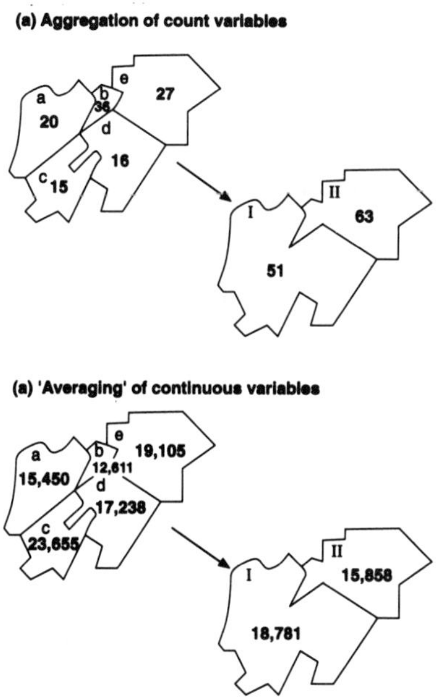

Figure 12.5 Illustration of the modifiable areal unit problem

16 and 27 households without a car (an illustrative population census variable). Areas a, c and d are joined to form intermediate area I, and b and e to create II. The frequency counts of the attribute for the two new areas are therefore 51 for I and 63 for II. Figure 12.5(b) illustrates how a similar procedure could be used to average the continuous variable mean household income. In areas a, c and d the mean income of all households is given as £15 450, £23 655 and £17 238, which would produce a mean value for I of £18 781.

Geographers regularly work with variables at different spatial scales and are therefore prone to suffer from the effects of the modifiable areal unit problem, which means that when the same two variables are correlated for different aggregation units widely contrasting coefficients may be produced. In Table 12.5 the hierarchical aggregation of 40 small areal units through four stages into five large areas is shown. Two variables, expenditure on job creation schemes and total number of people unemployed, are shown for each of the different types of spatial unit and their Pearson correlation coefficients are calculated. The coefficients show a positive relationship between the variables, although its strength decreases as the areas become larger, from +0.850 for the 40 smallest areal units to +0.587 for the five largest areas. One effect of the modifiable areal unit problem is that the ranges of X and Y values may change disproportionately as the units are aggregated. Furthermore, deviations from perfect linear correlation attributable to the influence of unexamined variables may to some extent cancel each other out, although their general effect is difficult to predict. Finally, an important aspect of this problem is that data for populations as well as samples are affected.

A further difficulty with correlation analysis concerns relationships which arise because the variables share some common element. This problem often occurs with ratio variables, which are calculated from the same denominator, but can also intrude into the analysis when variables are added, subtracted or multiplied, for example to produce new composite indicators. Variables sharing a common element in this way can produce *spurious correlations* in which the analysis appears to support the hypothesis of a strong relationship between the variables, but this result is in fact an artefact of the computations carried out on the data. Variables are often converted into ratios either because the X and Y variables have very different value ranges in numerical terms, or because there is a genuine substantive reason for relating three variables together. Some frequently used ratios in geographical investigations include per head, per cent or per 1000 of the population, per unit area and per year, month or week. When two ratio variables share the same denominator some of the differences between them can become muted or suppressed by the extent to which they both vary with respect to a third variable.

An agricultural geographer investigating mechanisation is likely to be interested in the levels of labour and machinery input on farms.

Table 12.5 The effect of modifiable areal units on product moment correlation coefficient

	Stage 1		Stage 2		Stage 3		Stage 4	
	X_1	Y_1	X_2	Y_2	X_3	Y_3	X_4	Y_4
1	35	9	29	6	30	7	22	5
2	23	3						
3	45	14	31	8				
4	17	2						
5	22	4	25	6	18	5		
6	34	8						
7	20	5						
8	9	3	10	4				
9	11	4						
10	12	1	19	4	4	19		
11	25	7						
12	13	3	21	6	33	11	38	11
13	29	9						
14	45	15	45	15				
15	54	14	44	10	44	10		
16	33	6						
17	13	2	23	11	23	9	23	10
18	26	6						
19	18	3						
20	33	10						
21	22	7	22	7				
22	14	8	22	10	22	10		
23	16	4						
24	36	7						
25	27	4	28	9	20	6	21	5
26	25	11						
27	23	9						
28	38	12						
29	12	2	12	2				
30	8	1	21	4	21	4		
31	21	4						
32	17	3						
33	38	8						

continued overleaf

Table 12.5 (*continued*)

	Stage 1		Stage 2		Stage 3		Stage 4	
	X_1	Y_1	X_2	Y_2	X_3	Y_3	X_4	Y_4
34	23	3						
35	49	10	36	7				
36	35	9						
					31	6	31	6
37	17	3						
38	34	8	25	5				
39	16	2						
40	35	8						
		$r = 0.850$		$r = 0.718$		$r = 0.601$		$r = 0.587$

Note: Columns headed X_1, X_2, X_3 and X_4 give the expenditure on job creation schemes for the 4 types of area; those headed Y_1, Y_2, Y_3 and Y_4 give the corresponding unemployment figures. Both variables are in thousands.

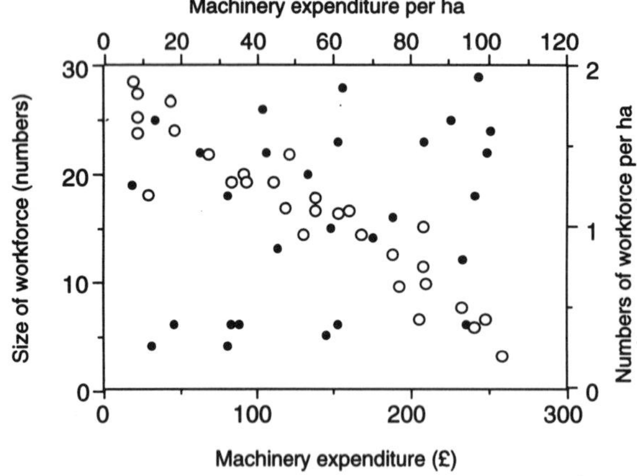

Figure 12.6 Effect of converting continuous variables to ratios

o - left and bottom axes

● - right and top axes

The general hypothesis is that farms with higher levels of machinery usage will have lower demand for labour input. The number of workers on farms in Britain rarely exceeds 30 people, whereas total expenditure on machinery in a year could be £100 000 or more. The value ranges are therefore numerically very different and the scattergram of the unconverted data, shown by the solid circles in Figure 12.6, shows a fairly random distribution. Some farms have a large workforce and high machinery expenditure, or small labour and machinery input, might exist because of variations in farm size and enterprise combinations. The figures are standardised by converting into two ratio variables, the number of workers per hectare and total expenditure on machinery per hectare. In the this example, the conversion process clearly distorts the strength and nature of the relationship between the variables and produces a reasonably strong negative relationship. The open circles in Figure 12.6 show the scatter of farms in respect of the two ratio variables. The number of workers and expenditure on machinery are themselves related to farm size and thus the conversion may have removed some of the random component in the scatter of observations. The Pearson product moment correlation coefficients for the two sets of data clearly suggest rather different conclusions about the nature of the relationship: in the first case $r = +0.206$ and in the second $r = -0.937$.

12.4 CORRELATION ANALYSIS IN EXEMPLAR PROJECTS

The analysis of the exemplar projects in the previous chapters has concentrated on the use of statistical tests in order to examine characteristics of the samples; so far no attempt has been made to explain the phenomena or to examine how one variable is related to another. The next stage in the analysis involves an examination of the possible relationships between selected variables. For example, in the land-use change project, is an increase in one type of land-use related to a decrease (or increase) in another? In the chalk weathering project, does any reduction in the weight of the chalk blocks vary with time between the different treatments? In the river pollution project, is the concentration of the various chemicals in the water samples affected by precipitation and temperature? And in the village communities project, is length of residence in the village associated with a particular attitude towards the proposed development? Correlation helps to provide statistical answers to these questions.

12.4.1 Land-use change

The process of land-use change is complex, and research has shown that in aggregate terms the changes occur relatively slowly (Best 1981). The expansion of built-up areas during the 20th century has produced only a relatively small increase in the percentage of land in Britain which is classified as urban. Changes in definition confound the issue, but a reasonable estimate is of urban land having increased from 6.7 to 9.9 per cent of the total land in England and Wales between 1931 and 1961 (Best 1981, p. 76), which is the period covered by the land-use change project. Changing the scale of analysis from the national to the local case-study area, as in the exemplar project, produces a more complex picture. The project is limited in so far as it simply provides a snapshot of the areal changes in each land use between two points in time: intermediate variations are ignored.

One of the important questions in land-use research has concerned the extent to which land in rural and rural-urban fringe areas, especially agricultural land, has been lost to urban uses during the present century. Within the confines of the exemplar project, certain aspects of this question can be examined. The places where a particular land use was dominant in the 1930s might also be where it remained important 30 years later. For example, those grid squares which had a large amount of woodland in the 1930s might also have relatively substantial areas of trees in the 1960s. In other words, the area of a particular land use at one point in time is related to the amount at another. This can be generalised into a null hypothesis which states that:

LU6 The areas of each of the seven land uses in the 1930s within the grid squares of sample B do not affect their areas in the 1960s. Any apparent relationship, which is indicated by a sample correlation coefficient other than zero, is the result of chance sampling.

Although the grid squares for sample B have been randomly sampled and the variables have been measured on the interval scale, the maximum area for any one land use for each observation (grid square) is 100 ha. In other words, the size of grid square artificially constrains the sum of the areas of the seven land uses to 100 ha. In this situation the product moment correlation analysis is not entirely suitable and Spearman's rank correlation is used.

The general procedure for calculating Spearman's rank correlation coefficient in MINITAB involves the following two commands:

```
MTB > RANK C1 INTO C5
MTB > RANK C2 INTO C6
MTB > CORRELATION C5 C6
```

where C1 and C2 are the columns containing the raw data and C5 and C6 are two new columns into which the rank scores will be placed before applying the CORRELATION command. The command simply reports the value of r_s without testing its significance nor displaying a scattergram of the data. If more than two ranked columns are specified on the CORRELATION command, thus:

```
MTB > CORRELATION C5 C6 C7 C8
```

then a correlation matrix is output showing the r_s coefficients for each pair of variables: in this instance the correlations of C5 with C6, C7 and C8; C6 with C7 and C8; and C7 with C8. The matrix may optionally be stored for future use, in which case it is not displayed.

The log of the MINITAB session for applying Spearman's rank correlation to investigate LU6 is given in Table 12.6. Once the worksheet (LANDB04.MTW) has been retrieved, the columns containing the raw data values for the areas of each land use in the two years are ranked into 14 new columns (C60 to C73). A series of CORRELATION commands calculate the r_s statistics for pairs of columns representing the areas of a land use in the 1930s and 1960s. The results of this correlation analysis (Box 12.1) suggest fairly strong positive relationships between the paired ranked land-use variables. In some cases the correlation coefficients are greater than +0.9. The weakest relationship was for rough grazing at +0.557. The significance of the various r coefficients has been determined by reference to Table 9 in Appendix IV. The minimum coefficient which is significant with 20 observations at

Table 12.6 Application of correlation analysis (Spearman's rank) to sample B in land-use project in MINITAB

```
MTB > OUTFILE 'land07'
MTB > RETRIEVE 'landb04'
MTB > RANK C4 C60
MTB > RANK C5 C61
MTB > RANK C6 C62
MTB > RANK C7 C63
MTB > RANK C8 C64
MTB > RANK C9 C65
MTB > RANK C10 C66
MTB > RANK C11 C67
MTB > RANK C12 C68
MTB > RANK C13 C69
MTB > RANK C14 C70
MTB > RANK C15 C71
MTB > RANK C16 C72
MTB > RANK C17 C73
MTB > CORRELATION C60 C67
MTB > CORRELATION C61 C68
MTB > CORRELATION C62 C69
MTB > CORRELATION C63 C70
MTB > CORRELATION C64 C71
MTB > CORRELATION C65 C72
MTB > CORRELATION C66 C73
MTB > NOOUTFILE
MTB > STOP
```

```
MTB > CORRELATION RankAg30 RankAg60
Correlation of RankAg30 and RankAg60 = 0.923
MTB > CORRELATION RankMG30 RankMG60
Correlation of RankMG30 and RankMG60 = 0.718
MTB > CORRELATION RankGr30 RankGr60
Correlation of RankGr30 and RankGr60 = 0.930
MTB > CORRELATION RankWo30 RankWo60
Correlation of RankWo30 and RankWo60 = 0.789
MTB > CORRELATION RankRG30 RankRG60
Correlation of RankRG30 and RankRG60 = 0.557
MTB > CORRELATION RankHs30 RankHs60
Correlation of RankHs30 and RankHs60 = 0.877
MTB > CORRELATION RankUA30 RankUA60
Correlation of RankUA30 and RankUA60 = 0.919
With 20 observations Spearman's rank correlation coefficients of 0.447
and 0.570 are significant at the 0.05 and 0.01 levels respectively.
```

Box 12.1 Spearman's rank correlation coefficient results for LU6 for each land-use (MINITAB output)

the 0.05 level is 0.447, and at the 0.01 level is 0.570. The coefficients for all land uses, with the exception of rough grazing at the 0.01 level, are greater than these critical values. The null hypotheses can therefore safely be rejected and the amount of land use at one point in time is highly correlated with its incidence at a later time, or vice versa.

12.4.2 Chalk weathering

The main research question in this project focuses on the factors influencing the weathering of chalk. The analysis of variance has demonstrated that the subsamples are significantly different in terms of their overall mean weight loss. The application of correlation analysis to the chalk weathering project investigates the relationship, for each experimental situation between the weight of the blocks and time. The purpose of the analysis is to see if the relationships vary between the types of treatment. Correlation analysis can identify the nature and strength of the relationship between the variables. In general terms the null hypothesis states:

CW6 The relationship between the weight of the chalk blocks and time is not significantly different between the nine types of treatment. Any apparent variation in the rate at which the samples of chalk blocks lost weight over time is the result of chance or sampling error.

The mean weight of the 12 blocks in the subsamples on each day is calculated and correlated with time, using Pearson's product moment coefficient. The MINITAB commands which manipulate the data and carry out the analysis are given in Table 12.7. The mean of the 12 blocks in each subsample for the 15 times when the weight measurements are taken must be calculated. This is carried out with the TABLE command, thus:

```
MTB > TABLE C2;
SUBC > MEANS C3 – C17.
```

where C2 contains the code for treatment type. These means are entered as nine additional data columns (one for each subsample), C31 – C39, together with another new column containing the time period to which the corresponding mean relates.

The correlation coefficients for the analysis have been summarised in Box 12.2 The relationships are clearly negative in all cases, it would have been improbable that the blocks gained weight during the experiment and therefore they provide an example of where a one-tailed test is appropriate. The results for the control treatments, where lower correlation coefficients have been obtained, make it clear that water is a vital element in the chalk weathering process, since, regardless of temperature regime, the three subsamples without any water showed virtually no change in weight. As far as the treatments involving saturated blocks are concerned, the relationships appear to be stronger when saline brine was used.

12.4.3 River pollution

The quality of river water and what causes this to vary is a complex issue reflecting the fact that the processes operating within a single

Table 12.7 Application of correlation analysis (product moment correlation coefficient) to chalk weathering project in MINITAB

```
MTB > OUTFILE 'chweat07'
MTB > RETRIEVE 'chweat03'
MTB > TABLE C2;
SUBC > MEANS C3 – C17.
MTB > READ C31 – C39
DATA > 30.004 29.971 29.968 29.984 30.083 30.032 30.007 29.995 29.989
DATA > 29.933 29.971 29.968 29.984 30.083 30.032 30.007 29.995 29.989
DATA > 29.778 29.874 29.968 29.984 30.083 30.030 30.005 29.983 29.987
DATA > 29.310 29.753 29.968 29.743 30.083 30.008 29.997 29.979 29.987
DATA > 28.640 29.393 29.968 29.457 30.083 30.028 30.819 29.962 29.957
DATA > 27.567 20.096 29.968 29.005 30.083 30.028 29.906 29.898 29.927
DATA > 26.956 27.900 29.968 28.420 29.949 29.935 29.864 29.838 29.903
DATA > 25.139 25.827 29.968 28.159 29.895 29.917 28.899 29.708 29.760
DATA > 23.443 22.347 29.960 27.626 29.700 29.982 29.763 29.530 29.722
DATA > 21.628 20.354 29.944 27.044 28.984 29.820 29.582 29.313 29.648
DATA > 19.266 17.492 29.858 26.532 26.926 29.608 29.308 29.228 29.586
DATA > 17.637 13.738 29.288 25.632 25.249 29.394 28.962 29.115 29.387
DATA > 16.487 10.276 28.904 24.861 22.484 29.180 28.681 29.006 29.344
DATA > 14.534  9.338 28.478 24.635 21.660 29.012 28.443 28.829 29.298
DATA > 12.373  8.658 28.247 24.384 21.140 28.839 28.201 28.751 29.253
DATA > END
MTB > SET C40
DATA> 1 2 3 4 5 6 7 8 9 10 11 12 13 14 15
DATA > END
MTB > CORRELATION C31 C40
MTB > CORRELATION C32 C40
MTB > CORRELATION C33 C40
MTB > CORRELATION C34 C40
MTB > CORRELATION C35 C40
MTB > CORRELATION C36 C40
MTB > CORRELATION C37 C40
MTB > CORRELATION C38 C40
MTB > CORRELATION C39 C40
MTB > NOOUTFILE
MTB > SAVE 'CHWEAT04'
MTB > STOP
```

river channel are part of a far larger hydrological system. The exemplar project is not really concerned with investigating the relationships within this system, but is a more applied project. It has sought to answer the empirical question of whether or not river quality has improved or deteriorated, rather than the causes of any change. In this light it is clear that correlation analysis, and for that matter regression, are not appropriate analytical techniques for the project. Nevertheless, it is appropriate to examine whether the concentrations of the different metallic ions, dissolved oxygen and ammonia were related to weather conditions.

It is reasonable to assume that the effects of temperature and rainfall in the preceding 24-hour period will not vary according to the previously determined river-quality class or flow-rate group. Thus the

```
MTB > CORRELATION T1 Time
Correlation of T1 and Time = −0.973
MTB > CORRELATION T2 Time
Correlation of T32 and Time = −0.936
MTB > CORRELATION T3 Time
Correlation of T3 and Time = −0.782
MTB > CORRELATION T4 Time
Correlation of T4 and Time = −0.980
MTB > CORRELATION T5 Time
Correlation of T5 and Time = −0.854
MTB > CORRELATION T6 Time
Correlation of T6 and Time = −0.877
MTB > CORRELATION T7 Time
Correlation of T7 and Time = −0.842
MTB > CORRELATION T8 Time
Correlation of CT and Time = −0.962
MTB > CORRELATION T9 Time
Correlation of T9 and Time = −0.958
```

Box 12.2 Product moment correlation results for CW6 for selected treatments of chalk blocks (MINITAB output)

correlation analysis can be carried out using the full set of 250 water samples in sample A and the 300 in sample B. The generic form of the null hypothesis is as follows:

RP6 Weather conditions in the period immediately before sampling took place has had no effect on the concentration of the different chemicals.

Acceptance of the null hypotheses implies that high levels of rainfall have not diluted the chemical concentrations or enhanced the dissolved oxygen levels. The log of MINITAB commands for plotting the pairs of variables and for carrying out these product moment correlation analyses is given in Table 12.8.

The results (see Box 12.3) for samples A and B reveal correlation coefficients which are very close to 0.0 in most instances, which is supported by the apparently random distributions of points across the scattergraphs. MINITAB does not allow a significance test to be applied directly to the columns of data. However, by way of an example, in the case of the correlation between precipitation and dissolved oxygen the coefficient ($r = 0.020$) can be converted into t thus:

$$t = \frac{0.020\sqrt{250-2}}{\sqrt{1-0.020}} = \frac{0.3150}{0.9899} = 0.318$$

An examination of the t distribution table in Appendix IV with $n-1$ degrees of freedom reveals that there is a high chance of having obtained this t value by chance and therefore the null hypothesis is accepted. The number of observations in both samples is so large and the r coefficients so close to 0.0 in all cases that further significance tests are not warranted.

Table 12.8 Application of correlation analysis (product moment coefficient) to river pollution project in MINITAB

```
MTB > OUTFILE 'river07'
MTB > RETRIEVE 'rivera03'
MTB > PLOT C10 C7
MTB > CORRELATE C10 C7
MTB > PLOT C10 C8
MTB > CORRELATE C10 C8
MTB > PLOT C10 C9
MTB > CORRELATE C10 C9
MTB > PLOT C11 C7
MTB > CORRELATE C11 C7
MTB > PLOT C11 C8
MTB > CORRELATE C11 C8
MTB > PLOT C11 C9
MTB > CORRELATE C11 C9
  ...
MTB > RESTART
MTB > RETRIEVE 'riverb03'
MTB > PLOT C9 C15
MTB > CORRELATE C9 C15
MTB > PLOT C10 C15
MTB > CORRELATE C10
MTB > PLOT C11 C15
MTB > CORRELATE C11 C15
MTB > PLOT C12 C15
MTB > CORRELATE C12 C15
MTB > PLOT C13 C15
MTB > CORRELATE C13 C15
MTB > PLOT C14 C15
MTB > CORRELATE C14 C15
MTB > PLOT C9 C16
MTB > CORRELATE C9 C16
MTB > PLOT C10 C16
MTB > CORRELATE C10 C16
MTB > PLOT C11 C16
MTB > CORRELATE C11 C16
MTB > PLOT C12 C16
MTB > CORRELATE C12 C16
MTB > PLOT C13 C16
MTB > CORRELATE C13 C16
MTB > PLOT C14 C16
MTB > CORRELATE C14 C16
MTB > NOOUTFILE
```

12.4.4 Village communities

12.4.4.1 The ϕ correlation coefficient

The main focus of the village communities project relates to differences in attitude to the proposed development among the indigenous and newcomer households. The survey of village residents has collected a range of information about the respondents, which helps to understand

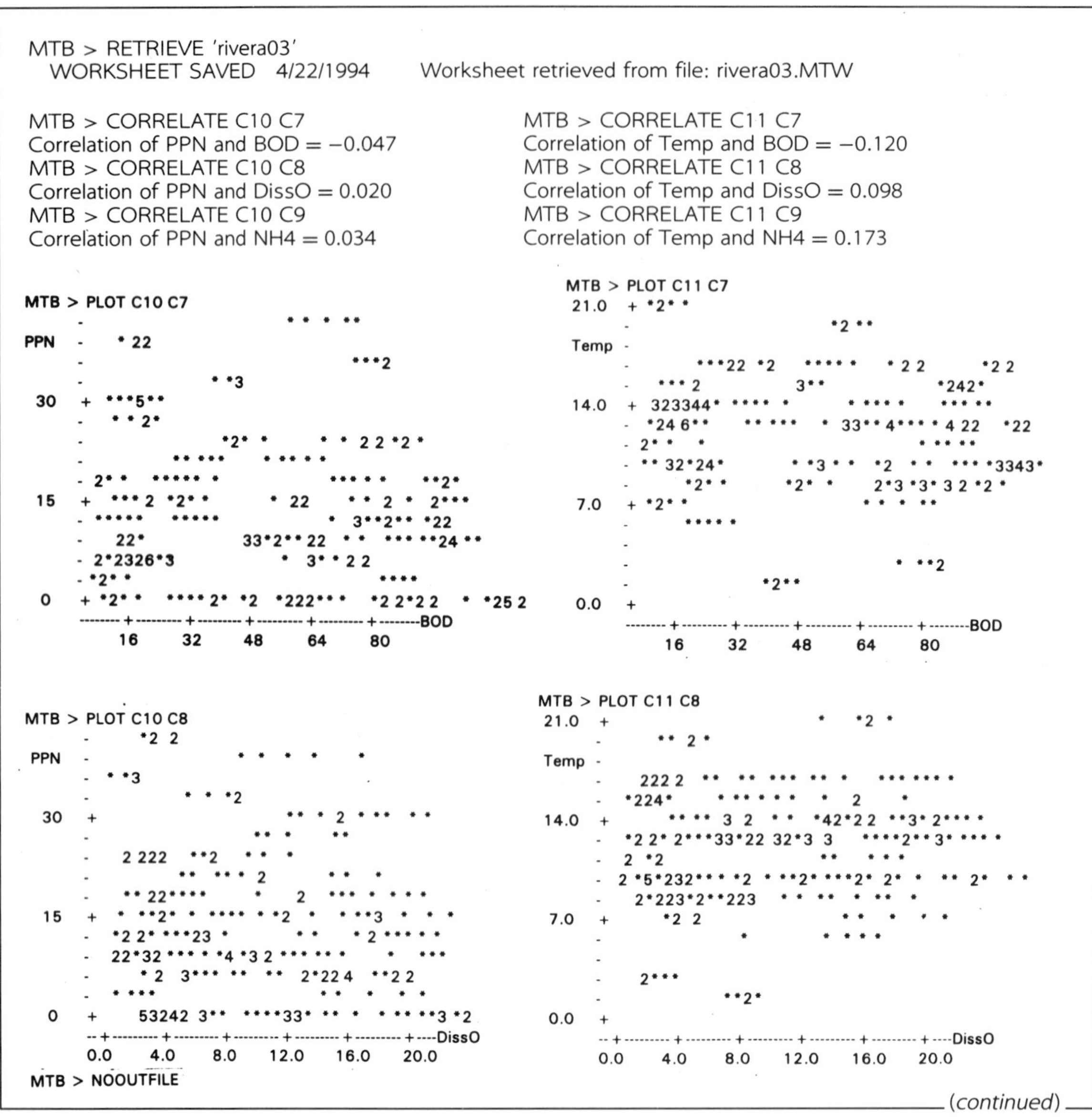

```
MTB > RETRIEVE 'rivera03'
  WORKSHEET SAVED   4/22/1994        Worksheet retrieved from file: rivera03.MTW

MTB > CORRELATE C10 C7                      MTB > CORRELATE C11 C7
Correlation of PPN and BOD = −0.047         Correlation of Temp and BOD = −0.120
MTB > CORRELATE C10 C8                      MTB > CORRELATE C11 C8
Correlation of PPN and DissO = 0.020        Correlation of Temp and DissO = 0.098
MTB > CORRELATE C10 C9                      MTB > CORRELATE C11 C9
Correlation of PPN and NH4 = 0.034          Correlation of Temp and NH4 = 0.173
```


(continued)

Box 12.3 Scatterplot and product moment correlation coefficient results for RP6 for river pollution Samples A and B (MINITAB output)

why some people are in favour of and others against the development. For instance, some individuals, with children who are about to leave school, might be in favour because they envisage that the industrial units will bring new jobs to the village. Such views may be held irrespective of length of residence. A comprehensive correlation analysis of the survey data could investigate a number of relevant null hypotheses; however, for the purpose of illustrating the ϕ correlation coefficient, the following example will suffice:

VC6 Any evidence from the sample to suggest that there is a relationship between people's length of residence in the village and

Box 12.3 *(continued)*

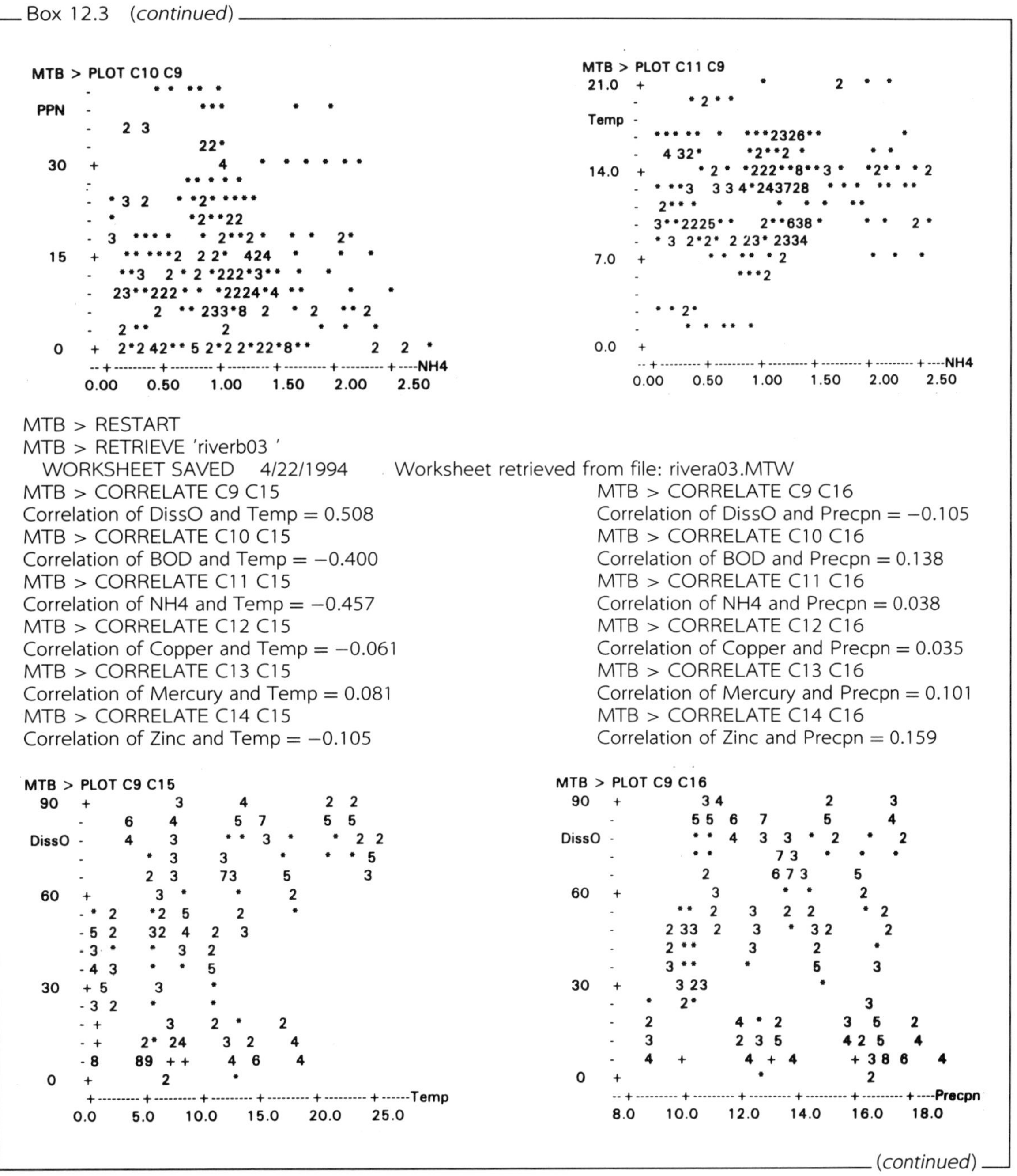


```
MTB > RESTART
MTB > RETRIEVE 'riverb03 '
  WORKSHEET SAVED    4/22/1994    Worksheet retrieved from file: rivera03.MTW
MTB > CORRELATE C9 C15
Correlation of DissO and Temp = 0.508
MTB > CORRELATE C10 C15
Correlation of BOD and Temp = −0.400
MTB > CORRELATE C11 C15
Correlation of NH4 and Temp = −0.457
MTB > CORRELATE C12 C15
Correlation of Copper and Temp = −0.061
MTB > CORRELATE C13 C15
Correlation of Mercury and Temp = 0.081
MTB > CORRELATE C14 C15
Correlation of Zinc and Temp = −0.105
MTB > CORRELATE C9 C16
Correlation of DissO and Precpn = −0.105
MTB > CORRELATE C10 C16
Correlation of BOD and Precpn = 0.138
MTB > CORRELATE C11 C16
Correlation of NH4 and Precpn = 0.038
MTB > CORRELATE C12 C16
Correlation of Copper and Precpn = 0.035
MTB > CORRELATE C13 C16
Correlation of Mercury and Precpn = 0.101
MTB > CORRELATE C14 C16
Correlation of Zinc and Precpn = 0.159
```


(continued)

their attitude towards the proposed development is misleading, having arisen purely as a result of chance.

The data for the village communities project are stored in an SPSS-X system file and only require a limited amount of manipulation in order to carry out the required statistical analyses. Attitude to the

Box 12.3 *(continued)*

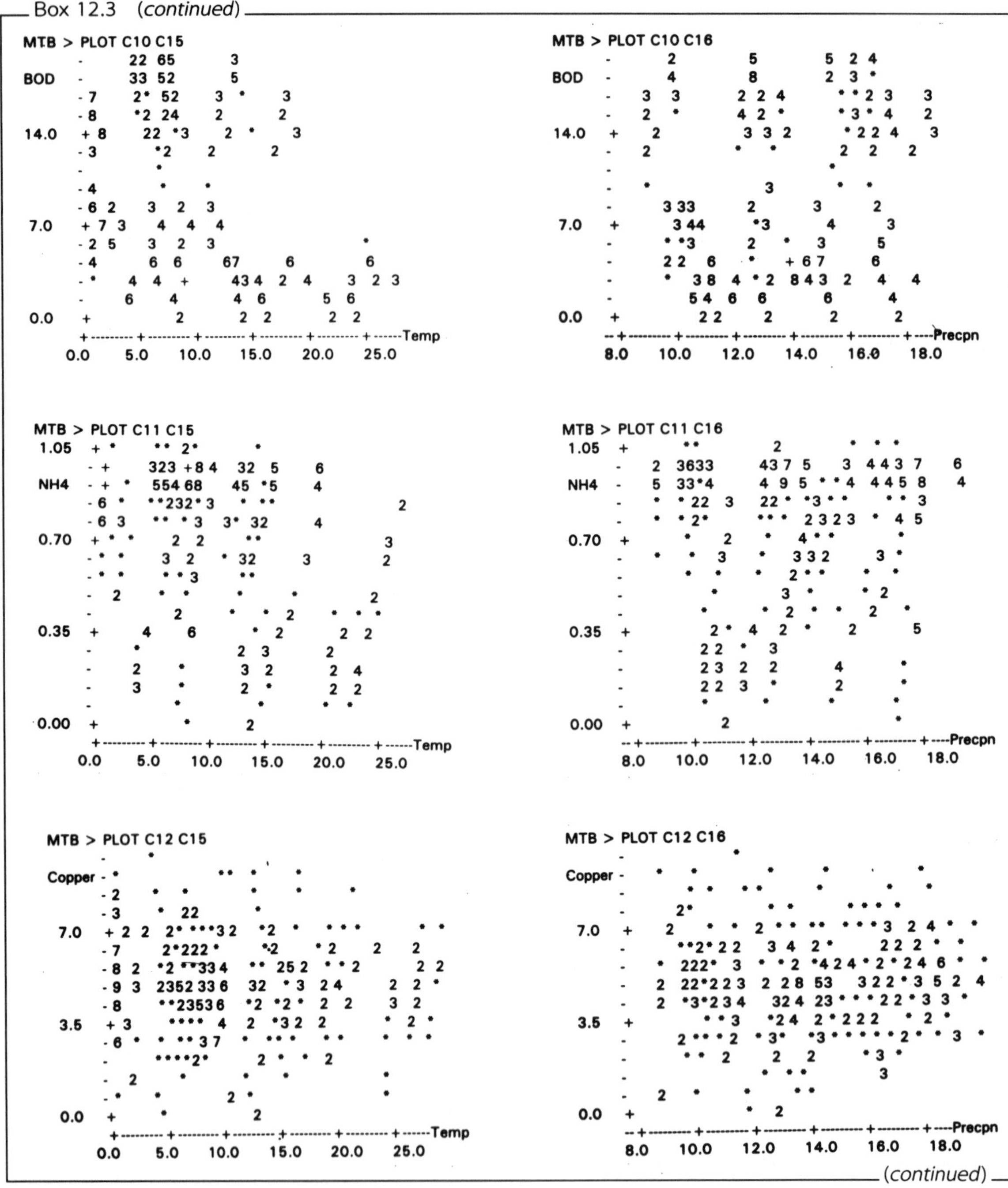

(continued)

Box 12.3 *(continued)*

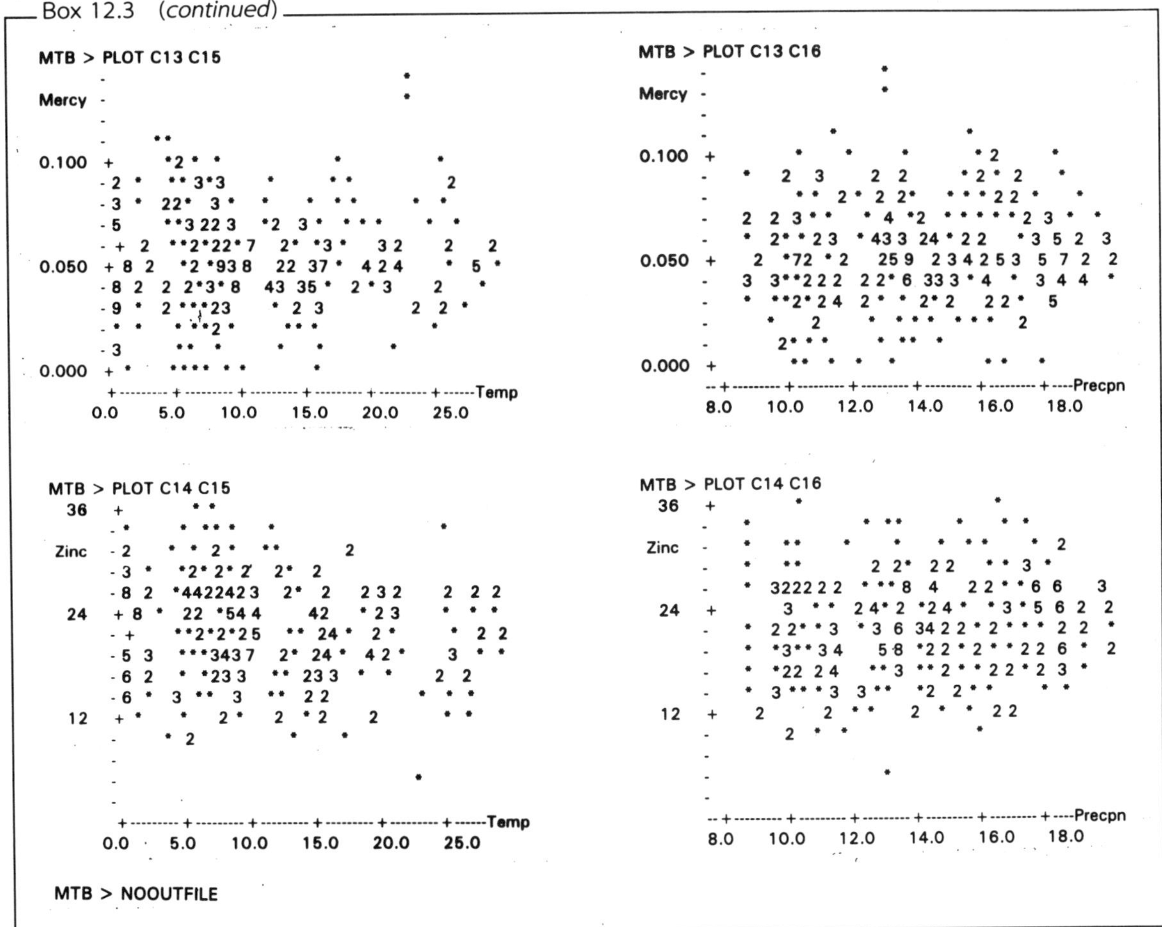

proposed development is already held in a dichotomous attribute (for or against). Length of residence has been grouped into seven classes as RELENGTH and is now recoded further in order to define newcomer and indigenous respondents in a dichotomous fashion: a cut-off point of 10 years was chosen for this purpose. The RECODE command (see Table 12.9) creates a new attribute, RESPTYPE. The ϕ correlation coefficient is available as one of the optional statistics on the CROSSTABS command thus:

```
CROSSTABS VARIABLES = RESPTYPE(1,2) FAVPROP(1,2)/
TABLES = FAVPROP BY RESTYPE/STATISTICS = PHI
```

The value of ϕ for this contingency table (Box 12.4) is 0.054 75, which has a probability of 0.5438 when converted to Pearson's chi-square. This indicates that ϕ is clearly not significant at the 0.05 level. The test result therefore indicates that the null hypothesis should be accepted with the conclusion that the survey offers no statistical evidence for a strong relationship between respondent type and attitude to the proposed development.

Table 12.9 Application of correlation analysis (ϕ and Spearman's rank) to village communities project in SPSS-X

```
FILE HANDLE SF / NAME = 'VILLAG01.SF'
GET FILE = SF
RECODE RELENGTH (1 = 1)(2 THRU HI = 2) INTO RESTYPE
CROSSTABS VARIABLES = RESTYPE(1,2) FAVPROP(1,2)/
  TABLES = FAVPROP BY RESTYPE /STATISTICS = PHI
NONPAR CORR VARIABLES = NFRIENDS LENGRES
  /PRINT = SPEARMAN
FINISH
```

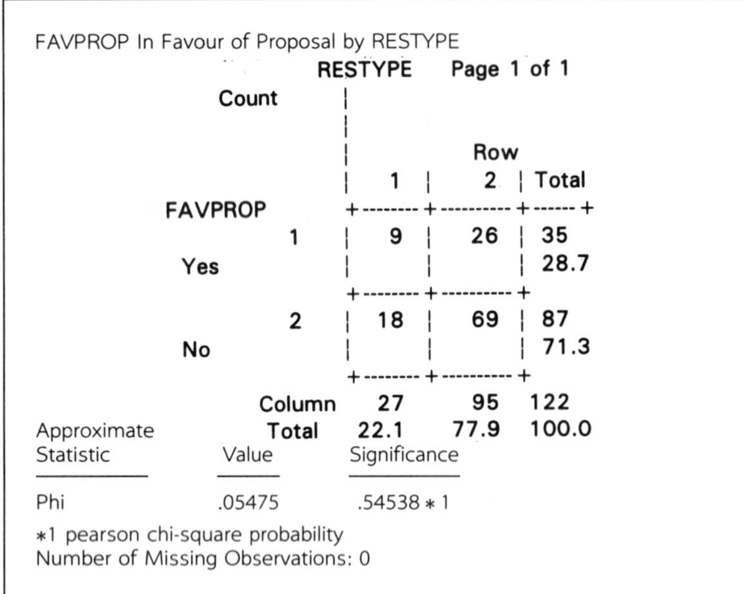

FAVPROP In Favour of Proposal by RESTYPE

RESTYPE Page 1 of 1

Count		1	2	Row Total
FAVPROP Yes	1	9	26	35 28.7
No	2	18	69	87 71.3
	Column Total	27 22.1	95 77.9	122 100.0

Statistic	Value	Approximate Significance
Phi	.05475	.54538 * 1

*1 pearson chi-square probability
Number of Missing Observations: 0

Box 12.4 Phi correlation results for VC6 in village communities project (SPSS-X output)

12.4.4.2 Spearman's rank correlation

Another relationship worthy of investigation is between people's length of residence and the number of friends in the village. Newcomers might find it difficult to assimilate into village life and a 'them and us' situation may develop. To consider the extent of this problem we can set up a null hypothesis, which states that:

VC7 The correlation coefficient for length of residence and the number of friends is actually zero; any figure other than this has occurred through sampling error.

Alternatively, friendship networks might develop within the newcomer and indigenous residental groups, which would obscure any distinction.

The product moment correlation procedure is inappropriate for these variables, since they are unlikely to conform to the bivariate normal

```
SPEARMAN CORRELATION COEFFICIENTS
LENGRES                          -.0286
                                 N( 120)
                                 SIG .378
                               NFRIENDS
" . " IS PRINTED IF A COEFFICIENT CANNOT BE COMPUTED.
```

Box 12.5 Spearman's rank correlation results for VC7 in village communities project (SPSS-X output)

distribution. The alternative, less demanding, Spearman's rank technique has been employed. The Spearman's rank correlation coefficient is calculated by the NONPAR CORR (non-parametric correlation) command in SPSS-X. The following extract from Table 12.9 illustrates the general syntax:

```
NONPAR CORR VARIABLES = NFRIENDS LENGRES
/PRINT = SPEARMAN
```

where the two variable names, NFRIENDS and LENGRES, denote the variables number of friends and the ungrouped length of residence, respectively. Spearman's rank correlation analysis is the default for this command, which outputs the number of cases and significance of the coefficient. The result of this analysis is shown in Box 12.5. The coefficient (−0.0286) has a significance of 0.378, which is greater than the chosen significance level or cut-off point (0.05). This result leads to the null hypothesis being accepted. A positive relationship between the two variables is not evident on the basis of the sample data. In other words, people who have lived in the village a long time are likely to have as many friends as those who had moved in more recently.

12.5 REVIEW OF SOFTWARE COMMANDS FOR CORRELATION ANALYSIS

The three types of correlation examined here are a selection of the techniques available for analysing relationships between variables. The full range includes not only other bivariate procedures, but also multivariate ones. Pearson's product moment and Spearman's rank correlation coefficients are by far the most frequently used, although the assumptions and limitations of the former should be noted. Table 12.10 summarises the MINITAB and SPSS-X commands for carrying out correlation analyses and associated statistical tests. The ϕ coefficient is less common, which is reflected by its absence from the MINITAB software. The bivariate correlation coefficients, r and r_s, are calculated by the same CORRELATION command in MINITAB, although the latter requires the user to issue commands that rank the data columns. Unfortunately the CORRELATION command does not perform a significance test on the coefficient.

A number of different commands in SPSS-X can be used to calculate Pearson's product moment correlation coefficient, although the most

Table 12.10 Comparison of software commands for performing bivariate correlation analyses

	MINITAB	SPSS-X
ϕ coefficient	Not available	CROSSTABS VARIABLES =/ /TABLES = /STATISTICS = PHI
Spearman's r_s	RANK C1 C2 C3 C4 CORRELATION C3 C4	NONPAR CORR VARIABLES = /PRINT = SPEARMAN
Pearson's r	CORRELATION C1 C2	CORRELATIONS VARIABLES = /PRINT = TWOTAIL

straightforward in the initial stages of using the software is CORRELATIONS. This command is followed by the keyword VARIABLES = and one or more lists of variable names. By default a one-tailed significance test will be carried out on the r coefficient, although the two-tailed version can be obtained by adding /PRINT = TWOTAIL to the command. The equivalent command for Spearman's r_s is NONPAR CORR followed by a variable list and /PRINT = SPEARMAN.

Chapter 13 Analysis of causation: regression

13.1 COMPARISON OF CORRELATION AND REGRESSION

The primary function of the correlation coefficients is to measure the direction and strength of any relationship between two variables. The values of the coefficients are mathematically constrained to lie between -1.0 and $+1.0$, which correspond to the delimiting situations in which there is either perfect negative or perfect positive correlation. Regression takes the analysis of point distributions a stage further by examining the *form of the relationship* between the two variables. The word 'form' in this context signifies the nature of the control that one variable exerts over the other: they are referred to respectively as the *independent* (X) and the *dependent variables* (Y). Regression analysis encapsulates the form of the relationship in mathematical terms, as an equation.

Sometimes the nature of the X variable's independence causes confusion. X is described as independent in the sense that any observation's value in respect of X is not controlled by its value for Y. Although X is described as the independent variable, it does not exist in isolation and may itself be dependent upon one or more other variables, which are not measured as part of the investigation. Such antecedent variables may be disregarded in a particular study because their controlling influence on variable X has already become part of established and uncontested scientific knowledge. Alternatively, such variables may be omitted because their effect is deemed to lie outside the limits of the study in question. Suppose that the position of the snout of a glacier has been accurately recorded over a number of years, from which calculations of its annual advance or retreat can be made. A corresponding series of mean annual temperature measurements in the vicinity of the glacier are also obtained. The study reaches the conclusion that, other things being equal, a higher mean annual temperature leads to greater glacial retreat. The simpler question of the effect of a temperature increase on ice is not examined, since the melting of ice as temperature rises is accepted as part of scientific law and does not require explanation. Similarly, as far as this study is defined, the cause of the temperature increase is not of any interest to the investigator.

The formula for the product moment correlation coefficient (R) is symmetrical and thus, from a computational point of view, it makes no difference which variable is designated as X and which as Y. Such a cavalier attitude is not permissible in regression analysis, since one of the variables causes, at least in part, the other. It is therefore necessary to theorise about the possible form of the relationship between the variables before attempting to represent this as a mathematical equation. In the previous example, it would have made little sense to suggest that the advance or retreat of the glacier caused the mean annual temperature change. In some investigations, the direction of the relationship, whether X causes Y, or Y causes X, or whether to some extent they cause each other, is not entirely obvious. Furthermore, one variable taken on its own may not be enough to explain the variations in the dependent variable and the concerted effort of a series of independent variables is taken into account. In this case multivariate regression techniques are required. Attention in this chapter will be focused on the more straightforward situation in which the dependent and independent variables can be specified unambiguously. In order to examine these, the bivariate regression technique known as the *simple linear regression model* will be employed.

13.2 SIMPLE LINEAR REGRESSION

13.2.1 Theoretical background

The theoretical starting point for simple linear regression is that for any known value of the dependent variable (X), the corresponding value of the independent variable (Y) can be determined either graphically or mathematically. The graphical determination of Y is achieved by virtue of the fact that the points denoting the intersection of the X values with their associated Y values lie along a straight line. Thus the value of Y for any known value of X can be read from the graph. The mathematical expression of the relationship between X and Y can be represented as an equation of the following generalised form:

$$Y = a + bX$$

where a and b are both constants. X signifies the known values of the controlling or independent variable, from which the values of Y can be calculated. Suppose the equation is computed for a series of X values, say 3.4, 7.5, 8.1, 8.5, 9.3, 10.8, and it is assumed that $a = 20.0$ and $b = 0.75$; then the six values of Y thus determined will lie along a straight line (shown by the solid line in Figure 13.1). The value of Y is always 20.0 plus three-quarters the value of X, remembering that it is X that controls Y. This can be written as the equation:

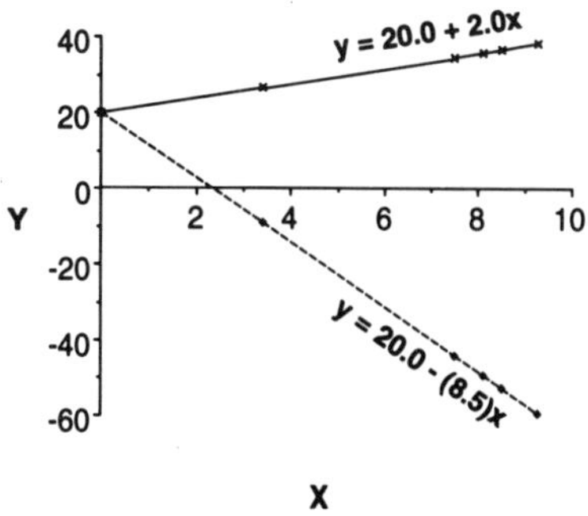

Figure 13.1 Simple linear regression

$$Y = 20.0 + 0.75X$$

Now suppose that the constant, b, in this hypothetical example is altered (say $b = -8.5$). The X values remain the unchanged but a new set of Y values can be calculated and the intersection of the X and Y values will fall along a different straight line, denoted by the broken line in Figure 13.1. The equation for this second line is:

$$Y = 20.0 - 8.5X$$

An examination of the equations and the straight lines passing through the known points in Figure 13.1 reveals a number of important general features about the equation for the linear regression model. The calculated value of Y always equals the distance of the regression line above or below the horizontal axis. The constant, a, is the value of Y when X equals 0 and the regression line cuts through the vertical axis: a is therefore referred to as the *intercept*. The *gradient* or *slope* of the line is given by the constant b, which is the amount that Y increases as X increases by 1 unit. From Figure 13.1, it is evident that a large b indicates a steep slope, while a small value for b denotes a gentle one. In the unlikely the event that b equals 0 the line is horizontal. The sign of the constant b provides information about the direction of the relationship. A positive value signifies that the straight line slopes from bottom left to top right, while a negative one means the line slopes from top left to bottom right. The sign of b has a similar implication to the sign of the product moment correlation coefficient.

A perfect linear relationship is of course unlikely to be encountered when investigating real-world phenomena: a straight line can rarely be drawn such that it passes through the points representing all the paired values for the X and Y variables in a population or sample. The problem is therefore to find the line which 'best fits' the scatter of points. A line which connects all the points for a realistic set of observations will usually zigzag across the graph (Figure 13.2), and is therefore not a feasible proposition. An infinite number of straight lines could be drawn, but the problem is to find the one which will best fit the scatter of points. But what does 'best fit' mean in this context? If

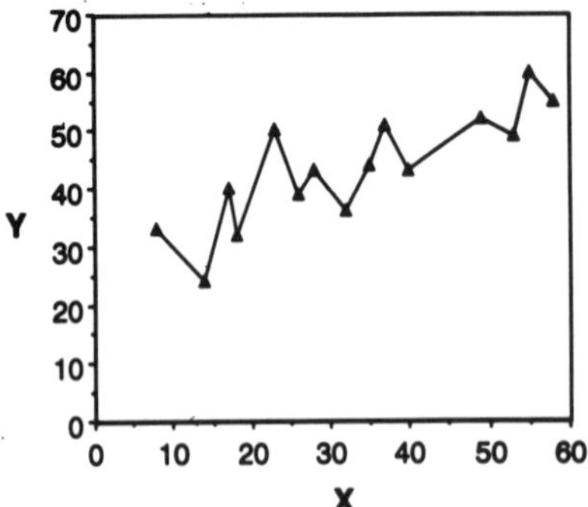

Figure 13.2 Direct linear connection between a scatter of points

the line cannot connect all the points, then a reasonable starting point is that the desired line should pass as close to as many points as possible and through the middle of the distribution. The point where $\bar{x}$ and $\bar{y}$ meet on the graph may be thought of as the middle or centroid of the points. Recalling that the linear regression equation calculates the values of Y for known values of X, when measurements for a real X variable fail to predict Y values on a line, the values are said to *deviate*. These deviations between the measured and predicted Y values can be positive or negative quantities.

The solution to the problem of identifying which straight line best fits a particular distribution of points would seem to be to select the line where the sum of the deviations from the line is zero: where the positive and negative deviations cancel each other out. Unfortunately, such deviations can be measured either vertically, horizontally, perpendicularly or at any other constant angle from each point to the line. The difficulty with this solution is that there are an infinite number of lines passing through the mean of X and Y from which the sum of the deviations is zero. The result is similar to taking the sum of the absolute differences between each observation and its mean, when trying to devise a measure of dispersion (see Chapter 5). The solution of this problem for calculating a univariate measure of dispersion suggests an answer in regression analysis, namely to minimise the sum of the squared of the deviations from the line. This eliminates some of the candidate lines, but the question remains, which deviations should be used: the vertical, horizontal or perpendicular ones. The vertical deviations should be used, since the basis of simple linear regression is that Y is dependent upon X, and not the other way around. Any deviation from the straight regression line is the result of variability in Y rather than X. This procedure for fitting a line to a scatter of points is known as the *method of least squares* and the line is referred to formally as the *linear regression of Y on X*.

The observed value of Y for a given value of X is likely to be different than that determined by reading across from the regression line to the Y axis. In other words, there are frequently discrepancies between the observed and predicted values of Y, which are equivalent to the deviations. Such deviations can occur because of errors in measurement, or because variables other than X also exert a controlling influence on Y. In simple linear regression these are assumed to be unimportant chance disturbances. Nevertheless, a consequence of this discrepancy is that the general straight-line regression equation is often rewritten as:

$$\hat{Y} = a + bX$$

where the 'hat' symbol over Y indicates that the values of Y on the straight line may be different to the actual value of Y as recorded in the sample.

The equivalent population regression equation is:

$$\mu = \alpha + \beta X$$

where α and β have the same meaning as the constants a and b. The use of μ, in place of $\hat{Y}$, is rather more significant and merits some comment. The symbol μ is usually employed to represent a population mean and its use in the population regression equation is likewise based on this principle. The values of Y falling on the regression line in a population are the means of the distributions of Y for each different value of X. Furthermore, according to the theory underpinning the simple linear regression model, these conditional distributions of Y are of an identical normal form. Thus $\hat{Y}$ can be regarded as the sample estimate of μ for any particular value of X.

The estimation of Y values in this way emphasises the predictive function of regression analysis. In addition to identifying cause and effect, regression is often used to predict the values of Y associated with values of X which lie outside the range covered by the sample. When $\hat{Y}$ is required for a value of X which lies within the range that has been measured, it is reasonable to argue that any deviation is the result of random variations. However, sometimes a prediction of Y is required at a value of X that lies outside the range actually included within the sample dataset, for example when trying to project a trend forwards in time: such an exercise is referred to as *extrapolation* and is problematic for two reasons. There is no guarantee that the straight-line relationship continues beyond the observed values of X; the line may start to curve or cease to exist. Even if a straight-line relationship is sustained beyond the range of measured values, then the sample means, $\bar{x}$ and $\bar{y}$, become less reliable as estimates for the true population means for the variables.

A straight line could be fitted to a scatter of observations according to the least-squares method by drawing vertical lines through all the points and a series of lines through the intersection of the means of X and Y. The deviations of the points from each of the lines would be measured, then squared and the minimum sum taken to indicate the best-fit line. In practical applications this operation is both tedious and prone to error. Fortunately, formulae exist which can be used to calculate the values of the constants a and b, thus:

$$b = \frac{n\Sigma XY - \Sigma X \Sigma Y}{n\Sigma X^2 - (\Sigma X)^2}$$

and

$$a = \frac{\Sigma Y}{n} - \frac{b\Sigma X}{n}$$

where n is the sample size or the number of pairs of X and Y values. The intercept, a, provides one known point for drawing the straight line and further points may be obtained by substitution into the standard linear equation, or by using the intersection of $\bar{x}$ and $\bar{y}$.

13.2.2 An example

In Chapter 12 the product moment correlation coefficient for the sample of farms in Yorkshire in respect of their area and net farm income was calculated as +0.8703, which was significant at the 0.05 level. But what is the form of the relationship? Theoretically farm size might be expected to control net farm income, but to what extent is this true? The scattergram in Figure 13.3 indicates that the points representing the farms in the sample tend to follow a straight line. Substitution of the appropriate figures into the formulae for a and b, most of which have been used in previous calculations, produces the following values for the constants:

Figure 13.3 Simple linear regression line for size and net farm income of sample farms in Yorkshire

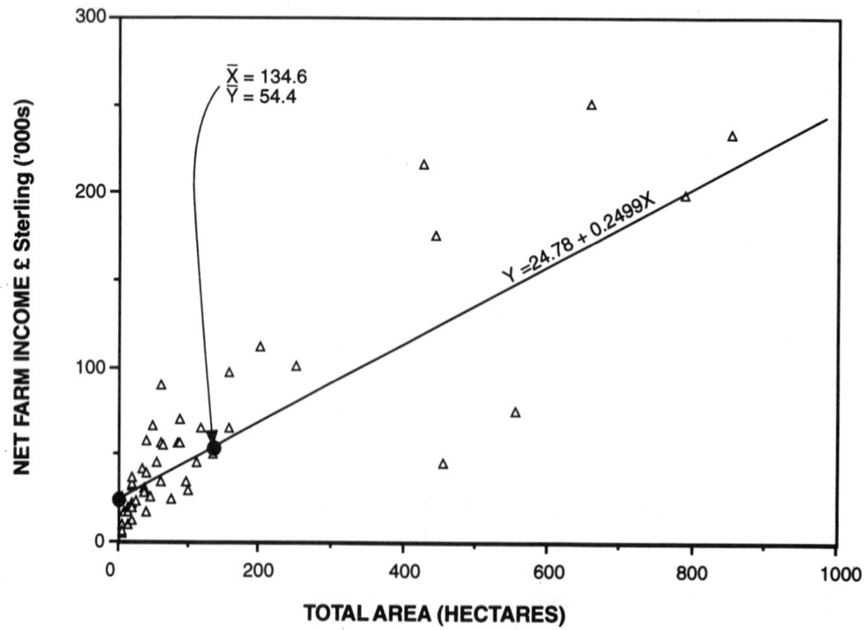

$$b = \frac{50 \times 906\,878.38 - 6730.7 \times 2921.4}{50 \times 2\,961\,034.50 - 6730.7^2}$$
$$= \frac{45\,343\,919 - 19\,661\,898.42}{148\,051\,725 - 45\,302\,322.49} = \frac{25\,682\,020.58}{102\,749\,402.5}$$
$$= 0.2499$$

and

$$a = \frac{2921.4}{50} - \frac{0.2499 \times 6730.7}{50}$$
$$= 24.78$$

The regression equation of Y on X is therefore

$$\hat{Y} = 24.78 + 0.2499X$$

The intercept, 24.78, and the intersection of the means, where $\bar{x} =$ 134.6 ha and $\bar{y} =$ £58 428 are sufficient to enable the regression line to be drawn on the graph. The low value of b, 0.2499, indicates that the slope of the line is fairly gentle. Net farm income measurements deviate vertically from the regression line, which may partly be accounted for by errors of measurement and partly by the effect of other variables.

The approach which has been adopted so far is to start from a scatter of points and to find out the regression equation and line which best fits that particular distribution. In other words, for any given distribution, there is one line which best fits the data according to the least-squares method. Unfortunately, the line itself is not unique and could be equally applicable to another scatter of points. Visually comparing the two distributions in Figure 13.4(a) and 13.4(b), to which the identical regression line and equation applies, makes it clear that the spread or dispersion of the points about the line is the key distinguishing feature of the two datasets. Thus some method is needed for representing this variability and the extent to which the line approximates to the data. The problem is similar to that when two sets of numbers have the same mean, but different dispersion.

The necessary quantity is known as the *standard error of the estimate*, $\sigma_{y \cdot x}$ for a population and $s_{y \cdot x}$ for a sample, and is in effect the standard deviation of the vertical differences of the points from the best-fit regression line. In the case of a population these vertical deviations are called *residuals* and are denoted by the Greek letter ϵ (epsilon); with a sample they are known as *error terms* and given the symbol d or e. The calculation of $\sigma_{y \cdot x}$ and $s_{y \cdot x}$ is relatively straightforward and based on the formulae for the population and sample standard deviations. The standard error of the estimate for a population is:

$$\sigma_{y \cdot x} = \sqrt{\frac{\Sigma(Y - \mu)^2}{N}} = \sqrt{\frac{\Sigma\epsilon^2}{N}}$$

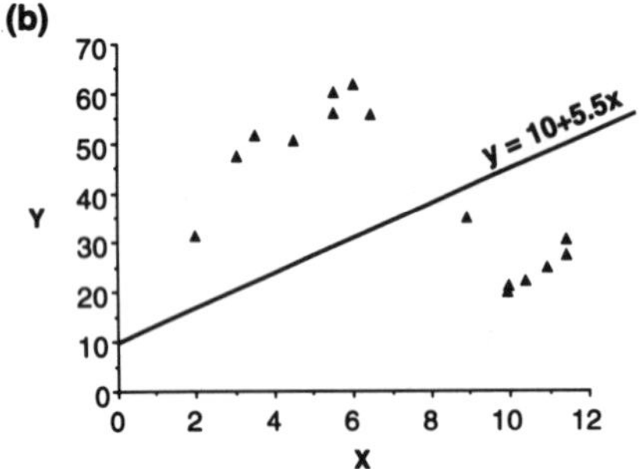

Figure 13.4 Contrasting scatterplots for identical regression line

and for a sample:

$$s_{y \cdot x} = \sqrt{\frac{\Sigma(Y - \hat{Y})^2}{n - 2}} = \sqrt{\frac{\Sigma d^2}{n - 2}}$$

where the sum of the squared deviations is divided by either N or $n - 2$.

In practical applications it may prove tedious to calculate the value of the residuals or deviations. In the example of the Yorkshire farms, 50 values for $\hat{Y}$ would be needed corresponding to the X values in the sample. Then the deviations from the observed Ys would have to be obtained $(Y - \hat{Y})$, squared and summed. Fortunately, there are alternative, more convenient formulae for obtaining the standard error of the estimate, which make use of quantities already employed in calculating the linear regression equation. The formula for a population may be written:

$$\sigma_{y \cdot x} = \sqrt{\frac{N\Sigma Y^2 - (\Sigma Y)^2 - \beta(N\Sigma XY - \Sigma X \Sigma Y)}{N^2}}$$

$$= \sqrt{\frac{\Sigma Y^2 - \alpha \Sigma Y - \beta \Sigma X \Sigma Y}{N}}$$

and that for a sample:

$$s_{y \cdot x} = \sqrt{\frac{n\Sigma Y^2 - (\Sigma Y)^2 - b(n\Sigma XY - \Sigma X\Sigma Y)}{n(n-2)}}$$

$$= \sqrt{\frac{\Sigma Y^2 - a\Sigma Y - b\Sigma X\Sigma Y}{n-2}}$$

Substituting the appropriate values from the Yorkshire farms example, the standard error of the estimate may be determined according to the first formula as follows:

$$s_{y \cdot x} = \sqrt{\frac{50 \times 340\,745.56 - 2921.4^2 - 0.2499(50 \times 906\,878.38 - 6730.7 \times 2921.4)}{50(50-2)}}$$

$$= \sqrt{\frac{17\,037\,278.00 - 8\,534\,577.96 - 0.2499(45\,343\,919 - 19\,663\,066.98)}{2400}}$$

$$= \frac{\overline{17\,037\,278.00 - 8\,534\,577.96 - 6\,417\,644.92}}{2400}$$

$$= \sqrt{868.77} = 29.47$$

or alternatively

$$s_{y \cdot x} = \frac{\overline{340\,745.56 - 24.78 \times 2921.4 - 0.2499 \times 906\,878.38}}{50 - 2}$$

$$= \frac{\overline{340\,745.56 - 72\,392.29 - 226\,628.91}}{48}$$

$$= \sqrt{869.26} = 29.48$$

The marginal difference between the values is due to rounding. The quantity 29.47 comprises a summary statistic which enables different samples to be compared in respect of the extent to which their points are scattered or dispersed about their regression line. It also allows distributions which share the same best-fit regression equation and line to be compared.

13.3 SIGNIFICANCE TESTING FOR SIMPLE LINEAR REGRESSION

The reference to 'one variable being controlled by or dependent upon another' may foster the misleading impression that the regression equation and its component parts (*a* and *b*) are somehow free from suspicion as to their reliability. Unfortunately, this is not the case. They are as likely to be influenced by sampling error and chance as any other statistical procedure. Thus it is necessary to consider techniques for significance testing in simple linear regression, and two basic approaches have been developed: one concentrates on the whole regression equation or model, while the other treats the constants a and b as separate statistics which require testing in much the same way as any other. Furthermore, regression analysis is frequently carried out on sample data in order to estimate the relationship between the dependent and independent variables in the population. Confidence intervals can be devised for the intercept and slope and for the best-fit regression line. These are analogous to the numerical limits either side of a sample mean within which the population mean will occur with a certain degree of confidence.

13.3.1 Analysis of variance

An adaptation of the oneway analysis of variance procedure yields a convenient technique for examining the reliability of the whole regression model. The null hypothesis under scrutiny is that no explanation of the variability in Y (the dependent variable) is provided by X (the independent variable). The total variance of the dependent variable $(\Sigma(Y - \bar{Y})^2/n - 1)$ is divided between that accounted for by the regression line and that associated with the residuals or deviations. These are known as the *regression* and *residual variances*, respectively; they are represented symbolically, for a population, as:

$$\sigma_{\mu}^2 \text{ and } \sigma_{\epsilon}^2$$

and for a sample as:

$$s_{\hat{Y}}^2 \text{ and } s_e^2$$

The values of these quantities are obtained by dividing the appropriate part of the total sum of the squares by the corresponding degrees of freedom thus:

$$s_{\hat{Y}}^2 = \frac{\Sigma(\hat{Y} - \bar{Y})^2}{k}$$

and

$$s_e^2 = \frac{\Sigma(\hat{Y} - \bar{Y})^2}{n - k - 1}$$

where k is the number of independent variables (always 1 in simple linear regression). Division of the resulting quantities yields the test statistic F:

$$F = \frac{s_{\hat{Y}}^2}{s_e^2}$$

The probability of having obtained the value of F or one greater derived from the sample data through chance may now be ascertained from the table of F distributions in Appendix IV Table 6, with k degrees of freedom for the numerator and $n - k - 1$ for the denominator.

The partition of the total variance into its regression and residual components gives some indication of the extent to which the variability of Y values is explained by the linear regression model or equation and how much is derived from the residuals or deviations. A large proportion of the total variance associated with the former suggests that the variable X and the regression equation together provide a good prediction of Y. But if the proportion of the variance derived from the residuals is high, then a low F will be obtained with the implication that other variables, unaccounted for, play an important part in explaining the variability of the dependent variable.

The relative magnitude of the regression and residual variances is a useful guide as to how the linear regression model works. For example, if the best-fit regression line is horizontal ($b = 0.0$), then $\hat{Y}$ is constant for all values of X and equal to the mean of $Y(\bar{Y})$. In this circumstance the regression equation becomes:

$$\hat{Y} = a + 0X = \bar{Y}$$

and every X value predicts $\hat{Y}$ as equalling $\bar{Y}$. When this happens the regression sum of squares and variance will be zero and thus the total variance equates with the residual variance. When the line is not horizontal and b less than or greater than 0, then some of the total sum of squares and variance of Y are accounted for by the regression model. In the unlikely event of the data points falling exactly on the regression line, the total sum of squares and variance of Y are entirely attributed to the model. The magnitude of the F ratio, therefore, helps to determine whether the amount of variability accounted for by the linear regression model is significant in comparison to that associated with the residuals.

One disadvantage of using the analysis of variance as a significance test for regression relates to the calculations involved. The values of $\hat{Y}$ predicted by the regression equation for each known X and the differences between these values and both $\bar{Y}$ and the known values of Y have to be calculated. The relevant calculations for the Yorkshire farms example (Table 13.1) highlight the complexities. The null hypothesis under examination in this case is that the regression equation fails to provide any explanation of the variation in Y, and any apparent causal relationship is merely the result of sampling error. The totals from the $(\hat{Y} - \bar{Y})^2$ and $(\hat{Y} - Y)^2$ columns can be substituted into the appropriate formulae in order to obtain $s^2_{\hat{Y}}$ and s^2_e thus:

$$s^2_{\hat{Y}} = \frac{128\,344.00}{1} = 128\,344.00$$

and

$$s^2_e = \frac{41\,685.25}{50 - 1 - 1} = 868.44$$

Dividing $s^2_{\hat{Y}}$ by s^2_e produces an F ratio of 147.77, which is far in excess of the critical value in the F distribution table in Appendix IV with 1

Table 13.1 Calculations for ANOVA significance test of simple linear regression for Yorkshire farms

(X)	(Y)	$(\hat{Y})$	$(\hat{Y}-\bar{Y})^2$	$(\hat{Y}-Y)^2$
456.8	45.6	138.93	6 481.27	8 711.30
45.6	25.3	36.18	495.18	118.28
20.5	12.2	29.90	813.68	313.39
7.8	17.6	26.73	1 004.81	83.34
250.2	101.4	87.30	833.88	198.67
134.6	50.3	58.42	0.00	65.88
75.8	24.1	43.72	216.25	385.04
96.7	34.3	48.95	89.92	214.49
13.6	10.2	28.18	915.02	323.23
100.8	30.0	49.97	71.54	398.80
112.5	45.5	52.89	30.63	54.67
19.5	20.1	29.65	828.00	91.26
20.5	37.5	29.90	813.68	57.72
6.4	6.2	26.38	1 027.12	407.21
555.2	75.6	163.52	11 045.27	7 730.71
60.3	56.6	39.85	345.18	280.60
156.9	96.8	63.99	30.93	1 076.54
854.8	233.5	238.39	32 387.95	23.96
60.3	34.7	39.85	345.18	26.51
15.7	19.8	28.70	883.55	79.27
19.4	22.2	29.63	829.44	55.18
86.0	56.7	46.27	147.78	108.76
425.6	216.7	131.14	5 286.66	7 320.95
50.8	66.2	37.47	439.03	825.13
5.3	10.1	26.10	1 044.81	256.14
788.5	199.3	221.83	26 698.96	507.43
65.4	55.4	41.12	299.45	203.82
39.1	27.8	34.55	570.11	45.58
88.7	70.2	46.95	131.83	540.74
4.5	5.3	25.90	1 057.77	424.55
16.2	20.1	28.83	876.14	76.18
39.0	30.4	34.53	571.30	17.02
19.5	31.7	29.65	828.00	4.19
40.5	57.6	34.90	553.52	515.25
115.6	65.4	53.67	22.65	137.63
88.7	56.3	46.95	131.83	87.49
20.3	33.7	29.85	816.53	14.80
34.6	41.9	33.43	625.07	71.80
156.5	65.0	63.89	29.83	1.23
40.5	16.7	34.90	553.52	331.27
62.6	89.7	40.42	324.15	2 428.15
657.2	250.6	189.01	17 052.78	3 792.80
55.1	45.8	38.55	395.15	52.57
40.5	39.5	34.90	553.52	21.15
25.0	23.4	31.03	750.79	58.18
14.5	16.7	28.40	901.47	136.97
443.6	175.6	135.64	5 961.02	1 597.15
6.7	25.6	26.45	1 022.32	0.73
13.8	17.2	28.23	912.00	121.63
202.5	111.3	75.38	287.53	1 289.91
6 730.7	2 921.4	1 706.78	128 334.00	41 685.25

and 48 degrees of freedom for the numerator and denominator, respectively. Thus the null hypothesis can confidently be rejected in favour of the alternative, which asserts that the controlling influence of farm size on net farm income evident from the sample data is statistically significant.

13.3.2 Testing elements of the linear regression equation and calculation of confidence intervals

The purpose of the tests is to determine the reliability of the constants a and b as estimates of α and β, the equivalent population parameters in the regression equation. The tests represent an alternative to the analysis of variance and will produce the same result overall in terms of whether the linear regression model can be relied upon as accounting for the causal relationship between the dependent and independent variables. Four key assumptions are made about the nature of the variables in the population from which the sample has been taken. These assumptions relate directly to the theoretical basis of simple linear regression and each varies slightly depending upon whether the population is infinite or finite in size. Each assumption has been given a name, and they are summarised in Table 13.2. Three of the assumptions concern the conditional distributions of Y values, which have already been referred to in respect of the product moment correlation coefficient. The four assumptions collectively define the linear regression model, which is a mathematical construct that is unlikely to be found in reality. However, provided the assumptions are not seriously violated, the model is generally regarded as reliable. The linear regression model does not require that the independent variable (X) is normally distributed, thus X values may be regular, for example every hour, 100 m or 5°C.

Table 13.2 Population assumptions of significance tests for the simple linear regression model

Assumption	Infinite population	Finite population
Linearity	Mean (μ) of each CD lies on regression line $\mu = \alpha + \beta X$.	Deviations of the mean (μ) of each CD of Y arise through chance.
Homoscedasticity/ Heteroscedasticity	Each CD of Y has same standard deviation ($\sigma_{y \cdot x}$)	Standard deviation of each CD of Y ($\sigma_{y \cdot x}$) might vary through chance.
Independence	Deviation of one Y value from the mean of Y is unrelated to the deviation of any other.	Correlations may occur by chance.
Normality	Each CD of Y is exactly normal	Some departure from normality may occur.

Note: CD = conditional distribution.

13.3.2.1 *The reliability of the slope coefficient* (b)

If an infinite number of samples were selected with replacement from a single population and the equations for the best-fit lines were determined, the result would be a set of slope constants, b values, each of which was an estimate of β. Their mean would also equal β and their standard error would be defined as:

$$\sigma_b = \frac{\sigma_{y \cdot x}}{\sqrt{\Sigma X^2 - (\Sigma X)^2/N}}$$

where $\sigma_{y \cdot x}$ is the standard deviation of Y values about the regression equation for the population (the standard error of the estimate). Unfortunately, this quantity can rarely be determined in practical applications, but the equivalent statistic ($s_{y \cdot x}$), derived from a single sample, provides an unbiased estimate for use in place of $\sigma_{y \cdot x}$ in the previous formula, thus:

$$s_b = \frac{s_{y \cdot x}}{\sqrt{\{\Sigma X^2 - [(\Sigma X)^2/n]\}}}$$

The standard error of b thus obtained can then be used in two ways. First, the confidence limits of b can be calculated. For example, the 95 per cent confidence interval of b lies between a lower limit of $b - t_{0.05}s_b$ and an upper limit of $b + t_{0.05}s_b$, with $n - 2$ degrees of freedom. Second, the standard error of b can be used in a t test to determine the probability that the difference between b and β has arisen through chance sampling error. The procedure is usually employed to test whether b is significantly different from $\beta = 0$, with the t-test statistic obtained as follows:

$$t = \frac{(b - \beta)}{s_b}$$

with $n - 2$ degrees of freedom. Thus the null hypothesis states that there is no relationship between the 'so-called' dependent and independent variables, and any evidence of a causal connection is purely illusory.

At first sight it might seem rather strange to test $\beta = 0$ rather than some other value. But what other value would be suitable? For the usual reasons it is unlikely that the parameter, β, can be calculated due to a lack of sufficient information about the population. If the information were adequate, then there would probably have been little point in taking a sample in the first place. The null hypothesis might specify that β equals some value other than zero, which may have been obtained from an earlier census of items in the population, which had included the same variables X and Y. In these circumstances the sample is intended to examine any change in the relationship.

Assuming that the population of farms in Yorkshire does not seriously contravene the four assumptions of the linear regression model, the confidence interval and test procedures can be applied to the sample. The null hypothesis states that any difference between b and β has arisen through sampling error and that $\beta = 0$ in the parent population.

The standard error of the estimate, $s_{y \cdot x}$, has already been calculated as 29.47, which can be substituted, together with the other appropriate quantities, into the formula for estimating the standard error to produce the following result:

$$s_b = \frac{29.47}{\sqrt{2\,961\,034.50 - 6730.7^2/50}}$$

$$= \frac{29.47}{\sqrt{2\,961\,034.50 - 906\,046.45}} = \frac{29.47}{1433.523} = 0.02056$$

The null hypothesis is tested by inserting the standard error into the t-test formula, which produces the following test statistic:

$$t = \frac{|0.2499 - 0|}{0.02056} = 12.152$$

With $n - 2$ degrees of freedom, here $50 - 2$, it may be estimated from the t-distribution table in Appendix IV reveals that the probability of having obtained a t value of 12.152 by chance is less than 0.000 1. In other words, the result is highly significant and the difference between b and a population $\beta = 0$ is more than would normally be expected. The null hypothesis can safely be rejected as untenable. The true β lies within the following 95 per cent confidence limits, with $t_{0.05}$ equalling approximately 2.009:

$$0.2499 - 2.009 \times 0.02056 \text{ to } 0.2499 + 2.009 \times 0.02056$$

$$\text{i.e. } 0.2086 \text{ to } 0.2912$$

Thus, on the basis of the information in the sample, the population slope coefficient, β, will lie outside these limits only 5 times in 100.

13.3.2.2 The reliability of the intercept (a)

According to the definition of the linear model, the intercept of the regression equation for a population, α, equals the mean of Y when $X = 0$ (i.e. $\mu_Y = \alpha$ for $X = 0$). If an infinite number of samples were to be taken from the population all with $X = 0$, their intercepts would be expected to have a mean of α and a standard error given by the formula:

$$\sigma_\alpha = \sigma_{y \cdot x}\sqrt{\frac{\Sigma X^2}{n\Sigma X^2 - (\Sigma X)^2}}$$

where $\sigma_{y \cdot x}$ is the standard deviation of the Y values about the regression line. The standard error of α can rarely be determined owing to only a single rather than infinite number of samples being available from the population. However, the equivalent sample statistic s_a provides an unbiased estimate of the parameter which can be used instead, and is defined as:

$$s_a = s_{y \cdot x}\sqrt{\frac{\Sigma X^2}{n\Sigma X^2 - (\Sigma X)^2}}$$

The t test for the intercept, a, and the calculation of the confidence limits now proceed in a similar fashion to those for b.

The standard error of a is used to carry out a t test in which the null hypothesis states that the difference between a and α is the result of sampling error and is not significant from a statistical point of view. The hypothesised value assigned to α is usually 0, since the sample which is being tested is the only evidence to suggest that the regression line does not pass through the origin of the graph where $X = 0$ and $Y = 0$. There are indeed some research situations where it is illogical to suggest that Y can take on a value other than zero when $X = 0$. For example, suppose an investigation of aeolian soil erosion is undertaken in which the independent and dependent variables are respectively wind speed and volume of soil removed. When wind speed drops to zero, it is reasonable to expect that no soil particles are removed. However, when appropriate sample data are collected and analysed this might not be the case. Such an eventuality can arise because of the confounding influence of other variables, inadequate theorising about the process or measurement inaccuracies. Nevertheless, from a hypothetical point of view the population intercept may be regarded as 0. The t-test statistic for a is calculated as follows:

$$t = \frac{|a - \alpha|}{s_a}$$

with $n - 2$ degrees of freedom. The probability associated with t is determined from the t-distribution table (Appendix IV). The 95 per cent confidence interval for a is defined as lying between $a - t_{0.05}s_a$ and $a + t_{0.05}s_a$. These limits define the interval within which the investigator can be confident that the population intercept, α, will fall 95 times in a 100. If this interval is relatively wide, then the sample is less reliable as an estimate for the population parameter.

The t-test and confidence interval procedures for the intercept (a) are now applied to the sample of farms in Yorkshire, which requires the standard error of a. The standard error of the estimate of a equals 29.47 and therefore s_a is:

$$\begin{aligned} s_a &= 29.47\sqrt{\frac{2\,961\,034.50}{50 \times 2\,961\,034.50 - 6730.7^2}} \\ &= 29.47\sqrt{\frac{2\,961\,034.5}{102\,749\,402.5}} \\ &= 5.003 \end{aligned}$$

The null hypothesis states that the intercept for the population of farms, α, is in fact 0 and the value of 24.78 generated from the sample data is the result of chance or sampling error. Substitution into the formula for t produces the test statistic:

$$\begin{aligned} t &= \frac{|24.78 - 0|}{5.003} \\ &= 4.953 \end{aligned}$$

With 48 degrees of freedom (50−2), the probability associated with $t = 4.953$ may be estimated from the t-distribution table in Appendix IV as less than 0.0001. The statistical test casts serious doubt on the null hypothesis, which may be rejected as extremely improbable. The 95 per cent confidence limits for the sample intercept are:

$$24.78 - 2.009 \times 5.003 \text{ to } 24.78 + 2.009 \times 5.003$$
$$\text{i.e. } 14.73 \text{ to } 34.83$$

The intercept for the population can confidently be expected to occur between these values for 95 samples in 100.

13.3.2.3 The reliability of $\hat{Y}$

The predicted values of the dependent variable associated with each X value are estimates of μ in the population, which, it will be recalled, are the means of the conditional distributions of Y. Unless the regression line happens to be horizontal, the value of $\hat{Y}$ varies along its length and each value has an upper and lower confidence limit. The calculation of these limits may be regarded as a generalisation of the procedure for the intercept, since the latter is effectively the value of $\hat{Y}$ where $X = 0$. The determination of these limits is particularly useful when the regression model is employed for predictive purposes.

In practice, the standard errors connected with $\hat{Y}$ are usually estimated from the sample observations, which involves some minor adaptation of the formula, thus:

$$s_{\hat{Y}} = s_{y \cdot x}\sqrt{\frac{1}{n} + \frac{n(X - \bar{X})^2}{n\Sigma X^2 - (\Sigma X)^2}}$$

where $s_{y \cdot x}$ is the standard deviation of the sampled items about the regression line. When the four assumptions of the regression model are satisfied, the quantity $|\hat{Y} - \mu|/s_{\hat{Y}}$ follows the t distribution with $n - 2$ degrees of freedom and the 95 per cent confidence limits for μ are:

$$\hat{Y} - t_{0.05}s_{\hat{Y}} \text{ and } \hat{Y} + t_{0.05}s_{\hat{Y}}$$

This interval defines the range within which the predicted value of μ will fall 95 times in a 100 for any chosen value of X.

There are of course as many values of $\hat{Y}$ as there are values of X and so the t-test statistic and confidence limits can be calculated for each value of the independent variable. When the confidence limits are plotted alongside the regression line on the scatter graph, they define two curved lines which are closest to the best-fit line at the point denoting the intersection of $\bar{X}$ and $\bar{Y}$. These confidence boundaries are curved because the more a particular value of X deviates from $\bar{X}$, the larger the standard error $s_{\hat{Y}}$ becomes.

The population of farms in Yorkshire may be regarded as conforming to the four assumptions of the regression model with the result that for farms of 100 and 250 ha, the predicted values of $\hat{Y}$ are:

$$\hat{Y} = 24.78 + 0.2499 \times 100 \qquad \hat{Y} = 24.78 + 0.2499 \times 250$$
$$= 49.77 \qquad\qquad = 87.26$$

These values can now be used to calculate the corresponding standard errors thus:

$$s_{\hat{Y}} = 49.77\sqrt{\frac{1}{50} + \frac{50(100 - 134.6)^2}{50 \times 2\,961\,034.5 - 6730.7^2}}$$
$$= 49.77\sqrt{\frac{1}{50} + \frac{59\,858}{102\,749\,401}}$$
$$= 49.77\sqrt{0.02 + 0.000\,583}$$
$$= 49.77\sqrt{0.020\,58}$$
$$= 7.14$$

$$s_{\hat{Y}} = 87.26\sqrt{\frac{1}{50} + \frac{50(250 - 134.6)^2}{50 \times 2\,961\,034.5 - 6730.7^2}}$$
$$= 87.26\sqrt{\frac{1}{50} + \frac{665\,858}{102\,749\,401}}$$

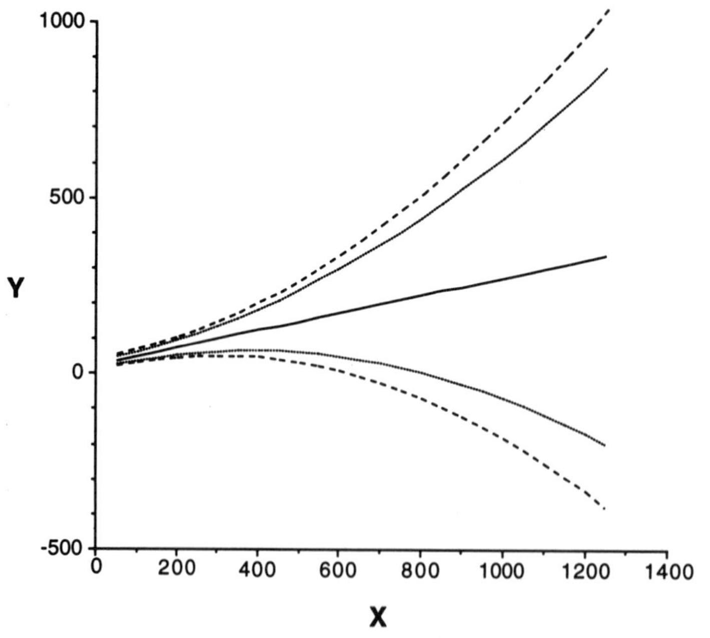

Figure 13.5 Confidence intervals (95 and 99 per cent) for simple linear regression

$$= 87.26\sqrt{0.02 + 0.006\,48}$$
$$= 87.26\sqrt{0.026\,48}$$
$$= 14.20$$

$s_{\hat{Y}}$ becomes larger the further X is from $\bar{X}$, and can be used to calculate the confidence limits for μ. With $n - 2$ degrees of freedom, in this case 48, the tabulated value of t at the 0.05 level with df = 50 is 2.009, thus the 95 confidence limits when $\hat{Y}$ equals 49.77 and 87.26 are respectively:

$$49.77 - 2.009 \times 7.14 \text{ to } 49.77 + 2.009 \times 7.14 = 35.43 \text{ to } 64.11$$

$$87.26 - 2.009 \times 14.20 \text{ to } 87.26 + 2.009 \times 14.20 = 58.73 \text{ to } 115.79$$

The 95 and 99 per cent confidence intervals for $\hat{Y}$ at regularly spaced values of X are shown in Figure 13.5. The curved nature of the lines is clear, and their interpretation is that for any given value of X the population mean μ will lie between the two lines 95 or 99 times in 100. The confidence limits thus define a convex 'lens', which is bisected by the regression line itself.

13.4 REGRESSION ANALYSIS IN EXEMPLAR PROJECTS

The correlation analysis of variables in the exemplar projects identified the strength and nature of selected relationships. The regression analysis will now attempt to consider whether such relationships can be regarded as causal and to demonstrate the practicalities of carrying out these procedures using MINITAB and SPSS-X. The full range of explanatory or independent variables has not been introduced in the projects, which have been defined within fairly narrow limits, but nevertheless they provide a useful introduction to the methods of investigating such causal relationships in certain areas of geography.

13.4.1 Land-use change

The correlation analysis of the land-use variables concentrated on the nature of any relationship between the area of a particular land use in a grid square in the 1930s and its area in the 1960s. The results showed that for most land uses this argument was supported by fairly strong and significant Spearman's rank correlation coefficients. The factors which cause land use to change are complex and include variables which lie outside the scope of the project, such as land value and the financial returns arising from different uses. One factor which may have an influence on whether urban- or rural-type land uses predominate in a particular area is distance from a large population centre or major transport route. The chi-square test, which has already been carried out on the land-use data, suggested that there was a significant difference between the rural-urban fringe and rural areas. The influence of distance can be examined further by adding this variable to the datasets and carrying out a regression analysis.

The study area for the project lies to the north of London in part of Hertfordshire, and so the obvious solution is to calculate the distances from each area of land use (sample A) or grid square (sample B) to the centre of London. However, London's influence is likely to permeate the whole of the study area and its differential impact on the plots and grid squares is expected to be fairly minimal. Therefore the distance used in this project is to the nearest interchange on the M1 motorway, on the principle that transport times and cost are an important controlling influence on land use. A null hypothesis, LU7, can be formulated to reflect this argument:

LU7 Any evidence from the sample datasets that distance to the M1 motorway in part determines the relative balance between the different land uses is simply the result of sampling error.

Simple straight-line distance is not the most satisfactory measurement to use; however, it has the advantage that the relevant figures can be calculated from the data already held in the MINITAB worksheets.

National Grid coordinates for the easting and northing of the sampled observations are stored in columns C1 and C2 in both worksheets. Using this information, the straight-line distance of each observation from a given point can be calculated using Pythagoras's theorem. Table 13.3 gives the log of the MINITAB session which carries out the data manipulation operations and the regression analysis for samples A

Table 13.3 Application of simple linear regression analysis to land-use project samples A and B in MINITAB

```
MTB > OUTFILE 'land08'
MTB > RETRIEVE 'landa04'
MTB > LET K1 = 092
MTB > LET K2 = 147
MTB > LET C27 = SQRT((C1 - K1) * *2 + (C2 - K2) * *2)
MTB > REGRESS C7 1 C27
MTB > RETRIEVE 'landb04'
MTB > LET K1 = 092
MTB > LET K2 = 147
MTB > LET C60 = SQRT((C1 - K1) * *2 + (C2 - K2) * *2)
MTB > REGRESS C11 1 C60
MTB > REGRESS C12 1 C60
MTB > REGRESS C13 1 C60
MTB > REGRESS C14 1 C60
MTB > REGRESS C15 1 C60
MTB > REGRESS C16 1 C60
MTB > REGRESS C17 1 C60
MTB > NOOUTFILE
MTB > STOP
```

and B. The following sequence of commands relates to sample A:

```
MTB > LET K1 = 092
MTB > LET K2 = 147
MTB > LET C27 = SQRT ((C1 − K1)* * 2 + (C2 − K2)* * 2)
```

The M1 motorway crosses the study area and the interchange to the west of Harpenden is used. The easting (092) and northing (147) of

Box 13.1 Regression analysis results for LU7 for each land use on distance to M1 in land-use project

$Y = a + bX$				t for a	P	t for b	P	ANOVA F	P
Sample A									
Area60s	=	51.4 − 0.07	Area30s	3.06	0.004	0.25	0.804	0.06	0.804
Sample B									
Arab60s	=	46.0 − 0.01	Arab30s	0.26	0.798	0.01	0.990	0.00	0.990
MkGd60s	=	96.6 − 0.60	MkGd30s	1.40	0.179	1.35	0.195	1.81	0.195
Gras60s	=	−124.0 + 0.95	Gras30s	0.88	0.392	1.04	0.314	1.07	0.314
Wood60s	=	−1.3 + 0.07	Wood30s	0.01	0.989	0.11	0.914	0.01	0.914
Heat60s	=	−32.9 + 0.23	Heat30s	0.53	0.601	0.58	0.570	0.34	0.570
Hous60s	=	55.0 − 0.31	Hous30s	0.47	0.642	0.42	0.680	0.18	0.680
AgUn60s	=	61.5 − 0.32	AgUn30s	0.85	0.407	0.69	0.498	0.48	0.498

Sample Output from REGRESS

Sample A

```
MTB > REGRESS Area60s 1 Distance
The regression equation is
Area60s = 51.4 − 0.068 Distance
Predictor        Coef          Stdev       t-ratio       p
Constant        51.40          16.81         3.06      0.004
Distance      −0.0676         0.2700        −0.25      0.804
s = 54.14     R − sq = 0.2%       R − sq(adj) = 0.0%
Analysis of Variance
SOURCE          DF          SS         MS          F          p
Regression       1         184        184       0.06      0.804
Error           38      111395       2931
Total           39      111579
Unusual Observations
Obs.  Distance   Area60s     Fit   Stdev.Fit   Residual   St.Resid
 24      46       178.00   48.31      8.82      129.69      2.43R
 29      37       178.00   48.87      9.62      129.13      2.42R
R denotes an obs. with a large st. resid.
```

Sample B

```
MTB > REGRESS Arab60s 1 Distance
The regression equation is
Arab60s = 46 − 0.01 Distance
Predictor        Coef        Stdev       t-ratio       p
Constant         46.0        177.0         0.26      0.798
Distance       −0.014        1.140        −0.01      0.990
s = 18.74     R − Sq = 0.0%     R − sq(adj) = 0.0%
Analysis of Variance
SOURCE          DF          SS         MS          F          p
Regression       1          0.1        0.1      0.00      0.990
Error           18       6318.5      351.0
Total           19       6318.6
```

the interchange are defined in MINITAB as constants K1 and K2 and the straight-line distance between each land-use plot or grid square and the junction is computed and stored in C27 for sample A and C60 for sample B. Once the distance columns have been created, the regression equation is obtained by means of the REGRESS command, which is used for both bivariate and multivariate regression. The general syntax of the command is:

MTB > REGRESS C1 1 C5 C98 C99

where C1 and C5 contain respectively the dependent and independent variables, and the 1 denotes that there is one predictor, which indicates that simple linear regression is required. The standardised residuals and $\hat{Y}$ values can be stored in two new columns, shown here as C98 and C99, if required. The REGRESS command automatically provides the t-test statistic and its associated probability for the intercept (a) and slope (b) coefficients. The analysis of variance table is also included, thus enabling the whole linear model to be tested.

The results of the regression analysis for samples A and B have been summarised in Box 13.1. In the case of sample A the relationship under scrutiny is between plot size and distance from the M1. The result indicates that the relationship is weak with the slope coefficient only equal to −0.07. Overall the linear model is not significant, which suggests that distance to the motorway did not play an important role in determining the area of plots. A different relationship is explored in sample B, where the areas of each land use per grid square (dependent variables) are regressed on distance to the M1 (the independent variable). None of the regression models is statistically significant, although the relationship between land-use area and distance is positive for three of the land-use categories (grass, wood and heather/rough grazing), whereas for the other four it is negative. It is worth noting that the only land use for which the relationship shows any inclination towards being significant is market gardening, where the probability of the F-test statistic is 0.195 in the analysis of variance.

13.4.2 Chalk weathering

The correlation analysis of the sub-samples of chalk blocks revealed that there was a fairly strong relationship between time and the degradation of the chalk, which remained fairly consistent between treatment types. The duration of the experiment is fairly restricted, and if continued further its linearity may start to change. Thus although it is appropriate to undertake a regression analysis comparable to the correlations carried out in the previous chapter, some caution must be exercised in attempting to extrapolate the rate of weight loss beyond the time period covered by the experiment. It is possible that the rate of loss for some or even all of the treatments changes after 14 days, with the result that the trend line starts to curve, and thus would require some form of curvilinear regression analysis. The aim of the regression analysis is to determine whether the relationships between mean weight and time can reasonably be described as causal. The general form of the null hypothesis is as follows:

CW7 The changes in the weight of the chalk blocks under the different treatments are not controlled by the elapsed time of the experiment.

Table 13.4 Application of simple linear regression analysis to chalk weathering project in MINITAB

```
MTB > OUTFILE 'chweat08'
MTB > RETRIEVE 'chweat04'
MTB > REGRESS C31 C40
MTB > REGRESS C32 C40
MTB > REGRESS C33 C40
MTB > REGRESS C34 C40
MTB > REGRESS C35 C40
MTB > REGRESS C36 C40
MTB > REGRESS C37 C40
MTB > REGRESS C38 C40
MTB > REGRESS C39 C40
MTB > NOOUTFILE
MTB > STOP
```

Box 13.2 Regression analysis results for CW7 for each treatment with time in chalk weathering project

$Y = a + bX$	*t* for *a*	*P*	*t* for *b*	*P*	ANOVA *F*	*P*
Trmt 1 = 34.2 − 1.33 Time	42.7	0.000	15.1	0.000	228.8	0.000
Trmt 2 = 35.3 − 1.70 Time	21.9	0.000	9.6	0.000	92.2	0.000
Trmt 3 = 30.5 − 0.11 Time	144.1	0.000	4.5	0.000	20.4	0.000
Trmt 4 = 31.3 − 0.45 Time	133.9	0.000	17.6	0.000	310.3	0.000
Trmt 5 = 33.0 − 0.65 Time	33.0	0.000	5.9	0.000	35.1	0.000
Trmt 6 = 30.4 − 0.08 Time	270.0	0.000	6.6	0.000	43.3	0.000
Trmt 7 = 30.6 − 0.14 Time	139.5	0.000	5.6	0.000	31.8	0.000
Trmt 8 = 30.3 − 0.10 Time	425.5	0.000	12.6	0.000	159.5	0.000
Trmt 9 = 30.2 − 0.06 Time	671.9	0.000	12.1	0.000	146.8	0.000

Sample output from REGRESS

```
MTB > REGRESS Trmt 1 1 Time
  The regression equation is
  Trmt 1 = 34.2 - 1.33 Time
  Predictor       Coef          Stdev        t-ratio        p
  Constant       34.1550        0.7996        42.72       0.000
  Time           -1.33025       0.08794      -15.13       0.000
  s = 1.472          R-sq = 94.6%              R-sq(adj) = 94.2%
  Analysis of Variance
  SOURCE        DF        SS          MS          F          p
  Regression     1      495.48      495.48      228.80     0.000
  Error         13       28.15        2.17
  Total         14      523.63
Unusual Observations
  Obs.     Time     Trmt 1      Fit      Stdev.Fit    Residual    St.Resid
    1       1.0     30.004     32.825      0.723       -2.821      -2.20R
  R denotes an obs. with a large st. resid.
```

The new columns created for the correlation analysis are now referenced on the REGRESS command (see the MINITAB log in Table 13.4). The columns C31 – C39 in CHWEAT04.MTW contain the 15 mean weights of the 12 blocks at times periods 0 to 15, with one column for each type of treatment. C40 contains the integers 1 to 15 to denote each time interval. The regression command is repeated for each type of treatment in order to compare the relationships.

The results are summarised in Box 13.2, which also includes a sample of the REGRESS output. The results include the significance of the analyses and show that for each treatment the null hypotheses would be rejected since the test statistics have probabilities which are well below the 0.05 or 0.01 thresholds. In all cases the signs of the *b* values are negative, which confirms that the passing of time leads to greater weight loss. The larger *b* (slope) values in the first two equations, representing the relationships between time as the independent variable and mean block weight each day for treatments 1 and 2, are stronger than in all other cases. This conclusion emphasises that it is a diurnal freeze–thaw regime which produces most weight loss in the blocks.

13.4.3 River pollution

The river pollution project is essentially concerned with two applied geographical questions: Has there been a change in the quality of river water? Are pollutant levels higher, lower or constant upstream and downstream of industrial premises occupying riparian locations? The statistical tests already carried out on the data have helped to answer these questions and the general absence of strong relationships between the climatic and chemical variables suggests that regression analysis is not appropriate.

13.4.4 Village communities

SPSS-X allows the linear regression equation to be calculated either by means of an option on the PLOT command or by the more sophisticated REGRESSION command. The PLOT command (see Chapter 7) is essentially concerned with generating scatterplots of variables; however, if the subcommand /FORMAT = REGRESSION is included, the regression equation of *Y* on *X* is provided as follows:

```
PLOT TITLE = 'BIRTH RATE REGRESSION'
  /VERTICAL = 'NATIONAL BIRTH RATE'
  /HORIZONTAL = 'NATIONAL GROSS DOMESTIC PRODUCT'
  /FORMAT = REGRESSION
  /PLOT = BIRRATE WITH GDP
```

The above sequence of SPSS-X commands will produce a labelled scatterplot (the details of the variables are self-explanatory) together with the regression statistics, *a* and *b*, and their standard errors. The output also includes the probability of the test statistic t for a two-tailed significance test.

The REGRESSION command is primarily designed for the more complex multiple regression analysis, where the regression model incorporates two or more independent variables as controlling or predicting the value of Y. The basic command may, however, be tailored to carry out simple linear regression. The REGRESSION command has a number of subcommands to accommodate the various permutations of multiple regression; however, the following sequence of commands will generate the simple linear regression model:

```
REGRESSION / VARIABLES = BIRRATE GDP
  /DEPENDENT = BIRRATE/METHOD = FORWARD GDP
  /SCATTERPLOT = (BIRRATE GDP)
```

In this format the command generates the default statistics, which include the analysis of variance for the whole regression model and the t tests for its different elements. The subcommand DEPENDENT defines the dependent variable and the METHOD = FORWARD subcommand specifies the independent variable, here GDP. SCATTERPLOT generates a plot of the observations standardised on the two variables according to the Z distribution. A scattergram of the raw data values can be obtained by means of the SCATTERPLOT subcommand. The main advantage of the REGRESSION over the PLOT command, as far as simple linear regression is concerned, is that a more comprehensive range of significance tests are carried out and it allows residuals and $\hat{Y}$ values to be stored in both a raw and standardised form.

Simple linear regression, and for that matter the more complex multiple regression, allows the independent variable to be recorded at discrete intervals, for example every 5 units, although the underlying measurement should be on either the ratio or interval scale. The dependent variable must be continuous. The majority of the variables in the village communities dataset fail to satisfy these requirements and the four assumptions of the linear regression model, since they are measured on the nominal scale.

Simple linear regression is therefore not an appropriate form of statistical analysis for most of the variables in the SPSS-X system file, which is a typical problem of research investigations in human geography and the social sciences. Nevertheless, by way of illustration, a regression analysis is carried out to determine whether the relationship between the number of friends a respondent has in the village and that person's length of residence can be regarded as causal. This is expressed in the following null hypothesis:

VC8 The relationship between the number of friends a respondent has in the village is not connected in a causal fashion with that person's length of residence. The intercept (a) and slope coefficient (b) derived from the sample survey are other than 0 simply because of sampling error.

The software commands to carry out this analysis appear in Table 13.5, which includes the instruction to produce a scattergram in order to view the data distribution. The results of the regression analysis (Box 13.3) confirm previous analytical tests by suggesting that there was not a strong relationship between length of residence and the number of friends a person had in the village. The regression equation is:

$$Y = 5.352 + 0.0179X$$

The low positive slope coefficient (0.0179) suggests that there is some tendency for long-term residents to have more friends, but the two-tailed significance test, where the probability is 0.5102, demonstrates

Box 13.3 Regression analysis results for VC8 in village communities project (SPSS-X output)

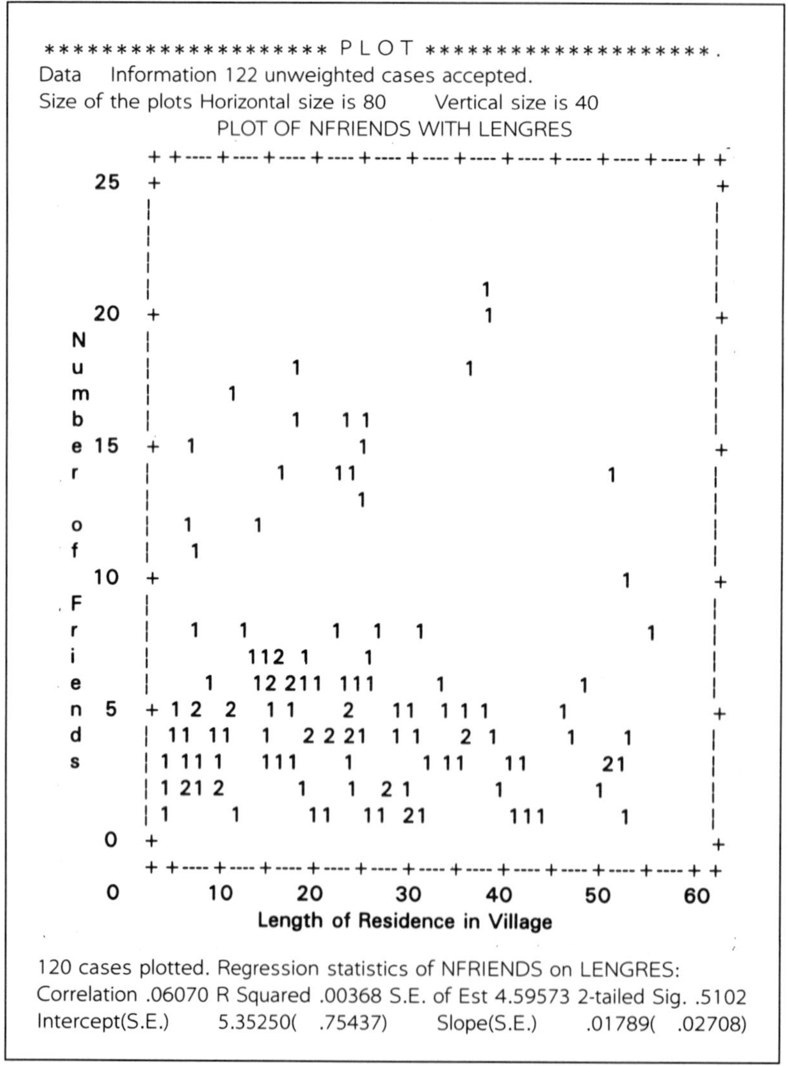

```
******************* P L O T *******************.
Data    Information 122 unweighted cases accepted.
Size of the plots Horizontal size is 80     Vertical size is 40
                    PLOT OF NFRIENDS WITH LENGRES
         ++----+----+----+----+----+----+----+----+----+----+----++
      25 +                                                         +
         |                                                         |
         |                                                         |
         |                                                         |
         |                                                         |
         |                                      1                  |
      20 +                                      1                  +
N        |                                                         |
u        |                 1                  1                    |
m        |          1                                              |
b        |                 1    1 1                                |
e     15 +  1                     1                                +
r        |               1     11                         1        |
         |                    1                                    |
o        |   1       1                                             |
f        |   1                                                     |
      10 +                                                  1      +
F        |                                                         |
r        |   1    1         1   1   1                          1   |
i        |          112 1     1                                    |
e        |      1   12 211  111     1              1               |
n      5 + 1 2  2   1 1    2   11  1 1 1       1                   +
d        | 11 11    1  2 2 21  1 1   2 1      1    1               |
s        | 1 11 1   111    1     1 11    11       21               |
         | 1 21 2      1   1 2 1        1      1                   |
         | 1      1    11   11 21         111     1                |
       0 +                                                         +
         ++----+----+----+----+----+----+----+----+----+----+----++
         0       10        20        30        40        50       60
                     Length of Residence in Village

120 cases plotted. Regression statistics of NFRIENDS on LENGRES:
Correlation .06070 R Squared .00368 S.E. of Est 4.59573 2-tailed Sig. .5102
Intercept(S.E.)     5.35250( .75437)     Slope(S.E.)     .01789( .02708)
```

Table 13.5 Application of simple linear regression analysis to village communities project in SPSS-X

```
FILE HANDLE SF/NAME = 'VILLAG01.SF'
GET FILE = SF
PLOT FORMAT = REGRESSION/PLOT = NFRIENDS WITH LENGRES
FINISH
```

that the null hypothesis should be accepted. The overall conclusion is that other variables exert a strong controlling influence on the number of friends that respondents claimed to have in the village.

Chapter 14
Spatial statistics

14.1 INTRODUCTION TO SPATIAL STATISTICS

The collection of techniques which have been examined in previous chapters is largely indistinguishable from the set which might be included in an introductory statistics text for most scientific disciplines. The examples and projects which have been used to elaborate these techniques are clearly drawn from the fields of human and physical geography, but the procedures themselves are generally applicable in a wide variety of situations. By placing such procedures within the context of the more familiar surroundings provided by geographical topics, the explanation of their purpose and computation is less daunting. However, the statistical analyses themselves and the underlying mathematical theories upon which they are based are as applicable to biology, economics, physics, psychology, sociology and other disciplines as they are to geography. The techniques are, as has already been outlined, an essential component of the scientific method of enquiry by means of which substantive, factual knowledge is accumulated and accredited.

The connection between geography and other scientific disciplines does not end with sharing the procedures of statistical analysis. The phenomena which are investigated by many other disciplines are often also of interest to the geographer. For example, the sociologist, economist, biologist and human geographer may share a common interest in ethnic groups within society. The sociologist may concentrate of the processes whereby such groups sustain a certain social cohesion and interact with other ethnic groups as well as the 'host' society. Parallels may also be made between the social success or failure of the same ethnic group in different locations, such as Asian communities in the English towns of Bradford and Leicester. The economist might investigate the propensity of these groups to take up employment in similar industries or set up their own businesses. The biologist might examine genetic differences and their contribution to physical characteristics. The geographer, on the other hand, while usually acknowledging the importance of these aspects, places the analysis in a spatial or locational framework, by asking such questions as:

- Why is the same ethnic group concentrated in similar areas in two or more different towns?
- Does the spatial distribution of individuals in immigrant groups change as successive generations grow up in the 'host' country?
- Why are some areas more favoured by immigrant groups than others?

The implication of these questions is that space and location are important concepts in geography, indeed the term 'geographical distribution' relates to the dispersion and pattern of phenomena across the space at or near to the earth's surface. Some dictionary definitions of geography state that it is 'the subject which describes the earth's surface' (Moore 1968).

The interest in geographical distributions is found in most branches of the discipline and is distilled into such concepts as spatial concentration, dispersal and regularity. Human geographers are often interested in whether a particular class of phenomena are more clustered in some locations than others, or whether their concentration has changed over time. For example, economic geographers have attempted to quantify the distributional changes occurring in different industrial sectors within a set of areas. Biogeographers have investigated whether the distribution of a particular species of plant is likely to have been produced by a random process. Occasionally phenomena seem to be regularly located in space, for instance rows of terraced housing in the valleys of South Wales or the gridiron pattern of streets in American cities, and spatial statistics may be used to confirm whether the pattern is as regimented as it appears.

It is manifestly obvious that all places are not identical and that they have unique locational coordinate references, such as according to the Cartesian or National Grid systems. Geography's main aim in the early part of the 20th century was to describe the unique assemblages of phenomena in different regions with the intention that ultimately some overall synthesis might be achieved. Disillusionment with this objective set in and a new approach to space emerged in which the spatial location and distribution of phenomena were themselves seen as important. This realignment was promoted as geography's salvation, leading the discipline out of the descriptive quagmire into the heady heights of nomothetic science, in which general laws of spatial location would be devised. With the benefit of hindsight, the hidden agenda behind this change was partly concerned with the difficulty of identifying a class of phenomena to which geography could claim sole research rights, and partly with a desire to attain scientific status.

One consequence of this reorientation, which occurred in conjunction with the quantification of the discipline, was the development of a collection of statistical techniques designed to investigate the spatial patterns displayed by various types of phenomena. These techniques are collectively known as *spatial statistics* or *geostatistics*. Spatial statistics analyses geographically distributed phenomena in three ways: first, through the derivation of numerical quantities to describe and compare them; second, by testing whether observed distributions are significantly different from some hypothesised pattern; and third, by examining the spatial relationships and connections between entities. These procedures were criticised for their overemphasis on the description and analysis of patterns rather than the explanation of processes. In due course this disadvantage led to spatial statistics becoming somewhat degraded as a worthwhile endeavour of geography. Real-world patterns appeared more chaotic than at first thought and lacked exact replication in different places. Furthermore, critics of generalised spatial modelling have argued that the models were frequently flawed and rarely reproduced in reality. In defence of the model-builders, most did not expect that reality would conform precisely with their models' predictions, since these were theoretical constructs whose value lay in isolating the key factors leading to general spatial patterns.

Having been criticised and to some extent discredited in the 1970s, spatial statistics has started to make a comeback during the late 1980s in parallel with an enhanced interest in geographical computing, particularly through GIS software. This re-emergence has brought with it new terminology, and these procedures are now sometimes referred to as *cartometric techniques*, and there is greater emphasis on understanding the processes which bring about the spatial patterns. Some introductory texts on the subject have been published (e.g. Unwin 1981), and this chapter is not a substitute for these more comprehensive discourses. Instead the purpose is to examine the underlying principles of a relatively discrete set of spatial statistics which are effectively an extension of the more general procedures already discussed.

14.2 SPATIAL STATISTICAL TECHNIQUES

The division of general statistical techniques into descriptive and inferential categories is also applicable to spatial statistics. Some spatial techniques produce a quantitative measure describing the central tendency or dispersion of the location of a class of entities, whereas others help to determine whether or not the distribution is random. The former sometimes go under the general heading of *centrographic* techniques, while the latter are called *pattern analysis*. In both cases the focus of attention is on the locational aspects of the entities, and techniques for points, lines and areas form a convenient basis for introducing the topic. The three main types of spatial distribution (clustered, regular and random) are illustrated in Figure 14.1, with respect to points, lines and areas. Real-world distributions are tested in relation to these ideal types.

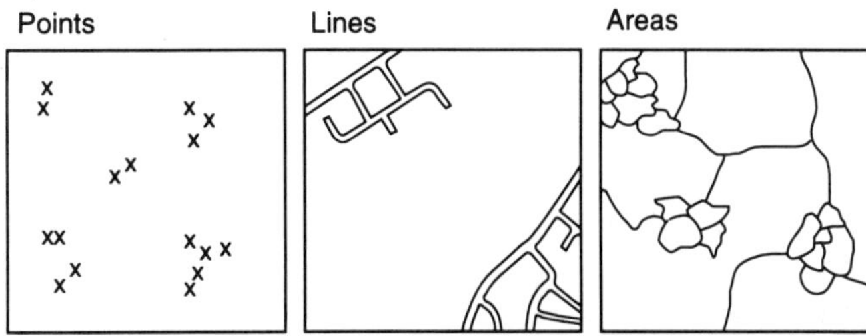

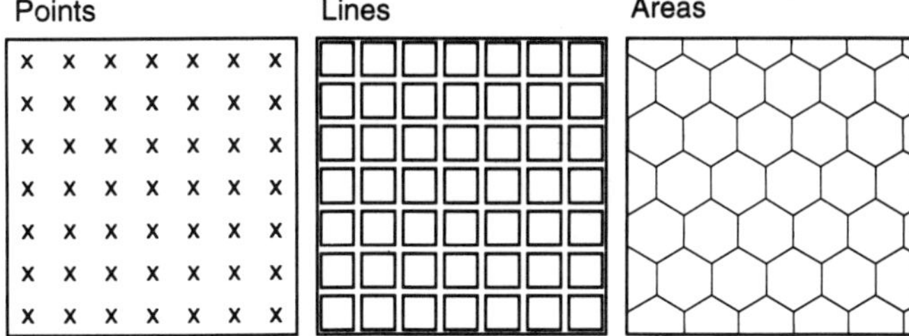

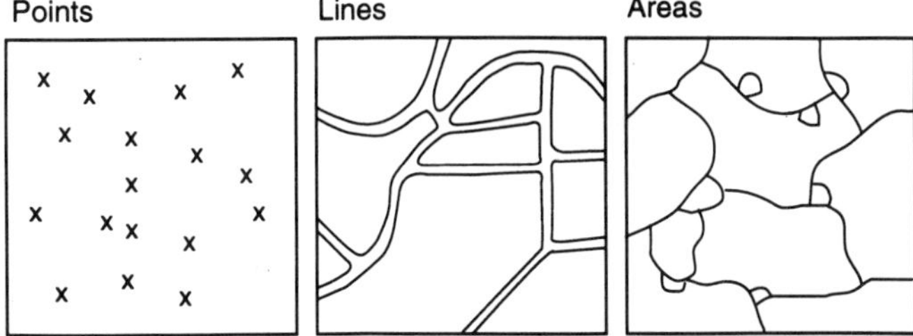

Figure 14.1 Distributions for points, lines and areas

The nature of the entities themselves and how they are represented on maps merit consideration before examining the techniques. The underlying assumption of spatial statistics is that, at a particular point in time, geographically distributed phenomena possess a fixed location, which can be identified by means of a spatial referencing system. The simplest system can be viewed as a two-dimensional numerical directory, which is rather like having both page and line number references to topics in the index of a book. A coordinate referencing system involves units of measurement which are shown to scale on a map. Thus the distance between phenomena and their density within an area can be determined.

The most frequently used referencing system places a grid over the curved surface of the earth and locates phenomena with reference to latitude and longitude, or X and Y, coordinates. When the study area is large or even global in scale, the sides of the grid cells are no longer parallel under some map projections, but converge towards the North and South Poles. In contrast, when the area of interest is sufficiently limited and an appropriate scale is chosen, the distortion caused by the curvature of the earth may be disregarded so that the grid is composed of a collection of regular squares of equal size. The National Grid used by the Ordnance Survey in Britain is an example of a coordinate system developed for a smaller area, which is tied in with the global latitude and longitude scheme. In order that the grid referencing system uniquely locates an entity, a known or generally accepted fixed datum is required for each axis of the grid: 0° longitude passes through the Greenwich meridian, London, and the equator is 0° latitude.

14.2.1 Points

A point is the most fundamental means of representing a geographical phenomenon and requires a single pair of coordinates. The degree of precision with which these locate a point depends upon the scale and resolution employed, and the purpose for which the map has been drawn. Most real-world phenomena have some areal extent, and they may occupy more or less area than the dimensions of the square unit denoted by the single pair of coordinates. At certain scales of resolution a take-away food shop may be adequately represented as a point on a map, but in reality it is a three-dimensional feature. Similarly, the locations of public telephones in rural areas are depicted on the Ordnance Survey 1:50 000 topographic maps by means of a letter 'T'. The surface area of telephone kiosks is estimated as approximately 2.25 m^2, yet a pair of four-figure National Grid coordinates to one of these T symbols (e.g. easting 5663 and northing 1125) identifies a square grid unit with sides 10 m long and therefore an area of 100 m^2. More precise locational references, for example 56635 and 11257, are impractical at the 1:50 000 scale. Points are also used to locate larger areal features, such as towns or factories, where the coordinates lie on one part of the entity concerned, for example its approximate centre of gravity (see Figure 14.2).

The description or analysis of point patterns refers to their density within a given area, to the determination of a central point and whether they tend towards a clustered, regular or random distribution. The density of points in an area (i.e. their number divided by the area in which they are contained) is a rather crude descriptive statistic, being highly dependent on how the study area's boundary is defined. The more useful spatial analytic techniques for points rely on calculating the distance between the points. Provided that the study area is relatively limited, the principles of Euclidean geometry can be applied, which assume a flat surface. Under this assumption the distance between two points can be determined by use of Pythagoras' theorem. Lines drawn between each pair of points form the hypotenuses of a series of right-angled triangles (Figure 14.3 includes two examples). The horizontal and vertical distances between the points lying at either end of each

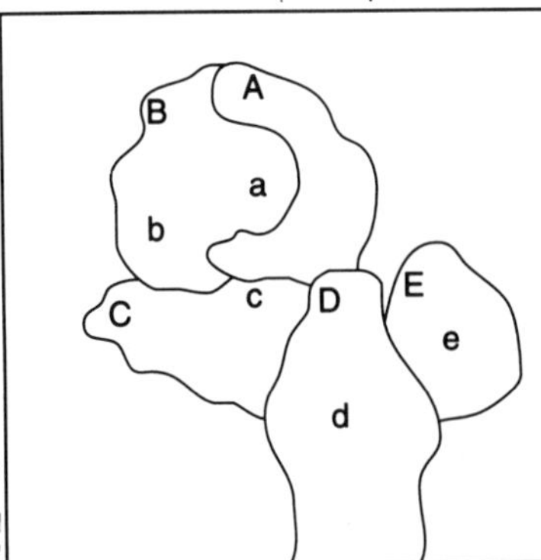

An area is labelled with a capital letter and the corresponding lowercase letter denotes the location of its centre of gravity (point where longest and shortest axis intersect)

Figure 14.2 Points as a location for a feature's centre of gravity: each area is labelled with a capital letter, the corresponding lower-case letter denoting the location of the area's centre of gravity (the point where the longest and shortest axes intersect)

Figure 14.3 Calculation of distance between two points using Pythagoras' theorem.

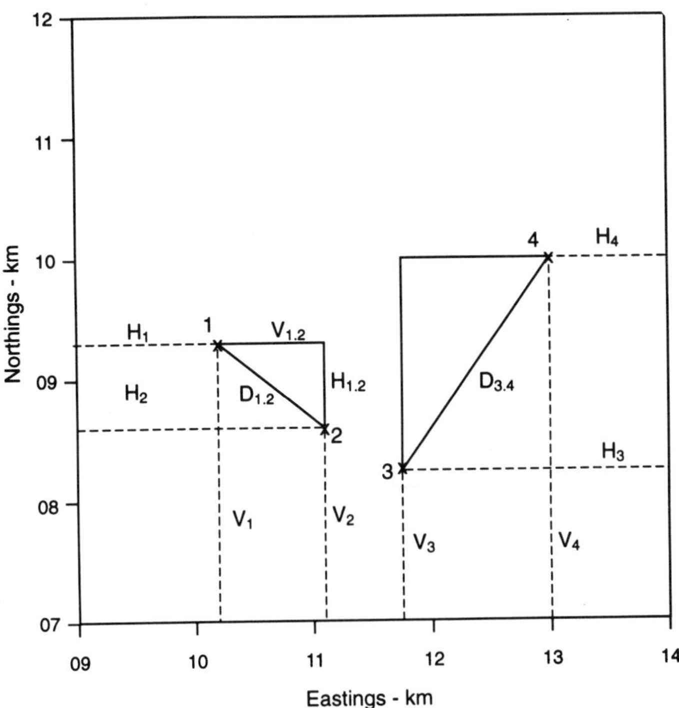

The distance between points 1 and 2 is calculated thus:

$$D_{1.2} = \sqrt{(V_2 - V_1)^2 + (H_1 - H_2)^2}$$

$$D_{1.2} = \sqrt{(111 - 102)^2 + (93 - 86)^2} = 11.40$$

hypotenuse provide the lengths of the other two sides of this triangle, which can be measured by reference to the regular grid. These are shown as lines $H_{1.2}$ and $V_{1.2}$ for one of the triangles in Figure 14.3, where the points are denoted by the numbers 1 and 2. The square root of the sum of the squares of these sides yields the length of the hypotenuse, which is the physical distance between the two points.

14.2.1.1 Descriptive statistics for points

The *mean centre* summarises the central tendency of a spatial distribution of points or of aggregate frequencies. The mean centre lies at the intersection of the means of the X and Y coordinates. Thus the first task is to sum the X and Y coordinates, as though they were simply numerical variables, and then divide ΣX and ΣY by the number of points, thus:

$$\bar{X} = \frac{\Sigma X}{n} \qquad \bar{Y} = \frac{\Sigma Y}{n}$$

The entities located at the points are often measured in some way and a rather more sophisticated measure of centrality can be devised which takes into account the magnitude of such a variable or frequency count in order to produce a *weighted mean centre*. The mean centre formula is adapted thus:

$$\bar{X} = \frac{\Sigma X_i W_i}{\Sigma W} \qquad \bar{Y} = \frac{\Sigma Y_i W_i}{\Sigma W}$$

where W represents the weighting variable for points $i = 1 \ldots n$ and ΣW is the sum of the weights. The procedure involves multiplying the coordinates by the value of the weighting factor for each point, summing the results and dividing by the sum of the weights. When data are held as an aggregate count of the number of points within a given set of grid squares, the mean centre is weighted by the frequency of points in each areal unit. The following formula is used:

$$\bar{X} = \frac{\Sigma X_i F_i}{N} \qquad \bar{Y} = \frac{\Sigma Y_i F_i}{N}$$

where N is the total number of grid squares containing points, X and Y are the coordinates of the grid squares and i goes from 1 to N.

The first two methods are illustrated in Figure 14.4, with the data in Table 14.1, for a scatter of 24 points. These points represent the location of tumuli on an area of the South Downs to the east of Brighton in East Sussex, England. A tumulus is an ancient burial mound, and each point locates one or more these features. The location of the mean centre for the tumuli is shown by an empty circle in Figure 14.4, and its coordinates are calculated thus:

$$\bar{X} = \frac{103\,135}{24} = 4297 \qquad \bar{Y} = \frac{12\,555}{24} = 523$$

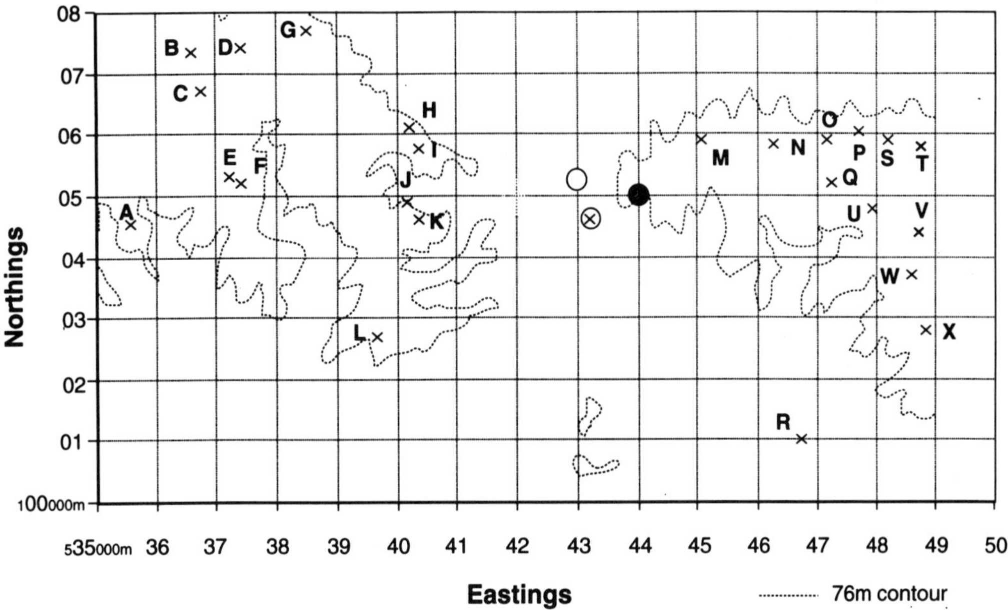

Figure 14.4 Point location of tumuli on the South Downs north-east of Brighton, East Sussex, showing mean centre

Table 14.1 Point data for South Downs tumuli

Point	*X*	*Y*	Number of tumuli (*W*)	*XW*	*YW*
A	3 560	455	1	3 560	455
B	3 660	735	1	3 660	735
C	3 675	670	1	3 675	670
D	3 740	740	1	3 740	740
E	3 720	530	4	14 880	2 120
F	3 740	520	2	7 480	1 040
G	3 850	770	2	7 700	1 540
H	4 020	610	1	4 020	610
I	4 035	575	1	4 035	575
J	4 015	490	1	4 015	490
K	4 035	460	1	2 105	1 380
L	3 965	270	1	3 965	270
M	4 505	590	1	4 505	590
N	4 625	585	1	4 625	585
O	4 715	590	2	9 430	1 180
P	4 770	605	5	23 850	3 025
Q	4 725	520	3	14 175	1 560
R	4 675	100	4	18 700	400
S	4 820	590	2	9 640	1 180
T	4 875	580	3	14 625	1 740
U	4 795	480	1	4 795	480
V	4 870	440	2	9 740	880
W	4 860	370	1	4 860	370
X	4 885	280	1	4 885	280
	103 135	12 555	43	188 595	21 975

Note: *X* and *Y* coordinates recorded to the nearest 10 m.

The weighted equivalent, using the number of tumuli at each point, is located with a solid circle in Figure 14.4 and has the following coordinates:

$$\bar{X} = \frac{188\,595}{43} \qquad \bar{Y} = \frac{21\,975}{43}$$
$$= 4386 \qquad\qquad = 511$$

The *aggregate mean centre* has only limited relevance in this example, since it would be more useful when most of the grid cells contain points. In this case only 19 of the 116 squares which are not over the sea contain at least one point. Nevertheless, its calculation is possible by taking the frequency count of tumuli for the 19 squares which contain one or more occurrences. The relevant data are given Table 14.2. The coordinates of the aggregate mean centre are calculated thus:

$$\bar{X} = \frac{1946}{19} \qquad \bar{Y} = \frac{208}{19}$$
$$= 43.20 \qquad\qquad = 4.6$$

and its location is shown by the crossed circle on Figure 14.4. The aggregate mean centre is approximately 5 km to the south of the other two central points, which indicates that there are slightly less occupied squares to the east.

The mean centre shares one problem with its counterpart, the arithmetic mean, namely the potential for distortion from extreme values.

Table 14.2 Aggregate grid square data for South Downs tumuli

X	Y	Number of tumuli (W)	XF	YF
35.0	4.0	1	35.0	4.0
36.0	7.0	1	36.0	7.0
36.0	6.0	1	36.0	6.0
37.0	7.0	1	37.0	7.0
37.0	5.0	6	222.0	30.0
38.0	7.0	2	76.0	14.0
39.0	2.0	1	39.0	2.0
40.0	6.0	1	40.0	6.0
40.0	5.0	1	40.0	5.0
40.0	4.0	4	160.0	16.0
45.0	5.0	1	45.0	5.0
46.0	5.0	1	46.0	5.0
46.0	1.0	4	184.0	4.0
47.0	5.0	5	235.0	25.0
47.0	6.0	5	235.0	30.0
48.0	5.0	5	240.0	25.0
48.0	4.0	3	144.0	12.0
48.0	3.0	1	48.0	3.0
48.0	2.0	1	48.0	2.0
			1946.0	208.0

Note: X and Y coordinates refer to 1 km grid squares.

The mean centre is a point within a rectangular area delimited by the extremities of the group of points in respect of their minimum and maximum easting and northing coordinates. If the actual points show marked clustering or possess a distinct shape, for instance covering a crescentic area, the mean centre might lie outside the scatter. This has occurred to some extent in the example, since there are two distinct clusters of points on either side of the study area. Figure 14.4 includes the 76 m contour and suggests that tumuli tend to be found above this altitude and generally away from low-lying land. However, the three different mean centres are located in the river valley and lie between the western and eastern clusters of points.

The spatial equivalent of the median can also be calculated to summarise the central tendency of a point distribution, although there is some divergence of opinion over its definition. The median divides a single set of numbers in half and is the value of the middle observation or the value of mid-way between the observations either side of the middle, whether or not this actually occurs within the set. The logical extension to finding the *median centre* of a collection of points is to draw two orthogonal lines (lines at right angles to each other), which pass through the medians of the X and Y coordinates. This method defines the median of the coordinates but not necessarily the median of the collection of points, since their distribution may be unbalanced between the quadrants. An alternative method divides the number of points into four equal-sized groups by means of a horizontal and a vertical line. The disadvantage of this approach is that several such lines could be drawn, which achieved the same result and yet gave the median centre different coordinates. The median centres provided by the both methods are shown respectively with solid and empty circles in Figure 14.5 for the scatter of tumuli over the same area of the South Downs. The mid-points of the X and Y coordinates are 4235 and 0553, which define the median centre according to the first method. An alternative median centre is located by means of the orthogonal broken lines, which locate the median centre at 4235, 0450.

The main centrographic measure of dispersion is *standard distance* (S_d), which is the spatial equivalent of the standard deviation. Standard distance measures dispersion around the mean centre, with larger values signifying that the points are more spread out. Standard distance is the square root of the sum of the standard deviations of the X and Y coordinates, and is measured in the same units as the distances between the points.

$$S_d = \sqrt{\frac{\Sigma(X - \bar{X})^2}{N} + \frac{\Sigma(Y - \bar{Y})^2}{N}}$$

The substitution of the relevant figures from the South Downs tumuli example (Table 14.3), gives a standard distance of:

$$S_d = \sqrt{\frac{5\,614\,849}{24} + \frac{556\,091}{24}}$$

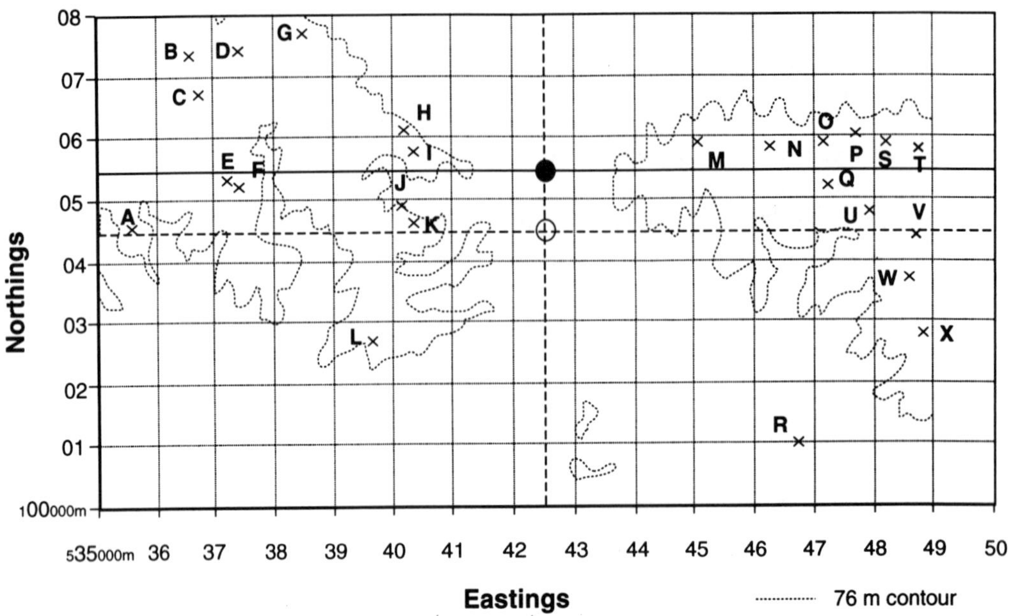

Figure 14.5 Alternative median centres for tumuli on the South Downs north-east of Brighton, East Sussex

Table 14.3 Point data for South Downs tumuli

Point	X	Y	Number of tumuli (W)	$(X - \bar{X})^2$	$(Y - \bar{Y})^2$
A	3560	455	1	543 169	4 624
B	3660	735	1	405 769	44 944
C	3675	670	1	386 884	21 609
D	3740	740	1	310 249	47 089
E	3720	530	4	332 929	49
F	3740	520	2	310 249	9
G	3850	770	2	199 809	61 009
H	4020	610	1	76 729	7 569
I	4035	575	1	68 644	2 704
J	4015	490	1	79 524	1 089
K	4035	460	1	68 644	3 969
L	3965	270	1	110 224	64 009
M	4505	590	1	43 264	4 489
N	4625	585	1	107 584	3 844
O	4715	590	2	174 724	4 489
P	4770	605	5	223 729	6 724
Q	4725	520	3	183 184	9
R	4675	100	4	142 884	178 929
S	4820	590	2	273 529	4 489
T	4875	580	3	334 084	3 249
U	4795	480	1	248 004	1 849
V	4870	440	2	328 329	6 889
W	4860	370	1	316 969	23 409
X	4885	280	1	345 744	59 049
				5 614 849	556 091

Note: X and Y coordinates relate to the nearest 10 m.

$$= \sqrt{233\,952 + 23\,170}$$

$$= 507.07$$

The standard distance of 5.071 km helps with interpreting the mean centre and may be used to compare with the distribution of the same phenomenon (i.e. tumuli) in different areas. Unfortunately, if the study areas are substantially different in size, then comparison of their absolute standard distance statistics is misleading and an adjustment should be made to obtain the relative standard distance. For example, Neft (1966) used the radius of a country to produce a relative measure in a study of population dispersion.

14.2.1.2 Inferential statistical tests for points

The spatial analytic techniques for analysing the processes by which point patterns are produced refer to mathematical probability distributions in the same way as the standard hypothesis testing procedures. The spatial techniques determine the probability that a particular distribution of points has been produced by a random process. The tests assess whether the difference between the expected random distribution and what has been observed is sufficiently large as to be unattributable to chance. The two most important types of hypothesis testing for examining point patterns are *quadrat* and *nearest-neighbour analysis.*

Quadrat analysis involves overlaying the study area with a regular square grid and counting the number of observations (points) falling in each of the squares. The complete grid must be sufficiently large for all occurrences of the phenomenon in question to fall in one of the squares, but is not necessarily rectangular. The count of observations per square gives a frequency distribution of the type which can be compared with the Poisson distribution (see Chapter 9). If the observed frequencies approximate to those predicted by the Poisson distribution then the pattern of the points can be attributed to a random process. The example discussed in Section 9.3 suggested that the pattern of road junctions in a 176 km^2 area of Hertfordshire was reasonably similar to that which would be expected according to the Poisson distribution.

There is a further important characteristic of the Poisson distribution, namely that its mean, μ, and variance, σ^2, are numerically equal, which forms the basis of a statistical test, known as the *variance–mean ratio* (VMR). A given pattern of points should be considered as a sample, even if all known occurrences of the phenomena in question have been counted, since the particular set of observations (points) is but one of many possible outcomes from an infinite number of points. Thus in the test the symbols λ and s^2 should be used to denote a sample mean and variance. The null hypothesis states that the point pattern is random and that $\lambda = s^2$. When the test is applied to a particular sample of observations, the numbers of points and grid squares are fixed, consequently the mean (λ) will be constant irrespective of whether the points are clustered, random or dispersed. It is therefore differences in the variance that indicate the nature of the point pattern. If the VMR is significantly greater than 1.0, then clustering of the points is indicated, whereas a value lower than 1.0 denotes dispersal or regularity. The null hypothesis can be tested by converting the sample ratio into either a t or χ^2 test statistic. Conversion into t requires the standard error of the VMR ratio, which is:

$$s_{\text{VMR}} = \frac{2^2}{k-1}$$

where k is the number of grid squares. This quantity can be used to produce a t-test statistic thus:

$$t = \frac{\dfrac{s^2}{\lambda} - 1}{s_{\text{VMR}}}$$

with $k - 1$ degrees of freedom. Alternatively the χ^2 test statistic can be calculated as VMR multiplied by the degrees of freedom, which is expressed in symbols as:

$$\chi^2 = (k-1)\frac{s^2}{\lambda}$$

In both cases the null hypothesis would usually be rejected, if the probability associated with the test statistic were less than the critical value (0.05).

Inspection of the pattern of points representing the tumuli on part of the South Downs suggests that they are clustered into two groups on either side of the river valley which bisects the study area (see Figure 14.4). Although the locations of all known tumuli within the area are shown, there could be some which have yet to be identified and others which have been obliterated by agricultural practices: thus the observed scatter is a sample. The null hypothesis states that the distribution of tumuli is random and any apparent tendency towards clustering away from the low-lying land of the valley bottom is the result of chance. The study area covers 116 grid squares with 45 tumuli, giving a mean (λ) of 0.388 per square (45/116). The variance is estimated from the following formula:

$$s^2 = \frac{1}{n-1}\left(\Sigma f_{\text{i}} X_{\text{i}}^2 - \frac{(\Sigma f_{\text{i}} X_{\text{i}})^2}{n}\right)$$

where X is the number of points in a square, f is the frequency of squares with that number of points, i goes from 0 to the maximum number of points in any square and n is the total number of points. Substituting the relevant figures from Table 14.4 produces a sample variance of 1.3004, thus:

$$s^2 = \frac{1}{115}\left(167 - \frac{45^2}{116}\right) = \frac{1}{115}(167 - 17.4569)$$

$$= 1.3004$$

Table 14.4 Frequency distribution for tumuli on an area of the South Downs, Sussex

No. tumuli per km² X	No. of squares f	fX	fX^2
0	97	0	0
1	11	11	11
2	1	2	4
3	1	3	9
4	2	8	32
5	3	15	75
6	1	6	36
		45	167

The variance and the mean of the sample enable the VMR to be calculated (s^2/λ):

$$\frac{s^2}{\lambda} = \frac{1.3004}{0.3879} = 3.3524$$

The large VMR ratio, 3.3524, provides evidence for clustering in the location of the tumuli and can be converted into either a t or χ^2 statistic in order to test for the significance of the result. The t test requires the standard error, which in this example is:

$$s_{\text{VMR}} = \frac{(2)^2}{(116-1)} = 0.0348$$

The t-test statistic is therefore

$$t = \frac{3.3524 - 1}{0.0348} = 67.6$$

The significance of the t statistic may be determined as usual from the t distribution table in Appendix IV with $k-1$ degrees of freedom. In this case the probability of having obtained such a large test statistic, and therefore a VMR value so different from 1.0, is lower than the smallest in the table, which clearly indicates that the null hypothesis can be dismissed as untenable. The alternative test statistic, χ^2, can be calculated thus:

$$\chi^2 = (116-1)\frac{1.3004}{0.3879} = (116-1)(3.3524) = 385.526$$

and reassuringly yields the same conclusion.

Quadrat analysis has some problems as an analytical technique, most of which derive from the arbitrary nature of the overlain grid. In the tumuli example, the 'default' 1 km National Grid system was used, but there is no reason why a grid with a larger unit size (e.g. 5 km), and a different orientation and base reference should not have been employed. The manipulation of the grid in these ways could clearly alter the variance–mean ratio. The underlying location of the points in relation to each other is unaffected by these adjustments, but the frequency of points per square can change.

Nearest-neighbour analysis concentrates on the spacing between points rather than their overall pattern and avoids some of the disadvantages of the quadrat approach. The procedure involves calculating the ratio between the observed and expected mean minimum distance between the points to produce the quantity R, which can lie either side of unity (1.0) within the range 0.0 to 2.1491. The former denotes perfect clustering, where all points lie on top of each other, and the latter signifies a regularly dispersed pattern, which forms a triangular lattice. An entirely random pattern would produce an index value of 1.0. The first stage in the analysis is to calculate the expected density (r_e) using the following formula:

$$r_e = 0.5\sqrt{(A/N)}$$

where A represents the area and N the number of points. The quantity A/N therefore denotes the density of points per unit area and is sometimes referred to as d, not to be confused with the use of this letter to denote a deviation or difference. The observed mean minimum distance (r_o) between the sample points is laborious to calculate by hand, since it requires the minimum distance between each point and its nearest-neighbour to be determined and their sum divided by the number of points in order to produce the mean. The nearest-neighbour index, R, is defined as:

$$R = r_o/r_e$$

The nearest-neighbour index is sometimes used simply as a descriptive statistic to compare the distributions of different phenomena within the same area. The index provides a quantitative summary of the spacing of different classes of phenomena of the same general type, for example between species of tree within a particular woodland area. The index value has of course been derived from a particular set of points, which should be regarded as a random sample of observations from a population of infinite size. The fact that the calculated R value is other than 1.0 does not on its own indicate that the points display some form of spatial preference; this could have occurred by chance. Consequently, it is sensible to carry out a significance test on the index value to determine whether or not the difference between r_o and r_e can reasonably be attributed to chance. The difference between the sample R and the value which would be obtained if the points were randomly distributed ($R = 1.0$) is examined by means a Z test. The null hypothesis states that the sample R is not 1.0 purely as a result of sampling error. The Z test requires that the standard deviation of the sampling distribution of d, otherwise known as its standard error, is calculated from the formula:

$$s_d = \frac{0.261\,36}{\sqrt{N(N/A)}}$$

where N and A have the same meaning as in the calculation of r_e. Having obtained the standard error of d, the Z-test statistic is:

$$Z = \frac{|r_o - r_e|}{s_d}$$

The probability associated with Z can then be assessed from the Z distribution table in Appendix IV. If the significance of the Z statistic is greater than the chosen significance level (larger than 0.05 or 0.01), then the null hypothesis of no difference should be accepted. Confidence limits for the value of R in the population can also be calculated so that, for example, 95 times in 100 R will lie between

$$R - 1.96s_d \text{ and } R + 1.96s_d$$

where 1.96 is the value of Z associated with 95 per cent probability.

The mean expected distance between the 24 points locating the South Downs tumuli to the nearest 10 m is

$$r_e = 0.5\sqrt{1\,160\,000/24} = 109.92$$

The calculation of the mean observed minimum distance between each point and its nearest neighbour may be carried out by using Pythagoras' theorem (see Section 13.4.1). Table 14.5 provides the results of these calculations for the distances between each pair of points in the study area. The minimum distance between each point and its nearest neighbour is shown in the right-hand column of the final section of the table. The column sums to 3083.2 giving a mean observed distance of 128.47 dm. Dividing r_o by r_e yields the nearest-neighbour statistic R, which in this example equals 1.1687. This value indicates some minor dispersal in the location of the tumuli, although since the data are for a sample of points, the statistical significance of the result should be assessed.

The null hypothesis states that the difference between the observed value of R, here 1.1687, and the value which would be produced if the points were located as a result of a random Poisson process (1.0) is the result of sampling error and of no statistical significance. The first stage in testing this hypothesis is to calculate the standard error, thus:

$$s_d = \frac{0.261\,36}{\sqrt{24 \times 24/1\,160\,000}} = 11.729$$

The associated Z-test statistic is:

$$Z = \frac{|128.47 - 109.92|}{11.729} = 1.582$$

The probability of having obtained a Z value of this order of magnitude by chance is 0.2282 (22.82 per cent). The null hypothesis should be accepted and the conclusion reached that tumuli sites on the South Downs near Brighton in Sussex tend to be slightly dispersed, although the R statistic is fairly close to 1.0 indicating a random pattern.

Table 14.5 Distances between South Downs tumuli

Point	2	3	4	5	6	7	8	9
1	297.3	243.8	337.1	176.7	191.4	428.2	485.4	489.9
2	*	66.7	80.2	213.6	229.4	193.2	381.1	407.7
3	*	*	95.5	147.1	163.5	201.6	350.2	372.3
4	*	*	*	211.0	220.0	114.0	308.7	338.0
5	*	*	*	*	22.4	272.9	310.5	318.2
6	*	*	*	*	*	273.1	294.1	300.1
7	*	*	*	*	*	*	233.5	268.8
8	*	*	*	*	*	*	*	38.1

Point	10	11	12	13	14	15	16	17
1	456.3	475.0	445.3	954.6	1072.9	1162.9	1219.3	1166.8
2	431.3	465.0	556.1	857.4	976.6	1064.9	1117.6	1086.5
3	384.7	416.8	494.1	833.8	953.8	1043.1	1096.9	1060.7
4	371.7	406.7	521.1	779.6	898.5	986.5	1038.8	1009.3
5	297.7	322.7	357.2	787.3	906.7	996.8	1052.7	1005.0
6	276.6	301.0	336.3	768.2	887.4	977.5	1033.5	985.0
7	325.0	361.0	513.1	679.3	796.8	883.5	934.7	910.0
8	120.1	150.7	344.4	485.4	605.5	695.3	750.0	710.7
9	87.3	115.0	312.9	470.2	590.1	680.2	735.6	692.2
10	*	36.1	225.6	500.1	617.4	707.1	763.7	710.6
11	*	*	202.5	487.6	603.1	692.3	749.2	692.2
12	*	*	*	627.7	731.3	815.4	871.9	800.1
13	*	*	*	*	120.1	230.9	518.7	230.9
14	*	*	*	*	*	90.1	146.4	119.3
15	*	*	*	*	*	*	57.0	70.7
16	*	*	*	*	*	*	*	96.2

Point	18	19	20	21	22	23	24	Minimum distance
1	1170.1	1267.2	1320.9	1235.3	1310.1	1302.8	1336.5	176.7
2	1197.3	1169.0	1224.8	1163.3	1245.4	1254.3	1306.8	66.7
3	1151.0	1147.8	1203.4	1136.0	1216.9	1222.4	1271.3	95.5
4	1133.1	1090.4	1146.2	1086.6	1169.1	1179.5	1233.9	114.0
5	1047.3	1101.6	1156.1	1076.2	1153.5	1151.2	1191.5	22.4
6	1025.0	1082.3	1136.6	1055.8	1132.8	1130.0	1169.9	273.1
7	1062.8	986.6	1042.5	988.5	1072.1	1086.3	1145.1	233.5
8	830.1	800.2	855.5	785.8	866.8	873.6	925.8	38.1
9	797.0	785.1	840.0	765.9	845.8	850.1	918.7	87.3
10	766.6	811.2	864.7	780.1	856.5	853.5	895.0	36.1
11	734.3	795.7	848.5	760.3	835.2	829.9	868.8	202.5
12	730.1	912.9	961.4	856.2	920.8	900.6	920.1	627.7
13	518.7	315.0	370.1	310.2	394.6	417.6	490.4	120.1
14	487.6	195.1	250.0	271.2	223.4	326.0	385.0	90.1
15	491.6	105.0	160.3	136.0	215.7	263.5	353.6	57.0
16	513.9	52.2	107.9	127.5	192.9	251.6	344.7	52.2
17	423.0	118.0	161.6	80.6	165.6	201.8	288.4	80.6
18	*	511.0	520.0	398.5	392.0	327.3	276.6	276.6
19	*	*	55.9	112.8	158.1	223.6	316.7	55.9
20	*	*	*	128.1	140.1	210.5	300.2	128.1
21	*	*	*	*	85.0	127.8	219.3	85.0
22	*	*	*	*	*	70.7	160.7	70.7
23	*	*	*	*	*	*	93.4	93.3
								3083.2

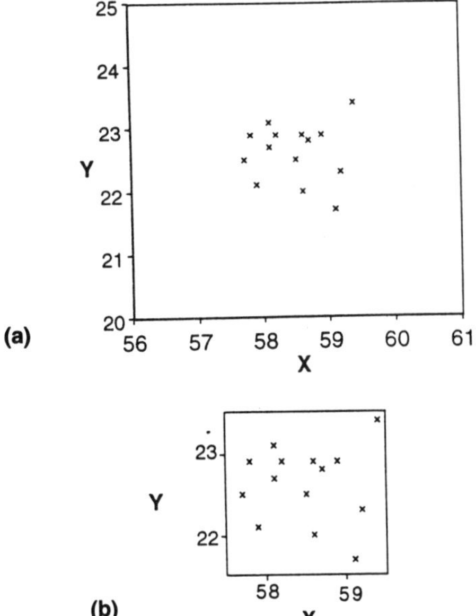

Figure 14.6 Effect of size of study area on the nearest-neighbour statistic, R. The same set of points produces a low value of R in (a) and a high value in (b)

Two main problems have been identified with nearest-neighbour analysis. The R statistic and its standard error are highly dependent upon the size of the study area and if the selected boundaries are inappropriate in relation to the distribution of points the value of R will be distorted. Figure 14.6(a) illustrates the situation where an artificially low value of R would be obtained because the study area is large in relation to the location of the points. In contrast, when the boundaries are more tightly drawn (Figure 14.6(b)) around the same points a more dispersed pattern would be indicated by a value of R above unity. A partial solution to this problem is to draw the boundaries with careful consideration for the phenomena under investigation. For example, in a study of the pattern of the location of take-away food shops in urban areas, the contiguous built-up area should delimit the study area, rather than some artificial rectangle drawn around the settlement in question. The second problem is that in some situations the minimum distance between the points is inappropriate for calculating the index, R. Where the points are distributed in a series of regularly spaced clusters, each with a similar number of points and distance between them, the nearest-neighbour distance will indicate a clustered pattern when in fact the groups of points are dispersed. In these circumstances, the second, third or fourth nearest neighbours may provide a more suitable means for analysis the overall pattern.

14.2.2 Lines

Lines are used on maps in two distinct, but nevertheless related, ways: to represent and locate inherently linear geographical phenomena, such as rivers, roads or pipelines; and to delimit areas and surfaces. As far as the description and analysis of line patterns is concerned, the first of these uses is of more interest. Some statistical techniques have been developed to analyse the patterns produced by linear features, but these tend to be used less frequently than those for points and areas. This section will outline the nature of such features, but the analytical techniques will be examined only briefly, since they are of limited relevance to the exemplar projects. Unwin (1981) gives the analysis of linear features more exhaustive treatment.

A line may be thought of as a 'second-order' spatial feature in terms of geometrical complexity, and its specification requires a minimum of two pairs of coordinates within the grid referencing system being used. When a line is represented by only two points, they denote its start and end locations and the path between them will necessarily be straight. Although only two pairs of coordinates are required to locate a straight line, it does of course traverse a set of intervening points lying along its path. Most lines on maps, even if the scale is large (e.g. 1:2500) exhibit varying amounts of *sinuosity*. A road link between two cities is unlikely to be straight, but will be routed to deviate around or approach towards other features. Similarly, it would be misleading to measure the straight-line distance between two confluences on a meandering river. A more sensible approach would involve measuring along the centre of the channel parallel to each bank. When a line follows a sinuous path in this fashion the number of points required to define its location increases. In principle an infinite number of coordinates could be used to track the path of such a line to an ever increasing level of accuracy depending upon the number of digits used in the referencing system. In practice, however, curved lines are regarded as being composed of a series of straight segments or arcs, which can be of either equal or variable length.

Section 14.2.1 indicated that the description and analysis of point patterns rely heavily on the measurement of distance between the discrete locations of the phenomena, but the individual points are not directly connected with each other. For example, the distance between any pair of tumuli points signifies how far apart they are, not that there is a line of this length between them. However, genuine lines track the path or route followed by the set of points which locate a linear feature. In the case of such phenomena, there is a direct and meaningful connection between the pairs of point coordinates which constitute the feature and the sum of the lengths between the points yields the distance between the start and end locations. Physical distance (for example, in metres or kilometres) is not a suitable measure in some investigations and alternatives, such as travel time or transport cost, are more suitable.

Two further concepts are important in the analysis of linear phenomena, namely direction and connection. The existence of connectivity between the set of points that constitutes a line means that their locations of are not independent of each other, but are linked to

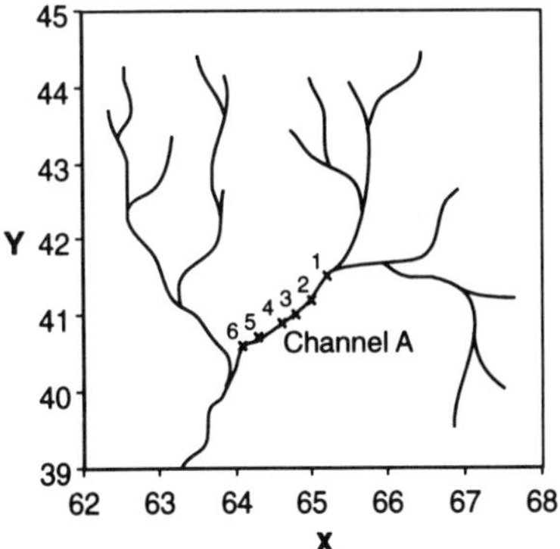

Sequence and co-ordinates of points in channel A:

1	652	415
2	650	412
3	648	410
4	646	409
5	643	407
6	641	406

Figure 14.7 Direction and connection in linear features

each other in a particular direction. The points defining a river channel system provide an clear example of these characteristics. The series points labelled 1, 2, 3, 4, 5 and 6, which lie along one channel (A) of the river system shown in Figure 14.7, are necessarily connected in this sequence, since any other order would imply that the river flowed in two directions or even away from the coast entirely.

14.2.2.1 Descriptive statistics and analysis of linear patterns

Three types of line pattern can be analysed: *simple paths*, *trees* and *circuits*. Simple paths treat lines as separate entities and the main focus is on their length. The 'standard' descriptive measures of central tendency and dispersion, such as mean path length and its standard deviation, may be calculated for a series of lines. Descriptive statistics for lines also focus on the departure of their paths from a straight path and their density and frequency within an area. The direction of a line can be recorded in terms of its bearing in degrees and minutes from a bench-mark point, usually north, or by reference to the nodes (start and end points) that it connects. Unwin (1981) has described in some detail the calculation of mean length and direction for a set of lines, which involves each line being treated as a separate vector with a magnitude and its angle recorded in degrees and minutes.

The description of tree and circuit line patterns is mainly concerned with the connectivity within a network of lines and nodes. In a tree pattern the lines form a series of connections between junctions or nodes without including any complete loops. Drainage basins provide the classic geographical examples of these tree-like structures, which are described in terms of their stream order (Horton 1945; Strahler 1952). Research with various types of branching system has shown that there is a negative relationship between stream order and the number of streams, with the slope of the line referred to as the 'bifurcation ratio'. Circuit line patterns include complete loops, and are clearly exemplified by reference to various types of transport network. The description of these linear patterns usually concentrates on the topological connections by means of a connectivity matrix. Such a matrix records the presence or absence of a direct connection between each pair of points in the network. The manipulation of such matrices helps to assess the overall connectivity of the circuit and its nodality in terms of the frequency of links of each node into the network. These measures enable different circuits to be compared and determine whether movement along the paths of the network between the various points is relatively constrained or uninhibited. Unwin (1981) outlines some of the indices which have been devised to summarise the extent of the connectivity within the network.

Some relatively specialised statistical analyses have been developed in order to investigate the various types of line pattern. The statistical question concerns whether the distribution of lines can reasonably be attributed to a random process. In other words, is the pattern significantly different from that which would occur by chance? The paths which cross an area can be analysed for the difference between their mean observed length and direction, their density and sinuosity and the frequency distribution of their lengths. Unfortunately, the binomial, Poisson and normal probability distributions, which have been applied to other statistical tests, are not suitable with lines for two reasons. A continuous probability density function is needed, since path lengths can possess any value and are not constrained to integer quantities as in the case of quadrat frequency counts for points. The shape and size of the study area also has a crucial influence on path length, and thus on the probability distribution. For example, paths across a rectangular shape are likely to have a strongly bimodal distribution, as their lengths tend towards those of the sides, giving these a higher probability of occurrence. Paths across a square are more likely to be unimodal. Most of the analytical procedures which have been developed only consider straight-line paths across an area. Relatively little attention has been paid to curved lines, whose lengths are not constrained by the maximum traverse across the area, or to lines which start and/or end within an area's boundaries.

The statistical analysis of tree patterns concentrates on the ordering of such networks. The basis of the procedure is to test whether the observed line pattern, for example four first-order, two second-order and one third-order stream (referred to as 4,2,1), is likely to have been produced by a random process given a known number of source channels. The first task is therefore to determine the total number of distinct outcomes, or *Topologically Distinct Channel*

Networks (TCDNs) — see Unwin (1981) — which could be produced from a known number of source lines. The principle underlying this operation is similar to that described in Chapter 9 in respect of the binomial distribution. Next, the number of ways in which the channel order profile for the observed network (say the 4,2,1 combination already mentioned) could be achieved by a random joining process is calculated. Dividing the number of such combinations by the total number of possible networks yields a proportion. This is interpreted as the probability of having obtained the observed channel order profile by chance.

The statistical analysis of circuit patterns proceeds in a similar fashion. In the case of a tree network the number of source lines in the observed system is used as the initial constraint for quantifying the ways in which they could join to produce one TDCN. The starting point with a circuit is the number of nodes and links in the observed network, which clearly has a critical influence on how many topologically distinct circuits can be defined. Therefore the statistical test focuses its attention on the nodality or inter-connectivity in the network: in other words, how frequently each node is connected into the network. For a given number of nodes and links the nodality can be expressed in numerical terms as a range from 0, meaning that a node is unconnected, to $n - 1$, where n is the number of nodes, which signifies that each node is directly connected to all the others. The probability of the observed nodality is then assessed against what might be expected if the nodes and links had been connected randomly.

The first problem is to determine the long-run random probability distribution. Whether one node is directly linked to another is essentially the same type of question as that dealt with by the binomial distribution (see Chapter 9): namely a phenomenon which has only two possible outcomes, connection present or absent. Because the total number of links in a network is also a constraint, the probability of one node being connected to another alters as the links are 'used up'. Unwin (1981) described the detailed procedure for calculating the *hypergeometric* probability distribution which is required in this case. The expected values are calculated from the following formula:

$$P(m, n, q) = \frac{\binom{q}{m}\binom{N-q}{n-1-m}}{\binom{N}{n-1}}$$

where n and q are the observed number of nodes and links, m is the desired nodality value and N is the total possible number of links. The observed nodality, N, is determined from the summation of the 0s and 1s in the rows of the connectivity matrix (omitting the 1s along the diagonal), where 1 and 0 indicate the presence and absence of a direct connection. The observed and expected nodality values can be expressed as absolute and cumulative frequency distributions and the maximum difference between their cumulative proportions provides the D test statistic, which can be examined through the Kolmogorov–Smirnov significance test.

14.2.3 Areas

Areas or polygons can be considered as third-order spatial units and are distinguished by the fact that they are spaces enclosed by lines. The partitioned space itself comprises a set of points which possess the common characteristic of being within the area rather than outside it. The size and location of an area can thus be changed by adding to or subtracting from the points which are enclosed within the boundary. The representation of such spatial features on maps by means of enclosing lines usually implies that they have some geographical meaning, forming for example natural features such as the coastline of an island or the extent of the built-up area of a settlement. The combination of various types of map symbolism allows different types of areal feature to be shown simultaneously. For instance, colour shading indicating the soil types occurring across a region might be overprinted with lines delimiting planning areas.

Individual polygons of the same type, for example local government areas, are often examined in relation to their neighbours or to more distant places, rather than being considered as isolated entities. Thus the topological concept of *adjacency*, the identification of which areas lie next to each other, is very important. Adjacency is particularly relevant in connection with the problem of spatial autocorrelation (see Chapter 12), in which geographically close or adjacent entities tend to possess either similar or dissimilar values in respect of a measured variable. A statistical procedure is available (Silk 1979), which enables the extent of autocorrelation to be quantified by looking at the number of adjacent areas which are classified in a similar or opposing fashion. The approach is most easily illustrated with respect to a set of areas categorised on a dichotomous attribute, but can be extended to more complex situations. The basis of the procedure is to determine the number of boundary line joins where the areas on either side are similar or dissimilar. For example, suppose that a set of areas are classified as high- or low-altitude; joins of the following types would be counted: high to high; low to low; high to low; and low to high. The observed and expected numbers of each type can be compared by means of the Z-test statistic. In this case, assuming the areas to be of equal size, the result of the significance test is likely to indicate a fairly high degree of autocorrelation, since areas of similar altitude would probably be close to each other, while dissimilar ones would be far apart. The determination of whether autocorrelation is present in a dataset to a significant degree is an important precursor for applying statistical techniques which assume that observations are independent of each other.

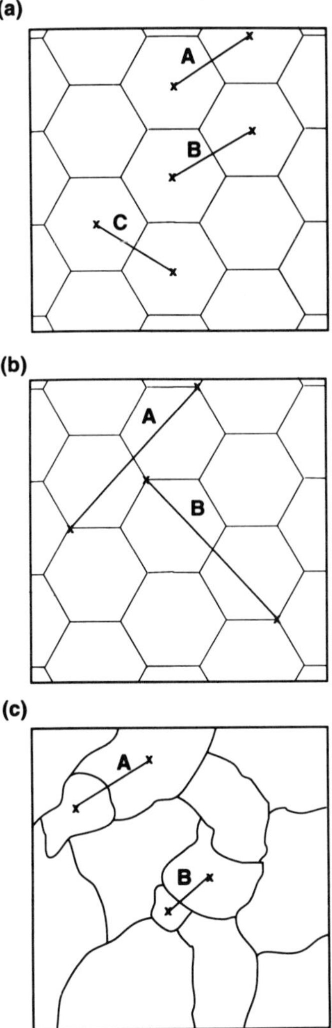

Figure 14.8 Measurement of distance between regular and irregular area features. (a) length of lines *A*, *B* and *C*, connecting the centres of 3 hexagons are equal; (b) Lines *A* and *B*, connecting opposite corners of adjacent hexagons, define the maximum distance between two areas. (c) Lines *A* and *B*, connecting the centroids of two pairs of adjacent areas, illustrate the variability of distance measures between irregularly shaped objects

The distance between areas is also relevant, but, since they can be of varying spatial extent with irregular boundaries, its measurement is more complicated than for points and lines. Figure 14.8 illustrates some of the problems. If the areas are regular, for example squares or hexagons with the same unit size, then the distance between the same relative location within each unit will be a constant (Figure 14.8(a)). The distance between any two points in adjacent areas cannot exceed the length of the line between their opposite corners (Figure 14.8(b)). Unfortunately, many geographical phenomena are irregular and unequal in size. In these circumstances the distance between two areas is highly variable (Figure 14.8(c)). The usual solution to this problem is to summarise the location of an area by means of a point at its geometrical centre, which occurs where the lines representing the maximum and minimum distance across an area intersect. These points are known as *centroids* and provide a convenient method for measuring the distance between areas.

Areas are not only important as geographical phenomena, possessing a certain shape, size and location, but also as being capable of measurement with respect to a wide variety of substantive or thematic variables and attributes. From a statistical point of view it might appear that the size of an areal spatial unit is just another variable, comparable with, for example, the number of people living within its boundaries. However, there is an important difference: the size and shape of an area can change, while the thematic variable remains the same. If the inhabitants of a series of adjacent areas mainly live in centrally located settlements, then changes in the boundaries of these areas may occur without seriously affecting their total population counts. On the other hand, their population density may alter dramatically. Figure 14.9(a) illustrates this type of change with three boundaries. In contrast, if population concentrations are close together, the physical shape of a polygon could change while its areal extent remains constant, and yet the population total might increase or decrease dramatically (Figure 14.9(b)).

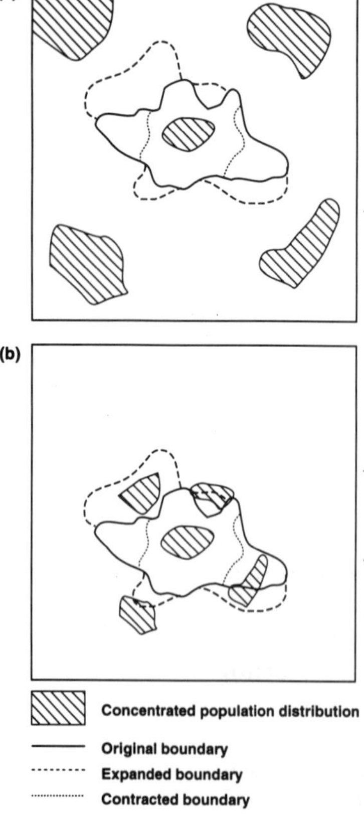

Figure 14.9 Effect of boundaries on the characteristics of area features: (a) boundary changes have no effect on the total population of the area; (b) boundary changes dramatically alter the total population of the area

14.2.1 Analysis of areal entities

Apart from looking for evidence of spatial autocorrelation, other techniques for analysing areal patterns do not on the whole involve significance testing. Part of the reason for this is the difficulty in devising a suitable probability distribution against which to test the sample data. An alternative approach has involved developing spatial indices, and two of these techniques will be considered here: first, the Lorenz curve for comparing spatial distributions over space or time; and second, location quotients for examining differences between an observed spatial distribution and a norm or standard.

Lorenz curves have been used in a number of geographical applications, as well as by researchers in other disciplines in respect of non-spatial data, to investigate such diverse topics as distributional change in the cultivation of potatoes in Great Britain (Britten and Ingersent 1964) and religious segregation in Northern Ireland (Poole and Boale 1973). The raw data for generating Lorenz curves in a geographical application comprise either the same variable recorded on two separate occasions (e.g. the number of service sector employees in the counties of Britain from the 1981 and 1991 Population Censuses), or two different variables measured at the same time for a set of spatial units (e.g. the amounts of derelict and residential land in the wards of a particular district).

Table 14.6 shows the frequency distributions of retail and community facilities which were recorded in village surveys in the 31 parishes of Colchester district in 1985 and 1990. A Lorenz curve for the data will indicate whether there is any evidence that the overall distribution has changed over the five-year period. The calculations and data manipulation for generating a Lorenz curve bear some resemblance to those required for the Kolmogorov–Smirnov test (see Chapter 10). Suppose the two variables are designated as X and Y, here denoting the data for 1985 and 1990, respectively. The ratio between X and Y is calculated and then the raw values are converted into percentages of their respective totals and the observations (parishes) are ranked according to the ratio (Table 14.6 shows the parishes already ranked by reference to the ratio). Finally, maintaining the ranked order, the cumulative percentage frequencies are calculated and plotted on the horizontal and vertical axes as a graph (curve). Figure 14.10 illustrates the Lorenz curve for the Colchester parish data and the deviation away from the diagonal suggests that there has been a slight reduction or shift in the number of facilities.

The plot of the paired percentages will follow the diagonal of the graph if there has been no change or there is no difference in the proportional distribution of the variables. When the Lorenz curve does not follow the diagonal, there has been a change in the spatial distribution of the variable, or the phenomena show some evidence of spatial separation. The point at which the perpendicular distance of the curve

Table 14.6 Calculation of Lorenz curve for parish facilities in Colchester, 1985 and 1990

						Cumulative		
Parish	1985	1990	Ratio	1985(%)	1990(%)	1985(%)	1990(%)	Difference
Mount Bures	12	17	0.71	2.6	3.8	2.6	3.8	1.2
Little Horkesley	5	7	0.71	1.1	1.6	3.7	5.3	1.7
Wakes Colne	13	17	0.76	2.8	3.8	6.5	9.1	2.6
Wormingford	20	24	0.83	4.3	5.3	0.8	4.4	3.7
Langham	7	8	0.88	1.5	1.8	12.3	16.2	3.9
Great Tey	10	11	0.91	2.2	2.4	14.4	18.7	4.2
Great Horkesley	24	26	0.92	5.2	5.8	19.6	24.4	4.8
Dedham	12	13	0.92	2.6	2.9	22.2	27.3	5.1
Boxted	23	24	0.96	5.0	5.3	27.2	32.7	5.5
Fordham	19	19	1.00	4.1	4.2	31.2	36.9	5.6
West Bergolt	24	24	1.00	5.2	5.3	36.4	42.2	5.8
Chappel	11	11	1.00	2.4	2.4	38.8	44.7	5.9
Aldham	16	16	1.00	3.4	3.6	42.2	48.2	6.0
Eight Ash Green	15	15	1.00	3.2	3.3	45.5	51.6	6.1
Birch	7	7	1.00	1.5	1.6	47.0	53.1	6.1
Layer de la Haye	7	7	1.00	1.5	1.6	48.5	54.7	6.2
Stanway	25	24	1.04	5.4	5.3	53.9	60.0	6.1
Marks Tey	21	20	1.05	4.5	4.4	58.4	64.4	6.0
Copford & Easthorpe	17	16	1.06	3.7	3.6	62.1	68.0	5.9
Layer Breton	14	13	1.08	3.0	2.9	65.1	70.9	5.8
Inworth & Messing	13	12	1.08	2.8	2.7	67.9	73.6	5.7
Tiptree	20	18	1.11	4.3	4.0	72.2	77.6	5.4
Layer Marney	19	17	1.12	4.1	3.8	76.3	81.3	5.0
East Donyland	15	12	1.25	3.2	2.7	79.5	84.0	4.5
West Mersea	14	11	1.27	3.0	2.4	82.5	86.4	3.9
Wivenhoe	18	14	1.29	3.9	3.1	86.4	89.6	3.1
Great Wigborough, Peldon & Salcott	13	10	1.30	2.8	2.2	89.2	91.8	2.6
Fingringhoe	17	13	1.31	3.7	2.9	92.9	95.5	1.8
Aberton & Langenhoe	16	12	1.33	3.4	2.6	96.3	98.1	0.8
East Mersea	17	12	1.42	3.7	1.9	100.0	100.0	1.8

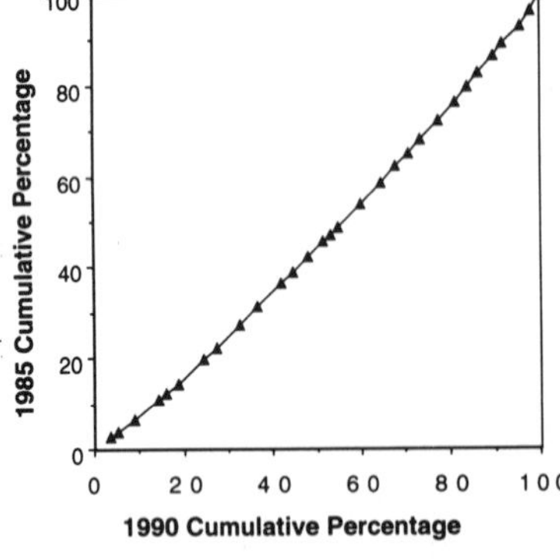

Figure 14.10 Lorenz curve for parish facilities

from the diagonal is greatest indicates the areas which are most dissimilar. This distance provides the index of dissimilarity, D_S, which may be obtained in three ways:

- by calculating the absolute differences between the two cumulative percentage frequencies;
- by measurement from an accurately drawn graph;
- by using the formula $D_S = \Sigma|X_i - Y_i|/2$, where X_i and Y_i denote the unaccumulated percentages for the two variables.

The dissimilarity index could be used for a series of matched variables in order to compare different areal patterns, but unfortunately it is influenced by changes in spatial boundaries and scale. A more serious problem from a spatial analytic point of view is that the technique operates without reference to the topological relationships between the areal units. In other words, the Lorenz curve concentrates on the aggregate distributional pattern, rather than the locational one. Furthermore, from a computational point of view it is feasible to use the technique with sample data, but if the sampled observations are unrepresentative of the population the analysis will be highly misleading. Finally, the technique requires that the data are held in the form of frequency counts for the two variables and therefore do not include any negative values.

An alternative spatial index, known as the *location quotient*, compares the distribution of a variable for a group of areas with some norm, such as the population mean. The purpose is to investigate the degree of concentration in the different areas. Suppose that the items in a population are capable of being classified into discrete categories with regard to a single variable, such as households by their tenure. The technique compares the proportion in a particular category within each of the areas in the study region with that for the whole area. Separate location quotients are calculated for each area. The technique can be used with absolute counts as well as relative (percentage) frequencies, although different formulae are employed. In the former case, using *LQ* to represent the location quotient, the index is calculated thus:

$$LQ = \frac{X_i/X}{Y_i/Y}$$

where X and Y refer respectively to the variable for the local and national areas, and i is a particular category of the classification variable (e.g. private rented tenure). Thus X_i denotes the number of items in an area categorised as i, and X is the total number of items within that area. Y_i and Y are the corresponding population figures, which can be regarded as a constant for each category in the classification scheme. If the data are held as percentages, then the location quotients can be calculated more directly thus:

$$LQ_i = \frac{X_i}{Y_i}$$

Table 14.7 Calculation of location quotients for parish facilities in Colchester, 1990

Parish	Retail	*LQ*	Social	*LQ*	Public	*LQ*
Aberton & Langenhoe	2	0.62	7	1.13	4	1.12
Aldham	0	0.00	7	1.33	4	1.32
Birch	3	0.76	8	1.05	5	1.13
Boxted	4	1.25	7	1.13	2	0.56
Chappel	0	0.00	9	1.45	4	1.12
Copford & Easthorpe	2	0.48	9	1.11	6	1.28
Dedham	6	1.22	8	0.84	6	1.09
East Donyland	6	1.28	7	0.77	6	1.15
East Mersea	3	1.11	5	0.95	3	0.99
Eight Ash Green	3	0.72	9	1.11	5	1.07
Fingringhoe	3	0.72	11	1.35	3	0.64
Fordham	2	0.68	7	1.22	3	0.91
Great Horkesley	4	1.16	5	0.75	5	1.30
Great Tey	1	0.37	7	1.33	3	0.99
Great Wigborough, Peldon & Salcott	2	0.68	8	1.40	2	0.60
Inworth & Messing	3	1.01	6	1.05	3	0.91
Langham	3	0.81	10	1.40	2	0.48
Layer Breton	2	1.01	4	1.05	2	0.91
Layer de la Haye	3	0.76	8	1.05	5	1.13
Layer Marney	3	1.74	3	0.90	1	0.52
Little Horkesley	0	0.00	5	1.50	2	1.04
Marks Tey	6	1.35	7	0.81	5	1.01
Mount Bures	0	0.00	5	1.50	2	1.04
Stanway	8	1.35	10	0.87	6	0.91
Tiptree	9	1.40	10	0.81	7	0.98
Wakes Colne	3	1.22	3	0.63	4	1.45
West Bergolt	8	1.35	10	0.87	6	0.91
West Mersea	10	1.69	7	0.61	7	1.06
Wivenhoe	9	1.54	8	0.70	7	1.06
Wormingford	3	1.01	5	0.87	4	1.21

where X_i and Y_i are respectively the local and national percentages for category i. Location quotients higher than 1.0 signify concentration of the phenomenon in the specific area and lower values the reverse.

The 1990 village facilities survey for the Colchester parishes demonstrates the technique. Rather than lumping the various services and facilities into one group they have been disaggregated into retail, social and public utilities in Table 14.7. The various location quotients are given alongside the frequency counts and the method of calculation can be exemplified by the case of the retail outlets in Wivenhoe, thus:

$$LQ = \frac{9/24}{134/552} = \frac{0.375}{0.243} = 1.54$$

Some parishes appear to be well placed with respect to the provision of retailing facilities — for instance Layer Marney, West Mersea and Wivenhoe have location quotients over 1.50 (1.5 times the norm). In contrast, parishes such as Aldham, Chappel and Great Tey are less well served in respect of retail outlets. Similar disparities can be identified for other types of facility (see Table 14.7).

There are two problems with the location quotient which detract from its attractiveness as a statistical technique. It shares the problem of many spatial indices that very little is known about its sampling distribution. Thus, if the data are based on a sample of observations, it is not possible to test the significance of the location quotients. If, for instance, only a sample of service and facility outlets had been counted in the Colchester parishes, the resulting location quotients might be misleading as estimates of the corresponding population parameters. The second difficulty is that, when items are less concentrated than in the population, the location quotients are constrained to lie between 0 and 1; on the other hand, there is no upper limit for the index above unity.

14.3 SPATIAL STATISTICS AND THE EXEMPLAR PROJECTS

Most general-purpose statistical software, such as MINITAB and SPSS-X, and even some of the newer geographical analysis and mapping software lack specific facilities for carrying out geostatistical analyses. Therefore the purpose of this section is to demonstrate, using the exemplar projects, how data manipulation and computation commands in MINITAB can be used to calculate a selection of the measures. Some of these operations are cumbersome, since the software may not be designed to manipulate data in the desired fashion. However, before looking at the practical issues, thc spatial characteristics of the data in the exemplar projects are briefly reviewed in each section in order to highlight the spatial statistics which are appropriate in each case. The land-use study, more than the other projects, lends itself to demonstrating some of the spatial statistics techniques.

14.3.1 Land-use change

The datasets for samples A and B in the land-use project include the National Grid eastings and northings for the sample points within the irregular plots and the bottom left-hand corner of the grid squares, thus enabling descriptive measures, such as the mean centre and standard distance between the sample sites, to be calculated. The computation of these measures is similar for the two samples. The log of the MINITAB session (Table 14.8) shows the application of the DESCRIBE command

Table 14.8 Calculation of mean centre and VMR for sample A and standard distance for sample B in land-use project in MINITAB

```
MTB > OUTFILE 'land09'
MTB > RETRIEVE 'landa04'
MTB > DESCRIBE C1 C2
MTB > CODE (000:019)0(020:039)2(040:059)4(060:079)6(080:099) 8 &
(100:119)10(120:139)12(140:159)14(160:179)16(180:199)18 C1 INTO C27
MTB > CODE (100:119)10(120:139)12(140:159)14(160:179)16(180:199) 18 &
C2 INTO C28
MTB > TABLE C27 C28
MTB > READ C29 C30
DATA > 0 22
DATA > 1 18
DATA > 2 9
DATA > 3 0
DATA > 4 1
DATA > END
MTB > LET C31 = C29*C30
MTB > LET C32 = (C29**2)*C30
MTB > LET K30 = SUM(C30)
MTB > LET K31 = SUM(C31)
MTB > LET K32 = SUM(C32)
MTB > LET K33 = K30 / K31
MTB > LET K34 = (1 / (K30 - 1))*(K32 - (K31**2) / K30)
MTB > LET K35 = K34 / K33
MTB > LET K36 = (K30 - 1)*K35
MTB > PRINT C29 - C32
MTB > PRINT K30 - K36
MTB > RETRIEVE 'landb04'
MTB > DESCRIBE C1 C2
MTB > LET K1 = SQRT(40.45+4.93)
MTB > PRINT K1
MTB > NOOUTFILE
MTB > STOP
MTB > LET K67 = (1 / (K63 - 1))*(K65 - (K64**2) / K63)
MTB > LET K68 = K67 / K66
MTB > LET K69 = (K63 - 1)*K68
MTB > PRINT C62 - C65
MTB > PRINT K63 - K69
MTB > NOOUTFILE
MTB > STOP
```

to C1 and C2 for sample A, which produces the easting and northing coordinates of the mean centre. The standard distance between the bottom left-hand corners of the grid squares in sample B is calculated by taking the square root of the sum of the variances of C1 and C2, thus:

MTB > LET K1 = SQRT(40.45+4.93)

where SQRT is the square root function and 40.45 and 4.93 are the variances which have been derived from the standard deviations (see Box 14.1).

The locational information relating to the observation units can also be used to decide which of the two samples provides more satisfactory

Box 14.1 (*Opposite*) Mean centre and VMR for sample points in sample A and standard distance for sample B in land-use project (extract from MINITAB output)

```
Sample A
MTB > Retrieve 'landa04'.
WORKSHEET SAVED 3/31/1993    Worksheet retrieved from file: landa04.mtw
MTB > DESCRIBE C1 C2
                N       MEAN     MEDIAN     TRMEAN     STDEV     SEMEAN
Easting        40      97.25      95.50      97.11     55.51       8.78
Northing       40     142.48     139.50     142.03     29.08       4.60
              MIN        MAX         Q1         Q3
Easting      3.00     193.00      59.50     122.75
Northing   102.00     195.00     113.00     173.25
MTB > CODE (000:019)0(020:039)2(040:059)4(060:079)6(080:099)8&
CONT > (100:119)10(120:139)12(140:159)14(160:179)16(180:199)18C1 INTO C27
MTB > CODE (100:119)10(120:139)12(140:159)14(160:179)16(180:199)18 C2 INTO C28
MTB > TABLE C27 C28
ROWS: C27     COLUMNS: C28
        10     12     14     16     18    ALL
                                                 CELL CONTENTS -
 0       2      1      0      1      0      4        COUNT
 2       2      0      0      0      1      3
 4       1      1      0      1      0      3
 6       0      2      1      0      1      4
 8       1      1      4      2      1      9
10       2      2      0      0      1      5
12       0      0      1      1      1      3
14       0      1      0      0      0      1
16       1      0      0      0      2      3
18       2      1      2      0      0      5
ALL     11      9      8      5      7     40
MTB > READ C29 C30
DATA > 0 22
DATA > 1 18
DATA > 2 9
DATA > 3 0
DATA > 4 1
DATA > END
MTB > LET C31 = C29 * C30
MTB > LET C32 = (C29**2) * C30
MTB > LET K30 = SUM(C30)
MTB > LET K31 = SUM(C31)
MTB > LET K32 = SUM(C32)
MTB > LET K33 = K30 / K31
MTB > LET K34 = (1 / (K30 - 1)) * (K32 - (K31**2) / K30)
MTB > LET K35 = K34 / K33
MTB > LET K36 = (K30 - 1)*K35
MTB > PRINT C29 - C32 [Respectively X, f, fX and fX^2]
ROW     C29     C30     C31     C32
  1       0      22       0       0
  2       1      18      18      18
  3       2       9      18      36
  4       3       0       0       0
  5       4       1       4      16
```

(continued)

Box 14.1 (*continued*)

```
MTB > PRINT K30 - K36
K30        50.0000        [ f ]
K31        40.0000        [ fX ]
K32        70.0000        [ fX² ]
K33         1.25000       [ ]
K34         0.775510      [ s² ]
K35         0.620408      [ VMR]
K36        30.4000        [ χ² ]
Sample B
  MTB > Retrieve 'landb04'.
  WORKSHEET SAVED 3/31/1993    Worksheet retrieved from file: LANDB04.MTW
  MTB > DESCRIBE C1 C2
                 N        MEAN      MEDIAN     TRMEAN     STDEV     SEMEAN
Easting         20       10.05       11.50      10.11      6.36       1.42
Northing        20       15.20       15.50      15.28      2.22       0.50
               MIN         MAX          Q1         Q3
Easting       0.00       19.00        4.25      15.00
Northing     10.00       19.00       14.00      17.00
  MTB > LET K1 = SQRT (40.45 + 4.93)
  MTB > PRINT K1 [Standard Distance in km]
        6.73
```

coverage of the study area. Although the samples have been drawn randomly, there may still be a tendency for clustering or regular spacing in the distribution of the points. The null hypothesis can be stated as:

LU8 The sample points/grid squares are randomly located across the study area and do not display any tendency for clustering or regularity in their distribution.

The hypothesis is examined by means of the variance–mean ratio test and nearest-neighbour analysis with respect to the observations in sample A. The Lorenz curve technique will be illustrated with the data for sample B.

14.3.1.1 Variance-mean ratio: sample A

The variance–mean ratio test requires the locational information for the sample sites to be expressed as a frequency distribution of the number of points per grid square. In this example the grid of 200 kilometre squares is too fine for only 40 points for sample A and the size of the grid squares is increased to 4 km^2. Several stages are required to convert the raw locational information, the X and Y coordinates, into a frequency distribution of points per grid square and then to calculate the desired statistics. The sequence of commands for sample A is shown in Table 14.8 (see also the sample output in Box 14.1). The first stage involves 'regridding' the points so that they fit within a grid of 50 squares. The three-figure coordinates for the eastings and northings in columns C1 and C2 are recoded into new columns C27 and C28 in the sample A worksheet LANDA04.MTW, thus:

```
MTB > CODE (000:019) 0 (020:039) 2 ... C1 INTO C27
MTB > CODE (100:119) 10 (120:139) 12 ... C2 INTO C28
```

For example, any point with an easting between 000 and 019 will be recoded as 0 and any between 020 and 039 will become 2. Similarly northings between 100 and 119 and between 120 and 139 are respectively reclassified as 10 and 12. The frequency count (cross-tabulation) for the 40 points across the new larger grid squares is obtained by means of the TABLE C27 C28 command. Two further new columns (C29 and C30) are added with the READ command, one of which contains the frequency class of points per square (i.e. 0, 1, 2, 3 and 4 points) and the other the frequency count of these occurrences (22,18,9,0 and 1). These columns correspond to those headed X and f in Table 14.4. Once these columns have been entered, two LET commands compute fX and fX^2 (see Table 14.4) as two further new columns, C31 and C32. The sums of columns C30, C31 and C32 are stored in constants K30, K31 and K32. The sample mean (λ) and variance (s^2) can now be calculated and placed in constants K33 and K34, thus:

```
MTB > LET K33 = K30 / K31
MTB > LET K34 = (1 / (K30 – 1)) * (K32 – (K31**2 / K30))
```

The VMR statistic is obtained by division and stored as K35, thus:

```
MTB > LET K35 = K34 / K33
```

Use of the PRINT command for the constants (K30 to K36) reveals the VMR ratio is 0.6204, which, being lower than than 1.0, suggests that the sample points tend towards regular dispersion. Finally the significance of the test statistic can be assessed by converting it into either a t statistic, which also requires the standard error of the VMR, or into a χ^2 statistic. The latter is more straightforward and calculated as:

```
MTB > LET K36 = (K30 – 1)*K35
```

The significance of the test statistic of 30.40 is estimated from the table of the chi-square distribution (Appendix IV) with 50 – 1 degrees of freedom. In this example the null hypothesis for sample A is accepted, since the probability of obtaining a χ^2 of 30.40 is greater than 0.05 and the apparent regularity indicated by the test statistic may be discounted as having occurred through chance (see Box 14.1).

14.3.1.2 Nearest-neighbour analysis: sample A

Nearest-neighbour analysis requires calculation of two quantities: the expected density of points (r_e) and the observed mean distance (r_o). An abbreviated sequence of commands for sample A is given in Table 14.9.

Table 14.9 Calculation of nearest-neighbour statistic for land-use project sample A in MINITAB

```
MTB > OUTFILE 'land10'
MTB > RETRIEVE 'landa04'
MTB > WRITE 'landa05' C1 C2
MTB > RESTART
MTB > READ 'landa05.dat' C1 C2
MTB > LET K1 = C1(1)
MTB > LET K2 = C1(2)
...
MTB > LET K40 = C1(40)
MTB > LET K41 = C2(1)
MTB > LET K42 = C2(2)
...
MTB > LET K80 = C2(40)
MTB > LET C3(1) = SQRT ((K1 - K2)**2 + (K41 - K42)**2)
MTB > LET C4(1) = SQRT ((K1 - K3)**2 + (K41 - K43)**2)
MTB > LET C5(1) = SQRT ((K1 - K4)**2 + (K41 - K44)**2)
...
MTB > LET C41(1) = SQRT ((K1 - K40)**2 + (K41 - K80)**2)
MTB > LET C4(2) = SQRT ((K2 - K3)**2 + (K42 - K43)**2)
MTB > LET C5(2) = SQRT ((K2 - K4)**2 + (K42 - K44)**2)
MTB > LET C6(2) = SQRT ((K2 - K5)**2 + (K42 - K45)**2)
...
MTB > LET C41(2) = SQRT ((K2 - K40)**2 + (K42 - K80)**2)
MTB > LET C5(3) = SQRT ((K3 - K4)**2 + (K43 - K44)**2)
MTB > LET C6(3) = SQRT ((K3 - K5)**2 + (K43 - K45)**2)
MTB > LET C7(3) = SQRT ((K3 - K6)**2 + (K43 - K46)**2)
...
MTB > LET C41(39) = SQRT ((K39 - K40)**2 + (K79 - K80)**2)
MTB > RMIN C3 - C41 C42
MTB > LET K42 = SUM(C42)
MTB > LET K43 = K42 / 40
MTB > LET K44 = SQRT(200/20)*0.5
MTB > LET K45 = K43 / K44
MTB > LET K46 = 0.26136/SQRT(20*(20/200))
MTB > LET K47 = ABS(K45 - K44) / K46
MTB > PRINT K42 - K47
MTB > NOOUTFILE
MTB > STOP
```

LANDA04.MTW is retrieved and the columns containing the eastings and northings, C1 and C2, are written out into a data file called LANDA05.DAT. The RESTART command is given to reload the software, so that these columns can be read into a new worksheet. This operation is required because the number of columns produced by the subsequent calculations when added to those already in worksheet LANDA04.MTW would exceed the number permitted in the software (100).

The expected density of points is obtained by a relatively simple LET command:

```
MTB > LET K44 = SQRT(200/20)*0.5
```

where 200 and 20 respectively denote the total area and the number of sampled points (see Table 14.9). The observed density of points entails lengthy and tedious computations in order to calculate the distance between each pair of points using Pythagoras' theorem and to store the results as a distance matrix. First the 20 individual easting and northing coordinates, which are held in columns C1 and C2, are spread so that each is stored as a separate constant, K1 to K8, thus:

```
MTB > LET K1 = C1(1)
MTB > LET K2 = C1(2)
MTB > LET K3 = C1(3)
...
MTB > LET K40 = C1(40)
MTB > LET K41 = C2(1)
MTB > LET K42 = C2(2)
MTB > LET K43 = C2(3)
...
MTB > LET K80 = C2(40)
```

The figures in brackets refer to the row numbers in columns C1 and C2; thus K1 will contain the easting for the first sample point, K2 the second, and so on up to K80 with the northing for the 20th point. The distances between each pair of easting and northing coordinates are calculated thus:

```
MTB > LET C3(1) = SQRT((K1 - K2)**2 + (K41 - K42)**2)
MTB > LET C4(1) = SQRT((K1 - K3)**2 + (K41 - K43)**2)
MTB > LET C5(1) = SQRT((K1 - K4)**2 + (K41 - K44)**2)
...
MTB > LET C41(1) = SQRT((K1 - K40)**2 + (K41 - K80)**2)
MTB > LET C4(2) = SQRT((K2 - K3)**2 + (K42 - K43)**2)
MTB > LET C5(2) = SQRT((K2 - K4)**2 + (K42 - K44)**2)
MTB > LET C6(2) = SQRT((K2 - K5)**2 + (K42 - K45)**2)
...
MTB > LET C41(2) = SQRT((K2 - K40)**2 + (K42 - K80)**2)
MTB > LET C5(3) = SQRT((K3 - K3)**2 + (K43 - K44)**2)
MTB > LET C6(3) = SQRT((K3 - K4)**2 + (K43 - K45)**2)
MTB > LET C7(3) = SQRT((K3 - K5)**2 + (K43 - K46)**2)
...
MTB > LET C41(39) = SQRT((K39 - K40)**2 + (K79 - K80)**2)
```

The first line in the sequence calculates the distance between sample points 1 and 2 and places the result in row 1 of C3, the second the distance between points 1 and 3 goes into row 1 of C4, and so on up to the distance between points 39 and 40 in row 39 of C41. This long series of LET commands produces a triangular matrix of distances stored in columns C3 to C41. The matrix contains a total of 820 pairs of measurements and has a similar form to the one given in Table 14.5. The next stage involves determining the row minima for columns C3 to C41, and storing them in a new column, C42, which can be achieved with the RMIN command, thus:

MTB > RMIN C3 – C41 INTO C42

The sum of the observed minimum distances is computed into K42 and their mean calculated as K43. The statistic *R* is also obtained as K45:

MTB > LET K42 = SUM(C42)
MTB > LET K43 = K42 / 40
MTB > LET K44 = SQRT(200/20)*0.5
MTB > LET K45 = K43 / K44

The value of *R* (K45) is 0.13949 (see Box 14.2), which suggests that the distribution of sample points is fairly clustered. Finally, a *Z* test

```
MTB > OUTFILE 'land10'
MTB > RETRIEVE 'landa04'
  Worksheet retrieved from file: landa04.mtw
MTB > WRITE 'landa05' C1 C2
MTB > RESTART
MTB > READ 'landa05.dat' C1 C2
MTB > LET K1 = C1(1)
MTB > LET K2 = C1(2)

MTB > LET K40 = C1(40)
MTB > LET K41 = C2(1)
MTB > LET K42 = C2(2)

MTB > LET K80 = C2(40)
MTB > LET C3(1) = SQRT((K1 – K2)**2 + (K41 – K42)**2)
MTB > LET C4(1) = SQRT((K1 – K3)**2 + (K41 – K43)**2)
MTB > LET C5(1) = SQRT((K1 – K4)**2 + (K41 – K44)**2)
MTB > LET C6(1) = SQRT((K1 – K5)**2 + (K41 – K45)**2)

MTB > LET C41(1) = SQRT((K1 – K40)**2 + (K41 – K80)**2)
MTB > LET C4(2) = SQRT((K2 – K3)**2 + (K42 – K43)**2)
MTB > LET C5(2) = SQRT((K2 – K4)**2 + (K42 – K44)**2)
MTB > LET C6(2) = SQRT((K2 – K5)**2 + (K42 – K45)**2)
MTB > LET C7(2) = SQRT((K2 – K6)**2 + (K42 – K46)**2)
MTB > LET C8(2) = SQRT((K2 – K7)**2 + (K42 – K47)**2)

MTB > LET C41(39) = SQRT((K39 – K40)**2 + (K79 – K80)**2)
MTB > RMIN C3 – C41 INTO C42
MTB > LET K42 = SUM(C42)
MTB > LET K43 = K42 / 40
MTB > LET K44 = SQRT(200/20)*0.5
MTB > K45 = K43 / K44
MTB > K46 = 0.26136/SQRT(20 * 20/200))
MTB > LET K47 = ABS(K45 – K44) / K46
MTB > PRINT K42 – K47
K42 8.82182 [Sum of nearest distances in km]
K43 0.22055 [ r_e in km]
K44 1.58114 [ r_o in km]
K45 0.13949 [ R ]
K46 0.18481 [ s_d ]
K47 7.80071 [ Z ]
MTB > NOOUTFILE
```

Box 14.2 Nearest-neighbour statistics for sample points in sample A in land-use project (MINITAB output)

may be carried out on the difference between r_o and r_e, which also requires the standard error to be calculated:

```
MTB > LET K46 = 0.26136/SQRT(20*(20/200))
MTB > LET K47 = ABS(K45 – K44) / K46
```

The probability associated with this test statistic (K47 = Z = 7.8007) may be assessed by reference to the Z distribution table in Appendix IV. In this case the high test value for Z has a low probability, which indicates that the null hypothesis LU8 for sample A can be rejected.

14.3.1.3 Lorenz curve: sample B

The standard statistical procedures have already examined whether the areal changes in the different types of land-use between the 1930s and 1960s are significant. A Lorenz curve indicates whether there is any evidence of spatial concentration. The technique is not suitable for use with sample A, since the boundaries of the irregular plots have changed between the 1930s and 1960s. Each areal unit in sample B is exactly the same size on the two occasions, and, although dealing with a sample, Lorenz curves can be calculated for each of the different land uses. The application of the technique in this project requires that the area measurements are treated as a frequency count of hectares. The sequence of commands for calculating the Lorenz curve for one category of land use, agriculture, which is stored in C4 and C11 for the 1930s and 1960s respectively (see Table 14.10), exemplifies the procedure. The ratio between the two columns is calculated by a LET command and their sums are stored as constants, thus:

```
MTB > LET C60 = C4 / C11
MTB > LET K4 = SUM(C4)
MTB > LET K11 = SUM(C11)
```

Then the counts in C4 and C11 are converted into percentages of their respective totals and placed in C61 and C62 and their ratio is computed into C63:

```
MTB > LET C61 = (C4*100) / K4
MTB > LET C62 = (C11*100) / K4
MTB > LET C63 = C61 / C62
```

The next stage entails sorting the rows with respect to this ratio and carrying across the ratio and the percentages (C63, C61 and C62) into three new columns:

```
MTB > SORT C63 C61 C62 INTO C64 C65 C66
```

The columns C65 and C66 contain the percentages correctly associated with their ratio value, which is held in C64. The final stage involves accumulating the percentage frequencies into columns C67

Table 14.10 Calculation of Lorenz curve for agricultural land for sample B in land-use project in MINITAB

```
MTB > OUTFILE 'land11'
MTB > RETRIEVE 'landb04'
MTB > LET C60 = C4 / C11
MTB > LET K4 = SUM(C4)
MTB > LET K11 = SUM(C11)
MTB > LET C61 = (C4*100) / K4
MTB > LET C62 = (C11*100) / K11
MTB > LET C63 = C61 / C62
MTB > SORT C63 C61 C62 INTO C64 C65 C66
MTB > LET C67(1) = C65(1)
MTB > LET C67(2) = C65(2) + C67(1)
MTB > LET C67(3) = C65(3) + C67(2)
MTB > LET C67(4) = C65(4) + C67(3)
MTB > LET C67(5) = C65(5) + C67(4)
...
MTB > LET C67(20) = C65(20) + C67(19)
MTB > LET C68(1) = C66(1)
MTB > LET C68(2) = C66(2) + C68(1)
MTB > LET C68(3) = C66(3) + C68(2)
MTB > LET C68(4) = C66(4) + C68(3)
MTB > LET C68(5) = C66(5) + C68(4)
...
MTB > LET C68(20) = C66(20) + C68(19)
MTB > PLOT C67 C68
MTB > NOOUTFILE
MTB > STOP
```

and C68 (for 1930s and 1960s, respectively) by means of a series of LET commands:

```
MTB > LET C67(1) = C65(1)
MTB > LET C67(2) = C65(2) + C67(1)
MTB > LET C67(3) = C65(3) + C67(2)
...
MTB > LET C67(20) = C65(20) + C67(19)
MTB > LET C68(1) = C66(1)
MTB > LET C68(2) = C66(2) + C68(1)
MTB > LET C68(3) = C66(3) + C68(2)
...
MTB > LET C68(20) = C66(20) + C68(19)
```

The values of C67 and C68 in row 20 should both equal 100.00 (per cent), although rounding may lead to some discrepancy. The cumulative percentages in these columns are plotted against each other with the PLOT command. The relatively primitive graphics in the mainframe version of MINITAB may, however, produce an unsatisfactory representation of the trend line of the Lorenz curve.

The results of the analysis (Box 14.3) show that the Lorenz curve is a useful method for investigating changes in the distribution of a

```
MTB > OUTFILE 'land11'
MTB > RETRIEVE 'landb04'
  Worksheet retrieved from file: landb04.mtw
MTB > LET C60 = C4 / C11
MTB > LET K4 = SUM(C4)
MTB > LET K11 = SUM(C11)
MTB > LET C61 = (C4 * 100) / K4
MTB > LET C62 = (C11 * 100) / K11
MTB > LET C63 = C61 / C62
MTB > SORT C63 C61 C62 INTO C64 C65 C66
MTB > LET C67(1) = C65(1)
MTB > LET C67(2) = C65(2) + C67(1)
MTB > LET C67(3) = C65(3) + C67(2)
MTB > LET C67(4) = C65(4) + C67(3)
MTB > LET C67(5) = C65(5) + C67(4)
MTB > LET C67(20) = C65(20) + C67(19)
MTB > LET C68(1) = C66(1)
MTB > LET C68(2) = C66(2) + C68(1)
MTB > LET C68(3) = C66(3) + C68(2)
MTB > LET C68(4) = C66(4) + C68(3)
MTB > LET C68(5) = C66(5) + C68(4)
MTB > LET C68(20) = C66(20) + C68(19)
MTB > PLOT C67 C68 [ Agriculture ]
      105 +
          -                                              * *
C67       -                                          * *
          -                                     *
          -                                   *
       70 +                                 * *
          -                            *
          -                        * *
          -                    *
          -                  *
       35 +                *
          -           *
          -       * *
          -     *
          -  * *
        0 +
          +---------+---------+---------+---------+---------+-------C68
          0        20        40        60        80       100
MTB > NOOUTFILE
```

Box 14.3 Lorenz curves for agriculture and grass land for sample B in land-use project (MINITAB output)

phenomenon. Agriculture and grass land, as recorded for sample B, reveal some shift in concentration over the period, but it is apparent that the curves lie close to the diagonal of the graph, which indicates no change in the relative percentages.

14.3.2 Chalk weathering

The chalk weathering project is a laboratory-based study, and therefore spatial analytical techniques are inappropriate.

14.3.3 River pollution

The river pollution project involves two randomly selected samples: the first is a set of points located on river channels, stratified according to their previous water-quality class; and the second is of 25 factories occupying riparian sites together with a further five control points, with measurements taken at a straight-line distance of 250 m upstream and downstream of the points. The rivers themselves are clearly linear features. However, their spatial pattern is not relevant to the pollution project, in which the data refer to samples of points. In the case of the first sample, the rivers are regarded as channels conveying chemical pollutants in solution rather than as spatial features: thus, provided that the sample sites are chosen at random, their location is immaterial.

There is one spatial issue worthy of examination with respect to the second sample. The samples of water are abstracted 250 m upstream and downstream of the factory and control sites. If the sinuosity of the rivers varies along these stretches then the distance between the abstraction points is likely to deviate around 500 m, which is the theoretical mean. Significant differences in the lengths of the river sections could distort the results of the chemical analyses, especially if they are not symmetrical about the sample site. Once the precise lengths of the stretches of rivers have been determined from the maps or from accurate field surveying, it might prove worthwhile to undertake a standard t test to see if their mean was significantly different from 500 m. A one-tailed test would be appropriate in this instance, since the mean sample distance between upstream and downstream sites cannot be less than 500 m.

14.3.4 Village communities

The observation units in the village communities project comprise a random sample of individuals in a particular settlement and therefore only limited spatial statistics are applicable. Careful random selection of the individuals has enabled standard statistical tests to be applied to the data, for example to determine whether distance from the development site affects people's attitude towards the proposal. Specific spatial analytic techniques are not appropriate.

14.4 REVIEW OF SPATIAL STATISTICS AND THE EXEMPLAR PROJECTS

With the exception of the land-use project, the exemplar projects were designed to illustrate the more general statistical procedures rather than the more specialised spatial statistics. The VMR and nearest-neighbour analyses of the spatial distributions of sample points have provided contrasting conclusions. These examples have emphasised that standard statistical software is often ill suited to undertaking geostatistical analyses. The data manipulation commands in MINITAB, which have been required to undertake these procedures, are quite complex and involve a number of repetitive operations, which makes the need for special software or command procedures abundantly obvious. Some of the software would have been more straightforward in SPSS-X. GIS software is now starting to face this challenge and to incorporate spatial analytical procedures.

Chapter 15
Summary of exemplar projects and conclusions

15.1 RESULTS FROM THE EXEMPLAR PROJECTS

Most statistics texts include realistic examples to illustrate the different techniques. Some books refer to the same example on a number of occasions, others use different data to demonstrate particular techniques. The four exemplar projects have attempted to go beyond this by looking at the whole process of geographical research and data analysis, and to emphasise that the purpose of using statistical techniques is to promote a scientific approach to the accumulation of geographical knowledge. In this regard, a statistical test which produces a non-significant result is still relevant. For instance, such a result might enable an investigator to conclude that two variables are unlikely to be related to each other, or that a group of sample means are only different through chance or sampling error. Such negative conclusions are of course disappointing, but should not be dismissed as worthless. It may be useful to know that two variables are uncorrelated, within the confines of the particular statistical technique and sample data, since it might enable one or both of them to be eliminated from the investigation, or at least to be regarded with some suspicion.

The projects have exemplified the application of various types of statistical analysis to geographical data and how computers can be used to undertake these analyses. Selected results from the projects have been presented in a piecemeal fashion at different stages in the text, but now, in the concluding chapter, these are drawn together into a more unified whole and reference is made to the projects' original aims and objectives. There are a number of additonal questions and hypotheses which could be asked of the project data (see Appendix III). One important aspect of academic research is that it should engender discussion and debate; in some instances the focus of such criticism is on methodological questions, while in others the interpretation of the results may be in dispute. Thus it is appropriate that the final two sections of this chapter attempt to look beyond the comparatively restricted confines of introductory statistical techniques. These sections consider any shortcomings in the projects and more advanced forms of statistical analysis which might be used to extend the basic projects.

15.1.1 Land-use project

The land-use project set out to examine patterns of land-use change in an area of Hertfordshire, north of London, by means of data from maps of the First and Second Land Utilisation Surveys, which were conducted in the 1930s and 1960s. The two samples reflected different approaches to spatial sampling and their results have been compared and contrasted. The project has also illustrated some of the difficulties which arise when using secondary sources of data. The results from the analyses are summarised in Table 15.1.

The Z- and t-test results indicate that both random samples were representative of the study area in relation to the mean area of arable land, and in the case of sample A also in respect of grass and agriculturally unproductive land, and for sample B for rough grazing. The changes in the areas of the seven land uses between the 1930s and 1960s proved to be highly significant, with very low probabilities for the W-test statistic. The land-use changes recorded by the two samples were compared and tested against each other by means of a Mann–Whitney test. Apart from agriculturally unproductive land and three land uses which were poorly represented in sample A, the two samples generated statistically consistent results. One particularly interesting result to emerge from sample B was that the rural-urban fringe and rural areas did not have significantly different mixes of land uses according to the Pearson's chi-square test. Strong positive Spearman's rank correlation coefficients were obtained for the relationship between the 1930s and 1960s areas of all seven land uses, which were significant at the 0.01 level except in the case of rough grazing. Straight line distance to an interchange on the M1 motorway was investigated as the independent variable for explaining the variability and distribution of plots sizes in sample A. Only a weak negative relationship was identified and the linear regression model was not significant.

15.1.2 Chalk weathering

The weathering of chalk is illustrative of the general processes of erosion, but is particularly prevalent where climatic controls exert a strong influence. A laboratory experiment was designed in order to eliminate the effect of certain confounding factors such the influence of vegetation or microstructures, which could have been problematic had field data been used. The project investigated three inter-connected factors: the effect of freeze–thaw temperature change; the role of water; and the influence of saline conditions. The analytical results are brought together in Table 15.2.

Table 15.1 Summary statistical analysis results for the land-use project

	Land uses						
	Arable	Permanent Grass	Orch'ds & M. Gard'g	Forest & Wood	R. Gr. & Moor	Hsg & Gardens	Agric Unprod.
LU1 (sample A)							
Test statistic (Z)	0.42	0.20	2.76	2.14	78.11	—	1.84
Probability (p)	0.67	0.84	0.01	0.03	<0.01	—	0.07
H_0 accept/reject	A	A	R	R	R	—	A
Apart from arable, permanent grass and agriculturally unproductive land uses, the sample means are significantly different from the population means.							
LU2 (sample B)							
Test statistic (t)	0.40	5.29	4.15	2.75	1.75	3.29	3.93
Probability (p)	0.70	<0.01	<0.01	0.01	0.10	<0.01	<0.01
H_0 accept/reject	A	R	R	R	A	R	R
Apart from arable, and rough grazing, heath and moorland, the sample means are significantly different from the population means.							
LU3 (sample B)							
Test statistic (W)	179.0	16.0	6.0	20.0	30.0	72.0	210.0
Probability (p)	<0.01	<0.01	<0.01	<0.01	0.02	0.01	<0.01
H_0 accept/reject	R	R	R	R	R	R	R
For all the land uses, there was a significant change in area between the 1930s and 1960s.							
LU4 (samples A and B)							
Test statistic (W)	416.0	284.0	—	—	—	246.0	249.0
Probability (p)	0.43	0.78	—	—	—	0.60	0.03
H_0 accept/reject	A	A	—	—	—	A	R
Only agriculturally unproductive land recorded a significantly different areal change between the 1930s and 1960s in samples A and B.							
LU5 (sample B)							
	Area type (urban-fringe and rural) by land use.						
Test statistic (χ^2)	9.32 (df = 6)						
Probability (p)	>0.10						
H_0 accept/reject	A						
There is no significant difference between the occurrence of the land uses and urban-fringe and rural locations.							
LU6 (sample B correlations between 1930s and 1960s areas)							
Correlation coefficient (r_s)	0.923	0.718	0.930	0.789	0.557	0.877	0.919
Significant r_s at 0.05 with 20 observations	0.447	0.447	0.447	0.447	0.447	0.447	0.447
H_0 accept/reject	R	R	R	R	R	R	R
For all land uses, the rank correlation coefficient is significant at the 0.05 level.							
LU7 (sample A)							
Regression equation: 1960s plot size = 51 − 0.07 (1930s plot size)							
Test statistic (F)	0.06						
Probability (p)	0.80						
H_0 accept/reject	A						
Plot size in the 1930s does not exert a significant controlling influence on plot size in the 1960s.							
LU7 (sample B regressions between 1930s area (independent) and 1960s area (dependent))							
Test statistic (F)	0.00	1.81	1.07	0.01	0.34	0.18	0.48
Probability (p)	0.99	0.20	0.31	0.91	0.57	0.68	0.50
H_0 accept/reject	A	A	A	A	A	A	A
For all land uses, the area in the 1930s does not exert a controlling influence on the area in the 1960s.							

Table 15.2 Summary statistical analysis results for chalk weathering project

	Treatments								
	1	2	3	4	5	6	7	8	9
CW1									
95% confidence intervals for mean total weight loss									
From:	16.1	19.6	0.9	4.7	7.7	0.8	1.2	0.9	0.4
To:	19.2	23.1	2.6	6.5	10.2	1.6	2.4	1.6	1.1
99% confidence intervals for mean total weight loss									
From:	15.9	18.9	0.5	4.3	7.2	0.6	1.0	0.8	0.3
To:	19.8	23.8	3.0	6.9	10.7	1.8	2.7	1.7	1.2
CW2									
Test statistic (t)	25.0	27.06	4.36	13.15	15.60	6.22	6.53	8.92	5.20
Probability (p)	<0.01	<0.01	<0.01	<0.01	<0.01	<0.01	<0.01	<0.01	<0.01
H_0 accept/reject	R	R	R	R	R	R	R	R	R

The loss of weight by the chalk blocks under the nine treatment regimes is significantly different from zero.

CW3					
Treatments	1 & 4	2 & 5	3 & 6	4 & 7	5 & 8
Test statistic (F)	2.74	1.87	4.24	2.37	16.91
Probability (p)	>0.10	>0.50	<0.05	>0.10	<0.01
H_0 accept/reject	A	A	R	A	R

The samples of chalk blocks which underwent treatments 3 and 6, and 5 and 8 come from populations which have significantly different variances with respect to weight loss.

CW4					
Treatments	1 & 4	2 & 5	3 & 6	4 & 7	5 & 8
Test statistic (t)	14.61	12.70	1.20	0.18	9.72
Probability (p)	<0.01	<0.01	0.24	0.86	<0.01
H_0 accept/reject	R	R	A	A	R

The mean weight losses of the samples of chalk blocks, which underwent treatments 1 and 4, 2 and 5, and 5 and 8, are significantly different.

CW5	
ANOVA on all sub-samples.	
Test statistic (F)	281.11
Probability (p)	<0.00
H_0 accept/reject	R

There is a significant difference in mean weight loss among the nine sub-samples.

CW6 (correlation of treatment by time)	1	2	3	4	5	6	7	8	9
Correlation coefficient (r)	−0.973	−0.936	−0.782	−0.980	−0.854	−0.877	−0.842	−0.962	−0.958

There are very strong negative relationships between weight loss and time for all treatments.

CW7 (regression of treatment (independent) on time (dependent))	1	2	3	4	5	6	7	8	9
Test statistic (F)	228.0	92.2	20.4	310.3	35.1	43.3	31.8	159.5	146.8
Probability (p)	<0.01	<0.01	<0.01	<0.01	<0.01	<0.01	<0.01	<0.01	<0.01
H_0 accept/reject	R	R	R	R	R	R	R	R	R

Time exerts a strong and significant controlling influence over the loss of weight by chalk blocks in all treatments.

The widths of the 95 and 99 per cent confidence intervals indicate that the different sub-samples were good estimators of the population. The weight losses which occurred over the 14 days of the experiment were in all cases significant, even for the control treatments, although for the latter the null hypotheses of no significant difference were only just rejected. The preliminary *F* tests carried out on the variances of selected pairs of treatment of sub-samples reveal that only in the case of treatments 5 and 8 was the probability low enough to conclude that the variances were significantly different. In the selection of tests there is clear evidence that the diurnal freeze–thaw temperature regime compared with a constant $-5\,°\mathrm{C}$ leads to greater weight loss. The oneway ANOVA on the nine sub-samples not surprisingly confirmed that the differences in weight loss were significant, although the procedure does not indicate whether one sub-sample is 'more different' than another. The weights of the blocks in the treatment of sub-samples declined as the experiment progressed, which resulted in a series of negative Pearson's product moment correlation coefficients. The control treatments displayed fairly weak relationships, with the strongest occurring for treatments involving saturated blocks. A similar conclusion emerged from the regression analysis of the same data, when time was used as the independent variable to predict weight loss.

15.1.3 River pollution

Degradation and despoliation of the environment have been on the geographer's research agenda for many years, although heightened public awareness in the subject might lead the unwary to conclude that it is of more recent origin. The impact of humankind's activities on the environment takes many forms, and the river pollution project has looked at one isolated aspect of the problem. The project has had two elements: first, the assessment of changes in the quality of river water; and second, the impact of industrial plants as sources of pollutant chemicals. Thus two related but separate samples were drawn in order to address these issues. Table 15.3 presents a summary of the statistical analysis carried out on Samples A and B.

Generally speaking, the differences in the concentrations of most of the chemicals between the 1985 national survey (population data) and the sampled water were significant according to the *t* tests for the five river-quality classes. The evidence from sample B clearly shows that water taken upstream and downstream of the factory sites did not have significantly different chemical concentrations. Water samples A and B were compared with respect to differences in the mean concentration of dissolved oxygen, biochemical demand and ammonia using the *t* test. The differences were not significant for the first two chemicals, but in the case of the mean concentrations of ammonia, which differed by 0.10 mg/l between the two samples, the result was significant at the 0.05 level. Both samples confirmed the clear association between flow rate and river-quality class with Pearson's chi-square statistics having probabilities lower than 0.001. The chemical concentrations in the water samples in sample B were tested statistically to determine whether current figures were connected with the river's class and flow-rate classification. Dissolved oxygen, biochemical oxygen demand and ammonia were clearly associated, whereas the metallic ions showed

Table 15.3 Summary statistical analysis results for river pollution project

	Chemical analysis					
	Dissolved oxygen	% Biochemical O_2 demand	Ammonia	Copper	Mercury	Zinc
RP1 (sample A)						
Quality class 1						
Test statistic (t)	2.15	0.18	3.81			
Probability (p)	0.36	0.86	<0.01			
H_0 accept/reject	A	A	R			
The mean concentration of ammonia is significantly different from the previous population figure for rivers in quality class 1.						
Quality class 2						
Test statistic (t)	2.61	11.92	4.47			
Probability (p)	0.01	<0.01	0.81			
H_0 accept/reject	R	R	A			
The mean levels of dissolved oxygen and biochemical oxygen demand are significantly different from the previous population figures for rivers in quality class 2.						
Quality class 3						
Test statistic (t)	2.37	11.95	0.25			
Probability (p)	0.02	<0.01	0.81			
H_0 accept/reject	R	R	A			
The mean levels of dissolved oxygen and biochemical oxygen demand are significantly different from the previous population figures for rivers in quality class 3.						
Quality class 4						
Test statistic (t)	4.58	14.47	3.65			
Probability (p)	<0.01	<0.01	<0.01			
H_0 accept/reject	R	R	R			
The mean levels of dissolved oxygen, biochemical oxygen demand and ammonia are significantly different from the previous population figures for rivers in quality class 4.						
Quality class 5						
Test statistic (t)	13.98	16.66	7.07			
Probability (p)	<0.01	<0.01	<0.01			
H_0 accept/reject	R	R	R			
The mean levels of dissolved oxygen, biochemical oxygen demand and ammonia are significantly different from the previous population figures for rivers in quality class 5.						
RP2 (sample B)						
Control samples						
Test statistic (t)	1.70	0.28	0.93			
Probability (p)	0.16	0.80	0.41			
H_0 accept/reject	A	A	A			
There is no significant difference in the mean concentration of the chemicals up/downstream of the sites.						
Other samples						
Test statistic (t)	0.97	0.99	1.01			
Probability (p)	0.34	0.33	0.29			
H_0 accept/reject	A	A	A			
There is no significant difference in the mean concentration of the chemicals up/downstream of the sites.						
RP3 (samples A and B)						
Test statistic (t)	1.90	1.20	2.77			
Probability (p)	0.06	0.23	0.01			
H_0 accept/reject	A	A	R			
There is a significant difference in the concentration of ammonia between samples A and B.						

continued overleaf

Table 15.3 (*continued*)

	Chemical analysis					
	Dissolved oxygen	% Biochemical O_2 demand	Ammonia	Copper	Mercury	Zinc
RP4 (sample A)						
	Flow rate by water-quality class					
Test statistic (χ^2)	90.77 DF = 32					
Probability (p)	<0.01					
H_0 accept/reject	R					
There is a significant association between flow rate and river-quality class in sample A.						
RP4 (sample B)						
	Flow rate by water-quality class					
Test statistic (χ^2)	552.13 DF = 28					
Probability (p)	<0.01					
H_0 accept/reject	R					
There is a significant association between flow rate and river-quality class in sample B.						
RP5 (sample B)						
Water-quality class						
Test statistic (H)	277.18	277.771	215.39	6.13	6.02	18.70
Probability (p)	<0.01	<0.01	<0.01	0.19	0.20	<0.01
H_0 accept/reject	R	R	R	A	A	R
Apart from copper and mercury, the median concentrations of the chemicals were significantly different between the five water-quality classes.						
Flow-rate class						
Test statistic (H)	191.01	190.53	148.27	9.83	5.86	27.01
Probability (p)	<0.01	<0.01	<0.01	0.20	0.56	<0.01
H_0 accept/reject	R	R	R	A	A	R
Apart from copper and mercury, the median concentrations of the chemicals were significantly different between the five flow rate classes.						
Up/downstream						
Test statistic (H)	9.84	0.00	0.50	61.58	84.52	142.17
Probability (p)	<0.01	0.99	0.48	<0.01	<0.01	<0.01
H_0 accept/reject	R	A	A	R	R	R
Apart from biochemical oxygen demand and ammonia, the median concentrations of the chemicals were significantly different between the up- and downstream sites.						
RP6 (sample A)						
By precipitation						
Correlation coefficient (r)	0.020	−0.047	0.034	—	—	—
By temperature						
Correlation coefficient (r)	0.098	−0.120	0.173	—	—	—
RP6 (sample B)						
By precipitation						
Correlation coefficient (r)	−0.105	−0.400	0.038	0.035	0.101	0.159
By temperature						
Correlation coefficient (r)	0.508	0.138	0.457	0.061	0.081	−0.105
Apart from between temperature and biochemical oxygen demand and ammonia in sample B, there are only weak relationships between the chemical concentrations and prior weather.						

Table 15.4 Summary statistical analysis results for the village communities project

VC1	Age of respondent	Housing tenure	Car availability	Economic position
Test statistic (χ^2)	152.32	36.53	0.02	19.23
Probability (p)	<0.01	<0.01	0.90	<0.01
H_0 accept/reject	R	R	A	R

The age, housing tenure and economic position frequency distributions in the sample of respondents are significantly different from those in the previous Population Census.

VC2	Distance from development
Test statistic (D/Z)	2.72
Probability (p)	<0.01
H_0 accept/reject	R

Respondents' residences are not randomly distributed in relation to the site for the proposed development.

VC3	Change of attitude
Test statistic (χ^2)	2.13
Probability (p)	0.14
H_0 accept/reject	A

Attendance at the public meeting has not significantly changed people's attitude to the proposed development.

VC4	Recoded length of residence by attitude to proposed development
Test statistic (χ^2)	1.00
Probability (p)	0.96
H_0 accept/reject	A

Length of residence is not significantly associated with people's attitude to the proposed development.

VC5	Economic position by attitude to proposed development controlling for housing tenure					
	Own outright	Buy with mortg.	LA rented	Pr rent	Tied	Other
Test statistic (χ^2)	3.164	6.827	3.943	0.900	2.000	2.000
Probability (p)	0.53	0.34	0.68	0.83	0.37	0.16
H_0 accept/reject	A	A	A	A	A	A

There is no significant association between these three variables.

VC6	Type of housing by attitude to proposed development
Correlation coefficient (ϕ)	0.06
Probability (p)	0.55
H_0 accept/reject	A

Type of housing and attitude to the proposed development are not significantly related to each other.

VC7	Length of residence by number of friends
Correlation coefficient (r_s)	−0.029
Probability (p)	0.378
H_0 accept/reject	A

continued overleaf

Table 15.4 (*continued*)

Length of residence and number of friends are not significantly related with each other.

VC8

Regression equation: Number of friends = 5.35 + 0.018 Length of residence	
Probability (p)	0.51
H_0 accept/reject	A

Length of residence does not exert a significant controlling influence on number of friends.

no such pattern. The correlation analysis of the chemical and climatic variables suggested conclusively that weather conditions in the period before the water samples were abstracted were not significantly related to the concentration levels.

15.1.4 Village communities

The last two or three decades have witnessed a reversal in the general trend for rural depopulation, which prevailed up to the middle of this century. The populations of many villages within commuting distance of employment centres or in attractive retirement locations have been growing as people move out of urban areas. A number of writers, going back as far as Pahl's *'Urbs in Rure'* study in Hertfordshire in the 1960s (Pahl 1965), have discussed the potential for conflict which exists between the newcomer and indigenous residents of rural areas. Such conflict may be manifested in residents' differential reactions to development proposals, which has been the subject of the village communities project. The summary results are shown in Table 15.4.

The sample survey produced a mix of respondents who were reasonably representative of the parent population according to the univariate Pearson's chi-square test, although there were significantly more elderly people and local authority households in the sample than in the village population. The Kolmogorov–Smirnov test, however, clearly shows that the interviewees were randomly distributed with respect to Cowper's Farm, the site proposed for the industrial development. Thus it appears that any spatial bias in the data has been avoided. Length of residence was hypothesised as an important determinant of attitude as far as the proposed development was concerned; however, residents in the village were undifferentiated with respect to this variable. Similarly, negative results were obtained when examining the respondent's housing tenure and economic position. The phi coefficient confirmed the previous results by failing to identify a significant relationship between newcomer/indigenous residents and attitude to the development. The development of friendships and social contacts within the village (dependent variable) also appears to have a negative relationship with length of residence. The survey results overall suggest that significant divisions do not exist within the study village. This may indicate a number of further avenues for investigation. Perhaps there has been so much in-migration to the village that truly indigenous inhabitants are no longer to be found. Alternatively, a narrower definition of 'newcomers' may be needed — for example, under 5 years' residence — in order to elicit evidence of social divisions.

15.2 COMPLEXITY OF REAL-WORLD PROBLEMS

Research questions in geography are intrinsically complex, linking together a number of different factors in an attempt to explain or understand the distribution of phenomena. Some simplification was inevitably necessary in the design of the four exemplar projects, and the analytical techniques already described could be used to answer different questions and be applied to other variables and attributes in the datasets. Equally, the questions which were investigated could have been looked at in other ways. The specification of a research problem or the definition of a topic to be investigated can be approached from either the theoretical or empirical direction. For simplicity, these can be thought of as equivalent to bottom-up or top-down approaches, although this analogy perhaps gives the false impression that they are necessarily opposing approaches, when this may not be the case.

The empirical approach is generally regarded as much more straightforward, since the investigator devises the research problem on the basis of observing something that appears to be interesting or different. But why is something interesting or different? If it is because its occurrence is unexpected or important, then this implies that some theoretical reference point has been used to determine what is expected or what is unimportant. For example, suppose a researcher notices that on average prices of properties in streets composed mainly of Victorian houses fell by less during the recent slump than those in roads where there are 20th-century properties. Is this difference unexpected or important, and therefore worthy of investigation? There are a number of reasons why the answer to this question might be yes. Perhaps people prefer to live in older houses and are thus prepared to pay more for them. Maybe Victorian houses have larger rooms and so they occupy more physical space. Newer properties may be more plentiful, leading to a surplus of supply over demand. These possible explanations clearly suggest an implicit reference to some anterior, theoretical information generally connected with the economic concepts of supply and demand. So even if research questions are posed on the basis of observation, they usually imply some theoretical foundation.

15.3 LIMITATIONS OF BASIC STATISTICAL TECHNIQUES

The book has followed a progression from the simpler to the more complicated statistical techniques. The move from description to explanation, from single- to multiple-sample investigations, and from univariate to bivariate procedures reflects this progression. The sequence can be taken further into an examination of a range of multivariate techniques involving one, two or more samples. In some respects, particularly as far as essential concepts are concerned, these more advanced techniques are but extensions to the principles which have been discussed in this volume. This final section is intended to whet the reader's appetite for taking statistical analysis into these new realms.

Research problems in geography, and indeed in other disciplines, are only partially resolved by the use of univariate or bivariate techniques. Multivariate procedures are required which can either summarise a larger number of variables in a descriptive fashion, or allow complex relationships between them to be explored and hypotheses to be tested. These two approaches form a convenient categorisation of multivariate techniques. Simple linear regression allows a relationship based on dependence between two variables to be examined, and other bivariate regression techniques permit non-linear relationships to be investigated, whereas regression analysis in its multivariate form takes the process further. The manner in which the values of a single variable are dependent upon those of two or more other variables can be expressed as a mathematical equation. In essence, the multiple regression equation is an extension of its simple linear counterpart. Superficially, it differs by the addition of slope coefficients for the extra independent variables, thus:

$$Y = a + b_1X_1 + b_2X_2 + b_3X_3 + \cdots + b_nX_n + e$$

where n represents the number of independent variables and e the residual or error. Multiple regression can be carried out in different ways: one approach considers all the independent variables together, while another allows them to be entered into the analysis one after the other. The latter enables the researcher to determine the relative importance of the different variables by an examination of their contribution to the change in r^2, the coefficient of determination. This statistic signifies the amount of the total variation which is explained. Canonical correlation is an alternative form of dependence analysis in which variables are examined in groups rather than individually.

Multivariate techniques in the second major group examine the interdependence between the individuals which make up either a population or sample of observations. The statistical procedures covered in the previous chapters have assumed that observations are independent or uncorrelated with each other. The variables were the main focus of attention. In the analysis of interdependence rather than one variable being explained by the others, and a causal relationship being hypothesised, all variables are regarded as sources of differentiation between the observations. The results of these statistical procedures are generally unsuited to hypothesis testing, so some debate has emerged over their usefulness and validity. The three interdependence techniques most often employed by geographers are factor analysis, cluster analysis and discriminant analysis.

Factor analysis comprises a group of related techniques including principal components analysis, which is sometimes the favoured option for geographical applications (e.g. Ilbery 1981; Hodge and Monk 1991). In brief, the different types of factor analysis have certain features in common. One comparatively large set of 'input' variables is reduced to a smaller set of factors or components, although the former term will be used for simplicity. The new factors are multi-dimensional, composite variables, which encapsulate, in a mathematical sense, certain aspects of the original variables from which they are derived. A factor is a mean variable, in the statistical sense, which is closely related to the originals and accounts for some of the variance between them. Factor analyses are iterative procedures, which produce a new composite factor that explains a little more of the overall variance at each successive iteration or pass through the data. The starting point for carrying out a factor analysis is the complete product moment correlation matrix between all the original variables. The sum of the correlation coefficients for each variable, including a value, usually 1.0, for its correlation with itself, are summed and divided by the square root of the total sum of the correlations. The resulting figures, known as *factor loadings*, which express the relationship between each 'input' variable and the new factor. The sum of the squared factor loadings provides a statistic, called an *eigenvalue*, which denotes the amount of the total variance explained by the factor. The eigenvalues become smaller with each successive factor that is derived, since the unexplained part of the total variance becomes progressively smaller. Once the eigenvalue falls below 1.0, the new factor does not account for any more of the total variance than a single input variable. Factor analyses therefore reduce a large number of variables to a smaller group of composite factors, and an important output from the procedure are *factor scores*. These provide a measure of the relationship between observations and the new factors. The factor scores are particularly useful in geographical investigations since they can be mapped to show the spatial distribution of values on the new factors. When derived from principal components analysis they can also be used as an input to cluster analysis.

Cluster analysis has also been used in a variety of geographical applications, particularly where a substantial number of observations or spatial units are to be classified. One notable example is the clustering of the 130 000 enumeration districts on a selection of variables from the 1981 Census of Population (Openshaw 1983; Charlton *et al.* 1985). Whereas factor analysis is concerned with reducing a potentially large set of variables into a more manageable number of factors, cluster analysis concentrates on collapsing the number observations into coherent and identifiable groups. Like factor analysis, cluster analysis refers to a collection of related techniques; Everitt's (1974) review still remains an invaluable account of the different forms. Most cluster analysis techniques are iterative and the clusters are identified according to one of two main strategies. The *agglomerative* approach starts by treating the individual observations as discrete entities, and each pass through the data results in one individual or a previously defined cluster being joined to another. Ultimately a single, undifferentiated cluster is produced of which all the observations are members. The *divisive* strategy works in the opposite direction: starting from a position where all entities have been assigned to one cluster, individuals or groups of its members are progressively removed. Finally, the number of clusters equals the number of individual observations.

A criterion is required in order to decide which individual should join another at each iteration. There would be little point in moving observations from one group to another in some random or arbitrary fashion. Several mathematical measures are available, which can all be thought of as measuring the similarity or dissimilarity between the entities. Two measures frequently used in geographical studies are *Euclidean distance* and the *sum of squares.* Euclidean distance essentially measures 'how far apart' two individuals are in n-dimensional space, where n equals the number of variables. The sum-of-squares measure or *Ward's method*, which has some similarity with Euclidean distance, concentrates on the sum of the squared deviations of each cluster from its centroid in n-dimensional space. Observations are joined to form groups of the basis of the minimum increase in the within-groups sum of squares, termed by Ward the *error sum of squares.* One problem with cluster analysis is that few satisfactory statistics are available to assist the analyst in deciding when to call a halt to the analysis and to accept the clusters which have been created.

Discriminant analysis tackles multivariate research questions from yet another point of view. Linear combinations of variables are used to distinguish between two or more groups of observations. The technique predicts into which group a particular case will fall according to its values on the set of variables. A particularly useful application of the procedure is to investigate whether a prior classification of cases into two or more groups is valid after some time has elapsed since the original allocation was made. Discriminant analysis finds the linear combination of variables which best allocates the observations to the prior groups in two ways: either by entering all variables directly into the analysis, or by including them in a stepwise fashion so that a set of variables is found which achieves the most satisfactory allocation of cases to the predefined groups. Discriminant analysis has not been used very widely by geographers, although given the fundamental interest in classification, which lies at the heart of much geographical research, greater use of the technique is perhaps warranted in the future.

Appendix I
Village communities project questionnaire

The questionnaire is addressed to individuals, but also includes questions relating to the respondent's household.

All information will be treated in strict confidence.

Interview Number ...... (1)

1. How many years have you lived in this village? ...... (2)

FOR THOSE MOVING IN WITHIN THE LAST 10 YEARS

2. What was your MAIN reason for moving:
    1. Retirement ...... (3)
    2. Employment
    3. Social
       (e.g. to be near friends/relatives)
    4. Other

    Check ONE only.

3. Which of the following characteristics of the village attracted you:
    1. its size ...... (4)
    2. its facilities
    3. its people ...... (5)
    4. its appearance
    5. something else

    Check ONE or TWO only.

    ASK ALL

4. How many people live in your household ...... (6)
    NOTE: A household is a group of people usually eating at least one meal a day together.

5. Does/is your household
    1. own its housing outright? ...... (7)
    2. purchasing its housing with a mortgage or other loan?
    3. renting from a local authority or housing association?
    4. renting privately (furnished or unfurnished)?
    5. tied to your work?
    6. of another type?

    Check ONE only.

6. Do you or any other member of your household have use of a car? Yes/No (8)

Interviewer to record respondent's sex. M/F (9)

7. In which of the following age groups are you? ...... (10)
   1. 18–24 yrs
   2. 25–44 yrs
   3. 45–54 yrs
   4. 55–64 yrs
   5. 65 yrs and over
8. What is your present economic position? ...... (11)
   1. Employer or self-employed
   2. Employee (full-time)
   3. Employee (part-time)
   4. Unemployed
   5. Housewife/househusband
   6. Retired
   7. Other (include student, etc.)

IF 1, 2 OR 3:

9. Do you work in this village? Yes/No (12)
10. How do you travel to work (main mode)? ...... (13)
    1. Car driver
    2. Car passenger
    3. Motor cycle
    4. Bus
    5. Train
    6. Cycle
    7. Other
11. Please indicate into which of the following broad bands your TOTAL ANNUAL HOUSEHOLD income falls ...... (14)
    1. Less than £10,000
    2. £10,000–£19,999
    3. £20,000–£29,999
    4. £30,000–£39,999
    5. £40,000–£49,999
    6. £50,000 and over
12. How far is your house from Cowper's Farm? (to the nearest 100 m) ...... (15)
13. How many people in this village would you regard as friends (i.e. see in either your house or their's at least once a week) ...... (16)
14. Do you feel that there are sufficient employment opportunities for young people in this village? Yes/No (17)

IF NO

15. Should employment opportunities be increased by: ...... (18)
    1. relaxing restriction on new development?
    2. encouraging existing employers to expand their activities?
    3. providing better public transport for commuters on weekday mornings and evenings?
    4. none of these

    Check ONE only.

16. Have you heard about the proposal to build a 15-unit industrial estate on Cowper's Farm? Yes/No (19)

IF YES at Q16

17. a) Are you in favour of the proposal? Yes/No (20)
    b) Have you discussed the proposal with any of the following:
       other members of your household? Yes/No (21)
       other people in the village? Yes/No (22)
       anyone else? Yes/No (23)
    c) Have you read about the proposal in the local newspaper? Yes/No (24)
    d) Have you attended any public meeting about the proposal? Yes/No (25)

IF YES AT 17 (d)

18. Did the meeting change your attitude to the proposed development? Yes/No (26)

IF NO AT 16

19. In general do you welcome such a development? Yes/No (27)
20. If you had known about the proposal would you have attended a public meeting? Yes/No (28)

TO ALL

21. What effect do you think such a development will have on the village?
    1. Encourage more people to live here ...... (29)
    2. Provide jobs for school leavers and young people
    3. Increase the amount of traffic
    4. Harm the character of the village
    5. Prevent the closure of local shops and facilities

    Check ONE only

Thank you for completing the questionnaire.

Notes for coding and data entry:

1. Unless otherwise indicated use:
   1 for Yes
   2 for No
   8 for Don't Know
   9 for Missing

2. Insert the appropriate code number(s) appearing alongside the choices in the space(s) provided.

3. Where a number is required (e.g. Q 1) record in the space provided by ... Enter these onto the computer as whole numbers (integers).

4. Variable numbers (1 to 29) are shown in brackets.

Appendix II
Random digits

6627282263	9159294694	7409383853	1364818195	8953861651
9707179631	7325790271	2961345919	6470207760	5675627204
6738720374	6348783314	1349273829	6584484976	8900018553
9927703459	8038851347	1910033799	4995926192	7171092938
5661347154	8281602977	8511180070	8267676825	3168968807
9029903446	7616637964	4146827806	6566783701	1494740731
4674213811	9053732937	5868846371	2329532256	7389702099
2951238056	7418388371	8041385328	0355608239	6577349807
6490733118	3262893645	4071256323	9433569010	0658802343
3425948478	5546877360	1772874995	4058630322	1237847912
2493791914	8265798927	3209226962	8361159206	2331009525
1536294366	6809813755	2130207454	0183094318	4973456235
0830754404	3463592947	2611437824	4852886157	2657905290
1581921425	9020386477	8837851328	7325870659	1213669837
8776396885	8835431596	3176145531	0107903889	1475665245
1831366638	5859792099	8785947841	1814697154	3077581438
0593750375	2628400580	7963933058	2875473203	5045100462
2381293477	7523901611	8494375239	2213429707	4999400311
5296572515	3261993155	7578368207	8931088617	8279499205
1893691768	1030790541	0199230897	5003003773	5768790965
5709252959	1567554893	3574733187	0345559774	7625943146
2879431610	5715951101	8656474428	7062942743	3976902807
0679758006	0285059485	3349826500	0600481334	3665560179
9999105232	3209893486	6082331612	0783403789	6247556396
6718667751	9550616035	4852682250	1856518014	5165551790
2987177880	2062022879	0157504529	6239466179	9194712436
5303760471	9298930474	8828282575	9606088158	7893113776
5882992717	7204779711	7067201546	9960748269	8773461390
3330319334	6330166688	5065211620	2892200589	0722698824
5542622907	6198220374	2905592121	1955965291	1038682222
5010694787	7995720461	4814491501	1399124815	9549477173
9297445493	3365815197	2659883360	4148582731	8941695667
1752753593	9619075200	4696136010	2509226368	7957189204
6060943605	1021401321	4562942290	9908638430	6049653189
8009266411	3683914633	6076565710	8113704464	3359373943

Appendix III
Details of the project datasets

The raw data for the projects can be read into either MINITAB or SPSS-X in order to replicate or experiment with statistical analysis techniques. In the following sections, the structures of the data records for the six datasets are illustrated by 3 sample records:

Sample Records for Land-Use Sample A

A	B	C	D	E	F	G
166	103	1	3	35	1	25
3	176	2	1	7	3	3
49	107	2	5	6	4	1

A = Easting, B = Northing, C = Urban/Rural code, D = Land-Use Code 1930s, E = Plot Area 1930s, F = Land-Use Code 1960s and G = Plot Area 1960s.

Raw data for land-use project sample A

166	103	1	3	35	1	25
3	176	2	1	7	3	3
49	107	2	5	6	4	1
173	195	2	4	14	3	47
59	177	2	3	65	1	53
193	144	1	3	46	3	34
189	112	1	2	17	2	4
106	125	1	4	5	6	14
98	165	1	3	23	3	44
122	140	1	2	27	1	55
88	141	1	3	16	1	40
64	137	2	1	10	1	16
94	182	2	2	6	1	10
190	104	2	1	57	1	100
23	109	2	1	30	1	21
123	186	1	4	17	3	9
15	107	2	7	3	7	4
96	162	1	1	39	6	1
61	122	2	1	43	1	122
78	145	1	6	2	6	2
15	105	2	3	65	3	150

83	134	1	1	75	1	142
96	116	1	4	30	1	142
100	102	1	1	100	1	178
191	154	2	2	23	1	52
120	177	1	5	12	1	153
7	139	2	1	20	1	29
173	181	2	1	50	1	56
105	112	1	3	45	1	178
152	123	1	1	28	1	21
55	133	2	1	30	1	34
118	183	1	3	43	3	2
33	184	2	1	5	1	18
186	136	1	2	9	1	41
85	157	2	4	25	1	53
88	153	2	3	65	3	9
21	103	2	1	25	1	17
95	159	1	7	4	7	4
107	129	1	1	8	1	8
70	180	2	3	31	1	19

Sample Records for Land-Use Sample B

A	B	C	D	E	F	G	H	I	J	K	L	M	N	O	P	Q
3	14	2	31	8	19	36	2	0	4	52	0	4	38	0	0	6
0	14	2	36	5	38	9	8	1	3	45	0	39	7	3	1	5
15	16	1	30	28	24	9	0	3	6	35	32	14	4	0	5	10

A = Easting, B = Northing, C = Urban/Rural code, D = Agriculture 1930s, E = Market Gardening 1930s, F = Grass 1930s, G = Woodland & Forestry 1930s, H = Heath and Rough Grazing 1930s, I = Housing and gardens 1930s, J = Agriculturally unproductive 1930s, K = Agriculture 1960s, L = Market Gardening 1960s, M = Grass 1960s, N = Woodland & Forestry 1960s, O = Heath and Rough Grazing 1960s, P = Housing and gardens 1960s, Q = Agriculturally unproductive 1960s.

Raw data for land-use project sample B

3	14	2	31	8	19	36	2	0	4	52	0	4	38	0	0	6
0	14	2	36	5	38	9	8	1	3	45	0	39	7	3	1	5
15	16	1	30	28	24	9	0	3	6	35	32	14	4	0	5	10
18	16	1	27	3	40	20	4	2	4	37	0	39	11	0	3	10
14	14	1	22	6	18	14	3	22	15	14	1	8	2	0	54	21
7	17	2	37	21	16	17	1	2	6	49	12	11	17	0	2	9
13	13	1	8	9	11	4	35	8	25	9	6	5	0	28	14	38
15	17	1	36	7	29	7	5	6	10	53	9	18	4	0	4	12
15	15	1	39	7	36	5	2	5	6	46	4	26	4	1	8	11
1	17	2	19	8	37	17	4	6	9	19	2	36	9	8	13	13
15	11	1	51	0	23	16	4	0	6	66	0	9	12	1	0	12
15	15	1	36	7	29	7	5	6	10	46	4	26	4	1	8	11
18	17	1	37	2	25	32	2	0	2	48	0	20	28	0	0	4
10	14	1	49	0	34	6	2	0	9	63	0	22	2	0	0	13
1	16	2	28	3	55	9	1	3	1	30	0	57	8	0	3	2
4	10	2	42	3	43	3	6	0	3	51	0	32	8	2	1	6
5	18	2	60	2	17	6	8	1	6	67	1	14	1	5	2	10
5	19	2	23	5	55	4	1	0	12	19	1	49	2	8	5	16

8 16 2 63 3 20 5 2 0 7 77 0 10 2 1 0 10
19 15 2 49 2 23 19 0 1 6 54 1 15 18 0 2 10

Sample Records for Chalk Weathering Experiment

A	B	C	D	E	F	G	H	I	J	K	L	M	N	O	P	Q
1130	.0129	.9929	.9729	.8328	.9527	.8226	.4123	.7822	.5421	.0919	.7818	.5216	.7615	.0410	.98	
2130	.0029	.8929	.6529	.0428	.5628	.0127	.9825	.9123	.4319	.9818	.4017	.4915	.8212	.32 9	.89	
3129	.9829	.9829	.8329	.5629	.3728	.9928	.9827	.6727	.4324	.4323	.0018	.0017	.5415	.4512	.56	

A = Block number, B = Treatment type, C to Q = Weight at time 0 (start) through to time 14 (end).

Raw data for chalk weathering project

```
1130.0129.9929.9729.8328.9527.8226.4123.7822.5421.0919.7818.5216.7615.0410.98
2130.0029.8929.6529.0428.5628.0127.9825.9123.4319.9818.4017.4915.8212.32 9.89
3129.9829.9829.8329.5629.3728.9928.9827.6727.4324.4323.0018.0017.5415.4512.56
4130.0230.0229.9929.6929.3528.9828.3227.6926.8325.2122.3221.8919.3217.0313.02
5130.0430.0429.7829.6729.5629.0328.3227.5627.0925.2121.4819.6719.4517.0615.43
6130.0029.8929.5629.3828.9828.3527.0725.5423.7823.4321.3419.6918.4516.0915.40
7129.9929.9929.9729.9529.9428.5427.8327.0024.8722.2919.5917.6516.7615.0412.05
8129.9729.9729.9529.9428.5627.9927.9826.8725.8723.4317.8816.8715.4313.219.89
9130.0030.0029.9728.4327.3425.3425.8922.0316.0415.3412.8911.159.058.937.65
10130.0030.0029.4329.5429.4328.3226.8225.6323.6723.5019.4318.4317.3216.1214.37
11129.9929.4329.3228.3527.3225.9825.3222.3421.4519.6519.4318.2117.8915.0714.89
12130.0530.0029.9128.3426.3223.4522.5519.6518.3215.9815.6514.0714.0613.0512.34
13229.9929.9929.9929.9929.9929.9929.9528.9927.4326.0319.4316.788.435.785.65
14230.1030.1030.1030.1030.0630.0029.6726.1919.3223.0018.0010.43 9.348.007.61
15230.0030.0030.0030.0030.0029.9929.9829.3428.6525.3219.4315.4813.6512.5712.09
16230.0530.0530.0530.0130.0029.7928.3726.8125.9319.9817.3212.729.718.986.45
17229.9329.9329.9329.9129.8029.5328.4926.4317.4515.3211.5711.5010.2110.069.87
18229.6829.6829.5429.2329.0828.1927.1826.0823.7122.5622.4319.0415.0213.0613.01
19230.0030.0030.0030.0029.9929.9929.9728.0723.0919.0116.2913.438.458.047.65
20230.1230.1230.1230.1230.1030.0929.3128.0924.0019.4316.3011.329.498.356.67
21230.0030.0030.0029.8329.6729.3528.0625.4222.3119.9219.5518.3211.0210.4310.11
22229.5529.5529.5429.5029.3428.3927.3726.1721.0619.4817.0210.398.878.798.77
23230.0030.0029.3228.4627.6527.4521.0019.1217.8917.5516.2710.326.076.004.56
24230.2330.2329.9029.8927.0426.3925.4519.2117.3216.6516.2915.1313.0512.0011.45
25330.0030.0030.0030.0030.0030.0030.0030.0029.9929.9226.8729.6629.3428.98
26330.0430.0430.0430.0430.0430.0430.0430.0430.0430.0129.8928.9628.3327.97
27329.8729.8729.8729.8729.8729.8729.8729.8729.8729.8729.8829.7628.2326.6626.45
28330.1230.1230.1230.1230.1230.1230.1230.1230.1029.9929.8928.6827.7126.7426.12
29330.0030.0030.0030.0030.0030.0030.0030.0030.0030.0029.9429.8728.9128.7328.67
30329.7129.7129.7129.7129.7129.7129.7129.7129.7129.7129.7029.5627.8526.8726.40
31329.8329.8329.8329.8329.8329.8329.8329.8229.8229.8029.6628.9528.7828.5628.00
32330.0230.0230.0230.0230.0230.0230.0230.0230.0230.0230.0130.0130.0030.0030.00
33330.0030.0030.0030.0030.0030.0030.0030.0029.9629.9429.4528.9827.9027.7827.67
34329.9929.9929.9929.9929.9929.9929.9929.9929.9929.9929.9829.9829.9729.9729.95
35330.0430.0430.0430.0430.0430.0430.0430.0430.0229.9929.8728.9328.9028.7828.78
36330.0030.0030.0030.0030.0030.0030.0030.0029.9929.9929.9829.9829.9829.9829.98
37430.0530.0529.9329.8929.8528.0628.0127.6127.5427.0726.9426.0124.2624.2524.21
38430.0130.0129.9529.9028.9028.7028.6128.0628.0127.4527.3527.0326.9426.9026.87
39429.8929.8929.8929.8929.8929.4028.3728.3528.3126.7226.5326.0726.0125.3625.34
```

40430.0130.0130.0129.1028.6528.5027.8327.3526.9826.7925.9825.3225.0525.0024.33
41430.0030.0029.6329.6229.3528.9928.9828.6528.3527.6127.4226.3225.7625.6925.68
42430.0030.0029.8929.8729.4429.3128.4428.3528.0427.7227.7226.0624.0624.0023.43
43429.8729.8729.8729.8729.8029.7828.9428.7528.7327.4926.0625.3221.9421.8921.67
44430.0330.0330.0330.0329.9929.8728.1928.0127.8427.3826.1726.0925.8025.6625.65
45430.0430.0430.0430.0429.8929.8729.0628.4525.3025.3025.3025.2524.6724.0223.98
46429.9329.9329.9329.9029.8528.6728.5528.3428.3127.5827.5426.0025.8325.0525.01
47429.9829.9829.5628.9027.9827.8827.3327.3227.0226.9826.3224.6624.5624.4024.32
48430.0030.0030.0029.9029.8929.0328.7328.6727.0826.4425.0523.4623.4523.4022.12
49530.0130.0130.0130.0130.0130.0130.0129.9929.0028.7827.4423.6721.0621.0020.98
50529.9929.9929.9929.9929.9929.9929.9929.9929.9929.0923.0721.9821.0020.0019.67
51530.0030.0030.0030.0030.0030.0030.0030.0029.8628.3424.9522.5019.6819.0518.99
52530.0630.0630.0630.0630.0630.0630.0630.0630.0630.0630.0630.0126.0024.6022.74
53530.1330.1330.1330.1330.1330.1330.1030.0430.0429.1926.7525.0824.0924.0023.45
54530.2530.2530.2530.2530.2530.2530.2530.2529.7629.7826.8925.6521.0621.0020.23
55530.5630.5630.5630.5630.5630.5630.0029.5029.0128.5426.3820.9019.6519.4519.44
56529.9929.9929.9929.9929.9929.9928.9828.9829.9829.9828.9028.4524.3224.3223.00
57530.0030.0030.0030.0030.0030.0030.0030.0030.0029.8927.0425.0024.2824.28
58530.0030.0030.0030.0030.0030.0030.0030.0028.9027.9822.7622.5019.6719.3218.23
59530.0230.0230.0230.0230.0230.0230.0230.0029.8927.1627.1226.3422.6522.3422.12
60529.9829.9829.9829.9829.9829.9829.9829.9329.9128.9128.9028.8725.6320.5620.55
61630.0030.0030.0030.0030.0030.0030.0030.0030.0029.9929.6529.0229.0128.9928.99
62630.0030.0030.0030.0030.0030.0030.0030.0030.0030.0030.0029.9929.7829.7729.76
63630.0030.0030.0030.0030.0030.0030.0030.0029.9329.9329.7129.6728.9028.6728.14
64629.7629.7629.7629.7629.7629.7629.7029.7029.6528.7128.6528.5428.0228.0228.00
65630.0030.0030.0030.0030.0030.0030.0030.0030.0030.0029.8929.3428.9928.5628.45
66630.0430.0430.0430.0430.0430.0430.0430.0430.0430.0430.0430.0430.0329.6629.14
67630.0530.0530.0530.0530.0530.0530.0530.0430.0329.9929.9829.6729.6729.5429.34
68630.0030.0029.9829.7229.9629.9528.9028.7229.7228.9828.6528.4327.9827.9827.98
69629.9929.9929.9929.9929.9929.9929.9929.9929.8929.7829.0128.4528.3428.3328.33
70630.4930.4930.4930.4930.4930.4930.4930.4930.4930.4730.0129.8929.7629.7229.70
71630.0530.0530.0530.0530.0530.0530.0530.0530.0530.0530.0230.0130.0130.0030.00
72630.0030.0030.0030.0030.0030.0030.0029.9829.9829.9829.6829.6829.6728.9028.24
73730.0030.0030.0030.0030.0030.0030.0030.0030.0029.9829.9829.9628.9527.4427.33
74730.0330.0330.0330.0330.0330.0330.0130.0029.9429.8329.6828.9928.9828.9828.98
75730.1230.1230.1230.1230.1230.1230.1120.1130.1030.0529.7628.5427.7227.6527.45
76730.0030.0029.9929.9929.9929.9629.9529.8929.8929.7429.9429.9428.8928.7628.65
77730.0030.0030.0030.0030.0030.0030.0030.0030.0030.0030.0030.0029.9029.6929.45
78729.7629.7629.7629.6829.6528.8728.6528.0628.9828.6127.9027.9027.8327.6727.33
79729.9929.9929.9929.9839.8929.7929.7829.0629.0028.9927.6627.6627.5427.0026.69
80730.0030.0030.0030.0030.0030.0030.0030.0030.0030.0029.6628.8428.8428.8228.78
81730.0730.0730.0630.0530.0429.9929.8929.8929.9329.8829.7329.7229.5729.5629.12
82730.1330.1330.1330.1330.1330.1330.1130.0829.8729.0029.0029.0028.9928.8828.76
83730.0030.0030.0030.0030.0030.0029.8929.7829.6729.5429.0528.0127.9827.8926.89
84729.9829.9829.9829.9829.9829.9829.9829.9229.7829.3629.3428.9928.9828.9828.98
85829.2929.2929.2929.2929.2529.0228.9828.7828.6728.4628.4328.5628.4327.6627.65
86830.0030.0030.0030.0030.0030.0030.0030.0030.0029.9429.8029.6629.6528.7828.65
87830.0030.0030.0030.0030.0030.0029.9829.8929.7829.6129.5629.3429.3429.2129.18
88830.0030.0029.9729.9529.8929.8429.7929.6729.0427.9827.8527.8427.8027.7127.68
89829.2829.2829.2829.2829.2829.2529.2029.1529.1529.1529.1028.6528.2128.2028.19
90830.0030.0030.0030.0030.0030.0030.0030.0029.9929.9929.9429.9029.8929.6729.51

```
91830.0630.0630.0630.0630.0530.0330.0029.9929.7129.6729.6629.6429.5429.5329.45
92830.1430.1430.1430.1430.1429.9529.9429.8829.4529.3229.3229.0228.9928.9828.79
93830.4830.4830.4830.4830.4830.4830.4829.9929.8929.7729.7629.6729.3529.3429.26
94830.0030.0029.8929.8729.7829.5629.0529.0329.0028.8928.7828.7828.6728.6728.66
95830.6930.6930.6930.6930.6930.6630.6630.4530.0129.9929.9929.7829.6629.6629.45
96830.0030.0030.0029.9929.9929.9929.9829.6729.6728.9928.5428.5428.5428.5428.54
97930.7830.7830.7830.7830.7830.7830.7830.7830.7830.7830.7830.4330.1230.0630.01
98930.9130.9130.9130.9130.9130.9130.8930.7830.6530.6530.0529.9929.9829.9829.79
99930.0030.0030.0030.0030.0029.9829.9829.6529.6529.6529.6528.9828.8828.7828.75
100930.0030.0030.0030.0029.9529.9429.8929.8829.8529.5429.5429.3329.3329.3029.29
101929.0029.0029.0029.0029.0029.0029.0028.9928.9928.9928.9928.9928.9828.9828.98
102930.0030.0030.0030.0030.0029.9929.9929.5629.5629.5629.5628.9928.9928.7428.49
103930.0930.0930.0930.0930.0730.0430.0330.0229.9929.6529.6529.6529.6429.6429.74
104930.0030.0029.9829.9829.9429.8329.8329.7829.7829.7829.6329.5629.5629.5629.56
105930.0630.0630.0630.0630.0630.0629.9929.9929.9229.9129.9129.8029.7529.7529.65
106930.0030.0030.0030.0030.0029.8829.7629.6629.5629.3429.3429.0029.0029.0028.99
107929.9829.9829.9829.9829.7229.6629.6529.0028.9028.9028.9028.9028.8828.7828.78
108929.0529.0529.0529.0529.0529.0529.0429.0329.0329.0329.0329.0229.0229.0129.01
```

Sample records for River Pollution Sample A

A	B	C	D	E	F	G	H	I	J	K
374	467	1	1	1	4	82.4	1.234	0.0078	25.1	8.5
374	467	1	1	2	4	77.8	2.765	0.0812	25.1	8.5
374	467	1	1	3	4	81.4	2.555	0.1045	25.1	8.5

A = Easting, B = Northing, C = 1985 river quality class, D = Site number, E = Water sample number, F = 1985 flow class, G = % Dissolved oxygen, H = Biochemical Oxygen Demand (mg/l), I = Ammonia (mg/l), J = Air temperature (°C) and K = Precipitation (mm)

Raw data for river pollution project sample A

374	467	1	1	1	4	82.4	1.234	0.0078	25.1	8.5
374	467	1	1	2	4	77.8	2.765	0.0812	25.1	8.5
374	467	1	1	3	4	81.4	2.555	0.1045	25.1	8.5
374	467	1	1	4	4	85.6	1.335	0.2345	25.1	8.5
374	467	1	1	5	4	83.9	1.909	0.0785	25.1	8.5
350	504	1	2	1	5	79.5	0.223	0.1294	8.2	11.0
350	504	1	2	2	5	84.5	0.561	0.0291	8.2	11.0
350	504	1	2	3	5	83.2	1.543	0.0910	8.2	11.0
350	504	1	2	4	5	87.4	2.030	0.2451	8.2	11.0
350	504	1	2	5	5	90.1	2.113	0.0549	8.2	11.0
331	525	1	3	1	6	83.2	1.564	0.2192	0.0	3.4
331	525	1	3	2	6	78.9	2.456	0.0910	0.0	3.4
331	525	1	3	3	6	85.6	2.678	0.2467	0.0	3.4
331	525	1	3	4	6	86.5	1.766	0.0012	0.0	3.4
331	525	1	3	5	6	84.3	1.998	0.2198	0.0	3.4
357	470	1	4	1	9	87.5	2.321	0.2194	17.5	10.1
357	470	1	4	2	9	86.7	2.899	0.0054	17.5	10.1
357	470	1	4	3	9	84.5	2.343	0.0001	17.5	10.1
357	470	1	4	4	9	83.4	1.655	0.0192	17.5	10.1
357	470	1	4	5	9	86.7	1.256	0.2341	17.5	10.1
346	402	1	5	1	4	81.2	0.655	0.1765	12.3	13.2
346	402	1	5	2	4	83.4	0.787	0.1902	12.3	13.2

346	402	1	5	3	4	80.3	1.544	0.1487	12.3	13.2
346	402	1	5	4	4	83.2	0.221	0.2154	12.3	13.2
346	402	1	5	5	4	81.2	1.540	0.1001	12.3	13.2
371	418	1	6	1	6	86.7	1.455	0.2176	0.0	15.0
371	418	1	6	2	6	88.2	1.113	0.1154	3.8	15.0
371	418	1	6	3	6	84.3	0.235	0.2092	3.8	15.0
371	418	1	6	4	6	83.6	2.001	0.2677	3.8	15.0
371	418	1	6	5	6	85.7	1.776	0.1005	3.8	15.0
305	531	1	7	1	9	88.9	1.452	0.0020	0.0	17.1
305	531	1	7	2	9	90.0	2.348	0.0329	0.0	17.1
305	531	1	7	3	9	86.5	2.161	0.1893	0.0	17.1
305	531	1	7	4	9	85.4	1.879	0.0903	0.0	17.1
305	531	1	7	5	9	87.2	1.458	0.2389	0.0	17.1
346	577	1	8	1	3	82.1	1.117	0.2780	35.3	9.4
346	577	1	8	2	3	79.5	1.003	0.3002	35.3	9.4
346	577	1	8	3	3	84.3	0.054	0.1388	35.3	9.4
346	577	1	8	4	3	85.3	0.658	0.1661	35.3	9.4
346	577	1	8	5	3	82.4	1.321	0.3021	35.3	9.4
368	416	1	9	1	3	84.3	0.982	0.2291	7.9	14.7
368	416	1	9	2	3	85.2	1.328	0.0820	7.9	14.7
368	416	1	9	3	3	81.2	1.536	0.1189	7.9	14.7
368	416	1	9	4	3	85.3	0.748	0.2771	7.9	14.7
368	416	1	9	5	3	83.2	1.467	0.1792	7.9	14.7
375	504	1	10	1	2	81.2	2.143	0.3005	16.3	9.5
375	504	1	10	2	2	84.3	2.069	0.2289	16.3	9.5
375	504	1	10	3	2	86.0	2.543	0.1812	16.3	9.5
375	504	1	10	4	2	81.3	1.143	0.0982	16.3	9.5
375	504	1	10	5	2	83.2	0.007	0.0381	16.3	9.5
374	445	2	1	1	7	75.6	2.454	0.6781	22.6	8.5
374	445	2	1	2	7	74.6	2.912	0.9456	22.6	8.5
374	445	2	1	3	7	77.8	5.116	0.2390	22.6	8.5
374	445	2	1	4	7	65.7	2.067	0.9763	22.6	8.5
374	445	2	1	5	7	70.1	4.657	0.5562	22.6	8.5
380	449	2	2	1	7	73.4	3.234	0.8650	9.1	10.2
380	449	2	2	2	7	76.6	2.778	0.4310	9.1	10.2
380	449	2	2	3	7	64.3	4.543	0.3429	9.1	10.2
380	449	2	2	4	7	75.3	5.303	0.2994	9.1	10.2
380	449	2	2	5	7	66.5	3.562	0.9005	9.1	10.2
351	487	2	3	1	8	71.2	2.657	0.9943	0.2	12.0
351	487	2	3	2	8	64.5	4.531	0.7391	0.2	12.0
351	487	2	3	3	8	71.2	4.876	0.5608	0.2	12.0
351	487	2	3	4	8	67.8	3.003	0.4529	0.2	12.0
351	487	2	3	5	8	67.3	2.657	0.4389	0.2	12.0
346	443	2	4	1	6	68.4	2.898	0.2791	16.8	8.3
346	443	2	4	2	6	65.6	3.549	0.6892	16.8	8.3
346	443	2	4	3	6	71.3	4.322	0.9206	16.8	8.3
346	443	2	4	4	6	63.2	3.852	0.3802	16.8	8.3
346	443	2	4	5	6	63.1	3.005	0.8431	16.8	8.3
385	456	2	5	1	7	67.7	2.794	0.4562	11.8	14.5
385	456	2	5	2	7	68.9	3.100	0.8721	11.8	14.5
385	456	2	5	3	7	74.3	4.388	0.7843	11.8	14.5

385	456	2	5	4	7	71.2	4.009	0.7623	11.8	14.5
385	456	2	5	5	7	75.4	5.456	0.4502	11.8	14.5
362	440	2	6	1	2	67.9	2.437	0.4556	5.9	16.7
362	440	2	6	2	2	63.2	3.121	0.8311	5.9	16.7
362	440	2	6	3	2	61.2	4.636	0.8008	5.9	16.7
362	440	2	6	4	2	67.3	3.010	0.7032	5.9	16.7
362	440	2	6	5	2	64.1	5.117	0.9321	5.9	16.7
402	497	2	7	1	3	61.2	4.231	0.4327	0.0	20.1
402	497	2	7	2	3	64.4	3.079	0.5658	0.0	20.1
402	497	2	7	3	3	60.4	4.241	0.3489	0.0	20.1
402	497	2	7	4	3	58.9	2.845	0.4548	0.0	20.1
402	497	2	7	5	3	65.3	5.043	0.6749	0.0	20.1
335	555	2	8	1	9	63.4	2.932	0.9112	41.8	7.1
335	555	2	8	2	9	75.6	2.436	0.4356	41.8	7.1
335	555	2	8	3	9	73.2	2.674	0.5562	41.8	7.1
335	555	2	8	4	9	68.2	3.995	0.6783	41.8	7.1
335	555	2	8	5	9	60.4	4.002	0.7311	41.8	7.1
348	540	2	9	1	3	61.3	3.421	0.6540	10.5	13.2
348	540	2	9	2	3	67.5	4.130	0.8741	10.5	13.2
348	540	2	9	3	3	71.4	2.114	0.8021	10.5	13.2
348	540	2	9	4	3	72.0	4.226	0.5436	10.5	13.2
348	540	2	9	5	3	67.4	4.318	0.6739	10.5	13.2
302	513	2	10	1	6	75.3	1.654	0.6729	16.3	8.7
302	513	2	10	2	6	69.8	5.436	0.9043	16.3	8.7
302	513	2	10	3	6	70.0	5.003	0.3453	16.3	8.7
302	513	2	10	4	6	62.7	3.547	0.3735	16.3	8.7
302	513	2	10	5	6	65.5	4.678	0.5629	16.3	8.7
392	483	3	1	1	2	43.2	5.678	0.6435	23.6	8.0
392	483	3	1	2	2	44.5	7.845	0.7655	23.6	8.0
392	483	3	1	3	2	49.1	10.561	0.8724	23.6	8.0
392	483	3	1	4	2	42.2	5.689	0.9004	23.6	8.0
392	483	3	1	5	2	43.2	8.765	0.6870	23.6	8.0
380	467	3	2	1	5	53.4	6.932	0.7509	10.1	14.1
380	467	3	2	2	5	46.4	9.021	0.6803	10.1	14.1
380	467	3	2	3	5	50.5	5.643	0.9032	10.1	14.1
380	467	3	2	4	5	56.1	6.887	0.8123	10.1	14.1
380	467	3	2	5	5	49.8	5.741	0.3451	10.1	14.1
375	455	3	3	1	1	42.1	8.657	0.3056	0.0	1.0
375	455	3	3	2	1	43.4	8.320	0.5988	0.0	1.0
375	455	3	3	3	1	44.5	7.902	0.4521	0.0	1.0
375	455	3	3	4	1	41.2	8.302	0.6493	0.0	1.0
375	455	3	3	5	1	39.8	7.655	0.7933	0.0	1.0
367	470	3	4	1	7	47.8	6.143	0.6654	14.2	12.6
367	470	3	4	2	7	50.1	8.451	0.5564	14.2	12.6
367	470	3	4	3	7	49.4	7.004	0.9876	14.2	12.6
367	470	3	4	4	7	47.5	8.421	0.8965	14.2	12.6
367	470	3	4	5	7	43.2	7.884	0.6754	14.2	12.6
367	335	3	5	1	9	48.9	10.154	0.9873	9.1	9.9
367	335	3	5	2	9	57.8	5.778	0.9876	9.1	9.9
367	335	3	5	3	9	45.8	8.994	1.0008	9.1	9.9
367	335	3	5	4	9	56.7	7.410	0.8765	9.1	9.9

367	335	3	5	5	9	57.9	10.400	0.7654	9.1	9.9
351	307	3	6	1	6	49.8	5.661	0.8769	5.6	12.1
351	307	3	6	2	6	56.7	4.772	0.4577	5.6	12.1
351	307	3	6	3	6	57.9	6.100	0.9878	5.6	12.1
351	307	3	6	4	6	55.4	7.603	0.6598	5.6	12.1
351	307	3	6	5	6	55.5	4.987	0.8099	5.6	12.1
345	470	3	7	1	4	51.2	6.870	0.7487	0.5	16.5
345	470	3	7	2	4	45.6	8.912	0.9876	0.5	16.5
345	470	3	7	3	4	47.4	8.543	1.0542	0.5	16.5
345	470	3	7	4	4	43.5	7.345	0.8763	0.5	16.5
345	470	3	7	5	4	46.5	9.001	0.8345	0.5	16.5
386	349	3	8	1	3	43.2	5.766	0.9765	33.0	10.1
386	349	3	8	2	3	42.5	8.554	0.8768	33.0	10.1
386	349	3	8	3	3	38.9	8.154	0.9342	33.0	10.1
386	349	3	8	4	3	41.2	6.932	0.9654	33.0	10.1
386	349	3	8	5	3	43.6	8.453	0.8996	33.0	10.1
356	416	3	9	1	4	45.7	8.256	1.1340	7.9	15.0
356	416	3	9	2	4	47.8	7.511	0.8732	7.9	15.0
356	416	3	9	3	4	45.3	5.663	0.8757	7.9	15.0
356	416	3	9	4	4	44.3	6.337	0.9554	7.9	15.0
356	416	3	9	5	4	45.5	6.836	0.8121	7.9	15.0
370	436	3	10	1	9	58.9	7.115	0.0000	19.8	12.3
370	436	3	10	2	9	47.8	8.317	0.8799	19.8	12.3
370	436	3	10	3	9	55.5	5.386	0.8343	19.8	12.3
370	436	3	10	4	9	53.2	7.492	0.9986	19.8	12.3
370	436	3	10	5	9	51.2	5.611	0.7652	19.8	12.3
383	393	4	1	1	8	15.4	12.435	1.0998	28.3	9.2
383	393	4	1	2	8	13.2	10.987	1.0083	28.3	9.2
383	393	4	1	3	8	17.6	15.765	0.7658	28.3	9.2
383	393	4	1	4	8	10.2	11.349	0.8769	28.3	9.2
383	393	4	1	5	8	15.6	16.098	0.7768	28.3	9.2
390	486	4	2	1	4	12.3	7.201	0.9987	6.4	13.2
390	486	4	2	2	4	13.4	9.789	0.8875	6.4	13.2
390	486	4	2	3	4	14.0	13.221	0.9121	6.4	13.2
390	486	4	2	4	4	12.3	15.765	0.8686	6.4	13.2
390	486	4	2	5	4	15.6	12.011	1.4350	6.4	13.2
374	467	4	3	1	6	25.6	15.432	0.9665	1.0	5.0
374	467	4	3	2	6	21.5	16.570	1.0097	1.0	5.0
374	467	4	3	3	6	23.0	17.091	0.8765	1.0	5.0
374	467	4	3	4	6	19.8	14.221	0.9945	1.0	5.0
374	467	4	3	5	6	17.6	8.776	0.8712	1.0	5.0
359	475	4	4	1	8	28.9	9.431	0.9484	20.6	12.8
359	475	4	4	2	8	27.6	15.210	0.9879	20.6	12.8
359	475	4	4	3	8	35.6	9.432	0.8131	20.6	12.8
359	475	4	4	4	8	33.0	17.010	0.8067	20.6	12.8
359	475	4	4	5	8	31.2	14.220	0.9567	20.6	12.8
360	429	4	5	1	5	28.1	11.001	0.9998	17.9	14.6
360	429	4	5	2	5	23.4	15.210	1.7550	17.9	14.6
360	429	4	5	3	5	19.1	13.001	0.9858	17.9	14.6
360	429	4	5	4	5	22.3	11.067	0.8711	17.9	14.6
360	429	4	5	5	5	21.5	8.548	0.9700	17.9	14.6

363	456	4	6	1	2	12.1	9.123	1.8711	4.7	15.2
363	456	4	6	2	2	16.5	16.456	0.9876	4.7	15.2
363	456	4	6	3	2	11.2	13.234	1.9987	4.7	15.2
363	456	4	6	4	2	10.3	11.001	0.9887	4.7	15.2
363	456	4	6	5	2	16.5	13.202	0.8445	4.7	15.2
383	412	4	7	1	7	31.2	10.956	1.9887	0.0	16.5
383	412	4	7	2	7	33.4	10.201	0.9877	0.0	16.5
383	412	4	7	3	7	27.6	11.989	0.9772	0.0	16.5
383	412	4	7	4	7	25.4	14.892	1.0885	0.0	16.5
383	412	4	7	5	7	33.0	17.567	1.0004	0.0	16.5
346	435	4	8	1	3	16.5	12.321	0.9443	39.2	10.4
346	435	4	8	2	3	15.4	9.764	0.8955	39.2	10.4
346	435	4	8	3	3	14.3	10.872	1.6794	39.2	10.4
346	435	4	8	4	3	11.5	13.902	2.0032	39.2	10.4
346	435	4	8	5	3	15.0	17.020	1.0034	39.2	10.4
380	434	4	9	1	7	21.5	15.998	0.9882	11.8	16.1
380	434	4	9	2	7	26.5	16.321	0.9621	11.8	16.1
380	434	4	9	3	7	24.0	14.328	0.8925	11.8	16.1
380	434	4	9	4	7	25.4	15.329	1.0043	11.8	16.1
380	434	4	9	5	7	22.3	16.910	0.9213	11.8	16.1
335	403	4	10	1	4	19.8	10.002	0.9322	15.4	8.3
335	403	4	10	2	4	23.3	13.650	0.9822	15.4	8.3
335	403	4	10	3	4	21.2	11.981	1.0091	15.4	8.3
335	403	4	10	4	4	17.1	13.210	0.9435	15.4	8.3
335	403	4	10	5	4	19.2	15.320	0.9889	15.4	8.3
367	328	5	1	1	4	5.5	17.564	2.0040	28.9	9.7
367	328	5	1	2	4	6.7	12.897	1.5640	28.9	9.7
367	328	5	1	3	4	8.9	19.234	0.9883	28.9	9.7
367	328	5	1	4	4	10.3	20.005	1.0070	28.9	9.7
367	328	5	1	5	4	11.2	17.042	2.1230	28.9	9.7
364	475	5	2	1	8	14.5	16.321	0.9987	10.1	13.5
364	475	5	2	2	8	12.2	11.210	0.5648	10.1	13.4
364	475	5	2	3	8	13.4	14.540	1.1998	10.1	13.4
364	475	5	2	4	8	11.6	16.910	1.6523	10.1	13.4
364	475	5	2	5	8	11.0	17.002	1.9872	10.1	13.4
344	332	5	3	1	1	3.4	19.034	0.9887	2.1	6.8
344	332	5	3	2	1	5.6	20.502	1.0043	2.1	6.8
344	332	5	3	3	1	7.1	14.556	2.3432	2.1	6.8
344	332	5	3	4	1	9.8	17.310	2.1172	2.1	6.8
344	332	5	3	5	1	5.5	15.210	1.8762	2.1	6.8
346	317	5	4	1	7	10.2	15.389	1.0992	12.8	14.3
346	317	5	4	2	7	11.3	11.432	1.5443	12.8	14.3
346	317	5	4	3	7	8.1	10.676	0.9921	12.8	14.3
346	317	5	4	4	7	7.0	17.548	1.0343	12.8	14.3
346	317	5	4	5	7	4.5	18.443	1.2840	12.8	14.3
373	494	5	5	1	9	9.8	12.891	0.8976	15.6	12.6
373	494	5	5	2	9	8.7	17.907	0.9221	15.6	12.6
373	494	5	5	3	9	6.5	13.543	1.6548	15.6	12.6
373	494	5	5	4	9	13.4	13.654	1.2341	15.6	12.6
373	494	5	5	5	9	12.1	16.756	1.8925	15.6	12.6
394	493	5	6	1	6	10.1	15.781	0.9899	6.2	13.9

394	493	5	6	2	6	7.6	13.210	1.0021	6.2	13.9
394	493	5	6	3	6	5.2	11.154	1.8872	6.2	13.9
394	493	5	6	4	6	7.8	12.478	2.0012	6.2	13.9
394	493	5	6	5	6	9.4	12.179	1.0034	6.2	13.9
376	495	5	7	1	2	4.5	16.273	2.2102	0.7	21.2
376	495	5	7	2	2	6.9	13.653	1.7621	0.7	21.2
376	495	5	7	3	2	9.5	17.652	0.9872	0.7	21.2
376	495	5	7	4	2	3.4	16.543	1.7621	0.7	21.2
376	495	5	7	5	2	5.6	15.821	2.0032	0.7	21.2
402	483	5	8	1	4	7.6	12.384	1.8721	31.2	12.7
402	483	5	8	2	4	8.8	15.176	1.0023	31.2	12.7
402	483	5	8	3	4	9.9	16.201	1.6754	31.2	12.7
402	483	5	8	4	4	10.0	14.002	0.9822	31.2	12.7
402	483	5	8	5	4	12.1	15.020	1.3452	31.2	12.7
385	497	5	9	1	3	10.5	14.892	1.2137	5.6	14.0
385	497	5	9	2	3	13.4	11.514	0.9897	5.6	14.0
385	497	5	9	3	3	12.6	12.319	1.6223	5.6	14.0
385	497	5	9	4	3	6.7	15.320	1.5852	5.6	14.0
385	497	5	9	5	3	4.5	16.438	1.2243	5.6	14.0
366	476	5	10	1	6	5.6	13.928	1.7775	18.5	11.6
366	476	5	10	2	6	17.6	17.210	1.3298	18.5	11.5
366	476	5	10	3	6	8.8	17.892	1.0991	18.5	11.5
366	476	5	10	4	6	6.5	13.456	1.5001	18.5	11.5
366	476	5	10	5	6	4.8	16.456	1.7721	18.5	11.5

Sample Records for River Pollution Sample B

A	B	C	D	E	F	G	H	I	J	K	L	M	N	O	P
377	514	1	1	1	1	1	5	85.4	2.341	0.2134	0.550	0.001	14.6	3.4	11.5
377	514	1	1	2	1	1	5	83.2	1.127	0.1213	4.760	0.025	13.5	3.4	11.5
377	514	1	1	3	1	1	5	86.9	1.768	0.1176	5.540	0.061	10.6	3.4	11.5

A = Easting, B = Northing, C = Site number, D = Upstream/downstream, E = Water sample number, F = Site type, G = 1985 river quality class, H = 1985 flow class, I = % Dissolved oxygen, J = Biochemical Oxygen Demand (mg/l), K = Ammonia (mg/l), L = Copper (ppb), M = Mercury (ppb), N = Zinc (ppb), O = Air temperature (°C) and P = Precipitation (mm)

Raw data for river pollution project sample B

377	514	1	1	1	1	1	5	85.4	2.341	0.2134	0.550	0.001	14.6	3.4	11.5
377	514	1	1	2	1	1	5	83.2	1.127	0.1213	4.760	0.025	13.5	3.4	11.5
377	514	1	1	3	1	1	5	86.9	1.768	0.1176	5.540	0.061	10.6	3.4	11.5
377	514	1	1	4	1	1	5	83.5	2.113	0.3502	3.100	0.040	14.2	3.4	11.5
377	514	1	1	5	1	1	5	82.1	2.004	0.3546	0.060	0.032	11.0	3.4	11.5
377	514	1	2	1	1	1	5	78.5	2.779	0.1123	6.710	0.099	25.3	3.4	11.5
377	514	1	2	2	1	1	5	77.5	1.120	0.2892	8.090	0.078	24.8	3.4	11.5
377	514	1	2	3	1	1	5	80.1	2.024	0.3841	9.870	0.083	30.1	3.4	11.5
377	514	1	2	4	1	1	5	78.9	1.515	0.3210	6.770	0.111	21.1	3.4	11.5
377	514	1	2	5	1	1	5	83.0	2.325	0.2098	4.590	0.035	23.9	3.4	11.5
374	440	2	1	1	1	2	6	74.3	4.238	0.4543	5.430	0.034	5.6	25.1	13.4
374	440	2	1	2	1	2	6	75.6	3.678	0.6789	3.120	0.045	12.3	25.1	13.4
374	440	2	1	3	1	2	6	70.3	2.998	0.8432	0.380	0.056	14.4	25.1	13.4
374	440	2	1	4	1	2	6	76.4	3.901	0.4564	1.220	0.094	21.1	25.1	13.4
374	440	2	1	5	1	2	6	73.0	4.555	0.6654	5.100	0.133	23.1	25.1	13.4

374	440	2	2	1	1	2	6	65.3	4.921	0.8123	5.770	0.452	25.6	25.1	13.4
374	440	2	2	2	1	2	6	73.5	3.451	0.5234	6.030	0.098	19.8	25.1	13.4
374	440	2	2	3	1	2	6	64.3	3.454	0.6785	7.190	0.087	34.5	25.1	13.4
374	440	2	2	4	1	2	6	67.8	4.550	0.6547	3.560	0.065	27.6	25.1	13.4
374	440	2	2	5	1	2	6	69.0	3.667	0.6123	6.470	0.043	22.5	25.1	13.4
396	487	3	1	1	1	3	3	50.8	7.894	0.7889	0.690	0.004	21.9	0.0	9.8
396	487	3	1	2	1	3	3	45.6	6.554	0.6578	5.470	0.012	20.1	0.0	9.8
396	487	3	1	3	1	3	3	44.5	3.665	0.9021	6.330	0.050	17.6	0.0	9.8
396	487	3	1	4	1	3	3	52.1	8.709	0.8222	2.510	0.033	14.5	0.0	9.8
396	487	3	1	5	1	3	3	45.5	8.065	1.0002	4.320	0.025	17.6	0.0	9.8
396	487	3	2	1	1	3	3	28.4	4.556	0.9921	6.490	0.006	27.9	0.0	9.8
396	487	3	2	2	1	3	3	25.6	6.771	0.5466	9.230	0.089	25.4	0.0	9.8
396	487	3	2	3	1	3	3	28.9	7.020	0.7387	4.660	0.053	21.4	0.0	9.8
396	487	3	2	4	1	3	3	23.6	7.511	0.8281	5.720	0.039	31.2	0.0	9.8
396	487	3	2	5	1	3	3	34.0	5.412	0.9921	8.100	0.087	26.5	0.0	9.8
388	391	4	1	1	1	4	3	15.6	12.600	0.9002	4.350	0.056	12.9	6.5	15.8
388	391	4	1	2	1	4	3	17.8	15.643	0.9821	5.690	0.071	16.8	6.5	15.8
388	391	4	1	3	1	4	3	14.5	9.113	1.0032	3.070	0.005	22.1	6.5	15.8
388	391	4	1	4	1	4	3	16.7	10.657	0.8221	6.110	0.021	18.7	6.5	15.8
388	391	4	1	5	1	4	3	13.2	16.502	0.5698	2.020	0.032	11.8	6.5	15.8
388	391	4	2	1	1	4	3	9.8	14.532	0.8776	5.440	0.078	19.8	6.5	15.8
388	391	4	2	2	1	4	3	8.7	15.022	0.9656	6.220	0.092	28.2	6.5	15.8
388	391	4	2	3	1	4	3	9.0	13.441	0.8932	5.040	0.904	31.4	6.5	15.8
388	391	4	2	4	1	4	3	5.6	15.661	0.8927	3.090	0.084	24.3	6.5	15.8
388	391	4	2	5	1	4	3	7.7	12.890	1.0111	7.910	0.096	25.6	6.5	15.8
365	325	5	1	1	1	5	2	11.2	17.659	0.9221	0.320	0.052	15.7	12.3	12.5
365	325	5	1	2	1	5	2	14.3	19.445	1.0121	5.780	0.043	18.9	12.3	12.5
365	325	5	1	3	1	5	2	16.5	13.822	1.1222	0.270	0.037	20.0	12.3	12.5
365	325	5	1	4	1	5	2	8.9	19.212	0.9912	3.720	0.060	16.7	12.3	12.5
365	325	5	1	5	1	5	2	6.9	17.655	0.8921	6.420	0.044	21.0	12.3	12.5
365	325	5	2	1	1	5	2	3.4	18.334	0.8954	9.020	0.071	23.4	12.3	12.5
365	325	5	2	2	1	5	2	5.6	19.003	0.9332	7.540	0.041	26.7	12.3	12.5
365	325	5	2	3	1	5	2	6.3	16.842	0.9821	3.960	0.053	22.1	12.3	12.5
365	325	5	2	4	1	5	2	1.4	17.886	0.9473	5.080	0.049	26.9	12.3	12.5
365	325	5	2	5	1	5	2	5.6	18.663	1.0054	6.230	0.073	19.9	12.3	12.5
354	513	6	1	1	1	1	8	89.4	1.234	0.3453	5.040	0.046	20.9	7.6	17.4
354	513	6	1	2	1	1	8	87.4	2.765	0.3782	4.920	0.003	14.7	7.6	17.4
354	513	6	1	3	1	1	8	83.7	0.998	0.1032	3.880	0.035	16.3	7.6	17.4
354	513	6	1	4	1	1	8	85.0	1.092	0.3214	3.010	0.042	18.1	7.6	17.4
354	513	6	1	5	1	1	8	91.6	2.020	0.2256	3.050	0.039	21.6	7.6	17.4
354	513	6	2	1	1	1	8	83.2	2.405	0.0122	5.430	0.056	24.2	7.6	17.4
354	513	6	2	2	1	1	8	75.6	2.121	0.3249	6.170	0.045	29.5	7.6	17.4
354	513	6	2	3	1	1	8	79.8	0.561	0.3892	7.200	0.062	30.6	7.6	17.4
354	513	6	2	4	1	1	8	74.3	0.054	0.3543	3.830	0.071	34.8	7.6	17.4
354	513	6	2	5	1	1	8	82.0	2.542	0.1237	2.970	0.040	24.5	7.6	17.4
348	485	7	1	1	1	2	6	67.8	3.310	0.4532	5.470	0.049	23.0	17.6	16.1
348	485	7	1	2	1	2	6	78.4	4.687	0.6549	3.080	0.061	12.0	17.6	16.1
348	385	7	1	3	1	2	6	65.8	3.456	0.6102	4.160	0.035	9.8	17.6	16.1
348	485	7	1	4	1	2	6	66.0	4.661	0.4302	2.240	0.045	15.8	17.6	16.1
348	485	7	1	5	1	2	6	74.3	3.429	0.7821	6.190	0.047	13.2	17.6	16.1
348	485	7	2	1	1	2	6	58.9	3.002	0.5006	5.340	0.066	26.1	17.6	16.1

348	485	7	2	2	1	2	6	63.2	4.050	0.7866	7.080	0.052	24.1	17.6	16.1
348	485	7	2	3	1	2	6	56.7	4.876	0.8043	6.250	0.043	18.8	17.6	16.1
348	485	7	2	4	1	2	6	64.2	3.829	0.7832	4.370	0.039	24.9	17.6	16.1
348	485	7	2	5	1	2	6	59.7	4.651	0.6032	2.050	0.061	26.8	17.6	16.1
370	452	8	1	1	1	3	6	47.8	6.895	0.7843	5.430	0.059	21.3	4.8	10.0
370	452	8	1	2	1	3	4	45.7	8.776	0.8332	3.680	0.033	18.1	4.8	10.0
370	452	8	1	3	1	3	4	51.2	5.661	0.9002	4.400	0.042	14.7	4.8	10.0
370	452	8	1	4	1	3	4	43.4	6.702	0.8921	2.190	0.003	9.7	4.8	10.0
370	452	8	1	5	1	3	4	45.4	8.093	0.9002	3.060	0.012	8.5	4.8	10.0
370	452	8	2	1	1	3	4	27.8	6.554	1.0010	6.010	0.067	26.5	4.8	10.0
370	452	8	2	2	1	3	4	33.3	6.234	0.8921	5.040	0.044	35.4	4.8	10.0
370	452	8	2	3	1	3	4	25.6	7.301	0.9921	4.770	0.067	30.2	4.8	10.0
370	452	8	2	4	1	3	4	28.9	5.443	0.8565	3.890	0.097	27.3	4.8	10.0
370	452	8	2	5	1	3	4	31.2	7.880	0.9943	6.930	0.071	28.4	4.8	10.0
396	482	9	1	1	1	4	3	17.8	13.260	0.9324	5.020	0.009	15.6	0.0	13.2
396	482	9	1	2	1	4	3	18.9	14.532	1.0025	5.120	0.032	19.3	0.0	13.2
396	482	9	1	3	1	4	3	13.4	15.667	0.8932	4.390	0.043	23.2	0.0	13.2
396	482	9	1	4	1	4	3	14.3	17.006	0.9304	4.310	0.037	20.7	0.0	13.2
396	482	9	1	5	1	4	3	11.3	16.112	0.8123	2.580	0.026	17.6	0.0	13.2
396	482	9	2	1	1	4	3	10.0	14.100	1.0021	5.040	0.064	30.1	0.0	13.2
396	482	9	2	2	1	4	3	7.6	10.200	0.9821	6.810	0.084	27.9	0.0	13.2
396	482	9	2	3	1	4	3	5.6	9.829	0.8951	7.923	0.063	21.7	0.0	13.2
396	482	9	2	4	1	4	3	8.9	10.341	0.9033	5.130	0.081	28.7	0.0	13.2
396	482	9	2	5	1	4	3	3.4	16.554	0.9801	5.680	0.072	34.6	0.0	13.2
339	336	10	1	1	1	5	1	11.3	16.789	1.0121	4.670	0.035	21.5	5.8	13.2
339	336	10	1	2	1	5	1	7.8	14.628	0.9991	5.320	0.051	18.9	5.8	16.7
339	336	10	1	3	1	5	1	8.9	17.004	0.8671	2.150	0.045	23.4	5.8	16.7
339	336	10	1	4	1	5	1	6.5	19.224	0.9021	4.020	0.025	25.6	5.8	16.7
339	336	10	1	5	1	5	1	10.3	15.640	1.1022	1.270	0.019	23.1	5.8	16.7
339	336	10	2	1	1	5	1	2.4	12.005	0.9881	5.980	0.066	29.8	5.8	16.7
339	336	10	2	2	1	5	1	3.5	18.965	0.8722	8.030	0.043	36.5	5.8	16.7
339	336	10	2	3	1	5	1	6.5	17.843	0.9543	6.760	0.069	33.5	5.8	16.7
339	336	10	2	4	1	5	1	1.6	20.221	0.8966	8.280	0.093	29.8	5.8	16.7
339	336	10	2	5	1	5	1	5.5	18.995	0.9405	4.540	0.061	27.1	5.8	16.7
370	416	11	1	1	1	1	4	87.6	1.768	0.3894	6.030	0.072	16.3	21.4	10.3
370	416	11	1	2	1	1	4	83.4	1.765	0.3254	3.910	0.043	15.4	21.4	10.3
370	416	11	1	3	1	1	4	93.2	0.435	0.2331	4.310	0.025	19.1	21.4	10.3
370	416	11	1	4	1	1	4	87.4	2.342	0.0921	2.890	0.031	20.1	21.4	10.3
370	416	11	1	5	1	1	4	82.1	1.987	0.1221	3.840	0.009	17.3	21.4	10.3
370	416	11	2	1	1	1	4	85.6	0.254	0.1659	4.990	0.056	21.8	21.4	10.3
370	416	11	2	2	1	1	4	83.2	2.445	0.3794	4.060	0.078	25.4	21.4	10.3
370	416	11	2	3	1	1	4	81.0	2.318	0.2802	5.070	0.035	27.6	21.4	10.3
370	416	11	2	4	1	1	4	77.8	2.022	0.2730	6.370	0.047	23.1	21.4	10.3
370	416	11	2	5	1	1	4	74.3	1.568	0.2190	8.110	0.062	20.1	21.4	10.3
387	459	12	1	1	1	2	5	65.8	3.445	0.3222	5.440	0.055	21.8	7.3	13.4
387	459	12	1	2	1	2	5	78.2	4.650	0.4356	3.710	0.023	13.2	7.3	13.4
387	459	12	1	3	1	2	5	64.3	3.437	0.6575	2.850	0.043	17.4	7.3	13.4
387	459	12	1	4	1	2	5	71.9	4.755	0.7832	4.030	0.012	15.2	7.3	13.4
387	459	12	1	5	1	2	5	72.2	4.255	0.5662	3.090	0.053	18.5	7.3	13.4
387	459	12	2	1	1	2	5	61.6	3.217	0.4554	5.120	0.067	23.5	7.3	13.4
387	459	12	2	2	1	2	5	55.7	2.998	0.7657	4.430	0.035	27.8	7.3	13.4

387	459	12	2	3	1	2	5	48.9	3.445	0.8112	5.070	0.066	26.5	7.3	13.4
387	459	12	2	4	1	2	5	56.7	3.676	0.5498	4.390	0.078	27.3	7.3	13.4
387	459	12	2	5	1	2	5	63.2	4.569	0.6665	5.670	0.062	22.8	7.3	13.4
369	332	13	1	1	1	3	4	43.0	5.892	0.7657	5.380	0.033	13.7	1.5	16.8
369	332	13	1	2	1	3	4	54.5	6.775	0.5004	2.890	0.021	15.9	1.5	16.8
369	332	13	1	3	1	3	4	47.6	7.881	0.6096	4.550	0.039	18.2	1.5	16.8
369	332	13	1	4	1	3	4	51.2	8.002	0.7403	1.220	0.045	16.0	1.5	16.8
369	332	13	1	5	1	3	4	48.9	7.141	0.8397	1.650	0.056	19.4	1.5	16.8
369	332	13	2	1	1	3	4	34.5	5.667	0.8043	4.550	0.076	20.2	1.5	16.8
369	332	13	2	2	1	3	4	25.7	5.612	0.7111	6.980	0.089	23.6	1.5	16.8
369	332	13	2	3	1	3	4	33.8	6.547	0.4711	7.040	0.045	28.7	1.5	16.8
369	332	13	2	4	1	3	4	34.4	5.489	0.8793	5.660	0.056	25.4	1.5	16.8
369	332	13	2	5	1	3	4	26.1	5.443	0.5430	4.990	0.043	26.7	1.5	16.8
353	479	14	1	1	1	4	3	18.9	9.880	0.6589	0.956	0.053	21.0	10.3	8.7
353	479	14	1	2	1	4	3	12.3	13.424	0.7765	1.002	0.043	11.2	10.3	8.7
353	479	14	1	3	1	4	3	16.2	16.548	0.8879	4.332	0.025	15.4	10.3	8.7
353	479	14	1	4	1	4	3	11.4	15.443	0.9332	5.102	0.061	16.8	10.3	8.7
353	479	14	1	5	1	4	3	21.7	13.221	0.8556	4.037	0.072	12.4	10.3	8.7
353	479	14	2	1	1	4	3	10.9	16.776	0.9043	4.721	0.066	19.8	10.3	8.7
353	479	14	2	2	1	4	3	5.6	13.443	0.8843	5.946	0.094	26.5	10.3	8.7
353	479	14	2	3	1	4	3	3.9	12.110	0.9232	8.932	0.043	29.6	10.3	8.7
353	479	14	2	4	1	4	3	8.8	15.305	0.9983	7.113	0.035	33.2	10.3	8.7
353	479	14	2	5	1	4	3	7.0	16.502	1.0001	6.664	0.050	31.2	10.3	8.7
397	491	15	1	1	1	5	2	6.7	16.004	0.9222	3.400	0.034	21.9	4.4	12.6
397	491	15	1	2	1	5	2	11.2	14.320	0.8795	5.042	0.003	20.8	4.4	12.6
397	491	15	1	3	1	5	2	8.9	17.876	0.7985	4.894	0.057	25.4	4.4	12.6
397	491	15	1	4	1	5	2	7.7	18.776	0.9954	5.072	0.045	27.6	4.4	12.6
397	491	15	1	5	1	5	2	7.2	16.554	1.0221	2.031	0.021	18.1	4.4	12.6
397	491	15	2	1	1	5	2	5.1	17.877	0.9212	6.403	0.072	34.5	4.4	12.6
397	491	15	2	2	1	5	2	5.6	13.443	0.8976	5.043	0.083	29.8	4.4	12.6
397	491	15	2	3	1	5	2	4.5	20.210	0.8491	4.043	0.091	26.1	4.4	12.6
397	491	15	2	4	1	5	2	3.2	19.221	0.9302	5.007	0.048	27.3	4.4	12.6
397	491	15	2	5	1	5	2	4.4	15.654	0.9888	6.108	0.061	28.9	4.4	12.6
347	402	16	1	1	1	1	7	87.5	1.768	0.2128	5.670	0.050	12.1	23.6	15.0
347	402	16	1	2	1	1	7	84.5	2.334	0.3920	4.530	0.045	17.6	23.6	15.0
347	402	16	1	3	1	1	7	81.2	0.987	0.2212	3.210	0.032	19.8	23.6	15.0
347	402	16	1	4	1	1	7	88.9	0.341	0.1543	5.920	0.049	15.4	23.6	15.0
347	402	16	1	5	1	1	7	86.5	2.334	0.0932	3.000	0.023	17.8	23.6	15.0
347	402	16	2	1	1	1	7	75.6	1.228	0.2143	5.210	0.054	21.2	23.6	15.0
347	402	16	2	2	1	1	7	73.4	1.259	0.3422	3.540	0.068	26.7	23.6	15.0
347	402	16	2	3	1	1	7	81.2	0.252	0.3332	4.470	0.034	23.4	23.6	15.0
347	402	16	2	4	1	1	7	76.8	0.986	0.1217	4.890	0.052	25.4	23.6	15.0
347	402	16	2	5	1	1	7	84.3	2.034	0.1821	7.100	0.075	22.0	23.6	15.0
366	447	17	1	1	1	2	5	76.8	4.540	0.5443	5.440	0.051	13.7	12.4	14.1
366	447	17	1	2	1	2	5	65.3	3.456	0.7665	3.480	0.048	18.7	12.4	14.1
366	447	17	1	3	1	2	5	67.7	4.350	0.6712	2.910	0.035	15.4	12.4	14.1
366	447	17	1	4	1	2	5	61.2	4.789	0.8665	5.830	0.021	12.1	12.4	14.1
366	447	17	1	5	1	2	5	65.7	3.224	0.4354	3.720	0.011	17.6	12.4	14.1
366	447	17	2	1	1	2	5	47.8	4.510	0.6576	5.670	0.065	23.4	12.4	14.1
366	447	17	2	2	1	2	5	51.2	3.033	0.6113	4.060	0.049	20.7	12.4	14.1
366	447	17	2	3	1	2	5	50.0	4.106	0.5067	7.030	0.064	28.7	12.4	14.1

366	447	17	2	4	1	2	5	56.7	4.043	0.8043	8.090	0.052	29.2	12.4	14.1
366	447	17	2	5	1	2	5	45.9	4.556	0.8902	5.420	0.070	21.4	12.4	14.1
341	465	18	1	1	1	3	3	43.5	8.776	0.7221	5.430	0.049	20.7	0.0	9.5
341	465	18	1	2	1	3	3	38.9	6.772	0.8992	3.090	0.036	16.5	0.0	9.5
341	465	18	1	3	1	3	3	47.8	8.703	0.9970	4.630	0.041	14.8	0.0	9.5
341	465	18	1	4	1	3	3	44.3	4.554	0.9008	5.820	0.021	13.9	0.0	9.5
341	465	18	1	5	1	3	3	45.1	3.055	0.7765	2.710	0.028	15.6	0.0	9.5
341	465	18	2	1	1	3	3	27.8	4.710	0.8876	5.010	0.056	21.3	0.0	9.5
341	465	18	2	2	1	3	3	35.6	8.023	0.9863	4.320	0.042	19.1	0.0	9.5
341	465	18	2	3	1	3	3	33.3	7.657	0.8721	6.090	0.067	25.4	0.0	9.5
341	465	18	2	4	1	3	3	29.8	6.558	0.9987	7.980	0.056	26.2	0.0	9.5
341	465	18	2	5	1	3	3	31.1	5.898	1.0911	8.020	0.073	27.4	0.0	9.5
366	451	19	1	1	1	4	6	15.4	16.504	0.9879	4.210	0.047	16.7	0.0	12.0
366	451	19	1	2	1	4	6	18.7	14.322	0.7865	3.610	0.059	21.0	0.0	12.0
366	451	19	1	3	1	4	6	12.2	15.667	0.9009	5.980	0.032	23.4	0.0	12.0
366	451	19	1	4	1	4	6	15.2	13.220	0.8654	4.030	0.045	14.5	0.0	12.0
366	451	19	1	5	1	4	6	17.6	17.004	0.9121	3.030	0.061	11.1	0.0	12.0
366	451	19	2	1	1	4	6	6.8	14.332	0.8951	2.650	0.083	23.7	0.0	12.0
366	451	19	2	2	1	4	6	9.8	14.333	0.9792	6.540	0.062	27.6	0.0	12.0
366	451	19	2	3	1	4	6	4.6	15.661	0.8831	8.540	0.059	22.3	0.0	12.0
366	451	19	2	4	1	4	6	5.5	14.981	0.8050	6.130	0.043	23.0	0.0	12.0
366	451	19	2	5	1	4	6	7.6	15.642	0.9932	4.350	0.067	23.1	0.0	12.0
369	471	20	1	1	1	5	6	8.7	16.530	0.9011	5.320	0.002	16.5	4.0	16.3
369	471	20	1	2	1	5	6	4.2	14.392	0.8099	4.470	0.045	19.8	4.0	16.3
369	471	20	1	3	1	5	2	8.8	16.923	0.9921	5.160	0.067	22.1	4.0	16.3
369	471	20	1	4	1	5	2	9.4	18.776	1.0211	3.660	0.065	23.4	4.0	16.3
369	471	20	1	5	1	5	2	10.9	14.556	0.9164	2.020	0.076	24.3	4.0	16.3
369	471	20	2	1	1	5	2	3.5	18.000	0.8922	4.560	0.078	25.4	4.0	16.3
369	471	20	2	2	1	5	2	6.6	19.887	0.9503	6.790	0.099	29.8	4.0	16.3
369	471	20	2	3	1	5	2	5.0	17.665	0.9033	4.980	0.087	27.1	4.0	16.3
369	471	20	2	4	1	5	2	7.3	15.667	0.8932	7.930	0.103	27.3	4.0	16.3
369	471	20	2	5	1	5	2	3.8	19.892	1.0021	5.620	0.112	26.8	4.0	16.3
369	411	21	1	1	1	1	4	83.4	0.343	0.2321	4.030	0.053	15.8	15.6	12.7
369	411	21	1	2	1	1	4	85.4	1.546	0.3902	1.120	0.045	19.3	15.6	12.7
369	411	21	1	3	1	1	4	86.2	2.334	0.2892	3.550	0.036	18.2	15.6	12.7
369	411	21	1	4	1	1	4	83.2	2.112	0.3421	2.010	0.011	20.8	15.6	12.7
369	411	21	1	5	1	1	4	81.6	2.002	0.1143	4.670	0.048	20.4	15.6	12.7
369	411	21	2	1	1	1	4	76.5	1.565	0.0922	3.270	0.076	23.4	15.6	12.7
369	411	21	2	2	1	1	4	78.8	1.201	0.2154	5.670	0.038	26.7	15.6	12.7
369	411	21	2	3	1	1	4	83.7	0.998	0.3216	7.320	0.072	25.2	15.6	12.7
369	411	21	2	4	1	1	4	82.6	1.502	0.2892	4.440	0.053	21.0	15.6	12.7
369	411	21	2	5	1	1	4	79.8	0.341	0.2917	5.030	0.094	20.1	15.6	12.7
330	555	22	1	1	1	2	6	73.2	3.445	0.4999	4.330	0.033	16.5	5.7	10.9
330	555	22	1	2	1	2	6	63.4	4.750	0.6541	3.980	0.021	14.7	5.7	10.9
330	555	22	1	3	1	2	6	66.5	3.443	0.8321	6.000	0.037	18.2	5.7	10.9
330	555	22	1	4	1	2	6	61.2	4.561	0.7265	3.050	0.056	19.8	5.7	10.9
330	555	22	1	5	1	2	6	62.1	4.332	0.6112	2.120	0.011	20.3	5.7	10.9
330	555	22	2	1	1	2	6	47.8	4.726	0.5412	3.450	0.054	24.1	5.7	10.9
330	555	22	2	2	1	2	6	56.7	3.412	0.6502	6.900	0.087	25.4	5.7	10.9
330	555	22	2	3	1	2	6	52.8	4.876	0.8743	6.040	0.059	22.3	5.7	10.9
330	555	22	2	4	1	2	6	59.0	4.501	0.7217	3.890	0.088	25.6	5.7	10.9

330	555	22	2	5	1	2	6	48.9	3.004	0.8322	5.660	0.091	20.8	5.7	10.9
359	417	23	1	1	1	3	3	46.5	5.443	0.8991	5.040	0.065	17.6	10.1	14.5
359	417	23	1	2	1	3	3	38.9	7.606	0.8911	4.530	0.047	19.4	10.1	14.5
359	417	23	1	3	1	3	3	44.4	6.120	0.7991	3.020	0.043	20.5	10.1	14.5
359	417	23	1	4	1	3	3	43.0	7.667	0.9002	3.780	0.035	15.1	10.1	14.5
359	417	23	1	5	1	3	3	48.2	5.691	0.9030	4.890	0.040	19.3	10.1	14.5
359	417	23	2	1	1	3	3	35.6	6.776	0.9822	6.870	0.044	29.8	10.1	14.5
359	417	23	2	2	1	3	3	29.8	8.776	0.7891	3.690	0.056	27.2	10.1	14.5
359	417	23	2	3	1	3	3	37.2	8.543	0.9811	5.280	0.078	31.2	10.1	14.5
359	417	23	2	4	1	3	3	35.4	8.102	0.7811	4.990	0.067	26.5	10.1	14.5
359	417	23	2	5	1	3	3	33.0	7.665	0.9821	9.430	0.053	29.6	10.1	14.5
348	476	24	1	1	1	4	2	12.6	14.556	0.9564	6.020	0.058	18.7	16.7	18.2
348	476	24	1	2	1	4	2	17.5	16.755	0.9743	4.840	0.045	19.1	16.7	18.2
348	476	24	1	3	1	4	2	11.1	14.332	0.9841	3.090	0.035	20.5	16.7	18.2
348	476	24	1	4	1	4	2	16.5	14.762	0.8968	5.030	0.051	23.4	16.7	18.2
348	476	24	1	5	1	4	2	13.2	16.554	0.9021	4.890	0.063	25.1	16.7	18.2
348	476	24	2	1	1	4	2	8.1	12.110	0.8772	5.670	0.098	27.6	16.7	18.2
348	476	24	2	2	1	4	2	9.8	13.442	0.9999	6.890	0.075	31.2	16.7	18.2
348	476	24	2	3	1	4	2	8.7	16.540	0.8922	9.180	0.065	30.9	16.7	18.2
348	476	24	2	4	1	4	2	7.3	12.002	1.0021	4.990	0.094	26.5	16.7	18.2
348	476	24	2	5	1	4	2	6.4	16.092	0.9882	8.560	0.067	25.8	16.7	18.2
406	489	25	1	1	1	5	2	8.1	15.121	0.9055	4.760	0.054	23.4	6.5	15.3
406	489	25	1	2	1	5	2	6.5	17.665	0.9807	3.890	0.035	17.6	6.5	15.3
406	489	25	1	3	1	5	2	7.3	19.820	0.9943	4.440	0.026	23.5	6.5	15.3
406	489	25	1	4	1	5	2	4.2	20.200	0.9916	4.620	0.032	17.2	6.5	15.3
406	489	25	1	5	1	5	2	6.5	14.550	0.8944	3.030	0.021	19.8	6.5	15.3
406	489	25	2	1	1	5	2	3.9	17.660	1.0212	5.550	0.054	23.4	6.5	15.3
406	489	25	2	2	1	5	2	3.4	18.904	0.9333	6.720	0.080	22.5	6.5	15.3
406	489	25	2	3	1	5	2	4.0	18.993	0.8923	7.520	0.045	33.7	6.5	15.3
406	489	25	2	4	1	5	2	5.4	19.322	0.7833	6.940	0.067	32.1	6.5	15.3
406	489	25	2	5	1	5	2	3.4	16.776	0.9965	6.710	0.087	25.6	6.5	15.3
346	572	26	1	1	2	1	6	86.6	0.192	0.3221	4.560	0.050	11.4	13.4	10.9
346	572	26	1	2	2	1	6	83.4	1.992	0.0127	5.170	0.043	9.8	13.4	10.9
346	572	26	1	3	2	1	6	89.8	2.342	0.1215	3.340	0.032	16.5	13.4	10.9
346	572	26	1	4	2	1	6	87.1	1.829	0.3125	4.450	0.003	15.4	13.4	10.9
346	572	26	1	5	2	1	6	78.9	1.892	0.3011	2.120	0.083	17.6	13.4	10.9
346	572	26	2	1	2	1	6	81.3	0.121	0.2102	2.870	0.032	18.7	13.4	10.9
346	572	26	2	2	2	1	6	84.4	1.554	0.0116	5.660	0.056	13.2	13.4	10.9
346	572	26	2	3	2	1	6	87.7	2.542	0.1456	3.430	0.034	15.6	13.4	10.9
346	572	26	2	4	2	1	6	88.0	2.118	0.1768	5.430	0.067	17.8	13.4	10.9
346	572	26	2	5	2	1	6	83.2	2.892	0.1815	4.770	0.021	20.7	13.4	10.9
304	512	27	1	1	2	2	6	71.3	3.443	0.5564	3.560	0.034	23.5	12.1	13.8
304	512	27	1	2	2	2	6	65.7	4.542	0.6783	4.530	0.045	21.0	12.1	13.8
304	512	27	1	3	2	2	6	66.8	3.725	0.6595	2.530	0.047	23.7	12.1	13.8
304	512	27	1	4	2	2	6	73.0	4.555	0.7611	5.460	0.041	19.1	12.1	13.8
304	512	27	1	5	2	2	6	63.2	3.333	0.8334	6.030	0.035	18.4	12.1	13.8
304	512	27	2	1	2	2	6	66.1	2.789	0.7832	5.400	0.053	24.1	12.1	13.8
304	512	27	2	2	2	2	6	66.0	3.445	0.6552	2.100	0.041	17.1	12.1	13.8
304	512	27	2	3	2	2	6	74.3	4.335	0.7892	0.990	0.058	16.3	12.1	13.8
304	512	27	2	4	2	2	6	63.8	4.102	0.8921	1.320	0.021	21.9	12.1	13.8
304	512	27	2	5	2	2	6	63.4	3.974	0.6202	1.760	0.029	23.7	12.1	13.8

376	439	28	1	1	2	3	4	53.2	7.334	0.8096	4.550	0.045	18.2	7.6	12.1
376	439	28	1	2	2	3	4	46.7	5.661	0.8407	6.660	0.037	19.3	7.3	12.1
376	439	28	1	3	2	3	4	51.3	8.659	0.9804	5.140	0.065	15.2	7.3	12.1
376	439	28	1	4	2	3	4	56.8	7.661	0.9843	4.440	0.045	18.4	7.3	12.1
376	439	28	1	5	2	3	4	45.6	5.432	0.5564	5.600	0.047	19.5	7.3	12.1
376	439	28	2	1	2	3	4	44.5	3.445	0.6437	3.450	0.061	16.0	7.3	12.1
376	439	28	2	2	2	3	4	48.7	4.556	0.7789	3.760	0.053	19.2	7.3	12.1
376	439	28	2	3	2	3	4	43.2	6.791	0.9987	4.470	0.058	23.7	7.3	12.1
376	439	28	2	4	2	3	4	42.5	8.113	0.6787	3.090	0.049	26.5	7.3	12.1
376	439	28	2	5	2	3	4	38.9	6.579	0.9987	2.870	0.041	21.3	7.3	12.0
376	432	29	1	1	2	4	5	22.0	15.665	0.9445	3.610	0.052	24.7	0.0	16.8
376	432	29	1	2	2	4	5	15.6	16.832	0.9933	4.560	0.043	26.2	0.0	16.8
376	432	29	1	3	2	4	5	11.0	14.553	0.8992	5.630	0.032	17.3	0.0	16.8
376	432	29	1	4	2	4	5	12.6	15.607	0.9935	4.090	0.067	19.7	0.0	16.8
376	432	29	1	5	2	4	5	16.7	16.099	0.8902	6.070	0.034	18.5	0.0	16.8
376	432	29	2	1	2	4	5	15.6	12.431	0.9540	4.890	0.055	23.7	0.0	16.8
376	432	29	2	2	2	4	5	13.3	14.543	0.8009	5.560	0.032	21.9	0.0	16.8
376	432	29	2	3	2	4	5	15.4	10.110	0.9112	3.330	0.047	25.6	0.0	16.8
376	432	29	2	4	2	4	5	12.6	13.679	0.7662	5.780	0.065	23.7	0.0	16.8
376	432	29	2	5	2	4	5	15.7	16.554	0.9921	7.030	0.052	20.9	0.0	16.8
359	471	30	1	1	2	5	2	8.9	16.312	0.9555	5.440	0.049	23.2	6.2	9.6
359	471	30	1	2	2	5	2	5.5	16.776	0.9988	4.300	0.050	18.7	6.2	9.6
359	471	30	1	3	2	5	2	6.4	15.102	1.0022	2.020	0.034	26.1	6.2	9.6
359	471	30	1	4	2	5	2	7.0	17.889	0.8992	4.440	0.046	20.3	6.2	9.6
359	471	30	1	5	2	5	2	8.4	18.772	0.9882	5.060	0.047	17.1	6.2	9.6
359	471	30	2	1	2	5	2	8.2	19.020	0.8775	7.610	0.048	19.4	6.2	9.6
359	471	30	2	2	2	5	2	6.5	21.430	0.9113	4.580	0.051	18.0	6.2	9.6
359	471	30	2	3	2	5	2	4.1	17.665	0.9871	5.930	0.039	23.6	6.2	9.6
359	471	30	2	4	2	5	2	5.6	18.634	1.0562	5.990	0.053	27.6	6.2	9.6
359	471	30	2	5	2	5	2	6.7	16.765	0.9822	4.030	0.056	24.1	6.2	9.6

Sample Records for Village Community Survey

26,0,1,4,3,3,2,1,5,6,1,9,9,3,650,3,1,9,1,2,1,2,2,1,2,9,9,9,1,
20,1,1,4,1,1,2,1,5,6,2,9,9,2,1000,5,1,9,1,2,2,1,2,1,2,9,9,9,1,
218,1,4,3,4,2,1,1,3,3,1,9,4,3,4350,1,1,9,1,1,1,2,1,2,2,9,9,9,5,

The 29 variables separated by commas on each record correspond to the questions on the questionnaire in Appendix I.

Raw data for village community project

26,0,1,4,3,3,2,1,5,6,1,9,9,3,650,3,1,9,1,2,1,2,2,1,2,9,9,9,1,
20,1,1,4,1,1,2,1,5,6,2,9,9,2,1000,5,1,9,1,2,2,1,2,1,2,9,9,9,1,
218,1,4,3,4,2,1,1,3,3,1,9,4,3,4350,1,1,9,1,1,1,2,1,2,2,9,9,9,5,
180,1,2,2,4,3,4,1,2,4,2,9,9,2,350,2,1,9,1,1,2,1,2,1,2,9,9,9,2,
154,2,2,2,1,4,2,1,2,5,2,9,9,2,50,3,1,9,1,2,2,2,2,1,1,1,9,9,3,
6,3,2,4,1,2,3,1,2,1,1,2,7,4,6400,15,1,9,1,2,1,1,2,2,2,9,9,9,3,
117,3,4,3,8,2,3,1,3,2,1,2,2,3,2050,5,1,9,1,1,1,2,2,2,2,9,9,9,5,
185,3,2,2,1,3,4,1,1,1,1,1,1,5,200,3,1,9,1,2,1,2,2,2,2,9,9,9,4,
129,3,1,2,1,3,2,1,5,6,2,9,9,4,3250,4,1,9,1,1,1,1,2,1,2,9,9,9,1,
196,3,2,1,2,4,3,1,1,2,1,2,5,3,1100,2,1,9,1,2,2,2,1,1,1,1,9,9,1,
210,4,2,3,2,5,2,1,2,2,1,2,2,3,600,2,1,9,1,2,2,2,2,1,1,2,9,9,1,
227,6,4,2,1,1,2,1,5,3,1,2,5,2,4750,4,1,9,1,1,2,1,2,2,2,9,9,9,2,

207,6,1,1,4,1,2,1,5,6,2,9,9,2,3050,2,1,9,1,2,2,1,2,1,2,9,9,9,3,
18,6,3,4,3,3,2,1,4,1,1,2,6,3,350,3,1,9,1,2,1,2,2,2,2,9,9,9,3,
289,7,1,3,1,1,2,1,3,3,1,1,7,1,650,6,1,9,1,2,2,1,2,1,2,9,9,9,4,
275,7,3,3,2,1,2,1,3,4,1,9,9,1,2050,5,1,9,1,1,2,1,2,1,2,9,9,9,2,
42,7,1,1,4,2,3,1,4,3,2,1,2,2,2300,4,1,9,1,2,2,2,2,1,1,2,9,9,3,
337,9,2,4,2,5,2,1,3,3,2,1,6,3,50,15,1,9,1,2,1,1,2,2,2,9,9,9,3,
209,10,9,9,9,1,2,2,2,1,1,2,1,2,250,17,1,9,1,1,2,1,2,1,2,9,9,9,2,
236,12,9,9,9,1,4,1,3,4,1,9,9,1,2050,4,1,9,1,2,2,1,1,2,2,9,9,9,4,
102,13,9,9,9,3,2,1,2,2,2,1,2,3,750,6,1,9,1,2,1,2,2,1,2,9,9,9,4,
62,13,9,9,9,4,1,1,2,2,1,1,1,3,500,7,1,9,1,2,1,1,2,2,2,9,9,9,4,
145,14,9,9,9,1,2,1,5,6,1,9,9,2,3050,3,1,9,1,2,2,2,2,2,1,2,9,9,4,
39,14,9,9,9,2,2,1,4,5,2,9,9,2,1250,6,1,9,1,1,2,2,2,1,2,9,9,9,2,
358,14,9,9,9,3,2,1,5,6,1,9,9,3,950,7,1,9,1,2,2,1,2,1,2,9,9,9,3,
167,14,9,9,9,4,2,1,2,2,2,2,3,3,650,5,1,9,1,2,2,1,2,1,1,1,9,9,3,
1,15,9,9,9,1,2,1,4,3,1,2,1,1,400,7,1,9,1,2,2,2,2,2,2,9,9,9,1,
295,16,9,9,9,4,2,1,4,2,1,2,2,2,500,6,1,9,1,2,1,1,2,2,2,9,9,9,3,
344,17,9,9,9,1,2,1,3,2,1,2,5,2,1000,4,1,9,1,2,2,1,2,2,2,9,9,9,1,
259,17,9,9,9,2,4,1,2,2,1,2,4,2,3100,4,1,9,1,1,2,2,2,2,2,9,9,9,2,
308,18,9,9,9,4,2,1,4,5,2,9,9,2,850,6,1,9,1,2,2,1,1,1,1,2,9,9,3,
55,19,9,9,9,3,2,1,2,7,2,9,9,3,850,16,1,9,1,1,2,1,1,1,1,1,9,9,5,
252,19,9,9,9,4,2,1,3,1,2,1,1,3,1250,4,1,9,1,1,1,2,2,2,2,9,9,9,2,
126,19,9,9,9,4,2,1,3,2,2,1,1,2,450,18,1,9,1,2,2,1,2,2,1,1,9,9,3,
168,19,9,9,9,4,2,1,4,2,1,2,5,3,750,4,1,9,1,2,1,1,2,1,2,9,9,9,4,
193,21,9,9,9,1,4,1,3,1,1,2,1,2,300,5,1,9,1,1,2,2,2,1,2,9,9,9,1,
182,21,9,9,9,1,3,1,5,6,2,9,9,2,1350,5,1,9,1,2,2,1,2,1,2,9,9,9,1,
187,21,9,9,9,2,1,1,3,2,1,2,7,4,2350,1,1,9,1,2,1,2,2,2,1,1,9,9,3,
144,21,9,9,9,2,3,1,5,6,2,9,9,3,950,4,1,9,1,2,1,2,1,2,2,9,9,9,3,
198,21,9,9,9,5,3,1,4,3,2,1,4,3,600,6,1,9,1,2,2,2,2,2,2,9,9,9,4,
49,22,9,9,9,4,6,1,3,4,2,9,9,1,100,4,1,9,1,1,2,1,2,1,2,9,9,9,5,
109,23,9,9,9,4,1,1,5,5,2,9,9,1,900,2,1,9,1,2,1,2,2,1,1,2,9,9,3,
219,24,9,9,9,3,2,1,3,4,2,9,9,1,150,14,1,9,1,2,2,1,1,1,1,2,9,9,3,
99,25,9,9,9,1,4,1,3,2,2,2,3,2,750,14,1,9,1,2,2,1,2,1,2,9,9,9,1,
335,26,9,9,9,1,2,2,3,2,1,2,1,4,800,15,1,9,1,2,2,1,2,1,2,9,9,9,1,
146,26,9,9,9,3,1,2,3,7,1,9,9,2,900,1,1,9,1,2,1,2,2,2,2,9,9,9,4,
234,26,9,9,9,4,3,1,3,2,2,2,1,3,350,4,1,9,1,1,2,2,2,2,2,9,9,9,1,
244,27,9,9,9,1,2,2,3,2,1,1,2,3,250,5,1,9,1,1,2,1,2,2,2,9,9,9,3,
73,27,9,9,9,4,2,1,5,6,2,9,9,2,800,1,1,9,1,2,1,2,2,1,2,9,9,9,4,
211,28,9,9,9,2,5,1,3,2,1,1,1,5,3150,5,1,9,1,2,1,1,2,2,2,9,9,9,4,
178,28,9,9,9,2,2,2,5,6,2,9,9,2,1350,8,1,9,1,2,1,2,2,1,1,1,9,9,1,
173,28,9,9,9,3,2,2,3,1,1,2,1,2,4350,4,1,9,1,1,1,2,2,1,1,1,9,9,2,
339,29,9,9,9,3,2,1,3,2,1,1,2,2,600,2,1,9,1,2,2,2,2,2,2,9,9,9,1,
261,30,9,9,9,1,3,2,4,2,1,2,4,3,300,1,1,9,1,2,2,2,2,1,2,9,9,9,1,
88,30,9,9,9,6,2,1,4,2,2,2,2,2,1000,1,1,9,1,1,2,1,2,1,1,1,9,9,5,
174,31,9,9,9,2,2,2,5,5,1,9,9,3,650,1,1,9,1,2,2,2,2,1,1,1,9,9,4,
286,31,9,9,9,4,3,1,3,2,2,2,1,2,200,3,1,9,1,2,1,2,2,2,2,9,9,9,4,
34,34,9,9,9,1,3,2,3,1,1,2,1,3,600,4,1,9,1,1,2,2,1,1,2,9,9,9,5,
314,34,9,9,9,2,2,2,3,2,2,2,5,2,5500,4,1,9,1,2,1,2,2,2,2,9,9,9,3,
3,34,9,9,9,2,3,1,5,6,2,9,9,2,1850,5,1,9,1,2,1,2,2,2,1,2,9,9,1,
169,36,9,9,9,4,1,1,3,2,2,2,3,2,150,5,1,9,1,2,2,2,2,2,2,9,9,9,3,
181,37,9,9,9,1,1,2,3,1,1,1,1,4,450,4,1,9,1,2,2,1,2,2,1,2,9,9,3,
239,41,9,9,9,2,3,1,3,4,2,9,9,1,200,3,1,9,1,2,1,2,2,2,2,9,9,9,4,

281,42,9,9,9,2,6,1,4,2,2,2,5,2,700,18,1,9,1,2,2,1,2,1,1,1,9,9,1,
52,44,9,9,9,3,2,1,3,2,2,2,4,3,600,20,1,9,1,2,1,1,2,2,2,9,9,9,2,
283,46,9,9,9,1,5,1,5,6,2,9,9,2,650,5,1,9,1,1,2,1,1,2,1,1,9,9,1,
273,51,9,9,9,2,2,1,5,1,1,2,7,4,450,6,1,9,1,2,2,2,2,2,2,9,9,9,2,
119,60,9,9,9,1,5,2,5,6,2,9,9,2,1500,14,1,9,1,2,2,1,2,1,2,9,9,9,3,
276,2,1,3,2,6,2,1,5,6,2,9,9,2,600,4,2,1,1,2,1,1,2,1,2,9,9,9,3,
112,3,1,4,3,1,2,1,5,6,1,9,9,1,200,5,2,4,1,1,2,2,2,1,2,9,9,9,2,
133,3,3,3,4,3,3,1,3,2,1,2,2,5,600,2,2,3,1,2,2,2,2,1,1,2,9,9,4,
21,4,3,4,3,2,5,1,4,1,1,2,1,3,2200,12,2,3,1,1,1,1,2,1,1,1,9,9,5,
348,5,1,2,1,1,2,1,5,6,2,9,9,1,2000,11,2,2,1,2,2,1,2,2,2,9,9,9,4,
195,5,2,3,1,5,1,1,2,1,2,1,1,2,250,8,2,3,1,2,1,2,2,2,2,9,9,9,4,
41,6,2,2,1,3,2,1,1,1,2,1,1,3,450,2,2,4,1,2,1,2,2,2,2,9,9,9,3,
192,7,4,3,1,2,2,1,2,5,2,9,9,3,950,5,2,4,1,1,2,1,1,2,2,9,9,9,2,
332,9,3,1,2,4,3,1,2,4,1,9,9,1,200,4,2,4,1,2,1,2,2,2,2,9,9,9,1,
269,10,9,9,9,6,4,1,2,2,2,2,1,3,1250,1,2,4,1,1,2,2,2,2,2,9,9,9,1,
336,11,9,9,9,3,2,1,5,6,2,9,9,2,4100,8,2,4,1,2,2,2,1,2,1,1,9,9,1,
5,12,9,9,9,2,2,1,3,3,1,2,7,2,2450,3,2,4,1,2,1,1,2,1,2,9,9,9,3,
25,12,9,9,9,2,2,1,4,5,2,9,9,3,1750,5,2,4,1,2,1,2,2,1,2,9,9,9,2,
94,13,9,9,9,1,2,1,2,2,1,2,1,2,1550,12,2,2,1,2,2,1,2,1,1,2,9,9,2,
162,13,9,9,9,2,4,2,5,6,2,9,9,1,6450,3,2,4,1,2,2,2,2,1,1,2,9,9,1,
78,14,9,9,9,1,2,1,5,6,2,9,9,1,400,6,2,3,1,2,2,1,1,2,2,9,9,9,1,
153,15,9,9,9,1,2,1,3,2,1,2,2,3,400,7,2,3,1,2,2,1,2,1,1,1,9,9,4,
312,16,9,9,9,1,2,1,4,7,1,9,9,1,2550,6,2,3,1,2,2,1,2,2,2,9,9,9,3,
103,17,9,9,9,2,2,1,3,2,1,2,2,3,4000,2,2,4,1,1,2,2,2,2,2,9,9,9,5,
70,17,9,9,9,2,3,2,4,7,1,9,9,1,900,14,2,4,1,2,1,1,1,1,2,9,9,9,4,
163,17,9,9,9,3,2,1,5,2,1,2,1,4,3400,6,2,3,1,1,1,2,2,2,2,9,9,9,5,
349,18,9,9,9,2,2,2,5,6,1,9,9,2,1250,7,2,1,1,1,2,1,2,2,1,1,9,9,2,
54,20,9,9,9,1,2,1,2,2,1,2,3,1,900,1,2,3,1,2,2,2,2,2,2,9,9,9,3,
256,21,9,9,9,1,2,1,4,5,2,9,9,1,950,3,2,4,1,1,2,2,2,2,2,9,9,9,2,
142,21,9,9,9,2,3,1,4,3,2,2,2,2,6700,4,2,4,1,2,1,2,2,1,2,9,9,9,1,
31,22,9,9,9,4,3,1,3,2,1,2,4,3,500,6,2,3,1,2,2,1,2,1,1,1,9,9,2,
100,23,9,9,9,3,2,1,3,2,1,2,2,2,650,6,2,2,1,2,1,1,2,2,2,9,9,9,3,
106,23,9,9,9,3,2,2,4,2,1,2,1,4,1500,8,2,4,1,2,2,1,2,1,1,2,9,9,3,
157,25,9,9,9,2,2,1,3,2,2,2,6,3,5150,16,2,3,1,2,1,1,2,2,1,2,9,9,3,
288,26,9,9,9,3,2,1,5,6,1,9,9,4,100,7,2,1,1,2,1,2,1,1,1,1,9,9,4,
240,27,9,9,9,2,4,1,3,2,1,2,2,4,4000,16,2,1,1,2,2,1,2,2,2,9,9,9,4,
324,27,9,9,9,2,3,1,5,5,1,9,9,4,150,2,2,3,1,2,1,2,2,1,1,2,9,9,3,
123,27,9,9,9,5,1,1,2,2,1,2,7,4,600,2,2,4,1,1,2,2,1,1,1,2,9,9,2,
285,28,9,9,9,4,1,1,3,2,1,2,2,3,1400,13,2,2,1,2,2,1,2,1,1,2,9,9,1,
302,32,9,9,9,1,2,1,3,2,2,2,2,2,450,5,2,4,1,1,2,1,2,1,2,9,9,9,2,
343,32,9,9,9,3,2,1,3,3,1,1,4,3,1650,6,2,3,1,1,1,2,2,1,2,9,9,9,1,
53,33,9,9,9,2,2,1,4,2,2,2,5,2,650,8,2,3,1,2,2,1,2,1,2,9,9,9,3,
108,33,9,9,9,2,3,1,5,6,2,9,9,1,250,3,2,3,1,2,1,2,1,1,2,9,9,9,3,
107,34,9,9,9,2,2,2,3,2,1,2,3,3,6350,3,2,3,1,2,2,2,2,1,2,9,9,9,3,
150,40,9,9,9,3,2,2,4,3,2,1,2,3,3050,3,2,4,1,1,2,2,2,1,1,1,9,9,2,
223,41,9,9,9,1,1,1,4,1,2,2,7,2,1100,2,2,3,1,1,2,2,2,2,1,1,9,9,5,
80,43,9,9,9,2,3,1,5,6,2,9,9,2,1700,1,2,3,1,1,1,2,2,2,1,2,9,9,5,
317,44,9,9,9,2,2,1,4,2,1,2,1,4,850,1,2,3,1,2,1,2,1,2,2,9,9,9,1,
65,45,9,9,9,1,1,2,4,2,1,2,1,3,800,21,2,3,1,2,2,1,2,1,2,9,9,9,3,
87,45,9,9,9,2,2,1,3,2,1,2,2,4,5550,1,2,2,1,2,1,2,2,2,1,1,9,9,3,
4,47,9,9,9,1,2,1,5,6,2,9,9,1,2950,4,2,2,1,2,2,1,1,1,2,9,9,9,2,

135,52,9,9,9,1,3,2,5,6,2,9,9,1,800,3,2,2,1,2,2,1,2,2,2,9,9,9,4,
318,52,9,9,9,1,3,1,5,6,2,9,9,2,5100,3,2,4,1,2,2,2,2,1,2,9,9,9,4,
311,53,9,9,9,2,2,1,4,4,1,9,9,2,650,3,2,1,1,1,1,1,2,2,2,9,9,9,5,
203,54,9,9,9,2,2,2,3,5,1,9,9,2,3500,4,2,3,1,2,2,2,2,2,1,1,9,9,3,
175,54,9,9,9,3,2,2,3,2,2,2,1,4,450,2,2,3,1,2,1,2,1,2,1,2,9,9,1,
327,56,9,9,9,2,1,1,4,2,2,2,2,2,2000,1,2,4,1,1,2,1,2,1,2,9,9,9,5,
321,63,9,9,9,2,3,2,5,5,2,9,9,2,850,10,2,2,1,2,1,1,1,2,1,1,9,9,2,
345,64,9,9,9,1,2,1,4,5,2,9,9,2,3000,8,2,1,1,2,2,1,2,2,1,2,9,9,3,
134,0,1,4,1,2,2,1,5,6,1,9,9,2,600,1,1,9,2,9,9,9,9,9,9,9,2,1,3,
179,0,1,2,1,2,2,1,5,6,1,9,9,1,450,0,1,9,2,9,9,9,9,9,9,9,2,2,4,
205,0,2,2,1,4,2,1,1,2,2,2,5,2,2450,1,1,9,2,9,9,9,9,9,9,9,1,1,2,
74,1,4,3,4,1,2,1,3,3,2,2,2,1,1750,2,1,9,2,9,9,9,9,9,9,9,1,2,5,
356,1,1,1,2,2,2,1,4,5,2,9,9,2,600,0,1,9,2,9,9,9,9,9,9,9,2,2,3,
19,1,2,2,1,5,3,1,2,2,2,2,1,3,400,2,1,9,2,9,9,9,9,9,9,9,2,1,3,
164,2,4,3,1,1,2,1,2,1,1,2,7,3,50,13,1,9,2,9,9,9,9,9,9,9,2,2,3,
2,2,3,3,8,3,2,1,3,5,2,9,9,2,1900,11,1,9,2,9,9,9,9,9,9,9,2,2,4,
40,3,3,3,2,2,2,1,4,2,1,1,6,3,2000,4,1,9,2,9,9,9,9,9,9,9,1,2,2,
355,4,2,2,3,1,5,2,2,2,1,2,4,3,3550,3,1,9,2,9,9,9,9,9,9,9,2,2,4,
128,4,1,4,2,1,2,1,5,6,2,9,9,2,2650,3,1,9,2,9,9,9,9,9,9,9,1,2,5,
59,4,1,2,1,2,2,1,5,6,2,9,9,2,200,6,1,9,2,9,9,9,9,9,9,9,2,2,4,
194,4,3,4,8,3,2,1,3,3,1,1,3,3,60,3,1,9,2,9,9,9,9,9,9,9,2,2,3,
58,4,2,2,1,4,2,1,2,2,2,2,2,3,300,6,1,9,2,9,9,9,9,9,9,9,2,1,1,
46,5,3,1,3,2,2,1,4,2,1,1,6,2,650,4,1,9,2,9,9,9,9,9,9,9,2,2,3,
22,5,1,3,1,2,4,1,5,5,2,9,9,2,350,1,1,9,2,9,9,9,9,9,9,9,2,2,3,
104,5,1,4,2,3,2,2,4,3,2,1,2,2,350,6,1,9,2,9,9,9,9,9,9,9,2,2,4,
200,6,4,3,2,3,3,1,3,2,2,2,4,5,100,1,1,9,2,9,9,9,9,9,9,9,1,2,5,
183,6,1,2,1,3,2,1,5,6,2,9,9,3,650,8,1,9,2,9,9,9,9,9,9,9,2,1,4,
352,6,2,2,4,4,1,1,1,4,1,9,9,1,350,7,1,9,2,9,9,9,9,9,9,9,2,2,3,
309,6,4,4,8,4,2,1,2,4,2,9,9,2,650,6,1,9,2,9,9,9,9,9,9,9,2,1,3,
8,7,4,3,8,1,2,2,1,2,1,2,6,1,650,5,1,9,2,9,9,9,9,9,9,9,2,2,3,
326,7,1,3,1,2,4,2,5,6,2,9,9,2,750,6,1,9,2,9,9,9,9,9,9,9,2,2,4,
115,7,1,1,4,3,2,1,5,6,1,9,9,3,1350,6,1,9,2,9,9,9,9,9,9,9,2,1,3,
84,8,3,1,3,1,2,1,4,3,1,2,2,1,3050,7,1,9,2,9,9,9,9,9,9,9,1,1,5,
44,8,2,2,3,4,2,1,1,2,2,2,1,4,600,6,1,9,2,9,9,9,9,9,9,9,2,2,3,
7,8,3,4,3,4,5,1,3,2,2,2,4,2,800,13,1,9,2,9,9,9,9,9,9,9,2,2,3,
132,10,9,9,9,2,3,1,5,6,2,9,9,1,950,20,1,9,2,9,9,9,9,9,9,9,2,2,3,
226,10,9,9,9,2,2,1,1,7,1,9,9,1,1950,3,1,9,2,9,9,9,9,9,9,9,2,2,4,
253,10,9,9,9,3,4,1,2,2,1,2,6,2,800,4,1,9,2,9,9,9,9,9,9,9,2,2,4,
230,11,9,9,9,1,2,1,4,2,1,2,7,3,3550,6,1,9,2,9,9,9,9,9,9,9,2,2,3,
300,11,9,9,9,2,2,1,4,2,2,2,7,3,700,6,1,9,2,9,9,9,9,9,9,9,2,1,3,
225,12,9,9,9,2,2,1,4,2,1,2,2,3,1550,151,9,2,9,9,9,9,9,9,9,2,2,1,
131,12,9,9,9,2,2,1,1,7,1,9,9,2,1650,14,1,9,2,9,9,9,9,9,9,9,2,2,1,
82,12,9,9,9,3,1,1,4,2,1,2,4,4,5300,4,1,9,2,9,9,9,9,9,9,9,2,2,3,
50,12,9,9,9,7,1,1,5,6,2,9,9,4,550,11,1,9,2,9,9,9,9,9,9,9,2,1,1,
23,13,9,9,9,2,2,1,3,2,1,2,5,2,1950,5,1,9,2,9,9,9,9,9,9,9,1,2,2,
224,13,9,9,9,3,2,1,2,3,1,1,4,3,650,5,1,9,2,9,9,9,9,9,9,9,1,2,5,
56,13,9,9,9,3,2,2,5,6,2,9,9,2,600,7,1,9,2,9,9,9,9,9,9,9,1,2,2,
96,13,9,9,9,7,2,1,1,3,2,2,7,3,450,6,1,9,2,9,9,9,9,9,9,9,1,2,5,
89,14,9,9,9,1,2,2,5,6,2,9,9,2,4500,4,1,9,2,9,9,9,9,9,9,9,2,1,3,
47,14,9,9,9,2,2,1,4,2,2,2,1,3,4550,5,1,9,2,9,9,9,9,9,9,9,1,1,5,
32,14,9,9,9,2,2,1,3,4,2,9,9,1,650,3,1,9,2,9,9,9,9,9,9,9,1,2,3,

97,14,9,9,9,2,2,1,4,5,2,9,9,3,200,6,1,9,2,9,9,9,9,9,9,9,2,1,3,
101,14,9,9,9,3,3,1,3,5,2,9,9,3,2050,7,1,9,2,9,9,9,9,9,9,9,2,2,4,
137,14,9,9,9,3,4,1,4,5,2,9,9,2,2800,4,1,9,2,9,9,9,9,9,9,9,1,2,2,
16,14,9,9,9,3,4,1,5,6,2,9,9,3,500,6,1,9,2,9,9,9,9,9,9,9,2,2,4,
323,14,9,9,9,4,2,1,4,2,2,1,2,1,200,8,1,9,2,9,9,9,9,9,9,9,2,2,4,
341,14,9,9,9,5,2,1,3,2,2,2,5,3,750,6,1,9,2,9,9,9,9,9,9,9,2,2,4,
13,15,9,9,9,1,2,1,3,2,2,2,3,3,2750,3,1,9,2,9,9,9,9,9,9,9,1,2,2,
116,15,9,9,9,1,2,1,4,2,1,2,1,4,2850,6,1,9,2,9,9,9,9,9,9,9,2,2,4,
60,15,9,9,9,1,2,1,5,3,2,2,5,2,3000,6,1,9,2,9,9,9,9,9,9,9,2,2,3,
243,15,9,9,9,2,2,1,2,2,1,2,3,4,950,7,1,9,2,9,9,9,9,9,9,9,1,2,5,
221,15,9,9,9,2,2,1,3,2,2,1,1,3,2900,6,1,9,2,9,9,9,9,9,9,9,2,2,1,
306,15,9,9,9,2,2,1,3,2,1,1,1,4,3500,9,1,9,2,9,9,9,9,9,9,9,2,2,1,
271,15,9,9,9,2,2,1,1,7,2,9,9,2,1100,11,1,9,2,9,9,9,9,9,9,9,2,2,3,
284,15,9,9,9,3,2,1,2,3,1,1,3,2,750,14,1,9,2,9,9,9,9,9,9,9,1,1,2,
189,15,9,9,9,4,2,1,3,2,1,2,2,3,750,15,1,9,2,9,9,9,9,9,9,9,1,2,5,
69,16,9,9,9,1,2,1,3,2,2,2,1,3,5000,7,1,9,2,9,9,9,9,9,9,9,2,2,3,
248,16,9,9,9,2,2,1,2,2,1,2,4,2,50,6,1,9,2,9,9,9,9,9,9,9,2,2,4,
264,16,9,9,9,3,2,1,3,3,1,1,2,3,2800,4,1,9,2,9,9,9,9,9,9,9,1,2,5,
222,17,9,9,9,1,1,2,4,1,2,2,7,3,400,6,1,9,2,9,9,9,9,9,9,9,2,1,3,
215,17,9,9,9,1,2,1,1,2,1,1,2,2,2500,4,1,9,2,9,9,9,9,9,9,9,2,1,3,
320,17,9,9,9,2,2,1,3,2,2,2,4,3,4150,9,1,9,2,9,9,9,9,9,9,9,2,1,3,
237,17,9,9,9,3,2,1,3,1,1,2,7,2,700,13,1,9,2,9,9,9,9,9,9,9,1,2,2,
347,17,9,9,9,3,2,1,4,2,2,2,4,3,1100,4,1,9,2,9,9,9,9,9,9,9,2,1,1,
291,17,9,9,9,4,1,1,3,2,2,2,3,2,950,7,1,9,2,9,9,9,9,9,9,9,2,2,1,
299,17,9,9,9,5,5,1,4,2,1,1,2,2,150,5,1,9,2,9,9,9,9,9,9,9,1,2,2,
297,18,9,9,9,2,2,1,3,3,2,2,1,2,2400,4,1,9,2,9,9,9,9,9,9,9,2,1,4,
158,18,9,9,9,2,3,1,3,5,2,9,9,3,1050,5,1,9,2,9,9,9,9,9,9,9,2,1,4,
138,18,9,9,9,5,2,1,2,2,2,2,2,4,700,8,1,9,2,9,9,9,9,9,9,9,1,1,2,
333,20,9,9,9,1,6,1,1,2,2,1,2,1,4000,5,1,9,2,9,9,9,9,9,9,9,2,2,4,
287,20,9,9,9,1,2,1,4,3,1,2,4,1,700,4,1,9,2,9,9,9,9,9,9,9,2,1,4,
310,20,9,9,9,3,1,1,5,6,2,9,9,3,100,6,1,9,2,9,9,9,9,9,9,9,2,2,3,
350,21,9,9,9,1,4,1,4,2,2,1,6,2,2000,4,1,9,2,9,9,9,9,9,9,9,2,1,4,
250,21,9,9,9,2,2,1,2,2,1,2,4,1,2700,6,1,9,2,9,9,9,9,9,9,9,2,2,3,
14,21,9,9,9,2,5,2,5,6,1,9,9,3,1300,3,1,9,2,9,9,9,9,9,9,9,1,1,5,
280,21,9,9,9,3,2,1,3,2,1,2,7,2,1700,3,1,9,2,9,9,9,9,9,9,9,2,1,3,
260,21,9,9,9,6,2,1,2,5,2,9,9,3,1250,5,1,9,2,9,9,9,9,9,9,9,2,1,1,
296,22,9,9,9,1,2,2,5,6,2,9,9,2,4000,1,1,9,2,9,9,9,9,9,9,9,1,2,1,
270,23,9,9,9,1,1,1,3,2,1,2,5,3,350,6,1,9,2,9,9,9,9,9,9,9,1,2,1,
228,23,9,9,9,1,2,1,4,2,1,1,3,3,3550,6,1,9,2,9,9,9,9,9,9,9,2,2,4,
149,23,9,9,9,2,1,1,1,7,2,9,9,2,1050,7,1,9,2,9,9,9,9,9,9,9,2,2,4,
79,23,9,9,9,3,2,2,4,3,1,1,4,2,2450,8,1,9,2,9,9,9,9,9,9,9,2,2,4,
38,23,9,9,9,3,4,1,5,6,2,9,9,2,250,3,1,9,2,9,9,9,9,9,9,9,1,1,1,
121,23,9,9,9,4,2,1,3,2,1,1,1,3,700,6,1,9,2,9,9,9,9,9,9,9,2,1,3,
48,23,9,9,9,4,2,1,4,2,1,2,2,1,800,17,1,9,2,9,9,9,9,9,9,9,1,2,2,
64,23,9,9,9,5,2,2,3,2,2,1,7,3,300,12,1,9,2,9,9,9,9,9,9,9,2,2,4,
217,24,9,9,9,3,2,1,2,1,1,1,1,4,650,19,1,9,2,9,9,9,9,9,9,9,1,2,5,
258,24,9,9,9,4,3,2,1,1,1,2,6,2,450,5,1,9,2,9,9,9,9,9,9,9,1,2,2,
139,25,9,9,9,1,2,2,4,2,1,2,4,3,2000,5,1,9,2,9,9,9,9,9,9,9,2,2,3,
35,25,9,9,9,2,5,1,5,5,2,9,9,2,200,15,1,9,2,9,9,9,9,9,9,9,1,2,2,
303,26,9,9,9,1,2,1,2,2,2,2,4,2,350,14,1,9,2,9,9,9,9,9,9,9,2,2,4,
85,26,9,9,9,1,2,1,3,7,2,9,9,1,3450,13,1,9,2,9,9,9,9,9,9,9,2,2,4,

```
161,26,9,9,9,2,2,1,2,2,2,1,5,1,3250,1,1,9,2,9,9,9,9,9,9,9,1,2,1,
201,26,9,9,9,2,2,1,4,2,1,2,3,1,250,1,1,9,2,9,9,9,9,9,9,9,1,1,2,
290,26,9,9,9,2,2,2,4,2,1,2,4,2,100,3,1,9,2,9,9,9,9,9,9,9,1,1,2,
151,26,9,9,9,2,2,1,3,3,1,2,4,3,2150,1,1,9,2,9,9,9,9,9,9,9,2,2,4,
357,26,9,9,9,2,2,1,4,3,1,1,6,3,1750,2,1,9,2,9,9,9,9,9,9,9,2,1,4,
274,26,9,9,9,3,2,1,5,1,1,1,1,3,600,5,1,9,2,9,9,9,9,9,9,9,2,1,4,
166,26,9,9,9,3,2,1,2,2,2,1,6,2,1250,1,1,9,2,9,9,9,9,9,9,9,2,1,3,
292,26,9,9,9,3,1,2,3,2,1,2,6,3,100,4,1,9,2,9,9,9,9,9,9,9,2,1,3,
220,26,9,9,9,3,2,1,4,2,1,1,2,5,1600,5,1,9,2,9,9,9,9,9,9,9,2,2,4,
266,26,9,9,9,3,4,1,4,2,1,2,5,4,1750,1,1,9,2,9,9,9,9,9,9,9,2,2,4,
176,26,9,9,9,4,1,1,2,1,1,1,1,3,300,2,1,9,2,9,9,9,9,9,9,9,2,2,4,
76,26,9,9,9,4,1,2,3,5,2,9,9,2,400,12,1,9,2,9,9,9,9,9,9,9,2,2,4,
113,27,9,9,9,6,3,1,3,2,1,2,2,3,2350,5,1,9,2,9,9,9,9,9,9,9,2,2,3,
160,28,9,9,9,2,2,1,4,2,1,2,4,1,50,14,1,9,2,9,9,9,9,9,9,9,2,2,4,
268,28,9,9,9,4,4,1,5,6,1,9,9,3,150,11,1,9,2,9,9,9,9,9,9,9,1,2,4,
130,29,9,9,9,3,1,1,4,3,1,1,7,1,1000,1,1,9,2,9,9,9,9,9,9,9,2,2,3,
12,30,9,9,9,4,2,2,3,2,1,1,2,3,350,5,1,9,2,9,9,9,9,9,9,9,2,2,3,
28,30,9,9,9,5,2,1,5,6,2,9,9,3,4000,8,1,9,2,9,9,9,9,9,9,9,2,2,4,
338,31,9,9,9,1,2,1,5,6,2,9,9,2,2700,2,1,9,2,9,9,9,9,9,9,9,2,1,1,
155,31,9,9,9,2,2,1,5,6,1,9,9,3,350,4,1,9,2,9,9,9,9,9,9,9,2,2,2,
329,32,9,9,9,2,2,1,3,1,1,2,7,2,2050,6,1,9,2,9,9,9,9,9,9,9,2,2,3,
114,32,9,9,9,2,3,2,4,2,1,2,2,3,550,5,1,9,2,9,9,9,9,9,9,9,1,1,1,
272,32,9,9,9,3,2,1,4,2,2,2,7,3,50,4,1,9,2,9,9,9,9,9,9,9,2,2,3,
136,33,9,9,9,1,1,1,4,2,1,2,5,2,150,4,1,9,2,9,9,9,9,9,9,9,1,2,2,
247,33,9,9,9,3,2,1,3,2,2,2,3,4,1350,7,1,9,2,9,9,9,9,9,9,9,1,1,2,
29,34,9,9,9,1,2,1,4,5,2,9,9,1,1000,4,1,9,2,9,9,9,9,9,9,9,1,2,5,
67,34,9,9,9,2,3,1,4,5,1,9,9,1,1000,2,1,9,2,9,9,9,9,9,9,9,2,2,4,
124,34,9,9,9,3,3,1,5,5,2,9,9,4,500,6,1,9,2,9,9,9,9,9,9,9,2,1,4,
91,35,9,9,9,2,3,1,3,2,1,1,6,2,2350,6,1,9,2,9,9,9,9,9,9,9,1,2,5,
51,35,9,9,9,4,5,1,2,2,2,2,2,2,250,3,1,9,2,9,9,9,9,9,9,9,2,2,3,
254,36,9,9,9,4,3,2,3,2,2,2,3,2,800,7,1,9,2,9,9,9,9,9,9,9,1,2,5,
125,37,9,9,9,1,2,1,3,2,1,2,2,2,700,3,1,9,2,9,9,9,9,9,9,9,1,2,2,
249,37,9,9,9,2,1,1,3,4,1,9,9,1,450,4,1,9,2,9,9,9,9,9,9,9,2,2,4,
353,37,9,9,9,2,4,1,5,6,1,9,9,3,1750,6,1,9,2,9,9,9,9,9,9,9,1,1,2,
140,37,9,9,9,3,2,1,3,2,2,1,7,5,1000,1,1,9,2,9,9,9,9,9,9,9,2,2,4,
212,42,9,9,9,1,5,1,3,2,1,1,4,3,3450,4,1,9,2,9,9,9,9,9,9,9,1,2,5,
93,43,9,9,9,3,2,2,4,7,2,9,9,2,700,4,1,9,2,9,9,9,9,9,9,9,2,2,1,
120,45,9,9,9,1,2,1,4,2,1,2,1,2,100,1,1,9,2,9,9,9,9,9,9,9,2,1,3,
319,45,9,9,9,1,2,1,5,6,1,9,9,1,500,3,1,9,2,9,9,9,9,9,9,9,1,2,2,
235,47,9,9,9,3,4,1,4,2,2,2,5,4,50,4,1,9,2,9,9,9,9,9,9,9,2,2,3,
315,47,9,9,9,4,3,1,3,2,2,1,1,2,1050,3,1,9,2,9,9,9,9,9,9,9,2,1,3,
214,48,9,9,9,2,1,1,5,6,2,9,9,2,2000,2,1,9,2,9,9,9,9,9,9,9,2,2,4,
241,48,9,9,9,3,2,1,2,2,2,2,1,2,1300,2,1,9,2,9,9,9,9,9,9,9,2,2,3,
188,49,9,9,9,1,2,1,3,2,1,2,2,3,1500,1,1,9,2,9,9,9,9,9,9,9,1,2,5,
105,51,9,9,9,1,2,2,4,2,2,2,3,2,3000,6,1,9,2,9,9,9,9,9,9,9,2,2,1,
81,51,9,9,9,2,2,2,3,2,2,1,2,3,3000,5,1,9,2,9,9,9,9,9,9,9,2,2,3,
152,51,9,9,9,2,2,1,4,2,2,1,1,2,350,4,1,9,2,9,9,9,9,9,9,9,1,2,5,
208,52,9,9,9,1,6,2,4,2,1,2,3,2,2950,2,1,9,2,9,9,9,9,9,9,9,1,2,5,
354,52,9,9,9,1,2,1,5,6,1,9,9,1,4050,1,1,9,2,9,9,9,9,9,9,9,1,2,1,
122,54,9,9,9,1,2,2,4,2,2,1,2,3,2000,3,1,9,2,9,9,9,9,9,9,9,2,2,4,
118,57,9,9,9,1,2,1,5,6,2,9,9,1,3050,4,1,9,2,9,9,9,9,9,9,9,1,2,5,
```

293,61,9,9,9,2,5,1,5,5,2,9,9,3,800,13,1,9,2,9,9,9,9,9,9,9,2,2,4,
278,63,9,9,9,3,6,2,3,2,2,1,6,3,2000,5,1,9,2,9,9,9,9,9,9,9,2,1,4,
197,2,1,4,1,2,1,1,4,5,2,9,9,3,1550,7,2,2,2,9,9,9,9,9,9,9,1,1,2,
57,3,4,1,4,1,2,1,3,2,2,2,1,3,400,2,2,3,2,9,9,9,9,9,9,9,2,2,3,
83,4,1,4,8,2,1,1,4,6,2,9,9,1,1200,6,2,3,2,9,9,9,9,9,9,9,2,2,3,
86,4,2,1,3,3,3,1,3,2,1,2,2,4,450,4,2,3,2,9,9,9,9,9,9,9,1,1,5,
265,5,3,4,3,1,2,1,3,2,2,1,4,1,650,15,2,4,2,9,9,9,9,9,9,9,2,1,1,
342,5,2,4,8,2,2,1,2,1,1,1,1,3,1450,13,2,1,2,9,9,9,9,9,9,9,2,2,1,
267,5,2,4,3,4,2,1,2,2,1,2,4,4,550,8,2,3,2,9,9,9,9,9,9,9,1,1,2,
17,5,2,1,8,6,2,1,3,3,2,2,5,2,450,15,2,2,2,9,9,9,9,9,9,9,1,2,5,
242,6,1,4,2,1,2,1,5,6,2,9,9,1,600,3,2,4,2,9,9,9,9,9,9,9,1,2,5,
334,7,2,1,4,3,2,1,2,2,1,2,5,4,750,4,2,4,2,9,9,9,9,9,9,9,1,1,1,
229,8,2,1,2,3,3,1,1,4,1,9,9,2,200,8,2,4,2,9,9,9,9,9,9,9,2,2,1,
43,8,1,1,2,3,5,1,5,6,1,9,9,3,250,3,2,3,2,9,9,9,9,9,9,9,2,2,3,
279,11,9,9,9,1,2,1,5,6,1,9,9,1,800,5,2,3,2,9,9,9,9,9,9,9,2,2,3,
232,12,9,9,9,1,3,1,3,3,2,1,3,2,1700,11,2,3,2,9,9,9,9,9,9,9,1,1,5,
98,12,9,9,9,2,1,2,2,3,1,2,5,2,6550,2,2,2,2,9,9,9,9,9,9,9,2,1,3,
9,12,9,9,9,2,2,1,3,4,1,9,9,3,400,7,2,3,2,9,9,9,9,9,9,9,2,1,4,
171,12,9,9,9,2,2,1,1,7,2,9,9,1,1250,1,2,1,2,9,9,9,9,9,9,9,2,2,4,
61,12,9,9,9,3,2,1,5,6,2,9,9,2,2000,6,2,4,2,9,9,9,9,9,9,9,1,2,5,
92,12,9,9,9,4,2,2,4,2,2,1,2,1,1400,13,2,1,2,9,9,9,9,9,9,9,2,2,1,
45,13,9,9,9,2,3,1,2,2,1,1,2,3,1050,3,2,4,2,9,9,9,9,9,9,9,2,2,1,
159,14,9,9,9,4,2,1,5,6,2,9,9,2,2500,8,2,4,2,9,9,9,9,9,9,9,2,1,1,
328,14,9,9,9,5,1,2,5,6,2,9,9,2,3300,5,2,3,2,9,9,9,9,9,9,9,2,1,1,
330,15,9,9,9,1,2,1,1,2,2,2,1,2,700,4,2,4,2,9,9,9,9,9,9,9,2,2,1,
172,15,9,9,9,3,2,1,3,2,1,2,1,3,1200,17,2,4,2,9,9,9,9,9,9,9,1,2,2,
27,16,9,9,9,1,2,1,2,2,1,2,2,1,850,3,2,2,2,9,9,9,9,9,9,9,2,1,1,
301,16,9,9,9,1,2,2,4,3,2,1,1,1,1050,4,2,4,2,9,9,9,9,9,9,9,1,1,5,
316,16,9,9,9,4,3,1,2,5,2,9,9,4,4050,8,2,2,2,9,9,9,9,9,9,9,1,1,5,
340,16,9,9,9,4,4,2,4,5,1,9,9,3,600,15,2,2,2,9,9,9,9,9,9,9,1,2,1,
304,16,9,9,9,6,1,1,2,1,2,2,7,4,2300,12,2,3,2,9,9,9,9,9,9,9,2,1,2,
110,17,9,9,9,1,5,2,4,2,1,1,2,3,1800,6,2,4,2,9,9,9,9,9,9,9,1,2,2,
331,17,9,9,9,1,2,1,4,2,1,2,5,3,3400,5,2,4,2,9,9,9,9,9,9,9,2,1,4,
177,17,9,9,9,2,5,2,4,2,1,2,1,4,3050,12,2,4,2,9,9,9,9,9,9,9,2,2,4,
351,17,9,9,9,3,2,2,5,6,2,9,9,2,350,5,2,3,2,9,9,9,9,9,9,9,1,2,5,
282,17,9,9,9,4,6,1,3,2,1,1,1,2,800,4,2,2,2,9,9,9,9,9,9,9,1,1,5,
33,17,9,9,9,4,3,1,5,3,2,2,5,2,400,3,2,4,2,9,9,9,9,9,9,9,2,2,4,
255,18,9,9,9,2,2,1,4,5,2,9,9,3,850,3,2,1,2,9,9,9,9,9,9,9,2,2,4,
147,18,9,9,9,6,3,1,4,3,2,2,2,3,2300,13,2,2,2,9,9,9,9,9,9,9,2,1,3,
111,19,9,9,9,4,2,1,5,6,2,9,9,2,350,1,2,2,2,9,9,9,9,9,9,9,1,2,1,
15,20,9,9,9,2,1,1,3,2,1,1,7,4,3850,2,2,2,2,9,9,9,9,9,9,9,2,2,3,
251,20,9,9,9,3,1,2,5,6,2,9,9,3,450,5,2,3,2,9,9,9,9,9,9,9,2,1,3,
190,21,9,9,9,2,4,1,4,2,2,2,5,2,4000,3,2,4,2,9,9,9,9,9,9,9,1,2,2,
322,21,9,9,9,2,5,1,4,5,2,9,9,4,750,1,2,3,2,9,9,9,9,9,9,9,2,1,4,
233,21,9,9,9,4,4,1,2,2,2,1,1,2,450,5,2,2,2,9,9,9,9,9,9,9,2,2,3,
263,22,9,9,9,3,2,1,3,5,1,9,9,3,1550,4,2,3,2,9,9,9,9,9,9,9,2,2,3,
202,22,9,9,9,3,4,1,4,5,2,9,9,4,5350,5,2,4,2,9,9,9,9,9,9,9,2,2,3,
305,23,9,9,9,2,2,1,2,2,1,2,4,1,5550,8,2,4,2,9,9,9,9,9,9,9,2,2,3,
68,23,9,9,9,2,2,1,5,5,2,9,9,1,4350,8,2,3,2,9,9,9,9,9,9,9,2,2,1,
346,23,9,9,9,3,2,1,3,2,1,1,7,3,250,7,2,4,2,9,9,9,9,9,9,9,2,1,4,
30,25,9,9,9,2,4,2,4,3,1,1,1,2,2600,2,2,4,2,9,9,9,9,9,9,9,2,2,4,

63,25,9,9,9,2,4,2,4,3,2,2,5,1,3650,4,2,3,2,9,9,9,9,9,9,1,2,5,
191,25,9,9,9,2,3,1,4,5,2,9,9,4,1950,5,2,3,2,9,9,9,9,9,9,1,1,2,
11,25,9,9,9,2,2,1,5,6,2,9,9,2,1050,3,2,2,2,9,9,9,9,9,9,2,2,3,
298,25,9,9,9,3,2,2,4,5,1,9,9,4,2000,3,2,1,2,9,9,9,9,9,9,1,1,5,
231,25,9,9,9,3,1,1,5,5,1,9,9,2,300,18,2,2,2,9,9,9,9,9,9,1,2,1,
156,27,9,9,9,1,2,1,2,2,2,2,2,2,200,12,2,2,2,9,9,9,9,9,9,2,2,3,
307,27,9,9,9,2,2,1,4,5,2,9,9,3,2000,1,2,2,2,9,9,9,9,9,9,2,2,3,
325,28,9,9,9,1,2,1,5,6,1,9,9,1,3850,2,2,3,2,9,9,9,9,9,9,2,2,3,
170,28,9,9,9,3,1,1,4,2,1,2,2,4,900,17,2,3,2,9,9,9,9,9,9,2,2,3,
77,28,9,9,9,3,1,1,5,6,2,9,9,3,700,15,2,3,2,9,9,9,9,9,9,1,1,5,
199,28,9,9,9,4,1,1,4,2,2,1,1,2,400,12,2,2,2,9,9,9,9,9,9,2,2,4,
257,29,9,9,9,5,1,1,3,1,2,2,6,3,450,5,2,3,2,9,9,9,9,9,9,2,2,4,
184,30,9,9,9,3,3,1,3,2,1,1,2,4,2300,2,2,4,2,9,9,9,9,9,9,2,1,4,
10,30,9,9,9,3,2,1,5,6,2,9,9,3,650,1,2,4,2,9,9,9,9,9,9,2,1,3,
294,33,9,9,9,1,3,1,5,6,2,9,9,1,3950,6,2,3,2,9,9,9,9,9,9,2,1,1,
72,35,9,9,9,2,2,1,2,2,1,1,1,3,4250,7,2,4,2,9,9,9,9,9,9,2,1,1,
143,35,9,9,9,4,3,2,3,3,1,2,5,2,200,1,2,3,2,9,9,9,9,9,9,1,2,2,
213,36,9,9,9,2,2,1,4,2,2,1,3,1,800,4,2,2,2,9,9,9,9,9,9,1,1,5,
186,37,9,9,9,1,4,1,2,3,2,2,3,2,450,1,2,3,2,9,9,9,9,9,9,1,1,5,
75,38,9,9,9,2,4,1,4,4,1,9,9,1,700,7,2,4,2,9,9,9,9,9,9,2,1,1,
37,40,9,9,9,1,3,1,4,2,2,2,5,2,450,12,2,3,2,9,9,9,9,9,9,1,2,1,
141,41,9,9,9,1,2,1,3,1,1,2,1,2,100,4,2,3,2,9,9,9,9,9,9,2,2,1,
246,41,9,9,9,2,4,1,4,2,1,2,5,3,650,2,2,2,2,9,9,9,9,9,9,1,1,5,
206,42,9,9,9,1,5,2,3,2,1,2,5,3,2900,1,2,2,2,9,9,9,9,9,9,2,2,4,
262,42,9,9,9,1,6,1,3,2,1,1,1,2,2650,6,2,3,2,9,9,9,9,9,9,1,1,5,
313,42,9,9,9,1,3,1,5,6,2,9,9,1,4000,8,2,3,2,9,9,9,9,9,9,2,1,3,
216,44,9,9,9,3,2,2,4,2,1,2,1,3,1250,19,2,3,2,9,9,9,9,9,9,2,2,4,
95,45,9,9,9,1,1,2,4,2,2,2,2,2,200,2,2,2,2,9,9,9,9,9,9,1,2,5,
24,45,9,9,9,1,2,2,3,4,1,9,9,1,300,2,2,2,2,9,9,9,9,9,9,1,2,5,
204,45,9,9,9,2,2,2,4,2,1,2,3,1,4450,7,2,3,2,9,9,9,9,9,9,1,2,5,
71,47,9,9,9,2,3,1,4,3,2,2,1,2,2950,5,2,3,2,9,9,9,9,9,9,2,1,3,
36,51,9,9,9,2,2,1,1,4,2,9,9,2,3400,3,2,3,2,9,9,9,9,9,9,1,2,2,
165,53,9,9,9,2,2,2,5,6,2,9,9,1,2350,3,2,1,2,9,9,9,9,9,9,1,2,5,
245,54,9,9,9,3,2,1,4,5,2,9,9,3,100,3,2,2,2,9,9,9,9,9,9,2,2,3,
66,56,9,9,9,1,2,1,4,5,2,9,9,2,5850,2,2,3,2,9,9,9,9,9,9,1,2,5,
127,58,9,9,9,1,4,2,3,2,1,2,4,3,600,5,2,3,2,9,9,9,9,9,9,2,1,3,
148,61,9,9,9,1,4,1,5,5,1,9,9,1,2700,8,2,4,2,9,9,9,9,9,9,2,1,3,
238,62,9,9,9,3,3,1,4,3,2,1,2,2,250,17,2,2,2,9,9,9,9,9,9,2,1,4,
90,18,9,9,9,4,1,1,2,1,1,2,7,4,650,8,1,9,9,9,9,9,9,9,9,2,1,3,
277,41,9,9,9,2,4,2,3,2,2,2,5,2,1550,1,1,9,9,9,9,9,9,9,9,1,1,4,

Appendix IV
Statistical tables

Table 1 Areas in the two tails beneath the standard normal curve (probabilities of Z) (Reproduced by permission of The Macmillan Press Ltd from Williams (1984))

Z	.00	.01	.02	.03	.04	.05	.06	.07	.08	.09
0.0	1.0000	0.9920	0.9840	0.9761	0.9681	0.9601	0.9522	0.9442	0.9362	0.9283
0.1	0.9203	0.9124	0.9045	0.8966	0.8887	0.8808	0.8729	0.8650	0.8572	0.8493
0.2	0.8415	0.8337	0.8259	0.8181	0.8103	0.8026	0.7949	0.7872	0.7795	0.7718
0.3	0.7642	0.7566	0.7490	0.7414	0.7339	0.7263	0.7188	0.7114	0.7039	0.6965
0.4	0.6892	0.6818	0.6745	0.6672	0.6599	0.6527	0.6455	0.6384	0.6312	0.6241
0.5	0.6171	0.6101	0.6031	0.5961	0.5892	0.5823	0.5755	0.5687	0.5619	0.5552
0.6	0.5485	0.5419	0.5353	0.5287	0.5222	0.5157	0.5093	0.5029	0.4965	0.4902
0.7	0.4839	0.4777	0.4715	0.4654	0.4593	0.4533	0.4473	0.4413	0.4354	0.4295
0.8	0.4237	0.4179	0.4122	0.4065	0.4009	0.3953	0.3898	0.3843	0.3789	0.3735
0.9	0.3681	0.3628	0.3576	0.3524	0.3472	0.3421	0.3371	0.3320	0.3271	0.3222
1.0	0.3173	0.3125	0.3077	0.3030	0.2983	0.2937	0.2891	0.2846	0.2801	0.2757
1.1	0.2713	0.2670	0.2627	0.2585	0.2543	0.2501	0.2460	0.2420	0.2380	0.2340
1.2	0.2301	0.2263	0.2225	0.2187	0.2150	0.2113	0.2077	0.2041	0.2005	0.1971
1.3	0.1936	0.1902	0.1868	0.1835	0.1802	0.1770	0.1738	0.1707	0.1676	0.1645
1.4	0.1615	0.1585	0.1556	0.1527	0.1499	0.1471	0.1443	0.1416	0.1389	0.1362
1.5	0.1336	0.1310	0.1285	0.1260	0.1236	0.1211	0.1188	0.1164	0.1141	0.1118
1.6	0.1096	0.1074	0.1052	0.1031	0.1010	0.0989	0.0969	0.0949	0.0930	0.0910
1.7	0.0891	0.0873	0.0854	0.0836	0.0819	0.0801	0.0784	0.0767	0.0751	0.0735
1.8	0.0719	0.0703	0.0688	0.0672	0.0658	0.0643	0.0629	0.0615	0.0601	0.0588
1.9	0.0574	0.0561	0.0549	0.0536	0.0524	0.0512	0.0500	0.0488	0.0477	0.0466
2.0	0.0455	0.0444	0.0434	0.0424	0.0414	0.0404	0.0394	0.0385	0.0375	0.0366
2.1	0.0357	0.0349	0.0340	0.0332	0.0324	0.0316	0.0308	0.0300	0.0293	0.0285
2.2	0.0278	0.0271	0.0264	0.0257	0.0251	0.0244	0.0238	0.0232	0.0226	0.0220
2.3	0.0214	0.0209	0.0203	0.0198	0.0193	0.0188	0.0183	0.0178	0.0173	0.0168
2.4	0.0164	0.0160	0.0155	0.0151	0.0147	0.0143	0.0139	0.0135	0.0131	0.0128
2.5	0.0124	0.0121	0.0117	0.0114	0.0111	0.0108	0.0105	0.0102	0.00988	0.00960
2.6	0.00932	0.00905	0.00879	0.00854	0.00829	0.00805	0.00781	0.00759	0.00736	0.00715
2.7	0.00693	0.00673	0.00653	0.00633	0.00614	0.00596	0.00578	0.00561	0.00544	0.00527
2.8	0.00511	0.00495	0.00480	0.00465	0.00451	0.00437	0.00424	0.00410	0.00398	0.00385
2.9	0.00373	0.00361	0.00350	0.00339	0.00328	0.00318	0.00308	0.00298	0.00288	0.00279
$Z =$	3.0	3.1	3.2	3.3	3.4	3.5	3.6	3.7	3.8	3.9
	0.00270	0.00194	0.00137	$0.0^{3}967$	$0.0^{3}674$	$0.0^{3}465$	$0.0^{3}318$	$0.0^{3}216$	$0.0^{3}145$	$0.0^{4}962$
$Z =$	4.0	4.1	4.2	4.3	4.4	4.5	4.6	4.7	4.8	4.9
	$0.0^{4}633$	$0.0^{4}413$	$0.0^{4}267$	$.0^{4}171$	$0.0^{4}108$	$0.0^{5}680$	$0.0^{5}422$	$0.0^{5}260$	$0.0^{5}159$	$0.0^{6}958$
$Z =$	5.0	5.1	5.2	5.3	5.4	5.5	5.6	5.7	5.8	5.9
	$0.0^{6}573$	$0.0^{6}340$	$0.0^{6}199$	$0.0^{6}166$	$0.0^{7}666$	$0.0^{7}380$	$0.0^{7}214$	$0.0^{7}120$	$0.0^{8}663$	$0.0^{8}364$
$Z =$	6.0	6.1	6.2	6.3	6.4	6.5	6.6	6.7	6.8	6.9
	$0.0^{8}197$	$0.0^{8}106$	$0.0^{9}565$	$0.0^{9}298$	$0.0^{9}155$	$0.0^{10}803$	$0.0^{10}411$	$0.0^{10}208$	$0.0^{10}105$	$0.0^{11}520$

The null hypothesis should be rejected if the probability of the test statistic is equal to or less than the specified significance level.

Table 2 Critical values of the t distribution (Reproduced by permission of The Macmillan Press Ltd from Williams (1984))

df	Significance levels (probabilities)								
	0.20	0.10	0.05	0.02	0.01	0.002	0.001	0.0002	0.0001
1	3.078	6.314	12.706	31.821	63.657	318.309	636.619	3,183.099	6,366.198
2	1.866	2.920	4.303	6.965	9.925	22.327	31.598	70.700	99.992
3	1.638	2.353	3.182	4.541	5.841	10.214	12.924	22.204	28.000
4	1.533	2.132	2.776	3.747	4.604	7.173	8.610	13.034	15.544
5	1.476	2.015	2.571	3.365	4.032	5.893	6.869	9.678	11.178
6	1.440	1.943	2.447	3.143	3.707	5.208	5.959	8.025	9.082
7	1.415	1.895	2.365	2.998	3.499	4.785	5.408	7.063	7.885
8	1.397	1.860	2.306	2.896	3.355	4.501	5.041	6.442	7.120
9	1.383	1.833	2.262	2.821	3.250	4.297	4.781	6.010	6.594
10	1.372	1.812	2.228	2.764	3.169	4.144	4.587	5.694	6.211
11	1.363	1.796	2.201	2.718	3.106	4.025	4.437	5.453	5.921
12	1.356	1.782	2.179	2.681	3.055	3.930	4.318	5.263	5.694
13	1.350	1.771	2.160	2.650	3.012	3.852	4.221	5.111	5.513
14	1.345	1.761	2.145	2.624	2.977	3.787	4.140	4.985	5.363
15	1.341	1.753	2.131	2.602	2.947	3.733	4.073	4.880	5.239
16	1.337	1.746	2.120	2.583	2.921	3.686	4.015	4.791	5.134
17	1.333	1.740	2.110	2.567	2.898	3.646	3.965	4.714	5.044
18	1.330	1.734	2.101	2.552	2.878	3.610	3.922	4.648	4.966
19	1.328	1.729	2.093	2.539	2.861	3.579	3.883	4.590	4.897
20	1.325	1.725	2.086	2.528	2.845	3.552	3.850	4.539	4.837
25	1.316	1.708	2.060	2.485	2.787	3.450	3.725	4.352	4.619
30	1.310	1.697	2.042	2.457	2.750	3.385	3.646	4.234	4.482
35	1.306	1.690	2.030	2.438	2.724	3.340	3.591	4.153	4.389
40	1.303	1.684	2.021	2.423	2.704	3.307	3.551	4.094	4.321
45	1.301	1.679	2.014	2.412	2.690	3.281	3.520	4.049	4.269
50	1.299	1.676	2.009	2.403	2.678	3.261	3.496	4.014	4.228
60	1.296	1.671	2.000	2.390	2.660	3.232	3.460	3.962	4.169
70	1.294	1.667	1.994	2.381	2.648	3.211	3.435	3.926	4.127
80	1.292	1.664	1.990	2.374	2.639	3.195	3.416	3.899	4.096
90	1.291	1.662	1.987	2.368	2.632	3.183	3.402	3.878	4.072
100	1.290	1.660	1.984	2.364	2.626	3.174	3.390	3.862	4.053
200	1.286	1.652	1.972	2.345	2.601	3.131	3.340	3.789	3.970
500	1.283	1.648	1.965	2.334	2.586	3.107	3.310	3.747	3.922
1,000	1.282	1.645	1.962	2.330	2.581	3.098	3.300	3.733	3.906

The null hypothesis should be rejected if the probability of the test statistic is equal to or less than the specified significance level. For a one-tailed test, the probabilities should be halved and the same t values used.

Table 3 Critical values of the chi-square distribution (Reproduced by permission of The Macmillan Press Ltd from Williams (1984))

df	Significance levels (probabilities)								
	0.50	0.20	0.10	0.05	0.025	0.02	0.01	0.005	0.001
1	0.455	1.642	2.706	3.841	5.024	5.412	6.635	7.879	10.827
2	1.386	3.219	4.605	5.991	7.378	7.824	9.210	10.597	13.815
3	2.366	4.642	6.251	7.815	9.348	9.837	11.345	12.838	16.268
4	3.357	5.989	7.779	9.488	11.143	11.668	13.277	14.860	18.465
5	4.351	7.289	9.236	11.070	12.832	13.388	15.086	16.750	20.517
6	5.348	8.558	10.645	12.592	14.449	15.033	16.812	18.548	22.457
7	6.346	9.803	12.017	14.067	16.013	16.622	18.475	20.278	24.322
8	7.344	11.030	13.362	15.507	17.535	18.168	20.090	21.955	26.125
9	8.343	12.242	14.684	16.919	19.023	19.679	21.666	23.589	27.877
10	9.342	13.442	15.987	18.307	20.483	21.161	23.209	25.188	29.588
11	10.341	14.631	17.275	19.675	21.920	22.618	24.725	26.757	31.264
12	11.340	15.812	18.549	21.026	23.337	24.054	26.217	28.300	32.909
13	12.340	16.985	19.812	22.362	24.736	25.472	27.688	29.819	34.528
14	13.339	18.151	21.064	23.685	26.119	26.873	29.141	31.319	36.123
15	14.339	19.311	22.307	24.996	27.488	28.529	30.578	32.801	37.697
16	15.338	20.465	23.542	26.296	28.845	29.633	32.000	34.267	39.252
17	16.338	21.615	24.769	27.587	30.191	30.995	33.409	35.718	40.790
18	17.338	22.760	25.989	28.869	31.526	32.346	34.805	37.156	42.312
19	18.338	23.900	27.204	30.144	32.852	33.687	36.191	38.582	43.820
20	19.337	25.038	28.412	31.410	34.170	35.020	37.566	39.997	45.315
25	24.337	30.675	34.382	37.652	40.646	41.566	44.314	46.928	52.620
30	29.336	36.250	40.256	43.773	46.979	47.962	50.892	53.672	59.703
40	39.335	47.269	51.805	55.759	59.342	60.436	63.691	66.766	73.402
50	49.335	58.164	63.167	67.505	71.420	72.613	76.154	79.490	86.661
60	59.335	68.972	74.397	79.082	83.298	84.580	88.379	91.952	99.607
70	69.334	79.715	85.527	90.531	95.023	96.388	100.425	104.215	112.317
80	79.334	90.405	96.578	101.880	106.629	108.069	112.329	116.321	124.839
90	89.334	101.054	107.565	113.145	118.136	119.648	124.116	128.299	137.208
100	99.334	111.667	118.498	124.342	129.561	131.142	135.807	140.170	149.449

The null hypothesis should be rejected if the test statistic is equal to or greater than the tabulated value for the corresponding degrees of freedom at the specified significance level.

Table 4 Critical values of the Kolmogorov–Smirnov D statistic

Sample Size	Two-tailed significance levels			
(n)	0.20	0.10	0.05	0.01
1	0.900	0.950	0.975	0.995
2	0.684	0.776	0.842	0.929
3	0.565	0.642	0.708	0.828
4	0.494	0.564	0.624	0.733
5	0.446	0.510	0.565	0.669
6	0.410	0.470	0.521	0.618
7	0.381	0.438	0.486	0.577
8	0.358	0.411	0.457	0.543
9	0.339	0.388	0.432	0.514
10	0.322	0.368	0.410	0.490
11	0.307	0.352	0.391	0.468
12	0.295	0.338	0.375	0.450
13	0.284	0.325	0.361	0.433
14	0.274	0.314	0.349	0.418
15	0.266	0.304	0.338	0.404
16	0.258	0.295	0.328	0.392
17	0.250	0.286	0.318	0.381
18	0.244	0.278	0.309	0.371
19	0.237	0.272	0.301	0.363
20	0.231	0.264	0.294	0.356
25	0.210	0.240	0.270	0.220
30	0.190	0.220	0.240	0.290
35	0.180	0.210	0.230	0.270
Over 35	$\frac{1.07}{\sqrt{n}}$	$\frac{1.22}{\sqrt{n}}$	$\frac{1.36}{\sqrt{n}}$	$\frac{1.63}{\sqrt{n}}$

The null hypothesis should be rejected if the test statistic is equal to or greater than the tabulated value for the corresponding sample size at the specified significance level.

Table 5 Probabilities for the Wilcoxon signed-ranks W statistic

n / W	1	2	3	4	5	6	7	8	9	10	11	12	13	14	15	16	17	18	19	20
0	.500	.250	.125	.063	.031	.016	.008	.004	.002	.001	.001	.000	.000	.000	.000	.000	.000	.000	.000	.000
1	1.000	.500	.250	.125	.063	.031	.016	.008	.004	.002	.001	.001	.000	.000	.000	.000	.000	.000	.000	.000
2		.750	.375	.188	.094	.047	.023	.012	.006	.003	.002	.001	.000	.000	.000	.000	.000	.000	.000	.000
3		1.000	.625	.313	.156	.078	.039	.019	.010	.005	.002	.001	.001	.000	.000	.000	.000	.000	.000	.000
4			.750	.438	.219	.109	.055	.027	.014	.007	.003	.002	.001	.000	.000	.000	.000	.000	.000	.000
5			.875	.563	.313	.156	.078	.039	.019	.010	.005	.002	.001	.001	.000	.000	.000	.000	.000	.000
6			1.000	.688	.406	.219	.109	.055	.027	.014	.007	.003	.002	.001	.000	.000	.000	.000	.000	.000
7				.813	.500	.281	.148	.074	.037	.019	.009	.005	.002	.002	.001	.000	.000	.000	.000	.000
8				.875	.594	.344	.188	.098	.049	.024	.012	.006	.003	.002	.001	.000	.000	.000	.000	.000
9				.938	.688	.422	.234	.125	.065	.032	.016	.008	.004	.002	.001	.001	.000	.000	.000	.000
10				1.000	.781	.500	.289	.156	.082	.042	.021	.011	.005	.003	.001	.001	.000	.000	.000	.000
11					.844	.578	.344	.191	.102	.053	.027	.013	.007	.003	.002	.000	.000	.000	.000	.000
12					.906	.656	.406	.231	.125	.065	.034	.017	.009	.004	.002	.001	.001	.000	.000	.000
13					.938	.719	.469	.273	.150	.080	.042	.021	.011	.005	.003	.001	.001	.000	.000	.000
14					.969	.781	.531	.320	.180	.097	.051	.026	.013	.007	.003	.002	.001	.000	.000	.000
15								.371	.213	.116	.062	.032	.016	.008	.004	.002	.001	.001	.000	.000
16								.422	.248	.138	.074	.039	.020	.010	.005	.003	.001	.001	.000	.000
17								.473	.285	.161	.087	.046	.024	.012	.006	.003	.002	.001	.000	.000
18								.527	.326	.188	.103	.055	.029	.015	.008	.004	.002	.001	.001	.000
19								.578	.362	.216	.120	.065	.034	.018	.009	.005	.002	.001	.001	.000
20								.629	.410	.246	.139	.076	.040	.021	.011	.001	.003	.001	.001	.000
21								.680	.455	.278	.160	.088	.047	.025	.013	.007	.003	.002	.001	.000
22								.727	.500	.313	.183	.102	.055	.029	.015	.008	.004	.002	.001	.001
23								.770	.545	.348	.207	.117	.064	.034	.018	.009	.005	.002	.001	.001
24								.809	.590	.385	.232	.133	.073	.039	.021	.011	.006	.003	.001	.001
25								.844	.633	.423	.260	.151	.084	.045	.024	.013	.006	.003	.002	.001
26								.875	.674	.461	.287	.170	.096	.052	.028	.015	.008	.004	.002	.001
27								.902	.715	.500	.319	.190	.108	.060	.032	.017	.009	.005	.002	.001
28								.926	.752	.539	.350	.212	.122	.068	.037	.019	.010	.005	.003	.001
29								.945	.787	.577	.382	.235	.137	.077	.042	.022	.012	.006	.003	.002
30								.961	.820	.615	.416	.259	.153	.086	.047	.025	.013	.007	.004	.002
31								.973	.850	.652	.449	.285	.170	.097	.054	.029	.015	.008	.004	.002
32								.981	.875	.688	.483	.311	.188	.108	.060	.033	.017	.009	.005	.002
33								.988	.898	.722	.517	.339	.207	.121	.068	.037	.020	.010	.005	.003
34								.992	.918	.754	.551	.367	.227	.134	.076	.042	.022	.012	.006	.003
35								.996	.936	.784	.585	.396	.249	.148	.084	.047	.025	.013	.007	.004
36								1.000	.951	.813	.618	.425	.271	.163	.094	.052	.028	.015	.000	.004
37									.963	.839	.650	.545	.294	.179	.104	.058	.032	.017	.009	.005
38									.973	.862	.681	.485	.318	.196	.115	.065	.046	.019	.010	.005
39									.981	.884	.711	.515	.342	.213	.126	.072	.040	.022	.012	.006

40	.986	.903	.740	.545	.368	.232	.138	.080	.044	.024	.013	.007
41	.990	.920	.768	.575	.393	.251	.151	.088	.049	.027	.015	.008
42	.994	.935	.794	.605	.420	.271	.165	.096	.054	.030	.016	.009
43	.996	.947	.817	.633	.446	.292	.180	.106	.060	.033	.018	.010
44	.998	.958	.840	.661	.473	.313	.195	.116	.066	.037	.020	.011
45	1.000	.968	.861	.689	.500	.335	.211	.126	.073	.041	.022	.012
46		.975	.880	.715	.527	.357	.227	.137	.080	.045	.025	.013
47		.981	.897	.741	.554	.380	.244	.149	.087	.049	.027	.015
48		.986	.913	.765	.580	.404	.262	.161	.095	.054	.030	.016
49		.990	.926	.788	.607	.428	.281	.174	.103	.059	.033	.018
50		.993	.939	.810	.632	.452	.300	.188	.112	.065	.036	.020
51		.995	.949	.830	.658	.476	.319	.202	.122	.071	.040	.022
52		.997	.959	.849	.682	.500	.339	.217	.132	.077	.044	.024
53							.360	.232	.142	.084	.048	.027
54							.381	.248	.153	.091	.052	.029
55							.402	.264	.165	.098	.057	.032
56							.424	.281	.176	.106	.062	.035
57							.445	.298	.189	.114	.067	.038
58							.467	.316	.202	.123	.072	.041
59							.489	.334	.215	.132	.078	.045
60							.511	.353	.229	.142	.084	.049
61							.533	.372	.244	.152	.091	.053
62							.555	.391	.259	.162	.098	.057
63							.577	.410	.274	.173	.105	.062
64							.598	.430	.290	.185	.113	.066
65							.619	.450	.306	.196	.121	.072
66							.640	.470	.322	.209	.129	.077
67							.661	.490	.339	.221	.138	.083
68							.681	.510	.356	.234	.147	.088
69							.700	.530	.373	.248	.156	.095
70							.719	.550	.391	.261	.166	.101

The null hypothesis should be rejected if the probability occurring at the entry corresponding to the intersection of the test statistic (w) and sample size (n) is equal to or less than the significance level. For a two-tailed test the probabilities should be doubled.

Table 6 Selected critical values of the F distribution (Reproduced by permission of The Macmillan Press Ltd from Williams (1984))

n_s	P \ n_l	1	2	3	4	5	6	7	8	9	10	15	20	30	40	50	60	100	Inf
4	0.10	7.71	6.94	6.59	6.39	6.26	6.16	6.09	6.04	6.00	5.96	5.86	5.80	5.75	5.72	5.70	5.69	5.66	5.63
	0.05	12.2	10.6	9.98	9.6	9.36	9.20	9.07	8.98	8.90	8.84	8.66	8.56	8.46	8.41	8.38	8.36	8.32	8.26
	0.01	31.3	26.3	24.3	23.2	22.5	22.0	21.6	21.4	21.1	21.0	20.4	20.2	19.9	19.8	19.7	19.6	19.5	19.30
5	0.10	6.61	5.79	5.41	5.19	5.05	4.95	4.88	4.82	4.77	4.74	4.62	4.56	4.50	4.46	4.44	4.43	4.41	4.36
	0.05	10.0	8.43	7.76	7.39	7.15	6.98	6.85	6.76	6.68	6.62	6.43	6.33	6.23	6.18	6.14	6.12	6.08	6.02
	0.01	22.8	18.3	16.5	15.6	14.9	14.5	14.2	14.0	13.8	13.6	13.1	12.9	12.7	12.5	12.5	12.4	12.3	12.1
6	0.10	5.99	5.14	4.76	4.53	4.39	4.28	4.21	4.15	4.10	4.06	3.94	3.87	3.81	3.77	3.75	3.74	3.71	3.67
	0.05	8.81	7.26	6.60	6.23	5.99	5.82	5.70	5.60	5.52	5.46	5.27	5.17	5.07	5.01	4.98	4.96	4.92	4.85
	0.01	18.6	14.5	12.9	12.0	11.5	11.1	10.8	10.6	10.4	10.2	9.81	9.59	9.36	9.24	9.17	9.12	9.03	8.88
7	0.10	5.59	4.74	4.35	4.12	3.97	3.87	3.79	3.73	3.68	3.64	3.51	3.44	3.38	3.34	3.32	3.30	3.27	3.23
	0.05	8.07	6.54	5.89	5.52	5.29	5.12	4.99	4.90	4.82	4.76	4.57	4.47	4.36	4.31	4.28	4.25	4.21	4.14
	0.01	16.2	12.4	10.9	10.0	9.52	9.16	8.89	8.68	8.51	8.38	7.97	7.75	7.53	7.42	7.35	7.31	7.22	7.08
8	0.10	5.32	4.46	4.07	3.84	3.69	3.58	3.50	3.44	3.39	3.35	3.22	3.15	3.08	3.04	3.02	3.01	2.97	2.93
	0.05	7.57	6.06	5.42	5.05	4.82	4.65	4.53	4.43	4.36	4.30	4.10	4.00	3.89	3.84	3.81	3.78	3.74	3.67
	0.01	14.7	11.0	9.60	8.81	8.30	7.95	7.69	7.50	7.34	7.21	6.81	6.61	6.40	6.29	6.22	6.18	6.09	5.95
9	0.10	5.12	4.26	3.86	3.63	3.48	3.37	3.29	3.23	3.18	3.14	3.01	2.91	2.86	2.83	2.80	2.79	2.76	2.71
	0.05	7.21	5.71	5.08	4.72	4.48	4.32	4.20	4.10	4.03	3.96	3.77	3.67	3.56	3.51	3.47	3.45	3.40	3.33
	0.01	13.6	10.1	8.72	7.96	7.47	7.13	6.88	6.96	6.54	6.42	6.03	5.83	5.62	5.52	5.45	5.41	5.32	5.19
10	0.10	4.96	4.10	3.71	3.48	3.33	3.22	3.14	3.07	3.02	2.98	2.85	2.77	2.70	2.66	2.64	2.62	2.59	2.54
	0.05	6.94	5.46	4.83	4.47	4.24	4.07	3.95	3.85	3.78	3.72	3.52	3.42	3.31	3.26	3.22	3.20	3.15	3.08
	0.01	12.8	9.43	8.08	7.34	6.87	6.54	6.30	6.12	5.97	5.85	5.47	5.27	5.07	4.97	4.90	4.86	4.77	6.64
15	0.10	4.54	3.98	3.59	3.36	3.20	3.09	3.01	2.95	2.90	2.85	2.72	2.65	2.57	2.53	2.51	2.49	2.46	2.40
	0.05	6.20	4.76	4.15	3.80	3.58	3.41	3.29	3.20	3.12	3.06	3.33	3.23	3.12	3.06	3.03	3.00	2.96	2.88
	0.01	10.8	7.70	6.48	5.80	5.37	5.07	4.85	4.67	4.54	4.42	5.05	4.86	4.65	4.55	4.49	4.45	4.36	4.23
20	0.10	4.35	3.49	3.10	2.87	2.71	2.60	2.51	2.45	2.39	2.35	2.20	2.12	2.04	1.99	1.97	1.95	1.91	1.84
	0.05	5.87	4.46	3.86	3.51	3.29	3.13	3.01	2.91	2.84	2.77	2.57	2.46	2.35	2.29	2.25	2.22	2.17	2.09
	0.01	9.94	6.99	5.82	5.17	4.76	4.47	4.26	4.09	3.96	3.85	3.50	3.32	3.12	3.02	2.96	2.92	2.83	2.69
30	0.10	4.17	3.32	2.92	2.69	2.53	2.42	2.33	2.27	2.21	2.16	2.01	1.93	1.84	1.79	1.76	1.74	1.70	1.62
	0.05	5.57	4.18	3.59	3.25	3.03	2.87	2.75	2.65	2.57	2.51	2.31	2.20	2.07	2.01	1.97	1.94	1.88	1.79
	0.01	9.18	6.35	5.24	4.62	4.23	3.95	3.74	3.58	3.45	3.34	3.01	2.82	2.63	2.52	2.46	2.42	2.32	2.18
40	0.10	4.08	3.23	2.84	2.61	2.45	2.34	2.25	2.18	2.12	2.08	1.92	1.84	1.74	1.69	1.66	1.64	1.59	1.51
	0.05	5.42	4.05	3.46	3.13	2.90	2.74	2.62	2.53	2.45	2.39	2.18	2.07	1.94	1.88	1.83	1.80	1.74	1.64
	0.01	8.83	6.07	4.98	4.37	3.99	3.71	3.51	3.35	3.22	3.12	2.78	2.60	2.40	2.30	2.23	2.18	2.09	1.93
60	0.10	4.00	3.15	2.76	2.53	2.37	2.25	2.17	2.10	2.04	1.99	1.84	1.75	1.65	1.59	1.56	1.53	1.48	1.39
	0.05	5.29	3.93	3.34	3.01	2.79	2.63	2.51	2.41	2.33	2.27	2.06	1.94	1.82	1.74	1.70	1.67	1.60	1.48
	0.01	8.49	5.80	4.73	4.14	3.76	3.49	3.29	3.13	3.01	2.90	2.57	2.39	2.19	2.08	2.01	1.96	1.86	1.69
120	0.10	3.92	3.07	2.68	2.45	2.29	2.18	2.09	2.02	1.96	1.91	1.75	1.66	1.55	1.50	1.46	1.43	1.37	1.25
	0.05	5.15	3.80	3.23	2.89	2.67	2.52	2.39	2.30	2.22	2.16	1.95	1.82	1.69	1.61	1.56	1.53	1.45	1.31
	0.01	8.18	5.54	4.50	3.92	3.55	3.28	3.09	2.93	2.81	2.71	2.37	2.19	1.98	1.87	1.80	1.75	1.64	1.43
Inf	0.10	3.84	3.00	2.60	2.37	2.21	2.10	2.01	1.94	1.88	1.83	1.67	1.57	1.46	1.39	1.35	1.32	1.24	1.00
	0.05	5.02	3.69	3.12	2.79	2.57	2.41	2.29	2.19	2.11	2.05	1.83	1.71	1.57	1.48	1.43	1.39	1.30	1.00
	0.01	7.88	5.30	4.28	3.72	3.35	3.09	2.90	2.74	2.62	2.52	2.19	2.00	1.79	1.67	1.59	1.53	1.40	1.00

The null hypothesis should be rejected if the test statistic is equal to or greater than the tabulated value for the corresponding sample size at the specified significance level. The columns for n_l denote the degrees of freedom for the sample yielding the larger variance. The rows for n_s represent the degrees of freedom for the sample with the smaller variance. These are respectively the numerator and denominator of the F test. For a one-tailed test the same F values are associated with halved probabilities.

Table 7 Probabilities for the Mann–Whitney U statistic (Reproduced by permission of The Macmillan Press Ltd from Williams (1984))
(a) Small-size samples

U	n_o \ n_r	1	2	3
0	3	0.250	0.100	0.050
1	3	0.500	0.200	0.100
2	3	0.750	0.400	0.200
3	3		0.600	0.350
4	3			0.500
5	3			0.650

U	n_o \ n_r	1	2	3	4
0	4	0.200	0.067	0.028	0.014
1	4	0.400	0.133	0.057	0.029
2	4	0.600	0.267	0.114	0.057
3	4		0.400	0.200	0.100
4	4		0.600	0.314	0.171
5	4			0.429	0.243
6	4			0.571	0.343
7	4				0.443

U	n_o \ n_r	1	2	3	4	5
0	5	0.167	0.047	0.018	0.008	0.004
1	5	0.333	0.095	0.036	0.016	0.008
2	5	0.500	0.190	0.071	0.032	0.016
3	5	0.667	0.286	0.125	0.056	0.028
4	5		0.429	0.196	0.095	0.048
5	5		0.571	0.286	0.143	0.075
6	5			0.393	0.206	0.111
7	5			0.500	0.278	0.155
8	5			0.607	0.365	0.210
9	5				0.452	0.274
10	5				0.548	0.345
11	5					0.421
12	5					0.500
13	5					0.579

U	n_o \ n_r	1	2	3	4	5	6
0	6	0.143	0.036	0.012	0.005	0.002	0.001
1	6	0.286	0.071	0.024	0.010	0.004	0.002
2	6	0.428	0.143	0.048	0.019	0.009	0.004
3	6	0.571	0.214	0.083	0.033	0.015	0.008
4	6		0.321	0.131	0.057	0.026	0.013
5	6		0.429	0.190	0.086	0.041	0.021
6	6		0.571	0.275	0.129	0.063	0.032
7	6			0.357	0.176	0.089	0.047
8	6			0.452	0.238	0.123	0.066
9	6			0.548	0.305	0.165	0.090
10	6				0.381	0.214	0.120
11	6				0.457	0.268	0.155
12	6				0.545	0.331	0.197
13	6					0.396	0.242
14	6					0.465	0.294
15	6					0.535	0.350
16	6						0.409
17	6						0.469

U	n_o \ n_r	1	2	3	4	5	6	7
0	7	0.125	0.028	0.008	0.003	0.001	0.001	0.000
1	7	0.250	0.056	0.017	0.006	0.003	0.001	0.001
2	7	0.375	0.111	0.033	0.012	0.005	0.002	0.001
3	7	0.500	0.167	0.058	0.021	0.009	0.004	0.002
4	7	0.625	0.250	0.092	0.036	0.015	0.007	0.003
5	7		0.333	0.133	0.055	0.024	0.011	0.006

U	n_o \ n_r	1	2	3	4	5	6	7	8
0	8	0.111	0.022	0.006	0.002	0.001	0.000	0.000	0.000
1	8	0.222	0.044	0.012	0.004	0.002	0.001	0.000	0.000
2	8	0.333	0.089	0.024	0.008	0.003	0.001	0.001	0.000
3	8	0.444	0.135	0.042	0.014	0.005	0.002	0.001	0.001
4	8	0.556	0.200	0.067	0.024	0.009	0.004	0.002	0.001
5	8		0.267	0.097	0.036	0.015	0.006	0.003	0.001

U	n_o	3	4	5	6	7	8	9
6	7		0.444	0.192	0.082	0.037	0.017	0.009
7	7		0.556	0.258	0.115	0.053	0.026	0.013
8	7			0.333	0.158	0.074	0.037	0.019
9	7			0.417	0.206	0.101	0.051	0.027
10	7			0.500	0.264	0.134	0.069	0.036
11	7			0.583	0.324	0.172	0.090	0.049
12	7				0.394	0.216	0.117	0.064
13	7				0.464	0.265	0.147	0.082
14	7				0.538	0.319	0.183	0.104
15	7					0.378	0.223	0.130
16	7					0.438	0.267	0.159
17	7					0.500	0.314	0.191
18	7					0.562	0.365	0.228
19	7						0.418	0.267
20	7						0.473	0.310
21	7						0.527	0.355
22	7							0.402
23	7							0.451
24	7							0.500

U	n_r / n_o	3	4	5	6	7	8	9
0	9	0.005	0.001	0.001	0.000	0.000	0.000	0.000
1	9	0.009	0.003	0.001	0.000	0.000	0.000	0.000
2	9	0.018	0.006	0.002	0.001	0.000	0.000	0.000
3	9	0.032	0.010	0.004	0.001	0.001	0.000	0.000
4	9	0.050	0.017	0.006	0.002	0.001	0.001	0.000
5	9	0.073	0.025	0.010	0.004	0.002	0.001	0.000
6	9	0.105	0.038	0.015	0.006	0.003	0.001	0.001
7	9	0.141	0.053	0.021	0.009	0.004	0.002	0.001
8	9	0.186	0.074	0.030	0.013	0.006	0.003	0.001
9	9	0.241	0.099	0.042	0.018	0.008	0.004	0.002
10	9	0.300	0.130	0.056	0.025	0.012	0.006	0.003
11	9	0.364	0.165	0.073	0.032	0.016	0.008	0.004
12	9	0.432	0.207	0.950	0.044	0.021	0.010	0.005
13	9	0.500	0.252	0.120	0.057	0.027	0.014	0.007

U	n_o	3	4	5	6	7	8	9	10
6	8		0.356	0.139	0.055	0.023	0.010	0.005	0.002
7	8		0.444	0.188	0.077	0.033	0.015	0.007	0.003
8	8		0.556	0.248	0.107	0.047	0.021	0.010	0.005
9	8			0.315	0.141	0.064	0.030	0.014	0.007
10	8			0.387	0.184	0.085	0.041	0.020	0.010
11	8			0.461	0.230	0.111	0.054	0.027	0.014
12	8			0.539	0.285	0.142	0.071	0.036	0.019
13	8				0.341	0.177	0.091	0.047	0.025
14	8				0.404	0.217	0.114	0.060	0.032
15	8				0.467	0.262	0.141	0.076	0.041
16	8				0.533	0.311	0.172	0.095	0.052
17	8					0.362	0.207	0.116	0.065
18	8					0.416	0.245	0.140	0.080
19	8					0.472	0.286	0.168	0.097
20	8					0.528	0.331	0.198	0.117
21	8						0.377	0.232	0.139
22	8						0.426	0.268	0.164
23	8						0.475	0.306	0.191
24	8						0.525	0.347	0.221
25	8							0.389	0.253
26	8							0.433	0.287
27	8							0.478	0.323
28	8							0.522	0.360
29	8								0.399
30	8								0.439
31	8								0.480
32	8								0.520

U	n_r / n_o	3	4	5	6	7	8	9	10
0	10	0.004	0.001	0.000	0.000	0.000	0.000	0.000	0.000
1	10	0.007	0.002	0.001	0.000	0.000	0.000	0.000	0.000
2	10	0.014	0.004	0.001	0.001	0.000	0.000	0.000	0.000
3	10	0.025	0.007	0.002	0.001	0.000	0.000	0.000	0.000
4	10	0.039	0.012	0.004	0.002	0.001	0.000	0.000	0.000
5	10	0.056	0.018	0.006	0.002	0.001	0.000	0.000	0.000
6	10	0.080	0.027	0.010	0.004	0.002	0.001	0.000	0.000
7	10	0.108	0.038	0.014	0.006	0.002	0.001	0.001	0.000
8	10	0.143	0.053	0.020	0.008	0.003	0.002	0.001	0.000
9	10	0.185	0.071	0.028	0.011	0.005	0.002	0.001	0.001
10	10	0.234	0.094	0.038	0.016	0.007	0.003	0.002	0.001
11	10	0.287	0.120	0.050	0.021	0.009	0.004	0.002	0.001
12	10	0.346	0.152	0.065	0.028	0.013	0.006	0.003	0.001
13	10	0.406	0.187	0.082	0.036	0.017	0.008	0.004	0.002

n_r	n_o								n_r	n_o								
14	9	0.568	0.302	0.149	0.072	0.036	0.018	0.009	14	10	0.469	0.227	0.103	0.047	0.022	0.010	0.005	0.003
15	9	0.636	0.355	0.182	0.091	0.045	0.023	0.012	15	10	0.532	0.270	0.127	0.059	0.028	0.013	0.007	0.003
16	9	0.700	0.413	0.219	0.112	0.057	0.030	0.016	16	10	0.594	0.318	0.155	0.074	0.035	0.017	0.009	0.005
17	9	0.759	0.470	0.259	0.136	0.071	0.037	0.020	17	10	0.654	0.367	0.186	0.090	0.044	0.022	0.011	0.006
18	9	0.814	0.530	0.303	0.164	0.087	0.046	0.025	18	10	0.713	0.420	0.220	0.110	0.054	0.027	0.014	0.007
19	9		0.587	0.350	0.194	0.105	0.057	0.031	19	10		0.473	0.257	0.132	0.067	0.034	0.018	0.009
20	9		0.645	0.399	0.228	0.126	0.069	0.039	20	10		0.528	0.297	0.157	0.081	0.042	0.022	0.012
21	9		0.698	0.449	0.264	0.150	0.084	0.047	21	10		0.580	0.339	0.184	0.100	0.051	0.027	0.014
22	9		0.748	0.500	0.304	0.176	0.100	0.057	22	10		0.633	0.384	0.214	0.115	0.061	0.033	0.018
23	9		0.793	0.551	0.345	0.204	0.118	0.068	23	10		0.682	0.430	0.246	0.135	0.073	0.039	0.022
24	9		0.835	0.601	0.388	0.235	0.138	0.081	24	10		0.730	0.477	0.281	0.157	0.086	0.047	0.026
25	9					0.268	0.161	0.095	25	10					0.182	0.102	0.056	0.032
26	9					0.303	0.185	0.111	26	10					0.209	0.119	0.067	0.038
27	9					0.340	0.212	0.129	27	10					0.237	0.137	0.078	0.045
28	9					0.379	0.240	0.149	28	10					0.269	0.180	0.091	0.053
29	9					0.419	0.271	0.170	29	10					0.300	0.204	0.106	0.062
30	9					0.459	0.303	0.193	30	10					0.335	0.230	0.121	0.072
31	9					0.500	0.337	0.218	31	10					0.370	0.257	0.139	0.083
32	9					0.541	0.372	0.245	32	10					0.406	0.286	0.158	0.095
33	9					0.582	0.407	0.273	33	10					0.481	0.317	0.178	0.109
34	9					0.621	0.444	0.302	34	10					0.519	0.348	0.200	0.124
35	9					0.660	0.481	0.333	35	10							0.224	0.140

The null hypothesis should be rejected if the tabulated probability associated with the test statistic and corresponding to the larger and smaller samples (n_r and n_o) is less than or equal to the significance level.

(b) Medium-sized samples

Two-tailed significance level 0.05 (0.025 one-tailed)

n_o \ n_r	10	11	12	13	14	15	16	17	18	19	20
3	4	4	5	5	6	6	7	7	8	8	9
4	6	7	8	9	10	11	12	12	13	14	15
5	9	10	12	13	14	15	16	18	19	20	21
6	12	14	15	17	18	20	22	23	25	26	28
7	15	17	19	21	23	25	27	29	31	33	35
8	18	20	23	25	27	30	32	35	37	39	42
9	21	24	27	29	32	35	38	40	43	46	49
10	24	27	30	34	37	40	43	46	49	53	56
11	27	31	34	38	41	45	48	52	56	59	63
12	30	34	38	42	46	50	54	58	62	66	70
13	34	38	42	46	51	55	60	64	68	73	77
14	37	41	46	51	56	60	65	70	75	79	84
15	40	45	50	55	60	65	71	76	81	86	91
16	43	48	54	60	65	71	76	82	87	93	99

17	46	52	58	64	70	76	82	88	94	100	106
18	49	56	62	68	75	81	87	94	100	107	113
19	53	59	66	73	79	86	93	100	107	114	120
20	56	63	70	77	84	91	99	106	113	120	128

Two-tailed significance level 0.01 (0.005 one-tailed)

n_r / n_0	10	11	12	13	14	15	16	17	18	19	20
3	1	1	2	2	2	3	3	3	3	4	4
4	3	3	4	4	5	6	6	7	7	8	9
5	5	6	7	8	8	9	10	11	12	13	14
6	7	8	10	11	12	13	14	16	17	18	19
7	10	11	13	14	16	17	19	20	22	23	25
8	12	14	16	18	19	21	23	25	27	29	31
9	14	17	19	21	23	25	28	30	32	34	37
10	17	19	22	25	27	30	32	35	38	40	43
11	19	22	25	28	31	34	37	40	43	46	49
12	22	25	28	32	35	38	42	45	48	52	55
13	25	28	32	35	39	43	46	50	54	58	61
14	27	31	35	39	43	47	51	55	59	64	68
15	30	34	38	43	47	52	56	61	65	70	74
16	32	37	42	46	51	56	61	66	71	75	80
17	35	40	45	50	55	61	66	71	76	82	87
18	38	43	48	54	59	65	71	76	82	88	93
19	40	46	52	58	64	70	75	82	88	94	100
20	43	49	55	61	68	74	80	87	93	100	106

The null hypothesis should be rejected if the test statistic is less than or equal to the tabulated value for the corresponding to the large and smaller samples (n_r and n_0) at the specified significance level.

Table 8 Critical values of the Kruskall–Wallis H statistic

Sample sizes			Significance level		
n_1	n_2	n_3	0.10	0.05	0.01
2	2	2	4.571		
3	2	1	4.286		
3	2	2	4.470	4.714	
3	3	1	4.571	5.145	
3	3	2	4.556	5.210	
3	3	3	4.622	5.600	6.489
4	2	1	4.199	4.822	5.702
4	2	2	4.458	5.125	6.000
4	3	2	4.444	5.400	6.300
4	3	3	4.700	5.727	6.746
4	4	1	4.066	4.966	6.667
4	4	2	4.555	5.300	6.875
4	4	3	4.477	5.586	7.144
4	4	4	4.581	5.692	7.490
5	2	1	4.170	5.000	6.210
5	2	2	4.342	5.071	6.373
5	3	1	3.982	4.915	6.400
5	3	2	4.495	5.205	6.822
5	3	3	4.503	5.580	7.030
5	4	1	3.974	4.923	6.885
5	4	2	4.522	5.268	7.110
5	4	3	4.542	5.631	7.440
5	4	4	4.619	5.618	7.752
5	5	1	4.056	5.018	7.073
5	5	2	4.508	5.339	7.269
5	5	3	4.545	5.642	7.543
5	5	4	4.521	5.643	7.791
5	5	5	4.560	5.720	7.980

The null hypothesis should be rejected if the calculated test statistic is equal to or greater than the tabulated value for the corresponding combination of sample sizes at the specified significance level.

Table 9 Critical values of the Spearman's rank correlation coefficient (r_s)

Sample size	Two-tailed significance levels			
(n)	0.10	0.05	0.02	0.01
5	0.900	1.000	1.000	
6	0.829	0.886	0.943	1.000
7	0.714	0.786	0.893	0.929
8	0.643	0.738	0.835	0.881
9	0.600	0.700	0.783	0.833
10	0.564	0.648	0.745	0.794
11	0.536	0.618	0.709	0.755
12	0.503	0.587	0.678	0.727
13	0.484	0.560	0.648	0.703
14	0.464	0.538	0.626	0.679
15	0.446	0.521	0.604	0.654
16	0.429	0.503	0.582	0.635
17	0.414	0.488	0.566	0.618
18	0.401	0.472	0.550	0.600
19	0.391	0.460	0.535	0.584
20	0.380	0.447	0.522	0.570
21	0.370	0.436	0.509	0.556
22	0.361	0.425	0.497	0.544
23	0.353	0.416	0.486	0.532
24	0.344	0.407	0.476	0.521
25	0.337	0.398	0.466	0.511
26	0.331	0.390	0.457	0.501
27	0.324	0.383	0.449	0.492
28	0.318	0.375	0.441	0.483
29	0.312	0.368	0.433	0.475
30	0.306	0.362	0.425	0.467
31	0.301	0.356	0.419	0.459
32	0.296	0.350	0.412	0.452
33	0.291	0.345	0.405	0.446
34	0.287	0.340	0.400	0.439
35	0.283	0.335	0.394	0.433
40	0.264	0.313	0.368	0.405
45	0.248	0.294	0.347	0.382
50	0.235	0.279	0.329	0.363
55	0.224	0.266	0.314	0.346
60	0.214	0.255	0.301	0.331
65	0.206	0.245	0.291	0.322
70	0.198	0.236	0.280	0.310
80	0.185	0.221	0.247	0.273
100	0.165	0.197	0.234	0.259

The correlation coefficient calculated from the sample data should be regarded as significant if it is greater than the tabulated value for the sample size at the specified significance level. For a one-tailed test the probabilities should be halved.

References and selected bibliography

Anderson, N.M. (1961) 'Scales and statistics: parametric and non-parametric', *Psychological Bulletin*, **58**, 305–316.

Ayer, A.J. (1964) *The foundations of empirical knowledge*. Macmillan: London.

Baker, A.R.H. (1973) 'Adjustments to distance between farmstead and fields: some findings from the southwestern Paris Basin in the nineteenth century', *Canadian Geographer*, **17**, 259–275.

Barber, G.M. (1988) *Elementary statistics for geographers*. Guildford Press: New York.

Barnett, V. (1974) *Elements of sampling theory*. Hodder & Stoughton: London.

Barnett, V. (1991) *Sample survey: principles and methods*. Edward Arnold: London.

Berdie, D.R., Anderson, J.F. and Niebuhr, M.A. (1986) *Questionnaires: design and use*. Methuen: London.

Berry, B.J.L. and Marble, F.F. (eds) (1968) *Spatial analysis: a reader in statistical geography*. Prentice Hall: Englewood Cliffs, NJ.

Best, R.H. (1981) *Land use and living space*. Methuen: London.

Best, R.H. and Coppock, J.T. (1962) *The changing use of land in Britain*. Faber & Faber: London.

Billinge, M., Gregory, D. and Martin, R. (1984) *Recollections of a revolution: geography and spatial science*. Macmillan: London.

Blalock, H.M. (1960) *Social statistics*. McGraw-Hill: New York.

Bracken, I. and Spooner, R. (1985) 'Interactive digitizing for computer assisted cartography', *Area*, **17**, 205–212.

Britten, D.K. and Ingersent, K. (1964) 'Trends in concentration in British agriculture', *Journal of Agricultural Economics*, **16**, 26–52.

Burrough, P. (1986) *Principles of geographical information systems*. Oxford University Press: Oxford.

Cable, D. and Rowe, B. (1987) *Software for statistical and survey analysis*. Study Group on Computers in Survey Analysis.

Campbell, J. (1991) *Map use and analysis*. Wm. C. Brown: Oxford.

Caws, P. (1965) *The philosophy of science*. Princeton University Press: Princeton, NJ.

Charlton, M., Openshaw, S. and Wymer, C. (1985) 'Some new classifications of census enumeration districts in Britain: a poor man's ACORN', *Journal of Economic and Social Measurement*, **13**, 69–96.

Chorley, R.J. and Haggett, P. (1967) 'Models, paradigms and the new geography', in Chorley, R.J. and Haggett, P. (eds) *Models in geography*. Methuen: London.

Clark, W.A.V. and Avery, K.L. (1976) 'The effects of data aggregation in statistical analysis', *Geographical Analysis*, **8**, 428–438.

Cohen, L. and Holliday, M. (1982) *Statistics for social sciences*. Harper and Row: London.

Colchester Borough Council (1985) *Village facilities survey*. Department of Planning, Colchester Borough Council.

Colchester Borough Council (1992) *Village facilities survey 1990*. Department of Planning and Development Services, Colchester Borough Council.

Cole, J.P. and King, C.A.M. (1968) *Quantitative geography*. Wiley: Chichester.

Coleman, A. (1961) 'The second land use survey: progress and prospect', *Geographical Journal*, **127** (2), 168–186.

Coleman, A. (1978) 'Agricultural land losses: the evidence from maps', in Rogers, A.W. (ed.) *Urban growth, farmland losses and planning*, Wye College for Institute of British Geographers.

Coleman, A. and Maggs, K.R. (1964) *Land use survey handbook* (4th edn), Isle of Thanet Geographical Association: Thanet.

Coppock, J.T. (1965) *Agricultural atlas of England and Wales*. Faber & Faber: London.

Dale, A., Arber, S. and Procter, M. (1988) *Doing secondary analysis*. Allen & Unwin: London.

Davis, J.C. (1973) *Statistics and data analysis in geology*. Wiley: New York.

Dawson, J.A. and Unwin, D.J. (1984) 'The integration of microcomputers into British geography', *Area*, **16**, 323–329.

Department of the Environment (1987) *River quality in England and Wales 1985: a report of the 1985 survey*. Department of the Environment and Welsh Office: London and Cardiff.

Department of the Environment (1990) *Environmental Pollution Act, 1990.* HMSO: London.

Department of the Environment (1992) *Royal Commission of Environmental Pollution, Sixteenth Report: Freshwater Quality*. Cm. 1966. HMSO: London.

Dixon, C. and Leach, B. (1978) *Questionnaires and interviews in geographical research.* Concepts and techniques in modern geography, No. 18. Geo Abstracts: Norwich.

Ebdon, D. (1985) *Statistics in geography.* Basil Blackwell: Oxford.

Evans, I.S. (1977) 'The selection of class intervals', *Transactions of the Institute of British Geographers* (new series), **2**, 98-124.

Everitt, B. (1974) *Cluster analysis.* Halsted Press: New York.

Fielding, A.J. (1982) 'Counterurbanisation in Western Europe', *Progress in Planning*, **17**, 3-52.

Forstner, U. and Wittmann, G.T.W. (1983) *Metal pollution in the aquatic environment* (2nd edn). Springer-Verlag: Heidelberg.

Freeman, T.W. (1961) *The geographer's craft.* Hutchinson: London.

Gardiner, V. and Gardiner, G. (1978) *Analysis of frequency distributions.* Concepts and techniques in modern geography, No. 19, Geo Abstracts: Norwich.

Gerrard, A.J. (1988) *Rocks and landforms.* Unwin Hyman: London.

Gould, P. (1970) 'Is *statistix inferens* the geographical name for a wild goose?', *Economic Geography*, **46**, 439-448.

Gregory, D. (1963) *Statistical methods and the geographer.* Longman: London.

Gregory, D. (1978) *Ideology, science and human geography.* Hutchinson: London.

Haggett, P. (1965) *Locational analysis.* London.

Hakim, C. (1982) *Secondary analysis in social research: a guide to data sources with examples.* Allen & Unwin: London.

Hammond, P. and McCullagh, P.S. (1978) *Quantitative techniques in geography.* Clarendon Press: Oxford.

Harvey, D.W. (1966) 'Geographical processes and the analysis of point patterns', *Transactions of the Institute of British Geographers*, **40**, 81-95.

Harvey, D.W. (1969) *Explanation in geography.* Edward Arnold: London.

Harvey, D.W. (1973) *Social justice and the city.* Edward Arnold: London.

Hodge, I. and Monk, S. (1991) *In search of a rural economy: patterns and differentiation in non-metropolitan England.* Local Economy Monograph No. 20, Department of Land Economy, University of Cambridge.

Horton, R.E. (1945) 'Erosional development of streams and their drainage basins: hydrophysical approach to quantitative morphology', *Bulletin, Geological Society of America*, **56**, 275-370.

Huff, D. (1973) *How to lie with statistics.* Penguin: Harmondsworth.

Ilbery, B. (1981) 'Dorset agriculture: a classification of regional types', *Transactions of the Institute of British Geographers* (new series), **6**(2), 214-227.

Johnston, R.J. (1979) *Geography and geographers: Anglo-American geography since 1945.* Edward Arnold: London.

Kendall, M. and Stuart, A. (1948) *The advanced theory of statistics*, Vol. I (4th edn). Charles Griffin: London.

Kuhn, T.S. (1962) *The structure of scientific revolutions.* Chicago University Press: Chicago.

Landis, J.D. (1985) 'Electronic spreadsheets in planning' *Journal of the American Planning Association*, **51**, 216-224.

MacDougal, E.B. (1976) *Computer programming for spatial problems.* Edward Arnold: London.

McFadden, F.R. and Hoffer, J.A. (1988) *Data Base Management.* (2nd edn). Benjamin/Cummings: California.

Maguire, D.J. (1985) 'Microcomputer graphics' *Bulletin of the Society of University Cartographers*, **19**, 94-96.

Maguire, D.J. (1986) 'Computer-drawn statistical graphics' *Bulletin of the Society of University Cartographers*, **20**, 36-38.

Maguire, D.J. (1989) *Computers in geography.* Harlow: Longman; and Wiley: New York.

Mather, A.S. (1986) *Land use.* Longman: London.

Mather, P.M. (1976) *Computers in geography: a practical approach.* Blackwell: Oxford.

Mather, P.M. (1991) *Computer applications in geography.* Wiley: Chichester.

Ministry of Agriculture, Fisheries and Food (annual) *Farm classification in England and Wales.* MAFF: London.

Minitab Inc. (1989) *MINITAB reference manual.* Minitab Inc., Philadelphia, USA.

Moore, W.G. (1968) *A dictionary of geography.* Harmondsworth: Penguin.

Moser, C.A. and Scott, W. (1961) *British towns.* Oliver and Boyd: London.

Nagel, E. (1961) *The structure of science.* New York.

Neft, D. (1966) *Statistical analysis for areal distributions*, Regional Science Institute Monograph 2, Philadelphia.

Norcliffe, G.B. (1977) *Inferential statistics for geographers.* Hutchinson: London.

O'Brien, L.G. (1986) 'Statistical software for microcomputers', *Area*, **18**, 39-42.

O'Brien, L.G. and Wrigley, N. (1980) 'Computer programms for the analysis of categorical data', *Area*, **12**, 263-268.

Openshaw, S. (1983) 'Multivariate analysis of census data: the classification of areas' in Rhind, D. (ed.) *A census user's handbook.* Methuen: London

Openshaw, S. (1984) *The modifiable areal unit problem.* Geo Books: Norwich.

Openshaw, S. and Taylor, P.J. (1981) 'The modifiable areal unit problem', in Wrigley, N. and Bennett, R.J.

(eds) *Quantitative geography: a British view*. Routledge & Kegan Paul: London, 60-69.

Openshaw, S., Carver, S. and Fernie, J. (1989) *Britain's nuclear waste: safety and siting*. Bellhaven: London.

Pahl, R.E. (1965) *'Urbs in Rure', Geographical Papers*, No. 2. London School of Economics and Political Science.

Poole, M.A. and Boale, F. (1973) 'Segregation in Belfast', in Clarke, B.M. and Cleave, M.B. (eds) *Social patterns in cities*. Institute of British Geographers, Special Publication, London.

Poole, M.A. and O'Farrell, O.N. (1971) 'The assumptions of the linear regression model', *Transactions of the Institute of British Geographers* (old series), **52**, 145-158.

Popper, K. (1965) *The logic of scientific discovery*. Harper Torchbooks: New York.

Potts, A.S. (1970) 'Frost action in rocks: some experimental data', *Transactions of the Institute of British Geographers* (old series), **49**, 109-124.

Reichmann, W.J. (1964) *Use and abuse of statistics*. Penguin: Harmondsworth.

Rhind, D. (1977) 'Computer aided cartography', *Transactions of the Institute of British Geographers* (New Series), **2**, 71-97.

Ripley, B.D. (1981) *Spatial statistics*. Wiley: Chichester.

Robinson, A.H. (1956) 'The necessity of weighting values in correlation analyses of areal data', *Annals of the Association of American Geographers*, **46**, 233-236.

Seymour, D.R. (1965) 'IBM 7600 program for locating bivariate means and bivariate medians', Technical Report No. 16, Department of Geography, Northwestern University.

Shaw, G. and Wheeler, D. (1985) *Statistical techniques in geographical analysis*. David Fulton: London.

Shepherd, I.D.H. (1985) 'Teaching geography with the computer: possibilities and problems', *Journal of Geography in Higher Education*, **9**, 3-23.

Siegel, S. (1956) *Nonparametric statistics for the behavioural sciences*. McGraw-Hill: New York.

Silk, J. (1979) *Statistical concepts in geography*. Allen & Unwin: London.

Smith, D.M. (1975) *Patterns in human geography*. Penguin: Harmondsworth.

Som, R.K. (1973) *A manual of sampling techniques*. Heinemann: London.

SPSS Inc. (1983) *SPSS-X user's guide*. McGraw-Hill: New York.

Stamp, L.D. (1948) *The land of Britain: its use and misuse* (3rd edn, 1962). Longman: London.

Star, J. and Estes, J. (1991) *Geographic information systems: an introduction*. Prentice Hall: Englewood Cliffs, NJ.

Stevens, S.S. (1946) 'On the theory of scales of measurement', *Science*, **103**, 677-680.

Strahler, A.N. (1952) 'Dynamic basis of geomorphology', *Bulletin, Geological Society of America*, **63**, 923-938.

Tannenbaum, E. (1980) 'Secondary analysis, data banks and geography, *Area*, **12**, 33-35.

Tennant-Smith, J. (1985) *Basic statistics*. Butterworth: Sevenoaks.

Theakstone, W.H. and Harrison, C. (1974) *The analysis of geographical data*. Heinemann: London.

Unwin, D.J. (1974) 'Hardware provision for quantitative geography in the United Kingdom', *Area*, **4**, 200-204.

Unwin, D.J. (1981) *Introductory spatial analysis*. Methuen: London.

Unwin D.J. and Dawson, J.A. (1984) *Computer programming for geographers*. Longman: Harlow.

Walford, N.S. and Hockey, A.E. (1991) *Social and economic restructuring in rural Britain: a methodology for contextual analysis*, ESRC Countryside Change Initiative, Working Paper No. 18.

Water Authorities Association (annual) *Water pollution from farm wastes (year): England and Wales*. Water Authorities Association: London.

Waugh, T.C. and McCalden, J.B. (1983) *Gimms Reference Manual: Release 4.5* Gimms Ltd.: Edinburgh.

Williams, R.B.G. (1984) *Introduction to statistics for geographers and earth scientists*. Macmillan: London.

Williams, R.B.G. (1985) *Intermediate statistics for geographers and earth scientists*. Macmillan: London.

Wood, W.F. (1955) 'Use of stratified random samples in land use study', *Annals of the Association of American Geographers*, **48**, 350-367.

Wrigley, N. (1985) *Categorical data analysis for geographers and environmental scientists*. Harlow: Longman.

Wrigley, N. and Bennett, R.J. (1981) *Quantitative geography: a British view*. Routledge & Kegan Paul: London.

Index